THE UNCERTAIN PROMISE OF SOUTHERN AFRICA

THE UNCERTAIN

PROMISE OF

SOUTHERN AFRICA

York Bradshaw and Stephen N. Ndegwa, editors

INDIANA UNIVERSITY PRESS   BLOOMINGTON AND INDIANAPOLIS

This book is a publication of

Indiana University Press

601 North Morton Street

Bloomington, IN 47404-3797 USA

http://www.indiana.edu/~iupress

Telephone orders 800-842-6796

Fax orders 812-855-7931

Orders by e-mail iuporder@indiana.edu

© 2000 by Indiana University Press

The paper used in this publication meets the minimum requirements of American National Standard for Information Sciences—Permanence of Paper for Printed Library Materials, ANSI Z39.48-1984.

Manufactured in the United States of America

Library of Congress Cataloging-in-Publication Data

The uncertain promise of Southern Africa / York Bradshaw and Stephen N. Ndegwa, editors.

p. cm.

Includes index.

ISBN 0-253-33827-1 (cl : alk. paper)—

ISBN 0-253-21424-6 (pa : alk. paper)

1. Africa, Southern—Politics and government—1975–1994. 2. Africa, Southern—Politics and government—1994–. 3. Africa, Southern—Economic conditions—1975–. 4. Africa, Southern, Social conditions—1975–. I. Bradshaw, York W., date II. Ndegwa, Stephen N.

DT1166.U53   2000

968'.0009'0511—dc21   00-040714

1 2 3 4 5   05 04 03 02 01 00

For Liezell, Chrystal, and Autymn

For Dorothy

CONTENTS

CONTENTS

TABLES

TABLES

ACKNOWLEDGMENTS

This book is the result of an international collaboration among several scholars in Africa, Europe, and the United States. The editors are particularly grateful to the authors for their commitment to the project and for their tireless and patient efforts to craft and update their chapters as events unfolded. The staff at Indiana University Press encouraged and nurtured this book, and was especially delightful to work with. The editors are particularly grateful to John Gallman, Jane Lyle, Janet Rabinowitch, and Kendra Boileau Stokes.

Several individuals and institutions made the completion of this book possible. The Department of Sociology at the University of Memphis provided space and support for the initial work on the manuscript, while the College of William and Mary provided support for completing the manuscript. The editors would like to particularly thank Professor John McGlennon, chair of the Department of Government, for his unfailing support for the project, including funding for editorial assistants. We also wish to thank Jennifer Lieb, Carolyn Ruff, and, especially, Sarah Bagley for their dedication and good cheer in their work to finalize the manuscript. Finally, several grants from the College of William and Mary and a research grant from the American Council of Learned Societies allowed Stephen Ndegwa to devote time to this project.

THE UNCERTAIN
PROMISE OF
SOUTHERN AFRICA

PART I.
INTRODUCTION

1. The Uncertain Promise of Southern Africa

York Bradshaw and Stephen N. Ndegwa

American college students built "shantytowns" during the 1980s to protest continued corporate investment in South Africa's morally bankrupt apartheid system. Even the most optimistic protester probably would not have predicted the pace of change in South Africa over the next decade. Economic sanctions, divestment, and violence within South Africa were strangling apartheid and making possible a new democracy of majority governance. The 1990s saw the release of Nelson Mandela from prison, his election as president, the writing of a new constitution, the formation of new political districts, the emergence of a new educational system, the retirement of Mandela as president, and a second round of successful majority-rule elections. Almost miraculously, these changes have occurred with relatively little violence. Aside from the former Soviet-bloc countries, no nation has experienced greater change than South Africa over the last decade.

In fact, southern Africa as a whole is a very different place than it was when the first and second editions of this book were published nearly two decades ago. In 1982, Zimbabwe had just become independent after a long and violent struggle, while the civil wars in Angola and Mozambique, fueled by the cold war, were raging, and the decade-long insurrection in apartheid South Africa was stewing in the townships. Ten or fifteen years ago, outside attention toward southern Africa focused on the superpower confrontation between the United States and the Soviet Union. South Africa proclaimed itself the last bastion of anti-communism in a region where the effects of late colonialism and long liberation wars carried forth without moral or material support from the West, thereby encouraging newly independent governments to embrace Soviet support and socialist designs. Today, by contrast, southern Africa commands attention more for its economic and investment potential rather than as a flash point of superpower rivalry. Some economies in the region are growing, and old single-party dictatorships and white minority governments have given way to democratic governments with varying degrees of success and maturity.

One of the most significant misconceptions in the West is that southern Africa, fresh from the overthrow of apartheid, is automatically "guaranteed" greater development, security, equality, and racial reconciliation. In fact, however, none of these characteristics is assured. Southern African countries face the challenge of simultaneous democratization and economic adjustment or recovery, amid high expectations—all arising out of the very fundamental changes experienced, and amid new constraints of a changed international context. As with other experiences of democratic and economic transition (e.g., Russia, Eastern Europe, and parts of sub-Saharan Africa), change in itself has produced immense expectations. But governments confront daunting challenges in meeting these expectations due to the deprivation experienced from years of racial domination and exploitation (South Africa, Namibia, Zimbabwe), civil wars (Angola, Mozambique), and mismanagement (Malawi, Zambia, and Zimbabwe). Alongside this, possibilities of quick transformation are limited by the nature of the negotiated transitions that preclude radical and revolutionary change and the reduced aid flows that have become the reality of the post–cold war dividend. The danger in this is the possibility that unmet expectations will lead to disappointment, disillusionment, and despair. While the authors in this volume are optimistic, the successful outcome of the current transition is by no means assured.

The purpose of this edited collection is to assess the current state of southern Africa in an era of uncertain promise. Changes experienced during the 1990s have been historic; at the same time, though, there are many challenges and even threats to continued development and reconciliation. The first part of the book examines the current political and development situation in six southern African countries—South Africa, Namibia, Botswana, Zimbabwe, Angola, and Mozambique. The second part of the book focuses on issues of enduring importance across the region—education, health, gender, the law, intra- and inter-regional power relations, international commerce, and popular culture. All of the authors were selected for their outstanding scholarship and years of experience living and working in southern Africa. Many of the authors are citizens of the countries about which they write. The others have lived in the region for substantial periods of time. Before turning our attention to these chapters, we examine several obstacles to continued reconciliation and development in southern Africa.

Regional Inequality and Competing Interests

Southern Africa is a region that exhibits varied levels of economic development, quality of life, and technological advancement. As discussed in chapter 15, which includes a compendium of data on southern Africa, the GNP per capita in southern Africa varies from a low of $200 in Malawi to a high of $3,600 in Botswana.

The under-five mortality rate (number of children that die before age five per 1,000 births) varies from a high of 224 in Malawi to a low of 65 in South Africa. And the number of Internet hosts (per 10,000 people) varies from a low of near 0 in several southern African countries to a high of nearly 35 in South Africa. These figures imply that southern Africa has countries with very different interests that emanate out of different histories and relationships.

The most developed country in the region is South Africa, which, with the end of apartheid, is expected to be the regional leader economically and politically. But South Africa (and every other country in the region) has its own problems and should not be expected to act altruistically toward its neighbors. In fact, the regional economies still suffer from an over-emphasis of the protectionism that emerged in the 1980s and persists today, even though the circumstances encouraging protectionism have largely disappeared. For South Africa, the linchpin economy in the region, protectionism was occasioned by the international and regional boycott that gave rise to subsidy-fed industries with protected markets. For its neighbors, especially the Frontline States, industry was geared toward reducing dependency on South Africa and also as part of the socialist commitment toward self-sufficiency. But these trends led to fairly inefficient industries, parastatals, and subsidy-fed commercial enterprises, including farming. Even with the recent transformation throughout the region, protectionism persists. The main reason is the pressure to maintain employment and, for countries other than South Africa, to avoid continued economic domination by the relatively more affluent, more efficient, and more capitalized economy of South Africa.

Two other important regional issues with economic implications are (1) natural resource and environmental concerns and (2) cross-border migration. Natural resource governance and, by extension, environmental management have not been priorities, partly because the countries in the region are well endowed with natural resources, especially minerals. However, in fact, southern Africa faces tremendous environmental stress, particularly in agriculture, due to recurrent drought. Water, which is critical to all aspects of development, is in short supply, and given that most rivers in southern Africa are shared among countries, water harvesting and pollution of rivers become more immediate cross-border concerns. The Namibian government's plans to dam the Epupa River, which also flows into Botswana and Angola, without consultations with its neighbors indicates the extent to which natural resource management, conservation, and environmental issues have implications for regional conflict. Moreover, this dam, which would be the largest in Africa, is expected to displace a small and marginalized community and has excited much opposition from environmentalists in Namibia and elsewhere in the region, especially South Africa. Similarly, another dispute involving Namibia is over a small wetland on its unmarked border with Botswana—described by one analyst as "a small patch of mud" but believed to hold potential mineral worth. The dispute has led to near military confrontation, leading Botswana to go on a military spending spree that threatened to escalate into a mini-arms race in the region.

A second critical issue is both legal and illegal cross-border migration, prompted by economic factors. This is over and above the rural-urban drift, which in southern Africa has been occurring steadily over the last half century such that it is the most urbanized region in Africa. Two migratory patterns are of particular interest. One is the movement of whites from South Africa in two waves, one leaving the region permanently—especially to Australia or New Zealand; the other is the movement of whites to the north in order to set up farming and commercial enterprises in countries within and beyond southern Africa. While other countries also have experienced increased mobility of capital and people to other areas, South Africa is the largest contributor given its economic predominance and the fact that white capital is by far the largest and most sophisticated in the region. Not irrelevant, white flight in the region is primarily from South Africa, the last bastion of conservatism to which white radicals fled from Mozambique, Zimbabwe, and Namibia as these countries became independent. It is too early to tell what effect this flight will have on the region. But the migration to the interior of the region and to East and Central Africa is likely to constitute the most significant plank in the private sector drive to integrate economies and energize industry and commerce in the north through South African expertise.

Of course, another dimension of cross-border migration involves the poorest citizens of the region who move into South Africa in search of work and an opportunity to escape their countries' battered economies. Even net out-migration countries in the region also absorb substantial numbers of citizens of less endowed neighbors. For instance, citizens of Angola have migrated into Namibia, while citizens from all countries migrate into Botswana where the standard of living is comparatively higher than elsewhere in the region except South Africa. Such cross-border migrations were impossible two decades ago and have become possible due to a number of factors, among them the peace that has returned to the region, the democratic transitions, and the ease of movement of people and goods across borders due to more open economic policies, especially the creation of common markets such as COMESA and SADC.

Migratory patterns have clear implications for the regional and internal dynamics of southern African countries. On the positive side, the mobility of human resources and capital sensitizes and may motivate governments to better manage national economies in order to attract and retain investment and labor. On the other hand, the noticeable presence of foreigners in commerce elicits antipathy bordering on xenophobia, which has been the case in South Africa where economic conditions for the black population remain depressed.

Political, Economic, and Social Change

Structural and institutional discontinuities are also evident in the political, economic, and social realms. Political power has shifted to the majority black populations in all southern African countries, but white dominance in the public realm has not entirely been overcome, although its caprice and exclusiveness has been broken. With particular reference to the three countries with more recent experiences of white domination (South Africa, Namibia, and Zimbabwe), economic power is still overwhelmingly in the hands of whites and especially concentrated in sectors such as manufacturing, banking, and farming. On the other hand, there is a fast-forming middle and entrepreneurial class of blacks, especially in South Africa, which follows the pattern of similar expansion of opportunity (first in the public sector and then in the private sector) for blacks in Zimbabwe and Namibia in the 1980s and 1990s and the other countries in the 1960s and 1970s. Tension is still evident in both political and economic relations (see below on race).

On the economic front, some movements have spawned contradictory outcomes. For instance, all countries are implementing some form of structural adjustment programs, regardless of the name given. They seek to reduce government regulation of the economy and to cut back on subsidies and unravel the welfare state. In the particular case of South Africa (and to a lesser extent Namibia and Mozambique), adjustment is being undertaken at the precise moment when the state needs to engage in redistributive policy to rectify cumulative inequality. However, these welfare states are being dismantled just at the time when the black majority has acquired power and become potential recipients of such subsidies, especially necessary to speedily secure economic and social equity. This break has implications for continued inequality, as the most needy and historically disadvantaged populations are unable to take advantage of the welfare state, which has already benefited whites who have now been displaced from power but who can more effectively compete in the markets.

Socially, the position of women is telling of the characteristic discontinuities and continuities that characterize the southern Africa transition and that most fundamentally suggest that the transition is by no means settled or complete and is instead a contested terrain. The struggle—for political power, economic equality, and social justice—in essence continues. For women, the practices of the past regimes that saw them marginalized in various sectors are beginning to change. For instance, disadvantages suffered by women in terms of access to credit and ownership of land have changed as women have become more organized, particularly as opportunities for political participation have opened and constitutions that assert equality between the sexes have been enacted. Not insignificantly, the cessation of civil wars and insurrections, whose major victims are women and children, have immensely increased the quality of lives. However, some negative trends persist: for example, in the continued acceptance of traditional authority structures as well as apartheid-era legal regimes that treated women as perpetual minors. Similarly, this shows up in government policies, such as land redistribution in Zimbabwe, where women are not considered as able to hold land.

Of course, social and economic advancement cannot occur in a climate of political conflict and warfare. Given that the region has been embroiled in armed conflict in all but the last five years of the preceding three decades, security issues remain paramount. While the major internal insurrections against racial domination ended in peaceful transitions and the civil wars have been extinguished by democratic pacts, the potential for internal and regional conflict persists. For instance, in Angola and Mozambique, the peace remains fragile and faces several challenges, including the tensions of former combatants co-existing as electoral winners and losers, sharing power, and the difficulties of economic recovery, which may be too slow for already impatient citizens and political actors. While conflict elsewhere in Africa is unlikely to directly affect fortunes in southern Africa, one country is an exception: the Congo. The Democratic Republic of Congo is important regionally in that occurrences in it would have reverberations through much of southern Africa due to refugee movements, spreading instability, and invitations to military adventures by neighboring countries. For instance, Zambia, which borders the Shaba province of Congo, has already suffered waves of refugee flows from the successive crises in the Congo in the 1990s, such as the state collapse in the waning days of the Mobutu regime and in the rebellion that toppled him. Similarly, Namibia, Angola, and Zimbabwe have sent troop contingents to bolster the regime of Laurent Kabila against rebel onslaughts, while South Africa, which has more economic interests in the Congo, has engaged in shuttle diplomacy at various points and made clear its displeasure in its neighbors' military interventions.

Race, Power, and Social Justice

The first author of this chapter has an outgoing toddler who has friends from many different races and ethnic groups. While visiting family in South Africa, she inadvertently broke the norms of a small town where white and black are still very segregated. The young child ran up to a small group of black children who were standing outside a store. She tried to "talk" with them and offered them a handful of French fries that she was eating. The children, though friendly, were uneasy and surprised at the advances of a young white child. Adults also appeared surprised and concerned as they looked around for the parents of the white girl. For a long moment, the author realized what many American towns were like prior to the 1960s (and some still are this way). No one said anything about the interaction between the children because, on the *surface,* the races get along reasonably well in South Africa. But the unspoken expressions revealed the people's real sentiments of fear and prejudice, underscoring that race is perhaps still the major issue in South Africa.

Indeed, race has been the fulcrum of southern African history of power, domination, and privilege; it remains the Achilles' heel of most of southern Africa. Two racial heritages exist in this region: one in which white settlement dating back to the middle of the seventeenth century proceeded on enduring notions of superiority and hegemony and sought to establish permanent settlement, and another, more recent one, which was carried forth as part of the continent-wide colonization by European powers starting in the late nineteenth century and concluding in the latter half of the twentieth century. In the first variety, South Africa and Namibia are the examples, while the rest of the region represents the second heritage. Race and the politics of racial exclusion, privilege, and domination have been more en-

8

during legacies in the former cases than in the latter. However, even those countries that were not occupied before the nineteenth century have been affected by the settler heritage trend in two ways. First, in some of the latter cases, colonialists attempted to replicate settler colonies (particularly in Zimbabwe), resulting in the longer period it took for these countries to become independent (Zimbabwe, Angola, Mozambique). Second, as the last wave of independence swept aside Portuguese colonies in the mid-1970s, direct military action and destabilization efforts by South Africa sought to ensure a buffer zone of white regimes (Namibia and Zimbabwe) or weakened African regimes (Mozambique) in their quest to sustain white hegemony in the region. The result has been the solidification of political, economic, and social cleavages along racial lines, given the nature of dominance in these countries' histories and particularly in the more recent formative struggles.

While power has ultimately shifted back to the majority black population under democratic rules, race remains a significant divide in political, economic, and social issues. This appears not only in the continued inequalities between the two races but also in the discourse over policy preferences. The racial debate has been most prominent in South Africa, and to a lesser extent in Zimbabwe and Namibia. This is not surprising since these three countries have had the most clear-cut racial domination in the recent past and transitions that have seen a majority of the white citizens choose to remain in the country. In South Africa, for instance, recently there has been a raging debate about the nature of the country's identity. For instance, new President Thabo Mbeki has described South Africa as two nations in one: one, white and privileged, the other black and deprived. The debate has found sharp definition in the attempts to pursue reconciliation and reconstruction, a theme that has been central to the peaceful and negotiated transitions in all three countries. For instance, the Truth and Reconciliation Commission, while providing some form of catharsis for the racial history, also revealed the depth of suspicion and resentment among whites at being singled out as the main culprits. Reflecting what is generally the mood of the transition, one white citizen wrote to the *Star's* editor, declaring that as a white, he was "a little tired of being the villain of the piece . . . and being considered an intruder in my own country."[1]

The slow pace of reconstruction (i.e., opportunities for blacks in the face of white privilege) and the presence of white power and privilege in state and economic institutions and constitutional protection as well as international pressure has made blacks realize that reconciliation does not equate with sacrifices on the part of whites. This has led to demands for more forceful redistribution of wealth and resources accumulated directly or indirectly through the historic privilege accorded to whites and the concomitant disadvantage faced by blacks. For example, some have argued for a forceful appropriation of land where the land market has not delivered enough land for redistribution (Zimbabwe), for affirmative action policies to enforce equal opportunity for blacks in industry and commerce that remain white controlled (South Africa), and for limits to be placed on land ownership to reduce foreign (putatively South African) and multiple ownership of farms in Namibia. However, as the *Star* editorial suggests, "it is not realistic to demand—in the name of nation-building—that people (both white and black) must simply surrender what they have."[2]

At the core of the race question are questions not only of economic and political opportunity, but also of identity and culture. Formerly disadvantaged groups are keen to acquire economic power and precedence following successful acquisition of political power. For the white minority populations, culture and language have become the rallying points for a broader struggle to preserve a way of life that is overwhelmed by the black majority and that, lacking political dominance, is likely to be whittled away over time. Thus, pursuits of preserving Afrikaner culture and language as an official language become the public face of the larger struggle to remain politically relevant while adjusting to minority status and to maintain economic power while losing the state's steady support. These struggles are much more pronounced in South Africa at the moment, but they have occurred in other countries in the last three decades, and range from battles about control, management, and content of resources such as public universities and radio stations, to breaking white dominance in state bureaucracies and sports, to reorienting policies in various social and economic fields in order to move from privileging a white minority to accommodating a broad base of citizens.

Given the wholehearted commitment with which all racially divided southern African governments have subscribed to reconciliation, this tension between the races will persist, especially in seeking to balance the pressures for redistribution and the opening up of opportunities for those historically disadvantaged with the protection of the rights, property, and equality of those who are currently and historically privileged. Achieving this delicate balance is by no means assured. Unaddressed, the racial divide will find particular resonance in continued inequality, exclusion, and minuscule opportunity for blacks and may give rise to a more radical politics seeking to redistribute wealth and a nationalist agenda. The Zimbabwe example is instructive. Faced with economic decline and persistent inequality, the ZANU(PF) government, under an increasingly unpopular President Robert Mugabe, chose to stoke racial resentment by claiming white sabotage of the economy, lack of quid pro quo in reconciliation efforts, and continued white dominance of the economy to the exclusion of blacks. With specific regard to the failure of land reform in two decades of independence, the government chose to declare its intention to forcefully acquire 1,500 white-owned farms for redistribution without compensation. While this threat was never carried out due to a variety of factors (including donor pressure and local opposition), it clearly indicates the possibility of more radical and uncompromising racial politics such as the land invasions in 2000.

Looking Ahead

Southern Africa continues to experience dramatic and exciting changes. The region has great promise; at the same time, however, there are a number of obstacles and pitfalls that could slow, or even stop, reconciliation and development in the region. This book discusses these issues in substantial detail. We turn first to a review of the balance of power in the region and to the chapters that investigate individual countries in southern Africa.

NOTES

1. "Tired of Being Villain," letter to the editor, *Star* (Johannesburg), 7 July 1998, p. 8.

2. "Our Divided Nation," editorial, *Star*, 5 June 1998, p. 8.

2. Balance of Power in Southern Africa

Colin Legum

When the signatories to the Rome Treaty embarked on their quest for a European Economic Community, they had the singular advantage that no member enjoyed complete economic domination over the others. This made it easier, though always difficult, to negotiate trade-off deals to satisfy the major interests and minimize suspicions within the nascent community. The situation is entirely different in southern Africa, where South Africa, the region's economic giant, casts a suspicious shadow over its neighbors as it continues to enlarge its dominance while at the same time carrying on negotiations to find agreement on economic, political, and military institutions capable of ensuring the region's stability in the twenty-first century. The negotiations were complicated by other factors. First, by South Africa's concurrent negotiations with the European Union—its biggest market—to reach agreement on an economic treaty that would also protect the interests of its partners in the SADC (Southern African Development Community). Second, by the contemporaneous phasing out of the Lomé Accord, which had implications for all South Africa's neighbors. Third, the different interests among the core group members of the SADC. Fourth, the lack of agreement within the South African political and financial establishment about the country's economic policy. Fifth, the pressures coming from an outer circle of sub-Saharan countries (e.g., Zaire, Tanzania, Uganda, Kenya , and Mauritius) to be involved in a larger type of economic union. And sixth, the need to find a consensus on how to react to globalization, which promised more to some of the core countries than to others.

In the region as a whole, South Africa accounts for less than one-third of the population but for more than 75 percent of the gross domestic product (GDP). Its economy is 3.4 times larger than the combined economies of the other members of the SADC, and 13.5 times larger than the second largest economy, that of Angola. Economists[1] have suggested that South Africa occupies a position in Africa

Table 2.1. Southern Africa GDP per capita 1984

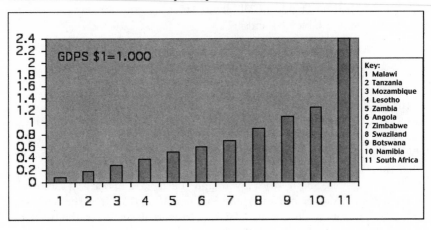

Table 2.2. Comparisons: South Africa, Southern Africa, and Africa, 1980s

	South Africa as % of		Southern Africa
	Southern Africa	Africa	as % of Africa
Surface area	20	4	20
Population (1990)	38	6	15
GNP (1986)	78	17	23
Export value (1988)	73	20	28
Import value (1988)	84	23	28
Installed electricity generating capacity (1988)	77	36	47
Electricity generated (1988)	89	54	60
Telephones in use (1987)	89	—	—
Cereal production (1988)	58	12	20
Maize production (1986)	58	26	45
Tractors in use (1987)	82	34	41
Motor vehicles in use (1987)	89	35	40
Paved roads (1987)	63	—	—
Rail lines (1987)	56	27	43
Coal mined (1985)	99	98	99
Cement produced (1987)	82	15	18
Steel produced (1987)	96	72	75

Source: Africa Institute of South Africa, Pretoria.

similar to the United States within the global economy. While the United States accounts for 26 percent of global GDP, South Africa accounts for about 44 percent of Africa's GDP (see Tables 2.1 and 2.2).

South Africa and Its Neighbors

The SADC's progenitor, the South African Development Coordination Conference (SADCC), was set up in 1980 by the Frontline African States as a bulwark against the apartheid regime's massive trans-border assaults. The SADC was established in August 1992, and was joined by the new South Africa two years later. It has twelve member states: Angola, Botswana, Lesotho, Malawi, Mozambique, Mauritius, Namibia, South Africa, Swaziland, Tanzania, Zambia, and Zimbabwe.

The Common Market for Eastern and Southern Africa (COMESA) has links with some SADC members—Botswana, Malawi, Mozambique, and Lesotho (the latter two withdrew in 1997). The COMESA's original membership extends south from Kenya and Uganda. Its main aim is to promote a free-trade area all the way down the east coast of Africa; but so long as it fails to win over South Africa and Botswana, its future remains unsure.

Frustration over this division with the COMESA and over the SADC's unsteady performance led to the creation in 1997 of an interim "parliamentary forum" composed of the SADC's core members. Initially it was not intended to be a parliamentary legislature with power to take binding decisions. Two of the principle issues before the "parliamentary forum" are questions of trade and South Africa's growing regional economic hegemony. Until the future of the parliamentary forum is decided, a separate body of political heads has been entrusted with monitoring political and military developments.

In a further development in February 1998, the SADC signed an agreement with three other continental regional economic groupings —the Economic Community for West African States (ECOWAS), the Intergovernmental Authority on Development (IGAD), and the COMESA—to coordinate their approach to Africa's problems of debt and development. Salim Salim, the secretary-general of the Organization of African Unity (OAU), described the agreement as a significant step in implementing the Abuja Treaty's objective to establish a single African Economic Community. It remains to be seen what role South Africa will play in promoting this important initiative, which would provide a leading edge to Thabo Mbeki's vision of African renaissance.

The SADC's agenda focuses on technological development, transformation of production organization, and subregional trading blocs. South Africa's contribution since joining the SADC has been unspectacular, probably because of its caution in not wishing to be seen as a dominating "new boy" member. But this explanation is not entirely convincing. Pretoria has clearly been having difficulty in deciding its own role as the engine of the region. Another possible reason for its foot-dragging is that countries like the United States have shown an interest in sign-

Table 2.3. Ratification of SADC Protocols as of January 1998

	Immunities and Privileges	Shared Watercourse Systems	Energy	Combatting Illicit Drug Trafficking	Transport Communication and Meteorology	Trade	Education and Training	Mining
Angola	●							
Botswana	●	●	●	●	●	●	●	●
Lesotho	●	●	●	●				
Malawi		●			●			
Mauritius	●	●	●	●	●	●		
Mozambique	●							
Namibia					●			
South Africa	●	●						
Swaziland	●	●	●			●		
Tanzania	●							
Zambia	●							
Zimbabwe			●					

ing a free-trade agreement with South Africa but not with the SADC as a whole. By January 1998, South Africa had ratified only one of the eight protocols adopted by the SADC. It was the only member that failed to ratify even the elementary protocol on immunities and privileges, which ensures the free movement of SADC officials within the region when traveling on a special passport. By mid-1998, only Botswana had ratified all eight protocols, as shown in Table 2.3.

It is difficult to read the mind of the South African government on the SADC and the other regional organizations. On the one hand, there is the reluctance to engage seriously with the SADC; and on the other, there are speeches like that delivered in February 1994 by the foreign minister, Alfred Nzo, who is also chairman of the SADC's Council of Ministers: "It is a matter of grave concern to me that at this stage of our cooperation we are still somewhat far from achieving the collective self-reliance necessary to make our region a major player in the global market."[2]

While seemingly dragging its feet, South Africa used its economic credibility and international prestige to press for financial assistance for SADC members. This approach was first shown in April 1998, when Vice President Thabo Mbeki was on an official visit to Japan. He pledged South Africa's surety for approved loans to SADC countries. As a beginning, his delegation gave guarantees for a $240 million loan for an aluminum smelting plant in Mozambique.

South Africa's Military and Economic Strength

South Africa's potential military strength is greater than that of the combined military forces of the other eleven countries in the region; the emphasis is on *potential,* for two reasons. The first is that budget cuts have reduced expenditure on the army, both personnel and weaponry, by over half (54 percent) since the African National Congress (ANC) came to power. A large part of the huge inherited war machines—tanks, aircraft, large guns, ships, and submarines—was either mothballed or left in a defective state.

The second reason for the deterioration in the strength of the South African Defence Force (SADF) is the altered priorities of the ANC government, which allocates 64 percent of its national budget expenditure to social services and education. Year by year, efforts by the Defence Ministry to halt the cut in military expenditure and to buy eight corvettes and two submarines needed to protect the nation's fishing grounds from foreign factory ships had been held up by the ANC caucus in parliament until mid-1998. Aside from the shift in National Budget priorities, the government displayed a lack of political will to become militarily involved even in peacekeeping efforts in the continent. For example, South Africa refused to provide any military units to help maintain order in the former Zaire after the overthrow of President Sese Seko Mobutu . Its approach to intervention in African conflicts is twofold: a preference for diplomacy over intervention; and a declared policy of making forces available only as part of an initiative by the OAU.

South Africa has also refused to participate with a number of other countries in the African Peacekeeping Initiative brokered by the United States. For all these reasons, South Africa, unlike Nigeria, has for the first time opted not to convert its potential military strength into effective power despite even urgent appeals for assistance by two of its SADC partners—Mozambique and Tanzania. Both had requested naval support to help protect their fishing grounds, which are being ravaged by foreign fishing factory ships. When South Africa refused Mozambique's request, the Maputo regime successfully invited Iran to supply submarines and corvettes. Tanzania subsequently warned it might have to follow suit. So, although South Africa is against foreign navies assuming a role around the continent's coasts, its own military stance has resulted in defeating this objective.

However, as the country with the largest arms industry in the continent, South Africa can, and does, play a military card by choosing its clients, thereby taking sides in conflict situations. But the role of arms deals has strong critics in the ANC on the principled ground that dealing in weaponry is immoral. For example, Jan van Eck, a former ANC member of parliament, wrote after the discovery that arms had been sold to the Rwanda government that "it is time we de-legitimize the use of force to settle political differences and re-legitimize the use of dialogue and negotiations. This was, after all, the essence of the so-called South African miracle."[3]

South Africa's economic outreach into and beyond the subregion grew substantially after the ending of apartheid, and shows every sign of continuing to do so. This economic outreach takes different forms: promoting two-way trade (all of it favoring South Africa), capital investment in African commercial firms, industrial enterprises, tourism, and, especially, mining and oil exploration. The list of South Africa's involvement in what has been described as "a constellation of Southern African economies led by private capital," enjoys the active encouragement of the South African government through its macro-economic Growth, Employment, and Redistribution (GEAR) policy.

Notwithstanding the acute shortage of investment capital at home, Africa has become a magnet for South African investment. Although the SADC and the near-captive Southern African Customs Union (SACU) provide the fastest growing markets for value-added exports—45.5 percent growth from 1990, 94 percent for the SACU alone—exports to the rest of the continent have begun growing even faster since the late 1980s—increasing from 27 percent in 1994 to 48 percent in 1995.

Many of South Africa's largest conglomerates, banks, and financial institutions have found openings for investment in some twenty countries in the north—from Mali and Ghana in West Africa to Eritrea, Kenya, Uganda, and Tanzania in the east, as well as tourist ventures in Indian Ocean islands, including the Comoros, Seychelles, Mauritius, and Madagascar. The countries of greatest immediate interest are Angola because of its oil and mineral resources, and the Democratic Republic of the Congo (formerly Zaire) with its huge potential for mining development. But even a country of relatively smaller economic interest like Ghana has attracted six of South Africa's biggest companies, like the mining giants Anglo-American, De Beers, and Gencor, and Standard Bank, in ventures ranging from gold mining and mineral exploration to banking. Zambia has attracted an even wider spread of commercial and financial interests, ranging from banking and brewing to shopping, milling, and tourism. In every country in the continent the sign is hung up, "South Africans Welcome," replacing the old forbidding sign of apartheid days: "No dogs or South Africans." The downside of South Africa's rapid economic expansion to its north is the growing imbalance of trade and investment with some of its SADC partners.

So far, and for the foreseeable future, this imbalance is the major cause of worry between South Africa and countries like Zimbabwe, Namibia, and Zambia. It is difficult, as yet, to see how the trade imbalance can be rectified, or what the political outcome will be if South Africa (like Japan in its trade relations with the United States) continues to be a net beneficiary of trade and capital investment in southern Africa. One predictable consequence is that the region may become polarized between an increasingly industrialized South Africa and an increasingly agricultural region to its north. This is already the trend, but if it worsens, incomes in the region will become more sharply unequal and employment opportunities in the largely agricultural societies will shrink, with the inevitable result that the pressure of immigration into South Africa will become more intense.

Networks and Corridors of Regional Integration

South Africa has already played a role, and is likely to play an even greater role, in advancing the SADC's rather tardy progress toward integrating roads and other communication systems in the region. It is able to use its technological superiority and its greater capacity to attract foreign capital to promote its own economic and security interests as well as to help its neighbors by hastening regional integration in the subcontinent. The Maputo Corridor—which is an ancillary to the earlier, more rudimentary Beira Corridor linking the south of Zimbabwe to Mozambican ports—was begun in 1997. It is planned not only as a road and rail link but also as a Spatial Development Initiative (SDI) involving public and private partnerships. Its aim as described by Paul Jourdan, South Africa's special projects coordinator, is to link up developing areas with economic potential. The corridor runs from Witbank, about 100 kilometers from Johannesburg and on the fringe of the East Rand gold and coal mining area, to the port of Maputo in Mozambique. Its design includes a new national toll road; industrial projects like the Mozel aluminum smelter; tourism attractions; agricultural projects like the Bushbuckridge coffee plantation; mining projects like the Tzaneen ilmenite plant, as well as gas and slurry pipelines. Two rail networks will link the corridor to Zimbabwe and Swaziland to facilitate the flow of trade between them and Mozambique. Eight more SDIs were on the drawing board in 1997. The aim of SDIs—according to the transport minister, Mac Maharaj, "is to promote investment opportunities and ensure optimal working relationships between the private and public sectors."[4] Amplifying this aim, Paul Jourdan said the objective can be spelled out in a four-letter word: Jobs.[5]

Another corridor is projected to link Namibia's Walvis Bay port to Angola's port at Namibe—and then on to Techamutete near Cassinga, the location of the region's biggest iron ore mines. Namibia, which is leading this project, seeks to make Walvis Bay the main port on the southwest Atlantic coast.

South Africa's flourishing electricity state corporation, Eskom, slated for privatization, has made considerable progress in developing a subcontinental grid system linking South Africa, Zimbabwe, Namibia, Botswana, and Mozambique, with the further aim of extending it as far north as Tanzania and to the Democratic Republic of the Congo where the Inga generating complex could, if "expanded," provide power for much of Africa. South Africa played a prominent role at a pan-African conference in 1998, which agreed on the necessity for a continent-wide integrated telecommunications system. As the possessor of the most advanced technology in this field, South Africa will almost certainly dominate such an integration process.

Although one of the SADC's eight protocols emphasizes the need for a regional water plan, the only significant progress in this area is the Highlands water and electrification scheme undertaken jointly by Lesotho and South Africa, mainly to meet the latter's water needs. Although the first phase attracted considerable controversy, there was tentative agreement in 1998 to move on to a second phase, subject to International Monetary Fund (IMF) funding.

The New White Trek to the North and the Black Push to the South

Two developments call for special attention. The first is the trans-border settlement of white farmers on land offered by African governments. This new "trek" began in the Eastern Transvaal bordering on Mozambique. After the end of Mozambique civil war in the late 1980s, the Mozambican government was keen to attract the skills of South Africa's flourishing agriculturalists to reclaim ravaged land (previously farmed by the Portuguese on a cash-economy basis), and to teach Mozambican peasants modern methods of farming. This arrangement, cautiously accepted by the South African government, was formally legalized by the Mozambique government, which specified that land would not be sold but would be farmed on a leasehold basis. The successful experimental start in Mozambique encouraged mainly Afrikaner farmers to move further north, as far as Congo-Brazzaville, the Central African Republic, and Uganda, as well as strengthening their numbers in Zambia. This new pattern of settlers (now still numbering fewer than 200) differs from that of the colonial period in three ways: the new settlers do not own the land they farm; they are obliged to pass on their skills to the peasants whose community owns the land; and the indigenous governments control the numbers and conditions of the immigrant white farmers, and benefit from their contribution to the local economy and through the training of peasants.

This opening up of Africa to white South Africans can turn out to be either a breakthrough in racial cooperation, benefiting adventurous white South African farmers, subsistence peasants, and the economy of host countries; or it can turn to tragedy. Initially, however, it is an African acknowledgment of the modern skills that, hopefully, can be transferred from South Africa. (*Sotto voce:* Why is this pattern of rural partnership not happening in South Africa itself? The answer, of course, is lack of trust.)

The other important development that can test South Africa's relationship to its neighbors to the limit is immigration within the region. There is no way of accurately gauging the number of "illegal" immigrants in South Africa: guesses vary from 2 to 8 million. The lower figure is probably nearer the mark; but the larger numbers represent the pressures of those hoping to escape the penury of their home environment and threaten to impose a considerable burden on South Africa's resources—such as the cost of maintaining security to try and halt the influx across several thousand miles of porous borders with Mozambique, Zimbabwe, and Angola; the expense of court cases and of repatriating illegals; and the pressure on already over-strained health and other social services. The government is faced with a trilemma: first, its neighbors remind the ANC of the sacrifices they made in playing host to the liberation movements, which resulted in heavy damage inflicted by the apartheid regime's trans-border attacks; second, there is pressure from humanitarian lobbies; and third, there is the animosity of black South Africans toward the "illegals" whom they accuse of taking their jobs by working for lower wages, and of competing as hawkers and for housing.

When the ANC government came to power, over half a million refugees were found to have become integrated into mainly local rural communities, some of them ethnic relations. After a survey, it was decided to grant citizenship to 400,000 of them. The debate is over how many more immigrants the country can absorb at a time when social and medical services and schooling are already strained, and unemployment is running from 20 to 30 percent; and over the likely number of immigrants if the door is not shut. The bright spot in this anguishing situation is that there is so little xenophobia. Nevertheless, there is already a problem, which threatens to become more acute. South Africa's much poorer neighbors (other than Botswana) look to an ANC government for benevolence; but like all governments, the ANC argues that benevolence begins at home.

Unless conditions improve in South Africa's neighboring countries, the problems of "illegal" immigrants will continue to grow as they have in Europe and the United States. It is an issue requiring regional cooperation if it is to be prevented from becoming a serious divisive issue within the region.

Diplomatic Leadership

For the three decades of the apartheid era, the region's diplomatic leadership was in the hands of the presidents of the Frontline African States—notably Julius Nyerere, Kenneth Kaunda, Robert Mugabe, and, until his martyrdom, Samora

Machel. After 1994, President Mandela stamped his personality on the region's foreign relations—a role taken over by his successor, Thabo Mbeki, who is the
confident champion of an African renaissance.

South Africa has punched well below its weight in its relations with the rest of
Africa, reflecting Mandela's personal style of leadership as well as that of his dauphin,
Thabo Mbeki, who quietly assumed the role of de facto foreign minister. Apart from
Pretoria's tactical decision not to throw its weight around, its foreign policy has
been distinguished by three main features: loyalty to the OAU; promoting regional
stability; and establishing cordial relations with countries like Cuba and Libya that
had supported Umkhonto we Sizwe's armed struggle, despite opposition from the
United States. Nevertheless, this did not impede the development of special relationships with the United States and Britain even though neither had special claims
to ANC friendship because of their policies in the most difficult days of the anti-
apartheid struggle.

The declared base of the ANC's foreign policy was "friendship to all, and refusal
to allow others to prescribe who should be the friends of the New South Africa."
The single exception to this all-inclusive policy was Taiwan, not because it had col-
luded with the apartheid regime, but because the Republic of China was potentially a much more important trading partner, while its support would be crucial
when the United Nations increases the permanent membership of the Security
Council to which South Africa aspires. None of these foreign policy objectives
conflict with those of Pretoria's regional partners.

Although a number of appeals were made to Pretoria to mediate in African
conflicts, South Africa responded only twice. The first was to offer police intervention, with Zimbabwe, in support of a joint mediation effort in Lesotho where
a split in the ruling party threatened the kingdom's security

The second intervention was of a different order. Mandela staked his personal
reputation when he played a lone hand in an effort to persuade General Mobutu
and Laurent Kabila to arrange an orderly transfer of power in Zaire. When his effort failed, Mandela led the field in giving unqualified recognition to Kabila as president. Because of the role played by Tutsis in Kabila's victory and continued Hutu
resistance in both Rwanda and Burundi, the entire Great Lakes area was plunged
into a dangerous crisis, which also drew in Uganda and Tanzania. South Africa continued to play a prominent mediation role in trying to establish security in the area.
Zaire (renamed the Democratic Republic of Congo) is seen to be of exceptional
economic and security importance to South Africa, but despite their strenuous mediation efforts, Mandela and Mbeki have found they lack the regional power to corral the warring parties.

▼▼▼▼

South Africa is a pivotal country in the continent. Depending on its success in maintaining political stability at home and achieving steady economic growth, it could

play an important part in helping to shape the continent's future, by demonstrating the value, necessity, and possibility of achieving a constitutional, inclusive, tolerant, and democratic political system through negotiations. It already inspires the programs of opposition parties in non-democratic states, and enables them to hold up South Africa as a model.

South Africa has demonstrated the value of a joint effort by the government and the private sector in promoting the country's economic interests; together they have succeeded in establishing a foothold for the country's business, financial, and industrial interests across a wide swathe of the continent, as well as in creating possibilities for a new inter-Africa trade pattern.

While most African countries warmly welcomed this new source of capital and enterprise, the downside has been to arouse suspicions among some of South Africa's closest neighbors about a perceived danger of a hegemonic economy threat to the development of their own economies, especially to their secondary industries. This is, perhaps, the single most likely source of possible disharmony within the region unless South Africa can find a way of harmonizing its expanding economic interests with its political and security interests as the regional power.

Unless there is a complete shift, as yet unforeseeable, in its military stance, South Africa is unlikely to play a military role, à la Nigeria, except, possibly, to contribute modestly to an OAU peacekeeping operation, and to provide naval ships to help patrol the seas around the subcontinent against illegal fishing. For the present, its approach to conflict situations like that in the Great Lakes area is based on its own experience: to put its faith in negotiations. But what if negotiations fail and the subcontinent's security becomes threatened?

So far from playing the Big Brother role in its region, the dominant attitude of the ANC is to maintain a low political profile and to discourage all military intervention. It is not easy to conceive that this position would hold should serious disorder break out in any of the border states and could be seen as a threat to South Africa's own security. At the close of the first five years of democratic government in May 1999—the Mandela era—there was reassuringly no evidence of any political pressure groups within the country pushing for the new South Africa to play a hegemonic role in its region.

To sum up, South Africa's three major interests in the continent are to help promote security in African states through support for possible OAU and SADC political, or peacekeeping, initiatives; to expand its trade and investment; and to promote regional integration through cooperation in infrastructural projects such as its imaginative Corridors of Peace.

NOTES

1. Patrick McGowan and Fred Ahwireng-Obeng, in *Global Dialogue* (Johannesburg, 1997).

2. *Business Day* (Johannesburg), 6 February 1994.

3. *Cape Argus* (Cape Town), 6 August 1997.

4. *Business Report* (Cape Town), 12 July 1997

5. *Business Day* (Johannesburg), 14 August 1998.

PART II.
COUNTRIES

3. | South Africa
Transition to Majority Rule, Transformation to Stable Democracy

Kenneth W. Grundy

On 10 May 1994, Nelson Mandela took the oath of office as the first president of the "new" South Africa. His inauguration marked a celebration of the end of a long and exhausting struggle to achieve a non-racial political regime and the beginning of an equally difficult and protracted process of state- and nation-building that is intended to lead eventually to the realization of a stable democracy.

Although such historical passages are significant, they cannot hide the fact that politics in South Africa, as elsewhere, is an ongoing process. Such dynamism must be appreciated before the analyst can begin to comment on the "success" or "failure" of a government or party or people in achieving their expressed goals. That said, it is possible to pronounce South Africa's decade of the 1990s a success. The diminution of political violence, the relatively peaceful transfer of power, the continuation of the transformation process, albeit painfully slow, can be regarded with pride and promise. These profound changes, tangible, practical as well as subjective, give the South African polity a special place in the annals of democracy, race relations, and Africa. But South Africa's membership in the community of democratic states is by no means complete and secure. This chapter seeks to address the tortuous process of social transformation, juridical transition, and further transformation. It is an interactive process in which base social changes contribute to political changes, which lead to further transformation that feeds further political change, and so forth. At each stage, the distribution of power changes, the political ground shifts, and the outcomes may differ with the intentions of the parties.

The Shifting Basis of Power

Long before the apartheid regime in Pretoria ever hinted at a willingness to negotiate a transfer of power or even a readiness to share power with the black majority, powerful socio-economic forces had been building that eventually made such concessions difficult to deny. Internal demographic and economic transformations had been set in motion that contributed to an inability of the white minority to hold on to power indefinitely. Perhaps the regime might have endured longer, but the price would have been a more persistent garrison state, a greater toll in blood and treasure for its own constituency, a willingness to suspend any pretense of defending "western, Christian values," a growing hostility from the world community, and a further decline in economic competitiveness and eventually in white material comfort and security. When, in August 1979, the prime minister warned his ruling National Party (NP) that South Africans must "adapt or die" and other white leaders said that "apartheid is dead," they were merely verbalizing the fundamental crisis in the apartheid state. In Antonio Gramsci's words, "the old is dying and the new cannot be born." The words of NP leaders were uttered as a rationalization for their penchant for cosmetic changes. But the fact remained: underlying revolutionary changes confronted the regime with dilemmas and provided its tormentors with opportunities they eventually exploited successfully.[1] And, of course, such objective changes prompted new perspectives on the future, themselves adding to the momentum for transformation.

Structural Economic Changes

The first of these changes worth considering were fundamental structural transformations in South Africa's economy.[2] South Africa's modern economy got its competitive start from mining, particularly gold mining, an industry that quickly became concentrated in the hands of a few firms and that raised itself to a level of almost unchallenged political power in the country. Mining depended on a migrant contract labor system that suppressed black wages. It also attracted Afrikaners to the cities in supervisory jobs. The whites on the mines were relatively well paid but still vulnerable to the vagaries of the economic cycles elsewhere in the world.

The agriculture sector was slow to commercialize and depended on land policies and labor tenancy that maintained at the bottom cheap, unskilled labor. Despite various government schemes to support white farming, commercial agriculture failed to prosper and whites moved from their farms to the cities, as did "superfluous" black farm workers, some of whom also settled in the homelands.

Manufacturing industry developed rapidly after the establishment of the gold mines. By the end of World War II, manufacturing had outstripped gold mining as the leading sector of the economy, and by 1965, manufacturing's contribution to the GDP exceeded that of agriculture and mining combined. The wages of workers in manufacturing were considerably higher than those paid mine and farm workers. Although corrections in this imbalance began in the 1970s, real wages in manufacturing remained higher. Urban areas where manufacturing was concentrated were also alive with political activity. Despite the regime's fear of an African proletariat and of widespread disorder and uprising, their chosen instrument for control, segregation, proved difficult and costly in the urban areas. Pushing Africans into well-demarcated segregated areas (so-called group areas, or townships) near cities provided a superficial and, in the end, short-term solution to white fears. The schemes of grand apartheid, that is, the demarcation of all of South Africa into white South Africa (some 87 percent of the land) and the creation of tribal homelands (the less promising rest) proved to be not viable. The uncontrolled growth of the urban black population,[3] fueled by the absence of economic opportunity in rural areas and the lure of jobs, insufficient in number nonetheless, unleashed pressures that exploded in the Soweto uprising (a generic term for nationwide political protest and unrest in 1976) and the smoldering civil war throughout the 1980s.[4]

The model of the homelands as labor reservoirs that were supposed to absorb excess labor during lean economic times and supply labor on demand during boom times, and of the rest of South Africa as essentially a white state in which black people reside in segregated group areas at the behest of the white power structure (political authorities and employers), simply did not work. A manufacturing-based economy requires a reliable, steady and secure, literate, and technically proficient workforce, something that "Bantu education" and apartheid's insecurities did not provide. Cheap labor is not necessarily efficient labor. Production costs grew as did the costs of the effort to enforce influx control (the policy of preventing the unauthorized movement of blacks into white designated areas) and group area segregation in the towns and cities (middle-level segregation of housing within the "white" territory). What is more, blacks began to organize politically and into trade unions and began to make compelling demands on the regime for a more equitable distribution of society's rewards and a voice in their own political future.[5]

The Evolution of the Afrikaner Nation

Even the once artificially cohesive Afrikaner community was subject to changes from the time its largely rural and blue-collar electorate had carried the NP to power in 1948. Through the years Afrikaners became better educated, more bilingual, more urbanized, and more involved in higher levels of finance, the professions, commerce, and industry. The very success of the Afrikaner nationalist policies aimed at bringing economic self-reliance to its people had sown the seeds of its own disintegration. The institutions of Afrikaner nationalism—the NP, the Dutch Reformed churches, the Broederbond, and a variety of social and cultural bodies—began to reflect the more open and diverse character of Afrikanerdom.

The NP, in particular, found itself increasingly the voice not of the rigid platteland farmers, but of the rising urbanized, university-trained, professional/commercial/industrial elite. And as the NP changed, segments of the Afrikaner population abandoned it, to the right, including the Herstigte National Party, the Conservative Party, and various para-military factions, and to the center, including the Progressive Federal Party and the so-called New Nats.[6] What once had been virtually automatic and comfortable NP majorities among the white electorate now became increasingly vulnerable. Many Afrikaners seemed to be losing faith in the rightness of their cause because now they viewed South Africa's social realities from a variety of perspectives, race being but one of them. The old cate-chisms of apartheid seemed, to many, dated and unconvincing. And those at the top of the *volk* knew that if they were to save their nation, new political structures were required.

The NP regime at first resisted the calls for reform articulated from within the system by the liberal minority parties and from outside by black radicals. By the late 1970s, however, even top government officials seemed prepared to entertain diluted reformist ideas, chiefly as a sop to obviate the need for more radical polit-ical concessions. Such "cosmetic" change was little more than a flexible or en-lightened (*verligte*) defense of the status quo. Reform from above, without the ac-tive involvement of bona fide popular, progressive black leaders would not suffice. Few popular black resistance leaders were prepared to accept the government's promises as good faith efforts to transform South Africa. The P. W. Botha reforms, such as the constitution of 1983 with its tricameral legislature and its more pow-erful state presidency, various trade union and local government reforms, and greater efforts to provide better services in selected communities (designed to defuse po-tentially explosive conditions) failed to lower political temperatures. But these re-forms inadvertently contributed to the buildup of pressure on government and on the economy. More black workers had a greater share of the disposable income. More were acquiring skills on which the modern economy depended, and although blacks were still disproportionately disadvantaged by the system, that system's de-pendence on them grew.

Rising Black Resistance

By the mid-1980s, the economy of South Africa had hit a wall. A combination of conditions contributed to a deep recession. These included a fall in gold prices beginning in 1982, balance of payments deficits, and the coming due of unprece-dented levels of foreign indebtedness, prolonged drought, mounting inflation, and rapid increases in unemployment, especially among those under age thirty, lead-ing to deep frustrations among the school-age population. School enrollments grew; graduates and school leavers streamed onto the job market (225,000 each year). Pressures on the urban poor were compounded by increases in food costs, taxes, rent, reduced government services, and a pattern of reward for unpopular black officials who cooperated with government. The budgetary crisis was magnified by the spiraling costs for police and defense, including cross-border raids to destabi-lize neighboring regimes and the war in Namibia-Angola.[7]

The cycle of township violence seemed unending. A political protest was or-ganized. The police or armed forces, fearing the demonstration might get out of hand, tried to end it by arresting leaders or dispersing the crowds. Demonstrators were shot and killed. This meant more funerals that provided the motive for more political demonstrations that again turned violent. Each successive stage of the strug-gle raised the levels of violence and suffering, with little end in sight. The symbolic struggle was being won by the forces of resistance. This brutal cycle continued until F. W. de Klerk became state president in August 1989.

Black resistance moved in three political directions.[8] One tendency, the so-called Africanist organizations, included those grouped under the rubric of "black consciousness." AZAPO (the Azanian Peoples Organization), affiliated student, youth, women, community, and trade union organizations, and later the Pan Africanist Congress (PAC) were in this camp. They stressed black self-reliance, cultural and community pride. and later, in the 1980s, class struggle, socialism, and racial confrontation. This tendency became identified, perhaps unfairly, with the rallying cry, "One settler, one bullet."

The second tendency might be regarded as traditional or ethnic. It sought to mobilize support by appealing to separate ethnic identities. In some instances traditionalists collaborated with the regime in the context of homeland governance and politics. In other instances, their role vis-à-vis the government was not clear. Some refused homeland "independence" even as they served in official positions and took salaries and budgetary support from Pretoria. Chief Mangosuthu Gatsha Buthelezi and his Inkatha Freedom Party (IFP) in KwaZulu, and political parties in other homelands, are examples of this form of political action.

Finally, and most importantly, the bulk of the focused resistance to apartheid was mounted by organizations identified with the Charterist movement—those organizations that accepted the principles of the Freedom Charter that had been adopted in 1955 by an alliance of Congress organizations. The successor to those organizations is the African National Congress (ANC), but since the ANC was illegal and operating in exile in the 1970s and 1980s, a less centralized coalition of organizations, to one degree or another following the guidelines established by the ANC and in close contact with that party, sought to unite and strengthen dissidents. They came together in 1983 as the United Democratic Front (UDF); a wide umbrella for some 565 bodies representing well over a million South Africans. This formidable but loose cluster of student, youth, worker, civic, women's, religious, and political bodies campaigned in 1983 and 1984 against Botha's constitutional "reforms," coordinating nationwide protests, consumer boycotts, rent strikes, people's education, and so forth. And in the background, giving direction to all this was the ANC in exile in Lusaka, Zambia. Its slogans and colors and symbols became the UDF's. It values and strategies were accepted by the UDF. The UDF and later the Mass Democratic Movement (a union of UDF and COSATU, Congress of South African Trade Unions), and the ANC, insofar as it was possible, coordinated their efforts. But the ANC did not control the UDF and neither did the UDF always control its own unruly affiliates. As long as they were marching in the same direction, the struggle built.

A culture of resistance became deeply embedded in the townships, particularly among the youth, a culture that in the 1990s the majority regime had difficulty containing. The ANC's determination to make the townships "ungovernable" in several respects had been realized. The insurrectionists were unable to seize power; but the regime could not end the insurrection and return to the apartheid order of the early 1970s. It was neither war nor peace. The regime held the military power; the resistance possessed the legitimacy. And the country was bedeviled by rising levels of crime, political violence, economic stagnation, and despair. It reached a point where neither side could see a total victory, no matter what resources it threw into the struggle. South Africa had arrived at what has been called a "hurting stalemate."

Changing Global Configuration of Power

The cold war, coinciding with the rise of the apartheid regime, had provided Pretoria with a modicum of protection from pressures from abroad and with tacit support for their efforts to resist reform and democracy in South Africa. By claiming to be committed to anti-communism, successive NP governments were able to sidestep or to stonewall their way through repeated international efforts to end apartheid, even to reform it.[9]

As it became increasingly apparent in the 1980s that the socialist world was pre-occupied with its own internal problems and hence was not in a position to provide much assistance or encouragement to South Africa's revolutionaries, the West itself saw little reason to stand behind the Pretoria regime as it sought to resist significant change. The communist bogey in southern Africa, if ever it posed a credible threat, was demonstrably less convincing. This was further reflected in the determination of the Western powers to reach a resolution of the Angolan civil war and the Namibian independence struggle. To do that required the diplomatic involvement of South Africa, even as it became clear that South Africa had become politically isolated in the region. Pretoria was still militarily dangerous and economically weighty, but nonetheless alone and with little credibility and legitimacy. Virtually everyone but the most convinced apartheid ideologue recognized this changing distribution of power. By this point, what was needed was to break down the conviction in the NP that somehow it could avoid surrendering ultimate power. To them, the new order was negotiable. Some still felt that by dint of careful political maneuvering, they might be able to fashion a regime in which they not only "shared" power but also exercised an effective veto over substantive state decisions. Change they must, but transform, never.

When South Africans took to the streets and the regime responded not with negotiation and compromise but with further repression, the world community, including conservative Western heads of government (e.g., Thatcher, Kohl, and Reagan) could no longer justify a hands-off policy.[10] Anti-apartheid organizations in the West began to pressure institutional investors (universities, churches, local and state governments with large portfolio pension funds) to divest, that is, to sell their shares of stock in corporations with operations in South Africa. Similarly, Western corporations found it difficult to maintain relations as usual with South Africa, and calls for disinvestment followed the failure of corporate codes of conduct to lead to major changes.[11] More than one-half of the U.S. firms with direct investments in South Africa withdrew between 1984 and 1989. The "hassle factor" proved irresistible. It appeared that those favoring the economic isolation of South Africa had gained the upper hand.

The regime and its economic partners had been able to avoid comprehensive sanctions. But the international community and individual states thereof had instituted a hodgepodge of policies designed to isolate South Africa economically and to demonstrate to their own politically active citizens and to outsiders that they were doing something against apartheid. Thus, albeit reluctantly in some cases, new investments were discouraged; commercial credits and bank loans were curtailed; dealings with South African governmental agencies were tightened; and trade in gold, gold coins, fissionable materials and nuclear technologies, steel, coal, textiles, agricultural products, petroleum, some computers, weaponry, and other products was embargoed.[12] By the end of 1986, South Africa was effectively denied access to international capital markets and considerable foreign capital prepared to pull out. In addition, a wide range of social, educational, and artistic boycotts were adopted to ostracize Pretoria, and efforts were made to support opponents of the regime and victims of apartheid. The economic sanctions slowly took their toll. Trade and investment declined, and even South Africans were forced to admit that the impact, on top of the profoundly unsettling domestic situation, was to discourage long-range economic growth.

Although the economic impact of sanctions was striking, the psychological rejection was equally telling. Economic and political uncertainty destroyed the regime's confidence and determination to persist. In the words of Robert M. Price, sanctions held "the potential to alter the white minority's 'risk calculus' in respect to the issue of majority versus minority rule."[13] If they perceived minority rule as a guarantee of white material well-being, and now minority rule was contributing to material decline, then perhaps whites should reconsider their stance. Not only was South Africa hurting economically, but this economic decline denied the regime the resources needed to sustain its carrot (enhanced economic and social services for collaborators) and stick ("total strategy") approach to putting down the insurrection. The very anemia of the economy heightened popular opposition to minority rule even as it brought the regime's constituents to question the efficacy of apartheid. In reality, the domestic political balance of forces was shifting.

The Process of Negotiation

The regime's top officials realized by the late 1980s that they had to come to terms with bona fide leaders of the black community, the ANC and its representatives in prison and in exile. Sham reform, co-optation, coercion, and repression had not worked. It was no longer a matter of "adapt or die." Rather, they would have to consider sharing power under the best terms possible for the white minority, with guaranteed protections and safeguards, and, if possible, a constitutional stake in the central government and the provinces, or else they would be forced to fight a protracted civil war in which all would lose, and ultimately the regime's supporters would lose all. Ferment in the white elite and electorate did not yet translate into a new consensus resigned to majority rule, and certainly not to a new regime identified with the popular black spokespersons. Those sea changes could come only as a part of a process already set in motion and gaining momentum. A journey's end point is not always the same as the destination. In societies in turmoil, unintended consequences have a way of happening.

Contacts with the ANC in Exile

Beginning in 1985, unofficial delegations of prominent South Africans traveled abroad to meet with officers of the ANC in exile. At first, participants were largely English speakers, white outsiders. Later, Afrikaners joined the "trek" and delegations were larger. Intimate meetings became conferences, and although the government publicly sought to discourage and prevent such meetings, they continued until the ANC was "unbanned" in 1990. The meetings contributed to a new perspective on the ANC and an appreciation of a common South African-ness amongst participants. Where Pretoria had for decades demonized the ANC as violent, bloodthirsty communists determined to chase white South Africans into the sea, the treks nullified the ANC's isolation. The ANC became humanized and legitimized, and this further eroded government credibility. It also contributed to further division in the white and Afrikaner polity. In the past, Afrikaner splits had been to the right—now some were splitting off to the left, and voices within Afrikaner ranks spoke openly about contacts with the ANC and the prospect of majority rule.[14]

Prison contacts. Against this background, secret contacts between government, the imprisoned ANC leaders (especially Nelson Mandela), and the ANC in exile were initiated. At first, the thought that Mandela might die while in custody disturbed the government for political reasons. Their opening approaches sought to release Mandela conditionally, provided he "unconditionally rejected violence as a political instrument." There was also the unrealistic hope that he would accept these terms and retire to the Transkei, thereby removing himself from national affairs. The government wanted to isolate Mandela from the ANC or drive wedges in the ANC over his unilateral dealings with government. When P. W. Botha offered Mandela his freedom in January 1985 on these terms, Mandela stood firm. Yet Mandela sensed that the time had arrived for ANC-government negotiations.[15]

While in the hospital for prostate surgery in November 1985, Mandela was visited briefly by Minister of Justice Kobie Coetsee. Mandela proposed talks about talks to Coetsee, but their next meeting did not take place until June 1986. This longer session was followed by silence from the government. Meanwhile, Mandela had visits from various outside parties, including a high-powered delegation of "eminent persons" from the Commonwealth. In addition, Mandela was taken on drives around the Cape Town area by prison officials. Eventually, at Coetsee's direction, a committee of senior officials, including Dr. Niel Barnard, head of the National Intelligence Service, began meeting with Mandela in May 1988. Their discussions ranged widely over issues such as the armed struggle, the nature of the ANC and its relations with the South African Communist Party (SACP), nationalization, the Freedom Charter, majority rule, and minority rights. These talks went on in the midst of unprecedented civil unrest, states of emergency, and growing international pressure on Pretoria. All along, Mandela sought to keep the ANC leadership informed about his contact with government and to ascertain the ANC's positions on these matters.

In December 1988, Mandela was moved to a cottage on the grounds of Victor Verster Prison in Paarl, where he was permitted frequent meetings with diverse political actors. He pressed Coetsee for a meeting with P. W. Botha, which came in the form of a courtesy call on Botha at Tuynhuys in July 1989. One month later Botha resigned as state president.

Mandela's high-level secret meetings with the negotiating committee continued. Government gestures, including (at Mandela's insistence) the release of ANC prisoners without conditions, enabled Mandela to prepare for a December 1989 meeting with the new state president, F. W. de Klerk. And this led to Mandela's celebrated release on 11 February 1990, after de Klerk's 2 February statement to parliament lifting the bans on the ANC, the PAC, the SACP, and numerous other "illegal" anti-apartheid organizations. As de Klerk said, "the time for negotiation has arrived." Mandela himself had outlined for de Klerk a "road map" for such negotiations.

Thus began a long, complex, often frustrating, seldom direct, but ultimately successful negotiated trek toward the handover of power from the minority NP government to a new, popularly elected Government of National Unity. It also marked a process of transition from a political struggle characterized by mass mobilization and confrontation (armed struggle and "total strategy" were the chosen modes of competition throughout the 1970s and 1980s) to a process chiefly relying on negotiation, symbol, propaganda, and coalition building.

Paralleling the national negotiations over the transition, the constitution, and the central institutions of state was a process throughout the country of negotiating forums at all levels. Many had been put into place before Mandela's release. In fact, they really gained momentum with the 1979 legislation that legalized black trade unions and ushered in collective bargaining. Negotiations were a major modus operandi in public affairs during and since the final stages of the overt struggle. But their efficacy and saliency grew after national negotiations had been legitimized. Practically every significant issue at all community levels was addressed by these often ad hoc procedures. Considering the rigidity of racial divisions and political structures during the earlier decades, this was an extensive and magnificent exercise in democracy, a useful educational and trust-building preparation for the larger issues that were to come.[16] In most instances, they involved diverse stakeholders, including government officers and established economic interests, as well as the "community" and progressive forces. And it was usually an interactive process in which participants regularly consulted with and sought mandates from their constituents. In these extensive negotiations an emerging civil society and a culture of democracy began to take root.

The National Negotiations

In Mandela's first year of freedom, the ANC and the government reached agreement on three accords—the Groote Schuur Minute (May 1990), the Pretoria Minute (August 1990), and the secret D. F. Malan Accord (February 1991). Essentially, these were the sorts of ground-rule understandings necessary to create a favorable environment for the constitutional talks to follow. For example, the ANC agreed to "suspend" the armed struggle and the government to release all political prisoners, allow the return of exiles, and amend the security laws.[17] But through 1991 this promising beginning began to break down. Despite a National Peace Accord (September 1991) signed by representatives of fifty political parties, business organizations, and public interest groups, there were signs of discord. Mandela, de Klerk, and Chief Buthelezi endorsed the accord, but it had little impact on the escalating violence.

On 20 December 1991, delegates from eighteen organizations assembled in Johannesburg for the CODESA I sessions (Convention for a Democratic South Africa). It was the broadest cross section of South African leaders ever to meet. But there were conspicuous absentees. Chief Buthelezi did not attend, although he sent an IFP delegation. The PAC and the right-wing Conservative Party and the extra-parliamentary radical right refused to take part. Participants were able to arrive at a Declaration of Intent that committed them to an undivided South Africa, peaceful constitutional change, a multi-party democracy with universal suffrage, separation of powers, and a bill of rights. They also agreed generally that there should be some form of interim government in place until a democratically elected body could draft the new constitution.

Although politics during the negotiation phase of South Africa's transition were different, a far cry from "armed struggle" and "total strategy," residual elements of confrontationalism were important to the process. The outcome of political negotiations at each stage still depended on the power of the participants. But how would one mobilize and express that power, without delegitimizing one's opponent's stance, thereby eroding trust? In such complex dealings, how can a party object to a minor point? The use of power tended to be crude (the protest, the boycott, the demonstration) and held the risk of threatening the negotiation process itself. For whites, the March 1992 referendum was such a symbolic gesture, in which 68.7 percent of an 86 percent turnout gave F. W. de Klerk a mandate to continue negotiations with the ANC.

At each successive venue and forum the question endlessly presented to the public was, "Are the negotiations on or off?"[18] Categorical choices are hardly the stuff of effective negotiation over complex issues. It necessitated decision-makers who were determined to see their way through to agreement.[19] In sum, negotiators sought to mobilize their supporters without bringing down the entire enterprise. Thus, the publics were largely excluded from the subtleties of the negotiations and were seen as armies in reserve to be deployed to threaten disruption. Keeping their constituents ready, holding the hotheads in tow, these were the twin responsibilities of leadership from 1990 until the 1994 elections. The end point was a democratic constitution, but the popular political culture was still confrontational. Miraculously, the compromisers succeeded despite important setbacks.

In early 1992 CODESA collapsed, thanks to the government's failure to prevent violence in the townships and possibly its or some of its operatives' collaboration in the unrest. For eight months no public negotiations took place. After a massacre of thirty-eight people at Boipatong, the ANC withdrew from the negotiations and launched a campaign of "rolling mass action." The state of emergency worsened, violence increased, and the ANC's policy culminated in an ill-advised march on Bisho, the capital of the Ciskei, and the shooting deaths of twenty-eight demonstrators.

But this renewed confrontation did reveal the conflicting short-term goals of the many parties. Inkatha and the NP sought agreement over the main points of a constitution before an elected constituent assembly could be put into place—that is, tried to force agreement that would tie the hands of a popular assembly. They also wanted to prolong the transition for at least ten years. The ANC, fully confident of dominating any elected constituent assembly and opposed to being locked into an interim government of indefinite duration, resisted too many pre-election commitments. It wanted to leave itself a relatively free hand to write the constitution and to control any future government.

There were costs for all sides in not negotiating. The economy flagged, violence worsened. Polls showed that NP popularity lessened and ANC support grew. Still, ANC organization was weak, almost entirely dependent on COSATU and the remaining UDF affiliates, and the ANC leaders knew this.[20]

Secretly, the ANC held bilateral talks with the government. Cyril Ramaphosa and Roelf Meyer took the lead, and by the end of 1992 announced a deal that was bitterly denounced by the excluded IFP. All parties would begin drafting an interim constitution and, at the NP's insistence, a bill of rights. These documents would include the essential principles on which the final constitution would be based. The ANC insisted on elections for a constituent assembly that would in turn serve as an interim parliament for five years (the NP's demand) and the basis for a government during which the final constitution would be drafted.

The ANC accepted an executive power-sharing arrangement for five years, too. All parties that received more than 5 percent of the votes were to be offered cabinet posts in proportion to their electoral strength. But Mandela was determined to reject anything that could be construed as a minority veto, and pressures on de Klerk from abroad as well as domestically eventually forced him to drop his various proposals for such an arrangement. A revolving presidency, an "inner cabinet" in which all major figures must agree on policy—none of these schemes were acceptable to the ANC. A persistent ANC and de Klerk were determined to have a deal. Even the April 1993 assassination of one of the ANC's most charismatic populists, Chris Hani, could not derail the negotiations. Indeed, the ANC used Hani's assassination to accelerate the pace of talks and to force the NP to establish a date for national elections. On 23 June 1993 the Multi-Party Negotiating Forum announced that elections would be conducted on 27 April 1994. Inkatha and the Conservative Party walked out of the talks in protest, and they never returned. But their absence served to expedite the work at the World Trade Center, where the forum established an array of committees to disaggregate the issues.

In session after seemingly endless session, South Africans debated, reasoned, and compromised their way toward agreement. Debating with one's enemies is tough enough. Afterward, each side had to return to its partisan caucus and convince it of the reasons for compromise. It was most difficult, and those who led their teams often were accused of "speaking the language of the enemy."[21] Meyer became the target of NP hard-liners and eventually, in 1996, quit the NP to create his own United Democratic Movement (UDM). Ramaphosa left ANC politics after the election to go into business, although he returned to the ANC national executive in 1997.

The interim constitution took shape. Its general outline included an enforceable bill of rights, the distribution of power between the national and provincial governments, a constitutional court to resolve disputes and to ensure that the constitution would be paramount, and a separation of powers at both central and provincial levels. It was to be a liberal democratic constitution, and its broad outlines were endorsed by both the NP and the ANC. A number of smaller compromises were meant to appease the NP and its constituents. The jobs and pensions of the largely white civil service, for example, were guaranteed. Some issues remained unresolved, deferring the final dispensation to the elected Constituent Assembly. Particularly the details of the devolution of power or power sharing were left pending. Although on the surface the NP seemed to make the most important compromises, the ANC was also prepared to live by the spirit of national unity.

Mandela was firm on insisting that the cabinet's decision should be decided by majority vote, but the wording was nonetheless vague. Both sides insisted that they got what they wanted—the ANC majority rule, the NP government by consensus. On balance, the ANC got its way.

In the end, de Klerk was outmaneuvered, largely because the shifting balance of forces in South African politics was to his disadvantage. He was not converted to majority rule. He knew, however, that he had little choice and hence he would have to take risks to salvage what he could. His timing was bad. He allowed his ego to get in the way. He overestimated his own party's national appeal and importance. But he did, after all, agree to move his people from a system based on minority rule to majority rule, and that was no mean accomplishment.

On 18 November 1993 an interim constitution was passed at the World Trade

Center, and with it the route to elections and majority rule was made clear. How to manage the elections now became the task of the Transitional Executive Council. A constant fear was that the militant white right posed a threat of civil war. They believed that de Klerk had betrayed the Afrikaner nation, and they seemed determined to upset the process.

Throughout 1992 and 1993, the ANC and Umkhonto we Sizwe (MK) officials had been meeting secretly with senior officers of the South African Defence Force (SADF) to assure their loyalty to the new regime. Working through General Constand Viljoen, the retired commanding officer of the SADF, the ANC also sought to make contact with the radical right, not just the Conservative Party and Viljoen's Afrikaner Volksfront, but also the militant right, chiefly identified with Eugene Terre'blanche and his Afrikaner Weerstandsbeweging (AWB), the largest para-military supremacist organization. The talks with the extremists got nowhere. In fact, the AWB virtually committed political suicide just before the elections. They had alienated some sympathetic followers by violently occupying the World Trade Center for a few hours while negotiations were in progress. Later they demonstrated their incompetence and unreliability by trying to prevent the overthrow of Lucas Mangope's government in Bophuthatswana, against Mangope's wishes. On 4 March 1994 AWB men drove through the streets of Mmabatho and Mafikeng shooting at bystanders and precipitating a Bophuthatswana army revolt, the very thing Mangope had sought to avoid. Flashing across television screens that night was the execution of three AWB white men by black troops, a sobering image for any who had expected white armed resistance to be easy.

The AWB bubble was burst, and General Viljoen immediately decided to register his Freedom Front candidates for the April elections. The real danger of military disruption of the election had fallen away. Despite Viljoen's unrealistic insistence on the creation of a white homeland, a *volkstaat,* a modus operandi was established. But no agreement on a *volkstaat* was forthcoming. The ANC was not prepared to divide South Africa territorially. It even had misgivings about federalism and relatively strong provincial governments. To give in to the Afrikaner nationalist demands would strengthen Inkatha's hand in demanding an autonomous KwaZulu-Natal.

The General Election of 1994

Almost until the last moment the question still remained: would there be an election?[22] Violence in KwaZulu-Natal was extensive, and Buthelezi's refusal to participate made it impossible for voting to take place in that region without his cooperation. One "independent" homeland had been wrenched into line (Bophuthatswana), the Freedom Front decided to contest the election, and the Ciskei government collapsed on 22 March 1994. Pressure mounted for Buthelezi to participate, too. On 19 April, a week before the first day of polling, Buthelezi took the

Table 3.1. 1994 and 1999 General Elections Results for the National Assembly

Party	1994			1999		
	Votes	% Votes	Seats	Votes	% Votes	Seats
African National Congress	12,237,655	62.6	252	10,601,330	66.35	266
National Party (NNP)	3,983,690	20.39	82	1,098,215	6.87	28
Inkatha Freedom Party	2,058,295	10.54	43	1,371,477	8.58	34
Freedom Front	424,555	2.17	9	127,217	0.80	3
Democratic Party	338,426	1.73	7	1,527,337	9.56	38
Pan Africanist Congress	243,478	1.25	5	113,125	0.71	3
African Christian Dem. Party	88,104	0.45	4	228,975	1.43	6
United Democratic Movement	—	—	—	546,790	3.42	14
United Christian Dem. Party	—	—	—	125,280	0.78	3
AZAPO	—	—	—	27,257	0.17	1
Federal Alliance	—	—	—	86,704	0.54	2
Afrikaner Eenheidsbeweging	—	—	—	46,292	0.29	1
Minority Front	—	—	—	48,277	0.30	1
12 other parties	159,296	0.82	0	28,866	0.18	0
Totals	19,726,579	100.00	400	15,977,142	100.0	400

IFP into the elections, launching an active campaign that indicated that perhaps all along he or his followers had intended to participate. Across the partisan spectrum, everyone except the Conservative Party and the AWB was now aboard. The way was clear for South Africa to go through with its first open exercise in electoral democracy.

For the record, from 26 through 28 April (the 29th in some areas), nearly 20 million citizens voted. Nineteen parties offered candidates for the National Assembly (a legislature that also sat jointly with the Senate as a constituent assembly to draft the new constitution). Nine provincial legislatures were also chosen. Because only white voters and a limited number of Indian and colored citizens had had any direct experience with national elections, people needed instruction on the mechanics and the meaning of the process, and reassurance about how the secret ballot worked. The electoral machinery—ballots, 80,000 voting booths at 12,343 voting stations, 5,000 election observers (2,000 from abroad), and 190,000 election workers—had to be coordinated by a newly formed Independent Electoral Commission (IEC), which had been given just three months to prepare for the polling. The logistics became even more complicated when the IFP joined at the last minute. Confusion and irregularities were commonplace. Over 500 complaints were registered with the IEC. Voter turnout was some 87 percent. In the end, the election satisfactorily met the demands for determining a consensus government.

During much of the campaign, political rhetoric was heated and not always open. Even though the elections were declared "free and fair" by a variety of observer and monitoring teams, multi-party democracy was under considerable strain.[23] Electioneering depended on mass mobilization, rhetoric was militaristic, there was little tolerance of opposing views, and each party sought to exclude its opponents from what it regarded as its home turf. Rallies were disrupted, signs destroyed, people intimidated. In the Western Cape, ANC versus NP contests were tense. In KwaZulu-Natal, the IFP-ANC fault line was dangerous. Rather than a dispersed multi-party pattern to the vote (seven parties gained seats in the assembly), there tended to be concentrations of single-party communities—a checkerboard pattern of voting rather than a salt and pepper one, with diverse voting sprinkled throughout the country. And, as expected, the parties tended to appeal to racially or ethnically exclusive constituencies. Subsequent surveys indicated that 94 percent of the ANC's voters were black African, 80–90 percent of the Democratic Party (DP) voters were white, and 85 percent of IFP support was African, mostly Zulu. The Freedom Front and the PAC were virtually 100 percent white and black, respectively (see Table 3.1).[24]

It was not the healthiest distribution of seats, especially with one party so close to garnering the two-thirds majority that would enable it, single-handedly, to write and amend the constitution.[25] In addition, the ANC was the only party that did well in all provinces. It captured power in seven provinces, and narrowly lost to the IFP in KwaZulu-Natal and to the NP in the Western Cape. In four provinces it had more than 80 percent of the vote, including 91 percent in the Northern Transvaal. Trends since the election indicate a weakening of opposition parties and a slight falloff in ANC support.[26]

The Government of
National Unity and Beyond

To compound the focus of power in parliament, major parties that would otherwise be regarded as the opposition were co-opted according to terms of the constitution into a quasi-coalition, known as the Government of National Unity (GNU). By joining the cabinet, they became responsible in a fashion for government policy, a policy largely determined by the ANC majority, and were thereby finessed into cooperation with the dominant party. As one scholar asks: "Where's the political opposition to be found in the new constitutional arrangements?"[27]

Presumably, by joining the government, smaller parties might be able to influence cabinet decisions. But they cannot prevent the ANC from pushing through policies should it desire. The operative clause in the interim constitution (in place until 1999) reads: "The cabinet shall function in a manner which gives consideration to the consensus-seeking spirit underlying the concept of a government of national unity as well as the need for effective government" (Art. 89 [2]). The majority party will, in the end, have its way. As Mandela said: "Majority rule will apply—we just hope we will never have to use it."[28]

In a proper coalition government, the votes of various minority parties may be necessary to enable the coalition to withstand challenges in parliament. Thus the minority parties have leverage by which they may pressure the dominant party to compromise. But in South Africa, the GNU was not, strictly speaking, a coalition government, and the chief incentive for the ANC to temper its policy preferences was to give the appearance that government was united. In the end, the majority party did not need the minority parties' votes for its government to stand. Until the defection of the NP from the GNU in May 1996, the opposition was little more than 23 MPs from those parties too small to be included in the GNU. By accepting an interim constitution in which only those parties gaining less than 5 percent of the vote were excluded from cabinet, South Africa assured itself of a very marginal opposition in parliament. With the dominant party garnering over 62 percent of the vote, being in opposition would have been difficult enough. But neutralizing another 31 percent of the voters in a GNU made the idea of a loyal opposition almost laughable.

That being said, despite the strains of continuing IFP-ANC violence in KwaZulu-Natal and the awkward situation of the NP signing on to policies that its constituents clearly disliked, all in the interest of cooperation and reconciliation, the GNU worked surprisingly well. The ambitious Reconstruction and Development Programme (RDP), the cabinet's chief policy achievement, emerged from the cabinet with widespread support and without crippling conflict. Few really divisive issues were introduced, no crises threatened to bring down government, and legitimacy and stability persist—the center held.[29]

In a fashion, the NP's early departure from the GNU in May 1996 might be regarded as an incremental step toward the sort of regime that replaced the interim constitution after the 1999 elections, a straight parliamentary majority rule system. As Vincent T. Maphai argues cogently, power sharing served South Africa well, as a confidence-building device for all concerned and as a requirement for stability. The very conditions that led to the unbanning of the anti-apartheid organizations and to the negotiated settlement also led to power sharing. Both the ANC and the NP accepted power sharing for strategic reasons. They saw it as a temporary provision, since neither could govern without the assistance of the other. But they were careful to include a "sunset clause" by which power sharing could be ended. As Maphai put it: "While government by grand coalition was necessary to bring about South Africa's transition to democratic rule, its continuation would hinder the institutionalization of the new regime."[30] Power sharing has served its usefulness, and now it can fall away.

The June 1999 national elections continued the pattern of overwhelming support for the ANC and widespread division among opposition parties (see Table 3.1). With a Government of National Unity no longer formalized constitutionally, the opposition party with the greatest parliamentary representation, the DP, chose not to participate in government. The IFP, however, has opted to be represented in what can be regarded as a coalition cabinet. It holds three of twenty-seven ministerial appointments. The DP went from seven to thirty-eight seats in parliament, from 1.73 percent to 9.56 percent of the vote. The UDM, in its first national contest, garnered 3.42 percent for fourteen seats. Although the ANC's proportion of the vote went up to 66.35 percent, it failed by one seat to obtain a two-thirds majority in parliament.

The big losers were the New National Party (formerly the NP), whose vote count fell from 20.39 percent to 6.87 percent and whose seats were reduced from eighty-two to twenty-eight. The Freedom Front, the PAC, and the IFP also lost support and parliamentary seats. In 1994 only six opposition parties made it to parliament. A dozen opposition parties hold seats after 1999.

Some Obstacles to a Smooth Transformation

Although numerous questions remain unanswered about the polity and its operations, the political transition from a race-based polity to one based on majority rule is nearly complete, yet subject to tensions. The non-racial democracy is in its infancy and still requires nurture and development. The next stage, according to the government, is to work toward social transformation, that is, to enable the great mass of disadvantaged South Africans to participate in the embryonic democracy by providing them with the skills and economic wherewithal and the social services they need to become contributing citizens. Social transformation is a vague and ill-defined concept, one about which there is a good deal of argument as to purpose, priority, and strategy, even within the ruling ANC alliance. The barriers to the realization of transformation are many.

KENNETH W. GRUNDY

National Power versus the Provinces

One of the issues about which the CODESA broke down in May 1992 was federalism. At base this had been a core dimension of constitutional rivalry: how far should the oppressed majority go to protect the political rights of the minority, and should those minority rights be protected in territorial terms?

The interim constitution and the 34 Constitutional Principles set out in schedule 4 of that constitution and adopted on 18 November 1993 sought to speak to the division of provincial and central government powers and responsibilities.[31] Among other things, these principles call for the constitution to define and protect provincial powers and boundaries.[32] National and provincial levels of government shall each have "exclusive and concurrent powers" and "appropriate and adequate legislative and executive powers and functions that will enable each level to function effectively." It goes on to set out how powers shall be allocated to each governmental level, and it calls for decision-making power to be placed where such decisions can be taken most effectively, in terms of rendering services. However, even the "exclusive" powers of the provinces are bounded by conditions under which national government is given the authority to intervene. Nonetheless, the central government is not to "exercise its powers so as to encroach upon the geographical, functional or institutional integrity of the provinces." All levels of government shall have constitutionally defined fiscal powers and functions and a "constitutional right" to an equitable share of revenue collected nationally.

These principles were open to various interpretations, and the issue troubled the Constituent Assembly. So, while on the surface South Africa appears to have a federal structure, a model not originally favored by the ANC, in reality the provinces have been granted relatively limited powers.[33] One can debate whether this is a decentralized unitary state or a centralized federal structure. A "faintly federal system" and "interdependent spheres" are other terms one hears applied. Simply put, what emerged is a mixed constitution.

The powers of the provinces and the role of the National Council of Provinces remained outstanding issues up to the deadline for the final draft, 10 May 1996. Agreements were reached through mutual adjustment of positions. Since the ANC had been the overwhelming victor in the 1994 election, their perspective on center-periphery relations won out. What emerges is a relatively centralized state. The powers granted to provincial legislatures are limited. "Exclusive" powers (schedule 5) are marginal. The "concurrent" powers (schedule 4) are more significant. They include agriculture, education, housing, police, tourism, trade, traditional leadership, and welfare. Strictly speaking, these are not "powers," but rather joint responsibilities. In regard to concurrent powers, the national government invariably provides the framework legislation; the specific content is left to the provinces. In cases of conflict between national and provincial legislation, uniform national legislation takes precedence (section 146). Section 100 allows central government (i.e., the national executive) to assume responsibility for a province when such province "cannot and does not fulfil an executive obligation in terms of legislation or the Constitution." It empowers the national government to step in to maintain "minimum standards of rendering service." This is exactly what the Presidential Review Commission recommended in March 1998, when it called on central government to intervene in the affairs of two provinces facing financial crisis.[34] Interestingly, both provinces are controlled by the ANC.

Provincial governments have practically no revenue-raising capacity (only gambling taxes and vehicle licensing). The central treasury supplied 96 percent of their combined budgets in 1997, and that, in turn, is the single largest item of governmental expenditure. That distribution is established according to a formula determined and administered by a national Financial and Fiscal Commission and upon which the provinces are well represented. But that does not please all provincial administrations. In 1995–96, for example, some 60 percent of national tax revenues were generated in Gauteng, yet Gauteng was allocated only 15 percent of the revenue pie.[35] When provinces overspend, the central government pays and misses its deficit targets. Occasionally provinces borrow from banks and incur debt. In reality, the provinces can do little on their own and, what is more, may hinder the delivery of services promised by the dominant party and the central government. The ANC may yet rue the day it ever compromised on even this weakened form of federalism.[36]

While some advocate giving provinces tax-raising powers, a few provincial administrations demonstrate little financial competence. Provincial officials lead in the number of cases of alleged public-sector corruption currently under investigation. A government audit of provincial administrations found the system chaotic and riddled with indiscipline, nepotism, and "grossly inadequate management."

The entire provincial system needs to be reordered, and that would necessitate constitutional change. Even within the ANC alliance, there is little agreement on the outlines for a new provincial system. At the center they agree in general that provincial autonomy, as limited as it may be, should be curbed even more. But provincial ANC leaders challenge these negative evaluations. The existence of provinces is rooted in constitutional principles that cannot be easily abandoned. But almost daily revelations of scandal could in time alienate the ANC from its constituents.

What would the ANC need to invest in provinces to make them viable? Would the people accept the transformation of provinces into administrative arms of national government? So far, the ANC's National Executive Committee has had some bruising battles with provincial leaders in the Free State, the Northern Province, the Eastern Cape, and Gauteng, and neither side gained in popularity or acceptance. The center-provincial struggle has just begun, and this is heated even when the same party, the ANC, is ostensibly in command at both levels. Such structural problems are amplified when one party controls the national government and other parties or coalitions of parties are responsible for particular provinces—power contests of a different sort.

KENNETH W. GRUNDY

Corruption in High and Low Places

It would be hard to detail even a fraction of the alleged instances of fraud and corruption in government. Hardly a day passes when the media is not reporting allegations, investigations, and revelations about public officials exploiting their public trust for private gain. Some accounts have the ring of partisan pleading. Some have been leaked and even fabricated for political advantage. Overbilling, bribes, kickbacks, "ghost" employees, retainers for relatives, excessive overtime claims, personal use of pension schemes, departmental credit cards, and state vehicles and equipment, misappropriation of state and donor funds, extravagant travel abroad for suspect state purposes, and falsification of public documents and records are just a few of the imaginative illegal practices that have come to light. We have no way of knowing how many officials are on the take, the magnitude of their avarice, or which modes of corruption are most common. All we can see are the outlines of practices that, at least all acknowledge, are serious and corrosive of governmental performance and legitimacy. Early on, Nobel Peace Prize winner Archbishop Desmond Tutu criticized the high salaries officials were awarding themselves. He quipped that the new government stopped the gravy train only long enough to clamber aboard. The ANC didn't like his words, but eventually Mandela forced pay cuts.

The fact remains that corruption has not reached the levels of elsewhere, nor has it sullied more than a few political careers. It seems most prevalent at the provincial level and most commonplace in ministries and departments with a large number of government contracts to let (e.g., education, housing). But it is growing. According to Transparency International, South Africa dropped from 21st place in 1995 to 23rd place in 1996 to 32nd in 1998 in their Corruption Perception Index. That survey seeks to measure the perceptions of the leaders of multi-national corporations.[37] It concentrated on "grand corruption," endemic and systematic graft worth millions of dollars to a country's economy.

The issue is not so much whether there is corruption, but rather what are the government and political parties doing about it. How the authorities view and act upon dishonesty sends unmistakable signals to other officials and to the people. If those at the top treat corruption lightly or, worse, protect those accused of it, it can spread rapidly throughout the polity. Is corruption a cancer metastasizing through society or is it being isolated and treated? The answer affects how the public regards its political leaders. The danger comes if the rot of cynicism sets in. If the people themselves adopt and rationalize the culture of entitlement and self-aggrandizement, then South Africa may sink into despondency.

Since South Africa is effectively a one-party dominant state, the ANC is responsible for setting the moral tone for the future. When corruption is uncovered, usually by the investigative press or thanks to politicians keen to undermine rivals, the ANC has on occasion appointed task groups and ordered audits to examine allegations. President Mandela has repeatedly called for campaigns to set the country on a "new moral footing."[38] Party leaders have spoken against "careerism" and the trend by some to carve the good life for themselves out of politics and government service at the expense of the masses. In November 1994 the ANC adopted a party Code of Conduct. It created a disciplinary committee to enforce the code. Failure to sign the code is supposed to amount to an MP forfeiting a place on ANC electoral lists. Elected officials are required to declare their family interests as well. Ministers have additional restrictions, such as surrendering corporate directorships, placing shares in "blind trusts," and playing no role in for-profit institutions.[39] Disclosure provisions were later extended to all MPs. The President's Office is also drafting legislation on ethics in government. This would include a statutory code of conduct for members of the executive at both national and provincial levels.

Despite its verbal commitments to clean government, the ANC has done little to remove from office and punish some high-profile culprits. A few provincial leaders have worked to root out sleaze and rampant bureaucratic overspending. Although these are exceptional cases, the results have not always been successful. In some instances the ANC has rebuked and even censured the whistle-blowers for alleged failure to follow ANC disciplinary procedures, and has used lateral movement ("redeployment" is a favorite word) as a way of silencing critics from within. There is a tendency for top figures in the party to rally around an embattled colleague rather than to make an example of him or her, or merely to remove the accused discreetly until charges can be examined. The public is looking for more outward evidence that the government is committed to combating the problem. There is still time to set a forthright moral tone from top to bottom.

Delivering on Promises

As its first major order of business, the ANC sought to consolidate and rationalize into a single comprehensive policy recommendation all of the many social welfare and upliftment proposals that it had championed. This was to be the culmination of its years in the struggle. The document that emerged was known as the Reconstruction and Development Programme (RDP), a set of goals held together by a number of policy promises and program proposals. The ANC asked to be judged in terms of its capacity to provide jobs, shelter, safe water, health care, nutrition, relevant education, and safety and security to all. Some very specific targets were set: for example, 200,000 housing units per year for five years, clean running water for 12 million, access to electricity for an additional 3.5 million households, free health care for all children under the age of six.[40]

Once in power, in a series of meetings, forums, consultations, and discussions, each ministry began to give flesh to the ANC's programs and general policy guidelines. Usually congeries of stakeholders were invited to become involved in the process. This was participatory democracy as envisioned by the ANC. In housing, for example, banks and lending institutions, construction firms, suppliers, developers, landowners, NGOs, union leaders, community and civic activists, the homeless, and government officials participated. Nearer to the drafting stages, top government officials sought to resolve differences and to ensure that all stakeholders were on board. It was, when it operated according to plan, an energizing experience that sought to galvanize all actors for the implementation stages. The reconstruction and development of South Africa will require a massive and complicated effort. Choices will have to be made and priorities ranked. Conflicts of interest are inevitable, and some groups and individuals will gain and others will lose out. To its credit, the GNU was determined to include almost everyone in the bargaining process. This was not policy from the top down.

But once the RDP became government policy, the actual fulfillment of its objectives proved to be more problematic. A cabinet level minister without portfolio in the President's Office was supposed to coordinate the overall program and to establish priorities and timing. Despite large budgetary appropriations, the government's program was marked by delays and wheel-spinning at the planning and initiation stages. In almost all areas, performance fell below goals. The capacity of the state to mobilize the necessary resources, the less-than-inspired contributions of key stakeholders, the sluggish national economic performance, the general inadequacies of the infrastructure and human resources left many expectations unfulfilled. It is not the limited financial resources alone that account for the shortfalls. The overall goals of the RDP—to satisfy basic needs, to develop human resources, to build the economy, and to democratize state and society—are widely accepted. These are all to be tackled in a "people centred," "people driven" way. The sheer magnitude of the undertaking overwhelmed the state's shallow managerial pool.

As is to be expected, performance has been uneven. On the plus side are a primary health care program that has already reduced infant mortality, half a million new electrical connections per year, three million people supplied with piped water, a slow spread of home ownership among the relatively poor, and wage increases that outpace the declining inflation rate. On the negative side are still high levels of crime and unemployment, poor school performance, a growing apathy toward government, and a parlous economy that is not generating enough revenue to finance the RDP projects. Given the magnitude of demands, it would be hard for any government to claim success.

With its less than sterling delivery, the RDP team was reorganized by the government in June 1996. Henceforth, RDP projects are to be funded and administered by the line ministries (e.g., housing, health, education). The government also realizes that unless it can turn around the economy, it will not be able to deliver on its promises. While it continues to put a positive spin on performance, it also downplays the earlier concentration on the RDP. It calls the RDP a "policy framework, not a blueprint, not a sacred text whose every sentence has to be implemented to the letter."[41]

The RDP had been the document on which the ANC contested the 1994 election. It had been "more than a vague list of election promises, and less than a fully elaborated programme of governance."[42] In June 1996 the government introduced with far less consultation a "macro-economic policy" that many said marked the eclipse of the RDP. It is not so much that the ANC has abandoned its social agenda.

Rather, it seeks at this time to lower expectations. The two programs dovetail. Growth, Employment and Redistribution (GEAR) is ostensibly the macro-economic framework to revitalize the economy and thereby to provide the funding for the RDP.[43] GEAR, in a nutshell, is a free-market oriented, economically liberal set of guidelines designed to encourage foreign and domestic investment and to stimulate economic growth. It emphasizes the need to achieve a 6 percent annual growth rate. GEAR resembles a voluntary structural adjustment program that seeks fiscal and budgetary discipline, privatization, and downsizing the state bureaucracy and civil service.[44] Many on the left in the ANC alliance and outside of it do not like the thrust and lean of GEAR and reject the secretive process by which it was created, and the fact that it was presented to the ANC national executive as "non-negotiable." COSATU and the SACP insist that "no policy is cast in stone," and they each put forward alternative economic documents.

COSATU produced its own "Programme for the Alliance" and threatened to reconsider the union federation's support for the ANC in the 1999 elections unless its program was accepted. It backed away from that threat. COSATU's program proposes the expansion of state housing financed through public borrowing, a national health program, comprehensive social security and public job creation, and an overall enlarged public sector—in other words, the welfare state alternative. The SACP tends to take a middle position between the fiscal conservatism of the ANC and COSATU's socialist model. It talks of the need for a "developmental state" to adopt some liberal precepts of "good governance." It could be accused of playing both sides of the street, agreeing to one course of action in ANC executive meetings and then as SACP officeholders criticizing ANC policies.

Jobs and Crime

South Africa, the Johannesburg region in particular, has long had a serious crime problem. It got little press largely because most crimes took place in the black townships and black Africans were the most frequent victims. In the apartheid years, the police were tasked to protect the regime and its principal beneficiaries, the whites. Government merely had police contain the black inhabitants so that they posed no threat to the nearby white areas. Large parts of the townships were "no-go" areas, effectively run by gangsters. The police and organized township criminals avoided one another. But once apartheid was ended, the new government was forced to confront crime problems its predecessor ignored. Gangs still control swaths of the former townships,[45] and organized criminals now also prey on the affluent white community. Burglary, car theft and car jacking, holdups, and muggings became more frequent and violent. The whites do not silently suffer their newfound attention. The world now knows about South Africa's crime problem.

In the early 1990s, Johannesburg came to be regarded as the murder capital of the world, with a per capita murder rate nearly 100 times that of a typical European capital and 7.5 times that of New York City. Two kinds of murders were common, political and criminal. Some 15 percent of all murders were regarded as political, the result of fighting among rival political, racial, or ethnic groups, of economic warfare with a political component (e.g., taxi wars), of conflict between citizens and the security forces, and of random and target killings by agents provocateurs out to destabilize the transition process. The rest are crimes of passion and greed. In the first years of this decade, all categories of crime except political crimes rose between 20 and 80 percent.

The rise in crime was practically inevitable. Poor black populations, lacking the basic human needs, live near affluent white neighborhoods. The old notions of order are eroding. Guns are easily available and cheap. There are 3.76 million licensed firearms in South Africa, and an estimated 4 million illegal weapons in circulation. Unemployment is rife. An entire generation of South Africans missed an opportunity for education in the 1980s. As a politicized and embittered youth, they heeded the call for revolution first, education later. Now, without skills and training, crime has become for many a reluctant career choice.

Crime increases, but the capacity of the police force to protect the populace has not improved. In 1996, according to a report by the Ministry of Safety and Security, close to 10,000 police officers were charged with offenses. Efforts to upgrade the force will take time. Some 30,000 officers have not completed junior high school. The actual level of crime may be higher than the figures indicate. So little confidence in the police exists that a 1996 crime report indicated that only some 450 out of every 1000 crimes committed were reported. Why bother?

There is no magic bullet to end the pernicious effects of pervasive crime. President Mandela has spoken of a "moral regeneration" to fight crime and solve other socio-economic challenges such as unemployment and the culture of entitlement, the idea that government and the system owes the disadvantaged free services. Why pay rent, license fees, electricity, and water bills? some ask. The state owes us these benefits. The culture of resistance that enabled the ANC to make apartheid ungovernable and to bring the ANC to power has been transferred, uncritically, to government in general. Such a generalized ethic of disobedience contributes to a fertile environment for other crimes.

The police today have had a difficult time designing and implementing a comprehensive anti-crime package. Top managers from private industry have been brought in to reorganize the police services. Modern managerial techniques are making a difference, but that has not stopped local civic organizations from calling for vigilante justice, a return to capital punishment, more stringent sentences, and tightened bail and prison procedures. In 1995 the South African Police Service Act consolidated eleven policing agencies into a single police service organized at the national and provincial levels. Crash training programs and a National Crime Prevention Strategy were launched. Reorganization, steady improvement of staff, equipment and procedures, removal of the deadwood of past regimes, greater efforts to enlist the community in police work, and a turnaround in popular attitudes toward crime, criminals, and the police are needed, coupled with an overall improvement in the economic situation. Both President Mandela and President Mbeki have criticized political opponents and the media for their tendency to exaggerate and distort the real crime situation. The fact is that, according to police statistics, the number of crimes has marginally declined, especially if population growth is factored in. The high-profile crimes of murder and attempted murder, public violence, abduction, and all categories of theft and robbery with aggravating circumstances have been reduced.

To many in South Africa there is a direct relationship between the employment picture and the level of crime in society. There is wide belief that if somehow government can manage to stimulate economic growth and create new jobs to sop up large numbers of the unemployed, violent and petty crime will naturally decline. In 1994, unemployment was estimated by the Central Statistical Service to be 32.6 percent. The rate among blacks was over 40 percent. Since then that figure has probably risen further. But the crime picture is so much in the news that a number of firms, local and foreign, have delayed decisions to invest. The tourist industry is also hurt by fear of crime. The argument has become circular—high unemployment leads to high crime, which depresses new investment, which means few new jobs, which contributes to high unemployment, and so forth. Crime and unemployment are indeed linked, but unfortunately in a negative spiral.

Where do they begin their economic renewal? In order to make South Africa attractive to investment, the ANC leadership has decided to take what one might call the IMF (International Monetary Fund) medicine. South Africa must make itself attractive by stabilizing the currency, balancing the state budget, privatizing state enterprises, and cracking down on cronyism, nepotism, and insider deals. The words "balancing the budget" cover a multitude of policies that have the short-term effect of reducing state involvement in the economy and reducing employment. The market, not government, it has been decided, must determine where money moves and how. But what this also means, in substance, is that jobs will be lost when parastatals are sold off and when government seeks to bring expenditures in line with revenues by applying modern principles of managerial efficiency.

The ANC is pulled in the direction of a low-wage economy to benefit its most vulnerable constituents. But it also finds itself eliminating redundant state jobs. This does not sit well with its alliance partners, especially with COSATU. For the moment, however, the perceived need to pursue short-term unpopular employment practices in order to make South Africa friendly to potential employers is deemed important. This is a slow, long-range approach to reconstruction, which the ANC seems prepared to stick with.[46] Rather than trying to provide for the basic needs of all, the government seems prepared for some compromises on those grand social-welfare schemes voiced during the transition period. Between 1992 and 1995 the ANC changed its economic stance significantly. Can it weather the political pressure those changed policies will unleash?

Fissures in the ANC Alliance

Indications are that the ANC will dominate politics for a long time. Although South Africa is a democracy, the ANC faces largely weak opponents, at least nationally. Unless an effective national party can emerge with wide appeal among the majority population, the ANC will stand unchallenged in this one-party dominant democracy. Parties that rule without viable opposition are tempted to abuse their power. Where will that opposition come from?[47] Many think that the most likely source of opposition to the national leadership of the ANC will come from within the ANC alliance itself.

The ANC leads a so-called tripartite alliance. Originally it consisted of the ANC and the SACP. COSATU joined later. The alliance was formed to improve the fortunes of the progressive forces in negotiations with the government and the NP and as a unified force to contest the 1994 general elections. The ANC has been historically involved in alliance politics, having led the Congress alliance of the 1950s, which brought together diverse Congress groups to adopt the Freedom Charter. There had long been cooperation between the ANC and the SACP in exile and its leaders formed interlocking networks in diverse organizations. There is an almost natural blending of skills and strengths, so much so that it is hard to tell who is ANC and who is SACP. Of course, it is possible to belong to both organizations at once.

In the tripartite alliance, the ANC needs the organizational capacities, material support, and membership of South Africa's largest trade union federation. COSATU needs a more complete policy agenda that can appeal beyond its 1.9 million members. The SACP is really a tiny organization, and reasons that its greatest impact can come by having its ideas integrated into the alliance platform. Many of the ANC's best thinkers, strategists, and most popular activists come from the SACP. Scattered throughout the polity are SACP members—large numbers of the National Assembly, cabinet ministers, deputy ministers, and provincial premiers. Its current membership is only 14,000,[48] but its real contribution to the alliance is its intellectual firepower and its legacy of unbending non-racial opposition to apartheid.

The introduction of GEAR in 1996 unleashed a firestorm of debate within the alliance. It has not died down. It is not just the content of GEAR that upsets the junior partners in the alliance, but also the way GEAR was developed and announced. Trade unionists question why they are in the alliance. If government is going to adopt "anti-worker" policies, maybe COSATU should rethink its role in the alliance and its support for the ANC-led government. One affiliate, the National Union of Steelworkers of South Africa, favored an immediate withdrawal from the alliance. The alliance had been established to bring to power a progressive, majoritarian government. Now that such a government is in place, if that government ignores COSATU's preferences in state policy, perhaps the time has come to distance itself from the alliance.

At its Sixth National Congress in September 1997, COSATU reviewed critically its role in the alliance.[49] An extensive report by its Commission on the Future of the Unions (headed by Connie September) sought to examine, among several things, the threats to unions posed by economic liberalization, and especially the irony that the government responsible for many of these economic changes is dominated by a party with which COSATU is allied. It warns that if the ANC continues its "right-wing" economic policies, the labor movement could be crushed. And it asks: how should COSATU rearrange its relationship with the ANC?

The September Report's answer is to recommend that COSATU establish greater autonomy within the alliance. "Flexible independence" it is called, which apparently means that COSATU should support the ANC when its takes progressive positions, should oppose the ANC when it adopts "anti-worker" positions, and should try to influence the ANC whenever it can. In order to strengthen its hand, COSATU must reach out to other key sectors of civil society, including the NGO movement, religious organizations, and progressive intellectuals. Although the Congress re-endorsed the tripartite alliance, it rejected GEAR but it did not demand that the ANC drop the policy. Interestingly, COSATU did vote to build the SACP and committed its funds to help finance the party and to share educational programs. This may be an effort to strengthen the left in the alliance to offset the liberal economic views there, or more significantly, to lay the groundwork for the emergence of a left-labor party. To re-endorse the alliance and to support the ANC in the 1999 elections demonstrate that for the moment the unions have nowhere to go. The ANC can expect growing protest from the unions, and the potential for disrupting the government's economic plans might jeopardize the ANC's desire to convince investors that South Africa is stable and will be a profitable outlet for their capital.

The SACP certainly wants to push the alliance leftward, too. "The kind of state that we are building needs to be interventionist, active and developmental in character." The SACP attacks the neo-liberal, minimalist conception of the state. On jobs: "we must ensure that big business does not, on this issue, turn government into a mere observer and arbiter between labour and business."[50] But without an alliance (whether it is with COSATU or with the ANC), the SACP is powerless.

For its part, the ANC is not ready to lose its ties with either labor or the SACP. It may not be ready to adopt the word "socialism" but neither has it pronounced its policies "capitalist." In reality, the ANC has not defined its economic policy definitively precisely because it is trying to satisfy a diverse set of interests. A mixed economy is about all it will admit at this point.[51] Its overall management of the economy has been liberal. But it also feels that the state must play a central role in economic growth and development.

The fact remains that tensions over policy could well lead to strains or a break. Deputy President Mbeki told a television audience during the ANC national conference that he could foresee a situation when the strategic alliance would collapse. "I think it will happen when racial issues cease to be a dominant feature and new issues come to the fore."[52] The following day, delegates reaffirmed formally the tripartite alliance.[53]

Of course, there are other sources of dissension within the alliance. Going into the ANC's Fiftieth National Conference in December 1997, there had been low morale among local and provincial delegates.[54] Open leadership battles alienated the rank and file from the national executive. The feeling was rife that the old modes of consultation had broken down. Vigorous debates marked the sessions. Occasionally the leadership's preferences for party office were rejected. But in the end, leadership got most of what it wanted and the delegates left with a renewed sense of party unity.

The ANC itself is a broad tent that includes diverse progressive tendencies, and a few non-democratic ones. Just to mention a few of the divisions: insiders versus outsiders, those who had been in exile and those who were active in the Mass Democratic Movement; Africanists versus non-racialists or Charterists, those who oppose non-Africans in important governmental and party positions and who favor a pro-active affirmative action agenda and those who feel that one's political and social contributions matter most, not one's genetic makeup; populists who favor immediate redistribution to the masses and who want to take the current leadership to task for its liberal economic policies and its policy of reconciliation versus the party's central organs of power, which stress discipline and unity. There is also some overlap among these sometimes fluid groupings. Winnie Madikizela-Mandela's failed candidacy for deputy president would appear to signal the primacy of Thabo Mbeki and the national party hierarchy, with some exceptions. Mbeki's candidates for chairman of the ANC and for deputy secretary-general both lost to popular candidates who lacked the leadership's endorsement. Thus, the election of Patrick "Terror" Lekota and Thenjiwe Mthintso shows that the spirit of dissent still lives. The organization prevailed on most issues; the rank and file showed their pluck—a healthy sign for party democracy. It is possible to envision a breakup of the ANC alliance and a reconstellation of the party system in South Africa. But for now, the realities of power make such a shift in party fortunes unlikely, indeed, politically ominous.

Some Questions about the Future: Transition Is Not Transformation

There are dozens of questions facing this new South African regime, only a few of which can be touched upon in a single chapter. Inter-ethnic relations, reliable water supply, economic diversification, educational improvement, the impact of AIDS, gender equality, civil-military relations, immigration from elsewhere in Africa, and links with organized crime abroad come to mind. Of necessity, coverage in this section is limited to topics that have been of particular and immediate interest to observers abroad, pressing topics to which the South African polity can add its unique voice.

The Truth and Reconciliation Commission

It may seem perverse to begin a section about South Africa's future with an examination of how South Africa is dealing with its past.[55] But if, at base, moving a country forward depends in large measure on the mindset of its peoples, then how people perceive of themselves matters. Do they respect and trust one another and their common institutions? Do they feel that they have a shared destiny? In fact,

South Africans have a long common history, and much of it does not easily lend itself to positive mutual reinforcement. Given the divisive character of apartheid, it is necessary for South Africans to redefine their national character, and facing up to the past is very much a part of that process.

The interim constitution stated that in order to advance reconciliation and reconstruction, amnesty shall be granted in respect to acts, omissions, and offenses associated with political objectives committed in the course of the political conflict of the past. But even more than amnesty for the perpetrators of political crimes, individual victims, their families, and the communities that have suffered as a result of human rights violations need succor. The assumption is that the truth is central to the healing process.

In June 1995 parliament passed an act enabling the creation of the Truth and Reconciliation Commission (TRC) and providing for procedures by which individuals responsible for gross violations of human rights committed between 1 March 1960 (when the ANC and other organizations were banned) and May 1994 (the inauguration of the GNU) can apply for amnesty.[56] They had to confess their political crimes if they wanted amnesty, and the commission had to be assured that their submissions were truthful and complete. Once amnesty is granted, there are to be no further sanctions against them. The TRC was at first to have a life of eighteen months, but later parliament formally extended the commission's life until April 1998. Its final, 3,500-page report went to the president in October 1998. Its publication was boycotted by the political parties, since all of them, to some extent, had been criticized therein.[57]

On the other side, victims and their relatives were encouraged to "tell their story" to a Committee on Human Rights Violations. This assumes that the very act of coming forth and unburdening oneself of the pain of victimization and human rights abuses contributes to an individual and social catharsis. Such testimony often revealed acts of abuse and the names of the abusers, some of whom themselves later applied for amnesty. In addition, although most of the victims have not requested elaborate compensation for their hurt, procedures are in place for making reparations to victims. A sum of R 100 million was included in the 1998–99 budget, and that slides to R 300 million for 2000–2001 for this purpose.

In its early days, the TRC hearings focused on victims as they offered moving and sometimes gruesome accounts of human cruelty, most of which were perpetrated by the security forces of the apartheid regime. For many whites this was an eye-opening experience, as some learned for the first time of the evil on which the old regime was based. Testimony demonstrates that the police operated only partially impeded by law and that they considered torture and murder of opponents of apartheid and the cover-up of those acts as legitimate and necessary. Many stories that had been hinted at earlier by the investigative press were confirmed. And as the hearings continued, evidence of high-level complicity in these abuses weakened the social fabric of minority rule further still. These powerful accounts led some to call the TRC "the Kleenex Commission," but witnesses confirm the healing effects on the participants and on the nation. These victim-oriented hearings ended in June 1997. Meanwhile, the commission took amnesty applications and its investigative team prepared for the hearings that followed.

The amnesty hearings proved more difficult, as some applicants resisted full disclosures. Contrition is a rare commodity. Many applicants behaved as if amnesty would be denied them; they and their lawyers sought to establish a record for a subsequent court proceeding that they assumed they would have to face. In all, the TRC received 15,000 statements from victims and over 7,000 amnesty applications. Between 10 and 15 percent of all the victims testified in public. As of October 1999, amnesty had been granted to 538 individuals. Another 5,412 applications have been rejected.

Did the TRC accomplish it aims? Not entirely. The volume of work was overwhelming and was not completed as scheduled. But as for educating the population and providing those victimized with a voice and a release, it apparently was successful. Still, there were numerous complaints about the TRC and its work. Only around one-half of all South Africans feel that the TRC was fair and unbiased.[58] The NP and the Freedom Front complained incessantly of the TRC's "witch-hunt" mentality. To them, the TRC did little to investigate abuses committed by members of the liberation movement and too easily granted amnesty to ANC "terrorists." The moral dilemma is nettlesome. Many feel that the evil of apartheid justified the violence of its opponents and that the abuses of those fighting for majority rule cannot be equated with the acts of those defending apartheid. Likewise, many on the left feel that the TRC was too soft on the applicants for amnesty and too preoccupied with reconciliation instead of with justice, as they see it. In reality, most perpetrators of political crimes did not bother to apply for amnesty, thumbing their noses at the entire process.

It would appear that the TRC was evenhanded and that large segments of South Africans were not pleased no matter what position the TRC took. A mid-1997 poll showed that 31 percent said the TRC favored or was hostile to some parties. Only 18 percent of the whites were satisfied with the TRC's fairness. Will the TRC achieve its larger purpose, to heal the nation? A mere 40 percent thought the TRC would bring South Africans closer together, and only 17 percent expected it to render people more willing to forgive. Some 24 percent expected people to feel more angry and bitter, and 23 percent said the TRC would cause more hurt and pain. And the TRC barely scratched the surface of the long-running violence in KwaZulu-Natal; so one can expect deep, almost irreconcilable wounds among IFP and ANC and now UDM victims there. In no major category of the population did a clearcut majority appear to believe that the TRC achieved reconciliation. These are depressing results after more than two years of high-profile testimony and hearings.

Affirmative Action

There are other ways in which the inequities and cruelties of the past can be addressed, as the majoritarian state establishes its policies and institutions.[59] The instruments of state power have been transferred to the new regime. But they do not yet reflect the character of the populace or the polity. Systematic efforts are afoot to change their composition. It is a matter of bringing in at managerial levels more personnel from traditionally disadvantaged communities as well as redressing racial imbalances among the rank and file. Of course, one important compromise leading up to the transfer of power was to guarantee the jobs and pensions of those employed by the apartheid state. Those terms present a major hurdle to rapid turnover, as do the slow economic recovery and the determination by economic planners to reduce budgetary deficits, including their desire to downsize the bureaucratic and security establishments.

This is one of those politically sensitive issues that seems to please no one—it never seems fast enough for those on the outside, and it is always unsettling for those historically privileged. Because of legal constraints, government seems most comfortable focusing first on the private sector of the economy. Its affirmative action proposals come in the form of the Employment Equity Bill. As it currently stands, each firm that employs more than fifty people must devise a transformation plan detailing how it intends to bring blacks and women into its workforce at various levels. That plan is then to be submitted to a national commission made up of various stakeholders who will accept the plan or require revisions to it. Once the plan is accepted, a company must meet its affirmative action targets or be subject to punitive fines. There is, however, the further danger that if a firm retrenches whites to meet the government's affirmative action requirements, it could face claims for unfair dismissal based on racial discrimination. It could be in a no-win situation. Corporate South Africa is critical of the bill and seeks to have it amended. But throughout the country, firms are being forced to rethink their employment practices. Most fear that they will not be able to identify and compete for the scarce pool of educated and experienced black talent. Hence, they complain of lowered standards and weakened competitiveness. Although many firms are making major efforts to alter the racial composition of their workforces at higher levels, it is not likely that many can move fast enough to satisfy political elements who feel responsible for favoring their impatient constituencies.

Transforming the governmental service employment picture is a more immediate challenge, since the people expect the ANC government to make good on its promises of jobs. Yet the ANC is hemmed in by a number of obligations, some of its own making. To begin with, governmental employees may not be removed simply because they were in place during the apartheid years. "Sunset clauses," job guarantees, and pension protection for white civil servants and security force members had been agreed to at the ANC's November 1992 executive committee meeting. These were seen as necessary conditions to get the white establishment to cooperate with the transition. If those positions are not available, where does one place new state employees without merely ballooning the budget? In fact, in the present mood of fiscal discipline, posts are being eliminated in almost all departments and agencies at national and some provincial establishments.

Meanwhile, at the top levels of the civil and security services efforts must be made to promote and to appoint blacks and women to key managerial positions, and to provide more than the appearance of affirmative action. This is particularly important in regard to the arms of state, where the government finds it embarrassing to have to rely on top officers from the ancien régime, especially since their unquestioning loyalty cannot be certain. By 1999 there were 195 generals and brigadiers of whom only 51 were black. Only one-third of all soldiers with rank are black, and only 16,000 former MK and APLA fighters had been incorporated into the South African National Defence Force (SANDF) in the first four years since integration began. There has been a pattern of reliance on natural attrition, severance packages, and retrenchment mechanisms, a slow, expensive, and politically unacceptable pace.[60] Similar efforts at the South African Police Service have produced similar results, a slow and unsatisfactory pace of change. It is a time of uncertainty for all groups, as the wrongs of the past are addressed, but fitfully.

The Mandela Factor

To many, the retirement of Nelson Mandela was a major turning point in South Africa's political history. Handley and Herbst labeled it the "postheroic phase" of its history.[61] In that Mandela is such a monumental figure, universally admired and respected, projecting wisdom and warmth, his decisions to step down as ANC leader in December 1997 and as president of South Africa at the end of his five-year term after the 1999 elections were seen by many, especially those outside South Africa, as worrisome.

The fact is that in many respects, even before the 1999 elections, the succession process was nearly complete. And it had been amazingly smooth. The ANC's Fiftieth National Conference in December 1997 provided ample evidence that the handover of power had been consummated. Thabo Mbeki was in firm command of the party's structure, and he demonstrated his capacity to oversee the consensual style of its executive organs and the disciplined "democratic centralism" of its unitary hierarchy.[62]

Before Mandela stepped down from the ANC's leadership, he also devolved to Deputy President Mbeki many of his political and presidential functions. Mbeki early on became Mandela's point man on key policy issues. Mandela, as president, was the master manipulator of symbols. Although he had become a figurehead rather than a hands-on president, he had accomplished this by choice. At the fiftieth conference Mbeki was officially named the ANC's candidate for president in 1999. Some dislike the idea of the president effectively choosing his own successor—not because they do not trust Mandela, but because it set a precedent they fear, in lesser hands, might lead to a self-perpetuating oligarchy. A politician's critical persona is stifled when his or her career depends on kowtowing to higher-ups.

In spite of some grassroots dissent from the delegates, and the return of the former ANC secretary-general, Cyril Ramaphosa, once seen as Mbeki's main rival for the presidency, as the largest vote-getter for the sixty directly elected seats on the national executive committee, the ANC hierarchy is firmly in Mbeki's camp. A good deal of this process was engineered by Mandela and Mbeki, together, as they sought to avoid an ugly party struggle for succession. Related to this process has been the much criticized practice of bringing people into government based on personal contacts and demonstrated loyalty to Mbeki. Insiders are favored. Clients are expected to stand by their patrons, no matter what. In some instances this means that blunderers and charlatans occupy important positions and are hard to displace. It also means that a number of talented people have been pushed out of active party roles.

That being said, there is wide agreement that Mbeki is a gifted politician, one able to organize and see actions through to completion. His management of national affairs as Mandela divested himself of presidential tasks had been deservedly praised. He lacks Mandela's charisma, his flair for the symbolic, and his capacity for fairness and sensitivity. Mbeki's style as president is different—more efficient, businesslike, more market friendly, less patient, less empathic. Things will get accomplished. To their credit, South Africans are prepared for the succession. That too can be attributed to Mandela's prescience. Unlike other leaders on the continent, Mandela realized that South Africa is more than one leader or even one major party. One hopes that he passed this mature perspective on to his successors. Part of Mandela's very greatness was his capacity to diminish the importance of the Mandela factor for the future.

Conflicting Visions of the Future: The Economic-Political Nexus

To say that the ANC leadership contest for the moment has been decided chiefly speaks to the personalities and the structural makeup of the party and most probably of the government. It tells us little about the policies that the government will feature and to what ends. Certainly, the ANC cannot be accused of failing to articulate its aims and objectives. Just look at rule 2 of the ANC constitution. Those aims include the end of "all forms of discrimination and national oppression," the transformation of South Africa into a "united, non-racial, non-sexist and democratic country," the elimination of "the vast inequalities" created by apartheid and national oppression, the building of a loyal and common society in which the diversity of the people is recognized, the promotion of "economic development for the benefit of all," and so forth.[63] And look at the numerous discussion papers, the party debates, and resolutions at all levels. In one respect the ANC is held afloat on a sea of words. And many in South Africa are not impressed by the ANC chorus, when the lyrics sung can mean different things to different people. While the goals are widely shared, even among those outside the ANC, there is little consensus on how best to achieve them.

Under Thabo Mbeki expect no major policy shifts. Continuity in leadership, he says, means continuity in policy. Yet he warns of a backlash against reconciliation unless whites do more to eliminate the apartheid-era disparities. "We are not one nation, but two nations," Mbeki has said. Some analysts hint that with Mandela's retirement the emphasis on reconciliation will be subdued. Even so, the substantive policies in place suggest continuity over all. And the thrust of those policies of late has been to encourage investment, entrepreneurship, economic stability, and steady growth. In doing so, the ANC is inclined to reduce government's role in the economy and to promote the private sector. Since the ANC is firmly in control of parliament and hence government, from where would the incentive come to change? There are some serious efforts made toward redistribution, especially in RDP projects, but increasingly the caution of managers is taking precedence over the ambitions of the revolutionaries. The ANC may want to call their programs "people centred" and to say that they are designed to "transform society" and to "liberate the vast mass of the poor from the shackles of poverty." But the government seems to be going about it in a way that first benefits those in a position to invest. In that sense there is a disconnect between ANC rhetoric and ANC performance. The activists mouth the words and even in some cases draft the programs; the managers run the show or else muddle through.

One might ask, will the fruits of an economic recovery come fast enough? And will they be shared widely enough to enable the polity to be stabilized? To begin, one might ask the question whether there has been an economic recovery. The real growth rate for 1997 was only 1.7 percent, down from 3.1 percent in 1996. A massive influx of foreign investment has not happened to fuel growth, and so much of government's plans seems to depend on achieving a growth rate of 6 percent by 2000. The prospects for that don't look good.

Profound problems bedevil the economy, and few look solvable fast and easily. They include high unemployment, a public debt the service of which sops up around 21 percent of the budget, slack gold prices that threaten to shut down marginal mines and to put another 100,000 out of work, weather conditions that put agricultural productivity in jeopardy for a few years, an unproductive and expensive labor force, and a world economy that suffers from the Asian slump. South Africa's commodity prices will fall under greater competition. South Africa's export picture had improved markedly over the last four years, but the world economy may reduce exports. Despite the advantages South Africa has over other African countries—a diversified economy, a rich and varied lode of minerals, a modern transportation and communications infrastructure, sophisticated financial institutions, and a well-trained and experienced cadre of professional lawyers, financiers, engineers, educators, and media workers—the confluence of problems does not suggest an early economic turnaround.

Increasingly, South Africa's black population is becoming stratified according to income and wealth. At the bottom are the unemployed, the squatters, those underemployed, and even some fully employed but who barely survive economically. Some 53 percent of black South Africans live below the $60 per month poverty line. With some 400,000 new job seekers coming onto the market each year and just 30,000 new jobs being created in the formal sector, this population segment will not shrink.

Then there is a growing middle class—clerks, teachers, civil servants, small business owners, skilled and semi-skilled workers—with an increasing stake in stability. Many have become property and home owners and some resist what they regard as unsettling gestures toward the poor. In general, they are doing fairly well, their salaries outpace inflation. As the white share of the country's total personal income drops (from 70 percent in 1960 to 53 percent in 1994) the black share rises (from 22 to 35 percent). Expressed another way, however, while racial inequality narrows, class inequality grows. The top 20 percent of blacks have increased their wealth significantly.[64] The middle class has become a powerful economic and political force.

Another segment of the black population has bought into the capitalist dream. In 1994 blacks owned and controlled only 0.3 percent of the market capitalization on the Johannesburg Stock Exchange. By 1998 they controlled and owned 10.3 percent.[65] These are the people in a position to cash in on the rhetoric of black empowerment—corporate restructuring, unbundling, affirmative action, strategic partnerships, cooperative agreements, and sales to black consortia of investors. Even some unions have entered into the market through corporate restructuring. Many powerful corporations, in the past exclusively white owned and controlled, are banking on co-opting black investors to their liberal conservative designs. There are a number of ways to promote black business interests, and not only do black businesses stand to benefit, the entire economy could gain.

Given the relatively recent conversion of the ANC economic thinkers to this market-based approach, there is a remarkable absence of ideological debate in South Africa. It is not so much that there is agreement as there is a voicelessness among the poor, who for so long had regarded the ANC as their voice. Many still do. The ANC tries to hold together that constituency, but the demands of governance have led it to try to shore up gross economic performance instead of making priorities of the social welfare agenda embodied in the RDP. It is a strategic decision that can be defended, provided that performance is realized.

Meanwhile, the people wait for results and some grow disheartened. Frustration with government often lacks focus and organization, and it is not easy to tell at this stage if and how these frustrations will be expressed. Who speaks for those left behind? In the current political party scheme, it would appear that no one has aggregated and articulated their interests, except for sections of the ANC. During the final apartheid years, the people (with the ANC's and the UDF's encouragement) developed a culture of protest and resistance. The ANC urged the people not to obey the white authorities. Under the slogan "Make the townships ungovernable," they called for widespread civil disobedience, boycotts, community self-defense and courts, refusals to pay rents and fees, and squatting on private and public land.

The ANC now must harvest what it has sown. President Mandela called on citizens, as their civic duty, to cooperate with government. Not all citizens comply. The ANC has without doubt made the transformation from liberation to administration. Since so far the fruits of liberation have been largely psychological, political, and organizational, increasing numbers of South Africans feel that there is an emerging gap between them and their government. Political elites at the center and citizens on the periphery are getting out of touch. The government has a limited capacity to govern, and there is a danger that it may focus on the issues that consolidate power in the center and that ignore its popular base.

What this government wants least is to be seen clashing with the disadvantaged. Yet clearing out squatter camps, collecting electricity fees, expelling students for failure to pay tuition, protecting the accused from vigilante groups, retrenching low-level government workers—these actions set up a "we-they" clash the ANC leaders do not relish.

Thus, it can be said that the ANC talks of equity and redistribution in the name of the poor, but pursues policies in the interest first of the emerging and increasingly powerful black middle and entrepreneurial classes. Contrary to external opinion, the ANC has become South Africa's stable center, restraining the underclass with promises and rhetoric and some social service improvements and programs in favor of growing the economy. If a market-based economy can bring about a self-sustaining growth in South Africa, then the ultimate test of ANC intentions will come when there is something more than crumbs to redistribute. A danger is posed should those who are benefiting from these interim growth strategies become entrenched in positions where they can resist the redistribution stages of the transformation. Immediate self-interest could offset enlightened self-interest as the propelling force in the political economy. In that way, the unarticulated ideology of personal need and want and self-aggrandizement could undermine the ANC's popular appeal and its "people centred" aspirations.[66] This is not an inevitable outcome, but it is a possibility that must be guarded against.

Seldom has the economic-political nexus been so transparently linked to a country's future. South Africa has high promise of becoming Africa's economic engine and its most stable and viable democracy. But for that to occur, economic development has to happen, and just as importantly it must flow throughout society. The people want badly for their chosen government to succeed. All South Africans, with a few exceptions, are committed to the new South Africa, or so they say. Many in the ANC government have thought carefully about the sort of regime and policies they want to pursue. The question now is whether the conditions, international and domestic, will allow these policies to bear fruit and whether those in positions of responsibility have the skill, experience, and integrity to carry them out.

NOTES

1. Robert M. Price, *The Apartheid State in Crisis: Political Transformation in South Africa, 1975–1990* (New York: Oxford University Press, 1991), esp. chap. 2.

2. For background, see Alf Stadler, *The Political Economy of Modern South Africa* (Cape Town: David Philip, 1987); and Ben Fine and Zavareh Rustomjee, *The Political Economy of South Africa: From Minerals-Energy Complex to Industrialization* (Boulder, Colo.: Westview Press, 1997).

3. Paul Maylam, "Explaining the Apartheid City: 20 Years of South African Urban History," *Journal of Southern African Studies* 21, no. 1 (March 1995): 19–38.

4. For background, see Gail Gerhart, *Black Power in South Africa: The Evolution of an Ideology* (Berkeley: University of California Press, 1978); Anthony W. Marx, *Lessons of Struggle: South African Internal Opposition, 1960–1990* (New York: Oxford University Press, 1992); and Stephen M. Davis, *Apartheid's Rebels: Inside South Africa's Hidden War* (New Haven, Conn.: Yale University Press, 1987).

5. See Rob Lambert and Eddie Webster, "The Reemergence of Political Unionism in Contemporary South Africa?" in William Cobbett and Robin Cohen, eds., *Popular Struggles in South Africa* (Trenton, N.J.: Africa World Press, 1988), pp. 20–41; and Jeremy Baskin, *Striking Back: A History of COSATU* (Johannesburg: Ravan Press, 1991).

6. Kenneth W. Grundy, "White Politics in Transition: Multidimensional Uncertainty," in R. Hunt Davis, Jr., ed., *Apartheid Unravels* (Gainesville: University of Florida Press, 1991), pp. 33–57.

7. Kenneth W. Grundy, *The Militarization of South African Politics*, rev. ed. (Oxford: Oxford University Press, 1988).

8. Tom Lodge and Bill Nasson, *All, Here, and Now: Black Politics in South Africa in the 1980s* (New York: Ford Foundation-Foreign Policy Association, 1991).

9. Kenneth W. Grundy, *South Africa: Domestic Crisis and Global Challenge* (Boulder, Colo.: Westview Press, 1991), esp. pp. 75–122.

10. Price, *Apartheid State*, chap. 7.

11. For example, for British-based firms (Code of Practice, 1974), U.S.-based firms (the Sullivan Principles, 1977), or European Community-based companies (1977). See Grundy, *South Africa*, chap. 4.

12. See Elna Schoeman, comp., *South African Sanctions Directory, 1946–1988: Actions by Governments, Banks, Churches, Trade Unions, Universities, International and Regional Organizations*, Bibliographical Series, no. 18 (Johannesburg: South African Institute of International Affairs, 1988).

13. Price, *Apartheid State*, p. 232.

14. See ibid., pp. 236–45.

15. This account of contacts is taken from Nelson Mandela, *Long Walk to Freedom: The Autobiography of Nelson Mandela* (Boston: Little, Brown, 1994), pp. 511–58; and Allister Sparks, *Tomorrow Is Another Country: The Inside Story of South Africa's Negotiated Revolution* (Sandton: Struik, 1994), pp. 1–67.

16. For one example of this grassroots enterprise, see Kenneth W. Grundy, "Cultural Politics in South Africa: An Inconclusive Transformation," *African Studies Review* 39, no. 1 (April 1996): 1–24.

17. Sparks, *Tomorrow*, pp. 120–30.

18. Mervyn Frost, "Democracy Delayed," *Indicator South Africa* 12, no. 1 (summer 1994): 21–26.

19. Hennie Kotzé and Pierre du Toit, "Reconciliation, Reconstruction and Identity Politics in South Africa: A 1994 Survey of Elite Attitudes after Apartheid," *Nationalism and Ethnic Politics* 2, no. 1 (spring 1996): 1–17.

20. For comprehensive coverage of negotiations until mid-1992, see Steven Friedman, ed., *The Long Journey: South Africa's Quest for a Negotiated Settlement* (Johannesburg: Ravan Press, 1993). Later events are analyzed in Steven Friedman and Doreen Atkinson, eds., *South African Review 7: The Small Miracle—South Africa's Negotiated Settlement* (Johannesburg: Ravan Press, 1994).

21. Frene Ginwala, quoted in Patti Waldmeir, *Anatomy of a Miracle: The End of Apartheid and the Birth of a New South Africa* (London: Viking, 1997), p. 227.

22. The election is reported and analyzed in Andrew Reynolds, ed., *Election '94 South Africa: The Campaigns, Results and Future Prospects* (New York: St. Martin's Press, 1994); Roger Southall, "The South African Elections of 1994: The Remaking of the Dominant Party State," *Journal of Modern African Studies* 32, no. 4 (December 1994): 629–56; Tom Lodge, "The South African General Election, April 1994: Results, Analysis and Implications," *African Affairs* 94, no. 377 (October 1995): 471–500; J. E. Spence, "'Everybody Has Won, So All Must Have Prizes': Reflections on the South African General Election," *Government and Opposition* 29 (autumn 1994): 434–55; R. W. Johnson and Lawrence Schlemmer, eds., *Launching Democracy in South Africa: The First Open Election, April 1994* (New Haven, Conn.: Yale University Press, 1996); and Robert Mattes, *The Election Book: Judgement and Choice in South Africa's 1994 Election* (Cape Town: Institute for Democracy in South Africa, 1995). An excellent review of this literature is Jeremy Seekings, "From the Ballot Box to the Bookshelf: Studies of the 1994 South African General Election," *Journal of Contemporary African Studies* 15, no. 2 (July 1997): 287–309.

23. Douglas G. Anglin, "International Monitoring of the Transition to Democracy in South Africa, 1992–1994," *African Affairs* 94, no. 377 (October 1995): 519–44.

24. Reynolds, ed., *Election '94*, pp. 190–99.

25. For pessimistic critiques of the party system, see Hermann Giliomee, "Democratization in South Africa," *Political Science Quarterly* 110, no. 1 (spring 1995): 83–104; and Adrian Guelke, "Dissecting the South African Miracle: African Parallels," *Nationalism and Ethnic Politics* 2, no. 1 (spring 1996): 141–54.

26. *Mail and Guardian* (Johannesburg), 29 May 1998, p. 6; IDASA survey in June–July 1997 and a MarkData survey released in December 1997, at

http://www. bibim.com/anc/nw19971007/41:IDASA-TRENDS

and

http://www.bibim.com/anc.nw19971203/65: STATEMENT ON RE . . .

27. Frost, "Democracy Delayed," p. 25.

28. Quoted in Waldmeir, *Anatomy of a Miracle,* p. 232.

29. Vincent T. Maphai, "A Season for Power-Sharing," *Journal of Democracy* 7, no. 1 (January 1996): 67–81.

30. Ibid., p. 67.

31. See appendix in Siri Gloppen, *South Africa: The Battle over the Constitution* (Aldershot, Dartmouth: Ashgate, 1997), pp. 277–83, esp. XVI–XXVII.

32. Political boundaries rarely coincide with areas of cultural and regional identity. There are fourteen disputed areas that could contribute to instability and conflict between provinces. See Richard A. Griggs, "Cultural Faultlines: South Africa's New Provincial Boundaries," *Indicator South Africa* 13, no. 1 (summer 1994): 7–12.

33. This interpretation is disputed in Hennie Kotzé, "Federalism: The State of the Debate in South Africa," *Politeia* 14, no. 2 (1995): 5–26.

34. *Pretoria News,* 28 February 1998, pp. 2, 20.

35. *Mail and Guardian,* 24 March 1995, pp. B1–2.

36. *Mail and Guardian,* 22 November 1996, p. 13; and 12 September 1997, p. 32.

37. *Mail and Guardian,* 1 August 1997, p. B1.

38. Most recently at his address at the opening of parliament. *Star* (Johannesburg), 7 February 1998, p. 11.

39. *Mail and Guardian,* 17 March 1995, p. 10.

40. African National Congress (ANC), *The Reconstruction and Development Programme: A Policy Framework* (Johannesburg: author, 1994); later it was put into a government document: Republic of South Africa, *Reconstruction and Development Programme White Paper* (Pretoria: Government Printer, September 1994).

41. ANC, *The Core Values of the RDP: A Discussion Document,* p. 6, at http://www.anc.org.za/ancdocs/discussion/rdp.html

42. ANC, *Core Values,* p. 1.

43. *Growth, Employment and Redistribution: A Macro-economic Strategy* (Pretoria: Ministry of Finance, 1996).

44. For a critique of GEAR, see Asghar Adelzadeh, "From the RDP to GEAR: The Gradual Embracing of New-Liberalism in Economic Policy," *Transformation,* no. 31 (1996): 66–95. See also Nicole Natrass, "Gambling on Investment: Competing Economic Strategies in South Africa," in the same issue, pp. 25–42.

45. A brief description of the impact of gangs on a community is in *Sunday Independent* (Johannesburg), 22 February 1998, p. 5.

46. R. Stephen Brent, "Tough Road to Prosperity," *Foreign Affairs* 75, no. 2 (March/April 1996): 113–27.

47. E.g., J. E. Spence, "Opposition in South Africa," *Government and Opposition* 32, no. 4 (autumn 1997): 522–40.

48. *Mail and Guardian,* 7 April 1995, p. 4; and 19 June 1998, p. 8.

49. Eddie Webster and Glenn Adler, "Which Way Labour? Cosatu's 6th Congress," *Southern Africa Report* 13, no. 1 (November 1997): 12–15, 32–33; and *Mail and Guardian,* 8 August 1997, p. 3.

50. "Only the Alliance Can Steer Our Country," *Umsebenzi,* September 1997, p. 1.

51. *Mail and Guardian,* 8 August 1997, p. 3. Mandela's speech to the SACP's 10th Congress:

http://www.bibim.com/anc/nw19980702/31:MANDELA-SACP

52. http://www.bibim.com/anc/nw19971220/48:ANC-MBEKI

53. http://www.bibim.com/anc/nw19971220/61:ANC-ALLIANCE

54. Tom Lodge, "Besieged in Mafikeng: The ANC Congress," *Southern Africa Report* 13, no. 1 (November 1997): 3–5.

55. Accounts by supporters of the process can be found in Kader Asmal, Louise Asmal, and Ronald Suresh Roberts, *Reconciliation through Truth: A Reckoning of Apartheid's Criminal Governance* (Cape Town: David Philip, 1996); and in a more comparative vein, Alex Boraine, Janet Levy, and Ronel Scheffer, eds., *Dealing with the Past: Truth and Reconciliation in South Africa* (Cape Town: IDASA, 1997). Also Andre du Toit, "No Rest for the Wicked: Assessing the Truth Commission," *Indicator South Africa* 14, no. 1 (summer 1997): 7–12; and Robert Price, "Race and Reconciliation in the New South Africa," *Politics and Society* 25 (June 1997): 149–78.

56. Promotion of National Unity and Reconciliation Act no. 34 of 1995; and amended as no. 87 of 1995.

57. The five-volume report is available as South Africa Truth and Reconciliation Commission, *Truth and Reconciliation Commission of South Africa Report* (London: Macmillan Reference, 1999).

58. Report on a MarkData poll at http://www.truth.org.za/sapa.9803/s980305d.htm

59. Kanya Adam, "The Politics of Redress: South African Style Affirmative Action,"

Journal of Modern African Studies 35, no. 2 (June 1997): 231–50; and Blade Nzimande and Mpumelelo Sikhosana, eds., *Affirmative Action and Transformation* (Durban: Education Policy Unit, University of Natal, March 1996).

60. See Ian Liebenberg, "The Integration of the Military in Post-Liberation South Africa: The Contribution of the Revolutionary Armies," *Armed Forces and Society* 24, no. 1 (fall 1997): 105–32; and for the 1999 data
http://www.bibim.com/anc/nw19991115/10:ARMY-RACISM

61. Antoinette Handley and Jeffrey Herbst, "South Africa: The Perils of Normalcy," *Current History* 96, no. 610 (May 1997): 222.

62. African National Congress, "Organizational Democracy and Discipline in the Movement," 08/06/97, at
http://www.anc.org.za/ancdocs/discussion/discipline.html

63. African National Congress, *Constitution: As Amended and Adopted at the ANC National Conference, December 1994* (Marshalltown, Gauteng: ANC Department of Information and Publicity, 1994), p. 4.

64. John Stremlau, *A House No Longer Divided: Progress and Prospects for Democratic Peace in South Africa* (New York: Carnegie Commission on Preventing Deadly Conflict, July 1997), p. 32.

65. *Sunday Independent,* 1 March 1998, bus. sec., p. 1.

66. See Heribert Adam, Kogila Moodley, and Frederick van Zyl Slabbert, *Comrades in Business: Post-Liberation Politics in South Africa* (Cape Town: Tafelberg, 1997).

4. | Zimbabwe
The Erosion of Authoritarianism and Prospects for Democracy

Masipula Sithole

This chapter attempts to show how authoritarianism in Zimbabwe was established in the decade of the 1980s and how it started eroding in the 1990s, beginning a process toward re-democratization. This process, though it may suffer some setbacks, is seen to be basically irreversible. Although Zimbabwe's opposition parties are still very weak, the ruling party has lost its hegemonic claim on the electorate, and a vibrant civil society has emerged and is likely to give impetus to the emergence of viable and democratic political parties. I argue that the decade of the 1980s, the first decade of independence, witnessed the consolidation of authoritarianism in post-colonial Zimbabwe, reaching an authoritarianism peak in the general and presidential elections of 1990. The erosion of this authoritarianism began to appear conspicuously in 1991, a continuing process that began much earlier. Further, I attempt to show that a democratic dispensation in Zimbabwe could either stem from a reformed/ transformed ruling party or be led by an emergent democratic opposition, the one being as likely as the other, and that civil society is a pivotal catalyst in democratizing either the ruling party or the emerging opposition.

Three Factors: A Preliminary Comment

There are basically three schools of thought on the issue of democratization "pressures" or "incentives" in Africa today. The "external factors" school expresses or emphasizes the view that the upsurge for liberal, multi-party, democratic change in Africa came in the 1990s as a result of changes in the international political climate that favored and demanded these changes on third world regimes in general, and those on the African continent in particular.[1] The "internal factors" school, on the other hand, rather than placing emphasis on external causal factors, suggests that the pressures for change were internal.[2] These internal factors gathered momentum on the continent itself for the past three decades and were only now releasing their accumulated energies. Finally, the third is the "synthetic factors" school, marrying the above two perspectives.[3]

The real question, however, is not whether one accepts one or the other school, but where one puts emphasis. That internal and external factors have been mutually reinforcing is a given. But unless democracy is sustained by the inner strength of a given society, the democracy project is built on quicksand and may last only as long as these favorable external conditions last. Democracy should find its sustainability from the inner strength of a society, not outside it. In this, we take the view that, basically, authoritarian regimes collapse due to constraints of conflicts and contradictions from within. But the reinforcing interplay between external and internal factors in the Zimbabwe political quagmire during the liberation struggle and after independence cannot be denied.[4]

The Erosion of Authoritarianism: A Theoretical Perspective

In his studies of authoritarian regimes and democratic transitions, Alfred Stepan suggests that we should not merely focus on the final collapse of authoritarian regimes,[5] but, and more importantly, we should focus on the "incremental process of 'authoritarian erosion' and the opposition's contribution to it."[6] Accordingly, he suggests that analysis of the breakdown of authoritarianism should focus on the dynamic relationship of five groups in a regime: (1) the core supporters of the regime; (2) the coercive apparatus that maintains the regime in power; (3) the regime's passive supporters; (4) the active opponents of the regime; and (5) the passive opponents of the regime.

The first group consists of the civilian supporters, who are characterized by a "siege mentality" and will see opposition as a "clear and present danger" to their interests. These will actively support repressive measures against any opposition. The second group, the military and security officers, will tend strongly to identify the interests of their organizations with those of the political regime. They may even conclude that national security positively requires that they run the government. Stepan's third group, the passive supporters, will submit to authoritarian hegemony under the weight of the first two groups. Constituting the middle classes, they will remain "quiescent and pliable," and may even be used by a "cohesive and self-confident authoritarianism." The remaining two groups are made up of the regime's detractors— the opposition. Among these, the activists will be few and virtually paralyzed and demobilized by the massive coercive force the regime is willing to use against them.

In the regime-erosion situation, on the other hand, all these groups will be found thinking and acting differently, suggests Stepan. With the fear that holds the regime together subsiding, the core group will start to fragment. Some will decide that the perpetuation of authoritarianism is not in their interest, and will go over to the opposition. Such a shift signals a newfound appreciation of democracy as a peaceful and predictable method for settling social and political conflicts.

Given the decisions among core supporters to withdraw their support, military resolve too may weaken. Some among them will then come to suspect that continued military support of an increasingly despised regime may be inimical to the interests of the military as a national institution. As these signs of weakening appear among the forces of authoritarianism, most of the passive supporters will quickly shift to passive opposition. It may also be expected that parts of key groups such as the clergy and the intellectuals generally will place themselves under the banner of active opposition.

With their ranks bolstered by growing defections from authoritarianism, the active regime opponents will find their days of paralysis at an end. The passive opposition will multiply as people no longer fear savage repression. Passive opponents will also lose their passivity, and coalesce and expand to the point where the "idea of redemocratization wrests hegemony away from authoritarianism."

Finally, and more importantly, Stepan suggests that authoritarian regimes are more likely to collapse under the strain of conflicts and contradictions that are purely internal, though exacerbated by an opposition that offers itself as the democratic successor regime.

Meanwhile, Stepan gives the opposition to the authoritarian regime five primary tasks, as follows: (1) resisting integration into the regime; (2) guarding zones of autonomy from it; (3) disputing its legitimacy; (4) raising the cost of authoritarian rule; and (5) creating a democratic alternative.[7]

In this regard, Stepan suggests that the first of these five tasks, resisting integration, is the sine qua non for the opposition, because if the cadres of the opposition allow themselves to become effectively demobilized and co-opted into authoritarian institutions and structures, the active opposition will have been compromised and will cease to exist. Therefore, the active opposition must protect its independence and autonomy jealously. Among the organizations to perform these tasks are opposition political parties, trade unions, churches, cultural associations, and civil society groups in general. The active opposition's main order of business, therefore, should be to "create non- or anti-regime subsystems":

> The more that new or pre-existing democratic trade unions, parties, or community movements take root and flourish, the less space is left for the implementation of new model authoritarian institutions. The larger and stronger the various non- or anti-authoritarian subsystems grow, the more effectively they can perform the other tasks of contesting the legitimacy of the authoritarian regime, raising the cost of maintaining it, and generally grinding it down while building support for a democratic alternative.[8]

Here I attempt to explain the process of the erosion of authoritarianism and prospects for democracy in Zimbabwe by examining the dynamic relationship of the above five groups in an authoritarian regime and the five strategic tasks of the opposition in Zimbabwe since 1980, using Alfred Stepan's theoretical framework.

MASIPULA SITHOLE

The Zimbabwe Case

Zimbabwe has experienced two authoritarian regimes, one colonial—spanning ninety years from 1890 to independence in 1980, and the other, post-colonial—spanning twenty years from 1980 to the present. Although Stepan's typology or model can be applied for analyzing both regime periods, this contribution treats only the post-colonial period, understandably a much briefer period.[9] But before we discuss authoritarianism in post-colonial Zimbabwe, let us begin by briefly outlining the important ethnic variable in Zimbabwe politics. This has to be done because this variable has been prominent in the Zimbabwe post-colonial state as in many other post-colonial African states.

The Ethnic Divide

As is typical of sub-Saharan Africa countries, Zimbabwe is ethnically heterogeneous, the two main ethnic groups or nationalities being the Shona, comprising nearly 80 percent of the black population, and the Ndebele, who are nearly 20 percent. The Ndebele are found mainly in the western part of the country around the regional capital, Bulawayo, the nation's second largest city; the rest of the country is mainly occupied by the Shona, although there is a mingling of the tribes in the Midlands province and in the larger cities such as Bulawayo and Harare. Whites are only 2 percent of the Zimbabwe population of nearly 12 million, but they (including the Asians) are the major actors in the economy. There are also subethnic groups among both the Shona and Ndebele, particularly the former, a factor that has made ethnic politics in Zimbabwe more complex than the Shona-Ndebele divide.[10]

The Ndebele, an offshoot of the Zulu of South Africa, dominated the Shona prior to the imposition of colonial rule on both groups in 1890. Unlike with the Tutsi minority who were used by the Germans and later Belgians to control the Hutu majority in Burundi and Rwanda, the Ndebele and Shona in Rhodesia had equal access to British colonial oppression and exploitation. But at independence in 1980 the Ndebele lost their pre-colonial dominance to the ascendant Shona, who were the beneficiaries of a democratizing process and had been largely responsible for defeating the white regime.

Nevertheless, and more importantly, the Ndebele-Shona divide meant the emergence of two ethnically and regionally based main political parties, the Zimbabwe African People's Union (ZAPU) founded in 1961, and the Zimbabwe African National Union (ZANU), formed as a splinter group from ZAPU in 1963. These parties in turn established parallel liberation armies, the Shona-based Zimbabwe African National Liberation Army (ZANLA) and the Ndebele-based Zimbabwe People's Revolutionary Army (ZIPRA), respectively, fighting a common colonial enemy in the 1960s and 1970s. Each grouping was always suspicious of the other, culminating in a ghastly civil strife after independence (1982–87) in Matebeleland

and in the Midlands—a strife that ended with the signing of a Unity Accord between Joshua Nkomo (Ndebele leader of PF-ZAPU) and Robert Mugabe (Shona leader of ZANU[PF]) on 22 December 1987 when PF-ZAPU was forced to merge into ZANU(PF), a Ndebele acceptance of the reality of a changed status. This ZANU(PF) hegemony led to an earnest drive toward the one-party state.[11]

One-Party Tendency and Constraints

After Zimbabwe achieved independence in 1980, there was a strong tendency toward a one-party state, thereby weakening the development of competition in the post-colonial political arena as had happened in the rest of post-colonial Africa. This development or tendency occupied the decade of the 1980s, not for lack of clarity and certainty in the leadership's preference for the one-party socialist state, but due to constraints in the 1980 constitution, negotiated under British mediation at the end of 1979 at Lancaster House to bring an end to the seven-year-long civil war between the liberation armies and the white minority regime of Ian Smith. The negotiated compromise embedded in this constitution provided for twenty "reserved" seats for whites for the first seven years of independence, and for multiparty politics entrenched for ten years.

Therefore, the one-party state seemed progressively imminent as Zimbabwe got nearer the 1990s, particularly after the 1987 expiry of the twenty "reserved" white seats and the announcement of the unity between ZANU(PF) and PF-ZAPU, traditionally the two major political parties in Zimbabwe nationalist politics, separately and jointly responsible for the liberation war. Although the formation of Zimbabwe Unity Movement (ZUM) by Edgar Tekere in early 1989 seemed to forestall the legislation of a one-party state, the crushing defeat of that party in the presidential and general elections of 1990 left no doubt in most observers' minds that legislation for the one-party state was around the corner. Then, in 1991, the fixation with the one-party state anachronism was abandoned.

What happened? What are the factors responsible for the change in direction? Was this change philosophical (principled) or political (tactical)? What is the state of health of the opposition in Zimbabwe? What are the future prospects for both the opposition and the ruling party? In other words, is authoritarianism eroding in Zimbabwe? What is the role of civil society in this erosion process and in building a democratic Zimbabwe? But first, let us consider the consolidation of authoritarianism in Zimbabwe.

Consolidating Authoritarianism: *Gukurahundi* Policy

How did ZANU(PF) establish its hegemony and authoritarianism?[12] Many authoritative accounts have been written on the fate of the opposition in Zimbabwe's one-party dominant regime.[13] These accounts have been critical of the ruling ZANU(PF) regime's attitude and behavior toward opposition parties during the ten years since independence (1980–90). The use of state institutions like the army (as in Matebeleland before the 1987 Unity Accord), the police, the Central Intelligence Organization (CIO), the media (daily newspapers, radio, and television) have been cited.

Also, up to mid-1992, the ruling party was financed from public funds through the now nominally defunct Ministry of Political Affairs, which received approximately Z$50 million every year and operated from a multi-story, multi-million dollar headquarters in Harare, the nation's capital. Under increasing criticism from opposition parties and civil society groups, this ministry was abolished in 1992, but the financing of the ruling party was immediately replaced by a self-serving Political Parties (Finance) Act under which a party that had at least fifteen seats in parliament was entitled to public funds. Currently, only three seats in parliament belong to the opposition; therefore it is not entitled to receive state funds.

Again under pressure from the opposition, the courts ruled that the Political Parties (Finance) Act of 1992 was "unconstitutional." This act was amended in 1997 to provide that any party that polled at least 5 percent in a general election should be entitled to state funds proportionately.[14] This in effect means that the ruling party, ZANU(PF), will continue to be the sole recipient of public funds until the next general elections, which are in the year 2000. But what accounts for weak opposition in Zimbabwe?

In order to appreciate why the Zimbabwe opposition has been weak, some critical background on how ZANU(PF) castrated the opposition and established an authoritarian regime is necessary. It can be said that the fate of the opposition was decided in 1979 and by the way that the Mugabe government dealt with PF-ZAPU as the party poised to offer viable opposition after independence.

In 1979, ZANU(PF) adopted the "*gukurahundi* policy" toward its opponents. *Gukurahundi* is a colloquial expression, which in Shona means "the storm that destroys everything." The peasants, from whom the expression or concept comes, use it with awe and fear because *gukurahundi* occurs during crop seasons and "destroys everything"—crops and weeds, huts and forests, the good and the bad, including people and beasts. After *gukurahundi,* usually nature brings a new ecological order. Such were the intended consequences of ZANU(PF)'s revolutionary policy as it evolved in the 1970s from the countryside.

Based in neighboring Mozambique (1975–79), ZANU(PF) "officially" adopted Marxism-Leninism as its ideology in 1977. It calendared and called the year 1979 "*Gore re Gukurahundi*" (The Year of the Storm)—the revolutionary storm that would finally destroy the white settler regime; the "internal settlement puppets";[15] and finally, the capitalist system. A new socio-economic and political order guided by Marxist-Leninist principles was to replace the "old order." *Gukurahundi* was a policy of annihilation, annihilating the opposition (black and white). Accordingly, an "enemies list" was published in mid-1979. It singled out ranking personalities of the "internal settlement" parties for liquidation.

The momentum of *gukurahundi* swept Mugabe and his party to power in the independence election of 1980. The instrument that ZANU(PF) used during the buildup to the election was ZANLA, its military wing. Subsequently, it used its youth and women leagues for political mobilization during and between successive general elections that have occurred every five years since the 1980 election, and presidential elections that have occurred every six years since 1990. Both these outfits have had a "commandist" political culture that is perpetuated by their paramilitary style of organization. Moreover, the youth wing is mostly led by former ZANLA combatants. But, by and large, the party lost many of its cadres into the army where, under British instructors, they were groomed into a "professional" rather than a "party" army. Hence, when faced with a PF-ZAPU opposition in Matebeleland (1982–87), Mugabe had to create the notorious Fifth Brigade trained by North Koreans instead of relying solely on the newly created national army. Significantly, the Fifth Brigade was commonly referred to as "Gukurahundi" with pride by its sponsors, and with resentment and fear by the recipients of the evil storm in Matebeleland.

Most leading personalities of PF-ZAPU and the former ZIPRA were sacked from government and from the national army, while others were detained. In 1984, Joshua Nkomo, the PF-ZAPU leader, fled into temporary exile in England in the wake of discoveries of arms caches in farms owned by PF-ZAPU. These farms and other properties were confiscated by the ZANU(PF) government in a hegemonic march into Matebeleland. Instructive to note in this process is the enormous and even enthusiastic support and approval the ZANU(PF) regime got from its civilian "core supporters" among the ethnic Shona. For instance, in the 1985 general election, held at the height of the Matebeleland conflict and *gukurahundi* excesses, ZANU(PF) increased its parliamentary majority by eight seats in a voter turnout of approximately 80 percent. Thus, with a "siege mentality," the Shona "core supporters" of the ZANU(PF) regime approved the "harsh and repressive measures" emitted by the regime in Matebeleland and the Midlands province.[16]

The Regime's Other Coercive Apparatus

At the Lancaster House constitutional talks in 1979, it was agreed that the task of reconstituting a national army for Zimbabwe be given to British officers. Thus, the present Zimbabwe National Army (ZNA) was created by the British by largely mixing "suitable" personnel from the three, hitherto warring armies of ZANLA, ZIPRA, and the Rhodesian Army. As a result, initially, the ZNA could not strongly identify its "corporate interests" with those of the emerging new political regime. Because of its chemistry, the loyalties were divided in three political directions: one (Rhodesian Army) went toward the old order; the second (ZANLA) toward the new order; and the third (ZIPRA) tended toward a regime that could have been. This underscores why, faced with the conflict in Matebeleland, as already mentioned, the new regime had to create the Fifth Brigade, its notoriety notwithstanding.

It was therefore unlikely that such a divided group could conclude that, in Stepan's formulation, "considerations of national security positively require that the armed forces run the government." Over the years, the ZNA has developed into a corporate entity with a professional image and interest in itself as an organization, such that today it possesses a professionalism rare in African armies and is unlikely to interfere in politics except in upholding the Zimbabwe constitution.[17]

The ZNA was more restrained than the Fifth Brigade in its approach to the conflict in Matebeleland. This could have been due as much to its emerging professionalism as to the neutralizing effect of its then divided loyalties. After the Matebeleland conflict, the ZNA's attention was quickly drawn to the conflict in neighboring Mozambique where Zimbabwe's economic lifeline and border security were in "clear and present danger" from activities of RENAMO (Resistencia Nacional Mocambicana), which sought to destabilize that country. The Zimbabwe army has also participated in peacekeeping missions under United Nations (UN) command in Somalia, Angola, and in Mozambique when peace finally came to that country. All objective reports indicate that the ZNA has undertaken its national and international duties and obligations with unsurpassed probity and professionalism. By keeping busy in the international front, armies have not been known to interfere in domestic politics, unless they began to incur unacceptable losses abroad. We will revisit this issue when we consider more recent events in Zimbabwe politics.

Unlike the army, the other security instruments—the Zimbabwe Republican Police (ZRP), and the Central Intelligence Organization (CIO)—have been perceived as political instruments of the ruling party, particularly the latter. The CIO was founded in 1964 by the Rhodesian Front politicians. While it served the Rhodesian state "secretly," it gained notoriety after independence when its agents served the Zimbabwe state "publicly," flashing their secret service identification cards in bars with the intent of striking terror in the people as ZANU(PF) consolidated authoritarian rule. The worst partisan bias of the CIO was displayed during the 1990 general and presidential elections when a ZUM candidate, Patrick Kombayi, contesting ZANU(PF) Vice President Simon Muzenda, was shot by CIO agents who were arrested, tried, found guilty, but later set free, the recipients of a presidential pardon.[18]

The Erosion of Authoritarianism

"The storm" succeeded in destroying PF-ZAPU, its main target after independence. But there are those who believe PF-ZAPU was not destroyed, but swallowed alive. By swallowing PF-ZAPU, ZANU(PF) swallowed a "moderating" pill. Unity had a "calming" effect on the hitherto high-pitched ideological and commandist tone of the ZANU(PF) regime. Although the unity accords had committed the "new"

Zimbabwe

party to a socialist ideology "guided by Marxist-Leninist principles," adopted by ZANU(PF) in exile in 1977 during the liberation struggle, and to the "establishment of a one-party state in the fullness of time,"[19] a position officially adopted by ZANU(PF) four years after independence at the party's 1984 National Congress, many observers had their doubts whether PF-ZAPU had their hearts in these aspects of the unity idea.

When the idea of the one-party state was introduced to the twenty-six-member Politburo after the 1990 general and presidential elections, none of the five in favor were former PF-ZAPU. These members were outspoken in their opposition to the one-party state. This gave courage to the majority members of the old ZANU(PF), who now also openly opposed the one-party state anachronism. Before unity, everything President Mugabe wanted from the Politburo he got. After unity, he did not always have his way.

The commitment to socialism went the same way. After unity, the socialist "leadership code" was taken off the agenda, even for theoretical discussion. At one time the committed President Mugabe posed the question to his Central Committee: "I am a socialist, what are you?" None answered, not even the "Simon Peters" of the party. Outside the context of unity, many would have lied and answered: "So am I, Mr. President," even against their inner convictions.

Accordingly, those who said PF-ZAPU was swallowed alive could have been right. If you swallow a living organism, one of four things is likely to happen: either (1) it (the organism) dies, or (2) it kills you, or (3) both die, or (4) both survive and become part of each other in a symbiotic relationship of sorts. The last scenario seems to have happened, and a new, moderate ZANU(PF) seems to be emerging, notwithstanding some setbacks. Thus, the view held by many that Joshua Nkomo (the 300-pound PF-ZAPU leader) was "too big to be swallowed" is probably correct. At eighty-two, he is now one of two vice presidents of both the country and the ruling party. Several former PF-ZAPU senior officials hold senior posts in both the party and government.

In successive cabinet reshuffles, particularly since the reshuffle of 1992, former PF-ZAPU leaders have made significant gains. These gains were further consolidated in the reshuffle of 1995 in what was believed to be President Mugabe's bid to contain a possible alliance between former PF-ZAPU and potential opponents within ZANU(PF) in Masvingo, home province of the Karanga, who are crucial in ZANU(PF) internal politics. (See note 3, and more will be said about this below.)

But it is the "moderating effect" that unity brought to Zimbabwe politics that should interest social scientists, from a processes point of view. Moreover, as Welshman Ncube has noted, unity opened up or broadened "democratic expression."[20] If external factors had something to do with this unity, then to that extent they were also a moderating factor. Significantly, there was no public outcry when the one-party state and socialism path were abandoned in 1991. Instead, there was public relief. The internal chemistry, both within the ruling party and in the mass public, had qualitatively changed. But this is not to deny that the international climate had also qualitatively changed.

75

Decline in "Elite Cohesion"

Edgar Tekere, the then outspoken former secretary-general of ZANU(PF), was the first leader to be expelled from the ruling party in 1987. He founded his Zimbabwe Unity Movement (ZUM) in 1989, the first party to be formed in nine years of independence, and the first party to cause a real challenge to ZANU(PF) after PF-ZAPU merged into ZANU(PF) in 1987. The Zimbabwe Unity Movement contested both the general and presidential elections of 1990, an election where the ZANU(PF) leadership had hoped to run unchallenged or win every seat and establish a one-party state unopposed. The violence perpetrated against the opposition during the 1990 election was the worst in an election year since independence, culminating in the shooting of Patrick Kombayi.

The decline in party "elite cohesion" continued to grow, as criticism of and challenge to the party from within persisted. Margaret Dongo, ZANU(PF) member in the 1990–95 parliament, defied the party after the Politburo refused her candidacy for the 1995 parliamentary elections. She ran as an independent candidate and lost, but cried foul. She petitioned the court and won. A by-election had to be called, and she won the Harare South constituency in the nation's capital by a three to one margin. Similarly, Lawrence Mudehwe defied the Politburo, contested the executive mayoral race in the important eastern border city of Mutare, and won against the favored party candidate. Following these victories, successful petitions were lodged through the courts for the nullification of executive mayoral election results on grounds that there were "irregularities" in these elections in the important cities of Masvingo, Bulawayo, and Harare, but all were won by ZANU(PF) candidates, though on a progressively poor poll.

Perhaps the most interesting (if not most important) manifestation of a rupture in "elite cohesion" is that championed by the charismatic Politburo member Dr. Eddison Zvobgo, from Masvingo, a province traditionally crucial to ZANU(PF) politics. In a widely read and debated speech delivered at an international conference in Harare in November 1995, Zvobgo called for the re-democratization of the Zimbabwe constitution,[21] particularly the aspects pertaining to the powers of the executive president—which, ironically, he drafted in 1987 when he was minister for legal and parliamentary affairs.

But in 1996 Zvobgo sustained serious leg injuries in a car accident, and was dropped from minister of mines to minister-without-portfolio in a cabinet reshuffle that took place in May following the April presidential election of 1996—ostensibly because he was in London getting medical attention. On his return, Zvobgo told the press that he was "fit for a cabinet post." He remains without portfolio to this day (2000).

The more recent manifestation of a breakdown in elite cohesion is the Dzikamayi Mavhaire and Cyril Ndebele incidents. In April 1998 a motion was introduced in the hitherto docile parliament calling for a limited presidential term of two five-year terms. Currently, the president can succeed himself indefinitely as long as he has the support of the electoral. Accordingly, President Mugabe is in his twentieth year in office, having succeeded himself three times since Zimbabwe became independent in 1980.[22] During the presidential term limit debate in parliament, Dzikamayi Mavhaire, a member of parliament representing the Masvingo Central constituency and who was also chairman of the ruling party in the Masvingo province, called on President Mugabe to retire. "The President must go," he said.[23]

An irate Mugabe called a Central Committee meeting of his party at which he had Mavhaire suspended from holding a position in the party for the next two years. The Speaker of the House, Cyril Ndebele, a former PF-ZAPU member, issued a certificate advising the party that Mavhaire expressed his views under "parliamentary immunity" and therefore should not be victimized.[24] President Mugabe denounced the Speaker's action as "rank madness." He attempted to purge his party of what he called "witches, administering noxious mixtures to our faithful ones." Cyril Ndebele would not rescind his stand and had the solid backing of former PF-ZAPU ranking officials in ZANU(PF). This created an impasse that began to threaten the unity of 1987 under circumstances of the recent publication by the Catholic Commission for Justice and Peace (CCJP) of the controversial *Breaking the Silence*,[25] an account of the Gukurahundi (Fifth Brigade) excesses and abuse of human rights during the Matebeleland conflict in the 1980s.[26] The "witch-hunt" or "purge" quickly fizzled out. The "case" against Ndebele died a political death for fear of reactivating past Shona-Ndebele conflict.[27]

In addition to the Shona-Ndebele divide, the ruling party suffers active intra-Shona and intra-regional cleavages and splits. Traditionally, there has been infighting between the Karanga, Manyika, and Zezuru in the pre-unity ZANU(PF).[28] Currently there is active tension within the party among these three major Shona subgroups, particularly between the Zezuru and the Karanga, for the control of the party leadership. Intra-regional infighting has also been rife, involving top-ranking members of the party in all three regions and subgroups. For instance, in Masvingo the party is split into the Zvobgo and Hungwe factions. (Dzikamayi Mavhaire belongs to the Zvobgo faction.) In the Mashonaland West province the Zezuru are split between supporters of Politburo member Nathan Shamuyarira and provincial chairman Swithen Mombeshora; while in Manicaland province the feud between senior Politburo member Dydimus Mutasa and provincial chairman Kumbirai Kangai seems permanent.[29]

In the circumstances of a fractionalized party leadership, the regime's instruments of coercion (the army, police, and CIO) must decide on two courses of action: either to get involved in faction politics (siding with particular politicians) or to protect their "professional interests" by being neutral unless protecting the constitutional position as interpreted by the courts.[30] Moreover, the incentive to become neutral and professional is increased by fear of a bloodbath should infighting start within these instruments of coercion themselves.

The tendency has been to expel critics and opponents from the party: Tekere in 1989; Dongo in 1995; Mudehwe in 1996. While Tekere formed his own party, ZUM, Dongo has not, at least not for now. But she is emerging as the rallying point for "independent candidates." She is chairperson of a new formation, the Movement for Independent Electoral Candidates (MEIC) formed in 1997. Whether Zvobgo and Mavhaire await the fate of Tekere and Dongo (being expelled from the party) remains to be seen.

Weak Opposition: Further Considerations

Opposition outside the ruling party has been very weak for reasons already mentioned, and since the ZANU(PF)–PF-ZAPU Unity Accord of 1987. However, there has been a proliferation of opposition parties since the 1990 elections such that currently there may be in excess of a dozen opposition parties in Zimbabwe, about seven of which are quoted in the local press from time to time.[31] They all suffer various levels of infiltration by the ruling party's intelligence agents, as well as from inept leadership often wasting its energies in internal wrangling, some of which is instigated by infiltrant agents provocateurs. These parties are often combinations, mutations, and permutations of previous formations.[32] The formation of more parties is predictable. Why so many opposition parties?

One is reminded here of a local joke, that if you were to put two Zimbabweans on the moon and visited them the next day, you would find that they have formed three political parties! The tendency toward many political parties must attest to the fact that Zimbabwe is a society of many political entrepreneurs. Moreover, the current "democracy friendly" international climate under harsh economic conditions of structural adjustment often encourages political entrepreneurship. "Form a party and there is always an international NGO to fund it," seems to be the calculation. But more often the incumbent regimes, on accepting the inevitability of multi-partyism, have sought to manage the transition from the one-party state by encouraging formation of "friendly" opposition parties, infiltrating others in order to keep them perpetually destabilized and weak. These strategies and techniques have been successfully employed by Daniel Arap Moi in Kenya, and by Mobutu Sese Seko before his ouster in a military insurrection from outside. But besides complaining about the use of the stick, the opposition in Zimbabwe has spent enormous energy quarreling and suspecting each other of "enemies within."

We have noted that Alfred Stepan tasks the "democratic opposition" with five functions: namely, resisting integration into the regime; guarding zones of autonomy from it; disputing its legitimacy; raising the cost of authoritarian rule; and creating a democratic alternative. As if to heed Stepan's call, a National Multi-Party Consultative Conference was convened in 1994 under the aegis of the now defunct Southern African Human Rights Foundation (SAHRF) based in the Midlands city of Kwekwe to work out a "common strategy" and approach to the 1995 parliamentary and 1996 presidential elections. Some six opposition parties were involved in this consultation.[33] In their communiqué, they called for the convening of a "National Multi-Party Constitutional Conference" to reform the "undemocratic" Zimbabwe constitution as amended severally since independence.[34] They de-

Table 4.1. Zimbabwe Parliamentary Election Results: 1979–1995

Parties	1979 Elections Votes	%	PR
UANC	1,212,639	67,27	51
NDU	18,175	1,00	0
ZANU	262,928	14,59	12
ZUPO	114,570	6,35	0
Total	1,802,758	100	72

Parties	1980 Elections Votes	%	PR
PF-ZAPU	638,879	24	20
UANC	219,307	8	3
ZANU	53,343	2	0
ZDP	28,181	1	0
NFZ	18,794	1	0
NDU	15,056	1	0
UNFP	5,796	0	0
UPAM	1,181	0	0
Total	2,649,529	100	80

Parties	1985 Elections Votes	%	SMD	PR
ZANU(PF)	2,233,320	77	64	60
ZANU	36,054	1	1	1
PF-ZAPU	558,771	20	15	16
UANC	64,764	2	0	1
Others	0,00	0	0	2

Partiess	1990 Elections Votes	%	SMD	PR
ZANU(PF)	1,690,071	81	117	98
ZUM	379,031	18	2	21
ZANU	19,448	1	1	1
Total	2,078,550	100	120	120

Parties	1995 Elections Votes	%	SMD	PR
FORUM	88,223	6	0	7
ZANU	93,546	6	2	7

Source: These tables were compiled from data supplied by the Office of the Registrar General of the Government of Zimbabwe.

nounced the country's Electoral Act of 1990, the Political Parties (Finance) Act of 1992, and other electoral practices as not providing the opposition an "even playing field."

For instance, the 1992 act entitled the ruling party access to some 50 million dollars for party activities, including payment of a full-time staff, offices, vehicles, the required deposit payment for every candidate contesting legislative and presidential elections, fees for booking meeting halls, paying for political advertising, and so on. Also, the registrar general, who is responsible for administering elections, and the chairman of the Electoral Supervisory Commission, charged with overseeing the impartiality of elections, have been "card-carrying" members of the ruling party. Further, the Zimbabwe radio and television are state owned, and therefore party controlled.

Accordingly, these opposition parties called for a boycott of the 1995 and 1996 elections. They boycotted and forfeited the elections to ZANU(PF), ZANU(Ndonga), and Independent, which won in the parliamentary elections 118, 2, and 1 seats, respectively, thereby confirming either the futility of playing on an uneven playing field, or that the opposition was not yet ready for an electoral combat, most likely the latter. Table 4.1 shows the weakness of the opposition in successive parliamentary elections, particularly after the 1987 Unity Accord between ZANU(PF) and PF-ZAPU. The 1979 and 1980 general elections were held under a "proportional representation" (PR) electoral system, while subsequent elections were held under the "single member district" (SMD) or constituency-based system. Although the data in these tables show the opposition would have come out better using the PR system, the ZANU(PF) electoral hegemony in both systems has been overwhelming. The opposition has had 3 seats in a parliament of 120 contested seats since the 1990 election.

However, of note is the fact that voter participation has declined significantly from a turnout of 93.6 percent in 1980 to 54 percent in 1995 for parliamentary elections, and from 53 percent in 1990 to 31 percent for the 1996 presidential elections—a record low since independence. Although the opposition might have been inclined to take credit for the low voter turnout in both the parliamentary and presidential elections of 1995 and 1996, respectively (in that they had called for a boycott), the explanation for voter apathy is likely to be the disillusionment with both the ruling party and the fractionalized opposition. Voter apathy is even higher in recent municipal elections, where the ruling party has been winning most contests in a voter turnout averaging 13 percent. Potential voters might, therefore, be waiting for an alternative, either within the ruling party or from outside it.

"Unity Accord" of Opposition Parties?

The question is often asked whether the existing weak opposition parties might sign a "unity accord" of their own, as did ZANU(PF) and PF-ZAPU in 1987. In politics anything is possible. But the more important question in this regard is whether such unity or coalition would make a difference. Would it attract the emergent "active majority" opponents of the ZANU(PF) regime presently looking for an alternative party? The answer is, probably not—for the following reasons.

There is a certain sustained threshold of support a party or parties should have (10 to 15 percent) in order to form a viable opposition. PF-ZAPU sustained this threshold (and better) until the 1987 unity with ZANU(PF). Even now, it maintains this threshold strength (or even better) in the ZANU(PF) unity.[35] Although ZUM and the Forum party had this threshold support in the 1990 and 1995 general elections, respectively, they failed to sustain it. Whether or not they were made to fail (through infiltration or lack of resources) is academic; the fact is that they failed to sustain the support, and their capacity to regain it now is doubtful.[36] The older opposition parties, the UANC/United Parties and ZANU(Ndonga), have failed to shed the stigma of the "internal settlement" politics of the late 1970s.[37] Again, it becomes academic whether they were fairly judged or not. As for the newer (post-1990) opposition parties, their threshold support is not known, since they have been boycotting elections, but the general suspicion is that they are as weak (if not weaker). Therefore, the present opposition parties are not only too many, but are so weak in their individual weakness that, if combined, they would make one weak opposition party. In all probability, that formation will not inspire the people into electoral participation. Then who will?

Civil Society and Struggle for Democracy

In Zimbabwe, as has happened elsewhere in Africa (Benin, Zambia, Kenya, Malawi, etc.), in the absence of strong opposition political parties, opposition to authoritarianism has been spearheaded largely by civil society. A viable opposition in Zimbabwe could well be inspired or brokered by civil society.

By the late 1980s the "core supporters" of the regime had begun to decline and the manifestations of demobilization and paralysis of "active opposition" to ZANU(PF) authoritarianism had started to show. For instance, the University of Zimbabwe students and intellectuals (Association of University Teachers), the Zimbabwe Law Society, clerics of the outspoken Zimbabwe Catholic Commission for Justice and Peace (ZCCJP) and the Zimbabwe Council of Churches (ZCC), the Zimbabwe Congress of Trade Unions (ZCTU), Zimbabwe Union of Journalists (ZUJ), and other organizations that have mushroomed in the 1990s, like the Zimbabwe Human Rights Association (Zimrights), the Foundation for Democracy in Zimbabwe (FODEZI), and Transparency International Zimbabwe—all led by people who were formerly the regime's "passive supporters"—began to oppose the ZANU(PF) regime openly. First, the demand was public accountability and disclosure of corruption, then opposition to plans for the establishment of the one-party state; now the demands include good governance, comprehensive constitutional reforms, transparency, and human rights.

The pressures against corruption led to President Mugabe establishing the San-dura Commission of 1987, which investigated corruption charges involving the sale of vehicles by party and government officials, apparently abusing a government facility at the Willowville Motor Industries in the outskirts of the capital Harare (hence "Willowgate" scandal!). Several senior party officials and cabinet ministers were found guilty and forced to resign.[38]

The ZCCJP spearheaded the campaign against the intended establishment of the one-party state after the elections of April 1990. In a strongly worded statement it said, in part: "We believe that a constitutionalised one party state is contrary to basic human rights; we believe that no generation has the right to make immutable decisions for the generations of the future. Therefore we recommend that: the ruling party abandons all plans to establish a legislated one party state in Zimbabwe."[39]

This position was immediately endorsed by the ZCC, the ZCTU, students, intellectuals, and former Zimbabwe president Canaan Banana. The message was heard from pulpits, factories, and classrooms. The ZCCJP inserted its full statement in several issues of the widely read *Herald* newspaper as a paid advertisement. The independent weeklies and monthly magazines published persuasive articles critical of the one-party state anachronism.[40] Zimbabwe intellectuals summed up their antipathy toward the one-party state in a contribution titled *The One-Party State and Democracy: The Zimbabwe Debate.*[41] The party's one-party state message had no "ghost of a chance" of penetrating to the people beyond its Harare headquarters. Instead the other message (anti-one-party state) finally penetrated party headquarters, and given an international climate equally hostile to the one-party state, the ruling party had to abandon the anachronistic idea.

Another unprecedented manifestation of resistance to authoritarianism was that spearheaded in November 1995 by Zimrights, Zimbabwe's leading human rights organization. Trouble started brewing in downtown Harare when police chasing two suspected thieves opened fire with assault rifles, killing two passersby and injuring the third. An infuriated crowd overturned a police van and set it ablaze, the first since independence. The police never showed remorse, merely calling the incident "unfortunate" and warning people to "keep away from scenes of crime." Zimrights denounced the callous shootings and response, and called a demonstration to commemorate the dead. Opposition politicians, other civic organizations, and university students and lecturers joined the demonstration. Zimrights organizers pledged to continue such demonstrations until the government started taking human rights seriously. But two hours later, a group of youths ran amok in the city, throwing bricks and overturning and burning eight government vehicles, an unprecedented show of anger at the state.

The "instruments of coercion" were restrained as they watched state property burn. No deaths were reported this time. Could it be because of disbelief, or because Stepan's scenario of an "increasingly despised regime" had started? Today, members of the CIO are more discreet in their "secret service" than in the past, probably the result of an incipient professionalism that is acquired in the process of growing up. But it might be the result of divided loyalties as "elite cohesion" within the ruling party has cracked, starting in the late 1980s with the casualties of the Sandura Commission, and the expulsion of Edgar Tekere mentioned above.

Yet another unprecedented event was the September 1996 civil service strike in which the government, out of character, had to succumb to demands for pay increments after a two-week work stoppage. Instead of listening to the strikers' claim that a basic 20 percent annual pay increase had not been included in their pay packets, the government resorted to its usual bullying response to such crises. The Public Service Association (PSA) called a nationwide civil servants strike. Public Service Minister Florence Chitauro issued them an ultimatum of two days to return to work; they didn't; they were fired, and seven thousand jobs were advertised to replace the striking workers. With characteristic arrogance, President Mugabe said he welcomed the opportunity to "trim down the size of the civil service."

An apparently intimidated and divided PSA leadership called off the strike. It was immediately replaced by a more militant faction calling itself the Unified Civil Service Negotiating Committee (UCSNC). It announced that the national strike should continue. They won the day when government backed down and agreed to the annual pay increase and other demands such as no victimization for those who had participated in the strike. This strike was reported as the "worst national strike in Zimbabwe's history," costing the nation over a billion dollars in lost revenue. It paralyzed all the essential services in the country, the most hard hit being health services and government itself. Army personnel had to be called in to provide emergency medical services.

With the hardships of economic adjustment programs, public sympathy was solidly behind the striking workers. Just a year before, the president and his cabinet had awarded themselves increments of more than double their salaries.[42] Several ZANU(PF) members of parliament were publicly sympathetic to the strikers. The police kept strictly to their law and order functions, and some were even heard remarking, in support, "We are civil servants too!" The "coercive apparatus that maintains the regime in power" was now beginning to have doubts.

The events of 1997 were even more dramatic. Around April 1997 there were press speculations about the abuse of the War Victims Compensation Fund, apparently based on information leaked to the paper by government employees of the Ministry of Labour and Social Services tasked with the administration of the fund. The fund was established by the Ian Smith regime in 1987 for the benefit of government victims of the liberation war. Its beneficiaries were mainly white supporters of the minority regime. But after independence, former freedom fighters (guerrillas) and civilians who were wounded or suffered some form of disability (physical and/or psychological) as a result of the liberation war were included as beneficiaries of the fund.

The information leaked to the press alleged that undeserving top government officials were drawing from the fund. After persistent reports and complaints, President Mugabe temporarily froze the administration of the fund and set up a commission (the Chidyausiku Commission) to investigate the alleged abuses. Members of the Liberation War Veterans Association (an organization of former guerrilla combatants) were the first to feel the effects of the freeze on the fund, as this was the only source of income for most of them. When their pleas fell on deaf ears, the Liberation War Veterans staged nationwide demonstrations in order to attract the attention of their patron, President Mugabe, who had insisted he would not see them; instead they were to put their complaint to the relevant Ministry of Labour and Social Services, which ministry had in turn insisted that they should wait for the outcome of the Chidyausiku Commission.

On Heroes Day celebrations (August 8), the Liberation War Veterans startled the nation when they disrupted President Mugabe's speech by singing war songs and beating war drums at the National Sports Stadium. The countrywide demonstrations continued, including at an international meeting addressed by Mugabe at the Harare International Conference Center, to which a riot squad was dispatched. The daring former combatants went as far as besieging the ruling ZANU(PF) party headquarters in Harare, holding some very senior Politburo officials until President Mugabe agreed to meet them. In the ensuing discussions they demanded compensation for liberating the country, until President Mugabe promised each of the nearly 50,000 former combatants a $50,000 lump sum gratuity and a pension of $2,000 per month payable until death. This undertaking was to cause another row in parliament, the party, and more importantly within civil society, particularly the trade union movement. The issue became: where was this money going to come from?

Government sought to impose a 5 percent War Veterans levy. Sensing the mood of an already over-taxed population, parliament rejected the Finance (Number 2) Bill, which was also subsequently rejected by a unanimous vote at the ruling party's Consultative National Assembly. An already outraged ZCTU called for a nationwide strike for December 9 to protest against heavy taxation and high cost of living. More than 3.5 million people took part in this unprecedented nationwide strike, which was violent in Harare, but peaceful in the rest of the country.[43] President Mugabe withdrew the proposed levy and had to come up with the money through other means, mainly by private sector borrowing, and selling shares in public enterprises. Commenting on the significance of the events of 1997, this writer stated:

> The year 1997 was Zimbabwe's "turning point," and it revealed that the country is in "acute danger." This was the year when, in an unprecedented move, president Robert Mugabe was forced to accede to the demands of former freedom fighters, a constituency crucial to the survival of his commandist party; this was the year when, in another unprecedented move, the Zimbabwe parliament woke up from seventeen years of sublime and shameful slumber and said "no" to a chief executive who had "privatized" the exercise of public office; this was the year when, in yet another unprecedented move, the ruling ZANU(PF) National Assembly unanimously said "no" to its "president-and-first-secretary" who appeared to have

lost touch with grassroots sentiment; this is the year when the "land question" aroused more anxieties and emotions than in any other period since independence; this was the year when the Zimbabwe dollar became *Zimkwacha*, a piece of paper, losing nearly a hundred percent of its value overnight; and, more significantly, 1997 was the year when the Zimbabwe people, by the nationwide demonstration against arbitrary taxation, rediscovered their "people's power." What a year 1997 was! It was, without a doubt, a "turning point."[44]

The Food Riots

The accumulated anger and frustration of 1997 burst asunder in the "New Year" when, on 19–22 January 1998, there were countrywide food riots, the first in Zimbabwe history. In some urban communities the army had to be called in to assist the police to stop the looting of shops and threat to life and property.[45] The government blamed the ZCTU and opposition parties for instigating the riots, but the ZCTU denied responsibility, putting the blame on the high cost of living. By most accounts, the food riots appeared spontaneous; no one organized them. As one opposition politician put it: "The stomach organized and coordinated these food riots. Hungry people need no one to organize them to look for food."[46]

Decidedly, the ZCTU has emerged as a force to reckon with in Zimbabwe politics. In April, it successfully called for a two-day, nationwide, stay-away strike and threatened another longer one if government did not drop taxes to tolerable levels. President Mugabe accuses the ZCTU of behaving like an opposition party and its leaders for having political ambitions.[47] In neighboring Zambia, the ruling party, Movement for Multi-Party Democracy (MMD), came to power in 1991 led by a trade unionist, Fredrick Chiluba, now that country's president. But, the first to effectively "destabilize" Mugabe's hold on power was the Liberation War Veterans Association.

The question is: Why did Mugabe not simply ignore and tire out the liberation war veterans? He tired and they wore him out, instead. Moreover, and most importantly, besides their unorthodox tactics of holding senior party officials hostage, the veterans constitute the backbone of the ruling party. They man the commandist infrastructure of the party without which it collapses. It is a case of the chickens coming home to roost, of political blackmail.

The success of the Liberation War Veterans Association opened up a Pandora's box in that it triggered the proliferation of liberation-war related pressure groups such as the Liberation War Collaborators Association; the Former Political Prisoners, Detainees and Restrictees Association; the Widows of Liberation War Heroes Association; and the Liberation War Recruitees Association. Each in turn demanded assistance from the state for their sacrifice during the liberation struggle. But of these, the first (liberation war collaborators) pose the greatest threat to ZANU(PF)'s hitherto impenetrable base in the countryside. The liberation war collaborators were most active in the rural areas during the liberation war of the 1970s. They were the conveyor belt between the armed guerrillas and the masses, an indispensable link without which any guerrilla war would not succeed.[48] The chairman of the Liberation War Collaborators Association threatened that his organization would start decampaigning Mugabe and his party in the rural areas if their demands for compensation were not met—yet another case of political blackmail![49] The rural population makes up about 75 percent of Zimbabwe's voters.

Continuing Student Unrest

The students remain intermittently on the street and in the classroom, demanding increases in financial support by the state and an end to corruption and mismanagement by public officials. Recently a University of Zimbabwe student was shot and seriously wounded by the police during a campus anti-corruption demonstration, resulting in a massive protest demonstration by the students in the city center on 29 April. By all accounts, this demonstration was the most peaceful and well organized ever staged by the University of Zimbabwe students.[50]

However, this was followed by another demonstration three weeks later that turned violent. Some of the demonstrators' placards called for President Mugabe to follow the example of Indonesia's President Suharto and resign, a case of the "contagion effect." The violence gave the authorities a pretext to close the university and the Harare Polytechnical College, indefinitely. The students have petitioned the courts, arguing that while the authorities may punish (including expelling) those who were involved in acts of violence, they have no jurisdiction to close the two institutions, penalizing the majority who either did not participate or were nonviolent in the demonstrations.

There is no doubt from the above accounts that the Mugabe regime has been beleaguered since the anti-police brutality demonstration of November 1995; the frequency with which anti-systemic manifestations have occurred and their intensity have increased. Alfred Stepan suggests that under challenge, the authoritarian regime may "lash back with heightened repression," but he adds, "such a backlash would carry its own risks."[51] Robert Dahl has argued that "The likelihood that a government will tolerate an opposition increases as the expected costs of suppression increases."[52]

A regime is able to effectively deal with its detractors only if it enjoys group elite cohesion. This is so because the instruments of coercion, to be effectively employed, must themselves be cohesive. This cohesiveness is directly proportional to the unity and cohesiveness of the regime's political elite. But, as we have seen, there has been a progressive decline in the ZANU(PF) elite cohesion, particularly in recent years. The costs are raised even higher by the prospects for infighting within the state "instruments of coercion" because of the sharp instruments they use. Meanwhile, there are two initiatives to reform or rewrite the Zimbabwe constitution to make it democratic.

Constitutional Reform Initiatives

The present Zimbabwe constitution was negotiated at the Lancaster House Conference in London in 1979 and enacted at independence in 1980. It separated the head of government (prime minister) from the head of state (president), and had a two-chamber legislature—a forty-member Senate and one hundred-member parliament, twenty of whom were to be elected by the white electorate for the first seven years. At the expiry of the seven years in 1987, the Constitutional Amendment No. 6 of 1987 abolished the twenty reserved white seats. Constitutional Amendment No. 7 of the same year introduced the current executive presidency that combined the functions of head of government (executive) with those of head of state (ceremonial). Constitutional Amendment No. 9 of 1989 abolished the bicameral legislative system and a 150-member unicameral parliament was introduced in which 120 seats are contested and the remaining 30 are appointed by the president.[53]

In all, there have been fourteen amendments to the Zimbabwe constitution since 1980, many of which have been self-serving to the president and the ruling party. Moreover, and more fundamentally, neither the Lancaster House constitution nor any of these amendments were put to the people of Zimbabwe as a whole for approval at referendum. Only through such a constitutional referendum can we say the Zimbabwe constitution has come from "We, The People," says University of Zimbabwe professor of public law Welshman Ncube.

Accordingly, there have been persistent calls by the opposition and civil society, particularly since 1994, for constitutional reforms. In January 1998, a formation calling itself the "National Constitutional Assembly" (NCA) was launched under the auspices of the ZCC. This initiative is the culmination of earlier initiatives by civil society groups, notably, the ZCC, ZCTU, ZimRights, ZCCJP, and others. All the parties, including the ruling party, were invited to the launch, but the ruling party officially declined. Significantly, the secretariat of the NCA Task Force is chaired by Morgan Tsvangirayi, secretary-general of the ZCTU. Essentially, the NCA's mission is to "democratize the Zimbabwe Constitution."[54]

Initially, the ruling party and government ignored the calls for reforms from the opposition parties. But recently, they have also taken initiatives of their own to reform the constitution, and have in turn invited the NCA or anyone interested to make representation to the "appropriate" party and government structures. So, essentially, there are two initiatives to reform the constitution: the one by the government, the other by civil society in the form of the NCA.

Therefore, the following three scenarios can be envisaged:

1. The government has adopted a strategy calculated at bringing the NCA to its "official" initiative in the constitutional reform process. For this to succeed, the ruling party and government would have to drastically change their attitude and approach. In this scenario, I see the assembly refusing to be co-opted into the government's initiative. (Recall Stepan's first task for the opposition: "resisting integration into the regime.") The possibility that some in the echelons of ZANU(PF) would

drift to the assembly forces is more than real, given the "decline in elite cohesion" noted earlier.

2. Alternatively, the assembly might well continue with its own initiative, parallel to that of the government, resulting in two new constitutions, one sponsored by government and the other by the assembly. The assembly will insist that these be taken to the people at a national referendum.[55] ZANU(PF) would prefer that the final version and vote on the constitution be taken in parliament, which it controls. So things could be headed toward a divisive impasse.

3. However, there is a third, perhaps less divisive alternative. An Independent Constitutional Reform Commission could be set up now or at the end of these parallel initiatives to reconcile the two views or approaches and come up with one constitution that would then be publicly debated and approved at a national referendum. Wise counsel suggests that the ZANU(PF) government should not be confrontational with the majority of the people who are now swelling the "active opponents" of the regime.

In these scenarios, ZANU(PF) has the option of either reforming/transforming itself to a democratic party, or remaining the undemocratic monster that it has been since independence, continuing to expel its internal critics until it expels itself from power. While many have doubts about ZANU(PF)'s ability to exorcise itself of its undemocratic culture of many years, some believe both options are equally open to it, given that the issues are essential to the survival of the party. Moreover, we have seen that party adjusting to an adverse climate both ideologically and in terms of the one-party idea. This is why some good and able people have not abandoned trying to reform the party from within. Yet the battle for succession looms large ahead.

Who Will Succeed Mugabe?

The answer to the question of who will succeed President Mugabe is one that those who know do not tell, and those who tell do not know. President Mugabe will be seventy-eight when his fourth term of office expires in 2002. Although he has announced he will quit only upon losing an election, most people in political circles do not see him running for a fifth term due to political pressure within and outside his party, much like in the President Suharto scenario in Indonesia. Press speculations frequently run the names of old guards, including Emmerson Mnangagwa (minister of justice and parliamentary affairs), Eddison Zvobgo (minister-without-portfolio), Nathan Shamuyarira (minister of trade and commerce), Dumiso Dabengwa (minister of home affairs), Kumbirai Kangai (minister of agriculture), and new arrivals like Ignatius Chombo (minister of higher education) and Simon Kaya Moyo (minister of tourism). The list is too long to make any sense. And Mugabe, typically, does not give any clue.

But the choice for his successor in the party could determine who will be able to galvanize the support of most of the opposition we have noted above, particularly the opposition in civil society. In this scenario, a viable opposition could come from a splinter group of the ruling ZANU(PF), not unlike with the major ZAPU-ZANU split of 1963. If the opposition galvanizes around a new personality outside the ruling party, he or she will cause a major split in the ruling party, to the same effect as the 1963 split. Thus, Zimbabwe would have traveled full circle. Hopefully, it will emerge the wiser and more democratic for the mistakes and experiences of the past.

Yet the triumph of the opposition is not the same thing as the triumph for democracy. Thus, crucial to Stepan's contribution, at least from our vantage point, is the notion of a "democratic opposition." While a viable opposition is the sine qua non of a democratic order in statecraft, unless it is a "democratic opposition," authoritarian regimes will alternate in the manner of musical chairs, and the struggle for democracy must begin again. In his seminal essay, Alfred Stepan advises the following: "The redemocratization of an authoritarian regime must combine erosion and construction. . . . If the opposition attends only to the task of erosion, as opposed to that of construction, then the odds are that any future change will merely be a shift from one authoritarian government to another, rather than a change from authoritarianism to democracy."[56] This is why the National Constitutional Assembly's present constitutional reform initiatives are a healthy sign. They may well constitute the manifesto of an emergent opposition party, or a thoroughly reformed ZANU(PF).[57]

NOTES

1. Most observers of transitions to democracy in Africa have noted the "contagion effect" of earlier transitions in the Soviet Union, Eastern Europe, and in formerly white-ruled South Africa, making the point that other authoritarian regimes in Africa could not sustain the credibility and legitimacy of their authoritarianism. Samuel P. Huntington calls this phenomenon the "snowballing" effect; see Huntington, "Democracy's Third Wave," in Larry Diamond and Marc F. Plattner, eds., *The Global Resurgence of Democracy* (Baltimore: Johns Hopkins University Press, 1993). For a critique of the external origin of democratic pressures on Africa, see Richard Joseph, "Africa: The Rebirth of Political Freedom," in Diamond and Plattner, eds., *Global Resurgence of Democracy,* pp. 307–9; Peter Anyang-Nyong'o, "Development and Democracy: The Debate Continues," *CODESRIA Bulletin* (Dakar), no. 2 (1991): 2; and Claude Ake, "Rethinking African Democracy," in Diamond and Plattner, eds., *Global Resurgence of Democracy.*

2. Ake, in "Rethinking African Democracy," p. 76, emphatically states: "Like development, democratization is not something that one people does for another. People must do it for themselves or it does not happen." The contributors to Anyang-Nyong'o's *Popular Struggles in Africa* (London: Zed Press, 1987), three years before the events in the Soviet Union and Eastern Europe as well as the release of Nelson Mandela in South Africa, are testimony to this thesis.

3. The psychological impact of similar events elsewhere on local events cannot be

underplayed. The nationalist movement that brought independence four decades ago was inspired by both internal and external factors. Ndabaningi Sithole's *African Nationalism* (London: Oxford University Press, 1968), pp. 47–74, makes this point.

4. For the early foundations of the international dimension of the nationalist movement, see J. Day, *International Nationalism: The Extra-Territorial Relations of Southern Rhodesian African Nationalists* (London: Routledge, 1968). For an analysis of later periods, see J. Davidow, *A Peace in Southern Africa: The Lancaster House Conference on Rhodesia* (Boulder, Colo.: Westview Press, 1984), and S. Stedman, *Peacemaking in Civil War: International Mediation in Zimbabwe, 1974–1980* (Boulder, Colo.: Lynne Rienner, 1991).

5. Alfred Stepan, "On the Tasks of a Democratic Opposition," in Diamond and Plattner, eds., *Global Resurgence of Democracy,* pp. 61–64.

6. I used the theoretical framework for this section in an earlier shorter article. See Masipula Sithole's "Zimbabwe's Eroding Authoritarianism," *Journal of Democracy* 8, no. 1 (January 1997): 127–41.

7. Ibid., pp. 64–67.

8. Ibid., p. 65.

9. A case can be made that the real period of colonial authoritarianism was during Ian Smith's Rhodesia Front regime of 1962–79, and that 1890–1962 was a period of less harsh "liberal" paternalism.

10. The Ndebele ethnic group is roughly 19 percent. However, the Shona further divide into subethnic groups: Karanga (22 percent), Zezuru (18 percent), Manyika (13 percent), Korekore (12 percent), Rozwi (9 percent), and Ndau (3 percent). For an analysis of the salience of ethnicity in Zimbabwe politics, see Masipula Sithole, "Ethnicity and Factionalism in Zimbabwe Nationalist Movement, 1957–1979," *Ethnic and Racial Studies* (January 1980); and Masipula Sithole, "Ethnicity and Democratization in Zimbabwe: From Confrontation to Accommodation," in H. Glickman, ed., *Ethnicity and Democratization in Africa* (Atlanta: ASA Press, 1995).

11. Many people not familiar with Zimbabwean politics have held the mistaken notion that, until of late, Zimbabwe was a one-party state. If anything, Zimbabwe has been a de facto one-party dominant state.

12. This section of the paper borrows heavily from Masipula Sithole, "Is Zimbabwe Poised on a Liberal Path: The State and Prospects of the Parties," *ISSUE: A Journal of Opinion* XXI, nos. 1/2 (1993): 35–43, but not in the context of Stepan's theoretical framework.

13. See R. Weitzer, "In Search of Regime Security: Zimbabwe Since Independence," *Journal of Modern African Studies* (December 1984); J. Moyo, *Voting for Democracy: Electoral Politics in Zimbabwe* (Harare: University of Zimbabwe Press, 1991); and A. Meldrum, "Drought, Death, and Dissidents," *Africa Report* (January/February 1993). The 1985 *Amnesty International Report* (London: Amnesty International), pp. 115–19, also documents these abuses of human rights.

14. The Political Parties (Finance) Act was amended in 1997 when the Supreme Court ruled it illegal following a petition by the United Parties for its repeal. See Supreme Court case no. SC 229/95 and Supreme Court judgment no. SC 139/97. For analysis of the genesis and implications of the amended act, see Masipula Sithole, *Zimbabwe's Public Eye: Political Essays* (Harare: Rujeko, 1997), pp. 1–3.

15. In 1978, the Rhodesian leader Ian Smith enticed Bishop Abel Muzorewa, the Reverend Ndabaningi Sithole, and Chief Jeremiah Chirau (leaders of three moderate/conservative parties) into an "internal settlement" that excluded the externally based

liberation movements led by Robert Mugabe and Joshua Nkomo, who regarded the three as "puppets" of Ian Smith.

16. In the aftermath of the 1985 election, ZANU(PF) held victory celebrations where a bull (PF-ZAPU's election symbol) was brutally axed to its death in front of a cheering crowd. A mock funeral procession was held in a separate incident to symbolize the death and burial of Joshua Nkomo, the PF-ZAPU leader. For an account of these elections, see Masipula Sithole, "Zimbabwe General Elections 1979–1985," in Ibbo Mandaza, ed., *Zimbabwe: The Political Economy of Transition* (Dakar: CODESTRIA, 1986).

17. See Masipula Sithole, "Why a Coup Is Unlikely in Zimbabwe," *Financial Gazette* (Harare), 5 March 1998.

18. A hospitalized Kombayi lost the election, which should have been postponed until he was well enough to contest it.

19. See the terms of the "Unity Accord" in C. Banana, *Turmoil and Tenacity: Zimbabwe 1890–1980* (Harare: College Press, 1989).

20. See Welshman Ncube in Banana, *Turmoil and Tenacity*, pp. 166–73.

21. See E. Zvobgo, "An Agenda for Democracy, Peace, and Sustainable Development in the SADC Region" (speech given to parliamentarians at the CPA/IPU Joint Dinner at the Meikles Hotel, Harare, 14 November 1995).

22. Mugabe served as prime minister from 1980 to 1987, when he became executive president. In 1989, changes were made to separate presidential elections from parliamentary elections and to make the presidential term six years (renewable) instead of five for parliament starting from 1990.

23. For the debate on the motion on "term limits," see Hansard, *Parliamentary Debates* 24, no. 5610 (February 1998). What infuriated President Mugabe is that Mavhaire is quoted as having said: "What I am saying is that the President must go."

24. Chapter 2.08 of the Privileges, Immunities and Powers of Parliament Act provides that, "There shall be freedom of speech and debate of proceedings in or before Parliament and any committee and such freedom shall not be liable to be impeached or questioned in any Court or place outside Parliament." Nevertheless, Mavhaire was barred from holding any position in the party for the next two years.

25. Harare: Catholic Commission for Justice and Peace and the Legal Resources Foundation, 1997.

26. Following the release of *Breaking the Silence: Yielding True Peace,* a pressure group calling itself "Imbovane Yamahlabezulu" was formed in the Matebeland capital of Bulawayo to demand government explanation and compensation for the atrocities and victims of the war in Matebeleland during the Gukurahundi (Fifth Brigade) terror in the 1980s.

27. Top ZANU(PF) stalwarts and members of that party's disciplinary committee, Dydimus Mutasa and Nathan Shamuyarira, had earlier insisted that Cyril Ndebele had a "case to answer," an interpretation that the chairman of the disciplinary committee and former PF-ZAPU vice president, Joseph Musika, firmly disputed. See "Party Heavyweights Clash Over Ndebele's Fate," *Financial Gazette,* 9 April 1998.

28. For a detailed account of infighting in the nationalist movement, see Masipula Sithole, *Zimbabwe Struggles-Within-the-Struggle* (Salisbury: Rujeko, 1979).

29. See "Serious Rifts in ZANU(PF) Erupt into Open," *Financial Gazette,* 12 March 1998; "Zvobgo Camp Under Fire," *Zimbabwe Mirror,* 13–19 March 1998; and "Intraparty Factionalism Thrives in Manicaland," *Financial Gazette,* 28 May 1998.

30. See note 17 above. Stepan has observed that the military may conclude that

"continued military support of an increasingly despised regime . . . may be inimical to the interests of the military as a national institution"; see Stepan, "On the Tasks of a Democratic Opposition," p. 63.

31. The opposition parties that appear in the press from time to time are the following: ZANU(Ndonga) (a splinter group from ZANU[PF]), the United Parties (formerly United African National Congress), the Zimbabwe Unity Movement, the Democratic Party, the Forum Party of Zimbabwe, the Front for Popular Democracy, and National Democratic Union. Although it has not formalized itself as a political party, the Movement for Independent Electoral Candidates is more often quoted by the press.

32. In 1991 was formed the Democratic Party (DP), an offshoot from ZUM; in 1992 was formed the FORUM Party of Zimbabwe (FPZ) an offshoot from ZUM, DP, UANC, ZAPU, ZANU, and FROLIZI (Front for the Liberation of Zimbabwe); in 1995 was formed the United Parties (UP) an offshoot from UANC, FORUM, ZANU(Ndonga), and CAZ (Conservative Alliance of Zimbabwe, formerly Ian Smith's Rhodesia Front); and again in 1995 was formed the PFD (Popular Front for Democracy), which was basically an offshoot from the original FORUM party.

33. The six participating political parties were the Democratic Party; the Front for Popular Democracy; the National Democratic Union; the United Front; the United Parties; and the Zimbabwe People's Party. ZANU(Ndonga), the FORUM Party of Zimbabwe, and the Zimbabwe Unity Movement did not take part.

34. Thus far, there have been fourteen amendments to the Zimbabwe Constitution. For a description of these amendments, see J. Reid-Rowland, "Amendments to Zimbabwe's Constitution," *Legal Forum* 6, no. 2 (1994).

35. While the elite cohesion of the original ZANU(PF) has declined, that of the former PF-ZAPU has remained steadfast, as witnessed in the Cyril Ndebele affair already detailed.

36. ZUM remains, but only in name. It lost sympathy with the people immediately following the 1990 elections when it became apparent that its leader, Edgar Tekere, lacked organizational capacity. See J. Moyo, "ZUM Plays Truant with Voters," *Parade,* January 1991, pp. 13, 49.

37. See note 15, above.

38. One minister, Maurice Nyagumbo, even committed suicide.

39. *Herald* (Harare), 11 April 1990.

40. Zimbabwe's influential independent weeklies include the *Financial Gazette,* the *Independent Standard,* and the *Mirror.* Monthly magazines include *Moto, Parade,* and *Horizon.*

41. Ibbo Mandaza and Lloyd Sachikonye, eds., *The One-Party State and Democracy: The Zimbabwe Debate* (Harare: SAPES Books, 1991). Some chapter titles in this book reveal the critical mood of these intellectuals: "Intolerance: The Bane of African Rulers"; "Should Zimbabwe Go Where Others Are Coming From"; "The Dialectic of National Unity and Democracy in Zimbabwe"; "A One-Party or a Multi-Party State"; "The One-Party, Socialism and Democratic Struggles in Zimbabwe"; "The Labour Movement and the One-Party State Debate"; and "Constitutionalism, Democracy and Political Practice in Zimbabwe."

42. The average salary for the "political class" in Zimbabwe is Z$35,000 per month, while for the average worker it is Z$1,000, below the poverty datum line of Z$1,332. (US$1 equals Z$18.)

43. Harare is the only city in which the police prohibited the demonstrations. This

was done because President Mugabe was giving his "State of the Nation" address to parliament in the City Center. Many observers believed that the prohibition was the reason for the violence in Harare. Incidentally, in his speech, President Mugabe never referred to the nationwide demonstrations.

44. See "Zimbabwe's Turning Point," *Financial Gazette,* 15 January 1998.

45. The food riots claimed eight lives, left ten wounded, and caused damage to property worth Z$75 million.

46. Margaret Dongo (independent member of parliament), interview by author, Harare, 21 June 1998.

47. In his 1998 "May Day" speech, the secretary-general of the ZCTU, Morgan Tsvangirayi, denied that his organization was involved in politics: "The only politics we are involved in is the politics of the stomach," he said. However, Tsvangirayi has his options open. See "Tsvangirayi Has His Options Open," *Financial Gazette,* 4 June 1998. Moreover, the law does not prohibit trade unionists from taking part in politics.

48. See "Some Comrades Are More Equal Than Others," *Financial Gazette,* 20 November 1997.

49. See "War Collaborators Threaten ZANU PF's Power Base," *Financial Gazette,* 28 May 1998. See also "Collaborators to Sue Government?" *Zimbabwe Mirror,* 12–18 June 1998.

50. See "Well Done *Herald* and ZBC," *Financial Gazette,* 7 May 1998.

51. Stepan, "On the Tasks of a Democratic Opposition," p. 68.

52. *Polyarchy: Participation and Opposition* (New Haven, Conn.: Yale University Press, 1971).

53. The constitution (as amended in 1989) provides for the appointment by the president of twelve non-constituency MPs, eight provincial governors, and ten traditional chiefs. The thirty also sit in parliament.

54. "The Constitution as Liability: Zimbabwe's Experience with the Bill of Rights," *Legal Forum* 7, no. 1 (1995).

55. For the "mission statement" of this organization, see *Debating the Constitution of Zimbabwe* (Harare: NCA Secretariat, Zimbabwe, 1997).

56. The Politburo of the ruling ZANU(PF) recently took a decision in favor of a referendum on the constitution. See "Politburo Agrees to Hold National Referendum on Constitution," *Financial Gazette,* 4 June 1998. See also "Party's Commitment to Reform Queried," *Financial Gazette,* 11 June 1998.

57. Stepan, "On the Tasks of a Democratic Opposition," p. 67.

5. | Democracy and Development in Post-Independence Namibia

Joshua Bernard Forrest

A lengthy national liberation struggle against South Africa's apartheid-based rule in Namibia was led by the South West African People's Organization (SWAPO) from 1966 through the 1980s and culminated in a December 1988 agreement brokered by the United Nations (UN) and the major Western powers. In that accord, South Africa agreed to withdraw peaceably from its former colony. Nearly one year later, in November 1989, relatively free and fair national elections democratically catapulted SWAPO into the position of majority political party in the country's transitional Constituent Assembly, in which MPs from six other political parties had also won seats. That assembly ironed out a new constitution and became the National Assembly at independence in March 1990.[1] Since that time, Namibia's democratic framework of government has remained remarkably stable despite lingering racial antagonisms and new political concerns. This stability in large measure reflects the continuing commitment to a free and fair electoral process, a rule-abiding parliament, vibrant local and regional councils, well-organized and active civic groups, and an army that is loyal to civilian rule. Nonetheless, underlying social and economic divisions remain unresolved and could provoke significant political problems in subsequent decades.

Institutional Context

The institutional framework of government established by the independence elections is a Westminster-style democracy in which the prime minister and his cabinet sit in parliament, and the majority party serves as the "ruling" party because it is able to pass laws without allying with opposition MPs. Since independence, SWAPO has enjoyed the position of ruling party; in the 1990–94 period, it held a 41-seat majority in the National Assembly, compared to 21 seats for the largest opposition party, the Democratic Turnhalle Alliance (DTA).[2] The SWAPO majority grew to 53 seats following the 1994 parliamentary election and to 55 seats in 1999 (discussed below).

Similarly to other Commonwealth legislative systems, ruling party and opposition MPs sit on opposing sides of the house floor; the Speaker of the National Assembly—currently Mosé Tjitendero—controls the discussion according to standard parliamentary rules. Substantial leeway is structured into debate time to allow for a wide range of off-the-cuff remarks.[3] Thus, although SWAPO's bills are eventually approved, this has often been preceded by substantial and lively argumentation that is reported in the print media, with highlights broadcast on national television.

Opposition party MPs have not felt inhibited to lambast ruling party policies. To cite one example of a critical outburst: on 3 March 1993, DTA MP Katuutire Kaura noted that he would hold the president and the prime minister accountable for "every child that starves to death, every house burglary, every killing of a farmer, for the stealing of government money, for poorly-trained doctors, for the shortage of medicines, for unemployment."[4] Moreover, care is taken to assure a generally balanced allocation of MP discussion time. Thus, for example, for the debate on a budgetary proposal, 660 minutes were set aside for SWAPO MPs, while opposition parties were granted nearly the same amount of speaking time—a total of 570 minutes (345 minutes for the DTA, 90 minutes for the UDF, with the NPF, FCN, and NNF each granted 45 minutes).[5]

At the same time, five national elections have been held since independence, assuring voters regular opportunities to choose their leaders at the local, regional, and national levels. In the 1992 regional and local council elections, balloting occurred smoothly and opposition parties ran candidates in most districts; SWAPO won control of nine of the thirteen newly established regional councils and thirty-two of the forty-five local councils.[6]

Two years later, in December 1994—five years from the 1989 vote, as required by the constitution—presidential and parliamentary elections were held, and they were declared free and fair by European observers, despite complaints by the opposition.[7] President Sam Nujoma confirmed his status as the country's intensely popular national leader by winning 74.5 percent of the presidential tally, while Mishake Muyongo, the DTA candidate, obtained 23.1 percent.[8] In the parliamentary balloting (conducted separately), SWAPO deepened its position as ruling party by winning a two-thirds-plus majority in the National Assembly with fifty-three seats and 72.7 percent of the votes. The DTA, the main opposition party, won only fifteen seats and 20.5 percent of the votes (down from 29 percent in 1989).[9] Three minor parties shared the remaining four seats.[10]

The country's third set of post-independence elections took place in February 1998 exclusively for local council seats; SWAPO won control of twenty-seven of the forty-five local councils, with the DTA attaining a majority on nine councils, the UDF controlling three councils, residents' associations obtaining control of two councils, and four councils being evenly divided.[11] The fact that two opposition political parties and urban residents' associations attained majority representation on a total of fourteen of the councils, with four additional councils being evenly divided, is especially noteworthy, as this helped to broaden political representation at the local level despite SWAPO's overall predominance. Moreover, in the fourth set of elections, the December 1998 vote for regional councils, the DTA won nearly one-quarter of the vote, and the UDF almost 5 percent, assuring a continued diversity of representation at the regional level, although SWAPO did win 67 percent of the vote and remained in control of ten of the thirteen regional councils.[12]

More generally, the elections of 1992, 1994, and 1998 functioned to further entrench the democratic process in Namibia because the voter registration and balloting processes were carried out entirely by Namibian political officials, whereas UN agencies had provided high levels of technical assistance during the independence elections of 1989. Political scientists generally view the holding of repeat free and fair elections (beyond the initial, "founding" elections) as critical tests of democratic durability.[13] Nonetheless, the 1994 national election result raised concerns in Namibia about shrinking popular support for opposition political parties, and the potentially negative impact on the country's multi-vocal National Assembly. In particular, the 1994 voting dramatized the fact that DTA head Mishake Muyongo had proved unable to rally the DTA's disparate component members into an organizationally unified and coherent opposition force.[14] The DTA loss of six parliamentary seats in the National Assembly clearly weakened its position as the primary opposition party. At the same time, however, alternative political parties[15] remained too small to wield much influence in the assembly, especially as they were reduced to three parties (down from five parties prior to 1994). This produced concern for the rise of a "one party dominant political system" in Namibia,[16] although the nineteen opposition members sustained lively debates and articulated anti-SWAPO positions during parliamentary sessions throughout the 1994–99 period.

The fifth set of national elections was held on 2–3 December 1999. In the presidential contest, Sam Nujoma won re-election to a third term with 72.5 percent of the vote, with Ben Ulenga, head of the newly created Congress of Democrats (CoD, discussed below) winning 12.1 percent and Katuutire Kaura of the DTA obtaining third with 11.7 percent. In the parliamentary balloting, SWAPO retained its two-thirds-plus majority with 55 of the 72 seats in the National Assembly, while the opposition vote was fragmented between the DTA, with 7 seats, and the CoD, which also obtained 7 seats. The vote made clear that SWAPO had held onto its solid support base in the populous far north and the major cities, while the CoD had pulled votes away from former DTA supporters without making inroads into the SWAPO voting block.

Meanwhile, the local and regional councils have proven particularly important in consolidating a grassroots linkage between the state and ordinary rural Namibians.[17] The local councils—consisting of municipal councils, town councils, and village councils—vary enormously in terms of administrative capacity and locally generated levels of financing, but generally have succeeded in facilitating democratic channels of community consultation and popular participation in local decision-making.[18] The regional councils have suffered from a lack of formal powers and financing, and some analysts believe that this may have contributed to declines in voter registration in some regions prior to the 1998 regional council elections.[19] However, through the 1990s, regional councillors have managed to work around administrative and budgeting difficulties and have become immersed in local development and social policy issues of deep concern to their mostly rural constituents. Their activities include lobbying for water piping and school-building projects and collaborating with development agencies and regional-level offices of government ministries to facilitate the implementation of drought relief programs. As a result of such activism, regional councillors have influenced the policy process within their respective regions and have provided villagers with an elected political voice that they have used to persistently press central government ministries for village-based programs.[20]

Moreover, the regional councils directly elected the "second" house of parliament—the National Council, which began functioning in February 1993. The Namibian constitution stipulates that the National Council cannot deny passage of a National Assembly bill, but it does not make clear whether the council has the power to amend bills or to propose new bills. The National Assembly has for the most part sought to take advantage of this constitutional confusion by treating the "second house" as an impotent institutional appendage. However, the National Council, despite the fact that it is overwhelmingly dominated by SWAPO national councillors (who hold nineteen of the twenty-six seats), has not acted as a quiescent, nominal institution. It has strongly criticized existing government policies, particularly regarding issues of concern to the predominantly rural regions, such as insisting on a speeding up of the National Assembly's consideration of land reform measures (see below), and demanding improvement in the quality of the government's pension check distribution program in the rural areas. The fact that all national councillors serve simultaneously as regional councillors, and that they commute regularly to their home districts to attend regional council meetings, provides the National Council with an especially representative character.[21]

Much of the vigor of the National Council's effort to establish itself as a viable second house of parliament is provided by Chairperson Kandindima Nehova, a long-time SWAPO partisan and (formerly) a trade union activist. Nehova commands significant respect within the party and within the politically influential Ongwediva constituency. Nehova's efforts to boost the National Council's standing have reaped notable dividends: since its creation in 1993 the National Council has achieved gradually augmenting political visibility and institutional stature. Some tension and a certain bicameral competitiveness between the National Council and National Assembly persist, but, promisingly, in the 1995–99 period the National Assembly accepted the National Council's proposed revisions of several bills, including one concerning a specification of the legal roles of traditional leaders.[22] In

JOSHUA BERNARD FORREST

February 1999, the councillors reconfirmed Nehova as National Council chairperson while electing a woman, Magreth Mensah, to serve as deputy chairperson.[23]

Beyond these parliamentary institutions, Namibia's military forces have thus far remained removed from domestic politics, which has added to an overall sense of national political stability. The Namibia Defence Force (NDF) represents a merger of the former People's Liberation Army of Namibia (PLAN), the armed forces of the nationalist liberation struggle, and the military units of the apartheid-era South West African state, the former South West Africa Territorial Force (SWATF). After some initial tensions the merger has functioned reasonably effectively, with the principal difficulty being the demobilization of former fighters who anticipated continued employment by the post-colonial state. Development Brigades were established to facilitate this process, with the intention that ex-soldiers would be re-mobilized for agricultural development work, but those brigades have thus far suffered from inadequate retraining and management problems. Nonetheless, the NDF has succeeded in shrinking its forces to approximately 8,000 soldiers,[24] while NDF generals appear to be fully devoted to the existing framework of government.

In 1999, the Namibian armed forces began to draw widespread political attention when the government decided to provide active military support to President Laurent Kabila of the Democratic Republic of Congo in his struggle against rebel forces. Although Namibian President Nujoma has defended this decision by reference to inter-African solidarity, his support for Kabila apparently also reflected longstanding personal and political ties between them that date to their common status as exiled political rebels in the 1960s and 1970s. In any case, at least several hundred Namibian soldiers were fighting alongside Congolese government forces beginning early 1999; by October 1999 a total of nineteen Namibian soldiers had been killed in Congo, provoking serious questions in Windhoek political circles about the reasons for Namibia's continued involvement in this war.

Meanwhile, the Namibian government's domestic record on human rights remains laudable on the whole, with a wide range of constitutionally protected freedoms being respected, including personal liberties, non-discrimination in employment, property rights, women's rights, and cultural rights.[25] Non-governmental organizations (NGOs) such as the Namibian Democratic Institute, Educational Publications Trust, and the Freidrich Ebert Institute have published and distributed educational literature concerning citizen's political and social rights, and these have been translated into local languages and aired over the radio.[26] The 1992 Labor Code stipulating workers' rights has been repeatedly distributed throughout the country, and commercial landowners have been forced to allow government-appointed labor commissioners to meet with farmworkers and to explain their new rights to them.[27] Namibia's Legal Aid Center (LAC), which played such a key role in documenting the apartheid government's human rights abuses during the 1980s, has enjoyed a free reign (unimpeded by the government) to work with independent rights advocates to promote research into and greater awareness of labor rights, women's rights, and police accountability,[28] and has continued to operate freely despite criticizing the SWAPO government in the late 1990s. Those criticisms involved concerns over strong government statements against certain newspaper stories, but the private media continues to operate unfettered and to launch diatribes against government policies. In this respect and in reflection of the five elections, the country has been ranked as the most democratic in all of southern Africa.[29]

Political Variables

Despite this impressive institutional context, since the early 1990s there has been growing concern about the increasingly evident centralist tendencies of the Namibian political leadership. This reflects the fact that, in the first place, President Sam Nujoma has asserted his personal power within the ruling party more fully than he did during his first term. For example, he appears to have been personally responsible for selecting the top thirty-two names on the ranked SWAPO party list presented to the Electoral Commission prior to the 1994 elections.[30] To be sure, this type of decision-making remains within the norms of the elected head of a parliamentary democracy. Nonetheless, additional signs of centralist tendencies have emerged in the 1994–99 period.

For example, the cabinet portfolios for defense and security were transferred to Nujoma in 1994, while the president also assumed personal responsibility for the home affairs (including domestic police) portfolio shortly prior to his inauguration for a second term in March 1995.[31] Also, some cabinet members have reinforced the centralized structure of the ministries that they each control. Moreover, the gap within SWAPO between the top leaders and ordinary party members appears to be widening, as the party leadership has grown comfortable with their role as national rulers while the younger, more "radical" wing of the party continues to press for greater attention to social problems. This gap adds to the perception of a concentration of power at the highest levels of the ruling party and of the state,[32] and helped fuel the emergence of a new opposition political party in 1999 (discussed below).

Also contributing to the concern over centralism are recent signs of a possible weakening of the national government's commitment to a pluralistic political culture, with particular regard to the freedom of operation of the country's privately controlled press.[33] It should be emphasized that, thus far, the Namibian media have provided a range of highly critical views on various policy issues in several different languages.[34] Five different newspapers consistently publish many stories that include searing critiques of government activities and policies. However, several SWAPO leaders, including President Nujoma, have repeatedly criticized what they view as overly harsh attacks by some columnists and reporters, and this has generated apprehension of a gradual movement toward governmental intolerance of press freedoms. This concern appeared confirmed when, in December 1996, the government passed a Privileges and Immunities of Parliament bill which made it illegal for MPs or reporters to publicly disclose policy information before it is officially presented within parliament.[35] However, this sparked loud protests from members of the media, and these protests in turn led the National Assembly to remove from the act the paragraph concerning reporters.[36] In large measure, it can be argued that, in effect, the democratic process functioned effectively to counteract the move toward centralism in respect to the free press, but strong suspicions regarding the government's eventual intentions continue to be voiced within Windhoek-based media circles.

Meanwhile, increasingly through the 1990s, some of the more potentially important civic groups such as trade unions, women's groups, and student organizations have been marked by growing fragmentation and internal fragility, which has added to the concern over the future of political pluralism in Namibia.[37] Most of these groups have become consolidated within larger federations that are formally or informally linked to the ruling political party. This raises the specter that a gradual shift toward centralized SWAPO rule, if sustained, may overly narrow the range of freely operating civic groups.[38]

One factor that has thus far functioned to partially moderate centralist tendencies has been the policy of "national reconciliation" adopted by the government at independence, although problems in the implementation of this policy have emerged. The origin of national reconciliation lies in the negotiations through which the independence constitution was forged during the course of the Constituent Assembly meetings in 1989–90. The policy of national reconciliation centers on overcoming past political grievances between previous political enemies (pro-apartheid vs. anti-apartheid) and among racial and ethnic groups. This policy emphasizes the importance of mutual respect between SWAPO and DTA politicians and among traditional leaders from various groups, as well as underlining the need for blacks to work together with (or at least to tolerate) the white populace despite their continued economic predominance.

In reflection of this policy of national reconciliation, since independence SWAPO's leadership has insisted on a full inclusion of the country's racial and ethnic groups in the national political system. The ruling party has made a special effort to ensure ethnic and racial representation across a broad spectrum of key political posts, from the cabinet level through the lower ranks of the civil service (this balance of ethnic representatives is similarly reproduced within SWAPO's own leadership structures). An ethnic breakdown of cabinet and of the top positions in each ministry reveals that Ovambo-speakers, despite a common perception that they dominate the political system, in fact hold only about one-quarter of the top and middle-range civil service posts even though they make up nearly half the Namibian populace[39] (although Ovambo-speakers do hold some of the most important positions, including the presidency, the ministership of trade and industry, and key army officer posts).

Meanwhile, the SWAPO leadership has been the target of strong and growing criticism both from among its members and from social, ethnic, and racial groups who continue to feel disenfranchised. Many of the more militant SWAPO party adherents have voiced concerns—at party congresses and in the media—that the policy of reconciliation in particular has meant that the party is turning its backs on key social problems such as landlessness and unemployment, while consolidating ties with privileged whites and other elites.[40] From a different perspective, many Kwanyama speakers in the north feel that the party leadership has also gone too far in extending its hand to non-Ovambo blacks, and they resent what they see as the unnecessary political eminence of the smaller ethnic groups, for example, in the assignments of some key posts to non-Ovambo. These posts have included the prime ministership (Hage Geingob, Damara), the National Assembly Speaker (Mosé Tjitendero, Herero), and until May 1997, the position of SWAPO secretary-general (the late Moses Garoeb, Damara).[41]

However, as already indicated, at the other end of this ethnic discontent there has been concern among some sectors of the non-Ovambo populace over what they perceive to be the undue political influence of Ovambo speakers, particularly Kwanyama. In fact, a small number of Herero and Damara traditional chiefs and a segment of the Reheboth Basters remain unconvinced of SWAPO's commitment to ethnic equanimity and have even called for ethno-regional separation from the Namibian state. It should be stressed here, however, that *most* Herero, Damara and Reheboth Basters, including traditional chiefs, have embraced Namibia's democratic order and reject the call for ethnic separatism. Nonetheless, some separatists loudly complain that SWAPO's multi-ethnic veneer masks Ovambo (especially Kwanyama) dominance, and that SWAPO leaders' personal links to the predominantly Ovambo far north assure this group enormous political influence. These ethnic critics remain a sharp thorn in the side of the government despite their failure to attract more than a small number of followers in their own communities.

Criticisms regarding Kwanyama/Ovambo predominance were articulated with particular concern when, in 1996, the SWAPO government allowed the restoration of the Kwanyama traditional kingship. However, it should be emphasized that this restoration took place only after other ethnic groups—including the Damara and Herero—had also been permitted to restore their kingships. It is the case that these kingships are largely nominal, that is, lacking in independent powers, but they do provide symbolic value to those Herero and Damara followers who resent SWAPO's overall drive to reduce the importance of ethnic politics. Moreover, precisely because the government has not wished to alienate popular traditional leaders, the Ministry of Regional and Local Government and Housing (MRLGH) has made a special effort to ensure the establishment of constructive ties with local chiefs and respected headmen.[42] This includes acknowledging the legitimate role of traditional leaders and including them on government-led negotiating teams and conferences to help resolve specific tensions at the regional levels.[43] A further example of ethnic inclusion has been the multi-ethnic national Council of Traditional Leaders, which incorporates key chiefs who work with the MRLGH to help adjudicate local disputes.[44]

These ethnic policies have helped to moderate concern among many Herero, Damara, Rehebothers, and other smaller groups regarding the charges of Ovambo predominance. Still, vote returns and exit polling suggests that many Namibians continue to cast ballots according to historical voting patterns, with SWAPO's political core base remaining centered in the far north (predominantly Ovambo-speaking) and the cities and larger towns (with large clusters of Ovambo speakers).[45] Moreover, SWAPO's ethno-political support in the south (Hardap and Karas regions) and in large sections of Omaheke and Otjozondjupa regions remains relatively superficial. Those regions are inhabited predominantly by Herero, Nama, Damara, and Rehebothers—many of whom strongly backed the component political parties of the DTA during the 1980s and in the 1989 independence election.

SWAPO did augment its vote totals slightly in those southern and east-central regions in the 1994 national election, and, importantly, the government has sought to promote various small livestock programs (such as drought relief) and other development programs there. However, it should be noted that many DTA supporters chose not to vote in 1994, in contrast to a rise in registration and voter turnout in pro-SWAPO regions.[46] Second, the relative disorganization of the DTA and other opposition parties contrasted starkly with the organizational advantages of the incumbent ruling party. DTA fragility combined with popular perceptions in various parts of the country that SWAPO is a predominantly Ovambo-speaking political party represents a lingering obstacle to the incorporation of all non-Ovambo Namibians into the national political process.

This potential roadblock became dramatized by the sudden appearance of a secessionist movement in Caprivi in late 1998, led by former DTA head Mishake Muyongo. This movement claimed a history of under-representation by Caprivians in Windhoek and of SWAPO-Ovambo control over and manipulation of key social institutions (especially hospitals and schools) in Caprivi. However, complicating this claim was the fact that Caprivians are divided ethno-politically between pro-SWAPO Basubia and pro-DTA Mafwe, even though both of these ethnic subgroups pertain to the broader Lozi ethnic group. Despite this strong intra-ethnic political division, secessionist leaders claim a common regional resentment against the Ovambo-dominated SWAPO government.[47]

Adding to a sense of crisis in the Caprivi was the DTA decision to boycott the regional council election of December 1998, asserting security forces had harassed their candidates; the boycott assured an all-SWAPO council.[48] Muyongo, who had already left Namibia for Botswana, then spearheaded the formation of a guerilla group that, in August 1999, returned to Namibia to attack a police station in the Caprivian capital city of Katima Mulilo. The rebels were immediately suppressed by the Namibian armed forces, who rounded up 200 suspects, tortured some of them, and held 85 for prosecution. Several additional guerillas were found and killed the following month, September 1999.[49] It is unclear how widespread support for secession remained within Caprivi, as some believe that Muyongo had the support of no more than several hundred Caprivians. From a security perspective, it appears that any remaining rebels pose little serious threat to the Namibian armed forces.

Moreover, there is no evidence that Muyongo has the support of Caprivi's traditional leaders. Indeed, it is important to re-emphasize, in regard to Caprivi as well as to all of Namibia's thirteen regions, that the government has treated most traditional and ethnic leaders with respect and has incorporated a variety of ethnic voices from rural areas into the nation-state. Most chiefs and headmen—Herero, Damara, Rehebothers, and others—have openly embraced the democratic order. Thus, overall, it is likely that the risk of ethno-political fragmentation has been minimized—a notable achievement of the government's policy of national reconciliation. At the same time, as indicated above, the regional councils and the National Council have played a constructive role in providing rural communities with access to the national political system in a democratic manner. Moreover, despite their diminished numbers as of the 1994 and 1999 national elections, opposition party members continue to voice substantial criticisms on the floor of the National Assembly, sustaining the vibrancy of parliamentary debates. These factors represent important counterbalances to the centralizing measures exhibited at the higher levels of the state while also providing momentum to continue the nation's progress, albeit gradual, toward national reconciliation.

Economic Divisions and Development Prospects

The issue of national reconciliation bears a special significance for the evolution of social class relations in post-independence Namibia. Here, it is important to emphasize that SWAPO has sought to forge alliances with socio-economic elites within the privileged "white" community, with successful black African urban traders, and with traditional elites in rural African communities. However, these alliances have raised a strong concern among some elements of the populace of the rise of a "political class" or "new bureaucratic bourgeoisie" reflecting the consolidation of post-independence economic interests among government, business, select traditional leaders, and commercial farmers.[50] These ruling class alliances could sow the seeds of social unrest by provoking mass resentment in the long term.[51]

Still, it can be argued that, thus far, these social class alliances have helped Namibia to achieve a relatively impressive degree of internal stability. More particularly, by respecting the village-level authority of many traditional leaders while also asserting the pre-eminent power of the SWAPO-controlled state, the government has effectively reduced the potential for serious unrest on the part of these traditional leaders. At the same time, however, in doing so, many peasants and observers fear the creation of a ruling class harmonization of interests through which the nation's political leadership has begun to distance itself from the majority of the country's rural and urban poor. This is especially the case as SWAPO has upheld a mixed state/market approach to economic development that allows for fundamentally free trade combined with targeted state investment to support certain economic sectors such as commercial agriculture.[52] SWAPO's continuing commitment to a market economy has helped to avoid a "mass flight" of indigenous whites, most of whom have remained in the country and have continued to contribute to its highly productive commercial cattle farming and industrial sectors. But while this policy choice has wielded substantial political stability and economic gains in the short term, this could be at the cost of longer-term social class quiescence.

More particularly, the growing consolidation of a new socio-economic political class has contributed to the sensitivity of what Namibians call "the land question," which could evolve into a significant source of social discontent. This land question involves two principal components: One is the fundamental and continuing division between the predominantly black African "communal" areas and the white-dominated "commercial" sectors. This bifurcation reflects the apartheid-era consolidation of some 32 million hectares of commercial farm land—most of the rural areas of central and southern Namibia—in the hands of 4,450 farmers,[53] the vast majority of whom are white. In contrast, more than one million black Africans live in the "communal areas," which total 33 million hectares in the far northern, eastern, and western regions.[54] The second aspect of the land question concerns conflicts over land scarcity between rich and poor farmers *within* the communal areas.

Both components of the land question—the commercial-communal division and the intra-communal area land conflicts—are viewed as exceptionally sensitive and politically charged issues in Namibia because of their significance for key social classes—the land-short peasantry, small landholders, large farmers, and commercial herders. SWAPO has sought to walk a fine line between responding to historically based demands to redistribute black African lands seized during the decades of white rule, and the concern to assure continuing political stability in the white-dominated cattle farming areas so as not to unbalance the lucrative commercial livestock sector. At the same time, within the communal areas, the government has sought to avoid exacerbating conflicts between poor peasants and wealthier farmers, and for this reason has been reluctant to approve a wholesale privatization of the land.

As a consequence of these conflicting and complex political pressures, the government has moved very cautiously regarding both segments of the land question, but some concrete steps have been initiated in order to address the communal-commercial division. In particular, the SWAPO leadership has undertaken a modest land redistribution within the commercial zones by purchasing farms offered for sale by private landholders and resettling landless peasants onto those farms. According to official government figures, between 1991 and mid-1997 approximately 20,000 landless communal farmers were relocated onto newly purchased farms in the commercial areas.[55] The number of commercial farms purchased by the government was minimal during the first five years of independence (seventeen commercial farms were acquired), but the pace of farm buying picked up substantially after the National Assembly passed the Commercial [Agricultural] Land Reform Act (the act was gazetted in March 1995).[56] Only farms already intended for sale have been considered for purchase, with the act permitting the government preferential purchasing rights, and compensation is based on existing market prices.[57] A total of thirty-nine commercial farms was obtained by the Ministry of Lands, Resettlement and Rehabilitation by mid-1997.[58]

The farms purchased in the 1991–97 period comprise a total of 240,935 hectares, and most are located within the central and southern regions of Oshikoto, Hardap, Karas, and Omaheke regions, with several farms also in Otjozondjupa and Kunene.[59] There are serious concerns regarding the technical ability of the newly transplanted communal farmers to maintain the productivity of the new farms.[60] However, the politically symbolic value of these resettlements—in initiating a land redistribution (however modest)—may prove even more important, at least in the short run, in demonstrating political concern by the government for the deep historical inequities between the communal and commercial areas.

Nonetheless, it is the case that barely a fraction of the 32 million hectares of commercial land has been redistributed. In early 1998, an additional N$20 million was allocated by the government expressly for land purchases and resettlement within the commercial areas,[61] but the pace of reform is likely to remain gradual. This cautious approach will help assure social peace for the time being, but eventually substantial discontent among the land-short peasantry could emerge if the redistribution process is not significantly widened.

Meanwhile, the second component of Namibia's "land question" reflects the fact that within the communal areas of the far northern regions—Oshana, Ohangwena, Oshikoto, Omusati, Kunene, Okavango—and in the central and eastern portions of Omaheke and Otjozondjupa regions, over-grazing of cattle and small stock combined with sustained droughts in the early and mid-1990s has produced an ecological and grazing land crisis. The reduction of grassland available to cattle combined with the reluctance of tens of thousands of herders to thin their stock herds sufficiently has exacerbated this crisis. Many economic elites and larger farmers have consequently carried out increasingly intensive "land-grabbing" campaigns that have marginalized growing numbers of poor peasants.[62] Conflicts have also broken out over access to water points, especially boreholes, with rising frequency and intensity especially in Omaheke and Otjozondjupa regions, and to a growing extent in Oshana and Omusati regions.[63]

This situation has been exacerbated by the government's hesitancy to enact and enforce a clear-cut new land law for the communal areas. The National Assembly deliberated the land question regarding the communal areas for much of the 1994–99 period; in July 1996 parliament drafted an Outline of a National Land Policy while also drafting a Communal Land Reform Bill.[64] Intense discussion and debate regarding the latter bill occurred throughout 1998 and 1999, with its final content yet to be determined, although skepticism has grown regarding the government's interest in protecting the land rights of poor farmers.[65] Indeed, it is not clear to what extent the growing schisms caused by land conflicts within the communal areas will be effectively eased by any new legislation. Overall, then, while the government's decision to undertake a modest land distribution in the commercial areas has at least begun to address the issue of communal-commercial farmer inequity, the increasing numbers of landless and land-short peasants *within* the communal areas could nonetheless eventually pose a major threat to social stability in those areas.

In contrast to the problematic land question, the country has made more notable strides in regard to agricultural development. After Namibia's independence in 1990, world markets became more accessible and the Namibian Meat Board was able to obtain higher prices for the country's substantial livestock exports.[66] Indeed, the commercial cattle and small stock sectors have remained highly productive, with at least US$200 million worth of beef, sheep, and goat products exported annually (mostly to South African markets). The export value of livestock and livestock products represented 16.7 percent of total exports, with 90 percent of Namibia's agricultural earnings derived from the livestock trade.[67] The commercial agriculture sector also continued to employ nearly 20 percent of all formal sector wage laborers, representing about 36,000 workers.[68] Namibia also developed a modest export niche in ostriches shortly after independence, which has continued to expand in the mid-to-late 1990s throughout the southern commercial regions, despite declining export ostrich prices.

At the same time, within most of Namibia's communal areas, a vibrant grassroots or "informal" trade involving an annual turnover of tens of thousands of head of cattle (and to a lesser extent goats and sheep) assures a relatively high level of capital accumulation among a broad cross section of small-scale livestock producers. The far north is characterized by cattle farmers each in possession of herds numbering between 13 and 21 head of livestock, while stock herds in Omaheke region tend to be somewhat larger, averaging 25–30 head per herd.[69] Thousands of herders sell several head of stock on a daily or weekly basis in many of the communal areas. In a single year, 13,257 head of cattle from the communal areas of Otjozondjupa and Omaheke regions and 19,450 small stock (goats) from communal areas in Karas and Hardap regions were sold on livestock markets.[70] It is furthermore common in the far north for herders to sell one or two head of cattle at what is called a "bush market" in the early morning hours, with marketers slaughtering animals on the spot and selling their remains throughout the day.

Moreover, more than 90 percent of rural Namibian families living in the regions of Oshana, Ohangwena, Omusati, and Okavango grow food grain crops (especially pearl millet, the staple food) and vegetables, often selling surpluses either privately or on local markets, further contributing to a modest scale of economic growth.[71] Other items such as handicrafts, locally produced vegetables and fruits, as well as imported foodstuffs are also sold at local markets in towns and villages throughout the rural areas in the far northern, eastern, and western regions and thereby contribute to the high levels of trade occurring within the communal areas. In addition, income from mine workers and farm workers, and remittances from urban migrants back to their extended families in these rural areas have been invested in productive economic activities such as farming, house building, and start-up costs for town-based micro-level businesses such as taxi driving, dry cleaning, artisanry, renting a market stall, or establishing a tavern. As a result, the economies of the predominantly communal area regions of Kunene, Oshana, Omusati, Oshikoto, Ohangwena, Okavango, Otjozondjupa, and Omaheke are bustling with hundreds of local markets that have contributed to substantial income gains for a significant proportion of rural Namibians.

At the same time, since independence in 1990 the government has invested considerable revenue into new food crop programs and irrigation and borehole construction projects within the previously ignored communal areas. Nearly three dozen agricultural development centers and new extension service offices have been established in rural farming areas by the Ministry of Agriculture, Water and Rural Development. Such programs have allowed livestock farmers to cull their herds at going market rates (although these prices are constantly disputed).[72] Two particularly dramatic improvements have been (1) the widespread distribution of newly developed and highly productive hybrid millet and maize seeds to peasant farmers, and (2) the provision of various drought relief services (such as cattle licks and feed) to communal area herds in an effort to preserve a portion of peasants' cattle stocks during extended droughts. These drought relief efforts were strengthened in June 1998 with the cabinet's approval of a total of N$80 million (US$16 million) for programs including emergency grazing for cattle and water supply.[73]

However, structural marketing problems, the ecological destruction caused by the drought crises, and high rates of rural unemployment make it difficult for many rural Namibians to take full advantage of these benefits. In the meantime, the land shortages described above, in combination with rising expectations of new jobs in the cities, have produced a strong influx of urban migrants who have added to concerns regarding overcrowded housing in Windhoek and in the regional capitals. A contributing problem is the fact that external investment from abroad has not flowed into Namibia to the extent anticipated at independence. Windhoek's economy remains relatively vibrant and stable, especially compared to other African capitals, but unemployment and underemployment have added noticeably to the growing class gap between rich and poor in much of the city.

At the same time, Namibia remains dependent on South Africa for approximately 75 percent of its imported goods, which some analysts believe contributes to the country's relatively weak position in the international economy.[74] Namibia's continuing participation in the Southern Africa Customs Union (SACU), while enabling the country to enjoy relatively low cost access to southern African markets and products, has also functioned to severely restrict the ability of Namibian firms to compete with South African companies that remain active within Namibia.[75] Thus, only 259 formally registered Namibian companies operate in the country, mostly located in the capital city (Windhoek) and related to the food-processing, textile, wood product, and mining sectors.[76] Potential value-adding sectors and industry in general remain dominated by South African production and trading companies, which enjoy high rates of market efficiency and easy access to marketing outlets within and outside Namibia.[77]

It should be stressed that while the development of "big industry" has certainly been restrained by SACU's influence, the proliferation of informal, small-scale businesses and local trading activities in communal areas (as noted above) provides a significant economic alternative for many rural Namibians. Still, the lack of national-scale integration of these locally oriented markets in combination with the impact of SACU has functioned to inhibit a fuller development of Namibia's industrial and commercial potential.

JOSHUA BERNARD FORREST

New Challenges to Namibian Democracy

The sections above make clear that Namibia has enjoyed some success in economic development, but it is important here to refocus our attention on national politics in order to take note of the generation of substantial discontent with the national government in recent years. Popular criticism has focused, among other issues, on the perceived lack of progress toward meaningful land reform, and, especially, on an apparent intensification of political centralism within SWAPO and the cabinet, along with an increasingly dismissive attitude of party leaders toward critiques from both within and outside the party. In March 1999, these factors provoked several leading SWAPO members to bolt the ruling party in order to create the new opposition political party, the CoD. This party represents intellectuals, students, youth, and disaffected former SWAPO members in Windhoek and in parts of the far north; it claims devotion to the promotion of social equity, land reform, a democratic culture and civic society, greater autonomy to regional governments, gender equity, and primary school improvement.[78] Its legitimacy is enhanced by the fact that it is led by Ben Ulenga, a former general secretary of the Mineworkers Union and former SWAPO higher-up, who enticed a purported 3,000 Namibians to join the party in 1999.[79]

The CoD's popularity is growing dramatically among young people as well as others who are committed to a more participatory style of governance, and their winning of 7 seats in the National Assembly in 1999 confirms the party's rising star status. The emergence of the CoD has already helped to further invigorate and strengthen Namibian democracy, as it provides a new and credible outlet for pro-democratic political activism that includes those with strong credentials as ex-SWAPO leaders, while adding political party diversity to Namibia's multi-party spectrum.

At the same time, it is important to turn our attention to one particular issue that contributed to the discontent that led to the formation of the CoD, and that may bear on the potential for Namibia's democratic consolidation. Here I refer to SWAPO's decision to allow President Nujoma to stand for a third presidential term. The Namibian leader's second term ended in 1999, and according to Article 29 of the Namibian constitution, no president may serve for more than two terms. However, in 1997, President Nujoma began to show signs of an interest in serving a third term,[80] and the May 1997 SWAPO party conference approved a proposal for a third term candidacy.[81] This decision was re-confirmed at the SWAPO Special Congress held 29–30 August 1998, and led to a constitutional amendment to legalize a third term presidency, which was virtually assured passage as a consequence of SWAPO's two-thirds-plus majority in both houses, and was approved on 4 November 1998 with fifty MPs voting in favor and fifteen opposed.[82]

Some members of the SWAPO leadership justified this decision by arguing that Nujoma's first term should not be counted because he was chosen to be president by the Constituent Assembly in February 1990, one month prior to the country's independence. From this perspective, promoted especially by SWAPO Secretary-

General Hifikepunye Pohamba, Nujoma should be considered to have begun his "second" term after the 1999 elections.[83]

Nonetheless, many analysts believe that SWAPO's treatment of this controversy suggested a worrisome trend toward ignoring the spirit of the constitutional framework. The problem, according to this view (shared especially by many Namibian intellectuals, human rights activists, and members of the media), is that Namibia's nascent political culture remains relatively fragile, and a formal contortion of the constitutional rules for the specific purpose of extending the president's time in office made it appear that the commitment of the nation's leaders to a democratic framework of government was weakening. Moreover, a third (or "second") term raised the unseemly specter of a presidential concentration of political power, adding to the centralist tendencies noted above.

However, it is possible that Nujoma's third term may in fact bear positively on Namibia's democratic prospects. In the first place, despite the departure of several party members to join the CoD, the large degree of respect for Nujoma held by SWAPO party leaders has enabled the president to hold together a factionalized ruling political party. Second, the president remains highly regarded even within traditionally anti-SWAPO political and ethnic circles, and this personal respect has contributed significantly to the country's overall stability and to national reconciliation efforts. I do not mean to suggest that Namibia's continuing success as a unified democracy is essentially conditional on Nujoma's presidency, but rather that the third term may enable his leadership to play a positive role in the country's continuing political development, despite the aforementioned centralist tendencies.

Here we may note that Nujoma's managerial style has changed considerably. During the early post-independence years (1990–93) he was viewed as exceptionally collaborative and non-interventionist: he generally preferred to allow the cabinet, the prime minister, parliament, and the civil service to govern the ministries and rarely interfered with their decision-making practices. During cabinet meetings, alternative views were actively solicited, and Nujoma made a point of not dominating the discussion or internal cabinet voting.[84] However, in the mid-to-late 1990s, his style of rule became increasingly less tolerant of alternative views, and junior SWAPO members as well as various Namibian intellectuals and activists became greatly concerned about Nujoma's and the cabinet's domination over the National Assembly and over the middle and lower ranks of the party.[85]

Still, it can be argued that this change in style remained within the bounds of Namibia's parliamentary system of government, as the executive branch of government, including the cabinet, is not separated from but rather is a part of the National Assembly. Thus, while appearance of growing "interference" in the affairs of parliament may well represent a real change in leadership style, this has not contravened the fundamental constitutional framework. In fact, Nujoma's tougher approach may actually add to SWAPO's popularity among key voting sectors in parts of the rural north and elsewhere.

For all these reasons, Nujoma's third term appears unlikely to threaten the basic framework of democracy in Namibia. Moreover, as emphasized above, local and regional councils have thus far helped to entrench participatory processes at the grassroots level in many parts of the country. Namibian NGOs and civic organizations, such as teachers' unions, communal farmers' organizations, and the urban residents' associations that won representation on a number of local councils in the February 1998 local elections, are likely to play a vibrant role in furthering a participation-oriented political culture.[86]

Moreover, despite the complaints by some political activists regarding the centralization of power, Namibia has thus far largely adhered to the protection of the personal and civic freedoms stipulated in the constitution.[87] We may note the result of a 1997 survey conducted by a non-profit international rights group (the Helen Suzman Foundation), which found that, in seven southern African nations, only in Namibia did most respondents declare that they were able to criticize their government and to hold public demonstrations without harassment by the state.[88] The harsh criticism of SWAPO leaders commonly voiced in public and in the media—including accusations by the CoD that Nujoma is moving toward "dictatorial" rule, and by some pro-DTA chiefs of SWAPO's "tribalist" policies—underlines the extent of Namibia's comparatively tolerant polity, in that it permits the articulation of such criticisms, as well the campaigning by anti-SWAPO candidates in local, regional, and national elections.

Nonetheless, over the long term, the deeply ingrained racial, ethnic, and class divisions created during the decades of apartheid rule remain problematic and could engender more serious conflicts if economic development efforts falter dramatically. The continuing vitality of Namibia's political institutions cannot alone sustain the progress thus far made toward reconciling the country's social classes and political factions. Comprehensive land reform in both commercial and communal areas, expansion of marketing opportunities for small-scale agriculturalists and traders, gains in job growth, and other development achievements are necessary to ensure the country's continuing progress toward nation-building and toward the integration (or at least continued mutual tolerance) of various political and social groups. Meanwhile, the overall institutional context, including a strong two-house parliamentary framework and a regularized electoral process, is likely to provide a reasonably stabilizing political environment for Namibia's still-young but promising democracy as the twenty-first century begins to unfold.

NOTES

1. For details of the liberation struggle and the transitional electoral process, see Lionel Cliffe (with Ray Bush, Jenny Lindsay, Brian Mokopakgosi, Donna Pankhurst, and Belefi Tsie), *The Transition to Independence in Namibia* (Boulder, Colo.: Lynne Rienner, 1994); and Colin Leys and John S. Saul (with Susan Brown, Philip Steenkamp, Sipho S. Maseko, Chris Tapscott, and Lauren Dobell), *Namibia's Liberation Struggle: The Two-Edged Sword* (London: James Currey; Athens: Ohio University Press, 1995).

2. The other opposition parties were the UDF (United Democratic Front), 4 seats; ACN (Action Christian National Party), 3 seats; NNF (Namibia National Front), 1 seat; NPF (National Patriotic Front), 1 seat; and FCN (Federal Convention of Namibia), 1 seat.

3. Author interviews with National Assembly Speaker Mosé Tjitendero, and observation of National Assembly sessions, Windhoek, 1993.

4. Citation in Tom Minney, "Sparks Fly in the NA," *Namibian* (Windhoek), 3, no. 115 (4 March 1993): 1–2.

5. This debate took place on 10 June 1992. Eve Black, "Time to Talk about Money," *NEW ERA* 1, no. 47 (11–17 June 1992): 3.

6. Joshua Bernard Forrest, *Namibia's Post-Apartheid Regional Institutions: The Founding Year* (Rochester, N.Y.: University of Rochester Press, 1998), chap. 2; William A. Lindeke and Winnie Wanzala, "Regional Elections in Namibia: Deepening Democracy and Gender Inclusion," *Africa Today* 41, no. 3 (1994): 5–14.

7. Heribert Weiland, "Landslide Victory for SWAPO in 1994: Many New Seats But Few New Votes," *Journal of Modern African Studies* 33, no. 2 (1995): 349–57, p. 351.

8. Ibid, p. 350, and report by Director of Elections Gerhard Tötemeyer and Chairman of Electoral Commission Johan Strydom, in *New Era* 1, no. 178 (16–21 December 1994): 7.

9. Ibid. (both).

10. These were the United Democratic Front (UDF), a predominantly Damara party, with two seats; the Monitor Action Group (MAG), conservative, largely white party, with one seat; and the Democratic Coalition of Namibia (DCN), an intelligentsia-based party previously called the National Patriotic Front (NPF), also with one seat.

11. Local associations won control of the Otavi and Rehoboth local councils, and hold the balance of power with one seat in Keetmanshoop (the other seats are evenly split between DTA and SWAPO) and in Omaruru (the other seats are evenly divided among the DTA, SWAPO, and UDF). In Gobabis, the local council was evenly split between seven SWAPO delegates and seven local residents' association delegates. Christof Maletsky and Graham Hopwood, "SWAPO Takes Elections" in *Mail and Guardian* (Johannesburg), 19 February 1998.

12. Two regional councils—Kunene and Hardap—were evenly divided between SWAPO and opposition parties; DTA won control of Omaheke region. *Namibian,* 11 December 1998; also, Gretchen Bauer, "Civil and Political Society Mobilized: The Struggle for Democracy in Namibia" (paper presented at the American Political Science Association meeting, Atlanta, September 1999), p. 8.

13. G. O'Donnell, P.C. Schmitter, and L. Whitehead, *Transitions from Authoritarian Rule: Tentative Conclusions about Uncertain Democracies* (Baltimore: Johns Hopkins University Press, 1986). A similar point is made in Weiland, "Landslide Victory," p. 349.

14. "Nujoma Consolidates Power on Eve of Namibia's Fifth Birthday," *Africa Report* 40, no. 3 (May/June 1995): 11; Mick Slatter, "Swapo Prepares for Second Win over Divided Opposition," *Africa Report* 3, no. 6 (November/December 1994): 6.

15. Referring to opposition parties apart from the DTA.

16. Gretchen Bauer, "Challenges to Democratic Consolidation in Namibia," in Richard Joseph, ed., *State, Conflict and Democracy in Africa* (Boulder, Colo.: Lynne Rienner, 1999), pp. 439–41.

17. Forrest, *Namibia's Post-Apartheid Regional Institutions*.

18. David Simon, "Restructuring the Local State in Post-Apartheid Cities: Namib-

ian Experience and Lessons for South Africa," *African Affairs* 95, no. 378 (January 1996): 51–85.

19. For example, see Christiaan Keulder's comments in Christof Maletsky, "Swapo's Share of Seats Exceeds Its Popularity," *Namibian,* 31 January 1999; and Bauer, "Civil and Political Society Mobilized," pp. 10–11.

20. Forrest, *Namibia's Post-Apartheid Regional Institutions.*

21. Ibid.

22. Victor Tonchi, "Voters and Governing in Independent Namibia" (paper presented at 38th Annual African Studies Meeting, Orlando, Florida, 3–6 November 1995).

23. "Nehova, Mensah Picked to Lead NC," *Namibian,* 16 February 1999.

24. Robert J. Griffiths, "Democratisation and Civil-Military Relations in Namibia, South Africa and Mozambique," *Third World Quarterly* 17, no. 3 (1996): 473–85, p. 478.

25. Claude E. Welch Jr., *Protecting Human Rights in Africa: Roles and Strategies of Non-Governmental Organizations* (Philadelphia: University of Pennsylvania Press, 1995), p. 19.

26. Ibid., p. 192.

27. Author interviews with labor commissioners, regional and local councillors in Hardap, Erongo, and Karas regions, 1993. It remains to be seen to what extent commercial farmworkers are able to take full advantage of those new rights.

28. Welch, *Protecting Human Rights,* p. 197, and see pp. 193–94.

29. "Governance and Human Development in Southern Africa," report by the Southern African Development Community, cited in Bauer, "Civil and Political Society Mobilized," p. 17 n. 5.

30. Slatter, "Swapo Prepares for Second Win," p. 6.

31. "Nujoma Consolidates Power," p. 11; Griffiths, "Democratisation and Civil-Military Relations," p. 482.

32. Bauer, "Civil and Political Society Mobilized," and Bauer, "Challenges to Democratic Consolidation"; John S. Saul and Colin Leys, "The Legacy: An Afterword," in Leys and Saul, *Namibia's Liberation Struggle,* pp. 196–206.

33. Gwen Lister, "Namibia Press: Under Attack," *Nieman Reports* 50, no. 1 (spring 1996): 65.

34. Mainly English but also Afrikaans and German, and several newspapers include sections in Oshiwambo, Herero, and other indigenous languages.

35. "Namibia," *IPI Report,* December/January 1996, p. 65.

36. Donald G. McNeil Jr. "Free Namibia Stumps the Naysayers," *New York Times,* 16 November 1997, p. 14.

37. For a detailed and convincing treatment of the role of the trade unions in this process of power centralization, see Gretchen Bauer, *Labor and Democracy in Namibia, 1971–1996* (Athens: Ohio University Press, 1998). Also, Bauer, "Challenges to Democratic Rule in Namibia" (paper presented to American Political Science Association meeting, Washington, D.C., August 1997), pp. 17–22.

38. Ibid.

39. Joshua Bernard Forrest, "Ethnic-State Political Relations in Post-Apartheid Namibia," *The Journal of Commonwealth and Comparative Politics* 32, no. 3 (1994): 300–323.

40. Chris Tapscott, "National Reconciliation, Social Equity and Class Formation in Independent Namibia," *Journal of Southern African Studies* 19, no. 1 (March 1993): 29–39.

41. In May 1997, due to his declining health, Garoeb was replaced as SWAPO secretary-general by Minister of Fisheries and Marine Resources Hifikepunye Pohamba.

42. Forrest, "Ethnic-State Political Relations."

43. For details, see ibid.

44. "Traditional Leaders," *Namibian,* 21 September 1999.

45. Weiland, "Landslide Victory."

46. Ibid, pp. 355–57.

47. "The Lozi Lost," *Economist,* 4 September 1999.

48. BBC Report, 3 December 1998.

49. "Three Rebels Killed," *Namibian,* 3 September 1999.

50. Chris Tapscott, "War, Peace and Social Classes," in Leys and Saul, *Namibia's Liberation Struggle,* pp. 153–70; William A. Lindeke, "Democratization in Namibia: Soft State, Hard Choices," *Studies in Comparative International Development* 30, no. 1 (spring 1995): 3–29, p. 22; Tapscott, "National Reconciliation."

51. Bauer, "Challenges to Democratic Rule."

52. For an insightful critique of this policy, see Lauren Dobell, "SWAPO in Office," in Leys and Saul, *Namibia's Liberation Struggle,* pp. 171–95.

53. National Planning Commission/Central Statistics Office, *Statistical Abstract* (Windhoek, 1992), Table 7.2, p. 56.

54. Pedro Belli, *Namibia: Poverty Alleviation with Sustainable Growth* (Washington, D.C.: World Bank, 1992), pp. xv, 12.

55. Wolfgang Werner, "Land Reform in Namibia: The First Seven Years," Basler Afrika Bibliographien Working Paper, no. 5 (Basel, Switzerland: September 1997), p. 11. Werner emphasizes that these figures have not been independently confirmed.

56. Ibid., p. 5.

57. Ibid., p. 6.

58. Ibid., p. 11.

59. Ibid., p. 13.

60. Ibid., p. 16.

61. *Namibian,* 4 June 1998.

62. Officials of the Ministry of Lands, Resettlement and Rehabilitation, interviews by author, 1993; see also Lindeke, "Democratization in Namibia," p. 18.

63. Concerning illegal fencing of communal lands in Namibia's Omusati region, see Oscar Johnson, "Fences March Across Namibia's North," *Mail and Guardian,* 23 October 1997. Regarding Omaheke region, see "Rich Farmers Urged to 'Leave Communal Land,'" *Namibian,* 16 September 1999.

64. Werner, "Land Reform in Namibia," p. 7.

65. "Unhappy Farmers to Head for State House," *Namibian,* 7 September 1999.

66. Operational Manager, Meat Board of Namibia, interview by author, Windhoek, 8 September 1993.

67. Herbert P. Schneider, *Animal Health and Veterinary Medicine in Namibia* (Windhoek: Agrivet, 1994), p. 3; Operational Manager, Meat Board, interview by author, Windhoek, September 1993. Meanwhile, mining represented 58.6 percent of Namibia's total exports, manufacturing 13.2 percent, and fishing 11.5 percent. All figures are from 1992–93; by 1999, these sector earnings had not changed significantly.

68. Belli, *Namibia,* p. 3.

69. "Land Related Issues in the Communal Areas," NEPRU Briefing Paper, in *National Conference on Land Reform* (Windhoek: NEPRU, 1991), p. 212.

70. Senior Manager for Operations, AGRA (a Namibian livestock marketing firm), interview by author, Windhoek, 9 September 1993. The year referred to was 1992.

71. Agricultural extension agents in the above cited communal areas (except Oka-vango), interviews by author, July–August 1993, and officials of the Ministry of Agriculture, Water and Rural Development, interviews by author, Windhoek, September–October 1993; also, see "Land Related Issues in the Communal Areas," in *National Conference on Land Reform* (Windhoek: NEPRU, 1991), p. 211.

72. Interviews by author, Windhoek, September– October 1993, and research visits to extension offices in Oshana, Omusati, Omaheke, Ohangwena, Hardap, and Karas regions, 1993.

73. *Namibian,* 26 June 1998. Those drought-relief programs also included substantial resources for the purchase and delivery of food supplies to drought-affected needy peasant families.

74. Lindeke, "Democratization in Namibia," p. 22; Steve Curry and Colin Stoneman, "Problems of Industrial Development and Market Integration in Namibia," *Journal of Southern African Studies* 19, no. 1 (March 1993): 40–59.

75. Curry and Stoneman, "Problems of Industrial Development," p. 51.

76. Ibid., pp. 43 and 49.

77. Ibid., p. 49.

78. "CoD Playing for Keeps," *Namibian,* 8 September 1999; "CoD Youth Take Issue with SWAPO," *Namibian,* 7 October 1999; Bauer, "Civil and Political Society Mobilized," p. 9.

79. "Thousands Flock to Democrats," *Namibian,* 6 April 1999, and Bauer, "Civil and Political Society Mobilized," p. 9.

80. Graham Hopwood, "Fears for Democracy in Namibia," *Weekly Mail and Guardian,* 15 July 1997; "Play It Again Sam: SWAPO Is Soon to Decide on the Future of a President," *Africa Confidential* 38, no. 4 (14 February 1997): 6–7.

81. Bauer, "Civil and Political Society Mobilized," p. 5; Bauer, "Challenges to Democratic Rule," p. 10.

82. BBC World Report, 6 November 1999; *Mail and Guardian,* 4 September 1998; PANA news agency reports, 6 and 8 July 1998.

83. *Mail and Guardian,* 3 September 1998.

84. Prime Minister Hage Geingob, interview by author, Windhoek, 1 December 1993, and personal communication with other cabinet members, Namibia, 1993.

85. Bauer, "Civil and Political Society Mobilized."

86. Bauer (ibid., p. 12) argues that NGOs and civic organizations have wielded a noteworthy impact on certain economic policies.

87. Welch, *Protecting Human Rights,* pp. 180 and 190–93.

88. McNeil, "Free Namibia," p. 14.

6. Democratizing the Administrative State in Botswana

John D. Holm and Staffan Darnolf

Introduction

Botswana is Africa's premier democracy. The country has held regular compet-itive elections for all major political offices since 1965. Political parties have been free to organize, hold meetings, and engage in intense criticism of one another and government officials. Civil society groups have formed in many sectors of society. Private newspapers have become persistent reporters and evaluators of government policies. Elected officials and civil servants attend a maze of public meetings, some of which result in serious dialogue between citizens and their rulers. The military has shown no inclination to undertake a coup. Indeed, military leaders have ob-tained political office only by resigning their commissions and becoming involved in party politics. Foreign governments have been fulsome in their praise of Botswana's democracy and rewarded the country with large amounts of foreign aid for its political progress.

Most interesting about Botswana's democracy is not its achievements but rather the process by which this new system of government is being embedded in the so-cial and political fabric of the country. Many analysts have tended to see Botswana as a deviant case relative to other African countries. While there is obvious truth in this observation, the fact remains that many Africans earnestly desire that their countries follow the Botswana path to democracy. Therefore, a close examination of the Botswana process of democratization is very relevant to Africa's future.

This essay explores the process of Botswana's democratization. A number of themes are emphasized. Most important is that the process has been slow rather than revolutionary. New structures and attitudes have emerged in response to tra-ditional Tswana views of politics, prolonged conflict between internal power cen-ters, economic change, and foreign influences. For the most part Botswana's democratization has involved citizens and elected officials influencing the *implementation* of policy and not its *formulation*. The civil service has continued, as was the case during colonial rule, to initiate policy proposals, debate them, and determine the options to be adopted. However, the balance of the fulcrum between the administrative state and public control is gradually shifting toward the latter. It is the process of this transformation which this essay addresses.

Each section of this chapter focuses on the character of democratization taking place in a particular political change dimension. The dimensions dealt with are as follows: political parties, executive-legislative relations, civil society, political communication, the administrative state, and international relations. Underlying the discussion of all these dimensions are some overriding themes regarding democratization. They involve two sets of generalizations. Contained in each set is a contradiction.

The first set relates to economic development. On the one hand, economic development in Botswana tends to facilitate democratization. Among other things, it breaks down ethnic ties, provides political parties and civil society groups with more opportunities to mobilize funds, increases the number of independent newspapers, and renders citizens more sensitive to regional political developments beyond Botswana's boarders. While none of these consequences ensures there will be democratization, each does increase its possibilities, as the case of Botswana demonstrates.

On the other hand, Botswana provides evidence that much democratization can take place at a fairly low level of economic growth. Botswana began holding competitive elections, respecting freedom of speech, and encouraging citizen participation in community decision-making in the first decade after independence (1966 to 1976), at a time when the country was one of the poorest in the world. At a minimum these developments were made possible by the willingness of various political elites to show a minimum of trust for each other and were facilitated by the considerable cultural homogeneity of the country's major ethnic groups, all but one of which are Tswana.[1]

The second set of generalizations concerns the connection of democratization and existing cultural traditions and institutions. From one perspective, it can be said that Botswana's democratic politics involves modifying existing institutions and behavior so they support citizen control over government. This means that widely accepted democratic forms, like the context of elections or the protections on free speech, operate in a way which has a distinctly Tswana flavor. In this regard, democratization tends to be much more syncretistic than other aspects of the development process such as industrialization. This syncretism is especially apparent in the early stages of Botswana's democratic development in that adapting traditional practices reduced both the resources required and rendered democratic practice much less strange. One consequence is that foreign experts are not all that critical in moving democratization forward. This kind of change is more dependent on what appears culturally appropriate than on what foreign advisers know on the basis of their experience with other countries.

At the same time, part of the democratization of Botswana has involved eroding cultural traditions which have been supportive of authoritarian decision-making. Thus many Batswana loathe public conflict, tend to treat elections as solely ethnic conflicts, and are submissive to authority figures, both traditional and modern, who are not subject to election and/or re-election. Overcoming these inclinations is a slow process which leaves top civil servants in charge of much of government's decision-making process from initiation to implementation. Democratization in this regard becomes very much a process of bringing about fundamental change in cultural beliefs. This process tends to be piecemeal and depend on the advent of new generations who are more educated and have greater wealth than their parents.

Before addressing the six dimensions of political change mentioned above, the next section of this paper details the basic socio-economic changes which have taken place in Botswana since independence. An overview of these changes is a critical precondition for understanding their impact on the political transformations which are the subject of this essay.

Socio-Economic Changes

Over the last four decades, Botswana has enjoyed one of the most rapid rates of growth in developing areas. In 1960 it was one of the poorest countries in the world, with a real GDP per capita of $474. By 1994, this figure had ballooned to $5,367. Only one African country had a higher real GDP per capita in 1994, Algeria at $5,442. (However, Algeria started with a figure of $1,676 in 1960.) In terms of growth rates for the per capita GNP, Botswana moved forward at a pace of 9.9 percent between 1965 and 1980. Between 1980 and 1993, it was 6.6 percent. The earlier rate was better than that of any other developing country for the same time period. The latter rate was exceeded only by China, Korea, and the Maldives. The impressive aspect of this growth process is that except for two relatively short recessions, it has been sustained for close to thirty years.[2]

The key factor in Botswana's growth has been diamond mining. The country's three major mines have developed to the point where they jointly produce more diamonds in dollar terms than any other economy in the world. They account for approximately one-third of the total GDP. Whenever the world demand for diamonds declines, Botswana's economy experiences a recession. In addition to diamonds, the country has also become a significant exporter of copper, nickel, and soda ash and greatly enhanced its capacity to export beef products in various forms. In the last decade, promotion of expensive safari tours has begun to bring impressive returns. Most recently, the manufacturing sector has begun to take off, led by Volvo and Hyundai assembly plants which export largely to South Africa.

Important in sustaining Botswana's growth has been the government's effective management of the development process. The Ministry of Finance economists have regularly drafted five-year plans which have focused public and private investment on high potential sectors. In addition, the government has operated with a minimum of corruption to distort investment choices, as for instance has happened in countries such as Nigeria. The country's political stability has helped to lure necessary foreign investments and loans.

The government has also succeeded in controlling the allocation of the income generated by the country's growth. Preference has been given to investment and a wide range of services for the entire population rather than increasing personal incomes. In particular, government has been concerned to restrict income increases for wage earners so as to make the country attractive for foreign investment. In order to compensate for a dramatic gap between higher and lower income groups, the government has allocated substantial funds to education, housing, and health and other social services. Altogether these areas received a total of 41 percent of the central government budget between 1992 and 1995. The consequences have been substantial in terms of an improved standard of living. Botswana ranks above all sub-Saharan African countries except South Africa on the United Nations Development Program (UNDP)'s Human Development Index (HDI), which is a measure of the standard of living for the population of a country as a whole. With respect to more specific indicators, Botswana's infant mortality rate (per 1,000 live births) dropped from 116 to 55 between 1960 and 1994; its adult literacy climbed from 41 percent in 1970 to 69 percent in 1994; and its life expectancy at birth increased from 45.5 years in 1960 to 59.8 in 1990. (Life expectancy dropped precipitously in the early 1990s due to AIDS, so that it is now 52.3.)[3]

While the government has reallocated some of the income from economic growth to improved services for low-income populations, the growth rate has been much more substantial than the improvement in the standard of living. This is reflected in the fact that Botswana ranks 97th on the UNDP's HDI index relative to the 175 countries for which the index was calculated, but it ranks 67th in terms of real per capita income among this same group of countries. This gap, which is one of the largest among developing countries, indicates that Botswana has "considerable scope for distributing the benefits of economic growth more equitably."[4] The designers of the government's strategy believe that as much of the country's increased income as possible should be reinvested in infrastructure and joint ventures with foreign capital. Their idea is that this approach will maximize the creation of jobs, maintain the country's high growth rate, and diversify Botswana's economic base from diamonds.[5] However, the ultimate consequence is that the government has done nothing to increase the proportion of the national income going to the poorest 40 percent of the population between the 1970s and current decade.[6]

Summary

Botswana's economy has developed at a world-class pace for almost three decades. The growth has been planned and managed by top economists in the Ministry of Finance. Although the living standards of the average citizens have increased and are among the best to be found in Africa, the government has not attempted to change the distribution of income among the population. As a result, the gap between rich and poor remains the same as it was in the late 1960s.

Party Competition and Elections

The development of democracy in a society canalizes the competition for power so that its outcome is critically dependent on popular elections. Since 1965, Botswana has regularly held such elections for parliament and local councils. There have been seven in all. They are relatively free. With a few exceptions, anyone can run for office by paying a minimal deposit and collecting a small number of signatures. Political parties face no legal constraints to their formation or holding meetings. The mass media carries candidate and party messages in a relatively unbiased fashion. The elections themselves involve infrequent irregularities. When there is evidence of serious errors, the courts step in and require a rerunning of the contest involved.

In spite of its track record as one of Africa's most democratic countries, serious doubts have been raised regarding the quality and significance of elections in Botswana. The central concern is the absence of competitive elections. While there have always been a number of opposition parties, no one party or coalition has shown itself able to threaten the domination of the Botswana Democratic Party (BDP) since the first elections in 1965. In essence, Botswana has been a de facto one-party state. The absence of a ruling party defeat at the ballot box raises the question as to whether elections and other forms of political competition make a significant difference in governance of the country. Could it be that elections are just window dressing for a ruling elite which is determined to continue in power by one means or another?

This section explores the extent to which Botswana has developed a basis for multi-party competition in future elections. Our argument is that electoral competition, while restricted, has after thirty years become increasingly embedded in the country's political fabric.

The BDP's Declining Majority

During its thirty plus years in power, the BDP has been challenged by three opposition parties at every poll—the Botswana National Front (BNF), the Botswana People's Party (BPP), and the Botswana Independence Party (BIP).[7] The BDP has managed to garner an absolute majority of the votes in each election (Table 6.1).

During the first five elections, the BDP obtained over two-thirds of the total vote. However, since 1984 the BDP's majority has been steadily falling. More important, beginning with 1984 the BNF emerged as a serious challenger for total votes. Between 1984 and 1994 it moved from one-fifth of the total vote to almost two-fifths. Most of this growth came in the urban centers where the BNF has been very ef-

Table 6.1. Percentage of Votes in Parliamentary Elections, 1965–1994

Party	1965	1969	1974	1979	1984	1989	1994
BDP	80	68.3	76.6	75.4	68	65	54.6
BNF	*	13.5	11.5	13.1	20.4	27.7	37.1
BPP	14	12.1	6.6	7.5	6.6	4	4.1
BIP	4.6	6	4.8	3.8	3.2	1.8	2.7

Source: Data from the *Mmegi* 10/21/94; Picard (1993).

* The party in question did not exist.
** After the 1989 election, the Botswana Independence Party (BIP) merged with Botswana Freedom Party (BFP), a party that was founded prior to the 1989 elections. The new party took the name Independence Freedom Party (IFP).

fective at articulating the discontents of wage earners, lower-level civil servants, and many self-employed workers. Given the very fast pace of Botswana's urbanization,[8] the BNF has been able to expand with very little need to change its appeal. The BPP and BIP meanwhile have become increasingly marginalized, dropping well under 10 percent of the vote in 1989 and 1994. They have become narrowly focused on the ethnic concerns of two non-Tswana groups, the Kalanga and the Bayei. In effect, urbanization has been gradually bringing about the emergence of a two-party state where the one represents predominantly the cities and other the rural areas.

Impact of the Electoral System

Botswana has a single-member district electoral system with no runoff election if one candidate does not receive a majority. Thus, the candidate winning a plurality of votes in a district wins the seat. Overall, the BDP has benefited from this system. In a number of constituencies where a majority voted against the government party candidate, either the BNF split into factions which both ran candidates, or one of the other opposition parties received sufficient votes to make the BDP candidate the plurality winner. Consequently, the BDP has always obtained more seats in parliament than its actual vote share, while the opposition parties have disproportionately received fewer seats than their share (Table 6.2). The most egregious result was in 1989 when the BDP won 65 percent of the vote but gained over 90 percent of the seats in parliament. In the last election, the spread was less dramatic but still significant, with the BDP winning 53 percent of the total votes but 68 percent of the contested seats.

Thus far the single-member district system has not prevented majority rule, in that the BDP has won a majority of the popular votes as well as a majority of the parliamentary seats. However, in the future, the outcome might be different. This possibility has to do with the delimitation of constituency boundaries, which will next occur in 2000. The rules require that within the rural areas electoral districts should be ethnically homogenous. The BDP has gained by this approach in that a

Table 6.2. Number of Parliamentary Seats Won by Political Parties, 1965–1994

Party	1965	1969	1974	1979	1984	1989	1994
BDP	28	24	27	29	28	31	27
BNF	*	3	2	2	5	3	13
BPP	3	3	2	1	1	0	0
BIP**	0	1	1	1	0	0	0

Source: See Table 6.1 for details.

number of smaller rural districts have been created in which the BDP has an advantage because of its identification with local ethnic groups. On other hand, the BNF's urban constituencies generally have been among the largest at the time of delimitation and have grown over the remainder of the decade. In the same period, many rural districts shrank. The result is that some urban constituencies have been double their rural counterparts by the end of a decade. Thus when elections are held in the penultimate year of the decade (e.g., 1999), the BNF has accumulated a proportionally much larger number of votes in winning its urban constituencies than the BDP has in the countryside. The only countervailing process is that urbanization in several areas has been spreading into previously ethnically homogenous rural areas, thereby increasing the BNF vote in rural districts which had been historically safe for the BDP.

Benefits of Being in Office

In most elections, officeholding almost always bestows some benefits on incumbents. These include easier access to campaign contributions from groups dependent on government contracts, the ability to use government resources for political purposes, and allocation of employment within the public sector. The BDP has benefited from all of these possibilities.

The BDP has obtained most of its political contributions from a few economic groups which are dependent on government favors. Most prominent have been the Indians, who play a dominant role in a number of retail sectors. For many years, a leader in the Indian business community, Mr. Dada, has been treasurer of the party. In return for this support, the BDP has shown little interest in supporting an expansion of small Tswana enterprises which compete with Indian businesses. European-owned corporations in Botswana have also channeled considerable funds into the BDP's coffers. Their primary concern is to obtain contracts and ensure they can employ sufficient expatriate staff.

The impact of these private contributions can be very dramatic. Because the country is so large and face-to-face campaigning is critical in the rural areas, the availability of motorized transportation greatly enhances candidate outreach to the voters. During the 1994 elections the BDP supplied each parliamentary candidate with one 4-by-4 vehicle for the duration of the campaign. This greatly increased BDP

Table 6.3. Percentage of Workforce Employed by Botswana Government, 1969–1994

	1969	1974	1977	1986	1989	1994
Local government employees	3.5	3.2	5.2	7.2	6.1	9.6
Central government employees	21.2	21.6	24.6	31.7	26	28.5
Total government employees*	24.7	24.8	29.8	38.9	32.7	38.1

*Excluding members of the Armed Forces

candidates' mobility as well as their status. Those representing other parties, on the other hand, had no such support and thus had to rely on their own resources, which in many cases meant borrowing vehicles from local supporters and gravely reducing the amount they traveled.

Government resources also play a role in campaigns. The BDP uses its control over government transport to expand its contacts with the voters. As an election approaches, the president spends considerable time touring villages all over the country in his "official" capacity. Local civil servants, teachers, and school children are given time off to swell the audience. Further expanding attendance is the use of government trucks to bring in people from surrounding villages to the president's meeting. In almost every case his entourage includes the BDP's candidates for office in the area. Usually, each public event focuses on the launching or completion of a project which will benefit the local area. Given the considerable development budget of government, this means there is always a long list of improvements on which the president can focus. Similar official tours by cabinet members ensure that few villages of any size are missed by the BDP leadership in the run-up to an election.

The overall importance of public employment cannot be underestimated as a factor in the BDP's success. Government is the single largest employer (Table 6.3). Over the last thirty years it has increased from constituting 25 percent of the formal workforce to almost 40 percent in the mid-1990s. This expansion has in part served to keep unemployment down in the formal sector, thus defusing a potentially dangerous election issue. In addition, government has been able to guarantee a considerable portion of the workforce a job for life. Also benefiting the BDP is the fact that government employees cannot by law participate in politics. This reduces the portion of the population which the opposition parties can mobilize. Even more chilling is the tacit assumption of many civil servants that their future advancement could be jeopardized if they display anything other than respect for the ruling BDP.

Government employment and contracts also have an impact on political competition. The BDP often seeks to co-opt its more effective critics by offering them attractive appointments to silence them. A difficult chief was made ambassador to Washington and later appointed to head the traditional court system; a feminist activist was appointed to the High Court; and several wealthy supporters of the

BNF have been given lucrative government contacts as long as they remain discreet in their support for opposition politicians.

A final telling example of the BDP's use of incumbency is its impressive headquarters—Solethsa House—located in the center of the capital city, Gaborone. This $1.6 million complex houses the BDP's administration offices and facilities for its social events. However, most of the space in the building is rented to government agencies and international aid projects. The rental income has thus covered the cost of the building's construction and upkeep over the last thirty years. By contrast, the BNF has its headquarters in a small rented house on the outskirts of Gaborone, where it is not easily reached by public transportation.

The BDP's Record: Thirty Years of Economic Growth

The level of party competition in a society can be influenced by an incumbent's performance in office. Often the ruling party is at a disadvantage. In the case of Botswana the reverse is true. As was detailed in the previous section, the country's citizens have experienced dramatic improvements in their standard of living during the BDP's tenure. At independence in 1966 Botswana was one of the poorest countries in the world. Thereafter the economic situation became even worse as the country experienced several years of severe droughts which required extensive outside aid. With the discovery of diamonds in the late 1960s, the situation changed dramatically. The profits from mining have fueled a real economic growth of around 8 percent per year. In spite of this record, income has remained extremely skewed. It is on par with Brazil, a country infamous for its huge slum areas and a small percentage of extremely rich families. [9] This situation might be expected to cause great political alienation among lower income groups, who would accordingly vote for the opposition. However, this has not happened in any decisive fashion. The major reason is that the government has used a considerable amount of its revenues for various programs which benefit the low-income population. These programs have included water drilling and reticulation for most villages, all sorts of village infrastructure schemes, universal education through elementary school, complete public subsidy of advanced education through the university, extensive public health programs, and extensive subsidies for housing construction. These programs have benefited not only the cities, as in many African countries, but also those living in the most remote rural areas. Most important, during the severe drought of the 1980s there were no reported cases of starvation. [10]

Such substantial and beneficial change in so short a time has placed the opposition parties in a difficult position with respect to making economic appeals. The BNF has concentrated mainly on claiming that it will increase the incomes of the wage-earning population and local Tswana entrepreneurs. Given the fact that the government has kept incomes down and provided extensive services, this appeal works much better in the cities where most of the population are wage earners. However, in the rural areas it has much less relevance, since most people are dependent on subsistence farming or are self-employed.

JOHN D. HOLM AND STAFFAN DARNOLF

Internal Feuds and Mushrooming of Political Parties

In a first-past-the-post electoral system, political parties need to create and sustain broad-based political alliances to win. Once again, the ruling BDP has succeeded much better than the opposition. Since its founding in 1962, the party has built and retained a sufficiently broad-based political coalition that it has not needed to ally with any other party in order to stay in power.

All major opposition parties have experienced prolonged internal conflicts. The decline in the BNF's fortunes in the 1970s was in part due to the fact that many of its urban supporters refused to campaign for the party since Chief Bathoen and some of his more conservative followers controlled the party platform and the party's strategy in parliament. In the 1980s the BNF's left wing reasserted itself and humiliated the party's more conservative members, leading to a decline in support in Bathoen's Bangwaketse constituencies.

In some opposition parties, defections by prominent members have triggered the founding of splinter parties which have drained their former party of a crucial segment of activists. The original BPP, the BDP's main competitor during the 1960s, split into three different sections before the 1965 election, effectively terminating its opportunity to become a viable opposition. During the 1970s and 1980s, BNF conflicts led to the creation of at least three small parties. While none succeeded in winning any seats, each helped to foster the image of the BNF as a party unable to handle serious conflict. The public acrimony within the party continued in the 1990s, this time with the moderate leadership expelling left wingers because of the latter's penchant to stir up class conflict.

Further compounding the problem of the opposition parties has been their failure to form an electoral coalition against the BDP. The desire to unite has tended to be particularly strong among opposition politicians immediately following an election defeat. Intense negotiations then take place between high-ranking representatives of the major opposition parties, and some or all agree to form an alliance for next election. Discussions begin on a common platform, and there are demonstrations of unity at several public meetings. But, as the next election draws near and it comes time to discuss which party will contest which constituency, the alliance collapses. No party constituency organization will sacrifice its chances to win a seat for the overall good of an opposition coalition.

Between 1989 and 1994 the same pattern occurred. To make a bad situation worse, less than seven weeks prior to polling day, three members of the BNF jumped ship and founded an additional three new parties. The opposition appeared to be in worse shape than ever before. For once, however, the ruling BDP was itself experiencing intense internal turmoil. This infighting was a result of the expectation that President Masire would resign his position sometime between 1994 and the next election. The two wings of the party were divided over a basic policy concern, namely the extent to which government resources should be used for local patronage versus development purposes. Some members of each side were determined to cause the defeat of candidates of the other faction so that they could win control of the BDP's parliamentary delegation. Masire finally managed to contain the struggle and limit his party's losses to the areas of its greatest political weakness, that is, the cities, Bangwaketse, and several minority tribes (Kalanga, Bushmen, and Bayei). Nevertheless, the BNF reduced the BDP's victory margin by twenty percentage points in 1994. This experience demonstrated a critical point concerning opposition parties in Botswana. The opposition cannot obtain power through its own efforts. It is only a serious threat in so far as the BDP becomes consumed by internal conflict. In effect, the development of the BNF into a competitive second party may have to await a decline in the organizational effectiveness of the BDP. In the foreseeable future, much will depend on the extent to which the BDP's new president, Festus Mogae, is effective in healing the wounds opened up by the struggle to succeed his predecessor.

Party Competition and Tswana Culture

The problem of developing party competition in Botswana faces two very serious cultural challenges. One is the strong Tswana aversion to public conflict, and the other is their inclination to interpret such conflict in ethnic terms.

In the Tswana political culture, it is imperative to minimize direct public confrontations by all means possible and to seek a consensus for major decisions. In pre-colonial politics, the chief discussed important matters in private meetings with his headsmen and advisers before conducting public discussions and making his decisions. These private dialogues would result in a consensus position which could be presented at *kgotla*, an assembly of all adult males.[11] At the *kgotla*, the chief's advisers would speak first, articulating their agreed-upon ideas. Others in the community were most respectful and circumspect if they chose to challenge the advisers. The chief would then announce his decision in a way which appeared to reflect a consensus.

▼▼▼▼

This high value placed on public agreement has continued to the present. There are two reactions to partisan conflict situations. One is amusement. Politicians in conflict are perceived to be engaged in tasteless behavior. Young people in particular attend political rallies out of a desire to be entertained by such deviance. The other reaction is a painful and intense yearning that the conflict be suppressed. This is reflected in attitudes toward the multi-party system. Many rural and illiterate Batswana, in spite of over three decades of elections, much prefer the idea of a one-party or no-party system to the present partisan conflict. This rejection of public partisan debate has made it difficult for the opposition parties to penetrate rural strongholds of the incumbent party by using issue appeals. The result is that Tswana inclinations to vote on an ethnic basis persist, as has been case since the first elections in 1965. To be sure, there has, for the first time, been some decline in ethnic voting in the 1990s.

The country's first president, Sir Seretse Khama, was widely seen as the rightful Paramount Chief of the largest of the eight Tswana ethnic groups (the Bamangwato). This made him a particularly appealing figure to people in this region, who constitutes over one-third of Botswana's population. During its first twenty years of existence, the BDP not only maintained overwhelming support (90 or more percent in eight of the twelve Ngwato constituencies) in the Bamangwato district, but the Bakwena, the second largest ethnic group in Botswana, gave the party nearly as large a vote (around 80 percent). Together these two groups constituted half the total population; thus, all the BDP needed to do was attract several other smaller tribes (e.g., the Bamalete, Bakgalagadi, Batawana, and Bakgatla) to have a comfortable margin. It did so repeatedly.[12]

After President Khama's death in 1980, Ketumile Masire was elected president. Masire not only lacked the traditional status of his predecessor but was a member of another much smaller Tswana group—the Bangwaketse—which tended to align with the BNF. Nevertheless, the BDP continued to hold a firm grip on the ethnic vote in its rural constituencies. Except in 1989, the BNF was able to retain its Bangwaketse support in spite of Masire's connections with this group. This persisting outcome, regardless of the president's ethnic affiliation, provides evidence that ethnicity in Botswana is becoming connected with particular political parties rather than individual politicians.

Still, changes have taken place in the electoral arena. Botswana can no longer be regarded as a de facto one-party state, but rather an emerging two-party system.[13] Part of this change reflects a slow process of declining association between partisanship and ethnicity. The 1994 elections provided the clearest evidence of this decline. In his analysis of the BDP heartland following the 1989 general elections, Parson found that opposition parties had not yet managed to make an inroad into constituencies where traditionally the ruling party had been strong.[14] By 1994 the situation was quite different. Instead of rural BDP politicians obtaining between 80 and 90 percent of the votes, they suddenly experienced dramatic drops ranging from ten to fifteen percentage points. Most revealing, BDP could no longer boast 90 percent support in any constituency. Moreover, the party dropped below 80 percent in nine of the Bamangwato constituencies for the first time. It could muster more than 80 percent in only four constituencies. Still, the BDP remained above the 70 percent mark in almost one in every four constituencies. Thus, it seems that the tendency among the electorate to vote according to ethnic lines is still very much alive in Botswana today, though it is in decline. Exactly what factors are intervening is not clear, except that there is a growing discontent with the BDP.

Summary

Electoral competition among the parties is gradually intensifying. The BNF is gaining votes steadily through urbanization. Ethnic voting in the rural areas is on a slow decline. And, internecine conflict within the ruling BDP has weakened its competitiveness. However, the BNF's ability to win is still compromised by the gerrymandering of district boundaries, its own internal conflicts, its inability to forge a electoral coalition of opposition parties, and the BDP's effective use of its incumbency. Moreover, the stronger the BNF becomes as a competitive opposition party, the more it may turn off Batswana who sincerely prize political consensus. If the BDP's new president can unite its two factions for the 1999 election, the BNF might actually win the popular vote but fail to gain control of parliament because of the concentration of its voters in the urban constituencies while the BDP remains in control of sufficient rural districts. At the very least the BNF, or its successor the BCP, should be a competitive second party, even if there is not a change of the party in power.

The Parliament: Its Role in Policy-Making

While Botswana is a "parliamentary" democracy, the role of members of parliament in the policy-making process is limited vis-à-vis the president. To be sure, the president is selected by the elected members of parliament. However, candidates for parliament must declare for whom they will vote at the time of their nomination. Since they are nominated by their party, this means they must pledge themselves to the party's candidate for president.

Once the president is elected, he appoints his cabinet without needing any approval from parliament. The president or cabinet members cannot be removed by parliament. If parliament does vote no confidence in the president, parliament is dissolved and a new election is held. In effect, in order to remove the president, parliament must go to the voters for approval. Thus far no president has even been threatened with a no-confidence vote.

In reality the first two presidents of Botswana have dominated the legislative process almost completely. There are several reasons. Most important is that members of parliament want to become ministers in the cabinet. And, if they are in the cabinet, they are concerned to head one of the more important ministries. Both these objectives mean that MPs work hard to remain in the president's good graces. Going against the president can easily mean being relegated to the political sidelines, as a backbencher or an assistant minister.

Also enhancing the president's position is that more than a majority of the elected members of the ruling party's delegation in parliament are cabinet ministers or assistant ministers. Once the president secures cabinet approval for a policy, the cabinet members are easily able through sheer numbers to determine the BDP parliamentary delegation's position on any vote. They need only a few backbenchers to prevail. Moreover, any MPs who bolt from the party line place themselves in danger of not being nominated as a candidate come the next election.

Further adding to the president's influence in parliament is that he nominates four "specially" elected members of the body. These persons are usually former civil servants or defeated BDP MP candidates. They owe a special loyalty to the president for their appointment given the limitations of their mass political base. With a few exceptions, this group of MPs have been among the most articulate in pushing the president's position with fellow legislators.

Even if a sizable group of MPs should want to challenge a president, they have a very difficult time seizing the initiative. Presidential policy proposals come to parliament after being developed by one or more ministries. The civil service undertakes extensive research, including the hiring of outside experts, and engages in wide-ranging consultation with other ministries and interested communities and organizations. In addition, the Ministry of Finance certifies that the necessary funds are available. In effect, a civil service proposal reflects a consensus of many if not most interested elites in the country.

Members of parliament who decide to challenge such well-prepared plans, on the other hand, have almost no resources at their disposal with which to criticize the program presented to them, let alone offer a convincing alternative approach. Parliament's Research Unit has only two staff members to serve forty-four members. Also, these staff members are career civil servants, who are not likely to help themselves in the long run by facilitating MP criticisms of executive proposals. Most of the time, MPs wait for groups in the public to develop a case against a cabinet proposal. Since, as we shall note later, most civil society groups have little policy analysis capacity or are already co-opted by the initiating ministry on the matter in question, it is rare that a public outcry is sufficient to lead to the withdrawal of legislation by the cabinet.

Further reducing the incentive of MPs to challenge the president and his cabinet is the fact that those from the rural areas know that their constituents are largely ignorant of the issues before parliament and more likely to vote for their MP on the basis of his personal reputation, most especially his family and ethnic background. In addition, there are few if any organized groups in the rural constituencies which keep track of their representative's voting record and report it to their members at election time. What is important for MPs is that they appear identified with their constituencies. They do this by regular tours on which they listen to voters' complaints about government programs in the area. When MPs return to parliament, they are interested in finding solutions to problems raised. One important option in this regard is the "Question Time" where they raise questions about complaints from their constituents. An MP can be easily persuaded to go along with a piece of legislation if the ministry in question will take care of a community's complaint with regard to one of its programs. In essence, parliament is more concerned with easing the pain constituents suffer with regard to current performance of government policies than in shaping future ones. In part, the president is chief policy-maker by default.

It is not likely that Botswana's MPs will become more policy oriented until civil society in Botswana becomes more involved in politics. The next section explores the extent to which this form of citizen participation has developed and become political.

Civil Society

The development of democracy requires more than elections and legislatures. In between the individual citizens and their elected representatives there needs to be a social network of organizations and forums through which the citizens engage in dialogue with their leaders. The first section below focuses on development of social organizations involved in this dialogue in Botswana.[15] The second section deals with the range of public forums of citizen-government interaction, ranging from public meetings to the mass media.

The Emergence of Civil Society

Civil society organization in Europe and North America partially preceded the emergence of political freedom and elections. Often civil society was a critical factor in beginning the process. In Botswana this situation is reversed. Citizens enjoyed elections and representation in parliament before beginning to participate extensively in social groups concerned with influencing government policy. Because of this lagged civil society development, a noticeable vacuum exists between elected officials and those they represent. Moreover, filling in this gap has been more a process of organizational development and cultural learning than it was in Europe and North America where it came as part of a struggle for political freedom. The discussion which follows begins with a consideration of the absence of civil society organizations in traditional Tswana society and then turns to the process by which civil society groups are building organizations and gaining access to and influence over decision-makers.

Historical Absence of Civil Society

In pre-colonial Botswana society, chiefs of the independent tribes were the primary locus of governmental power. The ordinary citizen accessed the chief through either the local headmen representing communities or elders speaking for their extended families. The chief for the most part determined when consultation took place and the topics to be discussed. Often, the chief's main concern was to mobilize support for decisions he had already made. Occasionally the chief met in *kgotla* with adult males; however, as with the headmen and elders, the chief set the agenda for issues to be discussed and made the final decision.

Colonial rule did little to change this process except that the chiefs now became the primary representatives of the public to the colonial government. In effect, until independence citizens spoke to government through tribal structures. They had no right to set up their own organizations to represent their common desires or concerns, whether these involved hunting, seeking expanded grazing areas, or migratory labor to South Africa.

The few interest groups which did emerge during the colonial period represented the educated class which found itself marginalized in the policy-making process. The most prominent groups were the Botswana Teachers Union (1937), Botswana Civil Servants Association (1941), the Red Cross (1948), and the YWCA (1962). The first two arose because their members felt exploited by European colleagues. The latter two sought to deal with the country's drought and poverty, conditions which many in the local population perceived as not taken seriously by the British.

When political parties arose in the 1960s to promote Botswana's independence and then to challenge each other for control of the new government, they created their own organization throughout the country. They did not foster independent civil society groups or seek to gain support from those few groups which did exist. For the most part, the parties viewed ethnic identity as their only credible basis for mass mobilization and thus showed no interest in promoting civil society groups which could interact with their organizations as well as government. For the most part, this attitude has continued to prevail into the 1990s.

The Organizational Growth of Civil Society

Government acts as a gatekeeper for the growth of civil society in Botswana. Supposedly government's role is a formality. The Societies Act requires that all organizations register before they undertake to fulfill their purposes. The Ministry of Interior, which is in charge of registration, requires that groups register only after they have written a constitution, elected their leaders, and shown a capacity to keep records and manage their financial affairs. While these conditions promote transparency, they also favor groups representing the more educated elements of the population. In rural areas, the effect of these conditions is that legal group formation can occur only when government officials decide to act as advisers to nascent groups. Needless to say, groups formed under such conditions tend to reflect the interests of a particular ministry such as agriculture or education.

The formal structure of most civil society groups is remarkably similar. There is an executive committee consisting of a president, vice president, secretary, and treasurer. The committee meets on the average of three times a year. In addition, there is an annual general meeting open to all members. This meeting elects officers for the coming year and hears reports from the executive committee and such committees as may be functioning.

In reality, Botswana's civil society groups tend to be on an organizational roller coaster. Groups form around a crisis experienced by their members and engage in a flourish of activity—meeting, seeking funds, producing some reports, seeking publicity in the newspapers, and petitioning the government. The more impressive ones undertake a project or two. Then, action declines to almost nothing for a number of years. Finally, members are galvanized to action by some new events. Sometimes, a split will occur, usually in regard to the kind of demands placed on the government and the degree of pressure employed. The result of such splits is two or even three groups operating in place of one. For instance, in education there are now groups representing elementary, secondary, and college teachers.

Elections rarely bring changes in the leadership of civil society groups. This lack of change is part of the reason for the decline in activity. Member demands for reactivation of the group sometimes lead to the election of a new slate of leaders. However, often a number of annual meetings transpire before dissidents are able to throw out entrenched leaders. In many cases, the members simply become alienated.

Somewhere around ten groups have managed to establish a full-time staff. When staff exist, they design and run group projects which are funded by the government, mobilize members for political action, and launch campaigns to attract new members. Most important staff spend considerable time lobbying the government for funds and policy changes. In almost every case, however, executive committees retain tight control over the development of their organizations so as not to allow the full-time staff to become the de facto leadership.

The membership size of civil society groups varies greatly. The unions by far have the most impressive numbers, with the stronger ones having over 50 percent of their potential supporters. This success derives from the geographic concentration of their following and their almost complete focus on income and benefits issues. Professional groups rally only a small proportion of their constituencies because of physical dispersion and less homogeneity of interest. Trade associations attract the larger businesses but receive little support from smaller ones, which are mostly African owned. Issue-oriented groups and charities have only a few members, most of whom are located in the capital.

A major problem for civil society organizations in Botswana is raising funds to sustain their activities. The most successful have been unions and trade associations. On the other hand, agricultural, issue-oriented, and charity groups are basically dependent on outside assistance, either from government or foreign aid, for their survival. Most of the members of these latter groups lack the willingness or income to make the necessary contributions. As a result, such organizations focus on activities which will bring in government monies. This often means providing services desired by government or aid agencies for group members or lower-income populations. As a result, self-sufficient civil society groups tend to be more aggressive in pushing member interests with the government. Those seeking government funds, in contrast, must tailor their ideas so as not to conflict too much with government policy objectives. The recent withdrawal of most foreign aid funds from Botswana has meant that groups lacking member financial support must rely totally on the government for their continued existence.

Access to and Influence over Decision-Makers

In a democracy, civil society groups are expected to gain access to and influence over decision-makers. This is not assured by the fact that elections are held on a regular basis or that the government recognizes citizen political rights, as is generally the case in Botswana. Groups must organize themselves to perform both activities.

In Botswana, almost all groups have made the civil service the target of their ac-

cess and influence activities. They have minimized contact with politicians and political parties. In part this choice stems from the fact that it is the civil service which
initiates and formulates most major government policies. At best, elected officials
have veto power. In such a situation, politicians become useful only as a last resort defense against change. In addition, the focus on the bureaucracy stems from
the fact that Botswana's civil society groups do not want to become part of partisan politics. Group leaders are seeking members regardless of ethnic identification,
and Botswana's political parties are to varying degrees associated with certain ethnic groups. Thus, civil society groups appear more non-ethnic if they avoid partisanship. Finally, there is the fact that political party leaders are not interested in
seeking the support of civil society groups. Their strategy is to build membership
on an individual basis through branch organizations and other means of direct contact. From this perspective civil society groups are likely to endanger party organization through independence of thought and action.

Top civil servants are aggressive in wanting to build a civil society which functions in a democratic corporatist style. They set up advisory bodies which include
relevant organized groups in civil society, but they use these bodies more to mobilize support for policies than as means to listen to the public regarding its problems and preferred solutions. To ensure that any votes come out right, the government stacks the membership of advisory bodies with civil servants and citizen
supporters. Most of the time the items on the agenda concern not problems or policy choices but options with regard to the implementation of a policy. Most group
leaders attend such advisory council meetings as a formality rather than with any
hope of having much impact on policy.

In this context, the most effective strategy civil society leaders have developed
for influencing government policy is to propose to some of the more understaffed
ministries that their group will take the initiative in formulating a particular policy. The group agrees to gather information and produce reports on a specific problem. The group receives funds from the government or from a foreign aid organization to hire consultants who collect the data and do the necessary analysis. If the
issue is really important, the group may organize a conference which brings together interested parties from government and the society to discuss the consultants' proposals. The conferences are by no means neutral venues; rather, most speakers are supportive of the solutions suggested by the consultants.

While the government finances this process of research and consultation, civil
society groups have considerable latitude to formulate policies which they can support. However, certain groups are excluded if they are considered unacceptable by
the relevant ministry. Thus, on education matters the secondary teachers organization is perceived as too radical in terms of demands for their involvement in curriculum decisions. Environmental groups having direct linkages with their counterparts in the developed countries are thought to be unconcerned with local needs.
In addition, some civil society groups are fearful of being co-opted by the government and consequently refuse to undertake joint policy development with ministries. The most resistant in this regard are trade union leaders. They believe that

the civil servants are so committed to weakening union power in the collective bargaining process that no basis for agreement on policy is possible.

Summary

Electoral democracy has not brought the flowering of civil society in Botswana. Indeed, civil society is only gradually moving beyond the traditional tribal process of consultation with the elders and headmen. Groups have emerged, but most have yet to mobilize the organizational resources required to be effective versus government. They tend to lack funds, staff, and often the membership. In the rural areas they are effectively led by government officials who keep their records and manage their finances. Those groups which do seek to affect policy have limited their influence by allowing themselves to be co-opted by ministries which finance the process whereby civil society groups formulate proposals. In effect, civil society exists as an extension of the bureaucracy rather than as a set of independent actors confronting politicians and civil servants.

Communication of Citizen Discontents

In developed societies, civil society organizations are an important channel of criticism of government policies. Since these organizations do not yet play this role in Botswana, most public discontent with government is expressed through the *kgotla,* freedom squares, and the private weekly newspapers. The first two consist of face-to-face communications and take place in Setswana. Both are open to the public as a whole and are critical to rural political communication. On the other hand, newspapers are mostly in English and thus only for the literate population, which is primarily urban. In effect, political communication tends to be bifurcated effectively into traditional and modern dimensions.

One caveat should be noted with respect to the discussion which follows. The government daily newspaper, the *Daily News,* and the government radio station, Radio Botswana, are not discussed. The primary responsibility of both as far as the government is concerned is to inform the public of program developments in the ministries and to stimulate citizen interest in participating. Neither provides citizens an opportunity to voice discontent. Thus, these mass media are not of interest in this section.

The *Kgotla*

As noted above, the *kgotla* was an important part of the traditional political system. Chiefs and headmen used it to manipulate public support for decisions for which a consensus had been developed among their advisers. At certain crucial junctions, however, dissent would break out in *kgotla,* usually involving disagreements within the royal family or among headmen representing different community interests. As a result, there has developed a tradition that the community in *kgotla* has a right to confront authority when members think they are being harmed. This critical function was preserved during the colonial period as a means by which the colonial government could check the behavior of the chief. Indeed, the British began requiring that the *kgotla* elect new chiefs instead of simply accepting primogeniture. When *kgotla* complaints became serious and prolonged with regard to sitting traditional authorities, colonial officials accepted requests from the *kgotla* for the removal of those authorities.

Since independence, the ministries have used the *kgotla* as a means to communicate with local communities on development projects. Everything from the location of schools and wells to privatization of communal grazing lands is discussed in *kgotla*. Effectively the *kgotla* is a place where government employees dialogue with their constituency. The traditional authority still chairs a *kgotla,* but for the most part civil servants are setting the agenda. The stronger and more independent minded a chief or headman, the more likely the *kgotla* is to become a center of serious criticism of local policies.

Kgotla meetings are now open to females, minorities, and young people. However, older male villagers still tend to dominate discussions, as was the case traditionally. There are exceptions. On matters of delivery of children's health services or the regulation of village crop lands, for instance, women are likely to attend in larger numbers and to have the most to say. On the other hand, older males will be the only ones speaking on issues related to cattle, and the more cattle one has, the more seriously one's remarks will be taken. When a minister or the president addresses a *kgotla,* a broad spectrum of the community attends. However, only those with more status will address questions on important local issues to a prominent guest. The local MPs and councillors most likely will be in attendance for all *kgotla* meetings, particularly if they are seeking to create an image of being attentive to village needs.

The chiefs and headmen make every attempt to keep partisan politics out of *kgotla*. Often party leaders at the local level will not participate in the discussion for this reason However, sometimes the opposition will encourage posing of questions which embarrass the government. Depending on the extent of tension between the BDP and local traditional authorities, the latter can shorten or extend such discussion. Sometimes, a chief or headman who is disgruntled with government will even encourage criticism. Civil servants generally do not appreciate such sensitivity to village concerns. In a few cases, the minister of local government and lands has reprimanded, suspended, or removed sitting chiefs who became too aggressive in fostering discontent. For over two decades, Linchwe II from Mochudi was extremely adroit at calling civil servants to account in his district *kgotla*. As a result, government appointed him to positions which removed him from the local scene. For the most part, traditional authorities are much more tame, being content to minimize conflict in *kgotla*.

In summary, the *kgotla* provides an opportunity for citizens to voice their concerns about proposed programs or to criticize functioning ones. With some leadership, particularly from a traditional authority, civil servants can be forced to explain their actions. At the very least, the government is given an opportunity to listen to a community while implementing policies.

The Freedom Square

Freedom squares are political meetings staged by one political party to promote its message in a community. They are most often on Saturday morning, though they may be scheduled during the week in small villages. They begin with choir music and local speakers. Then comes the featured outside speaker—an MP, a national organizer, or a cabinet minister. In order to ensure a good attendance, some end with a meal prepared by the local women's section of the party. The attendees are usually more young people, those in the community who enjoy music, and party activists. Members who own trucks often transport people from the surrounding areas to the event.

Freedom squares began at the time of independence because traditional authorities refused to allow politicians to campaign in *kgotla*. Some of the new politicians had seen such local rallies being held in the townships of South Africa and decided to replicate the experience in Botswana. The government regulates the meetings only in that the police must give approval for the site to be used. While freedom squares can be held anywhere in theory, in fact certain areas in most villages are recognized as *the* "freedom square" because of continued use. In effect, it is the community venue for party politics, just as the *kgotla* is where the people meet with civil servants and elected officials.

Freedom of speech in these village meetings is almost unlimited. During the first decade after independence, the government unsuccessfully prosecuted several opposition speakers for insulting the president. While there have been no prosecutions since 1980, the police still tape-record freedom squares on the grounds that they must be prepared for such cases. The effect of this police surveillance is minimal. Speakers say outrageous things with impunity. Character assassination has few limits. BDP speakers have compared the BNF to AIDS, and the BNF has returned the favor by accusing the BDP of being cannibals.[16] Insofar as policy issues are discussed, partisan rumor is often substituted for the facts.

This is not to say that the freedom squares do not provide useful information. When the Democracy Project at the University of Botswana asked citizens in 1987 how they received most of their information about party issue positions, close to a third (31 percent) said it was from freedom squares. The next most mentioned source was the radio and newspapers (11 percent each).[17] However, citizens come also for entertainment. They most enjoy the bantering which goes on when opposing activists show up to question and heckle the speakers. BDP politicians in particular can end up facing some challenging inquires in a village which feels neglected by government. The more effective freedom square speakers turn hostile queries into opportunities to embarrass their opponents.

Most freedom squares are held in the rural areas. They tend to increase in number as elections approach. Conflicts within a party almost always lead to each faction holding its own freedom square. As elections approach, the parties also hold rallies in the urban areas. Right before the election, it is not unusual for the two main parties each to hold two or three rallies in different parts of a major town on the same day. Attendance can reach several thousand, with the politically attentive moving from one party's meeting to that staged by the other.

Freedom squares are the one place in Botswana politics where citizens have become somewhat comfortable observing public conflict between their political leaders. In the long run, these meetings are likely to provide a model for the more open discussion of political issues in other parts of society. In the meantime, freedom squares serve to keep both local and national party leaders in direct contact with the mass of the population.

Private Newspapers

Private newspapers became a permanent part of Botswana politics with the founding of the *Guardian* in 1982. As literacy and purchasing power have increased among Batswana, the market for private newspapers and their number have expanded.[18] In 1998, there were four private weeklies (the *Midweek Sun,* the *Guardian, Mmegi,* the *Gazette*). The total circulation of the private press has more than doubled from the late 1980s when the circulation was 33,000 issues per week. By 1998, this figure was 72,000. In contrast, the state-run *Daily News* has a circulation of around 175,000 per week. However, it is free, whereas the private newspapers cost $0.30 a copy,

Private newspapers play a dominant role, much more than the opposition parties, in setting the agenda for serious political debate in the country. They criticize bills presented before parliament, disclose corruption among government agencies, and report on social and economic problems confronting various segments of society. On a number of occasions they have forced ministers and top civil servants to resign. Several times the government has withdrawn bills because of criticism from the newspapers. And, at certain points they have exposed conflicts going on within the leadership of the BDP, thus giving the consensus-oriented Batswana a lesson in the role of intra-party conflict in a democracy.

The relationship between the top echelon of the ruling party and the private press has always been tense in Botswana. The BDP's leadership regards newspaper criticism as the same as BNF propaganda. In part, this criticism is justified in that journalists have often played fast and loose with the facts and shown public glee while attacking a BDP politician. On the other hand, top government officials rarely grant interviews to private journalists, and when they do agree to be interviewed, they demand the questions in advance. Also, reporters are frustrated by the secrecy under which the government operates. This is particularly true in the area of national security. For instance, in 1998 a report on foreign-arms buying by African countries identified Botswana as the third largest purchaser on the continent. However, the Botswana government refused any comment on the report because the information was classified.[19]

When the South African and Zimbabwean civil wars in the 1970s and 1980s spilled over into Botswana, the government used the occasion to impose new restrictions on government information in the form of the 1986 National Security Act. The government subsequently prosecuted several private newspapers under the law. While none of these actions was successful, the newspapers spent considerable funds defending themselves. In addition, the president has expelled two immigrant journalists who wrote critical stories on the government. Under the law the president need not give any reason for his action.[20]

The end of the civil wars has not changed the tense relations between the government and the press. In 1997 the government presented parliament with a Mass Media and Communications Bill. The bill was intended to establish a National Broadcasting Board, a newspaper registration and accreditation system, and a press council. While these institutions are not alien to many established democracies, the Ministry of Information clearly sought to have sufficient authority to sanction reporters and newspapers displeasing the government. BNF MPs said little. However, editors, local journalistic groups, and international media and human rights institutions reacted with intense criticism.[21] A week later the government decided to withdraw the legislation.[22] This episode reflects the fact that the government and the press have yet to come to agreement as to the private press's role in Botswana democracy. Rather, there is a constant process of testing the limits, which breeds intermittent conflict over the meaning of freedom of the press in the country.

The private press does not leave the opposition parties unscathed. Their internal conflicts receive extensive coverage. The failures of election coalitions are reported. The ineffectiveness and self-serving nature of their criticism of government are revealed. And, the small attendance at some of their freedom square meetings does not go unnoticed.

The 1999 elections provided the private press with new opportunities to expand the literate public's interests in election politics. Its journalists covered more races outside of the capital. Editorials forced the parties to confront issue concerns of various civil society groups. Occasional articles highlighted possible weaknesses in ethnic political coalitions.

Summary

Citizen criticism of government policies and behavior has been established as an important element in Botswana's democracy. However, its impact is limited. The *kgotla* is controlled by the traditional authorities and the civil service. When the former in particular are concerned about citizen complaints, *kgotlas* offer important means to communicate public discontents. The freedom square is often a partisan affair with little opportunity for citizen input. However, it does allow political activists a chance to challenge the programs of the other parties and occasionally to articulate intra-party conflicts. The advantage of both these mechanisms is that the discussion is in Setswana and available to all citizens regardless of their literacy.

The private press provides a small group of literate and attentive citizens with a more sophisticated view of politics in Botswana. However, the tension between journalists and public officials has thus far prevented the latter from engaging in a constructive dialogue on most issues.

The Civil Service and Democracy

Before independence, colonial civil servants governed Botswana unrestrained by any democratic controls. At best, they sought popular support through the traditional chiefs and the *kgotlas* they might occasionally hold to seek ratification of a program in a given tribal area. Colonial rule was government by administrative domination.[23]

The Administrative State

The introduction of an elected parliament in 1965 and local councils the next year did little to change this situation. The first president, Sir Seretse Khama, viewed his political colleagues in the BDP and in parliament as having little or no vision relative to the country's development. He believed that the civil service generally and, most especially, a cadre of economists in the Ministry of Finance should be the ones to formulate a plan for the growth of the economy and then allocate the nation's resources to achieve this plan. To ensure that the government bureaucracy was effective, Khama supported the creation of a civil service run by rules and staffed with skilled personnel.

A firm line was drawn between politics and both policy formulation and implementation. Politicians could talk only to the highest responsible civil servant in a given government organization. At the national level this meant the permanent secretaries, whom Khama firmly supported in almost all cases in acting independent of political influences. Because Khama was the legitimate heir to the largest chieftaincy in Botswana, that of the Bamangwato, few politicians were prepared to challenge such a leader's approach to development of the post-independence government.[24] Indeed, BDP elected officials viewed him as the basis for their political survival rather than feeling any need to make the civil service sensitive to constituency desires.

President Khama also supported the civil service in establishing a personnel system isolated from the demands of political patronage and upholding highly professional standards of performance. Of necessity in this context, Africanization took place at a very slow rate. It was literally decades before Batswana could fill many technical positions. In the meantime, the government hired skilled North Americans, Europeans, and Indians on long-term contracts. Because of increasing demands for government services and regulation resulting from the growing Botswana economy, the absolute number of expatriates actually expanded for the first several decades after independence. Within the Tswana segment of the civil service, Khama and his top civil service advisers ruthlessly imposed a merit-driven promotion policy which created a relatively effective and confident group of top-level managers.

While the Office of the President directed growth of the personnel system, the Ministry of Finance and Development became the coordinator of policy development and implementation through its control of the planning process and the purse strings. The ministry obtained the most talented members of the civil service. It provided its staff with advanced training overseas and prolonged mentoring by experienced expatriates. The result was the emergence of a talented cadre of economic managers who sincerely believe they have a right to formulate and implement economic policy with only minimal input from other ministries, let alone receive direction from politicians and the citizenry.[25]

The presidential protection given the Ministry of Finance to plan and direct the economy is exceptional. With very little political intervention, top ministry officials regularly set goals for almost all areas of the economy from mining to social services, regulate wages and salaries for the public and private sectors, control prices through manipulation of foreign exchange rates, and determine housing and many food prices through government-owned enterprises. Private corporations at best play a cooperative role with the government in the more important sectors of the economy. Thus, De Beers, the international diamond marketing cartel, manages the diamond mines as a joint venture with the Botswana government. Parastatal corporations which are closely supervised by the Ministry of Finance run the major utilities, the country's airline, the national railroad, a massive housing corporation, and several slaughterhouses which process beef for export.[26]

Khama died in 1980 and was replaced by his vice president, Ketumile Masire. During Masire's tenure there was little change in the dominant role of the civil service in determining and implementing public policy. This is not surprising in that Masire served as minister of finance during Khama's rule. In this position, Masire came to both trust the ministry's top officials and understand many of the theories and strategies they used to conceive and implement their thinking. Indeed, both Masire and Khama regularly employed foreign and domestic economists to instruct ministers, MPs, and civil society leaders on the operation and development of Botswana's economy. The BDP has even adopted state planning objectives as the core of the economic section of its election manifestos.[27] In effect, for over three decades top development planners have been free to set the public agenda on economic questions. A regulation which prevents the implementation of new projects not in the development plan without a year-long review has allowed the Ministry of Finance to prevent almost all political end runs to its basic planning documents.[28]

Festus Mogae became Botswana's third president in March of 1998. He had held the top civil service positions in the Office of the President and the Ministry of Finance before joining the BDP and parliament. He quickly became the vice president and minister of finance under Masire. In these positions, he demonstrated an almost militant concern for keeping the politicians in line as far as interfering with the policy process or seeking patronage. He is widely respected, even by leading opposition politicians, for his unflinching willingness to stand up to even the most powerful BDP politicians. Thus, he is not likely to challenge the dominant role of the civil service.

Democracy by Veto

Since economic development is the main concern of the Botswana government, effectively its major policy decisions are taken in a most undemocratic fashion. In a very real sense, democratization of the policy process has involved challenging the bureaucracy through threat of a veto. This has meant that disgruntled groups must put political pressure on the president and his cabinet to review and overturn objectionable civil service decisions. The process by which this is done varies. Sometimes the more politically oriented ministers respond directly to constituency pressures. By far the most active in this regard has been the long-time secretary-general of the BDP, Daniel Kwelagobe. He spends considerable time traveling the country dealing with party discontents. Upon returning to the capital he often persuades the president and cabinet to delay, modify, or reverse civil service decisions affecting particular communities. Anything from the placement of a road or fence to regulations governing the development of commercial ranches has been changed as a result of the protests of BDP partisans. On other occasions, community groups may stage protests and enlist the support of ministries adversely affected by a project. Thus, a major dam building project pushed by the Ministry of Mineral Resources and Water Affairs for the Okavango waters was derailed by a coalition of environmental groups which mobilized the ministries of Local Government and Lands and Commerce and Industry on their behalf. On still other occasions, the protest is largely carried on in the private newspapers. This has been a particularly important factor when on several occasions civil servants have abused their authority to the point of benefiting personally from a specific development project.[29]

The Problem of Further Democratization

The belief of leaders of the civil service in their right to rule is well rationalized. From their perspective, the mass of the public is not sufficiently educated to understand its own best interests. When dealing with the public, top civil servants do not hesitate to show off their superior knowledge and skills in ways designed to cut off communication. Many in the civil service believe the main function of elected officials is to educate the public on the benefits of policies which have been developed for society by government. This basic confidence of government officials in their right to rule is reinforced by the fact that Tswana politicians, like all politicians, tend to be unabashedly self-serving in promoting their own interests and those of their constituency. By contrast, the civil servants perceive themselves as speaking for a higher national interest. Finally, the economic policies of government have been so successful, especially when compared to other countries in

Africa, that the civil servants are confident little can be gained by giving public opinion greater recognition in policy-making.

This authoritarian perspective places the civil service in a conundrum in that the Botswana state seeks its legitimacy primarily as a democracy. Therefore, the civil servants feel a need to appear democratic. Several factors are particularly critical in reinforcing the movement of the bureaucracy in this direction. One factor is the need to minimize elected officials' attempts to veto parts of policies. If a ministry can show that its policies have popular support, politicians become reluctant to go to the president and cabinet to block passage. Another factor is the government's desire to project itself on the international scene as a democracy. This image was a critical part of Botswana's attempt in the 1970s and 1980s to secure foreign aid by appearing to be a bastion of democracy confronting racist South Africa. Still another factor has been the insistence of foreign governments that their aid support only development projects with demonstrated community support.

The civil servants have developed a number of means to give their policies and programs a democratic veneer. Some of this veneer has an impact, particularly in the way policies are implemented. One is the constant use of public opinion polls and sociological analyses of project areas, particularly in establishing a community's needs and interests. Another device is the holding of a traditional *kgotla* in a community where interested citizens have an opportunity to give their opinions on a particular scheme before it is undertaken. At the national level, the government often holds conferences on a major policy question it is considering, for example, privatization, fencing grazing areas, and settling the hunter-gatherers. Persons are invited from various sectors of society as well as a few experts from overseas. For the most part, these gatherings end up focusing on how a new policy initiative should be implemented rather than whether something should be done or not. Finally, the civil servants have created a number of advisory councils related to such matters as wages and incomes, education, and labor relations. The councils consist of representatives of affected groups plus a substantial number of civil servants. Generally, top civil servants control the agenda, determine when meetings are called, and heavily influence the advice the councils give them.

The result of all these consultative processes is that civil servants generally launch their programs with the appearance of considerable public support. Sometimes significant changes are made to respond to community concerns. Moreover, the consultations induce many community leaders to feel they have a stake in the resulting program.

Thus far, however, neither political parties nor civil society groups have been able to give overall policy direction to the civil service on basic economic objectives and their implementation. Those wanting to make such a change are beginning to gather support within political party structures. The BDP itself is split into two wings. The dominant one to this point has supported the civil service's leadership on policy matters. Challenging it are members of BDP led by Secretary-General Kwelagobe and Party Chairman Ponatshego Kedikilwe. This group wants government policy and positions to become a source of local patronage, thus making government more of a tool for the BDP's continuation in power. At the same time, the opposition BNF has campaigned on a platform which basically promises that more of the returns from economic development will be distributed in the form of increased wages and services and less will go into capitalizing future growth. Also, the BNF seeks to reduce the influence of expatriate firms in Botswana's economy. If either or both of these groups of politicians were to gain control of the presidency, the continuing independence and policy domination of the civil service could be endangered.

Summary

Ultimately, the administrative state would appear to be doomed in Botswana. Privatization policies are increasing the size of the middle class, which is not dependent on the state for its survival. At present the civil service's domination survives because of the failure of the factions which oppose it, namely the rural and urban bourgeoisie, to form a coalition. The former continues to challenge the civil service from within the BDP, and the latter struggles to wrest control of the BNF from a collection of third world socialist visionaries. In effect, the civil service continues in power by default of its enemies and the success of its policies. In the process, democratization remains stalled.

The International System and the Development of Botswana's Democracy

As a developing country of only a million and a half people, Botswana has found itself subject to a myriad of international influences.[30] For the most part, these influences have not impacted the country's democracy. The political parties developed with little outside support; the more politically articulate private newspapers (i.e., *Mmegi* and the *Gazette*) are locally owned; the party primary system has largely been designed by party leaders to ensure that the local organization remains in contact with its constituency; and the freedom squares have emerged out of a need to have community space for face-to-face campaigning.[31]

This having been said, it is also true that foreign influences have played a role in extending popular control. Two sets of influences are most important: Western industrialized democracies, and the South African example. For the most part, the impact of each has been positive, although contrary effects are evident.

Western Industrialized Democracies

The shape Botswana's democracy took at its founding reflects many aspects of the British parliamentary system (executive dependent on legislature, single-member districts, and emphasis on political rights). In addition, in the negotiations before independence the British supported reducing the influence of the chieftaincy in its traditional form, which was clearly not democratic. However, the British also bequeathed to Botswana a strong civil service, which has, as noted above, dominated the policy-making process in a most undemocratic fashion.

The main device for subsequent Western influence on Botswana's democratization has been foreign assistance. Aid organizations have used their financial leverage to induce the civil service in particular and the politicians at times to be more attuned to community concerns. They have supported community participation in the design and implementation of local development projects. When communities have objected to central ministry plans, the aid agencies have often insisted on attending to local wishes. In some cases, these agencies have required that the Botswana government redesign social service, education, and drought relief programs so as to make minority groups, particularly the Bushmen and other remote area dwellers, major beneficiaries. The extension of such programs to minority populations has stimulated increased interest and participation on their part in party politics. Minorities have come to see that government policies can make a difference. In the case of the Bushmen, aid agencies have funded many of the activities of the principal groups putting pressure on the government for their right to participate on an equal basis in the electoral system and the economy.

Western democratic intentions have not always worked out in practice. Foreign aid to local organizations is given largely through central government ministries. Indeed, no aid project can continue for very long if there is not support for it from a ministry of the central government As a result, this aid gives the administrative state extra resources which can be held out to local communities and organizations as a carrot for cooperation on other matters. Also, top civil servants find ways to curtail the propensity of Western aid organizations to support local participation in development projects since such approaches challenge administrative domination. The resulting frustration on the part of the Swedish, Dutch, and Norwegian aid agencies is such that all are terminating their Bushman assistance programs. However, there is no doubt that the controversy they have generated in the remote areas has motivated the Bushmen to become for the first time a politically active part of the Botswana state.

Western aid to Botswana declined rapidly in the 1990s. It is now almost nonexistent. The reason for this decline is at least twofold: (1) Botswana's democracy is sufficiently institutionalized that in comparison with other nascent democracies in Africa it does not need help; and (2) the country is sufficiently developed to be able to sustain its own economic growth. The consequence, however, is that Western influence on Botswana's future democratization is likely to be relatively small. The impact will be limited to occasional outcries by Western diplomats when the Botswana government appears to abridge the political and economic rights of minorities, particularly the Bushmen.[32]

South African Democracy

Botswana has historically always been under the influence of developments in South Africa. Botswana's democratization is no exception. South Africa's impact in the realm of democratic change derives from the fact that its mass media reaches into all parts of Botswana. The only television available comes from South African stations. Literate Batswana read the South African newspapers and magazines. Many Batswana tune into South African radio stations. As a result, the more politically attentive are as conversant with the politics of South Africa as they are with that their own country. Of particular interest to this attentive group has been the way in which democracy has been institutionalized in South Africa.

Several aspects of this process have received particular attention. Most important is the political freedom granted the South African trade union movement. Under the apartheid system, unions became one of the most important internal factors pushing the whites to give up power. Since the advent of African rule, the unions have exercised considerable influence because of the close association of the union leadership with the ruling African National Congress (ANC). Batswana union leaders (and their members to a certain extent) have been very impressed and begun to ask themselves why they too should not be having a similar impact on their government. In addition, the climate of union-government cooperation in South Africa makes it harder for civil servants and BDP politicians to resist Botswana union demands for revision of the country's paternalistic labor laws. A major reform is thus likely to take place in the next few years. In the meantime, union leaders are beginning to debate various possibilities for becoming more active in election politics. They have observed how the unions helped the ANC oust the apartheid government and have begun to wonder if they should not try to do the same through Botswana's elections.

Other aspects of South Africa's active civil society have also impacted Botswana. For instance, the rise of a powerful women's coalition in Botswana appears in part to come from the example of such groups in South Africa. Religious groups in Botswana have been motivated to play an observer role in Botswana's elections by the success of the churches in monitoring the South African vote during the transition elections.

In the area of political participation, also, a series of influences is being felt. Even during the apartheid era, there was considerable freedom of press, especially in cases where the white government attempted to suppress liberal and African newspapers. As a result, there is recognition among more educated Batswana that a free press is not subversive to government or the national interest. The fact that the ANC government has continued to allow a free press has further emphasized this point. In addition, a number of other aspects of South African politics have at least gained respectability in Botswana. For the first time, the opposition in Botswana is advocating a proportional representation (PR) system of elections. The attractiveness of this idea comes from the fact that in the post-apartheid era, South African elections operate on the basis of PR. Also, the 1997 acceptance by the Botswana government of a constitutional amendment which allows persons between 18 and 21 to vote reflects a recognition that this group has been allowed to vote by the ANC.

South Africa's impact on Botswana's democracy has so far been relatively positive in the sense of generating issues which the Tswana governing elite has had to consider. The impact was not always so positive, in that during the apartheid era the relationship between the two countries was fraught with tensions. The BDP elite used this tension to justify fairly draconian security laws, particularly with respect to military and press affairs.[33] Should South Africa again move toward authoritarian rule because of a decline in political order, the impact is likely to be similarly negative. The falling back of their neighbor could justify slowing down on moves toward increasing pluralism, for fear that the same thing might happen in Botswana. Also, any violent opposition to an authoritarian South African regime could spill over into Botswana in the form of an influx of refugees and the country becoming the base for launching of cross-border attacks into South Africa. In such a situation, the Botswana government would feel a need to clamp down on organizations and persons with any appearance of supporting such activity.

Summary

Botswana's progress toward increasing democracy has been partially propelled forward by the impact of Western influences and the example of a multi-racial democracy in South Africa. The West has recently been important in awakening the Bushmen and other remote area dwellers to the politics of the modern state. South Africa has given the opposition motivation to challenge some of constraints the BDP government has used to maintain itself in power. This positive influence from abroad could turn negative in the future if South Africa moves back toward an authoritarian form of rule. However, for the most part Botswana's democratization has unfolded in response to the dynamics of domestic politics. Foreign influences have merely enhanced or, in the case of security laws, somewhat retarded the process.

Conclusions

Government accountability to its citizens requires democratic structures. However, establishment of these structures does not ensure that effective accountability results. Botswana's experience illustrates that for democratic structures to work, individuals and groups within society must have the will, resources, creativity, and political base to ensure accountability. Citizen control comes less because democracy is morally right than because those desiring particular democratic practices chose to accumulate power and use it to force acceptance of these practices.

Various groups in Botswana have made significant gains in political influence by promoting democratization. The traditional authorities have retained a role for themselves vis-à-vis the modern bureaucracy by chairing the *kgotla* and allowing it to be used for the voicing of citizen discontent. The private newspapers have regularly tested the boundaries of dissent and frustrated the BDP's attempts to limit critical dialogue. The BNF has mobilized the urban population at elections and through its leadership of a number of urban councils. The trade unions have increasingly organized wage earners for economic purposes, thus providing themselves with a future base with which to influence the politicians. The BDP leadership itself has been most effective at forging and maintaining a broad-based electoral coalition founded on ethnicity. The civil servants, in spite of their belief that they know what is best for Botswana's future, conscientiously hold consultations with groups and communities likely to be affected by implementation of particular policies.

In some regards, however, various groups in Botswana have not been successful in expanding their influence by promoting government accountability to the public. While the BNF leadership has been able to organize the urban population, it has done little to bring various rural ethnic constituencies into a broad-based coalition which could beat the BDP and thus provide Botswana with a competitive party system. Civil society groups, with the exception of the unions, have depended upon government and foreign-aid funding in order to survive, thus limiting the range of their influence in the policy process. The civil service has refused thus far to foster structures by which citizen influences can have a role in initiating policy proposals or negotiating over their content. The mass of the Tswana population has yet to recognize the importance of public political conflict in democratic decision-making processes.

Thus, while much remains to be accomplished, Botswana's democratization has often been viewed as so remarkable in Africa that it is termed "exceptional."[34] This description is true in the sense that no other African country has such a sustained record of political freedom over the last three decades. This record has been made possible in part by an equally exceptional record of economic development which has provided some critical opportunities for democratization. In particular, economic growth has propelled the urbanization which has broken down ethnic ties; it has provided funds for the development of political parties and some civil society groups (especially unions); it has created a middle class which could afford private local newspapers critical of government; and it has supported increasing linkages with South Africa and its democratization process.

On the other hand, much of the first two decades of Botswana's democratization took place without significant economic change. The country was among the least developed in the world. Yet, in this period, the *kgotla* was molded into an institution for checking the implementation of national policies at the local level; the freedom square emerged as an institution of almost unlimited freedom of speech for political party activists; political party activists learned to conduct political campaigns; and some civil society groups began organizing their members to influence the governing elites.

To understand this precocious aspect of Botswana's democracy, it is important to grasp the extent to which the country's political tradition has both persisted and been radically modified. This complex process of change has given Botswana's democracy—as is the case with others in Europe, the Americas, and Asia—its own unique or exceptional features while also producing some similarities with all democracies. This building of a democracy through cultural transmogrification and radical social change is most striking. It has been essential to the stability and dynamism which the polity has exhibited since political independence. Following are some of the key manifestations of these concurrent processes of renewal and transformation in the foregoing analysis:

• Political parties began in the 1960s representing traditional ethnic political identifications but have gradually sought to include groupings arising within the modernization process. The BNF has increasingly appealed for support from the lower-income groups in the city and small-scale entrepreneurs. The BDP has articulated the interests of the leaders of the bureaucratic state, cattle owners, and professionals.

• Rural elected representatives have functioned largely as defenders of traditional communities vis-à-vis the modernizing state. On the other hand, in order to retain their positions these representatives are being increasingly forced to recognize the legitimacy of the national party leadership and its policies as ultimately determining parliamentary votes on critical issues.

• Civil society groups are gradually organizing throughout modernized Botswana society; however, they have thus far concentrated on influencing the government decision-making and not on becoming involved in partisan politics. This fits in with the traditional Tswana desire to avoid public conflict. As the influence of these groups has become more secure, a few, such as women and unions, are beginning to explore ways of becoming involved in elections.

• Citizen communication with government has rested on traditional and modern bases. Village meetings, the *kgotla,* and freedom squares have provided a means for rural communities to interact with both politicians and civil servants. In the cities, private newspapers have since the 1980s emerged as the venue for much more frank discussions with government. With the spread of literacy, the newspapers will also become primary in the rural areas for conveying citizen discontent.[35]

• The civil service has recognized the need to interact with civil society organizations and local communities. As a consequence, it has established a tradition of listening to the mass of the population, very much in line with what the traditional authorities had done in *kgotla* in the pre-colonial period. While this listening appears sometimes to be a facade, it has forced the bureaucracy to become sensitive to community and group concerns in the implementation of some policies.

• In terms of looking abroad for inspiration with regard to democratization, Botswana seems to be moving away from the model it inherited from colonial rule, which its leaders had been exposed to since the beginning of the century, to considering alternative political structures being developed in neighboring South Africa with the advent of African rule. This new model is inspiring civil society activists to recognize the need for their groups to enter the realm of partisan politics, thus partially breaking down the traditional Tswana aversion to public conflict.

The result of all these processes of democratic change within Tswana society is a slow but steady shifting of the balance between administrative secretiveness and public accountability. Structures and beliefs are emerging in various parts of the political realm which encourage civil servants and ruling party politicians to respond to citizen demands. As of yet, the accumulation of citizen power has not reached the point where interest groups and political parties are negotiating with ministries or initiating policies; however, this change appears likely to come. The change will probably come as the result of a serious crisis, quite possibly an economic one triggered by a major recession in the diamond market. The model of South African democracy and its evolution will be most critical as a road map for this further democratization.

NOTES

1. The exception is the Kalanga who live in northeastern Botswana. The Tswana population is around 75 to 80 percent of total.

2. United Nations Development Programme, *Human Development Report 1997* (New York: Oxford University Press, 1997), pp. 147, 166, and 202–3.

3. Approximately one-quarter of the sexually active population is now HIV positive in Botswana. For the data in this paragraph see ibid., pp. 147, 166, 186; and UNDP, *Human Development Report 1991* (New York: Oxford University Press, 1991), p. 126.

4. UNDP, p. 46.

5. C. Harvey and S. R. Lewis, *Policy Choice and Development Performance in Botswana* (London: Macmillan Press, 1990).

6. Ibid., p. 281.

7. In July of 1998, a conflict between the BNF's founder and its Central Committee resulted in most of the elected officials and party activists (except those in the left wing and Koma's closest associates) joining together to establish a new party, the Botswana Congress Party (BCP). The new party should be better positioned to cope with the problems of the BNF discussed in this section, particularly those related to factional conflict.

8. Botswana's urbanization has been 12.3 percent per annum between 1960 and 1994, the fastest of any African country during this time period. See UNDP, *Human Development Report 1997,* pp. 192–93.

9. *World Development Indicators 1997* (Washington, D.C.: World Bank, 1997).

10. J. D. Holm and R. Morgan, "Coping with Drought in Botswana: An African Success," *Journal of Modern African Studies* 23, no. 3 (1985): 463–82.

11. Since independence, *kgotla* meetings include women and young people.

12. J. D. Holm, "Elections in Botswana: Institutionalization of a New System of Legitimacy," in F. Hayward, ed., *Elections in Independent Africa* (Boulder, Colo.: Westview Press, 1987), p. 138; J. Parson, "Liberal Democracy, the Liberal State, and the 1989 General Elections in Botswana," in S. J. Stedman, ed., *Botswana: The Political Economy of Democratic Development* (Boulder, Colo.: Lynne Rienner, 1993), pp. 73–79.

13. S. Darnolf, *Democratic Electioneering in Southern Africa: The Contrasting Cases of Botswana and Zimbabwe* (Göteborg: Göteborg University Press, 1997).

14. Parson, "Liberal Democracy," pp. 65–90.

15. For a more extensive treatment of the subjects covered in this section, see J. D. Holm, P. P. Molutsi, and G. Somolekae, "The Development of Civil Society in a Democratic State: The Botswana Model," *African Studies Review* 39, no. 2 (September 1996): 43–69.

16. Darnolf, *Democratic Electioneering,* p. 161.

17. See M. H. Lekorwe, "The Kgotla and the Freedom Square: One-way or Two-way communication," in J. D. Holm, and P. P. Molutsi, eds., *Democracy in Botswana: The Proceedings of a Symposium Held in Gaborone, 1–5 August 1988* (Athens: Ohio University Press, 1989), p. 225.

18. S. Grant and B. Egner, "The Private Press and Democracy," in Holm and Molutsi, eds., *Democracy in Botswana,* p. 254.

19. See *Mmegi,* 6–12 March 1998.

20. Grant and Egner, "Private Press," p. 262.

21. *Mail and Guardian* (Johannesburg), 8 July 1997 and 10 July 1997.

22. *IFEX Action Alert Service,* 9 July 1997.

23. L. A. Picard, *The Politics of Development in Botswana: A Model for Success?* (Boulder, Colo.: Lynne Rienner, 1987).

24. W. Henderson, "Seretse Khama and the Institutionalization of the Botswana State," in W. Henderson, ed., *Botswana: Education, Culture and Politics* (Edinburgh: Centre for African Studies, 1990), pp. 217–42.

25. For a most articulate statement of the policy perspective of civil servants in the Ministry of Finance, see S. R. Lewis, "Policymaking and Economic Performance: Botswana in Comparative Perspective," in Stedman, ed., *Botswana,* pp. 11–25.

26. For an excellent statement of the overall perspective of Botswana's planners and extent to which they realized their goals in the long term, see C. Harvey, and S. R. Lewis, *Policy Choice and Development Performance in Botswana* (Basingstoke: London, 1990).

27. See Ministry of Finance and Development Planning (MFDP), *National Development Plan 1979–1985* (Gaborone: The Government Printer, 1980) and *National Development Plan 1985–91* (Gaborone: The Government Printer) and compare them with the BDP election manifestos for 1984 and 1989, respectively.

28. J. D. Holm, "Development, Democracy and Civil Society in Botswana," in A. Leftwich, ed., *Development and Democracy* (Cambridge, Mass.: Polity, 1996), pp. 97–113.

29. The most famous occasion was the Leno affair when some top civil servants sought to obtain prime real estate in the center of Gaborone for an office building they wanted to construct as part of private investment.

30. R. Dale, *Botswana's Search for Autonomy in Southern Africa* (Westport, Conn.: Greenwood, 1995).

31. J. D. Holm, "Botswana: Lessons Learned Over Thirty Years of Democratic Development" (paper prepared for delivery at the 20th SAUSSC meetings in Lusaka, Zambia, 2 December 1997).

32. R. Hitchcock, and J. D. Holm, "Bureaucratic Domination of Hunter-Gatherer Societies: A Study of the San in Botswana," *Development and Change* 24 (April 1993): 305–38.

33. In response to a South African Defence Force raid into Botswana in 1985, the government of Botswana passed the National Security Act of 1986. The act allowed the

government to severely restrict the freedom of press in a manner not unlike the restraints imposed in South Africa at the time.

34. M. Bratton and D. Rothschild, "Institutional Bases of Governance in Africa," in G. Hyden and M. Bratton, eds., *Governance and Politics in Africa* (Boulder, Colo.: Lynne Rienner, 1992), p. 27.

35. Whether the government will ever allow independent radio or television stations to develop is an open question at this point.

7. Militarism, Warfare, and the Search for Peace in Angola

Horace G. Campbell

Introduction: Two Scenes of War and Resistance

Scene 1. Kuito, Bié

The battle for Kuito, Bié, in the heartland of Angola, raged on with artillery bombardment and a siege of the main urban administrative area for over nine months (January to September 1993). The Armed Forces for the Liberation of Angola (FALA, Forças Armadas para a Libertação de Angola), the army of the National Union for the Total Independence of Angola (UNITA, União Nacional para a Independência Total de Angola) and Jonas Savimbi, trained and equipped by a dying apartheid regime, had laid siege to this city in the central highlands of Angola. Siege is the oldest form of total war. (The long history of the siege of civilian populations in war had led to strict international rules regarding the entrapment and bombardment of unarmed civilians.) Yet, this was precisely the kind of warfare carried out by UNITA against the civilians of Kuito, Malanje, Huambo, and Uige between 1993 and 1994. The peoples of Kuito, whose memories of African military and cultural resistance to colonial pacification campaigns were still fresh, shared a history of resistance to colonialism with the other peoples of Angola. The electoral results of October 1992 had demonstrated that a significant number of these people had voted for UNITA in the historic elections. Jonas Savimbi, the leader of UNITA, claimed his lineage from Kuito and had pinned his hopes on a quick military victory in this town to reinforce the military occupation of over 65 percent of the administrative centers in Angola. After the fifty-five-day brutal siege of Huambo (the second largest city in Angola), from January to March 1993, UNITA had captured Huambo and wanted to add Kuito to demonstrate its capacity to dominate militarily the Angolan highlands. This siege was carried on at the same time as the "peace talks" in Abidjan, Ivory Coast. Savimbi had wanted to take Kuito in order to boost his ability to seize power by force. The army of UNITA had controlled most of the barrios of this city, but there were three barrios that were not taken. The barrio of Katonge had struggled to remain free of UNITA, and it was from this barrio on the Kuito River that the women seized the mobility to cross the river to forage for food.

The women of Kuito demonstrated exemplary courage in breaking the siege by going out at nights to forage for food. They used different techniques of dress, language, and trading patterns to bypass the soldiers of the government and UNITA. The army of UNITA had bombarded the city indiscriminately in the military confrontation, and on the radio deployed the ideals of Umbundu identity and family to legitimize the war. The civilian population lived in underground bunkers by day only to seize the night to find means to live. The wholesale bombardment had killed thousands, and it was unclear why UNITA wanted a victory that cost the lives of the very people they claimed they were fighting to defend. So many people died in the sieges of Kuito and Huambo that the dogs died from overeating cadavers. Bodies piled on the streets and the scenes of death forced the living to draw on their innermost strengths to find ways to survive. This sense of survival and solidarity by the women of Kuito helped weaken the army of UNITA. UNITA was forced to bargain for a cease-fire, called the Lusaka Protocol, after the forces of the government recaptured Huambo, the provincial capital, in November 1994. Then Jonas Savimbi retreated to Bailundo and claimed the support of the "traditional" leader of the Ovimbundu.

As I walked through the rubble of Kuito and Huambo in 1996, it became clear to me that the antidote to militarism had to be more profound than the signing of peace accords. UNITA had bombarded Kuito to save it, and the government had bombed Huambo from the air to save the people from UNITA. There had to be a conceptual grasp of the basis for militarism. The burning necessity for clarity was sharpened by the ways in which, in the process of cementing the identity of survival, the women and men of Kuito were at the same time unmasking the myth of ethnic solidarity and ethnic identity. This myth had been unleashed to demobilize and divide the peoples of Angola by militarists who had internalized what their colonial education had taught them—that Angola was a society of deep "tribal" rivalry. The experience of the siege of Kuito clarified the need for an understanding of UNITA beyond the literature that celebrated Jonas Savimbi as the tribal leader of the Ovimbundu people.[1] David Birmingham, a pre-eminent historian of Angola, pointed out that, "Savimbi was left traumatized with dismay that even his own highland people had not fully supported him."

African peasant women played a significant role in the failure of Jonas Savimbi to achieve his military objectives. The women of Kuito, like the women of Uige, Malanje, Huambo, and other cities invaded by UNITA, deepened the consciousness of resistance and struggle in order to breach battle lines to break the fetishism of war and masculine power that came to characterize the war of 1992–94. It was this same tenacity on the part of the ordinary citizens that prevented the military takeover by UNITA in 1999. Women in Kuito, like women all over Angola, fell back on the knowledge and skills of plants, medicine, and empirical sciences to subsist in a society where the governmental apparatus had been forced to deploy the resources of the society in the purchase of artillery pieces and jets. It was estimated that between 1992 and 1994 the government of Angola spent more than US$3.5 billion on weapons.[2] One international non-governmental organization (NGO) estimated that UNITA had expended more than US$3.7 billion dollars between 1992 and 1997. The expenditure on weapons by both the government and UNITA could be compared to the ways in which the women explained how pumpkin leaves became so central to the diet of those under siege. It forced me to look again at the knowledge African women had of food plants and medicine in Africa.

Scene 2. Courtroom in Luanda

The second scene took place in the courtroom in the overcrowded city of Luanda in February 1996. On trial was the police chief for Luanda, the capital city of Angola. The chief, a woman from a distinguished family in Cabinda, had achieved a very high rank in the security apparatus but had been tried for the abuse of authority. There was a rally for her in the court on the day of the sentencing by a coterie of professional women who declared that she was a scapegoat for the widespread corruption in the police and security forces. It was a contradictory moment in the history of the society for the professional women, many of whom had been active in the Organization of Angolan Women (OMA). They wanted to defend the independence of a police chief who was a woman, even if she was corrupt.

When the sentence was announced (five months), there was an uproar in the court and the small group of articulate women shouted that they would go on strike. The sentencing and the ensuing protests were broadcast over the state radio. There would be no cooking, no washing, no preparing of food, and no other support in the home (apparently a reference to a sexual boycott). Other boycotts by women in Africa had demonstrated that when women withdrew in mass from their partnership roles, men were left in a lurch. "Women knew that no society, nor men for that matter, could handle the trauma and chaos entailed by women's sudden withdrawal from social interaction. Elsewhere in Africa women had used the boycott to remind the community that no society can function without the duties and tasks performed by its women, namely, their spiritual, agrarian, economic and familial obligations."[3] The potential of a national strike by women in Angola was a powerful threat to the core of the power relations in Angola. However, the call for boycott by women in the courtroom was not followed up by any concrete action because the women attending court did not have organic links with the working women of Luanda, who struggled on a daily basis to survive in the stalemate between war and peace. The women of the professional strata did not have the material or political resources to effect their threat. In fact, many of the women in the courtroom disposed of the labor power of other women who worked in their household; hence their capacity to carry forward a strike over housework was limited. More importantly, the conditions of urbanization had over-taken the conditions of the village community where female-centered conscious-ness and solidarity could find an autonomous material base in the economic or-ganization of the village.

The women who had gathered in the courtroom did not lend overt support to the industrial action that was then under way by teachers who earned less than US$10 per month. This strike by SINPROF, the first independent trade union in Angola in the aftermath of the one-party phase of independence, had been led mainly by women, who dominated the teaching profession. In the same month, there had been a strike by health workers, the majority of whom were women. The call for a sex strike should be seen in the context of industrial actions then under way in a society led and organized by women. One could deduce from the shrill protests that the courtroom declaration of the professional women was a manifes-tation of the fact that they were themselves searching for new levers to escape the harsh economic conditions imposed by a society that was on a permanent war foot-ing, even though a peace protocol was in effect. The frustration over the inability of the government to confront the corrosive corruption of militarism and expen-diture on weapons could be overheard in private all over the city, but the profes-sional women failed to articulate this grievance in public. It was common knowl-edge in Luanda that millions of dollars were being made in commissions on the purchase of weapons by the top generals of the Angolan army.

These professional women who supported the police chief could be distin-guished from the teachers who defied the government and continued the strike until some of their demands were met. The teachers were striking not only for bet-ter pay but, more importantly, for schools to have buildings, desks, chairs, and other essential infrastructure to educate the young. On the other hand, the women in the courtroom wanted to oppose the fact that the police chief was being made a scapegoat for the widespread corruption taking over society. Their socialization and education had demobilized them in the sense that they did not see their task as building concrete political links with working women who were then involved in industrial disputes. Twice in the previous year there had been calls for a general strike by independent forces in the society who wanted the government to spend money on social services instead of the farcical no war–no peace standoff and meet-ings to conciliate Savimbi. The ruling party had warned those calling the general strike that only UNITA would benefit from a general strike. The general strike never materialized.

These two scenes of war captured the contradictions and challenges of the search for peace and a new mode of existence beyond militarism in Angola. The scenes of city sieges, war against civilians, underground bunkers, destroyed cities, barrios of resistance, industrial actions, calls for general strikes, and the tenacity of women were aspects of the militarism and warfare that no one in Angola could escape. An-gola has been a society torn by warfare for more than five hundred years. This chap-ter will try to focus on the issues generated by the past thirty-eight years (1961–99) of fighting. In many ways the two scenes described above are connected by the centrality of warfare in the history of Angolan society and the pivotal role of women in the struggles for peace.

As we reach the millennium, most popular and academic studies on Africa are preoccupied with the permanence of warfare and militarism. The writings on Africa suggest that warfare is endemic to the region. The existence of wars across the African continent (in Angola, Burundi, Congo Brazzaville, Democratic Republic of Congo, Eritrea, Ethiopia, Namibia-Caprivi Strip, Rwanda, Somalia, Sudan, Uganda, and parts of Nigeria) demand explanations beyond the simplistic notions of warlordism or the criminalization of the state in Africa. Frantz Fanon's prophetic words that the "last battle of the colonized against the colonizer will often be the fight of the colonized against each other" seem to be truer today than ever. How can one understand the massive expenditure on warfare in Africa in general and in particular in Angola? How could Angola continue a capital-intensive war for years while the conditions of human existence deteriorated? One of the more serious crises facing Africa relates to the fact that a search for a theory of society is no longer central to grasping the basis for militarism. It is becoming fashionable to view "tribal Africa" as being in a Hobbesian state of war. This is the dominant realist narrative of international relations. Institutions and organizations have been organized around this myth of chaos and anarchy. The National Security Review of the United States, number 30 of 1991, propagated the myth of endemic ethnic conflict without linking the prevalence of warfare to the cold-war investments in armaments. Treatises on the "coming anarchy" perpetuate this myth in the popular press.

The myth prevails so much that a search for alternative policy solutions devoid of all forms of militarism and arbitrariness has become difficult. Feminists who have deconstructed realism in the past thirty years have made fundamental critiques of the ideological and social processes at work that support and justify militarism. From these interventions, it is easier to understand the serious crisis facing Africa in relation to militarism. The dominant politics of the academy and the media emanate from the same forces that supported Jonas Savimbi and propelled the whole of Angola into the vortex of the cold war. The realism of Henry Kissinger initiated the massive investment in destabilizing Angola in 1975. This investment was reinforced during the twelve years of "constructive engagement" during the Reagan and Bush administrations in the United States.

One of the tasks of this chapter is to deconstruct militarism and warfare by starting from the position of social forces, with a vested interest in peace. The task is rendered all the more difficult because warfare has essentially developed its own narrative. Whether it is the narrative of conflict resolution or humanitarian or peace entrepreneurs, the conceptual work required to deal satisfactorily with the militarism in Angola and in Africa continues to be a bottleneck. Intellectual work that was supported and sustained by cold-war funding stifles critical inquiries into the warfare and destruction. Prescriptions emanating from the view of "tribal" Africa are fed into peace negotiations, making it difficult for many international diplomats to grasp the political and gender dynamics underlying the tragic history of militarism in Angola. Concepts of economic liberalization, ethnic nationalism, and destabilization are also found wanting. Feminist scholars in Africa now provide new lenses beyond the realist paradigms of conventional international relations.[4]

In Angola today, the strategies of the Angolan woman in the context of an escalation of warfare have ensured that the society reproduces itself under the most difficult circumstances. According to the World Bank, "throughout the post independence period, it has been estimated that three quarters of the economically active population in Angola have been involved in informal activities. Out of these people, about 85 percent work in agriculture and fishing and 10 percent in the parallel market, and 2–3 percent in informal industrial activities and handicrafts." The estimates of women engaged in this sector range from 60 to 80 percent. This chapter will not engage in the major debate on whether this sector actually supports self-exploitation. The informal sector has become politically recognized under the policies of liberalization. What the statistics demonstrate more than anything else is the fact that women have demonstrated that they are not *victims* but are willing to engage in whatever activity will keep body and soul together. Apart from the "informal sector," women are dominant in areas of formal employment, particularly in medicine and in education. While experts at the World Bank and others grudgingly recognize the fundamental role of women in the Angolan economy, the new humanitarian agencies seek to build on the male constructions of politics and society. The impact of this humanitarianism in relation to food and the integration of food aid into warfare will be one of the themes of militarism in this chapter. In so far as masculinity and violence are linked to concepts of patriarchy, the issue of the provision of food in a family setting becomes relevant, not only in relation to the well-being of the society but in the context of food as a weapon of war.

The idea of the nuclear family headed by the wage-earning male has been overtaken by new family structures, new social networks, and the creative social engineering of women. Dispersed by war, Angolan families—and society in general—have been forced to develop new social relations. Unfortunately, the legal basis for economic activities (in banking, international commerce, shipping, transportation, diamond trade, etc.) lags behind the social reality of the new family and economic forms. Thus, Angolan women are toiling daily at both the micro and macro level for the reorganization of the meaning of life and work in the society. This makes the field of social reproduction pregnant with possibilities for new directions in the politics of the society and the identity of the people

This chapter deals with the multiple wars against the Angolan peoples and the centrality of African women in moving away from warfare to new forms of social interaction. Angolan women have had to draw on the historic memory and practices of resistance and survival to maintain their dignity as human beings. The historical, linguistic, and psychological factors in the creation of the collective personality of a people offer important starting points in seeking to grasp the foundations for social transformation that must be the foundation for peace in Angola. The record of the spiritual, military, and cultural resistance of the peoples is manifest in the songs, dance, art, drawings, and other areas and continues to in-spire large sections of the population. The spirit of resistance has been manifest in numerous ways but nowhere as evident as in places such as Kuito. Despite the note-worthy presence of women in all spheres of existence, in the discussions on peace and reconstruction women are still marginalized. Peace is defined in negative terms—that is, as the absence of war. This negative definition derives from realist thinking that peace and security are achieved by shifting alliances, thereby pre-serving the balance of power between warring groups. In the specific case of An-gola, peace has been defined as a balance between the armies of UNITA and the FAA. If one were to measure the resources invested in reconciling warring parties as the basis for peace, one would then understand the limits of the present writ-ings on and peace accords in Angola. This is very evident from the study of the United Nations and its peace efforts in Angola.[5]

The social character of the war, the internationalization of the confrontation, and the impact on women forces a sharpening of the class and gendered nature of warfare in Angola. Scholars who are now theorizing on gender in international re-lations are bringing the questions of just, unjust, and senseless wars to the center of the discourse. Their interventions have substantially weakened the conceptions of "tribal war," since the argument has been made that the bodies of women are the spaces within which ethnic boundaries are conceived. The rules of war and the illegality of carrying war to civilian areas has been raised by feminist scholars; it is this feature of the city sieges in the last eight years that has stood out in the his-tory of warfare and militarism in Angola. The understanding of the gendered na-ture of warfare and violence is a crucial area of investigation being researched by scholars.[6] Whether in Beijing, at the United Nations, or at other international fo-rums, the issues of gender and peace are being placed on the table to move the dis-cussion on militarism to new terrain.

For this chapter, it is important from the outset to develop some periodization of the war and military confrontation in Angola to grasp how the nature of mili-tarism and warfare changed from the period of independence through the cold war and into the post–cold war era. There have been five main stages in the past thirty-seven years.

(1) The stage of the war against Portugal, 1961–75 (Alvor Accords).

(2) The 1975–81 consolidation of the government of Angola in the process of defeating the invasion and the destabilization by South Africa (UN resolutions call-ing for South African withdrawal from Angolan territory).

(3) The period of 1981 to 1988 and the threat against the society as a whole as the country was drawn into the cold war via constructive engagement and link-age. This was the period when the South Africans occupied the southern provinces of the country, and which ended with the military defeat of the South Africans at Cuito Cuanavale. The war continued between UNITA and the Popular Movement for the Liberation of Angola (MPLA, Movimento Popular da Libertação de Angola) up to the Bicesse Accord of 1991.

(4) The war after the 1992 elections and the takeover of two-thirds of the mu-

nicipalities in the country by UNITA. This period of war abated with the signing of the Lusaka Protocol in November 1994.

(5) The massive war that erupted in 1998, which was still raging at the beginning of the new millennium.

The war that began in 1998 was the fifth full-scale war in the country since it attained independence in 1975. Why has Angola been in a state of permanent war since 1975 when the Portuguese were forced to leave? What are the concrete lessons of the cold-war investments in Angola? These questions are examined in the context of the rampant militarism and the low respect for human life exhibited by the militarists in the society. This low respect for human life has led different leaders to think that armed confrontation is necessarily superior to social transformations through democratic, peaceful, persuasive, and community-based political interventions.

The Political Economy of Warfare and Militarism

Angola, with an estimated population of over 11 million, is a member of the Southern Africa Development Community (SADC). This country, the third largest in Africa, lies north of Namibia, dipping into the Caprivi Strip, and borders with Congo Brazzaville (the Republic of the Congo), the Democratic Republic of Congo, and Zambia. The country forms part of the Congo River Basin system, and the great Zambezi River starts in Angola. The many tributaries of these two wetland systems provide for a very rich biodiverse environment. Angola is one of the countries in Africa most endowed with water resources, with great rivers such as the Cuanza and the Cunene holding the potential for large-scale integrated hydroelectric, commercial, agricultural, and educational enterprises. The militarization of the water resources in Angola deepened after the South African government developed large-scale plans for irrigation of the dry areas of Namibia. It was from the Ruacaná Dam on the Cunene River that the South African Defence Force (SADF) launched its massive invasion of Angola in 1975, and it was to the dam at Calueque that the South Africans retreated in disorder after being trounced at Tchipa in 1988. The water resources of Angola, both inland and oceanic, form an essential component of the divide between war and peace because proper management of the water resources will serve the interests of the most oppressed section of the society, the women.

The large coastal area of Angola provides for fishing and offshore trading activities. It was this large border on the Atlantic Ocean that drew the Portuguese to Angola in the fifteenth century. Angola was governed by Portugal for three centuries. At the time of the Berlin West Africa Congress in 1884–85, Portugal was given the legal right to exploit the people and resources of this territory. Angola was one of the countries at the core of the scramble for Africa, as Portuguese, Belgian, French, German, and British interests clashed at the mouth of the Congo River.

Control of the river was one of the sources of contention between the various European powers at the Berlin congress. In this scramble, Portugal was bequeathed Angola, though as a backward and poor country, Portugal could not fully develop the rich natural resources. Angola went though five hundred years of warfare and nearly one hundred years of pacification campaigns. In every one of these campaigns there was violation of African women. The following description by a historian gives a vivid account of what pacification meant in Angola.

> To pacify meant to conquer militarily and force the African populations to submit to European sovereignty, as required for effective pacification. The campaigns were extremely bloody and involved the wholesale slaughter of entire villages. Success depended both on Portuguese technical superiority in firepower and on African auxiliaries, soldiers from rival tribes who were encouraged in the slaughter by the promise of booty, which was their early form of payment.[7]

The pacification campaigns meant that there were not simply military forays, but there had to be a corresponding body of ideas to justify imperial domination.

Oiling the War

The wealth of the country is now legendary. After 1975, the petroleum resources produced the anomaly of a "socialist" country dominated by the giants of the international oil industry. The petroleum industry in Angola began in 1955 when oil was discovered in the onshore Cuanza valley by Petrofina, which together with the Angolan government established the jointly owned company Fina Petroleos de Angola (Petrangol) and constructed a refinery at Luanda to process the oil. However, the main expansion of the country's upstream oil industry came in the late 1960s when the Cabinda Gulf Oil Company (CABGOC) discovered oil offshore of the Angolan coastal enclave of Cabinda . The Cabinda enclave had been ceded to Portugal at Berlin after diplomatic compromises to end the skirmishes between the European powers. In 1973 oil became Angola's principal export, and numerous subsequent discoveries have been made in the Cabinda area and in the Angolan offshore that have made Angola the second most important oil producer in Africa after Nigeria. The entire continental shelf of West Africa, from Nigeria, Cameroon, Gabon, and Equatorial Guinea to Congo Brazzaville and Angola, has been an area of oil exploration and production in the past ten years.

The petroleum industry is the economic mainstay of the ruling elements and constitutes Angola's most important economic activity from the point of view of the government. In 1960 oil accounted for less than 8 percent of gross domestic product, while agriculture contributed about 50 percent. By 1995, agriculture's share had fallen to 17 percent and that of oil had jumped to 40 percent. Crude oil accounts for 90 percent of total exports, more than 80 percent of government revenues, and 42 percent of the country's GDP. Oil output is expected to reach one million barrels per day by the year 2000. The country's known recoverable reserves are currently estimated to total almost 4 billion barrels, but continuing exploration finds new reserves at the same rate oil companies deplete old ones.

Year	Total Production (b/d)	Export Value (US$ million)
1985	232,000	1,191
1986	282,000	1,140
1987	359,000	2,100
1988	451,000	2,173
1989	453,000	2,682
1990	474,000	3,588
1991	494,000	3,078
1992	549,000	3,220
1993	503,000	n/a
1994	556,000	n/a
1995	673,000	5,000

▼▼▼

The table above shows that by 1995 the Angolan economy was exporting over US$5 billion dollars worth of oil.

New technologies in oil drilling have revealed extensive deposits of oil in Angola. The oil industry during the past decade has become a showplace of futuristic technologies. Producers can now find and produce oil with exceptional precision and at lower costs than was ever dreamed possible. Special sensors create three-dimensional maps of deep geological formations. Producers can drill horizontally for long distances, extracting oil trapped beneath towns. With computers guiding drill bits for miles underground, producers have resurrected numberless old fields long thought depleted. With the advent of new technology to drill in deep waters (approx. 1,500 meters deep), there has been extensive exploitation of the petroleum resources of Angola. The proximity of the oil blocks between the oil exploration at Pointe-Noire in Congo Brazzaville and Cabinda increases the contestation over the oil resources. The militarization of Congo Brazzaville and the political struggles in that society have been directly linked to the operations of U.S. and French oil companies. Angola has been drawn into this war because of the allegations that UNITA was using Congo Brazzaville as a rear base for resupply in the 1990s. The militarization of the oil-producing region of Angola is also manifest in the existence of a group, FLEC (Forças de Libertação do Estado de Cabinda, Front for the Liberation of Cabinda), fighting for the independence of Cabinda, the enclave where most of Angola's oil is produced.

The national oil company, Sociedade Nacional de Combustiveis de Angola (SONANGOL), was established in 1976 to manage all fuel production and distribution. In the late 1970s, the government had initiated a program to attract foreign oil companies. The Angolan coast, excluding Cabinda, was divided into thirteen exploration blocks, which were leased to foreign companies under production-sharing agreements. In 1978 the Angolan government authorized SONANGOL to acquire a 51 percent interest in all oil companies operating in Angola, although the management of operations remained under the control of foreign companies. The names of Chevron, Elf, Petrofina, BP, Texaco, and Petrobas dominated the extraction of petroleum. More than 7 percent of the oil imports of the United States emanates from Angola. The anomaly of a "Marxist" government protecting the oil companies was most manifest during the period of South African destabilization. Then, the Reagan administration pressured U.S. companies to leave Angola, but the profits were so huge that the companies defied the U.S. government. Hence, when the South African commandos attempted in 1985 to blow up the oil installations, it was the Cubans who were protecting the installations.

According to the U.S. Geological Survey in October 1999, "because of the opening of offshore lease blocks within the Angolan Exclusive Economic Zone in the past 4 years, there have been over ten world class oilfields discovered in Angola. The major oil companies involved, Elf, Chevron, Texaco and Mobil, plan on investing over $18 billion to double oil production over the next 4–5 years. The discoveries have been primarily petroleum and not much has been mentioned about natural gas." It is estimated that within ten years Angola will be producing more oil than Kuwait.

In light of the massive oil discoveries, the United States has established a bi-national commission with Angola. This commission supports further liberalization of the Angolan economy so that the vast wealth can still service external forces. The various publications of the business world, including the Economic Intelligence Unit, the *Wall Street Journal,* or the bulletins of the Department of Commerce of the United States, highlight the economic potential of Angola. The significant point that has to be reinforced is that transnational capital has always dominated the economy of Angola, even during the period when the MPLA proclaimed itself as a Marxist-Leninist party. One of the striking features of this period of warfare was that foreign capital intensified the extraction of minerals while there was untold destruction of human life in the society. Since the majority of primary oil fields are located offshore out of artillery range, exploration, development, and operations were able to continue throughout the long wars using offshore production and tanker loading facilities. War did not inhibit the extraction of oil or diamonds. Numerous external forces have coveted the wealth of this society, whose resources are summarized in the following passage from the Economist Intelligence Unit.

> In theory, Angola should be one of Africa's richest countries. Few parts of the continent have such a favourable resource endowment. Covering 1.25 mn Km (over five times the size of the UK), Angola has an abundance of land, only 4 per cent of which is currently estimated to be under cultivation. Climatic conditions are generally favourable for agriculture and a very wide range of crops can be grown. Besides feeding its own population, Angola could be a large net exporter of agricultural produce, and until the troubles of the last decade, it was the world's fourth largest producer of coffee. It also has large livestock resources in the more arid

south, extensive forest areas and, off its southern coast, some of the best fishing waters in Africa.

Angola is best known as an energy rich country. It has large deposits of oil and gas, and oil has been the main export since 1973. In addition, there is vast hydroelectric potential on the country's rivers, which one day could also provide the water for extensive irrigation. Furthermore the subsoil is a treasure ground of minerals, and Angola could eventually revert to its traditional role as one of the world's most valuable sources of diamonds. Before independence in 1975, there was a fast growing light manufacturing sector (roughly on par with Kenya) and there had been considerable investments in railways, roads and other infrastructure.[8]

Between 1975 and 1985, the Angolan economy was based on the command model of state centralization. After this period the government embarked on a policy of liberalization of the economy. Throughout both periods the revenue of the government was heavily dependent on its oil reserves. In the SADC region, Angola has the portfolio for energy and it has the potential to satisfy 86 percent of southern Africa's oil requirements. This oil sector has not been severely affected by militarism where the same oil has provided the resources to provide for militarism. Oil reserves are mainly located offshore of the northern Cabinda region and the northern coast, but also onshore around Soyo. The attack on Soyo by UNITA in 1993 brought a firm response from the U.S. government, and when the war broke out again in 1998 the U.S. government again warned UNITA not to attack oil installations. In 1997 and 1998 there were new oil discoveries, and it is estimated that Angola's oil production will double from the current production of 700,000 barrels per day. The war has meant that there are no beneficial backward and forward linkages in the Angolan economy from the exploration of oil. While natural gas is flared by the oil companies, the women in Angola spend hours looking for fuel wood. The oil refinery in the main city, Luanda, is in need of repair, and there has been a lack of proper infrastructure for the Angolan society to benefit positively from the production of oil. Instead, it is estimated that the Angolan government has spent over US$5 billion dollars on weapons since 1992 and has bartered oil futures for loans to buy weapons.

The majority of the population supplies their own subsistence needs and thus relies mainly on the skills and knowledge of women in agriculture, trade, fisheries, and other areas of economic intervention. The resilience of the women in this "informal sector," the "inner logic" of the economic operations, the price-setting mechanisms, and the general rules of the Candonga system befuddled traditional economists. Angolan women developed new rules for foreign exchange transactions that confounded central bankers and those that established exchange rates. By standard economic reporting, it is usually said that subsistence agriculture provides the main livelihood for 80–90 percent of the population but accounts for less than 15 percent of gross domestic product. The MPLA government failed to expend the oil resources on the population. After the fall of the Soviet Union in 1991, the leadership of the MPLA became openly bureaucratic and corrupt, losing its moral claims as the leaders of the struggle for independence. The corruption and bureaucratic culture of those with influence and power reinforced the powers of the international agencies and organizations. Lucio Lara, a veteran of the party, criticized the government in this way: "Once in the Council of Ministers I heard someone say that we must stop using the phrase, 'The important thing is to solve peoples problems.' I thought maybe he was right, because no one spoke out against him. In my opinion this was when the party began to collapse. The leaders felt they all had the right to be rich. That was the beginning of the destruction of our life. Our people are suffering and no one cares. If you talk to our people, they are all suffering. No one is smiling. But there is no preoccupation with this from the leadership."

Lara was critical of the preoccupation with business and enrichment by the leadership. He declared that the leaders of the country were too busy with business; they had no time to govern.[9] By 1992, the leadership treated the war as a business and did not consider political and moral ways of seizing the high ground from UNITA. Indiscriminate shelling and aerial bombardment by both sides exposed the disregard for human life. The government expended its energies on weapons and did not seek to use political measures to isolate UNITA. Instead, the government employed a private military company called Executive Outcomes to give support in the war. Executive Outcomes was made up of elements from the apartheid army that had established a private army for hire. The privatization of violence went hand in glove with the new politics of liberalization. By the end of the decade, the integration of the political economy of militarism into the globalized mercenary, diamond, banking, weapons, and war business was firm. While crude oil exports are known to account for 40 percent of the GDP, the amount of money from the sale of diamonds cannot be accounted for because the main diamond producing areas have been under the control of UNITA.

Diamonds and Warfare in Angola

The permanence of the war since 1975 is connected to both the interests of transitional capital and the reality that there are social forces in Angola who have been involved in war as a business. External domination of the economy has been a key factor in the politics of the society. The petroleum resources have been recycled for weapons by the ruling party, the MPLA, while the sale of diamonds has been dominated by UNITA. "Diamond revenues constitute the essential component of UNITA's capacity to wage war." These were the words of a special report to the Security Council of the United Nations by the committee established to assess the violation of UN sanctions by UNITA. This party has been able to continue the war after 1992 because of its control over the vast diamond fields in Lunda North Province. Before 1975, Angola was the world's fourth largest producer of diamonds. It has been estimated that Angola's alluvial reserves total between 40 and 130 million carats. In addition, there are untapped diamond reserves in volcanic pipes called kimberlites. Angola's six known kimberlite pipes, among the ten largest on earth, hold an estimated 180 million carats, worth several billion dollars. Currently, official and unofficial diamond production is estimated to be worth US$700 million per year. In 1999 the government of Angola announced changes to its production program that outlined its goal to produce more than 2 million carats of diamonds annually. The production of diamonds, like the exploration of oil, has been very much linked to militarism.

In 1998, a widely circulated report by Global Witness detailed the role of governments and companies in the Angolan war. The report, entitled *Rough Trade,* uncovered the role of diamonds in funding the war for UNITA.

> The importance of diamonds in funding UNITA's war effort over the last decade is well known and fairly well understood. Diamond revenue became increasingly important for a number of reasons including the political changes in the post–cold war era. Diamonds have provided the majority of UNITA's funding although gold, coffee and particularly in the late 1980's wildlife products and timber were all sources of funds. Between 1992 and 1998 UNITA obtained an estimated minimum revenue of US$3.72 billion from diamond sales. This does not include revenue from other sources, nor interest generated in overseas bank accounts. The international trade in diamonds has become a major obstacle to any possible progress towards peace; and has played the major role in enabling UNITA to restock its munitions and maintain a flow of supplies which in turn has enabled it to disregard the 1992 election results and to avoid meeting its obligations under the Lusaka Protocol.

Angola's diamonds, which are some of the best in the world, are in demand in the diamond business. Diamonds have been UNITA's major sources of revenue during the 1990s—gaining an estimated US$3.7 billion between 1992 and 1998—which has enabled UNITA to re-arm and maintain supplies despite the UN-sponsored peace process. UNITA has sold its diamonds on the unofficial, "outside" market and has found willing buyers within the diamond industry. The report identified the responsibility of the diamond trade and the complicity of De Beers in the war that had taken over half a million lives. The report stated that international sanctions imposed on the trade in non-authorized Angolan diamonds on 1 July 1998 did not have any significant impact on the capabilities of UNITA. And the report detailed the routes and the new countries that were brought into the global trade in diamonds and weapons.[10]

It can be estimated that the government and UNITA, together, have expended over US$8 billion on weapons since 1992. The legitimacy of the operations of the government has not been in question since the 1992 elections, but the revealing aspect of the political economy of militarism has been the way that UNITA as a non-state has been able to mobilize vast resources for war. The United Nations imposed sanctions on UNITA in 1993 (the first against a non-state), but UNITA was able through the international financial and trading system, namely liberalized markets, to procure weapons and market diamonds. Further sanctions were imposed in July 1998; however, the nature of the diamond industry in central and southern Africa assisted the war-making capabilities of UNITA. An energetic chairperson of the UN Sanctions Committee, set up to implement sanctions against UNITA, presented recommendations to the UN Security Council in 1999 on how to tighten existing sanctions, which have been flouted by UNITA. It was significant that the report submitted to the Security Council on 4 June 1999 called for the deployment of inspectors to report on sanctions violations for Ouagadougou, in Burkina Faso; Abidjan, in the Ivory Coast; Tshikapa, Dilolo, Kolwezi, and Lumumbashi, in the Democratic Republic of Congo; Nampula, in Mozambique; Rundu, in Namibia; Kigali, in Rwanda; Durban and the airfields in the northern portion of South Africa; Dar es Salaam, in the United Republic of Tanzania; Lomé, in Togo; Kyiv, in Ukraine; Entebbe and Kampala, in Uganda; Mansa, Mongu, Ndola, Livingstone, and Zambezi, in Zambia; as well as in Luanda and other Angolan ports. This impressive list exposed the truth that the investment of Jonas Savimbi in warfare and diamonds proved more attractive for many officials than respect for the resolutions of the Security Council of the United Nations. The vast web of the diamond trade and militarism in Angola spawned banks and financial institutions all over Africa, Europe, and Asia, weapons manufacturers in South Africa and Eastern Europe, traders and food procurers in South Africa, and front companies for the export of diamonds as far afield as Burkina Faso. [11]

The Jonas Savimbi model of warfare has been greatly facilitated by the liberalization of financial structures in the world. Hence, the movement of weapons, minerals, and fuel could continue without state oversight. It is this globalized economic structure that supports the warfare in Angola. In this context this chapter will identify Jonas Savimbi as a military entrepreneur in contradistinction to the conception of "warlord." As such, Savimbi developed a military capability that was beyond the capabilities of most governments in Africa. Elements from the army of UNITA fought on the side of the dying Mobutu government in 1997, and Savimbi was able to remobilize over 60,000 troops in 1998 after the United Nations had been through an expensive exercise of demobilizing the troops of UNITA under the Lusaka Protocol. The model of military entrepreneurship is one that operationalizes the control of resources within the territorial areas controlled militarily by the entrepreneur. These resources (in this case, diamonds) are set in motion to generate flows of cash, arms supplies, intelligence, and media resources. Such military operations, while appearing to be based more on an internal dynamic or internal civilian support, are in fact more dependent on external resources than internal resources. The military commercial model that developed in Angola can survive only when linked to international resource networks and globalized markets for weapons. It is this link between the external and the internal that makes it necessary to grasp the internationalization of the economy in the context of the internationalization and regionalization of warfare. The limitations of the liberation triumphalism have also been brought to the fore by the permanence of war in Angola.

Retreating from the Narrative of Military Victories

Between the five periods of warfare in Angola noted in the introduction, there was always euphoria after a peace accord. This was particularly the case in the period of optimism after the reversals of the South Africans in Angola in 1988, leading to the independence of Namibia. Between November 1987 and June 1988 the combined forces of the Angolan army, the Cuban internationalist forces, and elements of the South West African People's Organization (SWAPO) defeated the apartheid military forces of South Africa and UNITA at Cuito Cuanavale in Angola. In seeking to ensure that African youths in the future were inspired by this military battle that changed the recent history of Africa, some scholars embarked on bringing to the world the lessons of the "Military Defeat of the South Africans in Angola."[12] It was the view, then, that a people's consciousness is heightened by knowledge of the dignity and determination of their foreparents. It was necessary that place names and battles at Tchipa, Cuito Cuanavale, and Cunene should be common knowledge, just as the landing in Normandy in 1944 is seen as the turning point in the defeat of the fascism. The impetus of the anti-colonial discourse had encouraged intellectuals to be sympathetic to the military struggles of liberation movements, and in the process there was a whole output of literature to support armed struggles for independence.

The battles of Cuito Cuanavale and the subsequent independence of Namibia in 1990 were episodic events that strongly affected the military posture of the apartheid regime and forced the pace of negotiations in South Africa. However, these military confrontations did not end the full-scale war in Angola . Ten years later, the armies of an armed opposition, UNITA, were deployed in over 70 percent of Angolan territory, and a reserve army of UNITA was stationed in Zambia. The army of the government of Angola was fully mobilized and had undertaken two major military forays into the Democratic Republic of Congo (in 1997 and 1998) and in Congo Brazzaville. The immense deployment of both the troops of UNITA and the government of Angola made a mockery of the Lusaka Protocol of 1994, where both parties had undertaken to establish a framework for demobilization of troops and the creation of a government of national unity.

Full-scale war broke out again in 1998 after a period of intense diplomatic initiatives to end the war. The deployment of UN troops to Angola in 1996 and the desperate negotiating efforts of the UN special representative to Angola, Alioune Blondin Beye, failed to stem the planning and preparations for war. The UN special representative died in a plane crash in June 1998 at a time when he was seeking to halt the involvement of West African states in the sanctions-breaking activities of UNITA. A recent book on the whole process of negotiations detailed the painstaking work that was done to bring Jonas Savimbi into the political process by the United Nations, the United States, and the international community. Paul Hare, the U.S. special representative to the peace negotiations, has clarified the ways in which U.S. representatives placed their confidence in Jonas Savimbi. The conception of peace that has been promoted by the United States and institutions such as the U.S. Institute for Peace has been one that sought to place the just wars against colonialism below the cold-war priorities of the United States. At the end of 1999, it was revealed in documents of the *Bulletin of Atomic*

Scientists that the Pentagon had early in the cold war placed nuclear weapons on the Azores Islands. The aid to Portugal to fight liberation movements in Africa can now be seen in a wider context. The revelation clarified the commitment by successive U.S. administrations to the fascist government in Portugal. John Marcum summed up this early commitment to Portugal and to the cold war in this way: "One of the consequences of the American decision to choose NATO over Africa or the Azores over Angola, was to drag the cold war deeper into Angolan nationalist politics."

African nationalists had to fight the fascism of the Portuguese as well as the military linkages of the United States to governments such as Portugal and apartheid South Africa. These nationalists embarked on struggles of liberation to end the arrogance of colonial militarism and plunder, but the very process of armed struggles for liberation reinforced the traditions of militarism of the colonial order. The anti-colonial struggle was not predicated on transforming the colonial ideas of the scientific method, patriarchy, rugged individualism, and the warrior traditions in politics. The icon of the African soldier with the gun was supposed to be the hallmark of liberation and revolution. The decolonization generation of the 1960s grew up under the influence of the armed guerilla challenging the colonial overlords.[13] From Algeria to Kenya, down through to the white settler regimes of southern Africa, Africans had to resort to armed struggle to intervene in the political process. In the societies mentioned above, the ruling colonial and settler forces foreclosed peaceful resistance. However, by the end of the 1970s even cold war military planners were developing techniques of guerilla warfare as a component of low-intensity warfare. Thus the use of armed struggles by contra elements along with the patriarchal model of decolonization coincided with the exhaustion of the mystique of armed intervention in politics.

The use of the term *guerrilla* to characterize the military struggle for power, by leaders such as Charles Taylor in Liberia, Foday Sankoh in Sierra Leone, and Jonas Savimbi in Angola, made it difficult for a younger generation to fully grasp the difference between Amilcar Cabral and Samora Machel and the aforementioned fighters. That an organization such as RENAMO could call itself a liberation army meant that those fighting for a new order had to develop new means of political struggle. For these reasons, the limitations of armed resistance emerged in the South African struggle, and the mass democratic movement developed new strategies such as the mass strike, the stay-away, the school boycott, and other non-violent tactics of the United Democratic Front (UDF). These new tactics ensured the mix of mass action, armed struggles, sanctions, and international diplomacy for the removal of the white minority regime. It downplayed the use of armed struggle as the sole means of acquiring power.

The moral arguments on the justness of wars of liberation are being debated in a context where African women are coming forward to remind African leaders that in the fight for independence, while there were a few armed guerillas, there were millions of unarmed social forces who used different means to oppose colonial rule.[14]

There is now a developed literature that challenges the idea of Frantz Fanon that violence could be healing and therapeutic to former colonial subjects. The lesson of war in Africa is that warfare is hellish. Whether there were good intentions on the part of soldiers or political education, many people were killed. These feminists have pointed out the need to not only penetrate war as an act of force and the negative consequences of war but also to problematize the crisis of masculinity in the conditions of warfare and militarism. African feminists have deepened our understanding of how ethnicity and nationalism as backward-looking ideologies are anchored in a past based on male domination and masculine prowess. These scholars have been able to document how African women experience "nationalism and ethnicity as violation, war and conflict between men who appropriate the female body as the territory upon which they fight their vicious and destructive games—often in the name of national sovereignty and the search for peace among themselves."[15]

In Angola, as in many parts of Africa at war, it can now be said that the nationalist ideas of male leaders negated the positive aspects of the anti-colonial sacrifices. The reality was that well-intentioned wars deteriorated into massive warfare and destabilization because the leaders did not have autonomy over the course of warfare. More significant has been the widespread violation and violence against women. In the pervasive climate of war and destruction, women were more susceptible to multiple assaults and attacks. Increased violence in Angola meant that there was more sexual abuse of women, and there was a tendency for the militarism in the struggle for power to affect social relations. With the collapse of the economic infrastructure in Angola after 1992, the survival techniques of women kept the Angolan society together while billions from oil and diamonds were exchanged for weapons. Women and children in Angola felt the brunt of the shortages and hardships imposed by war, water shortages, chronic electricity shortages, shortages of food, high prices for shoddy goods, and the ravages of direct and domestic violence. The 1997 Human Development Report of the United Nations reported that over 82 percent of the population lived in absolute and relative poverty and two-thirds of the population lived on a dollar a day.

In a militarized society, where over 10 million land mines were planted, roads and village paths became danger zones. The limited transportation and economic infrastructure in the rural areas collapsed under the weight of the most massive bloodletting and dispersal since the slave trade. After the 1992 war, only the international "humanitarian" workers and "peacekeepers" enjoyed freedom of movement in the country. War and destruction served to unite cultural, structural, and direct violence as the centrality of women in keeping life together became more stressful and hazardous. With the breakdown of the limited health and sanitation infrastructure, working women as producers, caregivers, traders, healers, and mothers had to take on extensions of the role of the government. The large-scale movement and dispersal that had been precipitated by war and violence reflected the continuities in the centrality of force in the processes of production and social reproduction in Angola. More than 3 million persons were internally displaced inside Angola in the 1992–94 war.

Warfare and Peace Accords in Angola

It was in this context of war and dispersal that the Angolan people were search-ing for levers of participation in the society to end militarism, violence, and op-pression. The limitations of the peacekeeping exercise of the United Nations, and the peace that was ushered in by those who were "keeping peace in a rough neigh-bourhood" (the subtitle of Chester Crocker's *High Noon in Southern Africa*), forced the population to search for a new understanding of peace. African women were able to define the search for peace at the differing levels of warfare. The lessons of all the peace efforts served to clarify that peace involved far more than the techni-cal details of the mechanisms of the United Nations. The processes of militariza-tion and masculinization are now seen to be interwoven with the armaments cul-ture of the West, so that in the search for peace, there are many factors to consider.

The three major "peace accords" that were signed at Alvor in 1975, at Bicesse in 1991, and Lusaka in 1994 never ushered in peace in Angola. From the period of the Alvor agreement in 1975 to the Lusaka Protocol of 1994, the well-being of the Angolan people was never a consideration in the formulation of strategies for peace. In both cases, peace was an effort to create a government of national unity (in prac-tice bringing two armies together). The Tripartite Accords signed between the An-golans, Cubans, and South Africans in 1988 had brought about the withdrawal of the South African troops from Angola. The preoccupation of the United States with the presence of Cuban troops in Angola led to military cooperation between the United States and the apartheid government. It took the decisive trouncing of the South Africans to bring the withdrawal of the Cubans, despite the rewriting of his-tory to say that the accords came from the negotiating skills of Chester Crocker of the United States.[16] Before these accords, South Africa had signed a protocol in 1984 declaring that it would leave Angola, but this protocol was simply designed to give the South African army the time to beef up its militarization of Namibia. It was the defeat at Cuito Cuanavale that laid the basis for the implementation of Resolution 435 of the Security Council leading to the independence of Namibia. Under the Tripartite Accords, the UN Security Council under Resolution 626 of 1988 estab-lished UNAVEM 1 to oversee the withdrawal of the Cuban troops.

If the war to oppose South African aggression could be termed a just war in so far as apartheid was declared a crime against humanity by the United Nations, the war against UNITA after 1989 could be called a well-intentioned war. However, the independence of Namibia did not end the war for power in Angola nor the South African destabilization and destruction of the region of southern Africa. There were intensified battles in Angola between 1990 and 1991, especially the battles of Luena and Mavinga. The Bicesse peace accord was signed in Portugal in 1991 in the dying moments of the cold war on 31 May 1991, while on the previous day UN Security Council Resolution 696 of 1991 authorized the deployment of UN-AVEM 11. A cease-fire took effect two weeks later, and though there were continu-al violations of the cease-fire by UNITA, the Angolan government placed con-fidence in the United Nations to oversee the demobilization of the army of Jonas

Savimbi. This was in part because of the tremendous goodwill generated in southern Africa as a result of UN operations in Namibia to oversee the independence of Namibia following the withdrawal of the South African troops. The provisions of the Bicesse agreement of 1991 called for a cease-fire, the confinement of troops to assembly areas, demobilization of the Popular Forces for the Liberation of Angola (FAPLA, the army of the MPLA) and of FALA, and the creation of a new army. Elections were to take place after a period of registration and voting for a new government. However, less than three months after the Bicesse Accord, the Soviet Union had disintegrated and the pressures in the West to fully support the United Nations in the peace process to see that demilitarization took place disappeared.

The peace process was to be overseen by the United Nations along with three observer states: Portugal, Russia (replacing a disintegrated USSR), and the United States. The U.S. State Department was convinced that the details of the accord would support a victory for UNITA in the elections that were to take place in 1992. In keeping with the spirit of the accord, the Angolan government demobilized its army. The Bush administration in the United States provided technical and financial support to UNITA to win the elections. When UNITA forces finally moved into Luanda to participate in the electoral exercise, they arrived in new four-wheel vehicles made by General Motors. These vehicles were a visible sign of the partisanship of the United States during the elections. The Angolan government was pressured into an early election despite the fact that the infrastructure did not exist to carry out elections in a country with millions of land mines.

The monitoring system for the peace accords of Bicesse comprised soldiers from a Joint Political Military Commission, formed primarily of military men from UNITA and the MPLA. Men and women in Angola from other political parties, from churches and community formations who did not have an army behind them, had no say in this process. Similarly, non-military parties and institutions were not involved in the Joint Verification and Monitoring Commission (CMVF), which was responsible for the implementation of the peace. These accords broke down when UNITA lost the elections in 1992. The UNAVEM II mission to Angola proved to be an accessory to the renewed war in so far as the numerous meetings that were initiated "to bring Savimbi into the peace effort" never seriously affected the massive killings that went on between 1992 and 1994. It was for this reason that one journalist characterized the whole experience of the United Nations in Angola as that of *Promises and Lies*.[17] The narrative of the text on the promises of the United Nations and the lies of Savimbi were in marked contrast to the account of the peacekeeping role of the United Nations rendered by the special representative of the United Nations in the book *Orphans of the Cold War*.

The Lusaka Protocol of November 1994 formally marked the end of the war of 1992–94. In February 1995, the United Nations authorized the deployment of UNAVEM III, with the secretary-general of the United Nations supporting the deployment of more than 7,000 peacekeepers to Angola. The Lusaka Protocol should have ended the most brutal phase of the war since 1975. When the Angolans had fought the South Africans, there were set battles in conventional warfare with soldiers fighting soldiers. The "total war" concept of the apartheid army did not make distinctions between combatants and non-combatants in the areas under South African military occupation. Both the South African military and the United States trained the officer corps of UNITA as part of their contribution to fighting communism in Africa. These lessons were exercised with zeal by the army of UNITA. After 1992, most major cities were besieged. Starvation and disease, as well as deaths and injuries from bombing, shelling, and land mines resulted in an estimated 300,000 deaths. The UN Department of Humanitarian Affairs estimated that at the height of the city sieges by UNITA, over one thousand persons were dying every day in Angola. The barbarity inflicted on the civilian population could be compared to the brutal siege of Leningrad by the army of Germany during the Second World War in Europe. Under the rules of war, it had become part of international practice to set certain groups of people outside the permissible range of warfare, so that killing any of these people would not be a legitimate act of war but a crime. However, the general conception of war as a combat between combatants was discarded in the sieges of Kuito, Huambo, Malanje, and Uige. It was this reality that made the foraging of the women of Kuito so noteworthy in the history of Angola.

Throughout the period of the Lusaka Protocol, the sense of preparation for war could be felt in the society. Paul Hare, in his narrative on the attempts to bring Savimbi into the peace process, detailed the numerous trips taken by the secretary-general of the United Nations, by the U.S. representative to the United Nations, Madeleine Albright, and by Nelson Mandela to seek the support of Jonas Savimbi for the peace accords. It was significant that Jonas Savimbi did not sign the accord on behalf of UNITA. The representative of UNITA, Eugenio Ngolo Manuvakola, who signed the Lusaka Protocol was placed under arrest by UNITA. He later escaped to Luanda and assisted the formation of UNITA Renovado, a section of UNITA that opposed the continued war. Under the provisions of the Lusaka Protocol, the Bicesse process was to be completed, Savimbi was to be given a special status, and there was to be a government of National Unity and Reconciliation. On 11 April 1997, such a government was formed, with members of UNITA participating in the government. Many of the heads of government of SADC, including Nelson Mandela, attended the ceremony but Jonas Savimbi did not participate. The military wing of UNITA, led by Savimbi, was planning for war.

Throughout 1998 there were skirmishes between the army of Savimbi and the government. After five years of constant shuttle diplomacy, the UN special representative to Angola, Alioune Blondin Beye, decided to extend his activities to pressure the military wing of UNITA to hand over the civilian areas to state administration. The United Nations had decided that if state administration was not extended to four sensitive sites (Bailundo, Andulo, Mungo, and N'harea), there would be further financial and economic sanctions on UNITA. Alioune Blondin Beye undertook a trip to West Africa to pressure those states that were complicit in breaking UN sanctions against UNITA. His trip to West Africa took him to the Ivory Coast, Togo, and Burkina Faso. On 27 June 1998 the plane carrying Beye crashed in a mangrove swamp on its approach to the Abidjan airport. The death of Beye was like a symbol of the death of the Lusaka Protocol between the government and UNITA. Full-scale war broke out by December 1998, and within weeks UNITA was able to mobilize and arm over 60,000 troops. City sieges began all over, with the attacks on Malanje and Kuito taking the highest priority for the army of UNITA.

Though many in the United Nations expressed surprise at the ability of UNITA to rearm with sophisticated weaponry, the military capacity of Savimbi was common knowledge to those who followed his web of military entrepreneurship. UNITA remained a mobile military force with an army that could be deployed to fight on the side of the dying Mobutu regime in the Democratic Republic of Congo. The occupation of the administrative centers of the country by UNITA and the refusal by Savimbi to disarm dictated that more drastic measures were needed than those prescribed by international peace fixers. Peace institutes and conflict resolution centers that pontificate on peace building and peacekeeping from the safety of the societies that profit from warfare continued to argue that peace in Angola should include "dialogue" between Jonas Savimbi and the government. It was a view that believed in the need for ethnic balance. These conceptions of peace derived directly from the label of ethnic conflict to characterize liberation struggles and wars. In this process, this body of knowledge is intended to transform our understanding of the long process of military confrontation in Angola. From the perspective of the security experts, the armed struggle fought by the Angolans was not a national liberation struggle because of the divisions in the ranks of the liberation forces.

The Exhaustion of the Patriarchal Model of Liberation

The history of the Angolan independence battles is central to rehabilitating the sense of survival and struggle by all classes of Angolans and to begin to understand the gendered meanings of nationalism. The ways in which the leaders of these movements for liberation were trained had a bearing on the evolution of the liberation movements, their origins, ideological outlook, political orientation, and external support.[18] This training merged well with the subsequent documentation that reinforced the image of the ethnic map of Angola . All over southern Africa there has emerged a gendered analysis of the liberation process, which explores not only the contradictions between the colonialists and the colonized, but the gendered roles and values set in motion or accentuated by colonialism. This analysis has focused our attention on the images of masculinity and valor that have become part of the history of liberation. Some of the movements, such as FRELIMO, the MPLA, ZANU(PF), and the ANC, celebrate women who fought, and in Mozambique the picture of Josina Machel was prominently displayed as an icon of guerrilla war. In Angola, the MPLA celebrated Deodlina Rodriguez, and a square in Luanda was named after her.

As one of the three movements in Angola, the MPLA throughout its history sought to use the image of Queen Nzinga and other notable women of the past to inspire women and men in Angola. Through the medium of African cultural institutions, the youth are reminded of the centrality of African women in all phases of struggle. Through folktales, songs, references to spirit goddesses, and other narratives, African communities preserve the history of the centrality of women in struggle.

As the historic liberation movement, the MPLA had underscored the importance of Angolan women in the struggle by affirming that "the role of women, and the need for them to mobilize on their specific questions, was recognized from the start. In 1962, one year after the MPLA launched the armed struggle, the OMA was set up."[19]

For decades the MPLA used the Organization of Angolan Women (OMA) as an indicator of its commitment to the liberation of women. The formation of OMA and the legal initiatives of the MPLA on sex discrimination at work and in the payment of wages had underscored the prevailing position of the discussion of Angolan women, especially in the analysis of the importance of mass organs of the MPLA. The MPLA had been proud of its record and legislation with respect to the equality of women in the society. As one of the mass organs of the period of the single party, the MPLA, OMA had been established in 1962 to mobilize support for the national liberation struggles. All the written accounts of the war of national liberation pointed to the active participation of women in opposing colonial rule. Most of the literature on the role of women in the liberation struggles in Angola tended to highlight the military participation of the few women who were combatants, while presenting the majority of women as victims of war. The available literature tended to have two main depictions of women in resistance: aiders or supporters and victims. The former refers to women's roles as couriers, providers of protection, resources, and food for the guerillas. Women formed networks of caching and transporting supplies.

The roles of care, providing food, and transporting weapons were crucial to the success of the liberation movement. While it is important to demonstrate how women were central to the liberation process, it is also important to break the sense of liberation that was tied to armed struggle. Outside of the armed struggles, there were everyday forms of resistance in the society that complemented the military opposition to colonial rule. Yet, in many senses, the representation of the women in both UNITA and MPLA tended to concentrate on women only in supportive roles—that is, women as supporters of the male actors. More and more African feminists have drawn our attention to the deficiencies of the past writings on African liberation in general and on the struggles for peace in Angola in particular. The incomplete nature of this process forces a critical reappraisal of how the concept of liberation was presented. The inadequacies of the concept of liberation are most glaring when it appears as if women were only supporters and men were mainly responsible for the success of liberation movements.

The second characterization of women in liberation literature presents women as victims: victims of male sexual needs and desires for power, whether through rape by the guerillas or the forces of the oppressing regime. Women are positioned as helpless and powerless in the face of a male need to dominate and colonize them. The problem with this is that the portrayal of women as victims inherently implies helplessness and powerlessness. It subtly reinforces the view of women as "booty" or "canon fodder" for males in war. The Angolan novelist Pepetela has sought to bring out the problems of women in the frontline in the novel *Mayombe*. During the period of the war, in the ranks of the MPLA there was more openness about the oppression of women and the sexual abuses of women in the military camps. The existence of a vibrant women's organization ensured that the leadership of the MPLA had to pay attention to the issue of the oppression of women in the ranks of a liberation movement. No such openness existed in the ranks of UNITA, though it boasted its own women's organization, the League of Independent Women of Angola (LIMA, Liga de Mulheres Independentes de Angola).

In Angola, UNITA excelled in the principle of ethnization, or the practice of stamping ethnicity in the bodies of women. Many officials of UNITA have testified to the rituals that were initiated within the camps of UNITA to sanctify ethnic purity. The conception of women as booty and the fact that military commanders had unlimited access to the bodies of women became standard in territories held by UNITA. Sexual abuse and violence was the norm in the military camps, where women, especially the younger ones, had to be made available to the commanders. The traditional reproductive roles of women were seen as an extension of the war effort, since women produced the human labor necessary for UNITA to continue fighting. The exploitation of women by UNITA has been obscured by the positive images presented to the international media by the "mass organ" of UNITA, namely, LIMA.

The chronology of the impact of the policies of the movements on Angolan women has not been documented in a critical manner. In the past five years the social democratic societies of Scandinavia have supported attempts to publish *Country Gender Analysis of Angola* and other societies in the region. These studies reproduce the victim mentality where African women can only speak and act with external assistance.[20] These critiques of the liberation discourse force a richer concept of African liberation and decolonization than the simple narrative of settler and native, citizen and subject. At the outset of this chapter, I stated that the problem of militarism has posed a conceptual bottleneck for scholars. This bottleneck is nowhere more profound than in the androcentric approach to militarism and questions of national liberation. The question of androcentrism in theorization is deep and is linked to the contested theories of realism. The main writers on national liberation in Africa treated security and the state as if men were the only section of humanity. This is a profound limitation, and the crafting of politics with men in mind has had a devastating impact in solidifying patriarchy. Feminists have brought about fundamental rethinking of the categories that we employ and are bringing to our attention the pitfalls of androcentrism. Gerda Lerner, in the book *The Creation of Patriarchy,* wrote as follows:

> By making the term "man" subsume "woman" and arrogate to itself the representation of all of humanity, men have built a conceptual error of vast proportion into all of their thought. By taking the half for the whole, they have not only missed the essence of whatever they are describing, but they have distorted it in such a fashion that they cannot see it correctly. As long as men believed the earth to be

flat, they could not understand its reality, its function, and its actual relationship to other bodies in the universe. As long as men believe their experiences, their viewpoint, and their ideas represent all of human experience and all of human thought, they are not only unable to define correctly in the abstract, but they are unable to describe reality accurately.

The androcentric fallacy, which is built into all the mental contracts of western civilization, cannot be rectified simply by "adding women." What is demanded for rectification is a radical restructuring of thought and analysis which once and for all accepts the fact that humanity consists in equal parts of men and women and that the experiences, thoughts, and insights of both sexes must be represented in every generalization that is made about human beings.[21]

Nearly all of the well-known male nationalist leaders in Africa, even the most progressive, fell into the trap of speaking for men as if this represented all of the population. There were notable thinkers such as Amilcar Cabral and Samora Machel who argued that the liberation of the woman was fundamental to the national liberation process, but on the whole African liberation was represented as if the ideas of men represented all of human experience and all of human thought. Even the most progressive thinkers were not only unable to define correctly in the abstract but unable to describe reality accurately.

In this sense it is now possible to focus on the exhaustion of the patriarchal model of liberation. In the face of criticisms of male-centered discourse on liberation, there are those who seek to mainstream gender in southern Africa by developing programs to add women to various symbols of nationalism and liberation. Those who seek to extend the numbers of women in the liberation process are addressing the limitation of androcentrism. But this addresses only part of the problem. Reversing androcentrism cannot be accomplished simply by adding women; it requires a fundamental rethinking of the categories of gender, politics, citizenship, liberation, the state, and peace.

The methods of warfare employed by both the Angolan army and the army of UNITA have exposed the limits of a peace predicated on demobilizing male combatants. Moreover, the ways in which the war was carried to the civilian population, the use of the radio by UNITA, and the massive mobilization of economic resources demonstrated the way in which the army of UNITA had internalized the total war concept of the South African Defence Force. This total war concept was articulated as a total strategy involving (a) a political strategy, (b) an economic strategy, (c) psychological warfare, (d) a media and information strategy, and (e) a military strategy. The concept of total strategy reinforces the claim of the present chapter that warfare was not simply direct violence of military confrontations. UNITA continued the war in Angola all during the peace accords: holding administrative districts, blocking the free movement of the population, and holding more than half of the population under virtual hostage. This is where women felt the brunt of militarism, in the besieged areas. The war of UNITA involved all forms of warfare, and it is in this sense that the androcentrism of UNITA and the MPLA needs to be addressed.

The radical restructuring of thought and analysis demanded by those who seek to rise above androcentrism requires that the concepts used in problematizing militarism and peace be deconstructed. Categories such as ethnicity, mulattos, family, human rights, market, citizenship, tribe, and so on keep shifting without historical reference. While empirical data on warfare and peace accords are useful, the crucial conceptual problem has not been tackled satisfactorily. In the realist conception of peace, there is the continued demand for ethnic balancing in Angolan politics as the basis for peace. This realism compels a clarification of what is war. It was Clausewitz who argued that war is the continuation of politics by other means. This famous dictum can easily be applied to the warfare in Angola. I have already critically examined how the elections of 1992 were a continuation of the war in Angola by other means.[22] To understand the requirements of peace, it is necessary to grasp the concept of total war that was waged in Angola. Total war is not new, since in the history of the society, the intellectual war over the humanity of Africans provided the foundation for wanton destruction. It is here necessary to grasp how the war of ideas over the humanity of Africans legitimized the armed clashes in the society. The recent intense discussions over the multi-dimensional crisis in Africa provide the urgency for understanding the intellectual, moral, and spiritual dimensions of the current malaise of militarism in Africa.

Jonas Savimbi Fighting for Peace?

Jonas Savimbi has had such major impact on the history of Angola in the past forty years that it is difficult to treat any aspect of Angolan recent history without reference to the personality of Savimbi. His single-mindedness in the pursuit of power at all costs left him isolated even within the organization that he created. The legacies of the cold war media blitz accords to Savimbi an importance that enables the survival of an elaborate financial, military, and information system to perpetuate war. The history of Savimbi and UNITA provides an interesting glimpse of how the academy and the media have distorted the history of the liberation process in Africa. Savimbi had endeared himself to conservative and apartheid elements in his bid for power. He fought under the banner of anti-communism and "ethnic authenticity." The limits of his claim that he commanded the support of the Ovimbundu people were exposed when he lost the elections in 1992. David Birmingham wrote that, "The Angolan election was an unparalleled feat of democratic logistics. Its sequel however, was a war more savage, more destructive, more inhuman, than all the colonial wars, wars of intervention, and wars by proxy that had gone on before. The highland leaders were unwilling to accept that they had lost an election which the western world had confidently promised them that they would win."

Jonas Savimbi was left traumatized with dismay that even his own highland people had not supported him. The electoral process demonstrated that there was no homogenous Ovimbundu constituency. Savimbi's actions following his loss in the elections exposed the extent to which his political organization came to believe its own disinformation and propaganda that it was fighting for an ethnic majority.

Despite the rejection of Savimbi by the mass of the people, there remained powerful lobbies in the West that continued to support Savimbi and UNITA in the name of peace and the search for peace. One chapter in the book entitled *Cold War Guerrilla* was fittingly entitled "fighting for peace." The very same book detailed the considerable influence that Savimbi held among the conservative anti-communist and anti-Castro lobby in the United States. There was a similar lobby in South Africa, to the point where President Mandela also accepted that Savimbi had to be conciliated for peace to take hold in Angola. An indication of the importance placed on Savimbi can be seen from the recorded history of the UN mission in Angola and the details of the constant meetings with Savimbi after the Lusaka Protocol up to the time of the death of the UN special representative in 1998

After the 1992 elections, instead of declaring that the elections were free and fair, the then special representative of the United Nations dithered, writing to Savimbi, telephoning him, meeting him, and placing the demands of Savimbi over the stated wishes of the electorate. The full extent of this interaction is now recorded in the book *Orphans of the Cold War*.[23] In February 1996, on the thirtieth anniversary of the founding of UNITA, the glossy French publication *Jeune Afrique* carried a special issue on Savimbi as a fighter for peace. The information warfare of UNITA exposes how after thirty years the authors of disinformation have come to believe their own propaganda that Savimbi was a "key to Africa" (the title of Bridgland and Savimbi's 1986 book).[24] No other "liberation leader" in Africa had become so famous that Hollywood was moved to make a film of his fight for liberation (*Red Scorpion*).

Fred Bridgland, who wrote about Savimbi as a great African leader, was to later expose the atrocities carried out against dissenting UNITA members when the party operated under South African military cover in Jamba on the Namibian border. Prior to the 1992 elections, there were persistent stories in the Western media on the atrocities in the camps of UNITA. The disappearance of one of the top leaders of UNITA, Tito Chingunji, had created a temporary stir within the United States. However, the Pentagon continued its support. At the same time some Western television programs were showing the women of LIMA marching in bright red in support of the great leader Jonas Savimbi. The existence of LIMA and its appearance at international meetings on women's rights and peace demonstrated that there were women who would support their own oppression. Elaine Windrich in her book *The Cold War Guerrilla* chronicled the linkages between the propaganda and disinformation elements of the United States and the military machine of UNITA. By the end of the cold war the disinformation and propaganda on Savimbi had become so entrenched that citizens of the advanced capitalist countries did believe that Savimbi was a key to peace in Angola. This ensured that, despite sanctions by the United Nations, the elaborate banking, weapons procurement, and supply system for the military machine of UNITA continued to thrive.

The numerous efforts to conciliate Savimbi failed. There was, however, a price for this failure—the slow disintegration of UNITA. Early in 1991, leaders such as Nzau Puna, George Chicoty, and Tony Fernandes left the organization after the death of Chingunji. Some generals who had been integrated into the national army under the Lusaka agreement and had deserted the life of fighting repeatedly warned that Savimbi was acquiring more sophisticated weapons to return to war. When Savimbi refused to participate in the Government of National Unity and Reconciliation in 1997, most of the top leaders of UNITA who had been with the organization from the outset deserted Savimbi. Leaders such as Jorge Valentim, Abel Chivukuvuku, and Manuvakola turned their backs on the warfare of Savimbi and formed a reformed UNITA, dedicated to peaceful political interventions. By the end of 1998, the stubbornness of Savimbi had reached such proportions that only a new war could result. At the congress of the ruling party, the MPLA, in December 1998, President dos Santos reorganized the leadership and promoted the militaristic elements of the MPLA. When there was a formal declaration of war, Savimbi boasted that he could field over 60,000 soldiers with the most up-to-date artillery and conventional hardware. The heaviest fighting erupted around Cuito and revealed for the first time that UNITA possessed T-55 tanks. These tanks, made in the Ukraine, were operated by Ukrainian mercenaries. The government media reports stated that ninety tanks were brought into Andulo and Bailundo by air. Other war matériel recovered by FAA during December included sixteen BMP-2 armored personnel carriers, sixty RPG-7s, eleven anti-tank missiles, 850,000 AKM bullets, and eight cases of D-30 artillery ammunition. UNITA also had a range of other sophisticated weapons, including BM-21 medium-range artillery, South African G-5 howitzers, SAM missiles, and ground-to-air missiles.

The militarism of both the ruling party and UNITA politically marginalized non-military forces in the country. Despite the political divisions in UNITA and the atrocities carried out by the military wing of UNITA, sections of the media were still wedded to the idea of ethnic chaos if UNITA and Savimbi were not reconciled to some sort of power sharing. However, after the war in the Balkans, in Rwanda, and in the streets of Angola, a permanent international criminal tribunal is seeking to set up an international criminal court to establish new rules of war and engagement. At a meeting in Rome in 1998, there were deliberations to write into international law that it was a crime "if any military operation began in the knowledge that such attack [would] cause incidental loss of life and injury to civilians."[25] Under these new rules of war and engagement, the city sieges of 1993 would rank as war crimes and Jonas Savimbi would be considered a war criminal. At the summit of the leaders of the SADC in 1998, Savimbi was designated a war criminal.

In January of 1999 the secretary-general of the United Nations reported to the Security Council that, in light of the renewed war, the remaining peacekeepers were to be withdrawn from Angola. The failure of the United Nations has been directly linked to the pressures of the conservative forces in the United States and the influence of the ethnic narrative. The report was an admission of failure and was highly embarrassing to the United Nations, who had spent US$1.5 billion on operations in Angola that failed to bring Savimbi into the peace process. According to the *Guardian* newspaper, published in London on 19 January, the report by Kofi Annan "is an admission that the UN has had its most serious failure in Africa since the Congo debacle in the 1960's." The *Guardian* wrote that "for seven years the peacekeepers have, in effect, been a shield behind which UNITA troops have been able to hide and re-arm."

The writings of the UN and U.S. officials on their stewardship in Angola contain revealing insights into the reality that signing any peace agreement is only the first step and that the whole implementation process is more difficult. This is especially the case if elements from the Pentagon and the United States support one of the parties at war. Recent revelations on the reaction of the UN bureaucracy to the information on the impending genocide in Rwanda exposed the ways in which the West had internalized the "tribal" narrative. Once the genocide was constructed as ethnic violence between "Tutsi" and "Hutu," there was no need to invoke the 1948 United Nations convention on genocide. This is important, since all during 1993 the city sieges of UNITA were veritable acts of genocide for the civilian population in these cities, especially the women and children. The destruction and murder of tens of thousands going on in the Angolan countryside was tolerated because of the low value placed on African lives. This posture compounded the national security concept that there could be no effective peace in Angola without conciliating the ethnic forces of the Umbundu and the Kimbundu. In principle, this meant "keeping Jonas Savimbi aboard the peace process." These were the words of those in the U.S. State Department that had invested so heavily in the democratic credentials of Savimbi at the height of the cold war.

The public relations machinery of Savimbi in Europe, the United States, and South Africa had been effective. At the bases of UNITA, foreign dignitaries were shown pictures of Savimbi with Presidents Bush and Reagan of the United States and with the most important leaders of the West. Savimbi boasted that his friendship with the secretary-general of the United Nations dated back to their years together as students in Switzerland. The United Nations, the highest peacekeeping body in the world, failed to sanction UNITA prior to the elections when it (a) failed to allow the government to restore civilian control over one-third of the territory; (b) refused to surrender heavy weapons to the United Nations; and (c) failed to demobilize the most professional section of its hidden army. Even after the elections of 1992, the Security Council failed to take a firm position that Savimbi had lost the elections, and was involved in many meetings to "bring UNITA into a government of national unity." During this period, UNITA remobilized its army and set the stage for the most devastating war in the history of Angola. The farcical disengagement of troops was recognized for what it was when Savimbi was able to produce an army to occupy two-thirds of the country and start the war—once it was verified that he had been rejected by the majority of the people. The fact that Savimbi could repeat this feat again after the Lusaka peace agreement in 1994 demonstrated the complete failure of the United Nations. The return of Savimbi to war in 1998 with the massive armaments detailed above made a mockery of sanctions.

Savimbi was rewarded for returning to war by the United Nations expending millions of dollars in setting up peace talks to reconcile him. Various UN officials traveled to his army base in Andulo after 1994. The secretary-general of the United Nations, Boutros Boutros Ghali, joined the courting by traveling to Bailundo (in the province of Huambo) to hold discussions with Savimbi. When, four years later, the army of UNITA had made no move to hand over civilian areas for state administration, a new round of activities was started by Beye. Six years after the elections in 1992, Savimbi's forces returned to war. By the end of the following year, the Angolan government decided that only outright military victory would end the war. The capture of Bailundo and Andulo by the government forces in 1999 forced Savimbi to move his headquarters. At the age of sixty-five, Savimbi promised to continue by carrying the war to more civilian areas, especially Luanda.

Throughout the period of the Lusaka peace, the Department of Humanitarian Affairs of the United Nations made appeals for their de-mining program in Angola. But far from de-mining, new land mines were planted, and there were accusations that some companies were using the aid for de-mining to test the new land mine technology. The same companies that manufactured the land mines were bidding for tenders to carry out land mine clearance. The very sophisticated technology that could rid the society of land mines was not being used in Angola "because of cost." One of the most ironic aspects of the whole UN peace process was the way in which the military wing of UNITA could import and place land mines in the midst of sanctions and a highly publicized international campaign against land mines. The presence of anti-personnel land mines in Angola created and continues to create a crisis of massive proportions. Anti-personnel land mines pose a major obstacle for economic reconstruction, and without drastic intervention, agricultural production could be affected for another one hundred years. Problems of food production were most affected by the planting of land mines. In Angola, the reality of war and in particular of anti-personnel land mines continue to burden non-combatants, especially women and children. The presence of land mines reinforced the dependence of the population on imported food. Throughout the new war that escalated, one of the pressure points of the United Nations was for the maintenance of a "humanitarian" presence in Angola. This pressure emanated from the humanitarian/food lobby in international politics. The food lobby is part of a giant campaign to change the dietary habits of Africans and to make them dependent on foreign food. The war in Angola supports this campaign. Food as a weapon of war brings together the effects of both structural and direct violence in the lives of Angolan men, women, and children. The existence of over 10 million land mines prevents the regeneration of agriculture and provides the basis for future changes in property relations in the countryside.

Food as a Weapon of War against Women and Children in Angola

One of the more important "humanitarian activities" carried out in Angola by those who were supposed to be enforcing the Lusaka Protocol (keeping peace) had been the mandate to provide food for persons displaced by war. However, one of the areas that combatants attempt to control is the movement and supply of food.

From the time the South Africans occupied Jamba (in southern Angola), the U.S. State Department through the Office for Disaster Assistance provided food aid for UNITA so that Savimbi could feed his troops. NGOs were brought in to distribute food and medicines so that UNITA could extend its influence when the Angolan government agencies were already doing a better job at lower cost. In 1989, this was overtly political—USAID was carrying out official policy to weaken the government and to reduce its size.

The Angolan government had placed tremendous trust in the peacekeeping capabilities of the United Nations and gave undue support to the agencies of the United Nations in the period of the search for peace. The numerous agencies of the United Nations—WFP, WHO, UNICEF, UNDP, UNHCR, UNFPA—were involved in the first demobilization exercise (1992), in the organization of the elections (1992), and in the implementation of UN humanitarian programs between 1992 and 1999. It was during the period after the independence of Namibia that the secretary-general of the United Nations launched the Special Relief Program for Angola (SRPA). The first phase of SRPA had been in effect since October 1990, but the second phase of this appeal was launched after the Bicesse Accord, emphasizing rehabilitation over relief. The main objectives of SRPA had been the reintegration of 1.4 million displaced persons, returnees, and demobilized soldiers and their families; the improvement of basic services including water and sanitation; and the extension of immunization throughout the country. At the apex of this operation was World Food Programme (WFP). WFP distributed food throughout the country, provided logistics and support, and subcontracted relief work to international NGOs. In cases such as in Jamba where WFP did not have warehouses, NGOs stored food for WFP. In these areas, the distribution of food ensured the feeding of one set of combatants.

This situation meant that WFP has been one of the most important international agencies in Angola, operating with a budget of over US$100 million per year. All during the sieges of the 1992–94 war, UNITA used famine and hunger as a weapon of war. The skills of manipulating famine as propaganda had been honed with the help of the United States in the period between 1989 and 1992 after there was a decline in food supplies from South Africa. When the United Nations first declared sanctions after the departure of the Republicans from the White House in 1993, the skills of obtaining food aid increased. All during the city sieges, Savimbi was able to initiate meetings and contact with UN agencies to procure food when there were sanctions in place. The ostensible reason for the meetings in Kinshasa was to ensure that the trapped civilians of Kuito received food. However, the reality was that UNITA was being fed with imported food so that its soldiers could fight. UNITA was able to successfully manipulate the delivery of food by WFP because of its important ties with the UN secretary-general and supporters in the United States and Western Europe.

WFP functions as the food aid agency of the UN system, providing a central coordinating role in developing crop production estimates, food aid requirements, and logistics planning for major "relief" operations. With an annual budget of over

US$1.8 billion, it is the largest of the four UN organizations that operate at the front line of humanitarianism, the others being UNHCR, UNICEF, and UNDP. WFP signed a worldwide cooperative agreement with NGOs in 1995. One of the best places to get information on the operations of this "humanitarian" agency is to review its weekly summary of the military and humanitarian situation, its news releases, and its annual reports. Produced by the principal logistics organization in a country at war, the weekly summaries detailed the rhythm of the war in Angola. In its 1994 annual report, WFP said of itself that, "WFP and NGO operated in model collaboration in an emergency. WFP plays a leading role in coordination, programming, logistics of food and ensures the timely delivery of commodities. In turn, NGOs oversee efficient distribution of relief aid at the local level. WFP and NGOs conduct joint assessment and work together to provide a comprehensive system of monitoring food aid."

Recent studies on the massive manipulation of food by militarists in Somalia and eastern Congo have outlined how food can be used as a weapon of war against the people. Michael Maren's *The Road to Hell*, a study of the use of food to support military forces while the mass of people suffered, exposed the cooperation between international NGOs and militarists. Angolan women were able to experience firsthand the corresponding role of the WFP in Angola. By constructing Angolan women, men, and children as helpless victims, the WFP appealed for aid all over the world, while its food kept the soldiers of UNITA fighting. One appeal by WFP for support is outlined below.

WFP said that it was supporting 1,963,000 victims of drought and conflict for a period of six months in Angola.

Total number of beneficiaries	1,963,000
Total food	111,005 tons
Total WFP cost	US$69,227, 948
Duration	180 days

The chart below gives an indication of the budget of WFP in Angola in the period 1990–94.

WFP expenditure in Angola 1989–94 (in US$000):

Year	Development	Relief	Extra Budgetary	Total
1990	3,879	4,156	2,141	10,176
1991	4,261	15,082	6,682	26,024
1992	3,923	33,995	8,662	46,500
1993	1,381	37,277	18,705	57,360
1994	221	82,693	23,947	106,861

In Angola, WFP continued to act as the lead agency in the relief effort, handling 200,000 tons of food consignment in 1994. Access to many areas remained restricted owing to the fact that UNITA kept more than 60 per cent of the population under their military control. Consequently, almost half of total food supplies had to be transported by air. WFP also provided transport and logistics services to other UN agencies and over 40 NGOs. There is a WFP staff of 1500, developing an extensive delivery system, including port operations, warehousing, road convoy and train operations and a sophisticated workshop/maintenance unit to service all the equipment and vehicles. WFP is in a joint venture to open up main road corridors in areas of conflict, one connecting Malanje to Luanda and Kuito to Lobito.[26]

The above long excerpt from the WFP 1994 Annual Report gives some indication of the scope of the operation. The report also demonstrated that the WFP was organized along military lines in Angola.

The expenditure of US$106 million in Angola was the highest in Africa after Sudan, where US$110, 696,000 was spent. This is a country with three times the population of Angola. This meant that on a per capita basis, more money was being spent in Angola.

One can analyze this seemingly benign work in a number of ways. On the surface it would appear that the WFP was trying to ensure food as a basic right. However, a deeper examination would require that the supply of food in war-torn countries be placed in a larger debate on the future of food production and the role of genetically modified food. Current discussions on the long-term planning of biotech companies, the giant food transnational corporations, and the "elimination of the farmer" in the future are all germane to the debate on food aid. Jeremy Rifkin in his book on the *End of Work* brought out the aggressive role of giant food corporations in food production and the application of the techniques of genetic engineering in agricultural production. It is with this background that the work of WFP in Angola must be critically penetrated. Such a critical analysis would note that while food aid was urgent for displaced persons, the methods and the kind of food provided must be located in the larger context of the kinds of plans for postwar reconstruction in Angola.

A detailed study of the history of WFP would lead to many conclusions. The least charitable would be to question whether this organization has been intimately involved in the wars against the Angolan peoples at three levels:

- ideological with respect to the food and dietary habits of Africans, the effort to change these and make Africans more dependent on foreign supplies of food;

- logistical and military coordination as a weapon to support food, logistics, and supply of fuel for forces that international agencies support (in this case, the soldiers of UNITA); and

- to support political and social forces who are in agreement with particular sectional interests in the global struggle to dominate Africa and to create dependency. Angolan women were the ones who felt the brunt of this food war, since they were the ones burdened with the responsibility for providing food and care in the household and the community.

The documentation in the files of WFP from their work in Angola in 1993 shows that WFP was actually breaking the sanctions against UNITA. This occurred after the long negotiations between WFP and UNITA in Zaire in 1993, just before the UN Security Council was about to implement sanctions. The evidence so far shows that elements in WFP wanted to set up a clear logistical supply route with UNITA in case there were forces in the international community that were serious about sanctions. The matter of WFP support for UNITA continued to be very delicate, and it will not be possible to get a full record of the amount of fuel distributed by WFP in 1993 and to see what amount of this fuel ended up in the hands of UNITA. Moreover, WFP can claim that its negotiations to provide food for UNITA in 1993 (half the food for Huambo in return for half the food for Kuito) were conducted with the clear knowledge of both the government and the UN Security Council. This claim is predicated on the assumption that UNITA was providing food for the civilians held hostage in the areas under its control.

One concrete way of examining food as a weapon is to analyze the food that was distributed by WFP every month in Angola. The list of 35,062 metric tons of food supplied for one week in November 1994 is taken from the weekly reports of WFP. It states the kind of food and the country supplying this food. This author has replaced the quantity of food with the country supplying the food.

Maize	60 percent from U.S., 40 percent from EU.
Rice	Bought from Thailand or Vietnam.
Corn flour	Mostly from U.S.
Corn soya beans	From Netherlands. For children suffering from malnutrition.
Beans	From U.S., EU. Left over from drought relief in southern Africa.
Peas	From U.S.
Soup, minestrone	From Italy. Expensive; people do not know how to make this soup; link to elements in Socialist party; received from companies in the party.
Beef meat	From Scandinavia. Consists of tinned fish, tinned meat.
MRE	(Meals Ready to Eat) From U.S. Left over from Gulf War; in 1994 still 1 million metric tons after much was used for the demobilization in 1992. For the elections in 1992 and throughout the war. Primarily given to soldiers in battlefront positions.
Sugar	Source unknown
High protein biscuit	From Italy. Also high protein from the UK, Norway, and Netherlands.
Fruit juice	From Italy.
Salt	From Angola.

Of the 35,000 metric tons distributed for the month, more than 25,000 was of maize from the European Union (EU) and the United States, both of whom are proud of their record of supplying food for Angola. Charts can be provided by the UN Department of Humanitarian Affairs to show the donor community exactly how its money was spent. It can be seen that the only commodity secured from Africa was the salt. The regular appeals for food ensure that this is a major operation, and there is no great rush for the recovery of Angolan agriculture. In fact, this author was told of the example of one NGO suggesting that, in the north of Angola, WFP buy up the manioc crop as an incentive to returning farmers and a support of local cultivation. Manioc was a local crop, and the sale would have increased the price by boosting local productivity. This suggestion was turned down.

Manioc was not produced in the United States or the EU. Crops such as millet and sorghum, which are still produced and eaten by peasants throughout southern Africa, are not on the list of food distributed by the international food donors. Food aid from the United States and the EU is one means of disposing of the surpluses generated by agricultural protection in those Western countries. Presenting large amounts of food helps satisfy the large agricultural lobbies in both areas, while allowing the United States and EU to claim a moral superiority for feeding starving Africans. WFP was continuing an old colonial policy of promoting imported cereals into Africa. A fraction of this budget could be invested in improving productivity, storage, and processing of small grains such as sorghum and millet. Using this kind of evidence, future research will be able to reveal if WFP was at the forefront of an ideological war waged with food, not only in this current phase of war but in a long-range plan to change the dietary habits of Africans.

An important component of reconstruction in Angola is to explore how to assist women in the rural areas using the multi-sectoral approach. The starting point for this approach would be a conception of peace that involves community healing and transformation of the economic, military, and cultural bases of exploitation and militarization. Throughout the period of the Lusaka peace, the multi-sectoral approach to resettlement was aimed at demobilized soldiers. This was despite the fact that most reports indicated that UNITA was sending the old and ill as demobilized soldiers to the demobilization centers. The major thrust of the humanitarian efforts was the quartering of the soldiers of UNITA, the donors having staked their position and their future on this approach. Very few of the international NGOs are interested in the self-reliant activities of Angolan women. One commentator on the importation of food into Angola remarked that this was a tragedy since such a wide variety of food could be grown. However, there is intolerance of ideas that would lay the foundations for self-reliance in any sector of the Angolan society.

▼▼▼▼

The task of the long-term peace process in Angola must be to free the minds of the African from the complexes that have been fomented by militarism and the culture of violence. Thirty-eight years ago, Frantz Fanon penetrated the mental complexes associated with the psychological warfare, colonial war, and mental disorders. The challenge then, as now, was how to develop healthy minds in healthy bodies as the basis for peace and social collectivism. In this sense the spiritual health of a community cannot be divorced from issues of peace. Fanon took the question of peace out of the simplistic framework of the absence of armed conflict. He insisted that the mental health of a society is a prerequisite for decolonization and social development. Despite the profound impact of his work, women are exposing the androcentric nature of writers of his period.

Since the writings of Fanon, African women and peace activists have brought to the fore not only the impact of open conflict but the effects of structural and domestic violence in Africa. These forces have exposed the celebration of the warrior traditions in Africa. In the process of interrogating the issues of masculinity, sexuality, gendered concepts of peace, and warrior traditions, these women and activists have joined the debate on patriarchy in a way that will reinforce our understanding of the links between patriarchy and militarism.

NOTES

1. Fred Bridgland, *Jonas Savimbi: A Key to Africa* (Edinburgh: Mainstream, 1986). See also Leon Dash Jr., *Savimbi's 1977 Campaign against the Cubans and the MPLA,* Munger Africana Notes (Edinburgh: Mainstream, 1977); W. Martin James, *A Political History of the Civil War in Angola* (New Brunswick, N.J.: Transaction, 1992); Daniel Spikes, *Angola and the Politics of Intervention* (Jefferson, N.C.: McFarland, 1993); A. Klinghoffer, *The Angolan War: A Study in Soviet Policy in the Third World* (Boulder, Colo.: Westview Press, 1980). These books, written for audiences outside of Africa, justified the military support that went to UNITA from the Republican establishment in the United States.

2. *Angola: Between War and Peace* (Washington, D.C.: Human Rights Watch/Africa, February 1996). This publication was a sequel to the earlier 1994 study *Angola: Arms Trade and Violations of the Laws of War since the 1992 Elections.*

3. Nkiru Nzegwu, "Gender Equality in a Dual-Sex System: The Case of Onitsha," *Canadian Journal of Law and Jurisprudence* 7, no. 1 (January 1994): 75.

4. Ruth Meena, *Gender in Southern Africa* (Harare: SAPES Books, 1993). See also Jill Steans, *Gender and International Relations* (Cambridge, UK: Polity, 1998).

5. Margaret Anstee, *Orphans of the Cold War: The Inside Story of the Collapse of the Angolan Peace Process, 1992–1993* (New York: St. Martin's Press, 1996); and Paul Hare, *Angola's Last Chance for Peace* (Washington, D.C.: United States Institute for Peace, 1998).

6. Jacklyn Cock, *Colonels and Cadres: War and Gender in South Africa* (Cape Town: Oxford University Press, 1991).

7. Quoted from Rene Pélissier, *Les Guerres Grises: Resistance et Revoltes en Angola (1845–1947)* (Orgeval: Pélissier, 1977).

8. Tony Hodges, *Angola to the 1990's: The Potential for Recovery,* Special Report 1079, Economic Intelligence Unit (London: EIU, 1987). This report was updated as *Angola to 2000, Prospects for Recovery* (EIU, 1993).

9. Lucio Lara, published interview, *Jornal De Angola,* 16 December 1995.

10. *A Rough Trade: The Role of Companies and Governments in the Angolan Conflict* (London: Global Witness, 1998).

11. James Rupert, "Diamond Hunters Fuel Africa's Brutal Wars," *Washington Post,* 16 October 1999, p. 1.

12. Horace Campbell, "The Military Defeat of the South Africans in Angola," *Monthly Review,* April 1989, pp. 1–15.

13. Gerard Chailand, *Armed Struggle in Africa* (New York: Monthly Review Press, 1969). An indication of the range of organizations that could be called guerrillas in 1999 can be grasped from the book *African Guerrillas,* Christopher Claphamm, ed. (London: James Currey, 1998). Teresa Ann Barnes, "We Women Worked So Hard: Gender, Labour and Social Reproduction in Colonial Harare 1930–1956" (Ph.D. thesis, University of Zimbabwe, 1993).

14. Teresa A. Barnes, *We Women Worked So Hard: Gender, Urbanization, and Social Reproduction in Colonial Harare, Zimbabwe, 1930–1956* (Portsmouth: Heinemann 1999).

15. Patricia McFadden, "Women, War, and Militarism," *SAPEM,* 18 March 1981, p. 38.

16. Chester Crocker, *High Noon in Southern Africa: Keeping Peace in a Rough Neighborhood* (New York: Norton, 1992). Crocker has been one of the most consistent writers on the imperial version of peace. See among others his "Peacemaking in Southern Africa: The Namibia-Angola Settlement of 1988," *Diplomatic Record,* 1989/90, pp. 9–34.

17. Karl Maier, *Angola: Promises and Lies* (London: Serif, 1996).

18. One of the better accounts of the external orientation of the movements has been developed by Wamba dia Wamba, "Some Aspects of the Historical Background to National Liberation Struggles in Southern Africa: The Case of Angola" (University of Dar es Salaam, 1988, mimeograph). For an account that locates these movements as agents of ethnic nationalism, see John Marcum, *The Angolan Revolution,* vols. 1 and 2 (Cambridge, Mass.: MIT Press, 1969 and 1978).

19. Organization of Angolan Women, *Angolan Women Building the Future: From National Liberation to Women's Emancipation,* trans. Marga Holness (London: Zed Books, 1984), p. 14.

20. *Country Gender Analysis, Angola* (Stockholm: Swedish International Development Authority, 1992).

21. Gerda Lerner *The Creation of Patriarchy* (London: Oxford University Press, 1986), p. 220.

22. Horace Campbell, "Angolan Women and the Electoral Process in Angola, 1992," *Africa Development* 23, no. 2 (1993).

23. Anstee, *Orphans of the Cold War.* For a critical view of the role of the United Nations in Angola and its backhanded support for Jonas Savimbi, see Victoria Brittain, "Angolan Democracy: The International Betrayal," *Southern African Report,* January 1994, p. 25, and Victoria Brittain, "When Democracy Is Not Enough: Denying Angola's Election Result," *Southern African Report,* January/February 1993, pp. 41–45.

24. Bridgland, *Savimbi: A Key to Africa.*

25. Quoted in the *New York Times,* Op Ed, 10 June 1998.

26. World Food Program Annual Report 1994. See also WFP, *Angola* (Background Paper for round table discussion with donor representatives, February 1996).

8. Celebration and Confrontation, Resolution and Restructuring
Mozambique from Independence to the Millennium

M. Anne Pitcher

> For if the coming of formal independence has not altered substantially anything in many other African territories, this is unlikely to be the case in Mozambique. Here was a movement come to power with a clear sense of purpose, a firm popular base, and a cadre of leaders of the very highest caliber.[1]

These remarks eloquently convey the hope and jubilation that accompanied Mozambique's liberation from colonial rule in 1975. At that time, few observers could have imagined that the country would be near ruin two decades later. When the Front for the Liberation of Mozambique (FRELIMO, Frente de Libertação de Moçambique) concluded its bitter thirteen-year struggle against the oppressive Portuguese colonial regime, most Mozambicans cheered the movement and embraced its revolutionary agenda. Promising to end the "exploitation of man by man," FRELIMO gave a voice to workers and peasants, women and youth, who previously had been ignored, despised, and mistreated by the Portuguese. The new government nationalized many of the private companies that had formerly operated with such impunity across much of the country, and pledged to transform relations in rural areas through the creation of state farms, collectives, cooperatives, and communal villages. Furthermore, it aimed to improve living conditions for many urban Africans by offering free health care, a low-cost education, and subsidized housing. On independence day in 1975, there was every reason to be optimistic about Mozambique's future.

From Euphoria to Disappointment

FRELIMO achieved great strides in the initial years. Independence brought a release of creative energy by artists, musicians, poets, and playwrights who flourished and thrived in liberated Mozambique. A language of rights became a part of the national discourse as the government helped to organize women and workers to attain greater dignity and better conditions in the household and the workplace. A series of national literacy campaigns reduced the illiteracy rate by 20 percent in only five years. Primary school enrollments doubled, while the numbers of secondary school students went from 20,000 to 94,000 pupils between 1974 and 1982.[2] The government sponsored a nationwide vaccination program that vaccinated 96% of the population against measles, tetanus, tuberculosis, and smallpox by the end of the 1970s. It also delivered primary health care to the country: health posts and centers increased from 446 to 1,148 posts over a ten-year period.[3] In the countryside, many smallholders welcomed the opportunity to engage in the new forms of production introduced by state farms, collectives, and cooperatives. Many also responded enthusiastically to the services provided by communal villages. In urban areas, many Africans who had lived without water and electricity on the outskirts of cities and towns moved into well-constructed apartments that had been vacated by fleeing Portuguese settlers. Some of these apartments were located in city and town centers, and the new tenants paid only nominal rents to the government in order to live there.

Although FRELIMO's social accomplishments were impressive, they were also fleeting. By the late 1980s, over 50 percent of schools in five northern provinces were no longer functioning. The majority of teachers in the country lacked sufficient training, and approximately 95% of students in the country were taking longer than four years to complete the first four grades of primary school.[4] Even at the government level, only a very small percentage of personnel had higher education degrees.[5] In health care, life expectancy and infant mortality rates remained unchanged from the colonial period. Nearly one-fifth of the new health posts were no longer working.[6] Many smallholders abandoned communal villages and withdrew their labor from state farms and collectives. The urban housing stock deteriorated, while the numbers of new arrivals living in makeshift cane shacks on the margins of Maputo or Beira swelled.

Severe economic decline both accompanied the worsening social conditions and contributed to dwindling government resources available for ambitious development plans. By the 1980s, industrial production was half that of pre-independence levels, and industry was working at only a fraction of its capacity.[7] State farms were bankrupt. Exports had dropped by 75 percent, and official marketed agricultural production inside the country had reached appalling levels. Domestic food production was so low that Mozambique had to rely on massive food aid—sometimes as much as 90 percent of the total supply—to feed its population.[8] Resorting to imports to compensate for poor domestic output, Mozambique ran a substantial balance of trade deficit from the mid-1980s, which it was able to offset only by relying on international aid in the form of grants and loans. By mid-1992, half of Mozambique's budget came from donors.[9]

What explains the almost total collapse of FRELIMO's economic and social agenda after the impressive accomplishments of the initial years following independence? At least five factors contributed: the colonial legacy, poor weather conditions, the international setting, FRELIMO's own policies, and the coup de grâce—a prolonged and "low-intensity" war. Certainly, the colonial legacy presented innumerable obstacles to the struggling, new government—from the lack of east-west roads to a shortage of trained personnel; from the hasty departure of many Portuguese traders, who dominated the retail and wholesale commercial networks, to the sabotage of equipment by fleeing settlers. Almost anyone who has ever visited Maputo has been regaled with stories from the city's dwellers about how the Portuguese filled up elevator shafts with cement to prevent the new government from making good use of the buildings. With regard to infrastructure, social relations, technical skills, and financial capacity, the demands and negligence of the colonial past provided a harsh and unforgiving environment in which to forge a new society.

Secondly, adverse weather conditions delivered another blow to FRELIMO's ambitious economic policies. Three major rivers in southern and central Mozambique flooded after 1977, diverting scarce government funds to relief efforts for nearly half a million displaced victims. Severe droughts then followed in the early 1980s. The prolonged droughts reduced agricultural exports and sharply depleted domestic cereals production. Shortages of food directly affected around 10 percent of the population, many of whom suffered impoverishment and drought-related illnesses.[10] The government then had to resort to expensive imports and food aid to make up for the food deficit.

Thirdly, the international political and economic environment complicated FRELIMO's development agenda. When FRELIMO first came to power, the independence war in neighboring Zimbabwe (then Rhodesia) was still in full swing. To honor trade sanctions that had been passed by the United Nations against the Rhodesian colonial regime, FRELIMO prohibited the transit of trade through the Beira Corridor. The east-west corridor connected the port of Beira on Mozambique's coast with Zimbabwe and was a major transit route for Zimbabwe's imports and exports. To prohibit trade along the corridor severed the economic lifeline of the Rhodesian regime, but it also seriously affected the local economy in central Mozambique. Almost overnight, the amounts of trade through the port of Beira plunged, much to the dismay of most Beirans. They felt personally affronted that officials in Maputo had not even consulted them before taking a decision that ruined the city's economy.[11]

Just as trade through Beira began to resume following Zimbabwe's independence in 1980, tensions with South Africa escalated. Relations between South Africa and Mozambique had been strained after FRELIMO assumed power in 1975, but initially they were not characterized by "overt hostility," according to Hall and Young.[12] The consolidation of power by P. W. Botha changed relations markedly between the two countries. Under Botha's leadership, the South African government cut drastically the numbers of migrants to the gold mines and, in spite of associated increased costs, diverted transit trade that had formerly gone through Maputo to Durban and other ports in South Africa. To exacerbate matters, both the colonial regime in Zimbabwe and, later, South Africa supported efforts to destabilize Mozambique by financing the growth of a counter-revolutionary movement (see discussion below).

Globally, rising fuel prices and the prevailing cold war attitudes of many Western countries left Mozambique desperate for hard currency and diplomatically ostracized.[13] Aid by various Arab banks, and Scandinavian and Eastern European countries, offered some measure of compensation, but this aid often came with strings attached. For example, aid was linked to the purchase of food or materials from the donor or lending countries, even though particular donor items were inappropriate to conditions in Mozambique. Rusty cans of Bulgarian peaches in a country full of fresh fruit offer an illustration of the mismatch between Mozambique's needs and what outsiders were prepared to give. Scores of Eastern European trucks with broken axles provide another example. These vehicles were not made to cope with Mozambique's rough terrain. Yet even this support dwindled away with the collapse of the Soviet Union and its allies after 1989. Their departure left unfinished projects that dotted the countryside, from a Romanian cotton enterprise in Cabo Delgado to a sugar undertaking in Sofala province.

Fourthly, the policies enacted by the new government were also deeply flawed economically and politically. At least until 1983, the government privileged state farms over family farms, even though at independence family farms were responsible for the majority of agricultural production. Unfortunately, the state farms were expensive to run and lacked trained personnel.[14] They relied on unrealistic assessments about the availability and cost of labor. For example, Bowen writes that consumer goods shortages and a reliance on seasonal labor led to high absentee rates on the CAIL state farm in Gaza, a province in southern Mozambique. Similar problems plagued the cotton state farms in Nampula and Cabo Delgado provinces to the north.[15] Along with the droughts, these policies had a serious impact on FRELIMO's relationship with the family sector and subsequently undermined food production. Unable to purchase goods due to shortages and inadequate incomes, producers preferred to stay on their family farms cultivating their own crops rather than work on the state farms. As a result, marketed agricultural production declined. While Mozambique was largely self-sufficient in food at independence, by 1982 the government was importing 524,000 tons of maize, wheat, and rice to supply both urban and rural areas.[16]

Although some top government officials wanted to move away from state farms as early as 1978,[17] in subsequent years several government initiatives compounded rather than alleviated the difficulties and contributed to growing political tensions. For example, after President Samora Machel criticized urban overcrowding and goods shortages in the cities in a 1982 speech, local officials in Nampula city responded by detaining and deporting to the countryside anyone who could not prove his residency or employment in the city. A year later, a much broader national measure, Operation Production, followed this local initiative. It was designed to identify allegedly unemployed and/or itinerant persons in urban areas and relocate them for work in rural areas. In principle the program was meant to be voluntary, but in practice, government representatives used coercive tactics to corral and resettle suspected loafers and wanderers and those unlucky enough to be without employment.[18] Some Mozambicans who were rounded up in Maputo were resettled as far away as Cabo Delgado and Niassa provinces in the north. They were expected to take up farming even though many had no rural experience.

FRELIMO's social schemes for transforming the rural areas also faltered. Initially many rural peoples had enthusiastically greeted policies such as cooperatives, collective farms, and communal villages. These were presented as an attempt to improve their well-being and to foster some sense of collective involvement in the national effort to modernize Mozambique. But the excitement of rural people ebbed as they yearly confronted shortages of tools, inputs, services, and consumer goods, in addition to late payments for their produce. Farmers grew tired of government promises and resented the disruption caused by relocation to inadequate, unfinished communal villages. Moreover, many disliked government condemnation of their customary leaders and practices, and resented the constant moral invectives waged by what came to be known as the *abaixo* (down with) government because it denounced so many practices and attitudes. Some rural peoples throughout the country, but particularly in the northern and central zones, began clandestinely to rely on local, customary leaders, to practice witchcraft, to engage in ceremonies such as rainmaking and initiation rites, and to drift back to their ancestral lands or to migrate to other provinces and countries. Sometimes these activities occurred with the acquiescence of local FRELIMO party secretaries and government officials, either because they were sympathetic to customary practices or because they realized the tactical advantages of cooperating with local communities; at other times, such activities were harshly suppressed.[19] Taken together, the economic blunders, social insensitivity, and unpopular political ideas weakened support for the government and undermined its transformative agenda.

The External War Turns Internal

The final factor contributing to the country's near collapse was an escalating war against the FRELIMO government. The war turned mistakes of judgment or inexperience into enormous catastrophes and made major policy adjustments difficult. FRELIMO had to divert its attention to security concerns and lost the capacity and resources to reverse many of its errors. Defense spending equalled 35 percent of the state budget in 1985, diverting funds away from education and health.[20] Attempts to reorient agricultural production or improve industrial output had to be shelved while the government faced "low-intensity" but destructive conflicts in nearly all the provinces of Mozambique.

In the early years, external sources established, financed, and sustained the war against the FRELIMO government. Following independence, Africans who had formerly served under the Portuguese and deserters from FRELIMO created the MNR, the Mozambique National Resistance, from a base in Rhodesia, aided by Rhodesian intelligence agents.[21] The ostensible aim behind the group at this time was to punish the FRELIMO government for helping the Zimbabwe African National Union (ZANU) extend its armed struggle against the Rhodesian government. When Rhodesia/Zimbabwe became independent in 1980, however, South Africa stepped in to continue financing the MNR as a part of its commitment to "total strategy," a foreign policy approach based on regional destabilization. The policy sought to undermine nearby African regimes through a campaign of sabotage and subversion. Its purpose was to protect the white minority government in South Africa and weaken support for the African National Congress (ANC) by sympathetic African governments.[22] In Mozambique, South Africa launched several daring raids on suspected ANC safe houses and furnished military supplies to the MNR. Comprising approximately 10,000 troops by 1981, the MNR intentionally sabotaged accomplishments of the FRELIMO regime such as schools and health posts, took hostages to attract publicity, and bombed vital infrastructure such as roads, railroads, bridges, and ports.[23] Coinciding with unfavorable climactic conditions as well as FRELIMO's flawed policies for the countryside, the attacks particularly ravaged the south and center of Mozambique. Total production declined by 30 percent, while exports, the bulk of which were agricultural, dropped by 75 percent. Faced with debt and food shortages, Mozambique turned to international donors, many of whom used Mozambique's desperate situation to pursue blatantly political agendas such as structural adjustment and Western-style democratization.[24]

Brought nearly to its knees, the FRELIMO government under President Machel pursued negotiations with South Africa to settle any differences between the two countries in the hope that this would end support for the MNR. Both parties signed an agreement in 1984, known as the Nkomati Accord. Mozambique agreed to withdraw support for the ANC and received assurances from the white minority government in South Africa that it would no longer train and supply the Mozambican opposition group. Even before the ink was dry on the agreement, however, conditions worsened in Mozambique. Attacks, massacres, and kidnappings continued. The opposition also established military bases and/or made contact with local communities in nearly every province in the country.

There are several explanations for the source and degree of this increase in organization and strength. The MNR's continued reliance on external sources for military supplies and logistical aid seems beyond dispute. In addition to numerous sources of funding from throughout Europe and the United States, the movement depended on neighboring countries. It operated from bases in Malawi from 1984 to 1986 before international efforts forced the Malawian government to expel it. South Africa's involvement became more clandestine after 1984 but no less active. Though the matter has never been resolved, many suspect South African Defence Force (SADF) involvement in the death of Samora Machel in a 1986 plane crash in South Africa. Furthermore, Minter finds much evidence to suggest that South Africa supplied the rebels with military hardware, food, water, medicines, and instructions until the peace agreement in 1992.[25]

Equally, however, evidence points to increased efforts by the MNR to build a highly centralized and well-coordinated military organization and to attract domestic support. After 1984, it began using its Portuguese name and acronym of RENAMO (Resistência Nacional Moçambicana) rather than the English "Mozambique National Resistance" as previously, to signal that it had moved inside Mozambique and was Mozambican. Most of RENAMO's national and district political leadership entered the movement between 1984 and 1986, and the majority came from Manica, Sofala, Zambezia, and Tete provinces.[26] In contrast to government portrayals of RENAMO as "armed bandits," Vines argues that after Nkomati, RENAMO had re-fashioned itself militarily to function without the constant backing of South Africa, to operate more effectively within Mozambique (with the help of South African radio equipment), and to establish local bases.[27] It had a hierarchical, military command structure with well-coordinated and planned offensive maneuvers and good communications.[28]

Moreover, the movement began to adjust its strategy to suit domestic conditions and contingencies. Where support for FRELIMO remained strong, for example in the southern part of Mozambique, RENAMO's tactics replicated its earlier approach. The movement aimed to reduce morale through sabotage and torture because it could not gain a critical mass of support. In the center and north of the country, however, RENAMO incorporated ideological appeals and political persuasion into its violent repertoire, achieving varying levels of success in gaining local adherents or, at least, assuring neutrality. In one of the first works to document RENAMO's adaptation to local conditions, Christian Geffray examined Eráti district, Nampula.[29] Without denying RENAMO's continued reliance on terror to recruit members and humiliate populations, he argued that the movement had legitimate sources of local support in particular districts in Nampula in contrast to the then prevailing interpretation of RENAMO as a group of "armed bandits" who owed its existence mainly to external sources of support and finance. According to Geffray, hatred of communal village formation and displeasure with FRELIMO's condemnation of traditional leaders and customs fueled local rural resistance in parts of Nampula. This resistance was not simply expressed in individual acts of desertion or support for RENAMO, but manifested by collective efforts to avoid FRELIMO control, such that whole villages sometimes moved out of FRELIMO's jurisdiction.[30]

Owing to its focus on internal as opposed to external explanations for the conflict, Geffray's work aroused great controversy at the time of its publication in 1991, and it has been subsequently criticized for its tendency to "reify the distinction between state and rural society, misrepresent the dynamics of resistance in the South and downplay the importance of the economic crisis."[31] However, it did inspire other researchers to look more closely at domestic sources of discontent with the FRELIMO government and to consider specific historical, cultural, political, and socio-economic conditions that contributed to the support of, or neutrality with regard to, RENAMO. Work has now documented varied patterns of responses, tactics, and approaches to RENAMO within and among provinces in Mozambique.[32] For example, even within Manica province, much of which RENAMO reputedly controlled, the movement used widely varying strategies and confronted different re-actions by local communities.[33] These findings indicate that while RENAMO prob-ably could not have been sustained without South African aid, nevertheless, the opposition did attempt to establish local bases of support and authority often us-ing a mixture of coercion and incentives similar to that used by the colonial and FRELIMO governments. These efforts, combined with a drought, produced a stale-mate by the early 1990s, and both parties were ready to negotiate.

The End of War and the Peace Settlement

FRELIMO and RENAMO signed a peace accord on 4 October 1992. The agree-ment concluded twelve rounds of heated talks that had begun in July 1990 under the auspices of the Santo Egídio community in Rome. The choice of venue for the negotiations and agreements highlights the active role that both Protestant and Catholic churches played in bringing the two sides together.[34] A host of interna-tional observers from the United Nations to the European Community also closely monitored the peace process.

According to the terms of the agreement, the United Nations was responsible for overseeing the demobilization of FRELIMO and RENAMO troops and their in-corporation into a new 30,000-man army. The United Nations would also set up and monitor multi-party elections for the presidency and the Assembly of the Re-public. These elections were intended to take place a year after the accord was signed; in the event, they were delayed until October 1994.[35]

Several factors explain the timing of the accord and the decision of both parties to abide by it. First, the end of the cold war reduced and changed international support for each side. The collapse of the Soviet Union and its satellite of supporters such as Bulgaria and Romania abruptly cut the flow of military hardware to FRE-LIMO and left the government diplomatically and politically isolated. FRELIMO opted to strengthen ties with the West and Western donors: Machel had already laid the groundwork by visiting Washington just prior to his death in 1986. The price of greater ties with the West, however, was increased pressure to negotiate and to institute Western-style political and economic reforms. The decline of the Soviet Union equally softened South Africa's stance toward the FRELIMO govern-ment and weakened the link between South Africa and RENAMO. After F. W. de Klerk assumed the presidency in 1989, the South African government shifted its focus from foreign affairs to concentrate on resolving domestic conflicts. The gov-ernment released Nelson Mandela, unbanned political organizations, and began negotiations to bring democracy to the country: "total strategy" was forgotten. Al-though the SADF clandestinely and erratically continued to supply RENAMO, official South African policy was unfavorable to the rebel group.[36]

Secondly, a drought in 1992 affected most of Mozambique. Rivers ran bone-dry, and food production dwindled in the south and center of the country. Grain and water shortages threatened RENAMO's already precarious existence in the countryside. In FRELIMO-controlled areas, the drought further demoralized people and led to a high number of desertions from the army.[37] Battle fatigue on both sides prompted the leadership to negotiate for peace, but imaginative commitments by local communities to end the violence made peace a reality.[38] Third, the international community made promises to both sides to ensure that the agreement would be honored and that neither side would be humiliated or forgotten. The United Nations, using the acronym UNOMOZ, placed 7,000 peacekeeping forces in the country and spent several hundred million dollars to administer demobilization, maintain peace, and monitor elections.[39] Whereas formerly they had been denounced, religious groups now helped to educate inhabitants about the method and meaning of democratic elections. Several countries, notably the United States, agreed to underwrite the transformation of RENAMO into a political party, and to finance the purchase of homes and offices for RENAMO officials.[40] International funds were also pledged for the election campaign and as general economic aid. These funds were essential particularly since Mozambique's economy was almost completely destroyed by the war.

The Shift to a Market Economy

The arrival of peace allowed many economic policy shifts that were passed, but not implemented effectively during the war, to solidify and accelerate. These included a commitment to structural adjustment, the privatization of many important economic sectors, the generation of markets, and increased recognition of, and reliance on, smallholders. They reflected a government realization that state farms and other forms of state intervention were expensive and poorly managed. Further, they were an attempt to adopt several components of RENAMO's agenda as a way of both placating the opposition and undermining support for RENAMO. In addition, the policy shifts were a response to the demands by Western donors (who have become increasingly important since the mid-1980s) for a free-market economy and liberal democracy .

Known as the Economic Rehabilitation Program (ERP), the structural adjustment package adopted in 1987 eliminated price controls on most agricultural products, and reduced state subsidies and welfare programs. It devalued the metical, sought to privatize state assets, and liberalized trade. Through these measures, the ERP aimed to increase production for consumption and export, reduce the budget deficit, restore physical infrastructure, and improve the transit system.[41]

Economic indicators, particularly in industry, transport, and communications, showed some improvements in the three years after the ERP was passed. However, the withdrawal of subsidies on basic consumer items coupled with continuing unemployment and hardship imposed by the war had a negative impact on the poor.[42] Confronted with civil unrest and strikes, the government incorporated a social component into the structural adjustment package in 1989 to ameliorate its effects, changing the name to the Economic and Social Recovery Program (ESRP). These additions included a commitment to alleviate poverty through promoting employment, improving essential services such as health, education, and water, and guaranteeing at least a minimum income to the poorest in society. At the same time, the ESRP pledged to reduce the deficit, restore commercial networks, increase exports, prioritize the commercial and family sectors, and raise productivity in order to achieve self-sufficiency.[43]

In conjunction with laying the foundation for a market economy, the government decided to attract private investment and to sell state firms to the private sector. The process began slowly. After several years of poor output and reports of corruption, absenteeism, and mismanagement of state-owned assets, the government expressed a new appreciation at the Fourth FRELIMO Congress in 1983 of the role that the private sector could play in the development of Mozambique. It stated that "In agriculture and in industry, the private sector must contribute significantly towards supplying the people, increasing exports and developing the economy."[44] Further, the government passed a law on foreign investment in 1984; subsequent laws elaborated the conditions under which national and foreign investment could take place. However, substantial privatization occurred only with the peace accord in 1992: over half of the privatizations have taken place in the last six years.

The government has privatized approximately 840 companies out of 1,248 state companies as of the end of 1997. Agriculture and agro-industries (162 companies sold) and industry, commerce, and tourism sectors (434) account for the majority of companies privatized; construction (136) and transport (64) follow. Approximately 70 percent of the total investment, including new projects, is also in the agricultural and industrial sectors. Total pledged investment from 1985 to 1998 is around US$4 billion. Approved investment in 1997–98 is about $2.5 billion: the ongoing construction of an aluminum smelting plant outside Maputo accounts for much of this figure.[45]

Foreign investment accounts for the majority of the total investment. The sectors that nationals and foreigners are investing in do not vary significantly, but foreigners are concentrating on large-scale projects in key areas such as industry, mineral resources, and agriculture. The top three countries responsible for the majority of foreign investment are South Africa, Portugal, and Great Britain. South African investors have just started construction on one of the largest investments ever in Mozambique, a $1.3 billion aluminum smelting plant outside of Maputo. Additionally, South Africa has pledged around $100 million for 179 projects mostly in the south of Mozambique. While restrictions on capital export from South Africa may temper large investments,[46] South Africans are clearly interested in Mozambique's industrial, agricultural, tourist, and hotel sectors, and this interest is expected to continue.[47]

The Portuguese dominate the recently privatized banking sector and have large investments in the agricultural and industrial sectors. One Portuguese project is worth $25 million and entailed the purchase of Cimentos de Moçambique (Mozambique Cement) by CIMPOR, a Portuguese company. CIMPOR's bid won out over six other bids submitted by potential investors from South Africa, Portugal, Italy, and Norway. This company has three factories located in Maputo, Sofala, and Nampula provinces, and all three had completely stopped work at the time of purchase. When they are rehabilitated (at a cost of $96 million), they will supply most of the cement for the country.[48] Finally, the multi-national company Lonrho has provided most of the British investment. It operates in five provinces of Mozambique and has investments in coal and gold mining operations, hotels, air charter services, and agricultural enterprises. It also owns and controls the oil pipeline running from Beira to Zimbabwe.[49]

Domestic investors have also responded to the state's privatization initiative. The majority of the privatized companies are small and medium companies, and 90 percent of firms have been sold to nationals.[50] Five groups make up national capital. First, there are a few large companies such as Grupo do Madal, João Ferreira dos Santos (JFS), and Grupo Entreposto, which have historical roots in Mozambique. They are former colonial concessionary companies that remained after independence and have managed to recover and expand most of their holdings in the past few years. Although in some cases their directors are Portuguese and they have investments in Portugal, the government and their management consider them Mozambican. The justification for calling them Mozambican companies seems to be partly legal, partly numerical, and partly nostalgic. At the time of independence, these companies had the bulk of their capital in Mozambique. They were legally registered in Mozambique, and they were not subsidiaries of larger companies in Portugal. Any investments they had, or now have, in Portugal came as a result of their growth in Mozambique during the 1960s, not the other way around. Second, because the majority of their capital was in Mozambique and not Portugal at the time of independence, these companies decided to stay through the difficult period of state intervention. Their loyalty appears to have been rewarded. Today, JFS, Entreposto, and Madal are the largest national companies in Mozambique. They have considerable investments in Mozambique and are considerably diversified, but with privatization they also participate jointly with the government in several large undertakings.

Grupo do Madal, whose base is in Zambezia province, has been in Mozambique since the nineteenth century. It was one of the largest copra-producing concessions during the 1940s, making huge profits on the sale of copra to neutral countries during World War II.[51] It also expanded into cattle, tea, and timber by independence. Presently, it is engaged in joint ventures with the government in these same agricultural and agro-export enterprises as well as in mining.[52]

In the case of JFS, the state intervened in some of its companies following independence, but after 1986 began to reward JFS for its "loyalty" by giving it the options on state land that was going to be privatized. The current interests of JFS include sisal, rice, cotton, and tobacco production, industrial processing, marketing, and import/export trade. It wholly owns six companies, is a shareholder in several others, and is engaged in joint ventures with the state to produce tobacco, cotton, and other products throughout Mozambique.[53]

As for Grupo Entreposto, it was formed in the 1940s, and its major shareholders were the Mozambique Company, an old concessionary company dating from the nineteenth century, and the National Cotton Company, a large cotton concession in Manica and Sofala. It had industrial, commercial, and agricultural concerns throughout Mozambique by the 1960s. In 1968, it began to invest in Portugal and presently controls shares in twenty-five companies in Portugal in the auto industry and food distribution sectors. It also has investments in Spain and Brazil. Like JFS, it survived the nationalization period, and like JFS it has begun to diversify its investments in Mozambique. The company is now involved in timber, cotton, and cashew processing and the import-export trade. Alone and in association with the state, it participates in around eighteen companies in Mozambique.[54]

In addition to these very large national companies, the second group of national capitalists to emerge are made up largely of "Indians." These are actually second- and third-generation descendants of migrants from India, Pakistan, and several Arab countries. While they have links to families and firms outside of Mozambique, they hold Mozambican passports and consider themselves Mozambican. They are concentrated in the commercial sector, engaging in either import/export or trading networks in the rural areas. Several of the larger companies have expanded into industry and agriculture. For example, Grupo AGT, based in the north of the country, is the parent company for a number of different industrial, agricultural, and commercial operations controlled by the Gafar brothers. At the core of the firm is a trading company founded by Abdul Gani Tayob (the Gafars' grandfather) who came to Mozambique from British India in 1908. Now the firm has expanded into six of the country's ten provinces and has investments in cashew processing, salt extraction, food and beverages, livestock production, cotton, and cashew growing.[55]

Another Indian firm, Armazéns Hassam Nurmamade (ARNUR), began in 1938 and now trades agricultural, industrial, and construction products throughout the country. It operates in Niassa, has an office in Maputo, and works with associates in Portugal. It owns warehouses and purchases excess food from peasantry. It began to expand into cashew purchases in Nampula province in 1984 and Niassa province in 1991. Following the passage of legislation in 1993 that offered tax breaks for investment in less-developed provinces, ARNUR began to engage in agricultural production of beans and maize in Niassa province.[56]

The bulk of Indian companies are engaged in the commercial wholesale and retail sector, exporting and importing goods for urban and rural consumption. Smaller Indian traders go between Maputo in the south and Pemba in the north, to trade clothes, kitchen utensils, soap, oil, and other consumer items. Throughout the country they are mainly importers, exporters, and shopkeepers.

Third, Mozambique has its own version of "black empowerment"— the attempt to encourage black business interests that has become so popular in South Africa. Black Mozambicans are forming banks, appearing on boards, managing companies, and owning factories. They are shopkeepers, retail traders, industrialists, agricultural producers, and concessionaires. Some such as Egas Mussanhene, the president of the cooperative bank, CREDICOOP, or Americo Magaia, the director of FACIM (Mozambique's international trade fair) and a shareholder in a textile mill, have economics degrees, extensive business experience, and a genuine interest in running companies. Others are often front persons for foreign companies who want a Mozambican to make contacts for them. The vast majority, however, are neither high profile, well educated, nor fortunate enough to link up with a foreign company. Instead, they run small businesses, often in the informal sector, or small farms and marketing cooperatives in the rural areas. They depend on the market and are subject to its vicissitudes, but often they are overlooked in the literature on privatization.[57]

In spite of extensive privatization, the Mozambican state is still quite involved in the economy; thus these three groups have fashioned links with the state and rely on state officials for advice and special treatment. The larger companies also are involved in joint ventures with the state. But they have their own capital base and can and often do function independently of the state. This is not the case for two other groups who owe their existence to patronage and clientelistic networks. One group consists of many former and current national government members, local FRELIMO party officials, administrators, and supporters who have acquired companies and land. After a 1989 decree lifted restrictions on employing workers and owning businesses by FRELIMO members, the party's supporters have engaged in landgrabbing and industrial investment. In Gaza province, government officials at the district and provincial levels have benefited from the division of the CAIL state farm. Similarly, land in Sofala province was distributed not only to small producers but also to large commercial and agricultural interests and government officials. The former governor of Sofala is alleged to have 200 hectares in a cotton scheme near Búzi.[58] As far north as Cabo Delgado also, officials have allocated plots to themselves in the N'guri irrigation scheme on the Mueda plateau, while members of the military have received titles to "military warehouses, garages, and machine shops."[59]

Moreover, the current prime minister, Pascoal Mocumbi, owns shares in the Companhia Industrial de Matola, a large flour mill. He is on the board of directors of Lafinanciére Mozambique, one of four Mozambican companies to acquire a total share of 11 percent in the new company, which is a joint venture between the state (45 percent), Grupo Namib (a South African concern with 44 percent), and Lafinanciére. Lafinanciére engages in activities that benefit Promove, a project that helps former FRELIMO combatants.[60] Another member of the government, Armando Guebuza, who is the former transport minister and now the head of FRELIMO in the assembly, has invested in a company in Maputo. Mario Machungo, now the president of one of the largest private banks in Mozambique, held many ministerial portfolios from independence until his resignation in 1994. He is still a loyal member of the FRELIMO party. Moreover, from the provincial to the local level, governors as well as village administrators are receiving land grants as gifts. Some FRELIMO supporters and government officials have acquired these enterprises because of their connections and not necessarily because they have technical expertise.[61]

We do not know the full extent of investment by party and government members nor where they get the money to invest. One newspaper editorial claimed that civil servants are "using the taxes paid by the productive sector as the financial basis of their own businesses which, by and large, imply growing levels of extortion from the productive sector."[62] Moreover, although a 1990 law requires ministers to declare their assets to the minister of state administration, the minister is not required to make the information public. "Asked how members of the public could denounce corruption on the part of top officials, if they had no access to the lists of assets, Gamito (the former minister of state administration) replied, "'I have no idea. I don't know'."[63] One thing is certain, though: FRELIMO members are becoming part of the elite that they are creating.

The final group consists of the management of former state-owned enterprises who are now the private owners. In some cases, this is positive because the company may have been run well during the period of state ownership and the old management has experience. This is the case with Enacomo. It is a former state trading company that was privatized in 1993. Created by the state in 1976, it distributes goods all over the country and also is involved in importing and exporting commodities. It handled 50 percent of Mozambique's export earnings in 1982. Its new owners include the former marketing director who worked for the state for eighteen years, Kekobad Patel, who bought 30 percent of the company along with other members of the staff when the government decided to privatize it. As an article has claimed, "Enacomo's destiny is largely in the hands of those who formerly ran it for the government."[64] Yet many people are critical of the policy of selling state enterprises to the management because in many instances these same people ruined the company. For example, in Gaza, the former managers of the state farm there have benefited from the partition of the bankrupt CAIL state farm into smaller pieces.[65]

The rapid pace and large scope of the privatizations in Mozambique since 1992 have prompted the World Bank to call the undertaking "one of the most successful in Africa," but it is important to evaluate privatization within the context of the broader economic and political changes in Mozambique. From a macro-economic perspective, there are certainly some encouraging signs of recovery in Mozambique, but whether these can be attributed to structural adjustment, to the end of war, or to global forces is difficult to say. After soaring inflation rates in the early 1990s, inflation slowed to 4.3 percent in 1997. The Mozambican metical has stabilized too.[66] Until early 2000, favorable weather conditions have aided the growth of the agricultural sector, which saw a 9 percent rise in 1996 and continued expansion through 1999. With the revival of commercial networks, legal and illegal trade in the formal and informal sectors of rural and urban markets have increased dramatically. Overall, growth rates have averaged around 8 percent between 1993 and 1999. Some of the growth is related to recovery from the war, and until the floods in early 2000, it was expected to exceed 5 percent for the immediate future.[67]

Enormous obstacles also remain. Mozambique's external debt is still around $5½ billion.[68] The country has a severe trade deficit, with exports running about one-quarter of the value of imports. There is a $700 million deficit in the balance of payments, and 50 percent of the budget comes from donors.[69] Output has still not approximated pre-independence levels, and Mozambique is considered the poorest country in the world.[70] The Mozambican economy must still absorb hundreds of thousands of returnees—those who left for other parts of Mozambique or neighboring countries during the war—and gold miners who have lost jobs in South Africa owing to the restructuring there.[71] Furthermore, the privatization process is uneven and its effect is distorted. Most existing and proposed investment is centered in the Maputo-Matola-Machava area in the south, while areas in the north remain neglected. Social differentiation between urban and rural areas, between the elites and the poorest sectors of society, is widening. Foreigners, large capital concerns, and those tied to the government are securing the prime businesses in agriculture and industry, while Mozambican workers and smallholders may lose their jobs or their land. Trade liberalization has also brought hardships to firms in sectors as diverse as textiles and cashew processing. These firms cannot compete effectively against more modern, cost-efficient companies in other countries. Some companies have collapsed, while others run a continual deficit.[72] Plant closures, job losses, corruption, land conflicts, and environmental destruction—these too are aspects of the economic change that is now taking place in Mozambique.[73]

Democracy from Above, Tradition from Below?

At the same time that Mozambique is undergoing substantial shifts in its economic approach, political changes are under way. Mozambique held its first multiparty elections in October of 1994, municipal elections in thirty-three cities in June of 1998, and national elections again in December 1999. There are vibrant national and international non-government organizations (NGOs) active in almost every realm of society, from the health sector to the green zones around Maputo, Beira, and Nampula. However, while several democratic structures are in place, it is not clear that they are fulfilling the expectations of the electorate.

With the 1992 peace accord, the Mozambique government agreed to hold democratic elections. Elections for president and the Assembly of the Republic took place in October 1994 under the supervision of the United Nations and National Elections Commission. From 1992 to 1994, the United Nations oversaw both the demobilization of FRELIMO and RENAMO, the creation of a new army, as well as the staging of elections. The success of the UN operation in Mozambique has been contrasted sharply with its failure in Angola around the same period. The success can be attributed both to UN actions and to the specific conditions accompanying peace in Mozambique. The United Nations established a stronger, earlier presence in Mozambique than in Angola and poured millions of dollars into the transition process, not all of which was used productively and honestly.[74] Both RENAMO and FRELIMO had at least as many differences between them as UNITA and the MPLA in Angola. Yet both parties lacked the independent financial and organizational strength of those in Angola, and both were extremely reluctant to return to the battlefield. Divisions within FRELIMO and RENAMO allowed compromises to emerge on key issues regarding demobilization, the combined army, and the electoral process. Popular will to secure peace and participate in elections also played a large role.

Even though both parties effectively negotiated a peace accord and continued to work together on the National Elections Commission, the electoral process nearly did not reach a successful conclusion. Throughout the campaign, both sides engaged in intimidatory tactics against the other side.[75] Moreover, Afonso Dhlakama, the leader of RENAMO, repeatedly threatened to withdraw from the process unless he was paid more money.[76] On the eve of the elections, Dhlakama exasperated everyone by boycotting them. Fortunately, the remoteness of many rural areas and the use of obsolete radio transmitters to convey the message meant that many people did not hear that RENAMO had withdrawn. By the time negotiations brought RENAMO back into the process, people had already voted.

To identify those who were eligible to vote, the National Elections Commission hosted a registration campaign several months before the elections. Everyone age eighteen and over was allowed to vote. Voting took place at over 7,500 polling stations across the country over a three-day period. There were twelve candidates competing for the presidency, and twelve parties and two coalitions running for office in the Assembly of the Republic. Voters were given two ballot papers and instructed to make an "X" or place a fingerprint next to the candidate of their choice.[77]

The Mozambican election had a high level of participation, with approximately 87.8 percent of registered voters declaring their choice.[78] These included the literate as well as the illiterate, urban versus rural inhabitants, men and women. To educate voters about the electoral process, the radio, newspapers, churches, and other civic organizations conducted information sessions throughout the country in the months leading up to the elections. According to a number of focus groups that were organized to gauge voters' knowledge and opinions of the electoral process, the voter education campaigns were largely successful in explaining the mechanics of voting: where and when to vote and the number of ballots to be used. Moreover, voters understood the meaning of the secret ballot, although they had difficulty accepting that blind people could rely on a trusted friend or relative to mark the ballot for them.[79]

In spite of some irregularities, the United Nations declared the elections "free and fair" and validated the outcome.[80] Joaquim Chissano of the FRELIMO party captured the presidency with 53.5 percent vote in comparison with Dhlakama's 33.7 percent. However, RENAMO made a strong showing in the parliament by capturing half of the provinces in the country. These results gave RENAMO 119 assembly seats, only 10 fewer than FRELIMO. A third party, the Democratic Union, captured 9 seats, possibly because its placement on the parliamentary ballot was the same as that of Chissano on the presidential ballot, which confused some voters. FRELIMO basically captured the urban areas, the southern provinces, and its traditional stronghold in the north, Cabo Delgado, while RENAMO captured the bulk of the central and northern provinces of the country. In spite of RENAMO's strong showing, the 1990 constitution gave the ruling party the power to appoint all provincial governors; thus FRELIMO appointed the governors of even the provinces that RENAMO won.

By a minimum of criteria, Mozambique is now a democratic country. It has had multi-party elections, and prior to those elections political parties were allowed to organize and campaign more or less freely. Citizens enjoy the right to free speech, and journals and newspapers of every political persuasion proliferate—at least in the capital. There is an active and outspoken broadcast, print, fax, and even e-mail media to keep people informed of political developments. But at the end of the day the meaning of democracy is not that clear. As American college students sometimes do, voters in Mozambique equated the 1994 elections with the guarantee of all sorts of rights and privileges. When participants in various focus groups were asked what they thought elections would bring, they responded that elections would bring peace, jobs, and the free market; the elections would confer rights to land and restore "lost dignity." Furthermore, by bringing peace, elections would also eliminate hunger. According to focus group participants: "We made the war and God punished us with drought, which causes hunger. Elections will bring rain, and water will wash the blood of our brothers spread over our land. Then we will be able to cultivate our tillage and we will no longer starve."[81]

In addition to treating the electoral process as some kind of panacea for all the misfortunes that affected Mozambique, voters were also confused about the roles of the different national democratic institutions. For example, many voters were unclear about the responsibilities of the president versus the parliament and had very different expectations of the roles they should play.[82] Moreover, subsequent focus groups conducted several years after the 1994 elections suggest that a number of conditions necessary for a democratic culture to operate do not exist. Participants noted that corruption and the lack of regard for basic human rights continued, and questioned how a democracy could operate under those conditions. Voters also were not sure about their or the government's rights and responsibilities.[83] Additionally, they held high expectations about the capacity of their representatives to solve specific problems in their communities. Because the scope of the community's problems (e.g., more schools, hospitals, social services) exceeded the ability of the representative to resolve them, voters were invariably disappointed with their deputies. As one student in Chokwe remarked, "They listen to our problems, but they don't resolve them."[84] Of course, voters in countries with long histories of institutionalized democratic procedures have expressed the same exasperation. The difference in Mozambique is that democracy is not yet institutionalized. There is as yet no conviction that democracy is the "best" system, and thus the possibility of adopting another political system always exists if this one does not deliver.

Unfortunately, the 1999 elections offered no certain guide to democracy's future in Mozambique. Although most participants agreed that voting procedures were "free and fair," the legitimacy of the outcome was compromised by a lack of transparency in the tabulation of votes. In the Assembly of the Republic and especially in the presidential race, FRELIMO scored a narrow victory over RENAMO, but the high percentage of votes that were declared invalid prompted the press and RENAMO to demand a recount. The Supreme Court's decision to reject RENAMO's request for a recount followed the letter of the law, but left both the opposition and several observers disillusioned with the process. RENAMO members further contributed to a general feeling of disappointment by refusing to attend President Chissano's inauguration ceremony and by threatening to boycott the first sitting of the new parliament. In the end the opposition took its seats, but the tension and distrust between the two parties is evident.[85]

Further, torrential rains in the southern part of the country have followed the election result. Widespread flooding has dislodged land mines, killed hundreds of people, and displaced approximately one million residents. The coincidence of a highly contested election with heavy rains might lead some citizens to associate democracy with hardship, rather than with prosperity or dignity, as they did in the 1994 elections. Anxiety about the democratic process could undermine stability as much as unmet expectations. In the present environment of uncertainty and tragedy, the Mozambican government must proceed very carefully. Political mistakes at this juncture could prove costly.

While national elections decided the presidency and the Assembly of the Republic, they have left unclear the means of representation at the local level. One of RENAMO's central demands during the peace negotiations was the recognition of chiefs and other holders of customary power. Part pre-colonial, part colonial invention, chiefs were considered the lowest rung of the administrative ladder during the colonial period, and correspondingly, their reputation varied enormously across the country at independence. Many viewed them as collaborators with colonial officialdom in some parts of the south. In several central and northern provinces, however, many rural people saw chiefs as legitimate representatives, intermediaries who brokered the demands of the colonial state. FRELIMO denounced them as "obscurantist" after coming to power and officially eliminated them. In practice, however, as conditions worsened throughout the 1980s, local compromises between FRELIMO officials and important chiefs sometimes occurred, and in other cases local communities clandestinely supported chiefs and other holders of customary power, seeing in them a possible means to increase security and gain access to resources. Capitalizing on chiefs' resentment at their official condemnation, RENAMO used chiefs as a springboard to increase power and influence in some areas.[86] Faced with mounting pressure, FRELIMO decided to re-recognize "traditional authorities" in the 1990 constitution and agreed to re-assign them a role at the local level.

But over the last decade, the status of chiefs and other holders of customary authority has remained deliberately ambiguous. Following their re-recognition, chiefs around the country were told to "do the things they did before," and in several provinces they are doing just that. For example, in Nampula, local government administrators have contacted chiefs to adjudicate land conflicts, settle domestic disputes, and disseminate information about agricultural extension services or weather conditions. Private agro-export companies have also begun to rely on customary authorities to encourage cotton production.[87]

The national government is reluctant to go beyond the informal, ad hoc arrangements that have been concocted at the local level. While the 1994 Municipalities Law made references to an expanded role for "traditional authorities," the 1997 Municipalities Law that replaced it makes only a brief mention of "customary authorities."[88] Moreover, the hotly debated land law passed in July of 1997 contains only a few watered-down references to "customary norms and practices" that are to guide the allocation of land, and makes only indirect references to "traditional authorities." In June of 1998, municipal elections occurred in only thirty-three of the largest cities and towns, while no elections took place at the lowest administrative level. Thus, because the status of "traditional authorities" remains ambiguous, no standardized rules govern their selection process, no procedures of accountability direct their behavior, and they lack official power to act as interlocutors for their communities. In the interim, customary authorities are relying on a flawed colonial model as their guide for "governing" their communities.[89] The disjunction between the structures of representation at the local level and those at the national level remains as one of the central unresolved political issues in the country today.

Regional Stability and Integration

Much of what will transpire in Mozambique will depend on what goes on in the region and indeed in the world. Mozambique (especially southern Mozambique) is increasingly connected to South Africa, has joined the Commonwealth, and is improving its links with other countries of the Southern African Development Coordination Conference (SADCC). Greater regional integration means the greater use of Mozambique's transport networks by Zimbabwe, South Africa, and Malawi. Mozambique also supplies electricity from the Cahora Bassa Dam to South Africa and will be a key player in the construction of an electricity grid for Southern Africa. It offers potential development opportunities for regional and global investors in agro-export, industry, mining, and tourism. In addition, although it has shed its Eastern European connections, Mozambique is firmly in the orbit of Western powers and their representative institutions—the IMF, the World Bank, and Western donors. Philosophically and practically, it has embraced the Western values of democracy and the free market.

Yet, these are risky choices. Greater regionalization and globalization bring potential difficulties. Already there is concern about the loss of sovereignty as foreign investors acquire prime agricultural land and dominate key industries. For example, small Mozambican producers in Niassa province have criticized the governmental decision to allocate land there to white South African farmers. These concerns are as much political and cultural as they are economic. Food riots in Zimbabwe and student protests over university fees in South Africa are watched closely by Mozambicans of all political persuasions for their possible applicability and ramifications in this country. Moreover, even in the cultural arena, some observers have noted the growing Muslim influence in the country and have expressed fears that the Sudan may become quite influential.[90]

Challenges and Hopes Ahead

Looking at Mozambique today, it is difficult to encounter the euphoria and excitement that was present those first few years after independence. From a material perspective, conditions are not much better than they were at independence, and in some cases they are significantly worse. Much of the infrastructure that FRELIMO inherited was destroyed either by departing settlers or a senseless war. Unfortunate weather conditions, economic insecurity, and political instability have left many producers as impoverished as before. Flawed socialist policies embittered and disillusioned large sections of the population. Structural adjustment has exacerbated, not alleviated, social differentiation and worsened, not improved, infant mortality rates, educational levels, and other social indices. Privatization and liberalization have introduced new pressures and burdens for the country to overcome. But perhaps the most lasting achievements of a quarter century of independence are intangible rather than material. Liberation created a space for the development of a national identity and spirit. Through independence, women and youth, workers and rural producers found their voices and recovered their dignity. They learned to express and organize themselves, and to articulate their preferences and demands. The fruits of these efforts are evident in the numerous associations that have formed to represent every issue from the interests of children to that of land tenure. They are manifest in the free and critical press, and in the willingness of common citizens to stand up for their rights. They are reflected in the resilience and creativity of local communities. These are the accomplishments that link independence with the millennium, and their legacy will endure.

NOTES

1. J. Saul, *The State and Revolution in Eastern Africa* (New York: Monthly Review Press, 1979), p. 83.

2. A. Lind, *Adult Literacy Lessons and Promises: Mozambican Literacy Campaigns, 1978–1982,* Studies in Comparative and International Education, no. 12 (Stockholm: Institute of International Education, 1988), pp. 42, 46; Mozambique, National Planning Commission (NPC), *Economic Report,* January 1984, p. 26.

3. Mozambique, NPC, *Economic Report,* p. 27; see also A. Isaacman and B. Isaacman, *Mozambique: From Colonialism to Revolution, 1900–1982* (Boulder, Colo.: Westview Press, 1983), p. 139.

4. L. Graham, "The Dilemmas of Managing Transitions in Weak States: The Case of Mozambique," *Public Administration and Development* 13 (1993): 415.

5. Ibid., p. 418.

6. Ibid., p. 415.

7. H. Abrahamsson and A. Nilsson, *Mozambique: The Troubled Transition—From Socialist Construction to Free Market Capitalism* (Atlantic Highlands, N.J.: Zed Books, 1995), p. 56; and L. Caballero, T. Thomsen, and A. Andreasson, *Mozambique: Food and Agriculture Sector,* Rural Development Studies, no. 16 (Uppsala: Swedish University of Agriculture, 1984), p. 36.

8. A. Addison and I. MacDonald, "Rural Livelihoods and Poverty in Mozambique," background document for "The Poverty Reduction Strategy for Mozambique" prepared by the Poverty Alleviation Unit, Ministry of Planning and Finance (February 1995, mimeograph), p. 3.

9. United Nations Research Institute for Social Development, Programme for Strategic and International Security Studies, War Torn Societies Project, "Moçambique: Imagem do País" (Maputo: 5 January 1996), p. 7; and Abrahamsson and Nilsson, *Mozambique: The Troubled Transition,* pp. 126–27.

10. M. Hall and T. Young, *Confronting Leviathan: Mozambique since Independence* (Athens: Ohio University Press, 1997), p. 106.

11. W. Finnegan, *A Complicated War: The Harrowing of Mozambique* (Berkeley: University of California Press, 1992), pp. 91, 104.

12. Hall and Young, *Confronting Leviathan,* p. 114.

13. Abrahamsson and Nilsson, *Mozambique: The Troubled Transition,* p. 104; note that oil prices rose so high that oil went from 6.3 percent of the value of imports in 1973 to 25.5 percent of import values by 1982.

14. S. Kyle, "Economic Reform and Armed Conflict in Mozambique," *World Development* 19, no. 6 (1991): 638.

15. M. Bowen, "Socialist Transitions: Policy Reforms and Peasant Producers in Mozambique," in T. Bassett and D. Crumney, eds., *Land in African Agrarian Systems* (Madison: University of Wisconsin Press, 1993), p. 332, and M. A. Pitcher, "Recreating Colonialism or Reconstructing the State? Privatisation and Politics in Mozambique," *Journal of Southern African Studies* 22, no. 1 (March 1996): 57–58.

16. Caballero, Thomsen, and Andreasson, *Mozambique,* p. 75.

17. J. Barker, "Gaps in the Debates about Agriculture in Senegal, Tanzania and Mozambique," *World Development* 13, no. 1 (1985): 69.

18. B. Egero, *Mozambique: A Dream Undone—The Political Economy of Democracy, 1975–84* (Uppsala: Scandinavian Institute of African Studies, 1990), p. 188.

19. For a general discussion of some of the rural policies, see A. Casal, "A Crise da Produção Familiar e as Aldeias Comunais em Moçambique," *Revista Internacional de Estudos Africanos* 8–9 (January/December 1988): 157–91. FRELIMO efforts and local responses varied from province to province; for Cabo Delgado, the most northern province, see Y. Adam, "Mueda, 1917–1990: Resistência, Colonialismo, Libertação e Desenvolvimento," *Arquivo* 14 (October 1993): 44–76; H. West, "'This Neighbor Is Not My Uncle!': Changing Relations of Power and Authority on Mueda Plateau," *Journal of Southern African Studies* 24, no. 1 (March 1998): 156–57. West argues that villagers on the Mueda plateau in northern Cabo Delgado remained loyal to FRELIMO but still managed to sustain former settlement patterns and customary relations of authority within the communal villages. For efforts and responses in Nampula, see C. Geffray, *A causa*

das armas: Antropologia da guerra contemporanea em Moçambique (Oporto: Ediçoes Afrontamento, 1991), pp. 36–39, 48, 133; M. A. Pitcher, "Disruption without Transformation: Agrarian Relations and Livelihoods in Nampula Province, 1975–1995," *Journal of Southern African Studies* 24, no. 1 (March 1998): 129. In Tete, see J. Coelho, "State Resettlement Policies in Post-Colonial Rural Mozambique: The Impact of the Communal Village Programme on Tete Province, 1977–1982," *Journal of Southern African Studies* 24, no. 1 (March 1998): 61–91; and in Manica province, see J. Alexander, "The Local State in Post-War Mozambique: Political Practice and Ideas about Authority," *Africa* 67, no. 1 (1997): 4–5. Even in the south where FRELIMO was considered strong, resistance emerged, see J. McGregor, "Violence and Social Change in a Border Economy: War in the Maputo Hinterland, 1984–1992," *Journal of Southern African Studies* 24, no. 1 (March 1998): 41–47.

20. Abrahamsson and Nilsson, *Mozambique: The Troubled Transition*, p. 120.

21. W. Minter, *Apartheid's Contras: An Inquiry into the Roots of War in Angola and Mozambique* (Atlantic Highlands, N.J.: Zed Books, 1994), p. 32.

22. M. Murray, *South Africa: Time of Agony, Time of Destiny* (New York: Verso, 1987), pp. 48–50.

23. Minter, *Apartheid's Contras*, p. 41.

24. H. Abrahamsson, *Seizing the Opportunity: Power and Powerlessness in a Changing World Order—The Case of Mozambique* (Gothenburg: PADRIGU, 1997), p. 209.

25. Minter, *Apartheid's Contras*, pp. 186–88.

26. C. Manning, "Constructing Opposition in Mozambique: Renamo as Political Party," *Journal of Southern African Studies* 24, no. 1 (March 1998): 163, 168.

27. A. Vines, *Renamo: Terrorism in Mozambique* (Atlantic Highlands, N.J.: Zed Books, 1991), p. 30.

28. Vines, *Renamo*, pp. 80–87.

29. Geffray, *A causa das armas*.

30. Ibid., chap. 2–3.

31. J. McGregor, "Violence and Social Change," p. 42. Some of the criticisms and responses to Geffray can be found in B. O'Laughlin, "Interpretations Matter: Evaluating the War in Mozambique," *Southern Africa Report* 7, no. 3 (January 1992); and "A Base Social da Guerra em Moçambique," *Estudos Moçambicanos* 10 (1992): 107–42; J. Saul, *Recolonization and Resistance in Southern Africa in the 1990s* (Trenton, N.J.: Africa World Press, 1993); A. Dinerman, "In Search of Mozambique: The Imaginings of Christian Geffray in *La Cause des Armes au Mozambique Anthropologie d'une Guerre Civile*," *Journal of Southern African Studies* 20, no. 4 (December 1994): 569–86.

32. See, for example, O. Roesch, "Renamo and the Peasantry: A View from Gaza," *Southern Africa Report*, December 1990, pp. 21–25; Vines, *Renamo*; K. Wilson, "Cults of Violence and Counter-Violence in Mozambique," *Journal of Southern African Studies* 18, no. 3 (1992); M. Chingono, *The State, Violence and Development* (Aldershot: Avebury, 1996); Alexander, "Local State"; C. Manning, "Democratic Transition in Mozambique, 1992–1995: Beginning at the End?" (Ph.D. diss., University of California, Berkeley, 1997), chap. 4–6 and app. 1; Hall and Young, *Confronting Leviathan*, chap. 7; C. Nordstrom, *A Different Kind of War Story* (Philadelphia: University of Pennsylvania Press, 1997), chap. 3; and articles by J. McGregor, C. Manning, and M. A. Pitcher in the special issue on Mozambique, *Journal of Southern African Studies* 24, no. 1 (March 1998), and K. Wilson, personal communication with regard to Tete, 8 May 1998.

33. Alexander, "Local State," pp. 9–11.

34. Vines, "'No Democracy without Money': The Road to Peace in Mozambique (1982–1992)," CIIR briefing paper, April 1994, pp. 14–17; S. Chan and M. Venancio, *War and Peace in Mozambique* (New York: St. Martin's Press, 1998), chap. 1–2.

35. J. Ciment, *Angola and Mozambique: Post-Colonial Wars in Southern Africa* (New York: Facts on File, 1997), pp. 90–91; S. Chan and M. Venancio, *War and Peace,* chap. 3.

36. C. Alden and M. Simpson, "Mozambique: A Delicate Peace," *Journal of Modern African Studies* 31, no. 1 (1993): 88–89.

37. Vines, *No Democracy,* p. 29.

38. Nordstrom, *Different Kind,* chap. 7.

39. Vines, "Disarmament in Mozambique," pp. 191–205, and J. Schafer, "'A Baby Who Does Not Cry Will Not Be Suckled': AMODEG and the Reintegration of Demobilised Soldiers," *Journal of Southern African Studies* 24, no. 1 (March 1998): 207–22.

40. AWEPA, *Mozambique Peace Process Bulletin,* selected issues, 1993–94.

41. Kyle," Economic Reform," p. 644; Abrahamsson and Nilsson, *Mozambique: The Troubled Transition,* p. 112.

42. For a description of structural adjustment and its impact, see J. Marshall, "Structural Adjustment and Social Policy in Mozambique," *ROAPE* 47 (1990): 28–43; K. Hermele, *Mozambican Crossroads: Economics and Politics in the Era of Structural Adjustment* (Bergen: Chr Michelsen Institute, 1990), pp. 28–43; J. Hanlon, *Mozambique: Who Calls the Shots?* (Bloomington: Indiana University Press, 1991), pp. 145–66; M. Bowen, "Beyond Reform: Adjustment and Political Power in Contemporary Mozambique," *Journal of Modern African Studies* 30, no. 2 (1992): 266–67; J. Oppenheimer, "Cooperação para o desenvolvimento no contexto do ajustamento estrutural e da guerra: O caso de Moçambique," *Revista Internacional de Estudos Africanos* 16–17 (1992–94): 171–207.

43. Mozambique, Gabinete de Promoção de Investimento Estrangeiro (GPIE-Office for Foreign Investment Promotion), *Investor's Guide to Mozambique* (Maputo: GPIE, 1992), pp. 27–28; Kyle, "Economic Reform," pp. 637–49; V. Tickner, "Structural Adjustment and Agricultural Pricing in Mozambique," *ROAPE* 53 (1992): 25–42; Oppenheimer, "Cooperação para o desenvolvimento," pp. 197–200.

44. FRELIMO Party, *Frelimo Party Programme and Statutes,* IV FRELIMO Party Congress (Maputo: FRELIMO Party, 1983), p. 18.

45. Mozambique, Unidade Técnica para a Reestruturação de Empresas (UTRE-Technical Unit for Enterprise Restructuring), "Privatisation in Mozambique," *UTRE Information Bulletin,* no. 5 (March 1998): 4–6; Mozambique, Centro de Promoção de Investimentos (CPI-Investment Promotion Centre), "Situação de projectos autorizados," 15 January 1998, p. 5. The rest of this section is based on research I conducted for a forthcoming book on privatization in Mozambique.

46. S. Nhantumbo, "Finance Minister Views Economy, Foreign Investment," *Notícias,* 24 May 1994, in U.S. Foreign Broadcast Information Service, *Daily Report. Sub-Saharan Africa* (Washington, D.C.: The Service), 15 June 1994, p. 12.

47. C. Morna, "Mozambique," *Institutional Investor,* sponsored section (n.d.), p. 16; Mozambique, CPI, "Situação de investimento autorizado em 1998," Table 5.

48. T. Angelo, "Nova empresa de cimentos aposta no mercado regional," *Africa Hoje,* ano X, no. 79 (December 1994): 64–65.

49. Hanlon, *Mozambique: Who Calls the Shots?* p. 244; Mozambique, CPI, "Investidores" (15 March 1997, mimeograph).

50. Mozambique, UTRE, "Privatisation in Mozambique," p. 6.

51. L. Vail and L. White, *Capitalism and Colonialism in Mozambique* (London: Heinemann, 1980), p. 256.

52. Rogerio Henriques, Regional Director, Madal Company, interview by Anne Pitcher and Scott Kloeck-Jenson, Quelimane, Mozambique, 21 May 1998.

53. João Ferreira dos Santos, "Brief Presentation of João Ferreira dos Santos Group" (n.p., n.d., mimeograph).

54. "Grupo Entreposto-expanding in Mozambique," *International Review for Chief Executive Officers* (n.p., 1994).

55. "Ikbal Gafar nasceu para ser empresário," Savana, 5 July 1996.

56. "Armazéns Hassam Nurmamade," *Economia,* ano 6, no. 18 (July/August 1993): 49.

57. The material presented here is based on selected newspaper and journal articles from *Savana, Demos, Notícias,* and *Tempo* covering the years 1994–98.

58. G. Myers, J. Eliseu, and E. Nhachungue, "Segurança e conflito em Moçambique. Estudos de caso sobre acesso á terra no período do pós-guerra" (University of Wisconsin and Ministry of Agriculture Land Tenure Center, December 1993), pp. 29, 64, 89.

59. H. West, "Creative Destruction and Sorcery of Construction," *Cahiers d'Etudes Africaines* 147, XXXVII-3 (1997): 687.

60. "CIM privatizada," *Mediafax,* 29 December 1994.

61. "Onde estão os empresários moçambicanos?" *Notícias,* 21 December 1994.

62. "E caríssimo investir em Moçambique," *Mediafax,* 6 July 1995, p. 2.

63. "Ministers' Assets," *Mozambiquefile,* no. 224 (March 1995): 20.

64. Morna, "Mozambique," p. 10.

65. G. Myers, "Competitive Rights, Competitive Claims: Land Access in Post-War Mozambique," *Journal of Southern African Studies* 20, no. 4 (December 1994): 621.

66. Mozambique, "Plano Económico e Social para 1998," September 1997, p. 16.

67. Mozambique, "Plano," p. 6.

68. Banco de Mozambique, *Statistical Bulletin,* ano 5, no. 16 (September 1997), p. 21.

69. Banco de Mozambique, *Statistical Bulletin,* ano 5, no. 16 (September 1997), p. 19, and Abrahamsson, *Seizing the Opportunity,* p. 227.

70. Abrahamsson, *Seizing the Opportunity,* p. 225.

71. J. Head, "Migrant Mine Labour from Mozambique: Employment Prospects and Policy Options in the 1990s," *Journal of Contemporary African Studies* 13, no. 1 (1995): 91–120.

72. For a discussion of the cashew debacle, see J. Hanlon, *Peace without Profit: How the IMF Blocks Rebuilding in Mozambique* (Portsmouth, N.H.: Heinemann, 1996), and the informative article by C. Cramer, "Can Africa Industrialize by Processing Primary Commodities? The Case of Mozambican Cashew Nuts," *World Development* 27, no. 7 (1999): 1247–66. For a discussion of textiles, see B. Langa, "Sul-africanos sustentam indústria de confeccões," *Domingo,* 29 March 1998, pp. 12–13.

73. On the many land conflicts generated by the concessioning and privatization of state assets in agriculture, see the work by Myers, Eliseu, and Nhachungue. For a fascinating account of the gendered aspects of land conflicts and land management, see also H. Gengenbach, "'I'll Bury You in the Border': Women's Land Struggles in Post-War Facazisse (Magude District), Mozambique," *Journal of Southern African Studies* 24, no. 1 (March 1998): 7–36. A. Isaacman relates the harmful environmental effects of

cotton growing in "Historical Amnesia, or, the Logic of Capital Accumulation: Cotton Production in Colonial and Postcolonial Mozambique," *Environment and Planning D: Society and Space* 15 (1997): 757–90. G. Harrison explores the different forms of corruption in "Corruption as 'Boundary Politics': The State, Democratisation, and Mozambique's Unstable Liberalisation," *Third World Quarterly* 20, no. 3 (1999): 537–50.

74. West, "Creative Destruction," p. 692; Vines, "Disarmament in Mozambique."

75. West, "Creative Destruction," p. 690.

76. AWEPA, *Mozambique Peace Process Bulletin,* selected issues, 1993–94.

77. K. Sheldon, "Justice and Reconciliation: A Report from Mozambique's First National Multi-Party Elections," *Democratic Left* 23, no. 1 (January/February 1995): 26.

78. Sheldon, "Justice and Reconciliation," p. 26.

79. Claim/Louis Harris International, "Vota Moçambique," prepared for National Democratic Institute (n.p., September 1994, mimeograph).

80. AWEPA, *Mozambique Peace Process Bulletin,* 14 (February 1995): 4.

81. Claim/Louis Harris International, "Vota Moçambique."

82. Claim/Louis Harris International, "Vota Moçambique."

83. E. Saraiva, "Civic Education: A Report on Focus Group Research in Mozambique," prepared for National Democratic Institute (August 1997), p. 19.

84. Saraiva, "Civic Education," p. 11.

85. C. Manning, personal communication, 10 March 2000; "Dhlakama quer contar tudo de novo," *Metical,* no. 631, 22 December 1999; "Imbróglios Eleitorais," *Metical,* no. 638, 1 January 2000; "Deputies Take Their Seats," Agencia de Informação de Moçambique (AIM-Mozambique Information Agency), e-mail text, 14 January 2000; "Opposition Boycotts Chissano's Investiture," AIM, e-mail text, 15 January 2000.

86. On issues concerning "traditional" authorities, customary practices, and state power, etc., see M. Cahen, "Etat et pouvoir populaire dans le Mozambique indépendent," *Politique Africaine* 19: 36–60; "Le Mozambique: Une nation africaine de langue officielle portugaise?" *Canadian Journal of African Studies* 24, no. 3: 315–47; Geffray, *A causa das armas;* Alexander, "Local State"; Mozambique, Ministério da Administração Estatal, Projeto "Autoridade/Poder Tradicional," "Algumas Considerações sobre a Sociedade Amakhuwa" by I. Lundin (August 1992).

87. M. A. Pitcher, "Recreating Colonialism or Reconstructing the State? Privatisation and Politics in Mozambique," *Journal of Southern African Studies* 22, no. 1 (March 1996): 70–71.

88. The 1994 Municipalities Law was declared unconstitutional.

89. Alexander, "Local State," pp. 18–19. Some customary authorities are even demanding their old colonial uniforms, as I observed in Nampula in 1994 and 1995.

90. *Savana,* 1 August 1997.

PART III.
THEMES

9. Popular Culture in Southern Africa

David B. Coplan

Having successfully passed the temporally arbitrary but culturally popular "end of the millennium,"[1] it appears we may at last spare ourselves further consideration of the differences between "popular" and other discursive but specious qualifiers of the concept *culture* such as "traditional," "folk," "mass," "high," or (my favorite) "capitalist." This merciful change in the terms of the debate around popular culture comes about with the recognition that socio-economic processes labeled "modernization," "(post)industrialization," "urbanization," "social differentiation" (class formation), and even "capitalist expansion" are neither the determinants nor the defining correlates of cultural transmission, stylization, or creativity. Nor, even in Africa, can categorical differences between forms of culture be based any longer on romantic but misconstrued distinctions between organic, autonomous, self-reproducing communities and the individualistic, mobile, class-structured, globalized social arena that results from migration, urbanization, and wage labor. This mythic, totalizing opposition of gemeinschaft and gesellschaft had as its cultural correlate the static dichotomies of the traditional and the modern, the indigenous and the Western, the local and the global. As Barber argues, popular genres can be identified as those that do not so much hybridize as destabilize and consume those stereotypical categories and their opposition altogether.[2] It is these dynamic, anything goes (together) contemporary forms that engage the self-expressiveness of the vast majority of people in Africa today, and that shatter the common misconception that there is somewhere in the West a cultural capital of the global. Indeed, while the majority of southern Africa's dispossessed still look to modernism, not post-modernism, for a post-colonial social narrative,[3] it is in popular genres that people's own reified and essentialized concepts and self-concepts of culture are disputed and falsified in intuitive experience.

The reality, in any event, is that in much of southern Africa it has been well over

DAVID B. COPLAN

a century since any such (implicitly moralizing) substantive dichotomies have borne any relation to the situation on the African ground. Rural people are thoroughly integrated into the market and wage economy even if they are not labor migrants, and in South Africa and Zimbabwe, forced population movements created as well the oxymoronic marginalization and squalor of "rural urbanization." Under the hegemony of forms of European settler colonialism that distinguished southern Africa and Kenya from the rest of sub-Saharan Africa, urban hybridizations transformed, albeit unevenly, rural consciousness and cultural practice. In the towns, rural inflows have remained wellsprings for urban identity politics and cultural self-redefinition and synthesis. While rural-derived styles of urban performance, for example, have been maintained and elaborated by people for whom home (as opposed to residence) will always be somewhere in the countryside, "home" itself may have assumed more an ideological and imaginative than social or geographical location. Even social differentiation, today as much a feature of rural as of urban social landscapes, does not attach itself by way of the putative identification of the "popular" with the (working) "people's" culture. Elites in every sector and community also create, participate in, and identify with forms popularly thought of as popular culture.

Nor can we usefully continue to argue, as have Marxists, over whether popular culture represents the falsification of popular consciousness through the hegemonic transmission of alienating cultural representations in the capitalist or state-sponsored mass media or, mutatis mutandis, the irrepressible simmering up of popular identities and aspirations and the subversion of ideologically dominant expressive regimes. Popular culture is both alienating and subversive and neither, but it is nothing if not the paradoxical product of what Johannes Fabian has recognized as dialogical "moments of freedom."[4] In his remarkable, thoroughly original study of popular theatrical processes in Shaba, (then) Zaire, Fabian addresses his definitional powers more directly to the African predicament: "The kind of performances we find in popular culture have become for the people involved more than ever ways to preserve some self-respect in the face of constant humiliation, and to set the wealth of artistic creativity against an environment of utter poverty. All this is not to be dismissed off-hand as escape from reality; it is realistic praxis under the concrete political and economic conditions that reign."[5]

Critical theorists are quite correct, then, in presuming that popular genres represent more than what Barber terms "the work of local cultural producers speaking to local audiences about pressing concerns, experiences, and struggles."[6] It is vital to our understanding of popular culture in southern Africa that it be seen not only to span but to mutually implicate state-sponsored and other public ideological programs, productions for the commercial culture market, and organic efflorescences of popular consciousness that, in African-American novelist Ishmael Reed's phrase, "Jes' Grew." All of these are imbricated, as local, categorical, national, and transnational expressive forms, in the wider social contradictions and movements in the politics of the modernist post-colony. In southern Africa as elsewhere, popular culture is by any definition born of contestations over consciousness and self-representation, and its protean investments by power appear, transpose, and disappear, Foucault-like, in multiple structural locations. By this token then, local language television and radio serials, re-interpreted American soap operas, folkloric astonishments in city newspapers,[7] religious cults and street preaching, wall paintings, anti-witchcraft movements, "festivals of smuggling" at border markets, political rumor, mythology, and cults of personality, the "beautiful deaths" of celebratory Mozambican funerals, South Africa's kangaroo "people's courts" as well as its Truth and Reconciliation Commission (TRC)—these are all as much popular culture as the region's eclectic musical recording styles and artists.

What must be emphasized strongly as well is that the most widely disseminated and influential forms of popular culture in southern Africa include not only those produced for mass print or broadcast media but also the oral or more properly *aural* popular genres that thrive quite apart from them.[8] True, in industrialized South Africa, television can now claim to be a universally available if not fully dominant national mass cultural medium. As Hall points out, however, TV does not obliterate other media but reconstitutes their uses (and vice versa). Likewise with radio: as the South African government has begun to decentralize its ownership and control, the reality of pluralistic language communities has strongly reinforced that medium's transformation from a national into a regional or local community voice.[9] Further, the broadcast media, whether national or local, are not only located in but help to fertilize and cultivate a landscape of "live popular genres produced by small-scale, localized artisanal methods, and disseminated on a face to face basis."[10] So, for example, any address to Africa's popular literature must begin with the study of the imaginative history of existing, vital aural genres. As Michael Fischer observes, "the infusion of fiction with oral culture, family stories, creates a collective voice of the people; the both historical and eternal quality that comes from shared experience, and of which curers and grandparents are sources.[11] My own extensive analysis of the poetic songs of South Africa's Basotho mineworkers and bar maids brings to the surface just such a self-conscious genre.[12] While these songs are broadcast today over Sesotho-language radio and in "traditional music" programs on television, mine migrants have elaborated and sponsored this form for over a century without these media. Indeed Barber's recent collection foregrounds a range of such irrepressible genres, from the visual arts and bodily adornment on offer in the open-air markets to political cartoons to critical popular song and dance styles to oral poetry and urban political theater.[13]

While recognizing popular culture in southern Africa then, simply stated, as the culture of southern Africans, processes of cultural production remain crucial to participation in popular cultural creation, stylistic elaboration, communication, consumption, and discourse. So if categories and practices of culture are to be qualified as popular, this can only be through an understanding of how categories (forms, genres, styles, instances) of expression are produced, distributed, and consumed; by and for whom, with what resources, under whose direction, within what institutions, against what background of history and cultural memory, constituting what images of self-recognition, questioning what answers, both responding to and creating what conditions.[14] Further, it is crucial to recognize differences in the power available to intervene in the process of cultural production.[15] As Yonah Seleti observes of the mediation of the mass media between the "national" and the "popular," all mass media "take the nation for granted as their audience [and] seek to create a particular national identity based obviously on what they imagine to be the ideal national identity."[16] An example of this ideal is the imagined South African patriotic non-racial sports fan, who supports the national side and local league attentively whether the game be soccer, rugby, or cricket. Set against this, in reality, is lack of support for soccer among whites, lack of interest in cricket among blacks, and rugby as the jealous preserve and secular religion of the Afrikaner (with its English acolytes), scornfully keeping potential black interest at bay. But as Stuart Hall warns of the discourse of nationalism:

> When we constitute an identity which leaves some voices more marginal and leaves some voices out, that which is excluded almost always picks itself up off the floor, gets itself together, and walks around to the back door, breaks a window and comes back in. It comes back in to trouble the fixed, settled, well-ordered structure of who-is-in and who-is-out. Be careful that in that moment of constituting the us we don't forget to hear the them. Who is the them being left out? Who is in the margin? Who is excluded? The excluded aren't going to be excluded all the time! They are going to come back and trouble the way in which we are trying to organize and classify the world.[17]

In practice, "the national" consists of multiple language cultures and registers encoded in distinctive generic forms. These forms range from the implicit rhetorical referencing in ordinary figurative speech, including gossip and humor, to culturally marked genres of poetry, song, and folk narrative, to more inter-cultural, formalized modes of narration such as the dramatistic testimony of the court room or the dialogic recounting of events in public settings, to the models, archetypal images and story forms of print and electronic news media, to post-colonial idioms or genres of popular literature in English, Portuguese, and the indigenous languages. Indeed, in South Africa the interposition of "the colonial language in the indigenous terrain raises issues about English as the lingua franca or the language of the state; the significance of oral cultures and the status of indigenous languages in conditions of modernity are central concerns."[18] In the midst of this, the hegemony of standard English in daily discourse is breaking down due to the new acceptability of both black dialects of South African English and of black "vernaculars," the alternative press and media, popular music, dance, fashion, styles of humor, bodily expression, and implicit culture.[19] Across the old divide, rural and urban working-class Afrikaners (including the "coloured people" of mixed racial descent) are now positively revaluing and historicizing games, cuisine, and styles of folk speech, performance, and sociability that were strongly influenced by Khoisan forebears and other indigenous people among whom they have lived and upon whose labor they depended. It is indeed encouraging that, despite grumbling from the Afrikaans cultural right, with the formal dismantling of apartheid, Afrikaans culture is being liberated from its fitfully hegemonic, racially exclusive governmentality and jostling with renewed creative energy for a place among the other indigenous language cultures of the land. In the cultural *potjiekos* (potluck stew) of Johannesburg, the local music group with the best new name is certainly jazz-fusion virtuoso Paul Hamner's Unofficial Language.

The cultural production of the national is likewise central to self-conscious efforts at "reconciliation and development" in southern Africa. Given the current situation in the region, both these terms are over-burdened, and we might realistically write of "working misunderstandings" rather than reconciliation, reconstruction rather than development. While it is easy enough to see that most such efforts are generating more heat than light, more divisive rhetoric than social vision or consensus, one must sympathize with anxious nation-builders compelled to whistle shrilly in the dark. Today, glancing sidelong south of the equator, Kinshasa braces for a second post-Mobutu coup as the hinterland slips into armed anarchy. Meantime, the city's many world-famous popular musical artists have all relocated to Paris. Angolans seem determined to prove most tragically yet again the subcontinental applicability of the French Luba proverb, *Le pouvoir se mange entier,* "power is eaten whole."[20] In Zambia, the culture of democracy survives among the masses but is rudely violated by those, led ironically by a trade unionist, they latterly brought to power under the banner of the Movement for Multi-Party Democracy(!). Zimbabwe's dictatorship revels in self-congratulation over the many and varied "popular" culture groups it sponsors or promotes, but by this very means keeps watch over and interferes in popular cultural life down to its very grass roots, suppressing any expression or movement that smacks of organic popular self-expression or seeks to operate outside the national culture ideology of the state. Mozambique, recovering from civil war and showing impressive growth rates, has successfully managed to market the rich potential of its southern provinces to foreign corporate investors backed by the World Bank. As significant tourism returns to a Maputo with dreams of one day again resembling Laurenço Marques, perhaps popular music and dance will experience a rebirth already evident in the city's popular literature in Portuguese. For this to happen, in Mozambique as elsewhere in the region, money that might confidently be spent on the consumption of culture must somehow find its way into the pockets of the popular classes, for it is in this way that reconciliation, development, and popular culture are clearly interdependent.

Lesotho, after experimenting hopefully once again with democracy in 1993 after a twenty-three year hiatus, apparently botched the 1998 elections, castrated multi-party politics, invited political chaos, and put itself on course for de jure as well as de facto devolution into South Africa. Fortunately, such political haplessness has less effect on Basotho society than might be the case elsewhere. This is because what happens in the political world of the capital, Maseru, has little meaning or impact on the country's workers and farmers, whose lives are focused on their local homesteads and communities and across the border in South Africa.[21] Then too, the underlying stability of Lesotho beneath the level of the fractured political and military elites is due not a little to *Sesotho,* seen as a people's culture of considerable oral historical purchase and elaboration, focused on the ideology of chieftaincy, national symbols, genres of popular song, dance, and poetry, traditional medicine, initiation schools, popular Christianity, and the imagined continuity of *mekhoa le meetlo ea Basotho,* "Basotho ways and understandings." Swaziland, currently unable to properly face, let alone solve, the crisis of its monarchy, entrenched aristocracy, and governance, may find itself in straits parallel to those of Lesotho sooner rather than later.

Powerful, economically viable South Africa might envy these tiny neighbors, or at least the cohesion and rootedness of their popular national cultures. Post-apartheid society is as racially and culturally divided as its predecessor. Old accusations, resentments, and misunderstandings blend dangerously with disappointed expectations and overblown notions of social and personal entitlement in every region, black/white town, and walk of life. Pre-liberation social gulfs yawn as widely as ever, now exacerbated by the extraordinary rise of a black and brown haute bourgeoisie with little practical empathy with the plight of the poor who make up the vast majority of the population. Quite apart from the world's highest levels of violent crime, intra- and inter-community violence is endemic.

In the Free State, the daily murders of white farm families are ascribed by the government to "simple" criminality, thinly concealing the understandable but deep-seated, mutually destructive popular hatred of white farmers by black rural people who labored under rural apartheid only to be summarily evicted and warehoused in rural slums when basic rights of occupation and employment were legislated. What is needed are changes in popular consciousness on both sides of the fences to bring about a cross-racial community partnership upon the land, without which a democratic government can do little to find a solution. At present, impotent government and security officials can only repeat the empty mantra warning white farmers (of all groups!) not to "take the law into their own hands." Meantime, white farmers can only suspect a black populist political conspiracy to drive them off the land, a conspiracy ignored by a ruling party leadership that may privately share the belief, popular with many Africans, that the "Boer" farmers have asked for what they are getting.

Malice aforethought was no less prevalent in relations among political leaders and brokers in KwaZulu-Natal, as murder became an increasingly important source of employment in the Natal midlands once again in the run-up to the 1999 elections. This time there was a new political actor in the form of the United Democratic Movement (UDM), an aggressive Xhosa/Zulu/Afrikaner alliance attacking the African National Congress (ANC) with the tacit support of Chief Buthelezi's Inkatha Freedom Party. Not new are the politically metaphorical witchcraft accusations of "third [security] force" involvement, accusations to which the national police commissioner has given credence in the most bitterly ironic measure of the post-apartheid security crisis: In order to contain the spiraling political killings in Richmond, Natal, said the commissioner, he was closing the little town's police station and transferring its 150 officers elsewhere. One could say more, but is there the need?

The popular culture of violence in South Africa is not confined to the arenas of political or racial contest, but finds expression in diverse settings. So the featured attractions of hastily marketed tours introducing daring tourists to the "authentic" Soweto include argumentative taverns with their volatile mix of alcohol and amour propre, car hijackers at home, "semi-retired" gangland notables, and disgruntled castaways of the struggle. Returning to the popular violence of the supernatural, stagnant growth and the economic suppression of the majority have made non-metaphorical witchcraft accusations as much a social currency in urban townships as in the rural valleys of Mpumalanga and the Northern Province. Inchoate fears of the malevolence of one's neighbors and associates pervade township life and provide explanations for misfortune and dashed expectations. Up in the northern low veld, power struggles among African independent church movements, local political brokers, and extended family networks have led to hundreds of gruesome burnings and killings of accused witches since 1994, with survivors losing their property and taking refuge in locally reviled "witch villages."

The forms of popular culture, then, in whatever sphere of social action they engage, and whatever cultural authority or reflexive status they may or may not possess, arise, flourish, melt away, and surprisingly re-appear as the conditions for their production and the constitution of their audience are progressively transformed. Witchcraft accusations and the peculiarly South African institution of "ritual [medicine] murders" wax and wane like popular dances,[22] albeit for quite different reasons. The connection between the quality of political consciousness and popular creative self-expression, for example, is illustrated by the recent history of popular "township" theater. From the 1960s to the 1980s, popular musical theater developed and flourished in South Africa's urban African townships, despite (or because of?) the most draconian censorship and suppression. Mobile, inexpensive, fluid, boisterously political—township theater companies required no set written scripts, elaborate scenery, costumes, or lighting to cast up an image larger and even more searing than township life. Indeed, so engaged were township audiences fresh to theater, that creators, works, and performances themselves became social agents, an active part of the politics of black urban life as well as an expression of them.[23] Such politicizing melodramas were difficult for the agents of the state to censor or even physically lay their hands on, and they provided more gripping, Brechtian self-dramatizing entertainment than anything state-controlled media could possibly offer. By the early 1990s, however, the political necessities that had mothered theatrical invention in the townships had changed. Now rather condescendingly dubbed "protest theater," popular political musical drama in the townships seemed to disappear more rapidly than it had arisen; the bright hand-painted banners of upcoming shows no longer festooned township brick expanses and guy wires. Over the past several years, theater that traces its social and stylistic roots to township plays of the "struggle" period has transmuted into new forms, some of them more thoughtful, innovative, and theatrically realized than their vital but disorderly, burlesquing, self-indulgent predecessors. Such productions include Bheki Mkhwane's *Sitting Around the Fire* and single-handed tour de force *Solomon's Pride* at the Civic in Johannesburg (1999), and more notably, the Third World Bunfight Company's

1997 Grahamstown sensation *iMumbo Jumbo,* characterized thus in the production's press release:

> a dramatic ritual recounting the true, intrepid, sacred and quixotic 1996 quest of
> Chief Nicholas Tilana Gcaleka (sangoma [healer], priest, liquor salesman, guru)
> to Scotland to retrieve the skull of his ancestor, King Hintsa kaPhalo Paramount
> Chief of the AmaXhosa (treacherously beheaded whilst attempting to escape A
> Colonial Posse in 1836) and thereby to usher in an era of New South African peace
> and fertility. Performed by witchdoctors, ancestors, prophets, musicians, hill tribes,
> media hounds and other animals.

The surrealism of this wild, fun-house mirror portrayal was enhanced by the
real-life theatrics of Gcaleka (not his real name) who was neither a chief nor a de-
scendant of Hintsa. Despite the lack of any real evidence that Hintsa's head had either been cut off or shipped to Scotland, Gcaleka managed to convince corporate
sponsors to pay his fare, and he was duly presented with a skull with a hole in the
temple taken from the mantelpiece of a sympathetic Scottish family. Upon examination in South Africa, the skull turned out to be that of a twentieth-century British
woman. It is regrettable that performances of such innovative productions are largely
confined to formal institutional performance venues in the commercial heart of the
major cities and the National Arts Festival in Grahamstown.

Not that community theater has ceased to exist, and in forms that more faith-
fully justify the term than did many previous projects in the pre-liberation era. I
shall mention but one example, the Sibikwa players, founded by Phyllis Klotz and
Small Indaba over a decade ago and well known for successful and provocative
productions at the "fringe" section of the Grahamstown National Arts Festival. Now
located in a disused factory on the outskirts of the East Rand industrial town of
Benoni, Sibikwa survives (barely) on the dedication of its staff and intermittent
grants from private sponsors and the Gauteng Provincial Department of Education. Notably absent from Sibikwa's list of sponsors are the national and provincial
Departments of Arts, Culture, Science, and Technology, but at Sibikwa, hopes of
formal ministerial support spring eternal. In the meantime, Sibikwa uses veteran
black actors such as Percy Mtwa, star of *Woza Albert* and *Bopha!* to train community people as actors in projects that derive from donor or sponsor support. These
include teacher-training programs in the teaching and the uses of drama in the classroom; *Isintu,* a play produced for the Civic and sold to sponsors as a form of youth
employment; and an eagerness to engage in "theatre for development" efforts if only
sponsorship would appear. Staff at Sibikwa have spoken of the need to re-create a
community-based black theater audience now that "township theater" at the old
community halls has died. The professionalization of black theater and the full,
regular availability of the formal downtown commercial venues that accommodate
it are a good development, they agree, but the problem remains of how to expose
an audience beyond that of the new middle class to theater once again. Sibikwa
staff also have observed quite cogently that the nature of theater as a participatory
and interactive, *socially embedded* art form give it a developmental role different

from and potentially more effective than that of television. They acknowledge, however, that realizing such a potential role depends on direct linkages between community workshops such as Sibikwa, school drama programs and festivals, professional theater, and the broadcast media that have yet to be forged. One staffer bemoaned the government's unwillingness to regard theater as a cultural resource entitled to public funding, but Percy Mtwa argued that official support is often artistically constraining and professionally debilitating. Mtwa noted that artists with a single-minded thirst for and dedication to creating plays, such as Mkwane or the four directors showcased in the Market's Young Directors Festival, could get their work produced, and that it was this kind of work that would in time constitute its own paying audiences. He admitted that it might be some time before township people were "ready for good shows"—that is, provided with a view of theater as both a pleasurable and important form of cultural sustenance and a valid claimant on their limited entertainment budgets.

There is yet another side to the issue. One of the great virtues of professionalized, in this case university-sponsored, productions such as *Love and Crime in Johannesburg,* is that their sophistication provides access to what cultural philosopher Raymond Williams calls the "structure of feeling": an articulation of experience with broader social forces and expressions of ideology; of emotions, perceptions, and reflections with the structure of reality.[24] The Market's 1999 Young Directors Festival, for example, features plays about the dreams of homeless immigrants to Johannesburg, the violence and disorganization in the urban black taxi industry, the fate of a young girl accused of spying by both sides in the political violence in Alexandra township in the early 1990s, the local game of football portrayed through choreography and dialogue, life in a remote village in Mpumalanga province and in the streets of the notorious, seedy Johannesburg district of Hillbrow. Intensely authentic and acted with an athletic freshness and superb gift for mimicry, these plays are both moving and fun to watch. But they are not related to the larger forces that structure these situations in the true lives of "the people," because their creators simply do not know or do not know how to portray how the larger world is organized in relation to their characters' thoughts, feelings, and experiences—what, behind or above the world of appearances, is really *going on.* It is this link, the ability to entertain these articulations, that the professional urban theater of companies like Junction Avenue in South Africa reveals and portrays so well, and not just its superior production values, that makes it, in the end, more *entertaining.*

The political transformation of South Africa is certainly one cause for the loss of impetus and direction in popular theater, as the often morally ambiguous political contradictions of the current era have yet to provide a social canvas for the medium's inherently broad, stereotypifying brush. Another more obvious reason for popular theater's decline, however, is the migration of its concerns, enactments, and most important, its audiences, to television now that this state-sponsored (if not state-controlled) mass medium is both universally available and actively concerned with dramatizing popular self-concepts and imagination. The majority of South Africans now, in Stuart Hall's term, *recognize* themselves and their worlds in the evening video dramas scripted in any one or several of the local languages and shown on two of the three government service (SATV) channels. As Hall explains, these dramas encode those different ways in which "people have addressed us, have called us, and the recognitions this implies of yes, that is me."[25] The media, he continues, "are crucial not just because they put out information about us but because they trade in images of us, in possible identifications. The media ask us to assent to them and in return they promise to recognize us. Our emotional or psychological security is partly dependent on the way we are *represented*."[26] Where television in southern Africa fails in this project—as in Zimbabwe, for example, where political self-expression is repressed and, despite the huge expense, not exactly legal satellite dishes bloom in visible protest of the vacuous drollery of state television—popular live theater remains vital and self-sustaining.

As a field of inquiry, cultural studies of local evening television dramas—soap operas, if you will—in southern Africa would repay the effort in insight into social self-images, provided that processes of cultural production are incorporated into the analysis. Support for such a proposal comes from other studies of national media in Africa and elsewhere. In Nigeria, for example, local African or English-language dramas, expensive to make despite their low production values, are universally preferred to news or to programming imported from North America, Britain, and Australia.[27] In southern Africa, too, people are more entertained and engaged by representations of scenes, situations, and characterizations in which they recognize themselves.

This is as much the case with broadcast advertising as with program content. South African television advertising, for example, currently recognized internationally as among the industry's most innovative, has been forced to be so because advertisements imported directly from North America or Europe have for the most part failed on the local market. Agencies whose marketing campaigns have "gone local" with instantly recognizable South African visual, audio, textual, and narrative symbols and images have experienced measurable success, even in a depressed consumer market. What have not been successful in this genre, however, are local advertisements that base their appeal on politically aspirational or socially idealized situations or relationships. People in places doing things we might ideally like to see do not work as local content in South African television, as they impose an inauthenticity of experience with which audiences have strikingly little patience. Perhaps ruling party politicians still trying to sell "rainbow nationalism" at home and "the South African miracle" abroad would benefit equally from the advertising industry's market-oriented "reality testing."

In neighboring countries, as I have suggested, the problem of inadequate quality and quantity in local television is addressed through pay-per-view services and equipment that allows for reception of satellite and South African channels. In South Africa, apart from the MNET subscription service offering primarily sports and Hollywood films, the audience is constituted almost entirely around the three state-sponsored channels, one entirely in English and the other two in a rotating variety of all eleven official languages. Afrikaans, once linguistic queen of SATV, has since

1996 been reduced to a mere 3 percent of programming, all on TV2, while "Southern Sotho" gets 6 percent. This proportion is peculiar in view of the prevalence of Afrikaans as a home language in many black as well as white communities and as the most widely used lingua franca after English. Local programming, while popular, experiences problems because of its relative cost—between eight and sixteen times more per episode than the purchase of a popular imported series—the small size and under-capitalization of local production houses, and the interlocking managements of SATV and a favored minority of programming companies. The government's attempt to fund television through a system of individual television monitor licenses similar to that used in Britain has met with conspicuous resistance. Despite a continuing campaign of alternating threats and incentives, less than 40 percent of television owners actually pay their annual license fee. Characteristically, the two mixed-language channels and specifically TV1, the channel for the multi-cultural youth audience, have marketed their vivacious, culturally fashion-conscious, and physically striking "continuity presenters"—male/female pairs who provide a conversational link between scheduled program offerings—more successfully than their programs. Hugely popular, too, are the "hosts" of local music, game, and variety shows. Despite its 40 million people, South Africa behaves like a smaller society in which audiences establish a sense of personal connection to local media personalities, and the social networks of media centers of Johannesburg and to a lesser extent Cape Town reverberate with rumor and gossip about such celebrities, whom just about everyone it seems (including the author) has met at some public event or venue.

In the case of radio, virtually all African countries of course have a historical commitment to "national" state broadcasting services that have played a central role in post-independence political and cultural life, and in the over-determination of nationalist consciousness as the ideological program of the ruling elite. In the post–cold war period of "democratization" in Africa, some diversification in service and programming has been introduced, although news and information have remained largely controlled. In southern Africa, as elsewhere on the continent, one aspect of this control is a relentless rhetoric of administrative direction and involvement, despite the decreasing capacity of governments to preside over anything except neo-colonial interference in the lives of their citizens. So a popular term for hourly radio news bulletins is "Minister Said," reflecting the tendency for virtually every sentence read by announcers to begin with the phrase "The minister said. . . ."

In South Africa, both before and after 1994, this tendency has been similarly noticeable, but the country's radio services have had a more diverse and responsive history. Radio began as municipal services in the major cities of South Africa in 1924. No programming of any kind, however, was directed at the black majority until 1941, when a daily five-minute war bulletin in Zulu was introduced in Durban. This concession was intended to counter rumors said to be spreading among the city's African domestic workers of all the blessings to be expected "when Hitler comes."[28] Very slowly over the next two decades, programming for Africans increased. The hodgepodge of vernacular voice dramas and traditional and urban, foreign-influenced, and religious music intended to attract the mix of migrants, urban workers, and petit bourgeoisie that made up the urban black population pleased hardly anyone. Still, the use of the full range of whatever the fledgling black-oriented recording industry and the "transcription service" of the SABC studios themselves could find to record did demonstrate an attempt to provide entertainment that the newly forming black urban audience might want to hear.

Afrikaans- and English-speaking services were provided for whites, the English services conspicuously oriented to British cultural concerns and featuring announcers with self-consciously British accents. In the 1960s, under the policy of "separate development," regionally based radio services in seven of the African languages were instituted under the collective management of the SABC's "Radio Bantu." Music, drama, news, and information were linguistically segregated grammatically and lexically "purified," by frequency and location, in an effort to inculcate ideologies of cultural difference not only between black and white, but also ethnically among blacks. Programming was "ruralized" as much as possible consistent with commercial appeal (something of a contradiction in itself in view of black urbanization), in an effort to promote identification with insular language communities and with ethnic "homelands" in which blacks resident in urban areas were supposed to find political self-expression. "Coloured" people had to make do with the white stations, and Indians had limited programming in Indian languages in Natal. Language separation aside, programming on SABC was remarkably narrow overall, with a mix of musical styles and other programming material on "national" stations for each group, rather than the demographic/stylistic "format" stations common in Western countries. As a result, South African radio before the mid-1980s was disliked by virtually everyone except those who hadn't imagined the alternatives, and more liberated and responsive services from Swaziland and some of the quasi-independent homelands became instantly popular.

The introduction of television was famously resisted by Nationalist minister J. B. Herzog who, probably correctly, saw it as at once a threat to social morality and as a source of information about the world beyond South Africa, with potentially negative impacts on the hegemony of apartheid. So the medium did not make its appearance in South Africa until 1976, and then only for white viewers, with no black people appearing in the strange television of apartheid's white nationalist panopticon. Later, two limited-broadcast channels, one for Zulu/Xhosa and one for Sotho/Tswana viewers, were instituted, along the same segregating ideological lines as radio. Thus viewers of white services were treated to multi-racial and multi-cultural programs from overseas mixed with local series portraying a South Africa devoid of black people and their languages. Black channels, conversely, showed a South Africa in which black people never encountered a person who spoke even a different language, let alone of another race.

Needless to say, the progressive collapse of the Nationalist regime was accompanied by strenuous demands that resulted in a receptive program for the reform and diversification of television in South Africa. As liberation approached, television began to play a leading role in the conscious development of new popular cultural models for a self-creating society. The transformation of SATV into a service that genuinely attempts to be a *popular* public broadcaster has not simply democratized language programming to better serve all of the country's language groups (Afrikaans excepted). It has also sponsored the scripting and production of local programming that at least occasionally focuses, sincerely if somewhat naively, on salient issues of a tumultuous and dynamic democratizing society.

After a period of uncertainty over the direction change should take, SATV has achieved, within severe financial constraints, a balance the corporation finds satisfactory between addressing its "mandate" as a public service broadcaster and the commercial necessity of providing popular entertainment. In 1998, the Independent Broadcasting Authority finally licensed the first free-to-air private-sector channel. Interestingly, some local cultural programming, in particular music, survived the successive reworkings at SATV over the past decade. *Ezodumo,* a multi-ethnic program of neo-traditional guitar band music popular with black viewers of small-town and rural origin, has retained its slot over this period and still today has the third highest ratings of any regular feature on SATV. A more urban youth-oriented live music show, *Ezimtoti,* is also popular, as are a range of programs featuring both local and imported contemporary music videos. A new late-night offering, *African Jukebox,* features music videos from around sub-Saharan Africa.

As the challenge to apartheid gained momentum in the 1980s, the cultural isolation of South Africa had already begun, willy-nilly, to erode. Styles of music, forms of arrangement, and a near revolution in performance and recording technologies poured in from all over the world of popular music. Exchanges with the English-speaking Caribbean, the United States, the United Kingdom, and, importantly, the rest of sub-Saharan Africa led the way. South African Lucky Dube is currently one of the world's leading exponents of Jamaican reggae. *Soukous* (now locally known as *kwasa-kwasa*) from Zaire has achieved its own local expressions and adaptations right alongside those of the ubiquitous funk and rap/hip-hop of black America. Pride and resurgent interest in the contemporary possibilities of indigenous traditional music accompanied these influences. Groups such as Harari, led by the talented composer and multi-instrumentalist Sipho Mabuse, successfully blended Zulu dance-song, American "soul," and rock. Noise Khanyile blended Mahlathini's neo-traditional Zulu *mbaqanga* with Zairian *soukous.* Urban traditional vocal harmony group Ladysmith Black Mambazo teamed up with Paul Simon and revived the American pop singer-composer's career.

Perhaps most significant of all was the emergence, from humble origins, of a new style of South African popular dance balladry with a distinctive African "township" beat that re-established local artists as viable competitors with American and British imports in the industry. The basis of this style, unfortunately called "bubblegum" in the 1970s, or alternatively, "Soweto soul," was the modernized, sophisticated choral jazz of Miriam Makeba and Letta Mbuli, blended in with solo popular balladry by vocalists like Steve Kekana and a host of others. In the 1980s, popular dance vocalists Brenda Fassie, Chicco (Sello Twala), Sipho Mabuse, and more recently Rebecca Malope gradually outgrew their "bubblegum" beginnings and innovated a fulsome, richly textured new style of popular dance song that combined a range of some of the most musically interesting local and imported qualities with lyrics that on occasion provided thought-provoking political and social commentary.

In music radio, indeed, diversification and responsiveness to audience demand has been far more effective and far-reaching than in television. Simply to balance its books, SA Radio sold a number of its stations to private sector investors after 1994. Those stations that were retained were in most cases radically reformed in line with audience preferences. One result of this effort has been a new cultural dynamism among the vernacular language stations, with Radio Lesedi (southern Sesotho), Radio Thobela (northern Sesotho), and Radio Ukhozi (Zulu) among Johannesburg's most popular.

The greatest surge in popularity, not surprisingly, occurred among stations providing absolutely contemporary popular music to black urban youth, such as Johannesburg's Yfm. Significantly, this audience was not constituted only or even primarily around imported black contemporary youth styles from the United States, although a major SABC station, Radio Metro, bases its national appeal on such material. After years of lobbying by local musicians, a quota was introduced requiring 30 percent local content in all music programming. New narrow-market stations such as Cape Town's Fine Music Radio, specializing in European classical and American classic jazz music, addressed the requirement by programming sophisticated South African jazz. While broadcasters at first feared a falloff in listenership, the result was rather a post-apartheid renaissance in local music in all its splendid variety. As wider opportunities for recording opened up, local musicians rushed to create new ensembles, sounds, and styles. While much of what could now be heard was not particularly polished, a lot of interesting and original music that would otherwise never have been recorded suddenly appeared over the airwaves. A new youth style called *kwaito,* derived from 1980s township soul ("bubble gum"), "drum 'n bass," and American hip-hop, surged to the forefront of the industry with a heavily rhythmic combination of teenage sexual urgency and lyrical social commentary. In 1996, the recording industry produced over one thousand new albums in the *kwaito* genre.

Since then, commercial Darwinism has taken its selective toll, and only the most creative, well-managed *kwaito* groups have managed to maintain their popularity and sales. These successful artists all feature an innovative mix of overtly sexual popular dancing, stage (media) presence, and engaging vocal work, and include such groups as Boom Shaka, Abashante, Arthur, and M'du. Other briefly popular ensembles have fallen by the wayside, in part because South Africa's stagnant economy cannot currently sustain volume or diversity in the recording industry. The township market is still primarily for cassette tapes rather than compact discs, but even cassettes haven't proved inexpensive enough. As elsewhere in Africa, for every original CD or tape purchased, hundreds more are pirated and sold as cheap, poor quality cassette copies on township street corners. The middle-class white and black audiences are simply not large or forthcoming enough to support the industry in such circumstances, and there is little cross-fertilization or crossover in stylistic preferences. So no matter how appealing and well publicized an album by the top white rock groups, its sales are unlikely to exceed 25,000. The many hopeful young black artists that ought to be sustained by the township consumer are forced to walk the plank by pirates. In July 1998, the South African recording industry posted the lowest sales figures since before the democratic transformation.

A final note on youth: In the decades when the right to urban residence and the construction of an urban African set of identities were themselves forms of resistance, black popular culture was produced and organized around markers of transforming social identity and the display of cultural capital necessary for the establishment of claims to urbanized status and social class. So in the 1970s and 1980s, the meaning of "popular" in South African black culture shifted political gear from the expression of social reality to its active rejection. The youth culture of the time, fueled by the "black consciousness" of its African-American materials and models, made modernist rebellion into a nationalist cultural style. The expressions of this style not only in performance but in dress, funerals, leisure, education, and political activity played a large role in creating the modes of solidarity that kept the anti-apartheid Mass Democratic Movement moving through the dark and torturous tunnel of the 1970s and 1980s to the light of the 1990s.

As the struggle for liberation began to achieve its political (if not yet social) aims, the energies of militant township youth that had been absorbed in this struggle found in part a new focus in the creation of a new, performance and media-oriented youth popular culture. "Culture clubs" and youth clubs sprang up in black communities throughout the country's urban areas, and by the early 1990s almost half of township youth were involved in associations of this kind. Their hope is that the educational, vocational, and cultural programs of these clubs can make up in some measure for the failings of their schools, and offer at least the possibility of a way out of the cycle of violence, poverty, and stagnation that rules life in the townships and shantytowns in the midst of South Africa's remarkable political renaissance. In sum, popular culture must become a focus and a crucible for the forging of a distinctly social self-consciousness among young southern Africans. Without such social consciousness, there is only the intensifying poverty of spirit that posts no high road to reconciliation or development.[29]

NOTES

1. Based on an inaccurate estimation of the year of the birth of the Christian prophet, Jesus of Nazareth, even the popular concept of the onset of the third millennium is wrong: officially it begins at midnight, 1 January 2001.

2. Karin Barber, "Introduction," in K. Barber, ed., *Readings in African Popular Culture* (Oxford: James Currey; Bloomington: Indiana University Press, 1997), pp. 1–2.

3. Graham Pechey, "Post-Apartheid Narratives," in F. Barker, P. Hulme, and M. Iversen, eds., *Colonial Discourse/Postcolonial Theory* (Manchester: Manchester University Press, 1993), p.156.

4. Johannes Fabian, *Moments of Freedom* (Charlottesville: University of Virginia Press, 1998).

5. Ibid., p. 19.

6. Karin Barber, *I Could Speak until Tomorrow* (Edinburgh: International African Institute, 1993), p. 2.

7. In a forthcoming doctoral thesis at the University of Cape Town, journalistic anthropologist Lesley Fordred shows that folkloric forms are beginning to attain the status of "news" in mass-circulation print journalism.

8. David B. Coplan, *In the Time of Cannibals: The World Music of South Africa's Basotho Migrants* (Chicago: University of Chicago Press; Johannesburg: University of Witwatersrand Press, 1994), pp. 8–10.

9. Stuart Hall, "Random Thoughts Provoked by the Conference 'Identities, Democracy, Culture, and Communication in Southern Africa,'" *Critical Arts* 11, no. 1/2 (1997): 1–16.

10. Barber, "Introduction," p. 4.

11. Michael Fischer, "Ethnicity and the Arts of Memory," in G. Marcus and J. Clifford, eds., *Writing Cultures* (Chicago: University of Chicago Press, 1986), p. 221.

12. See *In the Time of the Cannibals;* and *Lyrics of the Basotho Migrants* (Madison: University of Wisconsin Press, 1995).

13. Barber, ed., *Readings in African Popular Culture.*

14. Johannes Fabian, "Popular Culture in Africa," *Africa* (London) 48, no. 4 (1978): 316.

15. Ruth Teer-Tomaselli, "Shifting Spaces: Popular Culture and National Culture (Introduction)," *Critical Arts* 11, no. 1/2 (1997): ix.

16. Quoted in ibid., xii.

17. Hall, "Random Thoughts," 14.

18. Michael Chapman, "South Africa in the Global Neighbourhood: Towards a Method of Cultural Analysis," *Critical Arts* 11, no. 1/2 (1997): 19.

19. Pechey, *Post-Apartheid Narratives,* p. 161.

20. Fabian, *Power and Performance,* pp. 3, 21ff.

21. David B. Coplan and Tim Quinlan, "A Chief by the People: Nation versus State in Lesotho," *Africa* (London) 67, no. 1 (1997): 27–61.

22. G. I. Jones, *Basutoland Medicine Murder* (London: His Majesty's Stationary Office, 1951).

23. David B. Coplan, *In Township Tonight! South Africa's Black City Music and Theatre* (London and New York: Longman; Johannesburg: Ravan, 1985); and David B. Coplan, "Ideology and Tradition in South African Black Popular Theatre," *Journal of American Folklore* 99, no. 392 (1986): 151–76.

24. Hall, "Random Thoughts," p. 11.

25. Ibid., p. 13.

26. Oluyinka A. Esan, cited in Barber, "Introduction," p. 7.

27. Hugh Tracey, personal communication, 1975; Coplan, *In Township Tonight!* p. 160–61.

10.   Gendered Terrains

Negotiating Land and Development,
Whose Reality Counts?

Jean Davison

The winds of political change initiated by Zimbabwe's independence in 1980 became a gale in the last decade of the twentieth century. The result is a far different landscape. The creation of a democratic state in Namibia in 1990 and pivotal multi-party elections in Zambia that ousted the sole president, Kenneth Kaunda, signaled demands for a new, more democratic order. These demands swept across Malawi and Mozambique with a multi-party fervor that led to the demise of pre-existing orders in both countries, and finally swept South Africa clean, dislodging the recalcitrant apartheid state that had held the majority of South Africans ransom for over fifty years. Democracy, American style, became a symbolic indicator of development in the region. It was integrally linked with economic development in the minds of the newly enfranchised.

Eager to experience the benefits of development touted by their new leaders and the G-8 nations, marginalized groups across the region began clambering for a share. These groups included impoverished peasants, the landless, and women, often but not always one and the same. Women became more strident, insisting that their reality counted. Political wisdom dictated their inclusion; they are the numerical majority in most southern African states. Gender, a concept virtually unknown two decades earlier, assumed center stage as a crucial socio-political dimension of development. Fueling the storm of regional change, gender politics has left no nation untouched.

This chapter looks at gender within a participatory development framework. This approach emphasizes maximum participation in community-oriented rural development. Its goal is greater empowerment. More particularly, the chapter examines gender inequities and measures to overcome them in one development sector—rural agriculture. As the vast majority of the population in the region continues to live in rural areas earning a living from the land, this critical resource is at the heart of the inquiry. Further, in countries such as Zambia and Zimbabwe where making ends meet in the urban sector is becoming increasingly untenable, a trend in reverse migration is developing as people head back to the land in hopes of improving their lot. In post-apartheid South Africa, land has become a veritable lightning rod for the development aspirations of the forgotten and neglected. Regardless of the type of land tenure practiced, gender is implicated. We cannot look at state efforts to redistribute land without examining who allocates land, who uses it and maintains its productivity, and who profits from its output. For these reasons, and because succeeding chapters in this volume take up other aspects of development, I have chosen to narrow my focus to the agriculture-land nexus.

Gender Meanings:
The Social and the Political

Gender is *socially* constructed rather than biologically determined. Sex, which sometimes gets confused with gender, is *biologically* constructed. It refers to biological differences determined by chromosomes, hormones, and anatomy. Gender is the way the categories of female and male are culturally defined. Looking at development through the prism of gender means examining the socio-cultural factors that influence constructions of male and female. These factors include the network of beliefs, attitudes, customs, behaviors, and activities that determine gender categories in a particular society. No two societies construct gender in quite the same way. In most societies, males and females have attached to their gender a set of ever-changing, socially defined characteristics that include sexual orientation, reproductive values, and social norms through which individuals and groups interact and provide for their economic and social survival.

Gender perceptions, attitudes, and behaviors are learned through a process of socialization that begins in the home, is carried on in the community and school, and is reinforced by various other social institutions. Individual and institutional beliefs contribute to the process. Gender-specific roles, behaviors, and even stereotypes are reinforced by myths and stories, proverbs and customs to the point where they can become internalized. However, because they are *learned* behaviors and attitudes, they can also be changed to bring about more positive behaviors that benefit women and men equally.

To some people, gender implies women; "gender roles" is used synonymously to mean women's roles. This is too narrow a focus, and is inaccurate; it deletes men from the gender equation. Gender is a comparative, relational concept. Concentrating solely on males or solely on females excludes one-half of the human experience. Both are needed in planning, implementing, and evaluating development policies and programs.

Related to the way gender is constructed are other intertwined modalities, including social variables such as race, ethnicity, class, religion, age, and education. Regional and national variations also impinge on gender identities and behavior.[1]

Each of these modalities, singly or in combination, interacts dialectically with gender in a given society at a particular point in time.

Definitions of gender depend heavily on positionality. Attacking Eurocentric feminist constructions of gender, Chandra Mohanty critiques Western feminists for essentializing women's experience regardless of race, class, or nationality.[2] She argues that liberal Western feminists psychologize complex and often contradictory historical and cultural realities that mark differences among women. Included is the effect of colonialist-imperialist ideologies that oppress indigenous cultures and races, and privilege white masculinity as the norm. The differences that result need to be engaged rather than ignored or transcended. African women, in particular, have been characterized by scholars and development practitioners in the North as victims. As Zimbabwean scholar Rudo Gaidzanwa points out, this characterization is demeaning and ignores the significant role women played in pre-colonial southern Africa and in their historical struggles alongside men for liberation from colonial rule.[3] In objectifying women as victims, we lose sight of individual agency as well as geographical and historical particularities.

Gaidzanwa critiques European notions of gender rooted in the European experience.[4] She maintains that colonial gender politics in southern Africa closely reflected gender developments in Britain such that suffrage was extended first to those in privileged positions, mainly white males, then to men of color in the laboring classes, then to white women, and lastly to black women.[5] Class and race, articulated as they were in the colonial experience, were the primary factors shaping gender in southern Africa. Gaidzanwa's work demonstrates that historical, regional, and national circumstances together influence constructions of gender.

The colonial gender paradigm was not based on a static set of principles, however. It was subject to change. But too often, as Gaidzanwa points out, post-colonial states adopted a modified model that privileged elite black men, ignoring the needs of women, certain ethnic groups, and the most impoverished peasants. With the dramatic shifts that have been occurring in the last decade, the masculinist model has come under scrutiny and its precepts are being challenged.[6] For instance, new constitutions in South Africa, Malawi, and Mozambique have upended institutions that previously privileged males, black or white. These new constitutions recognize explicitly the rights of both genders. Based on this new equity ideal, steps are being taken to ensure that women at all levels share power and authority with men. Efficacy is the goal, rather than merely integrating women as the earlier WID (Women in Development) approach advocated.[7] Alternative models of development that are culturally and nationally appropriate, as well as being environmentally sustainable, are given priority.

Gender Analysis and Development

Gender analysis refers to a systematic study of differences between men and women in a given society. Most gender analysis frameworks ask the same basic questions:

1. Who does what? (looking at the division of activities between men and women)
2. Who has what? (access to and control of resources)
3. What factors influence this gender arrangement? (cultural prescriptions, laws, economic and political factors) Are changes occurring in these factors? If so, are they amenable to changes in the present gender situation? Where are the points of resistance?
4. How are public resources distributed? Who gets what? What institutional structures are used? How equitable are they? How effective? How efficient? What can be done to make them equally responsible to women and men?

Gender analysis provides critical contextual data, including information about the obstacles and opportunities that women and men experience in the context of their own locality and within a particular sector. The results are used in planning, monitoring, and evaluating development programs. The three models most frequently used by gender analysts are (1) the Harvard Analytical Framework, (2) the Moser Model, and (3) the Empowerment Model based on the work of Zambian researcher Sarah Longwe.

The Harvard Analytical Framework

The Harvard framework, the earliest model, consists of three diagnostic tools to assist practitioners in developing a description and analysis of gender relations in a community. The model examines who does what, who owns what, and who controls what within a given community. The framework applies gender analysis to a needs assessment. Given a gender profile of the community, what does each gender need from the particular program or project to be designed? A component of the framework assists practitioners and community participants to design a gender-sensitive project. The final component gives guidelines for evaluating the extent to which the original needs of the females and males in the community have been met.[8]

The Moser Analytical Model

In the Moser Analytical Model, Caroline Moser isolates two types of needs related to development: practical and strategic needs. *Practical* needs refer to short-term, immediate needs for fulfilling women's and men's physical needs: for example, better sanitation, improved maternal health, a potable, proximate water supply. *Strategic* needs refer to long-term needs that require structural changes in a society: for example, increasing women's voting power in the national legislature, increasing opportunities for both women and men to own property, and increasing the number of women managers or male nurses. Moser argues that, in the past, development agencies have concentrated on women's practical needs because they are less politically contentious than strategic needs.[9] Meeting strategic needs often involves reordering the way a society structures gender from the top to the bottom—from national ministries to households. Moser's model is designed to analyze whether projects meet just one set of needs or both. The objective of her model is to make sure that a policy or project includes initiatives that will enhance gender equity. This means including measures designed to meet women's strategic needs.

Moser recommends including an analysis of what she perceives to be women's triple roles. These are

1. productive roles (agriculture, business, professions);
2. reproductive roles (procreation, child care, family care, home manager); and
3. community organization roles (kin work, organizing weddings, funerals, sitting on development committees, community development project work).

Often in analyzing women's roles, development practitioners concentrate on either of the first two roles and do not include the third, which is equally important and time consuming.

The Empowerment Model (Longwe)

Zambian scholar Sarah Longwe's empowerment model is useful because it addresses the issue of gender equity head-on. She conceptualizes the process of development as a continuum leading toward ever-increasing levels of empowerment.[10] The least empowering is the *welfare* level, which addresses women as passive recipients of development rather than as active participants. The next level up, the level of *access,* enables the disadvantaged to leverage key technical, social, and natural resources, but does not empower recipients in a critical way. At the intermediary level, gender *conscientization,* active consciousness of gender disparities, knowledge building, and the articulation of strategies for change begin to take place. The *participation* level is crucial because it is at this level that the disadvantaged become active, defining their own development. The quantity and quality of their participation makes the difference. At the apex is *control.* At this highest level women, as well as men, assume control of resources, problem solving, decision-making, and leadership. They assume control and authority for agricultural production, including control of land, labor, and income from production. The model is useful because it draws attention to what the disadvantaged gender needs to increase its power at each level, with the final result being full empowerment. It also amplifies the importance of participation. Within the context of southern Africa, Longwe's model is most appropriate for analyzing the extent to which women have gained equality with men in all sectors. My discussion is limited to an analysis of gender differences in access to and control of land for agricultural production.

JEAN DAVISON

Gender Disparities in Access to and Control of Land

This section looks at historical antecedents and continuing customary practices and laws that affect, in particular, women's development rights to land in the region.

Historical Antecedents

The extent to which men and women have access to land for production varies from country to country, and within countries by region and culture. We know something about pre-colonial land use patterns, gleaned from the records of colonial travelers, missionaries, agricultural officers, and colonial anthropologists. However, as these documents were largely written from the perspective of European white males, the validity of their observations about indigenous practices is questionable. For example, Landeg White in a historical study of a matrilineal village in southern Malawi, illustrates that male missionaries in the latter part of the nineteenth century had very little understanding of or use for a land tenure system that privileged women.[11] Among the Mang'anja, land was often controlled by women and passed down to matrikin, usually daughters or granddaughters. Coming from a European culture that solely recognized land/man relationships, British colonials found it difficult to alter their perceptual lens so that women's agricultural rights and responsibilities as well as men's were acknowledged and their needs addressed. Similar examples of colonial insensitivity to matrilineal gender relations exist for Zambia[12] and northern Mozambique.[13] The masculinist bias was reinforced by agricultural officers throughout most of the twentieth century, regardless of pre-existing systems.[14]

For the region as a whole, southern Africa historically was predominantly patrilineal and patriarchal, with women heavily involved in growing food on land largely controlled by men. However, there were class differences among men, and those who did not have sufficient resources to accumulate the necessary bridewealth in cattle and other goods could become *vakwasha,* "sons-in-laws" as they were known in Shona, by contributing their labor to a future father-in-law through bride service.[15] By pledging his labor to a wealthier man who had a marriageable daughter, a less fortunate man gained both access to land for cultivation and the opportunity to establish his own homestead with a new wife once he completed his bride service obligations to his future father-in-law.

Contrary to indigenous practice, colonial agricultural officers assumed that production was largely a male domain. Such was not the case, particularly after the penetration of European capital and the institutionalization, through indirect rule, of the onerous hut tax to underwrite colonial administrations. The need for cash to pay the hut tax eventually led, but not without resistance, to an invasive and pervasive system of trade in male labor across the region. The boldest and the brawniest men were either forced, as in Mozambique and Angola, or were coerced, as in Zambia, Malawi, and Lesotho, to leave home to support mining capital and commercial agriculture in South Africa and the Rhodesias. These men often left behind a father, a wife, or a sister acting as guardian of their land. As long as their land was cultivated, it was protected from appropriation.

Women who were left behind, usually those with children and the elderly, picked up the slack and increased their own labor on the land, or they devised new strategies for meeting their families' needs by diversifying production and expanding into other areas—selling cooked food or beer brewing, for instance.[16] That southern Africa's rural areas have been disrupted and inextricably altered by this vast sea of shifting, often cyclical, migratory labor is indisputable. It is a pattern that has persisted and expanded in the last two decades of the twentieth century as southern African nations have become increasingly obligated to global capitalism, including its financial institutions, world markets, and trade policies.

Laws of the Land

In most southern African countries, two systems of law governing the use, trade, and leasing of land co-exist. One is "customary law," a colonial appellation designating indigenous practices. The other falls under the rubric of "general" or common law, depending on whether the statutory system traces its descent from Roman-Dutch and British common law, or is a reinvented system of codified laws crafted in the post-colonial period. Each country with a dual system has its own labels. In most countries the two systems have separate courts, but in Botswana these exist in a single hierarchy, moving from the lower and higher customary courts to customary courts of appeal, various grades of magistrates courts, and, at the top, the final Court of Appeals.[17] All of Botswana's courts can apply customary law in the appropriate cases under the guidance of the Customary Law Act. Where customary law is not applicable, the courts apply the common law. A similar hierarchy operates in Swaziland.[18]

Of the former British colonies, Zambia's statutory legal system has most closely resembled the British system until very recently when efforts were undertaken to reform it. Malawi, Zambia, Namibia, and South Africa continue to have dual systems, as do Lesotho and Swaziland at the lower levels. Mozambique and Angola made concerted efforts at the time of independence to replace the colonial system of Portuguese law, bringing all courts under one unified system, from people's courts at the local level to the Supreme People's Court. All land was brought under the direct control of the state, although pre-existing occupants were allowed to keep their land provided it was used productively, according to the state's criteria.[19]

After Zimbabwe independence, responsibility for arbitration of customary law was transferred from chiefs' courts to new local bodies appointed by the Ministry of Justice. Chiefs and headmen were replaced by district councils and primary courts. Since then, chiefs have often represented themselves as the official voices for the defense of "tradition" in the Communal Areas, and conflicts between chiefs and district councils over land allocation are notorious.[20] In most of southern Africa, land is theoretically held in trust by a titular ruler, be it the Swazi king or the president of Zimbabwe. Holding land in trust enables the state to undertake land reforms designed to optimize production and, ideally, to improve the lot of the displaced and disadvantaged. It also has led to unprecedented land accumulation by members of a ruling indigenous class, as happened in Swaziland after independence.[21]

In South Africa, where most indigenous groups were patrilineal, land allocation historically was the responsibility of male heads of clans and villages. This role was formalized through the notion of a "chief," or "traditional authority" under colonial rule to expedite the notion of a customary land tenure system.[22] To some extent in the former homelands, chiefs still have a deciding role in arbitrating land matters. However, a tension exists in post-apartheid South Africa over whether customary practices related to land ought to be codified into law or not. Control over arable land has become the terrain for contestations for political space and power that involve local male chiefs and male-dominated vested interests. In such arenas, women have little voice, though the gender factor is constantly raised and debated, and women's equal access to land is a tenet of the government's Reconstruction and Development Program (RDP).

Various types of land are recognized in each country and are treated differently depending on "customary" and general law. Land typically falls into three categories: (1) customary land, which is controlled and allocated by village heads (men or women), chiefs, or other designed traditional authorities; (2) private land legally registered with a deed, either freehold (owned outright) or leasehold, whereby land owned by the state or a public body is leased for a specified number of years by an individual or organization; (3) public land acquired or set aside by the state for public purposes, such as roads, railways, state hospitals and schools, public markets, and national parks. It is the first two types of land that raise gender issues related to development.

Customary Land and Gender

Formerly designated by colonial administrators as "tribal reserves," customary land falls under the jurisdiction of "customary law" with its accompanying system of customary courts (sometimes known as "chiefs' courts"). Within customary areas, land cannot be sold. It is perceived as a bundle of resources rather than a geometric area.[23] Indigenous wisdom had it that as long as a parcel of land was cultivated, proprietary rights to its use were not in question. If it fell fallow for several years, however, it was subject to redistribution by a village head or chief. This flexibility of tenure remains in force in areas where land scarcity is not an issue. However, increasing population density and depleted soil in many of the former "reserves" have led to dwindling parcels of arable land and with that a growing trend toward commercialization and informal leasing. As Worby found, in a study of Communal Areas in Gokwe, Zimbabwe, within areas deemed "customary" there has been an increase in the lease of usufructory rights as pressure on arable land has escalated.[24]

Land that falls under customary law is often perceived to be communal land. In Zimbabwe, for example, the areas that encompass the former tribal reserves and fall under customary jurisdiction are referred to as Communal Areas (CAs). However, the term is misleading because in the CAs, most land is allocated to specific heads of families, almost exclusively male, or their individual sons. Occasionally a woman may inherit land from her father if she does not have brothers or she is unmarried with children. But this is unusual. Land in the CAs is not held communally except for grazing land or water rights. This is also the pattern for similar areas in Botswana, Lesotho, South Africa, and Swaziland, although, as Peters points out with a case study from tiny Kgatleng district in Botswana, instances of private claims to grazing land and boreholes are emerging.[25] Whether this is an anomaly or a trend is difficult to determine without more evidence. Because customary law in the majority of southern African countries is based on an ideology of patrilineal authority and control, women have few formally recognized rights to land under such systems.

It is believed that "a woman is child of a man."[26] In other words, it is expected that a woman's father or husband will be her guardian.[27] Women most often gain access to land for food production through husbands (and occasionally through fathers). A married woman is expected to contribute her labor to her husband's family land whether he is in residence or not. With the high incidence of male emigration in many rural areas, wives of out-migrating husbands find themselves managing and working their husband's land in his absence. Yet few reap the benefits of production; their husbands control the proceeds. What income they earn comes from optimizing land they've been allocated by their husband for cultivation. Furthermore, when a divorce occurs, a woman is expected to return to her parents' home, leaving her children, often, with her husband's relatives. In Swaziland, in cases where a woman is unmarried and has no family, a woman may go to the chief of her area for advice or "adoption" in order to gain access to land.[28] The case of widows throughout the region is more complex and will be taken up in a later section.

Having painted this overview of women's access to customary land in patrilineal areas, there is one caveat. Under certain circumstances, women may achieve access to land through strategies that make use of both customary and general law. In other words, there is some flexibility, some room for manipulation of the customary system on a case by case basis. A study in Swaziland of rural women's access to land carried out by Laurel Rose illustrates how some women gained access to and control over land by leveraging both customary courts and the "modern" legal system (Roman-Dutch law) to obtain their objectives.[29] Under the customary system, they used avoidance strategies (avoiding people unsympathetic to their position or avoiding unfavorable chiefs' courts by resorting to "forum shopping"). Or they used deception strategies under the customary system, lying about their personal circumstances or deceiving the legal institutions about their land rights. Using the statutory legal system, they also used avoidance tactics until they found a court sympathetic to their goals, or they used control strategies like recruiting assistance from a sympathetic government official, or maintaining dual residences. Similarly, Pankhurst and Jacobs demonstrate how women in one Communal Area in Zimbabwe use avoidance and deception strategies that negotiate both systems of law.[30]

The scenario is slightly different in customary matrilineal areas where a woman marries virilocally, following her husband to his village once the bridewealth is negotiated and the marriage a certainty. It is vastly different in matrilineal areas where women marry uxorilocally, remaining in their own natal villages where they have access to land through their matrikin, while their husbands relocate to join them. In areas where bridewealth has been transferred and women marry virilocally, as among the Tonga in northern Zimbabwe, southern Zambia, and a portion of Malawi, and in other parts of central and western Zambia, a woman leaves her natal home on marriage and cultivates her husband's land. Should there be a divorce, she may be forced to return to her natal home where she may or may not have access to land through matrikin.

In theory, Zambian women have equal legal rights with men under statutory law. They can acquire, hold, or dispose of property, including land, in their own right under customary law. And once married, a woman has a right to hold property she acquired either through gift or inheritance prior to marriage in her own name, separate from her husband's property.[31] But Namasiku Ilukena argues, with regard to land, that in many rural areas local customs persist that treat women as minors to their husbands and adult male relatives.[32] Consequently, Zambian women's equal access to and control of land spelled out in civil law depends on the extent to which these laws are known and adhered to in rural areas. Unless women are aware of their legal rights and demand equal treatment with men, they are in danger of having their rights ignored or trampled by expediency.

In large parts of southern and central Malawi, some parts of northern Zambia, and in northern Mozambique, women in matrilineal groups where uxorilocality is practiced such that a man leaves his home when he marries to take up residence in his wife's village, women have direct access to and authority over land in most rural areas.[33] A husband has to "beg land" from his wife's matrikin or a matrilineal village head if he wants land to till. He usually joins his wife in cultivating her land, or he may become a wage earner joining the migrant labor throng. Land under customary jurisdiction is cultivated by husband and wife together with children, or by the wife with the occasional assistance of matrikin in her husband's absence. In any case, should there be a divorce, the husband is expected to return to his original village, leaving the children with his wife in her home, as they belong to her matrilineage. She has security of land, which a man usually does not have. In Malawi, the Land Act and the Lands Acquisition Act do not discriminate against either sex. Women and men have equal rights to land.[34] The situation is similar in Mozambique. In short, whether a person is disadvantaged or not under customary law depends on the lineage ideologies and residential practices that operate in local areas. Opportunities for agricultural development are shaped by these gendered relationships to land.

Gendered Terrains

One characteristic of indigenous tenure practices is their flexibility and adaptability. Linked to this flexibility, however, is a certain amount of ambiguity. The way that "customary law" gets applied in various localities and situations can intensify gender biases. Yassine Fall notes that "Interpretation, codification or transcription of customary laws may lead to mistakes."[35] She points out that the "complexity and sometimes incompatibility of different sets of rights, responsibilities or obligations, may have contributed in creating gender biases." Ambiguities in tenure practices, especially in periods of rapid change, provide opportunities for misinterpretation and manipulation. Land reforms designed to codify customary practices in the interests of advancing cash-crop production have created new gender disparities that disadvantage women.[36] Land that falls under customary jurisdiction, then, is vulnerable to competing gender claims.

Private Freehold or Leasehold Land

Private freehold land is limited to special areas where, during the colonial period, land was set aside for African "master" or "progressive" farmers with a certain level of assets and agricultural training to encourage increased production with initial inputs from the state. In South Africa, upwardly mobile Africans purchased freehold land before 1913 and farmed it until they were expelled from their land under the apartheid regime beginning in the 1960s. In Zimbabwe, once black-owned farms now make up the Small-Scale Commercial Farming areas where much of the land is privately held. More recently, across southern Africa, freehold titles to land have, and are being, extended to individuals who buy land adjacent to or within urban areas.

Leasehold land refers to land that is leased for a long term, such as a ninety-nine-year lease, or for a short term (for example, five- to ten-year leases). The longer-term leases are awarded to local commercial farmers for large-scale production or often to multi-national corporations for commercial purposes. In some cases, a corporation that leases land will in turn contract out most of the land to individual, small commercial growers. A contract is signed between the private company and an individual producer guaranteeing the grower exclusive use of a portion of land in return for growing a specified cash-value crop such as cotton, sugar, or tea, which is then sold to the company for a set price. These contract schemes provide resource-poor farmers a means of acquiring land for cash-crop production in areas where it is scarce.[37] In almost all cases, contracts are signed with male farmers. Short-term leases are allocated to farmers in resettlement schemes or in designated, state-sponsored progressive agricultural schemes. The latter are usually tied to expectations of increased production.

In the vast majority of cases, freehold and leasehold land is controlled by male owners, regardless of pre-existing, customary practices—in other words, regardless of lineage ideology and residency practices. It is only within the last decade that state entities have begun to recognize the advantages of female entitlement to land. In Malawi, the Registered Land Act prohibits gender discrimination, but it took two decades before the state (and development agencies) began encouraging women to become titleholders. Women in post-apartheid South Africa are beginning to leverage similar laws prohibiting gender bias in property ownership. And under the Government of National Unity's Reconstruction and Development Program (RDP), women's needs for greater equity in land is fully recognized.

First to benefit from changes in land tenure laws across the region are women who head their own households and have dependents: single mothers, divorced women, and widows. Married women and single women without children in countries like Zimbabwe, Lesotho, and Swaziland rarely are able to obtain title to freehold or leasehold land, a pattern that has been noticeably resistant to change. These women remain disadvantaged in most resettlement areas and agricultural schemes, even where a woman, herself, has earned the Master Farmer status that makes it possible for her family to get land in the scheme.[38] Ncube observes of Zimbabwe that the person who holds or owns the land has the authority to control the labor of other family members.[39]

It is a rare occasion when a woman has the financial resources to purchase freehold land in her own name. Lack of financial resources acts as one obstacle. Relatedly, it is nearly impossible for women to secure the necessary loan to purchase land because they lack the prerequisite collateral. Therefore, for the vast majority of women, married or single, owning freehold land is nothing more than a distant dream.

Marital Status and Claims to Land

Marital status has everything to do with whether an individual gains access to and controls rights in land. In areas where customary law prevails, most unmarried individuals—male or female—have limited access to land unless they have children. They gain access to land through their mothers or fathers as they demonstrate their knowledge of how to till and care for the land. Or occasionally they may obtain land from a local chief. But they don't have recognized rights to land in the same way a married person does. Thus, young unmarried adults of either sex are disadvantaged under customary land jurisdiction.

Married individuals have specific rights to land. Ideally, once a man marries and begins to have a family, his father or maternal uncle will give him a parcel of land. In turn he will allocate part of that land to his wife or wives for food production. However, in areas of land scarcity, a father may not have enough land to go around. In such cases, it is often the oldest son who gets the land and younger sons must move on or purchase land in other areas. A similar situation exists for women in matrilineal groups. A woman gets land through her mother or grandmother. Sometimes she gets it through a chief. But if land is scarce, there may not be enough to go around. In such cases, tensions can erupt between sisters. One or more of them may be forced to move to a different area, or take up an urban occupation.

Widows (and widowers in matrilineal groups) have precarious rights to land and property, depending on customary law. They have more rights under statutory law. The way customary laws treat widows varies greatly from country to country, with the worst case scenario being Zimbabwe. In most countries, the patrikin or matrikin of the deceased man or woman have claims to certain property rights.

Mozambique

In Mozambique, a woman under the civil code of the family law has a right to half her husband's matrimonial property independent of whether there are extended family heirs (descendants, ascendants, collatorals) with claims or not.[40] This applies to both women married under the civil code (only 10 percent in the late 1980s) and women married under customary law or living in consensual unions. Even a woman whose husband has left her nothing in his will is entitled to half the property, and for the other half, she is fourth in line under Mozambican family law.

Malawi

In Malawi succession rights vary by district and circumstances. Generally, in cases where a husband has left no will and the property is worth less than MK 10,000, a wife must make an application to the traditional court in which the couple resided to act as executor of her husband's estate. A similar situation holds for a widower. The house and all household belongings go automatically to a widow. Throughout much of Malawi, two-fifths of the estate goes to the widow, the children of the deceased, and other direct dependents.[41] The shares are equally divided unless the deceased has expressed other wishes, or the spouse has made a contribution to the estate, in which case her/his share will be larger. The remaining three-fifths is divided among relatives who under customary law are entitled to a share, matrikin in matrilineal areas and patrikin in the patrilineal north. In the Northern Region and several districts in the Central and Southern Regions, the unequal division of property has been changed so that a widow and her children get half the estate. There is a movement to make this a nationwide change. One of the continuing problems in Malawi is the claims made on a deceased person's property by matrilineal or patrilineal kin without first ensuring that the widow has ample financial resources to maintain herself and her children. Land may or may not be an issue, as most women in rural areas have access to some land they have inherited or acquired from matrikin.

Botswana

In Botswana, cattle are as important a property as land. Under the dual marriage system, a person can be married either under customary or under civil law. Under customary law, *bogadi* (bridewealth), usually in the form of cattle and goats, is transferred to the bride's family on an incremental basis, giving the husband specific rights over his wife's labor—both productive and reproductive—unless the couple separates and the *bogadi* is returned by her family.[42] As in much of southern

Africa, customary marriage is perceived to be a union between two families rather than two individuals. Customary law legitimates the practice of polygyny, whereby a husband may take more than one wife provided bridewealth is transferred in each instance. In contrast, under Botswana's civil Marriage Act, marriage banns must be published by the individuals and a civil ceremony is required legally recognizing the marriage. *Bogadi* may or may not be transferred. A civil marriage discourages polygyny, thus avoiding the problems of multiple widows' claims.

Marital practices are changing unevenly; much is left to family heads and clan leaders among the Batswana. One positive change is that family heads tend to reduce the amount of their estate, especially in cattle, by transferring portions of it over time to children and other living heirs. Particularly among the Bakgatla, changes favoring equal inheritance for women (including daughters) have been initiated through innovative customary court decisions.[43] In 1987, there was a move to make equal inheritance the nationwide legal standard, a proposal that is gaining gradual support.

Two types of property rights are recognized under Botswana's Marriage Act, community of property and individual property. If a woman marries with community of property, she can claim one-half of her deceased husband's estate under the Succession Act of 1970, and can claim maintenance for herself and her children. Under customary law a widow is left unprotected. She has a right to inherit some property from her deceased spouse, but her rights as a widow are circumscribed and depend on the generosity of her in-laws, who are the main arbitrators of customary succession.[44]

Lesotho and Swaziland

Lesotho and Swaziland have very similar sets of customary and general laws that pertain to marriage and inheritance of property. Under customary law, similar to in Botswana, marriage is a transaction between two patrilineal families in which bridewealth is transferred from the man's family to the woman's family. Additionally, in Swaziland a Swazi custom known as *libovu*—in which the intended husband's female relatives capture a visiting bride and smear her face with red ochre to legitimate the marriage, sometimes against her will—further complicates customary marriages.[45] In both countries, customary marriages may be polygynous. In contrast, under the civil code, a marriage can only be monogamous.

Under the civil succession law in Lesotho, a widow is included with her children to receive an equal share. If there are no children, the widow receives one-half of the estate. The rest of the estate goes to patrilineal male heirs, and if there are no male heirs, the widow and any female children are still ineligible to receive the remaining share. The decision as to who will benefit is made by a family council.[46] The widow's share of the land is divided by surviving sons on her death.[47] But in cases where an unmarried woman has died, under customary law her estate has devolved to her father rather than her sons.[48]

However, this generic patriarchal portrait for Lesotho masks inverted gender scenarios where a woman may be the landholder and a man finds himself among the growing landless.[49] Lawry, in a case study of Basotho sharecroppers in an area under customary tenure, demonstrates that men and women with differing scarce resources have opportunities for pooling their resources through share-cropping arrangements.[50] In Lawry's sample, the majority of households that con-tributed land for cultivation (sharing out) were headed by older women (63 per-cent of the thirty households). Though Lawry doesn't tell us, presumably these were widows, divorced, or single women. The average age of those sharing out was sixty-three years. These households had less than half the annual income of the households gaining access to land by sharing in, all headed by men who were on average fifty years of age and most of whom had formerly worked in mines in South Africa. Of the ten men sharing in, only two had access to land, in each case one small portion. The rest were landless. In contrast, over 43 percent of those sharing out owned two fields, 13 percent owned three fields, and 3.4 owned four fields.[51]

The men sharing in had enough financial resources to hire a tractor (60 per-cent) or owned oxen. Thus they were able to provide plowing services that those providing land in the sharecropping arrangement could not afford. This benefited the largely female landowners who were older and had a scarcity of resident adult labor for cultivation. Hence "half-share plowing," as it's known in Lesotho, enables landless men to gain access to land while it affords women who hold arable land but lack other scarce resources (labor and cash) access to tractors or plows needed to cultivate their fields. Under such half-share arrangements, those sharing out and those sharing in divide the crop equally. Lawry's study demonstrates that, contrary to the generic gender pattern, cases exist in Lesotho where older women are land-holders and men are landless, and that in such cases the two parties are likely to pool their resources under customary arrangements that benefit both, increasing their mutual control over production.

Whether a woman is married in community property or out of it also makes a difference in both Lesotho and Swaziland. The most disadvantaged woman is one who has married in community of property, because she has no *locus standi in ju-dicio* (she cannot represent herself in a court of law, but instead must be represented by her husband or a male relative), and she has little control over the joint prop-erty of the marriage, whether land or cattle.[52] Under customary law, all property is controlled by the husband, whereas under general law a wife and husband may choose whether to have community of property or separate property. A marriage with separate property means that a woman retains her full contractual and pro-prietary rights, similar to a single woman. She can purchase and register freehold land in her own name.[53] This gives her an advantage over women married in com-munity of property who are under the control of their husbands. In Swaziland, however, overlapping jurisdictions in the two court systems at the lower levels af-ford women under community of property more options and legal forums for se-curing access to land and other property.

Zimbabwe

The situation of Zimbabwe is, on the surface, similar to that of Lesotho and Swaziland. At independence, Zimbabwean women were still viewed as virtual minors in this patriarchal, patrilineal country, despite a law passed in 1982 rescinding women's minority status and giving them equal adult status with men at age eighteen. However, resistance to gender equality persists at all levels, and it was not until 1991 that legislation was finally passed guaranteeing a woman's right to secure a loan without her husband's permission.

Similar to Lesotho and Swaziland, two types of marriage exist, one under the African Marriages Act that applies solely to Africans, and one under the general Marriage Act. Under the African Marriages Act, which codified customary law, bridewealth is transferred and the marriage may be polygynous. Under the general Marriage Act, only monogamous marriages are recognized. However, there is one catch: the proprietary rights of Africans married under the Marriage Act are subject to customary law.[54]

Marriages under general law are contracted either in community of property or out of it, with many women opting for out of community as it allows them to maintain their individual rights to property throughout a marriage. In cases of divorce, the Matrimonial Causes Act empowers the general court to make an equitable reallocation of property held individually during the marriage. Land in Communal Areas, however, is inherited by an eldest son or returns to the husband's patrikin. Even in Resettlement Areas and Small-Scale Commercial Areas, land is most often passed on to sons. Patriarchal attitudes toward women die hard in Zimbabwe, and this is nowhere more true than in matters of land.

South Africa

Marriage laws in South Africa stem from the apartheid era. The Matrimonial Affairs Act no. 37 of 1953 and the Marriage Act no. 25 of 1961 set out the legal perimeters.[55] These laws cover who is authorized to officiate at marriages, proof of age of majority (eighteen years), and marriage between a person and relatives of his or her deceased or divorced spouse, which mainly covers leviratic marriages. In 1968, in keeping with the racial segregation that marked the apartheid system, a law was passed prohibiting marriages between people of different races. But it has been rescinded.

The Divorce Act no. 70 of 1979 provides for the dissolution of a marriage either on grounds of an "irretrievable break-down of the marriage" or "the mental illness or continuous unconsciousness" of a spouse.[56] Irretrievable breakdown is defined as (a) a situation where parties have not lived together continuously for a period of at least one year; (b) one spouse has committed adultery and the other finds it irreconcilable with a continued marital relationship; (c) a spouse has been legally declared a habitual criminal and is imprisoned. The Divorce Amendment Act no. 7 of 1989 enables a spouse in a divorce action to share in the pension interest of the other spouse. Marital relations between spouses began to shift in 1984 when a chapter on the Abolition of Marital Power in the Matrimonial Property Act removed restrictions on the capacity of a wife to contract and litigate business, and abolished the common law rule that had previously given a husband marital power over the person and property of his wife. Further loosening came with the Domicile Act of 1992, which recognizes a person's right to choose a domicile, regardless of sex or marital status.

Laws affecting matrimonial property recognize two systems: community of property and out of community property. Most marriages are undertaken in community of property. The Matrimonial Property Act of 1984 significantly altered the way control of communal property in marriage is ordered. It gives to a wife the same powers as her husband regarding the disposal of assets of their joint estate. It prohibits either spouse from alienating, mortgaging, burdening with servitude, or conferring any other right in immovable property, mainly land, without the consent of the other spouse. Proof of consent is required. The law applies to every marriage in community of property irrespective of whether the marriage occurred before 1984 or subsequently. In cases of divorce, property held communally is divided equally between spouses, taking into consideration any marital inputs.

The law makes out of community property marriages subject to an accrual system. The accrual of a spouse's assets is defined in the 1984 statute as "the amount by which the net value of *his* [author's emphasis] estate at the dissolution of his marriage exceeds the net value of his estate at the commencement of that marriage."[57] The assumption is that the husband is the primary accruer of property and other assets. The first part of the 1984 act deals mainly with exclusions in calculating the accrual's net worth at the time of a marital dissolution. These exclusions include individual inheritances (including land), legacies, and donations. Donations between spouses are not included in assessing the worth of an accrual. The court has the right to order division of the accrual where a spouse who is subject to the accrual system confirms his or her right to a share of the accrual at dissolution. To protect the property rights of a widow or widower under this system, the statute stipulates that the accrual of the estate of a deceased spouse should be determined before any testamentary disposition is heard, donation *mortis causa* made, or intestate succession initiated.

The overall effect of the 1984 Matrimonial Property Act was to provide the means for implementing gender equity in community of property. To change the matrimonial property system under which a husband and wife are married, the couple may jointly apply to a court to change the system, regardless of whether they were married before passage of the 1984 act or not. This statute is particularly important to wives married in community of property, as it protects their rights to an equal share of the joint estate.

South Africa, since the transition in 1994, has been preoccupied with forming a new government and designing an innovative non-racist, non-sexist constitution that provides the framework for a more equitable distribution of rights and resources. The remainder of this chapter narrows the regional lens to look at gender issues linked to land reform in the two countries where land tenure is most contentious—Zimbabwe and South Africa.

Deliberations over Land in Zimbabwe: The Missing Link

Land is a provocative issue in Zimbabwe. Part of the problem lies in the legacy left by colonialism; indigenous groups were dispossessed of their arable land, and it was incorporated into a capitalist system of tenure that separated the races and privileged white farmers and mining interests. After independence in 1980, a swelling tide of ex-combatants, urban unemployed, and marginal peasants, eager for retribution, began demanding land. The state responded with a program of redistribution and resettlement that saw over fifty thousand impoverished families resettled in the first ten years.[58] Land provided a safety valve for rising expectations. More recently, it has become the approved solution of choice for addressing Zimbabwe's poverty problems. Small wonder that excluded women see land as the answer to overcoming their inequitable position and expanding their capabilities and freedom.

Periodically since independence, President Robert Mugabe has appointed land commissions to study the hard issues surrounding redistribution and come up with recommendations designed to meet demand and at the same time increase overall agricultural output. The most recent land commission was appointed by Mugabe in 1993 to evaluate the viability of Zimbabwe's various tenure systems and make suggestions for reforms to optimize production under each system. Achieving gender equity was not a priority. Yet an analysis of the commission's work illuminates gender issues that surfaced that affect Zimbabwean women's economic security and continue to impede their progress in agricultural development. It also illustrates what happens when women are not included in the development process as planners and participants. It's a case of missed opportunities.

The Work of the Commission

Zimbabwe recognizes four systems of land tenure: communal (customary), resettlement, leasehold, and freehold title. The Commission of Inquiry into Appropriate Agricultural Land Tenure Systems (Land Tenure Commission) set up in 1993 was charged with evaluating the appropriateness of each system in relation to sustainable resource management, farm productivity and investment, and making recommendations for change. It was also charged with examining the existing inheritance system in each subsector of agriculture (Communal Areas, Resettlement Areas, Small-Scale Commercial Farm Areas, and Large-Scale Commercial Farm Areas) and recommending appropriate inheritance procedures to be followed. Relatedly, the commission was asked to assess the extent to which fragmentation of plots into unviable economic units under customary inheritance patterns was occurring, and determine its impact on agricultural production. From this assessment, the commission was expected to recommend an appropriate farm size per household under each farming system and in each ecological region. Finally, the commission was asked to consider new legislative measures needed to initiate and sustain the recommended land reforms under each system. It was a tall order.

In January of 1994, the commission, composed of twelve members of which only one was a woman and four were chiefs, requested oral and written public evidence. Among the groups that responded was the Zimbabwe Women's Resource Centre and Network (ZWRCN). The organization carried out a gender analysis of existing tenure and inheritance practices and submitted a written report to the commission outlining its findings and suggesting changes to protect and equalize women's rights to land and security of inheritance under each system. For example, in the Communal Areas, ZWRCN recommended that

1. women have access to land in their own right, as single or married women, disabled, ex-combatants or unemployed women;
2. wives and husbands have joint access to land, regardless of the type of marriage;
3. if a husband decides to take another wife/wives, he should acquire separate land for each wife or share his own half-share with them, and the first wife retains her original half share; and
4. in cases of polygynous marriages, if a husband dies each wife should keep the portion of land that was allocated to her prior to her husband's death.[59]

ZWRCN made similar recommendations for the other subsectors and tenure areas, and recommended that a legal framework be initiated for extending such legal rights to women.

The Commission's Report and the Response

The commission issued a report on 1 November 1994 outlining its findings and making recommendations. The report provoked controversy and debate, especially with regard to women's tenure rights and security in land. Welshman Ncube, a respected law professor and specialist in land tenure rights, after reviewing the report, observed that although there was plenty of leeway in the commission's Terms of Reference to address the gender dimensions of each tenure system, the commission had "failed to systematically and clearly focus and then make recommendations on women's access to and control of land and/or land rights."[60] Only on the issue of inheritance had it carried out "some significant gender analysis" and made gender-related recommendations. He concluded: "Questions of women's lack of fair and equitable access and control of land in all the tenure systems remained largely unaddressed as if these have no bearing on the optimum utilization of land and also on land productivity, the twin main concerns of the Land Commission."[61]

Ncube found that the relationship between general marriage laws and customary laws and practices, on the one hand, and women's access to land, on the other, was only fleetingly referred to, and that existing laws and customary practices that clearly discriminate against women were ignored, in contradiction to Zimbabwe's commitment to honor the UN Convention on the Elimination of All Forms of Discrimination Against Women.

Ncube was not the only critic. The ZWRCN found that few of their recommendations for reform were addressed. The only recommendation accepted was on the issue of inheritance in cases of polygynous marriage; the commission agreed that co-wives should be treated equally. A look at the situation and commission's recommendations in each tenure system pinpoints the gender gaps in access to and allocation of land and factors that influence gender inequities.

The Situation in the Communal Areas

A key factor affecting women's access to land in the Communal Areas is married men's grip on land under patrilineal precepts. Customarily, arable and residential land is allocated only to married men, which perpetuates the practice of limiting women's access to vital resources, as they acquire land mainly through their husbands. Although land is allocated to wives for cultivation, it is held by the husband and should there be a marital separation, a wife's continued occupation of the land becomes tenuous.[62] If a legal divorce follows, the woman loses her use rights to the land and must leave her husband's homestead. In case of a husband's death, a woman's occupation of the plot she was allocated at marriage becomes dependent on the good will of her husband's family under "customary law."

If the commission had acknowledged the socio-cultural constraints that determine women's precarious access to land in communal areas, a recommendation might have been forthcoming to recognize the land rights of both husband and wife. Furthermore, in cases of divorce, it should have recommended an equitable adjustment to ensure continued access by both partners.[63] With regard to inheritance rights, to achieve greater equity for widows, the commission should have recommended that the surviving spouse retain the tenure rights of the deceased. But the commission chose to sidestep cultural issues that adversely affect married women rather than antagonize local chiefs who wield power at the local level. As a result, the commission fell back on traditional explanations. As Ncube notes, hiding behind the elusive concept of family, the commission's report "strengthened traditional structures and institutions for dispute settlement."[64] By playing the "tradition" trump card and leaving it up to patriarchal family heads and chiefs to decide land matters, the commission left married women with no more rights than they previously held in the Communal Areas. The patriarchal prerogative was left intact. The commission suggested that customary inheritance law be codified to clarify ambiguities. But Ncube argues that codifying customary law would serve no other purpose than to further entrench male rights to land.

The commission did make one concession. It recommended that all widows affected by polygynous marriages should retain their pre-existing land. Where a widow is threatened with eviction, the commission suggested that the village customary council intervene, and if the council failed to take action, the widow would have the right of appeal through the general courts. Only in this one instance was the commission amenable to change.

The commission's recommendations regarding administrative institutions responsible for land allocation and arbitration in Communal Areas merely served to reinforce patriarchal traditionalism by doing nothing to change the leadership structure. Chiefs and kraal heads at the community level and on Land Boards retain authority for making decisions about land and arbitrating disputes. Since women are rarely chosen to fill these leadership roles, they have little opportunity to participate in land decisions.[65] By adhering to a traditional gender structure that privileges men rather than opting for an elected leadership that might open opportunities for women's participation, in turn meeting one of their strategic needs, the commission missed a chance for greater gender equity and increased production.

The Situation in the Resettlement Areas

Looking at Resettlement Areas, women's security of tenure is also precarious. In the case of married persons, land is allocated to a husband. Therefore, the land use permit bears his name. This situation was largely ignored by the Land Tenure Commission. What the ZWRCN recommended, and the commission needed to spell out, is that for married persons the permit (and under a future system of leasehold, the lease) should be issued jointly in the names of both spouses, and on the death of one spouse, the other should inherit all the deceased's rights related to the permit or lease. As it stands, if a male settler dies, his widow is usually allowed to maintain the holding, "not as a matter of right but as a matter of administrative discretion on the part of the scheme administrators."[66] Therefore, security of tenure for these women is not guaranteed but is subject to the discretion of male administrators who may or may not be sympathetic to a widow.

Instead of advocating a joint permit that would sustain a widow's rights after her husband's death, the commission fudged by recommending that inheritance in resettlement areas fall under the purview of "common law." The trouble is, as Ncube (1996) points out, inheritance under "common law" excludes a widow from inheriting her husband's property; it is inherited by the deceased's children, usually an eldest son.[67] It is under general law that spouses have rights to inherit from one another.[68] A confusion over legal terms confounded the commission's recommendation on inheritance.

Another problem overlooked by the commission is the current method of selecting resettlement participants. The 1985 Ministry of Land, Agriculture and Rural Resettlement policy explicitly stated that in Resettlement Areas women should be assigned to land in their own right, but it excluded married women. Settler selection criteria give priority to widows and other female heads of households based on their poverty and the disadvantages they experience in the Communal Areas, but it does not take into consideration the needs of impoverished married women.[69]

Consequently, intra-gender differences in marital status that affect control of resources have not been addressed. Had women been given a participatory role in formulating resettlement policy, this conundrum would likely have been avoided.

In the Resettlement Areas, because married men hold the permits to land, they retain the authority to use land as collateral for credit even when absent from the household and working in another area. This disadvantages married women who might have occasion to seek loans to improve their production. Overall, then, the most disadvantaged category of women in the Resettlement Areas is married women. They neither hold a permit to the land and with it the right to income from its production, nor have the right to use that land as collateral to secure a loan. Since many of these women cultivate and manage the land in their husband's absence, they are doubly disadvantaged. In sum, the redistribution of a public resource, land, although well intended, led to new inequities that were reinforced by the institutional structures set up to implement and manage resettlement schemes.

Tenure Issues in the Commercial Farm Areas

In Small-Scale Commercial Farm Areas, which constitute the former African Purchase Areas, the problems of ownership and inheritance are formidable for women. On the death of the lessee or owner, the eldest son usually succeeds to ownership of the property regardless of a widow's contributions to production or her wishes. In order to qualify for a title deed or leasehold in these areas, a member of the family must have minimum farming skills. Even where the wife, rather than the husband, has the required skills to qualify, the title is awarded to the woman's husband. This practice disadvantages married females for the same reasons spelled out for Resettlement Areas. Consequently, married women in the Small-Scale Commercial Farm areas are no better off than their sisters in Resettlement Areas. They must depend on the good will of a husband, and on his death of his male relatives, to maintain their usufruct rights in land. The following case study from Gokwe illustrates the problem that a married woman faces should her husband die. It voices her realities.

"This Land, My Sister," So Begins the Song: The Case of Ratidzai

Ratidzai, a mother of five, married at age seventeen and educated to grade seven, sits at Murombedzi growth point selling tomatoes and kale to support her five children.[70] None are going to school, as she cannot afford the school fees. The four younger children mind the vegetable stand when she goes with Rumbidzai, her oldest daughter, to order vegetables to sell from the commercial farms. She has become a squatter on her parents' land in Zvimba, having been dispossessed of her "own" land in Gokwe. She knows she has no claim to her father's land—it belongs to her brothers, who farm it with their families.

Gendered Terrains

A year ago she would have laughed at the thought of having to buy vegetables and fruits to sell. She was a farmer then on her own land in Gokwe, which she had tilled for over fifteen years. She was married to Philemon, a rural bus driver who came home once or twice a month as his driving schedule permitted. Ratidzai and her children tilled the land and made the homestead a home with their own hands. She had two oxen, which she harnessed at 5:00 A.M., and with Rumbidzai leading the oxen, she'd plow their six-acre plot, sow the cotton seed, and spray it. "There wasn't anything she didn't know about cotton. . . . Her life was the land."[71]

She built a hut for her sons with the proceeds from the cotton she cultivated. She was fortunate. Usually a husband decides what will be done with the proceeds—he may buy a new scotch cart or get a second wife. He's the one who has ultimate control over the proceeds of her labor.

Then tragedy struck. Ratidzai's husband died of HIV/AIDS. A widow now, after the funeral Ratidzai prepared the land for the next season's crop. Then her father-in-law stepped in. "This is my son's field," he told Ratidzai. "Now that he is dead, take your children and go back to your home in Zvimba." As the law stands, customary practices and the law dictate that a woman cannot own land in her own name, nor jointly with her husband. So when Ratidzai's father-in-law and his six grown sons approached her, she had no option but to pack up and go home.

The case of Ratidzai, which came to my attention in a Zimbabwean newspaper, amplifies the precarious situation of married women and widows in the Small-Scale Commercial Areas. They are subject to seemingly intractable customary practices and common laws over which they have no control. Yet, as Ratidzai's case illustrates, these women are very resourceful. During the 1991–92 and 1993–94 droughts, when land stood parched and dry and the cotton withered, women in Makaha turned to panning gold to augment their income.[72] They did what Zimbabwean women have been doing for millennia during periods of drought: they diversified, combining agriculture with alternative strategies for survival.

During the same month that Ratidzai was dispossessed of her land by in-laws, Zimbabwe's Agricultural Finance Corporation (AFC) was applying to the Ministry of Lands, Agriculture and Water Development for permission to foreclose on the large-scale farms of twenty black male commercial farmers. The reason given by these farmers for failing to repay the loans they'd secured from the AFC for purchasing land and underwriting inputs was several poor growing seasons brought on by the droughts of the early 1990s.[73] On behalf of the debt-laden farmers, the all-male Indigenous Commercial Farmers' Association sought help from the state to forestall the foreclosures. The association was successful in getting the Ministry of Lands, Agriculture and Water Development to suspend the foreclosures.

The case of Ratidzai, on the one hand, and the twenty large-scale farmers, on the other, illuminates an enormous gender gap not only in economic scale but in political power. Gaidzanwa's argument that colonial gender politics in Southern Africa mirrors the suffrage movement in Britain in extending rights first to men based on color, and then to white women, with black women getting them last, also applies to gender politics in independent Zimbabwe[74]—black women are still

253

struggling to achieve basic rights that black men and whites (former Rhodesians) take for granted. Married white women in the freehold areas are far more likely to have security in land through legal means than black women, whose voices have been largely silenced in the debate over indigenization and equity in landholding. That men have the political clout to influence state decisions affecting land, but women farmers like Ratidzai have little power to change laws that dispossess them of their land is an issue the Land Tenure Commission was negligent in addressing.

If the commission had recognized indigenous women's realities by addressing their tenuous position and lack of access to financial resources and collateral to obtain the necessary loans to purchase land in their own right, it would have initiated a set of recommendations designed to empower female commercial farmers by enabling women to purchase farmland in the Small-Scale and Large-Scale Commercial Areas. The commission's suggestions might have included an innovative rural loan scheme targeting women. It has certainly been demonstrated that given the necessary resources (including land and labor), adequate inputs, and access to credit, women farmers are as efficient and productive as male farmers.[75] However, women's realities were ignored.

Equally important, had the commission taken into consideration women's as well as men's needs for security of succession under leasehold and freehold tenure systems, a widow's rights to inherit land would not have been relegated to the dubious realm of "common law," which privileges male heirs over female heirs. As a state-appointed body, the commission had the authority to suggest substantive changes in gender-related land tenure practices, but it did not use its authority to advance women's property rights. As such, women's empowerment was stymied. Neither Ncube nor ZWRCN was satisfied with the commission's findings.[76] Nor were other groups concerned with achieving gender parity. Partly the problem lay in the composition of the commission.

Composition of the Commission
and Its Influence over the Outcome

The lessons of the Land Tenure Commission illustrate how entrenched notions of "custom" and "tradition" are manipulated by holders of power to circumvent equal gender access to land and its inheritance under different tenure systems. These defenders of the status quo largely ignored women farmers' realities. The makeup of the commission's membership had a direct bearing on the outcome. A third of the commissioners were chiefs who most often are identified with patriarchal traditionalism.[77] Their staunch defense of "customary practices," through which they exercise local control, accounts for some of the body's lack of interest in and resistance to making changes that would empower women. Any suggestion that entailed reordering gender property relations at the local level was viewed as undercutting the power of traditional authorities.

That only one woman was represented on the commission with little voice to oppose the male majority undoubtedly was another factor. Certainly the recommendations of the ZWRCN, as well as those of other women's groups, were largely ignored. Part of the problem may have been their political stance—these groups took a *reactive* rather than a *pro-active* stance designed to maximize input. Had they insisted *prior* to the appointment of the commission that: (1) there be gender parity in the commission's membership or minimally a critical mass of women; and (2) among the commissioners appointed at least two be included who were qualified in gender analysis, the results might have reflected greater attention to solving gender issues under each tenure system. Certainly the survival of the agricultural sector depends on it, and flagging agriculture was a key issue of the commission.[78]

If the interested groups had organized politically to achieve the above objectives, mobilizing both men and women conversant with gender disparities in land matters and using various strategies (including use of the media) to draw attention to the inequities with one voice, greater headway might have been made. Women, who are the numerical majority in Zimbabwe (51 percent), need to constantly reassess their role in Zimbabwe's gender politics to ensure that their numbers and voices are heard. Having won the war against colonialism, their struggles to achieve equity in land continue. In neighboring South Africa, where land is equally an evocative issue, the gender dimensions are more readily acknowledged.

Gender Equity and Land: Reinventing South Africa

South Africa, similar to Zimbabwe, has been grappling with popular demands for land and its redistribution since the demise of the apartheid regime. Under that regime, beginning in 1951, the National Party set aside prescribed areas, labeled *bantustans* for African (indigenous) development. Under the goals of "separate development," all *bantustans* were eventually to become "independent" states. Only four, Transkei, Bophuthatswana, Venda, and Ciskei, achieved that dubious status. Over 3.5 million black Africans were forcefully removed from their land and were sent to *bantustans* over a period of thirty-three years.[79] Among them were those living in white farming areas and African freeholders who had purchased land in the first decade of the century. By 1980, 54 percent of South Africa's black population lived in *bantustans,* often under crowded conditions.[80]

During the 1980s, there were increasing signs that as an institution apartheid had outlived its time. With the price of gold dropping precipitously in the early 1980s and an accompanying devaluation of the rand, an economic recession escalated into a crisis that pushed the National Party leadership into a defensive position by the mid-1980s. It was, however, Chase Manhattan Bank's decision to withdraw, based on the apartheid regime's economic instability and political unrest, that pushed South Africa over the brink.[81] Once Chase Manhattan left, other banks followed and called in their short-term loans. The government declared bankruptcy, with a unilateral moratorium on repayment of its foreign debts. Widespread unemployment and increased poverty followed. By August 1985, per capita GDP (gross domestic product) had fallen to mid-1970s levels, and as a result, a growing tide of blacks from the rural areas began migrating back to the urban areas, forming rings of shack settlements on the fringes.[82] It was a tide that the floundering apartheid state could not prevent. To compound the festering problems, international and bilateral sanctions followed. P. W. Botha, then president and National Party leader, responded by tightening security on opposition groups like the African National Congress (ANC) and hunkering down. A state of emergency was declared.

It took another five years for the National Party to realize that its only survival lay in joining with the ANC leadership in designing a government of national unity that was more equitable. A new order was in the making. With the election of F. W. de Klerk in 1989 and the release of Nelson Mandela in February 1990 began an unsettling reactionary period of violence as tensions between the ANC leadership and Mangosuthu Buthelezi, leader of the Inkatha Freedom Party (IFP), escalated over the IFP's place in the new order.[83] Aided and abetted by what came to be known as a "the third force," a government-backed police initiative to destabilize ANC support by fueling Inkatha "warriors"—whether township youth or migrant workers—with weapons and turning a blind eye to the bloodshed that resulted, the eighteen-month cycle of violence that erupted in the dying days of apartheid left an indelible psychological mark on the social fabric of South Africa's black communities, especially its children and youth. They are still struggling to overcome the consequences.

After a hasty referendum called by de Klerk in 1992 confirmed that the large majority of white voters (68.7 percent) wanted peace and a new, more democratic non-racial order, the machinery was set in place for general elections. The elections of April 1994 initiated that new order, with Nelson Mandela becoming president and the ANC taking the majority of seats in parliament. The results ushered in a transitional Government of National Unity (GNU). To tackle the overwhelming problems that faced the previously disenfranchised and disadvantaged majority, the GNU launched the Reconstruction and Development Program (RDP). The GNU also made a commitment to promoting women's rights, including their land rights.[84] Gender became a key concern.

The Place of Gender in the New Order

Similar to Zimbabwe, South Africa had no history or tradition recognizing gender conflict as a political issue. South Africans were preoccupied with the struggle against apartheid; gender was not in the political consciousness of most opposition leaders (or their groups), as evidenced by the lack of women in the ANC's leadership. The ANC's energy was focused primarily on race and class. As Charman and colleagues observed at the beginning of the 1990s, "The reality of current conditions within the national liberation movement impose specific constraints on the intent to legitimate gender struggles and eliminate gender oppressive relationships in South Africa. Gender issues and politics may well compete and conflict with the process of creating a new nation."[85]

Table 10.1. Breakdown of National Assembly Membership by Party and Gender, 1996

Party	No. of Seats	No. of Women	%
African National Congress	252	78	31
National Party	82	10	12
Inkatha Freedom Party	43	10	24
Democratic Party	7	1	14
Pan Africanist Congress	5	1	20
Others	11	0	0
Total	400	100	101*

*Rounded

Source: Republic of South Africa, 1996.

Gender took a backseat until late 1991 when a women's coalition was formed made up of women's groups, women's wings in labor unions, feminist academics, and representatives of other activist organizations in which women were central. The coalition began a campaign for the inclusion of gender as a separate political category in the new constitution and for advancing women in political office. Their efforts paid off.

Prior to the 1994 elections, although women made up 54 percent of South Africa's voting population, they held only 2 percent of the seats in parliament. After the national elections in 1994 they held 25 percent of the seats (see Table 10.1), and the Speaker of the National Assembly is a woman, Dr. Frene Ginwala. Although the increased participation doesn't quite reach the 30 percent minimum proportion recommended in 1990 by the UN Commission on the Status of Women, it is a noteworthy gain for the region.

The new legislative power has enabled South African women to move gender issues from the periphery to the center of politics. Only in one other Southern African nation do women have comparable legislative clout. In Mozambique, women constitute 26 percent of the National Assembly. By comparison, women are only 14.3 percent of Angola's parliament and 13.3 percent of Zimbabwe's National Assembly. They make up a much smaller proportion in the other states of the region.[86]

On taking office as president in April 1994, Nelson Mandela acknowledged the tremendous gender inequities that still existed in South Africa, with women bearing the brunt of those inequities. He became an advocate for the inclusion of women in the new political order. On 24 May 1994, in his first State of the Nation address, he declared,

> It is vitally important that all structures of Government, including the President himself, should understand fully that freedom cannot be achieved unless the women have been emancipated from all forms of oppression. All of us must take this on board that the objectives of the Reconstruction and Development Pro-

gramme will not have been realized unless we see in visible practical terms that the condition of women in our country has radically changed for the better and that they have been empowered to intervene in all aspects of life as equals with any other member of society.[87]

In the constitutional negotiations that served to ensure the democratization of the state, gender equality became a specific goal. It is made explicit in chapter 2 of the constitution, the Bill of Rights.

Equality includes the full and equal enjoyment of all rights and freedoms. To promote the achievement of equality, legislative and other measures designed to protect or advance persons, or categories of persons, disadvantaged by unfair discrimination may be taken. . . . The state may not unfairly discriminate directly or indirectly against anyone on one or more grounds, including race, gender, sex, pregnancy, marital status, ethnic or social origin, colour, sexual orientation, age, disability, religion, conscience, belief, culture, language and birth.[88]

Chapter 9 of the constitution provides for the establishment of a Commission for Gender Equality with the express purpose of evaluating any law passed by the national legislature, or any other legislature, that affects gender equality or the status of women to ensure that the overarching gender goal of a non-sexist society is achieved. More generally the body's functions include "the power to monitor, investigate, research, educate, lobby, advise and report on issues concerning gender equality."[89] The commission was set up by Act 39 in 1996 after the constitution was adopted in May.

In addition to the commission, an Office on the Status of Women (OSW) was established in the Office of the Deputy President. Its function is to ensure that the constitutional imperatives outlining gender equality and the government's resulting political commitments are translated into real and meaningful programs. Thabo Mbeki, then deputy president and heir to Nelson Mandela, firmly supported the work of the OSW.

Another indicator of the post-apartheid state's commitment to achieving gender equality is the participation of more women at the cabinet level. Out of a total of twenty-seven ministers appointed by Mandela, four were women (roughly 15 percent), and half of the deputy ministers were women (eight out of fifteen). It was a beginning.

Although the need to include women and equalize gender in every aspect of the RDP has been officially recognized by the GNU, implementing gender equity on the ground, as it were, is a far greater task. Patriarchy is palpable, especially in rural areas.

The Land Legacy: Agriculture and Gendered Terrains

An abundance of evidence exists for South Africa, dating back to the observations of Portuguese explorers in the early seventeenth century, that women in indigenous groups did much of the hard labor in agriculture—digging, planting and tilling, threshing, and even constructing their own homes with mud and wattle—

while men built kraals for their cattle and milked the cows.[90] As time went on, women found themselves increasingly challenged as they intensified production on a gradually diminishing land base. Colonialism and white settler expansion contributed to the process of land dispossession, which changed social relationships in the beginning of the late nineteenth century. The outcome of this process was that young men engaged in wage labor away from their rural communities while women engaged in unwaged productive and reproductive labor.[91] Women responded to male migration by reorganizing agricultural production.[92] Through inter-cropping, they intensified use of the land, and switched from labor-intensive crops like sorghum and millet to maize. Although the latter resulted in higher yields, nonetheless it was more susceptible to drought, a consequence that continues to plague rural subsistence, particularly when a *series* of droughts, such as those in the early 1990s, occurs.

The pattern of male emigration still holds for much of South Africa. For example, in Nhlangwini in rural KwaZulu, Murphy found in 1989–90 that only 25 percent of the men enumerated in her sample resided at home; 75 percent had migrated out.[93] Of the 25 percent who were resident, the majority were commercial farmers. Porter and Howard found a similar pattern in Transkei and Natal.[94]

The Zulu are the predominant ethnic group in what now is KwaZulu-Natal. Under Zulu patrilineal rules, arable and residential land is allocated by indigenous authorities, often an *nduna* (traditional leader). It is allocated to a man for his household once he marries. However, Levin and Weiner argue,[95] similar to Ranger, that the notion of a chief being custodian or trustee of the land is partially a colonial invention produced by an expedient search for a system of customary land tenure. Regardless of theory, in practice women's principal route to land is through husbands when they marry.

Zulu women in Nhlangwini, where Murphy carried out her fieldwork, often find themselves with a shortage of arable land. The way they increase their access is by leasing or renting private land as a group—something they might not have had the financial resources to do as individuals. Women band together to hire a large enough plot that they can cultivate communally. Then they split the proceeds of their labor equally.[96] However, what they earn goes toward family maintenance, with little left to reinvest in agriculture. As such, this form of communal agriculture is related to subsistence rather than realizing a profit.

Among the Zulu, the *induna* are the pivotal political decision-makers. Women would not seek to become an *nduna* because, as several women told Murphy, it would be interpreted as a challenge to the Zulu (patriarchal) system. They are well aware that the system is dominated by men. An elaborate code of respect exists, incorporated in the Zulu concept of *ukuhlonipha*. It extends to gender relations; women are expected to show great deference and humility where men are concerned. As one woman confided to Murphy, when asked about the possibility of becoming an *nduna*, "Men do not like women to be in charge."[97]

I found a similar ethic espoused when, during a visit to South Africa for the Kellogg Foundation in 1996, I watched several *amakozi* (Xhosa word for traditional leader) engaged in a debate on indigenous politics versus one-person, one-vote democracy on a nationally televised program called "Future Imperfect." The program featured a panel of legal specialists, government representatives, and several chiefs. The central question being asked was, "Do traditional customs have a place in the new South Africa?" The debate ranged widely as to whether a consensual form of politics, as exists in most indigenous political arenas, or a democratic process is better in rural South Africa. At stake was whether *amakozi* should be appointed by consensus, as in the past, or elected in the future. A Zulu chief, who strongly favored consensus at all levels, "within the family and the tribe," when asked about the place of women in politics, stated that women do take part in decision-making, "just a little below the men." It was a telling remark. Nombaniso Caba, a Xhosa, observed that among the Xhosa there are some traditional leaders who are women. None were on the panel.

The panel also debated the question of land, and most agreed that men and women should have access to basic resources, as stipulated under the property section in chapter 2 of the constitution: "The state must take reasonable legislative and other measures, within its available resources, to foster conditions which enable citizens to gain access to land on an equitable basis."[98]

Noting that under "customary law," land belongs to men—married men—there was some debate about the efficacy of changing the present system in the former homelands. If a man abuses his wife, one chief argued, under customary law the *amakozi* can take action to discipline the man as "the home is for the children of the wife." If customary practice became codified law, he further argued, the home might be declared "private property" and the *amakozi* would have no right to intervene. As Levin and Weiner observe, competition for power and political space around issues of land involve grappling with local power dynamics and vested interests, including the interests of women.[99]

Various speakers on the panel noted that customary practices are not cast in stone but change over time to accommodate changing circumstances. There was general agreement that codifying customary land law could have negative consequences; it might lead to women's further oppression with regard to property, because once the patrilineally based customs were codified, they might prove difficult to change. What was unique about the panel is that gender issues were consistently engaged during the debate.

The land question in post-apartheid South Africa is littered with obstacles. The reason lies in politics. Bernstein argues that the configuration of political forces that emerged after the 1994 elections is the result of an alliance between the ANC and "progressive" chiefs.[100] He doesn't explain what he means by "progressive," but I assume he means *amakozi* who are willing to exchange customary practices for the benefits of development, whatever form it may take. Levin and Weiner agree that an alliance between the ANC and traditional leaders emerged.[101] They argue that it led to the ANC's eventual divorce from the masses. The ANC ended up wooing the "progressives" among the chiefs and ignored the others.

South Africa's rural areas are fragmented ethnically and differentiated along lines of class, gender, generation, and lineage, as Levin and Weiner observe.[102] All these factors influence the tenor of land reform. As Bernstein points out, the ANC did not grapple with the implications of changing gender relations in the former homelands, especially with reference to male urban migration.[103] From their outposts abroad or within South Africa, the leaders' eyes were focused on the urban areas. Meanwhile, households in the former homelands became more differentiated and fragmented under the male migrant labor regime. And land scarcity intensified with consequences for women's food production, as Murphy's study in Nhlangwini indicates.[104]

Popular demands for land redistribution in rural areas have been only partially addressed. The whole notion of land reform is a tricky business, not only because much arable land is in the hands of white South Africans, whom Mandela made every attempt not to alienate, but because land allocation is the material basis on which the power and authority of the *amakozi*, the traditional leaders, rest.[105] It is not wholly surprising that land reforms outlined in the RDP have been limited, both politically and economically, by "ethical discourse" and a "narrow technocratic view of redistribution," as Bernstein contends.[106] Multiple categories of people are involved. The debate over land tenure, as the televised program "Future Imperfect" indicated, enjoins the institution of chieftaincy. It implicates "customary" rights over land allocation that chiefs have historically held. It also embraces gender, which touches every household in the rural areas.

The ANC's National Land Commission was set up in 1994, and in November 1994 the Restitution of Lands Act was passed. In negotiating the authority of the Lands Claims Commission and the courts in arbitrating claims, the government softened its position on land dispossession to assuage the concerns of white farmers over their property rights. The Department of Land Affairs (DLA), in line with the RDP, distinguishes between land restitution to victims of forced removals and land redistribution to meet the economic needs of rural dwellers.[107] However, as an article in a Johannesburg daily pointed out, the Restitution of Lands Act turned out to be a work-in-progress; it had to be amended in 1996 to "weed out dubious claims."[108]

By the end of April 1996, 7,000 claims had been made, with more than 60 percent of them coming from KwaZulu-Natal and the Western Cape.[109] The Transvaal Agricultural Union, dominated by white commercial farmers, began complaining that published claims were having an adverse effect, devaluing land. It contended that many of the claims appearing in print were fraudulent. Claims by farmers who lost land to homeland development were being ignored, it was asserted, and regional land commissioners, overburdened by the sheer number of claims, were not communicating with the claimants. As a consequence, the land question has become a catalyst for bringing to the surface racial and class tensions that promise to plague the new non-racial nation for some time to come.

The DLA responded to the concerns of the Agricultural Union by advocating amendments to the Restitution Act that would empower the Land Claims Commission to throw out invalid claims rather than leaving such decisions to the courts.

Accordingly, the whole issue of land reform has become bogged down not only by a backlog of competing claims but by bureaucratic disputes over jurisdictional power. Relatively muted in all these disputes are the voices of women whose needs for land and land security have been drowned out by the more strident voices of both white and black male farmers demanding that justice be served. Yet Murphy's study in Nhlangwini[110] and my own research in Lenyenye (next section) indicate that women desperately need land.

Women's Needs for Land in Two Rural Areas

Land scarcity is beginning to take its toll on women farmers, who account for the bulk of agricultural production in rural areas, as the vast majority of men are engaged in cyclical labor migration. This section looks at two case studies, one from Lenyenye in Northern Transvaal and the other from North Pondoland in Transkei. The first case is based on fieldwork I carried out in April–May 1996, and the other is based on the work of Porter and Howard in two contract farming schemes in a former homeland in the mid-1990s.[111]

Ithusheng Community Association in Lenyenye

Located in the northeast corner of Northern Transvaal, halfway between Pietersburg and Kruger National Park, is an isolated rural township. It is the home of Ithusheng Community Association (ICA). Ithusheng is the inspiration of Mamphela Ramphele, who was banished by the apartheid regime to this remote area as a result of her work with her partner, the late Steve Biko, in the Black Consciousness Movement in the 1970s. Headquartered in the township of Lenyenye, ICA, or simply Ithusheng, serves rural communities within a sixty-kilometer radius. Dr. Ramphele began by establishing a much-needed clinic in 1977. She observed that many of the children who visited the clinic with their mothers were malnourished. In response, she initiated a child care facility, with nutrition being a major focus. As a result, Ithusheng grew out of the nutrition needs of local children.

Ithusheng began with communal gardens as a strategy for teaching mothers how to grow nutritious foods at little cost. A South African Christian Council spin-off, Victims of Apartheid, was ICA's first major donor. It supported the project for eleven years. In the meantime, a variety of international voluntary assistance organizations, foundations, and private companies in South Africa also helped to fund the project. A community center was built at Lenyenye in 1992. It functions as a multiservice center. As of mid-1996, ICA had three major programs in operation in addition to the communal gardens: a child care program, a health care center and village health program, and an income-generating program, under which exist a tractor outreach project and a communal brickmaking project. In addition, communities in the surrounding areas have local projects that ICA supports with professional advice and occasional inputs. The management board of ICA is participatory in that it includes community member representatives, three men and three women, involved in the community-based projects.

Most of the land surrounding Lenyenye is semi-arid farming land. It is "owned" by male household heads under customary tenure practices. The average holding is three to five hectares, but some are much smaller. Men grow cash-value crops such as maize on their plots. Women gain access to land usually through their husbands. For some women, the parcels they are allocated prove to be too small to raise sufficient and nutritious food for their families. Other women, especially those heading their own households, are landless. For these reasons, the ICA leases land on the edge of the township, which it turns over to mainly women's groups to cultivate on a communal basis. The land I observed being cultivated by one group was roughly a half hectare. The crops cultivated were maize, peanuts, and yugo beans. The nine women involved, who came from Mohlaflareng area, included three widows and six older women on state pensions. Originally there had been seventeen women, but half had dropped out between 1994–95 due to the drought—it adversely affected the group's productivity. The rest of the women stayed in because, as they related, they had no alternative. The women had first heard about Ithusheng from other women. They learned that ICA was willing to help women's groups establish communal gardens and would provide land and manure (fertilizer) to help them get started. The women buy their own seed.

ICA has two tractors and has trained two men to operate them, one in his 50s and the other in his 20s. When we asked about women operating the tractors, we were told that "women are not interested in driving tractors." Ithusheng charges a fee for plowing the fields of both members and non-members. However, the first plowing for a communal garden belonging to ICA members is free. Thereafter the price is R 128 ($31 in 1996 dollars) per plowing. The cost to non-members, usually male farmers, is R 160 ($37). Sixty-two non-member farmers in the surrounding area hired the tractor service between mid-1995 and mid-1996. One non-member farmer interviewed, who was employed as a civil servant, said that he uses the ICA plowing service twice a year. He grows maize, tomatoes, and spinach, which he sells commercially. He indicated that he annually earns R 2,800 ($651) on mealies (dried maize) and R 4,300 ($1,000) on tomatoes. He earns less on spinach—he couldn't remember the exact amount. He related that access to a tractor had enabled him to cultivate a larger area than he used to, and because the plow cut deeper, the land was better for growing maize. As a result, his yield had improved.

In contrast to the civil servant/farmer, who not only had a regular income for inputs like plowing, but access to sufficient land to produce three cash-value crops, the Ithusheng communal garden groups have more difficulty realizing a profit. As of 1996, there were six groups involving roughly 10–15 members each. The purpose of the gardens, from ICA's perspective, is to improve the nutritional status of marginal families. Most members of the groups are women who are landless or have handkerchief-size plots. They depend on the crops they raise in communal gardens to supplement other sources of food they either raise at home or buy for their families. Depending on climatic factors, the groups may or may not have a surplus. In drought years they barely have enough to supplement the diet of their own families. In 1996, however, when there were abundant rains, at least one group had a bumper crop in peanuts. Eight of the nine members were in the process of bagging the last of the peanuts for sale at the time of my research. From the harvest's initial proceeds, they'd bought new vegetable seeds. Neat rows of spinach and carrot seedlings were sprouting in a "nursery," a large rectangle shaded by a dried grass structure to protect the infant vegetables. The women had hopes of increasing their profits with the new crops. How would they use the profits? First they would make sure they had plenty of seed. Then they would set aside R 128 for the next season's plowing. Any extra would be divided between them.

The case of Ithusheng points to the consequences for family nutrition of gender inequities in access to land. Women in and around Lenyenye still have far fewer chances for access to and control of land than men. In order to meet their families' needs, and possibly earn some income, landless women and those with minimal plots, similar to the Zulu women in Murphy's study,[112] search for alternative ways to secure land. One of the benefits of ICA's communal gardens is that not only does the project enable impoverished women, including those on a minimal government pension, to leverage land, but the gardens provide a chance to increase the nutritional status of their families. As a bonus, they may earn a little income in a good year. ICA provides a means for women to improve family subsistence levels, but it is unable to provide a strategy for earning income on a sustained basis because the amount of land cultivated is too small and the weather conditions too variable.

The crux of the gender gap in Lenyenye lies in land discrepancies. Compared to many of their male counterparts, women have meager access to arable land. Underlying this inequity are cultural prescriptions that are not amenable to change without state intervention. The government through the RDP is committed to increasing women's rights in land. Laws covering community of property for married women exist. But in Lenyenye knowledge of these laws is vague, and the development mechanisms for women seeking greater equity in land through the RDP remain undefined. Rather than tackle the underlying structural reasons for the disparity by advocating changes in local land tenure practices and educating women as to their property rights, both of which would provide them with a greater sense of efficacy, ICA continues to address women's immediate practical needs.

North Pondoland: Women, Land, and Contract Labor

At the opposite end of South Africa from Lenyenye, in the Mpondo area of Transkei on the southern Indian Ocean, is a sugar scheme that dates back to the early 1980s.[113] North Pondoland Sugar Ltd. began as a resettlement scheme in 1982. The land to launch the scheme was appropriated from local communities in the former homeland of Transkei without adequate compensation. In 1996, 30,000 people, largely Xhosa speakers, lived on the North Pondoland Sugar estate. Only a few households in the original communities that "donated" the land had the resources to become involved in the scheme. As a result, the sugar cane venture intensified growing economic disparities between households in pre-existing communities. Those with more resources became contract growers; others did not. Moreover, some women were particularly disadvantaged by the scheme because it involved land that they had cultivated prior to the scheme's inception. For men, the scheme became a strategy for acquiring land in a region of extreme land pressure.[114]

The total scheme consists of 130 plots devoted to cane production and a core estate where the sugar refinery is located. Those who settled on scheme plots to grow sugar cane gained access to parcels that average ten hectares.[115] The contract with the mostly male household heads in the scheme (there were only 30 female growers out of a total 130 in 1995) specifies that the plot must be planted in cane. However, women farmers found that when the cane is young, they can intercrop beans between the rows of immature cane, thus maximizing the land's capacity. Maize for home consumption is restricted to one hectare adjacent to the homestead. These gardens are usually located in the hilltop areas. Women account for 70 percent of the labor on the sugar cane plots because the majority of male growers are migrant workers or are involved in off-estate enterprise.

Indigenous farmers are attracted to outgrowing cane because it affords a consistent cash income and some availability of inputs, such as credit and fertilizer, that may be unavailable or costly. Related to the cost of inputs, Porter and Howard note that diversion of scheme inputs to non-contract crops is not unusual.[116] Women stretch the contractor's inputs to cover food crops as well as cane.

The North Pondoland Sugar scheme is managed by three white males (a British administrator and two South Africans). The only black male involved at the management level is a Xhosa liaison manager who comes from the region. He speaks the language of the growers, is sympathetic to their needs—often visiting them with an extension worker—and even settles marital disputes that arise between male growers and their wives. His own wife runs a small business at the edge of the estate that the growers patronize. Thus a race/class matrix exists between management and growers on the scheme, with the Xhosa liaison manager the only one bridging the gap.

Under new loan conditions in 1994, men now hold title to their plots unless a woman has no husband. Title is essential for access to credit. Frequently women (wives and daughters) work all year on a cane plot, but it is the husband who goes to the sugar factory to collect the cane check at the end of harvest. And he retains control of the funds, distributing money to his wife for house maintenance, clothing, and school fees.

A bone of gender contention on the North Pondoland estate is that the cane check is in a husband's name, but his wife and children do most of the work. In cases of absentee male plot holders, a man may be gone for months and appear only to collect the cane check. If the husband is sympathetic to his family's needs and provides for its members, no problems arise. Tensions flair, however, in situations where an absentee husband continuously cheats his wife or wives out of the proceeds of the cane check. Porter and Howard describe two complaints brought by wives against their absentee grower husbands.[117] In each case, the woman took her problem to the Growers' Association, a body that acts as a conduit for communication between growers and a contracting company such as North Pondoland. As the primary producer, each woman argued, she should have control of the cane check because she did most of the work and her husband had proved irresponsible.

After hearing their separate cases, the Growers' Association agreed to intervene on the women's behalf and approached North Pondoland: the cane land was re-registered in each wife's name as was the contract, with the result that from then on these women controlled the proceeds of their own production. They were successful because they had used an alternative forum to present their cases, and by engaging the support of the mostly male Growers' Association they were able to reach the Pondoland management and resolve the inequity.

As the Government of National Unity is committed to promoting women's land rights, it is likely that as more women contest their situations, local land boards will be forced to hear their cases. The alternative is for women to withdraw their labor from production, a form of protest that is gaining popularity throughout Africa.[118] The result of this protest strategy is reduced production and wasted resources, as Porter and Howard note. Corbridge points out that exploitation in contract farming is based ultimately on an undefended and unequal distribution of property rights.[119] This is nowhere more true than in Transkei on the North Pondoland Sugar estate where gender struggles over control of land and its proceeds are bound to escalate.

Whose Reality Counts? Some Conclusions

Chambers, in a recent issue of *World Development,* posits that changes in the language of development over time have helped to shift our thinking about the development enterprise.[120] By introducing and stressing new terms, combining them in innovative ways, and by listing and disaggregating them, we alter our mindsets.[121] In proposing a new combination, "responsible well-being," Chambers draws on the experiences of participatory research practitioners and Participatory Poverty Assessment (PPA) advocates, who ask the fundamental question, "Whose reality counts?"[122] By asking such a question, we shift our perspective from a top-down to a bottom-up approach. The question raises issues about gender equity and efficacy. It enables marginal women and the most impoverished men to articulate their realities. It provokes questions about social and economic exclusion.

Unless we are willing to listen to married women on the North Pondoland Sugar estate who have a solution to the deprivation they feel over not being able to control land and the contract for growing cane; unless we understand the strategies women in the former homelands use as groups to leverage land for communal production; until we hear the stories of women in Zimbabwe who risk losing land they've tilled for fifteen years on their husband's death because patrilineal precepts give power to their fathers-in-law to decide, and support their quest for changing inheritance patterns; unless we listen to older women in Lesotho who know how to use their land to gain access to other scarce resources such as tractors, and women in Swaziland who know how to negotiate two sets of courts to leverage land for increased production, we are in danger of missing realities that ground development.

By the same token, we need to listen to men—to married men in the former homelands of South Africa whose land has become marginal and so in contract farming have found an alternative; to aging chiefs in Zimbabwe's Communal Areas who fear a loss of authority and the opportunity to settle family squabbles should rights to land allocation be transferred to a distant claims commission or the state; to single men in Lesotho with little or no land who use other resources such as a tractor to leverage access to cropland by "half-sharing" with older women who have land; to young men in northern Mozambique and southern Malawi who have little direct access to land, and so must "beg land" from their wives' matrikin or sell their labor on plantations owned by multi-national corporations.

Participatory development allows spaces for hearing other people's realities, for learning about the strategies they use to overcome obstacles that prevent them from gaining access to land or optimizing its use. It allows us to learn how women, as active agents, negotiate their way through competing systems of law, taking advantage of both. It informs our understanding of the underlying sets of gender relationships that order who allocates land, who uses it and maintains it, and who benefits most from its production, and where these sets of relationships need to change to increase people's overall efficacy. It amplifies the connections between community action and the need for shifts in public policy at the national level. But an awareness of women's realities is not a sufficient condition for change.

As the case of the Land Tenure Commission in Zimbabwe demonstrates, institutional structures designed to facilitate development do not always honor rural women's realities. They may sidestep gender issues rather than create innovative strategies for achieving more efficacious gender relations. The South Africa's RDP has taken a positive first step in addressing gender inequalities in property. However, the RDP will only be as effective as its actions; it is one thing to articulate the need to increase women's rights in land and quite another to design measures with sufficient teeth to make it happen. Until the government implements specific policies whereby women, particularly in the former homelands, are guaranteed equal access to land and the means to hang onto it regardless of local "customs," and until they gain access along with men to the means to improve production (including technical inputs and credit), and are able to benefit directly from the land's output, the good intentions of the RDP will remain at the level of rhetoric rather than reality.

As I indicated at the beginning of this chapter, knowing who does what and who has what is a beginning in assessing gender inequalities in access to resources. Acknowledging the factors that influence women's (and men's) realities, including cultural prescriptions, laws, and political obstacles that shape their chances for full empowerment is an important next step. But key to the process of transforming gender relations is the institutional structures at all levels that perpetu-ate gender inequalities and yet have the potential to change them. Until concrete measures are taken to restructure strategic institutions—from land tenure com-missions and local tenure committees to producers' associations and management teams—to make them more gender appropriate and sensitive to women's strate-gic as well as their practical needs, women's quest for full empowerment with men will be stymied.

The cases in this chapter demonstrate that social categories of development elude us if we oversimplify, if we essentialize all women and all men into single cate-gories. Similarly, we miss something if we overlook the ways women and men work together to solve their problems, like the gender pooling of resources that occurs in rural Lesotho, or the efforts of the male Growers' Association in South Africa to help women on the North Pondoland estate to solve their tenure problems. We need to carry out gender analyses to pinpoint inequities, but we also need to look at gender collaborative strategies that have worked in southern Africa and else-where, and build toward a future in which gender collaboration becomes an an-swer to questions that continue to plague development practitioners. The voices of the excluded often suggest the very answers we're looking for.

NOTES

1. I. Amadiume, *Male Daughters, Female Husbands* (London: Zed Press, 1987); R. Meena, "Gender Research/Studies in Southern Africa: An Overview," in R. Meena, ed., *Gender in Southern Africa: Conceptual and Theoretical Issues* (Harare: SAPES Books, 1992); R. Gaidzanwa, "Bourgeois Theories of Gender and Feminism and Their Shortcomings with Reference to Southern African Countries," in Meena, ed., *Gender in Southern Africa;* and C. Mannathoki, "Feminist Theories and the Study of Gender in Southern Africa," in Meena., ed., *Gender in Southern Africa.*

2. "Feminist Encounter: Locating the Politics of Experience," in M. Barrett and A. Phillips, eds., *Destabilizing Theory: Contemporary Feminist Debates* (Stanford, Calif.: Stan-ford University Press, 1992); "Introduction: Cartographies of Struggle," in C. Mohanty, ed., *Third World Women and the Politics of Feminism* (Bloomington: Indiana University Press, 1993); and "Under Western Eyes: Feminist Scholarship and Colonial Dis-courses," in Mohanty, ed., *Third World Women and the Politics of Feminism.*

3. Gaidzanwa, "Bourgeois Theories of Gender and Feminism."

4. Ibid.; R. Gaidzanwa, "Women's Land Rights in Zimbabwe: An Overview," Oc-casional Paper, no. 13, Department of Rural and Urban Planning, University of Zim-babwe (Harare: University of Zimbabwe, 1988).

5. Gaidzanwa, "Bourgeois Theories of Gender and Feminism," p. 100.

6. See S. H. Longwe, "From Welfare to Empowerment: The Situation of Women in Development in Africa: A Post UN Women's Decade Update and Future Directions," Women in Development Series Working Paper, no. 204 (Ann Arbor: Michigan State University, 1990).

7. Amartya Sen in *Development as Freedom* (New York: Knopf, 1999) argues that women's capabilities for developing resources have been constrained by a narrow focus on economic aspects, while ignoring social aspects that prevent women's agency and freedom.

8. C. Overholt, M. Anderson, K. Cloud, and E. Austin, *Gender Roles in Development Projects* (West Hartford, Conn.: Kumarian Press, 1985).

9. Caroline Moser, "Practical Gender Needs and Strategic Needs in Development," *World Development* 17, no. 2 (1989): 1799–1825; and Caroline Moser, *Gender Planning and Development: Theory, Practice, and Training* (New York and London: Routledge, 1993).

10. Longwe, "From Welfare to Empowerment."

11. Landeg White, *Magomero: Portrait of an African Village* (Cambridge: Cambridge University Press, 1987).

12. A. Richards, *Land, Labour and Diet in Northern Rhodesia* (Oxford: Oxford University Press, 1939); A. Richards, "Some Types of Family Structures Amoungst the Central Bantu," in R. Radcliffe-Brown and D. Forde, eds., *African Systems of Kinship and Marriage* (Oxford: Oxford University Press, 1950); E. Colson, "The Plateau Tonga," E. Colson and M. Gluckman, eds., *Seven Tribes of British Central Africa* (Manchester: Manchester University Press, 1951); K. O. Poewe, *Matrilineal Ideology* (New York: Academic Press, 1981); P. Stromgaard, "A Subsistence Society under Pressure: The Bemba of Northern Zambia," *Africa* 55, no. 1 (1985): 39–58; and K. Crehan, "Land, Labor and Gender: Matriliny in 1980s Rural Zambia" (paper presented at the annual African Studies Association meetings, Toronto, 3–6 November 1994).

13. N. Hafkin, "Trade, Society, and Politics in Northern Mozambique, c. 1753–1913" (Ph.D. diss., Boston University, 1973); S. Amfred, "Women in Mozambique: Gender Struggle and Gender Politics," *Review of African Political Economy* 41 (1988): 5–12; and A. Pitcher, "Conflict and Cooperation: Gendered Roles and Responsibilities Amoungst Cotton Households in Northern Mozambique" (Cornell University, Ithaca, 1995, mimeograph).

14. For instance, G. Kay, *Changing Patterns of Settlement and Land Use in the Eastern Province of Northern Rhodesia* (Yorkshire: University of Hull, 1965); and R. W. Kettlewell, *Agricultural Change in Nyasaland, 1945–1960* (Stanford, Calif.: Food Research Institute, Stanford University, 1965). See critiques in M. Wright, "Technology, Marriage, and Women's Work in the History of Maize Growers in Mazabuka, Zambia: A Reconnaissance," *Journal of Southern African Studies* 10, no. 1 (1983): 71–85; J. May, *Zimbabwean Women in Colonial and Customary Law* (Gweru: Mambo Press, 1983); Gaidzanwa, "Women's Land Rights in Zimbabwe"; J. Bruce, "Do Indigenous Land Tenure Systems Constrain Agricultural Development?" in T. J. Bassett and D. E. Crummey, eds., *Land in African Agrarian Systems* (Madison: University of Wisconsin Press, 1993); A. Spring, *Agricultural Development and Gender Issues in Malawi* (Latham, Md.: University Press of America, 1995).

15. E. Worby, "What Does Agrarian Wage-Labour Signify? Cotton, Commoditisation and Social Form in Gokwe, Zimbabwe," *Peasant Studies* 21, no. 1 (1995): 1–23.

16. E. Skjonsberg, *Change in an African Village: Kefa Speaks* (West Hartford, Conn.: Kumarian Press, 1989); E. Schmidt, *Peasants, Traders and Wives: Shona Women in the History of Zimbabwe, 1870–1939* (Portsmouth: Heinemann, 1992); H. Moore and M. Vaughan, *Cutting Down Trees: Gender, Nutrition and Agricultural Change in the Northern Province of Zambia: 1890–1990* (Portsmouth, N.H.: Heinemann, 1994); and Crehan, "Land, Labour, and Gender."

17. A. Molokomme, "Women's Law in Botswana," in J. Stewart and A. Armstrong, eds., *The Legal Situation of Women in Southern Africa* (Harare: University of Zimbabwe Publications, 1990).

18. R. T. Nhlapo, "The Legal Situation of Women in Swaziland and Some Thoughts on Research," in Stewart and Armstrong, eds., *Legal Situation of Women in Southern Africa.*

19. B. O'Laughlin, "Through a Divided Glass: Dualism, Class and the Agrarian Question in Mozambique," *Journal of Peasant Studies* 23, no. 4 (1996): 1–39.

20. T. Ranger, "The Communal Areas of Zimbabwe," in Bassett and Crummey, eds., *Land in African Agrarian Systems,* p. 363.

21. H. S. Simelane, "The Post-Colonial State, Class, and the Land Question in Swaziland," *Journal of Contemporary African Studies* 11, no. 1 (1992): 22–50.

22. R. Levin and D. Weiner, "The Politics of Land Reform in South Africa," *Journal of Peasant Studies* 23, no. 2/3 (1996): 94–115.

23. E. Sjaastad and D. W. Bromley, "Indigenous Land Rights in Sub-Saharan Africa: Appropriation, Security and Investment Demand," *World Development* 25, no. 4 (1997): 549–62.

24. Worby, "What Does Agrarian Wage-Labour Signify?"

25. P. Peters, "Manoeuvres and Debates in the Interpretation of Land Rights in Botswana," *Africa* 62, no. 3 (1992): 413.

26. Molokomme, "Women's Law in Botswana," p. 13.

27. S. M. Seeiso, L. Kanono, N. Tsotsi, and T. Monaphathi, "The Legal Situation of Women in Lesotho," in Stewart and Armstrong, eds., *Legal Situation of Women in Southern Africa;* Nhlapo, "Legal Situation of Women in Swaziland"; and W. Ncube, "The Matrimonial Property Rights of Women During and After Marriage in Zimbabwe: A Study of Property Relations, Domestic Labour and Power Relations Within the Family" (M.A. diss., University of Zimbabwe, 1986).

28. L. Rose, "A Woman Is Like a Field: Women's Strategies for Land Access in Swaziland," in J. Davison, ed., *Agriculture, Women and Land: The African Experience* (Boulder, Colo.: Westview Press, 1988), p. 200.

29. Rose, "A Woman Is Like a Field."

30. D. Pankhurst and S. Jacobs, "Land Tenure, Gender Relations, and Agricultural Production: The Case of Zimbabwe's Peasantry," in Davison, ed., *Agriculture, Women and Land.*

31. C. N. Himonga, K. A. Turner, and C. S. Beyani, "An Outline of the Legal Status of Women in Zambia," in Stewart and Armstrong, eds., *Legal Situation of Women in Southern Africa.*

32. N. Ilukena, "Women, Land, and the Environment," *Women Plus* 1, no. 1 (1996): 25–26.

33. J. Davison, "Tenacious Women: Clinging to Banja Household Production in the Face of Changing Gender Relations in Malawi," *Journal of Southern African Studies* 19, no. 3 (1993): 405–21; J. Davison, *Gender, Lineage, and Ethnicity in Southern Africa* (Boulder, Colo.: Westview Press/Harper Collins, 1997); P. Peters, "Against the Odds: Matriliny, Land and Gender in the Shire Highlands of Malawi," *Critique of Anthropology* 17, no. 2 (1997): 189–210; Stromgaard, "Subsistence Society"; Crehan, "Land, Labour and Gender"; Arnfred, "Women in Mozambique"; and A. Pitcher, "Lineage, Gender, and Cash: Women and Cotton in Northern Mozambique" (paper presented at the annual meetings of the African Studies Association, Boston, 4–7 December 1993).

34. National Commission on Women in Development (NCWID), *Women and the Law in Malawi* (Lilongwe: NCWID, 1993).

35. "Gender Relations in the Democratization Process: An Analysis of Agrarian Policies in Africa," *Issue: A Journal of Opinion* 25, no. 2 (1997): 10.

36. Gaidzanwa, "Women's Land Rights in Zimbabwe"; H. W. O. Okoth-Ogendo, "Agrarian Reform in Sub-Saharan Africa: An Assessment of State Responses to the African Agrarian Crisis and Their Implications for Agricultural Development" in Bassett and Crummey, eds., *Land in African Agrarian Systems;* W. Ncube, "Women's Access to and Control of Land," *Women Plus* 1, no. 1 (1996): 21–23; and C. Brantley, "Through Ngoni Eyes," *Critique of Anthropology* 17, no. 2: 147–69.

37. G. Porter and K. P. Howard, "Comparing Contracts: An Evaluation of Contract Farming Schemes in Africa," *World Development* 25, no. 2 (1997): 227–38.

38. S. Mvududu, "The Dynamics of Gender Structuring in Resettlement Schemes," *Women Plus* 1, no. 1 (1996): 12–15.

39. Ncube, "Matrimonial Property Rights of Women," p. 1.

40. I. Casimiro, I. Chicalia, and A. Pessoa, "The Legal Situation of Women in Mozambique," in Stewart and Armstrong, eds., *Legal Situation of Women in Southern Africa.*

41. NCWID, *Women and the Law in Malawi.*

42. Molokomme, "Women's Law in Botswana."

43. Ibid.

44. Ibid.

45. Nhlapo, "Legal Situation of Women in Swaziland."

46. Ibid.

47. S. W. Lawry, "Transactions in Cropland Held Under Customary Tenure in Lesotho," in Bassett and Crummey, eds., *Land in African Agrarian Systems.*

48. Nhlapo, "Legal Situation of Women in Swaziland."

49. Commercialization and increasing landlessness have brought new pressures for land reform by donor agencies and commercial farmers in areas of customary tenure, but so far the state, backed by elites and traditional leaders, has resisted changes that would undermine customary rights. See Lawry, "Transactions in Cropland."

50. Ibid.

51. Ibid., p. 232.

52. Nhlapo, "Legal Situation of Women in Swaziland," p. 114.

53. Seeiso et al., "Legal Situation of Women in Lesotho"; and Nhalpo, "Legal Situation of Women in Swaziland."

54. J. Stewart, W. Ncube, M. Maboreke, and A. Armstrong, "The Legal Situation of Women in Zimbabwe," in Stewart and Armstrong, eds., *Legal Situation of Women in Southern Africa.*

55. Republic of South Africa, *Statutes: Husbands and Wives* (Pretoria: Republic of South Africa, 1979), p. 423.

56. Ibid.

57. Republic of South Africa, *Statutes: Husbands and Wives* (Pretoria: Republic of South Africa, 1984), p. 487.

58. E. Moyo, "Women and the Soil," *Woman Plus* 1, no. 1 (1996): 3–5.

59. Zimbabwe Women's Resource Centre and Network (ZWRCN), "About the Land Tenure Commission," *Woman Plus* 1, no. 1 (1996): 5.

60. Ncube, "Women's Access to and Control of Land," p. 21.

61. Ibid.

62. S. Moyo, *The Land Question in Zimbabwe* (Harare: SAPES Books, 1995).

63. Ncube, "Women's Access to and Control of Land."

64. Ibid., p. 62.

65. E. Moyo, "Women and the Soil."

66. Mvududu, "Dynamics of Gender Structuring," p. 12.

67. Ncube, "Matrimonial Property Rights of Women."

68. Ibid., p. 22.

69. Mvududu, "Dynamics of Gender Structuring."

70. This case study comes from an anonymous article published in Zimbabwe's *Sunday Gazette,* 12 February 1995, p. 11.

71. Ibid.

72. J. L. Mavunga and C. Mugedeza, "Women Turn to Mining When Land Fails to Produce," *Women Plus* 1, no. 1: 19–20. In "Coping with Drought in Zimbabwe: Survey Evidence on Responses of Rural Households to Risk," *World Development* 26, no. 2 (1998): 19–20, Kinsey, Burger, and Gunning found that the majority of male household heads (63 percent) in three resettlement schemes responded to the same two droughts by selling off one or two head of cattle, and some turned to temporary wage work (roughly 40 percent) before turning to panning gold (11 percent).

73. Agricultural Reporter, "AFC Sale of 20 Black-Owned Farms Blocked," *Herald* (Harare), 23 February 1995, p. 1.

74. Gaidzanwa, "Bourgeois Theories of Gender and Feminism."

75. See A. R. Quisumbling, "Male-Female Differences in Agricultural Productivity: Methodological Issues and Empirical Evidence," *World Development* 24, no. 10 (1996): 1579–95.

76. W. Ncube, "Women's Access to and Control of Land"; and ZWRCN, "About the Land Tenure Commission."

77. Ranger, "The Communal Areas of Zimbabwe."

78. The growing number of cases throughout Africa of wives withdrawing their labor from production as a form of protest on their husband's land, with detrimental consequences for production, should be a wake-up call for land tenure commissions that ignore the gender dimensions of land issues. See J. Carney, "Struggles Over Land and Crops in an Irrigated Rice Scheme: The Gambia," in Davison, ed., *Agriculture, Women, and Land;* S.O. Babalola and Dennis, "Returns to Women's Labour in Cash Crop Production: Tobacco in Igboho, Oyo State, Nigeria," in Davison, ed., *Agriculture, Women, and Land;* D. von Bulow and A. Sorenson, "Gender and Contract Farming: Tea Grower Schemes in Kenya," *Review of African Political Economy* 56, no. 3 (1993): 38–52; and Porter and Howard, "Comparing Contracts."

79. H. Bernstein, "South Africa's Agrarian Question: Extreme and Exceptional?" *Journal of Peasant Studies* 23, no. 2/3: 1–52.

80. Ibid., 13.

81. P. Waldmeir, *Anatomy of a Miracle: The End of Apartheid and the Birth of the New South Africa* (New York: Norton, 1997).

82. Bernstein, "South Africa's Agrarian Question."

83. Waldmeir, *Anatomy of a Miracle.*

84. Porter and Howard, "Comparing Contracts."

85. A. Charman, C. deSwardt, and M. Simons, "The Politics of Gender: A Discussion of the Malibongwe Conference Papers and Other Current Papers of the ANC" (pa-

per presented at the first Conference on Women and Gender in Southern Africa, University of Natal, Durban, 30 January–2 February 1991).

86. The percentages in the other countries range from 7 percent in Zambia and Namibia down to 5 percent in Botswana. In comparison with Mozambique and South Africa, the proportion of women in the U.S. Congress is far less, only 11 percent of the total membership, even less than in Angola and Zimbabwe. In only five countries have women gained or surpassed the 30 percent minimum proportion recommended by the United Nations: Sweden—41 percent; Norway—39 percent; Finland—34 percent; Denmark—33 percent; and the Netherlands—30 percent. See N. Neft and A. D. Levine, *Where Women Stand: An International Report on the Status of Women in 140 Countries* (New York: Random House, 1997).

87. Republic of South Africa, *Constitution of Republic of South Africa, 1996* (Pretoria: Constitutional Assembly, 1996).

88. Ibid., p. 6.

89. Ibid., p. 56.

90. See C. White, "'Close to Home in Johannesburg: Sexism in Township Households" (paper presented at the first Conference on Women in Gender in Southern Africa, University of Natal, Durban, South Africa, 30 January to 2 February 1991) for a review.

91. Charman, "The Politics of Gender."

92. C. Walker, *Women and Gender in Southern Africa to 1945* (Cape Town and London: James Currey, 1990).

93. C. Murphy, "Gender Constraints to Increased Agricultural Production—A Case Study of Women in KwaZulu" (paper presented at the first Conference on Women and Gender in Southern Africa, University of Natal, Durban, South Africa, 30 January to 2 February 1991).

94. Porter and Howard, "Comparing Contracts."

95. Levin and Weiner, "The Politics of Land Reform in Southern Africa," p. 104; Ranger, "The Communal Areas of Zimbabwe."

96. Murphy, "Women and the Soil."

97. Ibid., 11.

98. Republic of South Africa, *Constitution,* p. 9.

99. Levin and Weiner, "Politics of Land Reform," p. 100.

100. Bernstein, "South Africa's Agrarian Question."

101. Levin and Weiner, "Politics of Land Reform."

102. Ibid.

103. Bernstein, "South Africa's Agrarian Question."

104. "Gender Constraints to Increased Agricultural Production."

105. Levin and Weiner, "Politics of Land Reform," p. 105.

106. Bernstein, "South Africa's Agrarian Question," p. 15.

107. Levin and Weiner, "Politics of Land Reform."

108. L. Cook, "Government Moves to Block Dubious Land Claims," *Business Day* (Johannesburg), 26 April 1996, p. 1.

109. Ibid.

110. Murphy, "Gender Constraints to Increased Agricultural Production."

111. Porter and Howard, "Comparing Contracts."

112. Murphy, "Gender Constraints to Increased Agricultural Production."

113. This section is based on a study of contract farming carried out by G. Porter

and K. P. Howard in the mid-1990s (see "Comparing Contracts"). The purpose of the research was to look at power relations and the way they are negotiated in contract farming schemes. Mainly they were concerned with microlevel issues. They studied two contract farming schemes in Transkei, one for sugar production and the other for tea. In addition, they examined two sugar schemes in Natal by way of comparison. This section makes use of the data and researchers' observations for only one of the four schemes, the North Pondoland Sugar scheme.

114. Porter and Howard, "Comparing Contracts," p. 232.

115. Porter and Howard, "Comparing Contracts."

116. Ibid., p. 229.

117. Porter and Howard, "Comparing Contracts."

118. See n. 76.

119. S. Corbridge, "Marxisms, Modernities, and Moralities: Development Praxis and the Claims of Distant Strangers," *Environment and Planning: Society and Space* 11, no. 3 (1993): 449–72, quoted in Porter and Howard, "Comparing Contracts," p. 228.

120. R. Chambers, "Editorial: Responsible Well-Being—A Personal Agenda for Development," *World Development* 25, no. 11 (1997): 1743–54.

121. Ibid., 1745.

122. Ibid., 1747.

11. Law and Gender in Southern Africa
Human Rights and Family Law

Chuma Himonga

Studies on gender in Africa[1] reveal that due to the differential effects of post-colonial macro-economic policies and legislation on men and women, gender in-equality continues in different degrees in all systems of law—received common law, customary law, and systems of religious law. Gender inequality is therefore still a prevalent feature of African legal systems today, although there have been some notable improvements since the mid-1980s.[2] Following especially the coming into force of the Convention on the Elimination of All Forms of Discrimination Against Women (CEDAW)[3] and increased activism in civil society in support of women's rights, human rights norms have increasingly moved to center stage as African legal systems revisit the subject of gender inequality.

The 1990s have therefore witnessed the adoption in southern Africa of a number of national and international human rights instruments, entrenching, among other things, the equal rights of men and women in many aspects of life. In addition, courts in the region have relied on international human rights norms enshrined in treaties, sometimes even where the states concerned are not parties to the treaty.[4] The result is that guarantees of equality between men and women are becoming a common feature in the legal systems of southern Africa, albeit in varying degrees. Alongside these human rights instruments are a considerable array of ordinary legislation attempts to foster equal rights between men and women, especially in the fields of family law (e.g., marriage, parent-child relationship, and inheritance) and private status generally. In fact, owing to their specificity, most of these ordinary statutory rights are considered to offer women the best protection, in comparison to internationally and constitutionally protected rights.[5] Examples are laws that confer majority status on men and women on an equal basis,[6] and laws that give men and women equal rights to inherit property.[7] These laws are, therefore, an integral and important part of efforts directed at the enhancement of gender equality in southern Africa. They provide the means of evaluating the impact of state intervention in the various enclaves of gender inequality on a level different from that of human rights.

This chapter seeks to analyze the impact of human rights on gender inequality in southern Africa, focusing particularly on the Republic of South Africa, Namibia, Zimbabwe, and Zambia. The first two countries represent the new democracies,[8] which are considered to have the best and most extensive equality provisions in Africa.[9] On the other hand, Zambia and Zimbabwe represent the older constitutional democracies[10] with less benign equality provisions. Apart from examining the legal provisions on equality and non-discrimination, the chapter also considers factors that impinge on the implementation of these provisions. It is obvious that egalitarian ideals of equality for their own sake are of little value unless they are translated into de facto equality for men and women. This necessitates a consideration of the enforcement of statutory provisions by the courts and the factors that limit the effectiveness of these legal provisions.

The chapter shows that reasonable attempts have been made to address gender inequality in the legal provisions. However, serious challenges and problems remain at the level of implementation of these provisions. Of particular significance are problems rooted in the structure of state institutions charged with the responsibility of implementing rights and the challenges created by the application of law in pluralistic legal systems. These challenges clearly indicate the relationship between law and society and the limitation of law as an instrument of social change.

The study of gender equality in this chapter is confined mostly to family law, including succession law. This is because, first, family law provides a point of focus. Second, and most importantly, this branch of law is a window through which we might view gender relations in more than one area of life in which gender inequalities occur. For example, because family law is the site where the public and private spheres of life intersect,[11] a study of issues of gender in family law opens a way to understanding the position of men and women with regard to employment, access to productive resources, and participation in the economic and political spheres of life generally. Furthermore, family law goes to the very heart of the legal subjectivity of a woman. Coverture, in most societies, makes women non-persons.[12] In African customary law systems this is compounded by the fact that a woman's legal capacity is circumscribed by coverture as well as kinship. According to some versions of customary law, women are considered to be perpetual minors under the guardianship of their male relatives before marriage and of the husband after marriage.[13]

This chapter explores the above issues in seven sections, starting with the application of human rights to private relations. Sections three and four examine gender equality by reference to constitutional provisions and international human rights instruments, respectively. Then follows a discussion on the instrumentality of law in relation to gender equality. Section six deals with the impact of human rights in family law legislation and court decisions. This analysis is carried into section seven where the problems and challenges of achieving gender equality in practice are considered. The chapter concludes by noting that while substantial provision is made for gender equality in the domestic and international rights instruments in southern Africa, the implementation of the legal provision is limited by various factors.

Application of Human Rights

Two issues are pertinent to the application and enforcement of human rights in national legal systems. The first is the application of the Bills of Rights contained in the constitutions to private persons in their private relations (i.e., horizontal application). The second is the domestic application to gender equality of international human rights treaties ratified by the countries of southern Africa.

Horizontal Application of the Bills of Rights

The horizontal application of the Bills of Rights is important because many inequalities between men and women are found in the private spheres of family law, land law, and succession law. In African legal systems, the common law (as opposed to legislation), customary laws, and religious systems of law dominate the regulation of private relations.

In Western jurisprudence, with only a few exceptions, the rights contained in the Bills of Rights have only a vertical application. In other words, they protect the citizen against the exercise of state power in its various manifestations.[14] They do not, therefore, apply horizontally, to protect individuals in their relationships with each other, and to be invoked by them in their private law disputes. This means that unless the constitutions contain specific provisions for the horizontal application of human rights, these rights apply only vertically.

Although there is apparently no clear answer to the question of the horizontal application of the Bills of Rights in southern Africa,[15] there are examples of provisions for the limited application of the Bills of Rights to private relations. In South Africa, the Constitutional Court[16] decided in *Du Plessis*[17] that although the Bill of Rights in the interim constitution[18] was not in general capable of application to private relations, it had "an influence on the development of the common law as it governs relations between individuals."[19] This entitles the courts to apply the Bill of Rights in the interpretation or development of the common law where the state is not involved, but not to declare the rule of law in question unconstitutional.[20] Furthermore, the court seems to have underscored the Bill of Rights as a basis for the courts to adapt all systems of law to changing social values and socio-economic conditions, including those that have a bearing on gender equality. It stated in this regard as follows: "Judges can and should adapt the common law to reflect the changing social, moral and economic fabric of the country. Judges should not be quick to perpetuate rules whose social foundation has long since disappeared."

It has been asserted that the final constitution of South Africa[21] contains a clearer principle of horizontal application of the Bill of Rights than its predecessor, the interim constitution.[22] At least certain rights, including the right to equality and equal protection and benefit of the law, are said to have direct application to private relations.[23] It is, therefore, possible to argue that in South Africa, private relations, whether governed by legislation, common law, customary law, or religious systems of law, are not shielded from the application of the equality provisions of the Bill of Rights.

Zambia is another interesting example, as far as concerns the role of judicial activism in advancing gender equality with regard to the horizontal application of the Bill of Rights. Even though the provisions of the constitution on the horizontal application of the Bill of Rights are less clear than those of South Africa,[24] the High Court for Zambia has applied the Bill of Rights to private relations. In *Sara Longwe*[25] the High Court enforced, albeit tenuously,[26] the constitution's anti-discrimination clause to protect the applicant, a woman, from being discriminated against by a hotel, a private company. Explaining his reasoning for this decision, the judge stated that "what started as regulations to control the powers of the rulers, have with the passage of time . . . come to cover the activities of even private individuals or institutions."[27]

Kankasa-Mabula has questioned the correctness of this decision.[28] It is, obviously, beyond the scope of this chapter to enter into this debate. Suffice it to say that a more technical interpretation of the provision concerned than that adopted by her may be necessary to determine the meaning of the constitutional provision in question and, therefore, the correctness of the decision of the High Court. The experience of South Africa in the interpretation of the provisions of the interim constitution concerning the horizontal application of the Bill of Rights clearly shows the complexity and highly contentious nature of the horizontal application of the Bill of Rights when the constitution is lacking in clarity.[29]

Be that as it may, the High Court's decision in *Sara Longwe* is, for our present purposes, worth noting as a laudable attempt by a human rights conscious judge to interpret the constitution broadly, in order to rid society of gender-based discriminatory practices and laws. This approach is consistent with the approach taken by courts in southern Africa in the question of the domestic application of international human rights instruments to advance gender equality, discussed in the next section. Furthermore, the decision of the High Court in *Sara Longwe* represents, in my view, an important development in relation to gender issues. This is considering the lack of constitutional protection from discrimination based on gender, as shown later in this chapter.

The Domestic Application of International Human Rights Instruments

International human rights norms carry a certain political clout, but most importantly they fill significant gaps in domestic law. Many African constitutions do not, for example, contain comprehensive gender equality provisions. The extent to which international human rights norms are applied in these countries is therefore critical to the advancement of gender equality.

In most southern African countries, ratification of a treaty alone is not sufficient; legislation is required to make an international treaty a part of the country's domestic law.[30] No country has so far legislated any of the major treaties on gender equality, such as the CEDAW, into their domestic law. However, some constitutions in the region explicitly provide for the interpretation of their constitutional Bills of Rights by reference to both public international law and comparable foreign case law,[31] and this would include treaties providing for gender equality. Furthermore, there is an emerging body of jurisprudence from the courts indicating that judges draw upon international conventions in their interpretation of domestic law no matter whether or not the relevant convention has been ratified by that country.[32] In this way the application of conventions affecting gender equality has been extended to some countries. In this connection two cases are of special note, namely, *Unity Dow*[33] and *Longwe*.[34] These cases are important not only because they incorporate international human rights norms into domestic law, but because they are landmark decisions posing a challenge to gender discrimination in the common law and social practice in their respective jurisdictions[35] and in southern Africa generally.[36]

In *Dow* a citizen of Botswana, Unity Dow, sued the state to challenge a citizenship law that excluded the children of her marriage to an American citizen from acquiring Botswana citizenship. The children were born in Botswana but were ineligible to acquire Botswana citizenship because their father was a foreigner. Unity Dow claimed, among other things, that by denying her the right to pass citizenship to her children, the law in question denied her the equal protection of the law, and that she was discriminated against on the ground of her sex, contrary to the provisions of the Botswana constitution. Children of Botswana men married to foreign women were not similarly excluded from acquiring Botswana citizenship. Among the contentions of the state was that because Botswana society was patrilineal (and patriarchal), it was necessarily tolerant of gender discrimination. Outlawing such discrimination would therefore leave nothing of the customary law of Botswana. At the bottom of this contention was clearly the suggestion that it was necessary to uphold discriminatory laws in Botswana in order to preserve the traditions and customs of the people.

These contentions were not acceptable to the Court of Appeal,[37] which held on this point that "Custom and tradition have never been static. . . . They have always yielded to express legislation. Custom and tradition must *a fortiori* . . . yield to the Constitution of Botswana. A constitutional guarantee [of rights, including those of equality] cannot be overridden by custom." The court then said that courts in Botswana would endeavor to interpret tradition and custom creatively to conform to the constitution, but where this goal could not be achieved, "it is the custom not the constitution which must go." Accordingly, the court upheld Unity Dow's claim that the citizenship law was unconstitutional.

It is significant, for the present purposes, that in reaching this decision the court "placed particular reliance on the provisions of international human rights [treaties] concerning non-discrimination, equal protection of the law and elimination of discrimination against women."[38] Some of these treaties had not been ratified by Botswana, while others had been ratified but not as yet incorporated into domestic law. Thus referring, for example, to CEDAW, which had not yet been ratified, Judge Ammissah said that such conventions could be used to aid the interpretation of constitutional provisions pertaining to gender equality. He stated:

> I take it that a Court in this country is obliged to look at the Convention of this nature which has created an international regime when called upon to interpret a provision of the Constitution which is so much in doubt to see whether that Constitution permits discrimination against women as has been canvassed in this case.

In relation to the African Charter on Human and People's Rights,[39] which had been ratified but not incorporated into domestic law, the judge stated:

> There is a clear obligation on this country like on all other African states signatories to the Charter to ensure the elimination of every form of discrimination against their women folk. . . . It is the clear duty of this court when faced with the difficult task of the construction of provisions of the Constitution to keep in mind the international obligation. If the constitutional provisions are such as can be construed to ensure the compliance of the state with its international obligations then they must be so construed.

In *Sara Longwe*,[40] the High Court for Zambia similarly relied on a convention (CEDAW) that, though ratified, had not as yet been incorporated into Zambian domestic law. In this case, Sara Longwe was refused entry to a specified bar of the Intercontinental Hotel on the ground that she was not accompanied by a male. Only females accompanied by male patrons were, according to the hotel's regulations, allowed to enter the bar in question. There was no similar restriction of entry to unaccompanied male patrons. Sara sued the hotel in the Zambian High Court. She claimed, inter alia, that her exclusion from the bar amounted to discrimination against her based on her sex, contrary to the constitution. In support of her claim she relied, inter alia, on CEDAW.

Judge Musamali, as he then was, accepted Sara Longwe's contention. The influence of CEDAW on his decision is indicated by the following statement:

> I have to say something about the effect of International Treaties . . . which the Republic of Zambia enters into and ratifies. . . . The Convention on the Elimination of All Forms of Discrimination Against Women . . . is such an example. . . . Ratification of such documents by a nation state without reservation is a clear testimony of the willingness by that state to be bound by the provisions of such a document. Since there is that willingness, if an issue comes before this court which would not be covered by local legislation but would be covered by such international documents, I would take judicial notice of that Treaty or Convention in my resolution of the dispute.

Partly relying on CEDAW, the court decided that the denial of access to Sara Longwe to the hotel's bar discriminated against her on the ground of gender, and that the regulations of the hotel justifying this discrimination breached Sara Longwe's fundamental freedom of assembly and of movement contrary to the constitution. The court accordingly ordered the offending regulations of the hotel to be "scrapped forthwith."

Thus although most of the countries of southern Africa have not taken steps to make the conventions they have ratified part of their domestic law, the courts consider them relevant to the interpretation of domestic law. Despite the doctrinal position in the various countries that have not incorporated the international conventions in issue into domestic law, the courts in practice go about their business as though these conventions were part of domestic law (even though they may not use them to the full extent). And as can be seen from *Dow* and *Longwe,* this approach of the courts has tremendously helped to advance gender equality in the region.

Finally, mention must be made of the Bangalore Principles, emanating from a colloquium of senior Commonwealth judges in 1988.[41] These principles pertain to the domestic application of international human rights norms. Two of them deserve special mention. The first states that a treaty that has been ratified but not yet incorporated into domestic law may still be taken into account by a court when dealing with a case where domestic law (i.e., constitutional, statute, or common law) is ambiguous. The second principle requires judges not to interpret statutes in a manner that violates international law.[42] These principles clearly support judges who draw upon international human rights norms to enhance gender equality.

Gender Equality in Constitutional Provisions

The equality provisions are among the most prominent rights and freedoms in the constitutions of southern Africa.[43] The ideal equality provisions affirm the right of every person "to equality before the law and to equal protection of the law" and that "no person shall be unfairly discriminated against."[44] Some countries have more generous and comprehensive provisions than others. Thus the South African and Namibian provisions fall on the generous side, while the Zimbabwean and Zambian provisions are less generous.

The South African constitution introduces its Bill of Rights, which it declares to be the cornerstone of democracy, with an affirmation of the "democratic values of human dignity, *equality* and freedom"[45] (italics supplied). It then goes on to guarantee the right of equality of all persons before the law and to proscribe discrimination on grounds, inter alia, of gender and sex.[46]

One of the early cases dealing with the principle of equality decided by the South African Constitutional Court[47] was *Fraser.*[48] The court entertained an application by Fraser, the father of an extra-marital child. The child's mother gave him up for adoption against his father's wishes. She did this according to a law governing children[49] that gave the mother of an extra-marital child, but not the father, the right to consent to the adoption of the child. Fraser challenged the constitutionality of this law, alleging that it was discriminatory, contrary to the equality provisions of the Bill of Rights in the constitution.[50] The court decided that the relevant law was, indeed, discriminatory in that it drew an unacceptable distinction between, inter alia, the fathers and mothers of extra-marital children without any regard to the best interests of the child.[51]

For our present discussion, it is also important to note the court's emphasis on the importance of the principle of equality in the constitutional framework of South Africa. It stated that the guarantee of equality "lies at the very heart of the Constitution. It permeates and defines the very ethos upon which the Constitution is premised."[52] The Constitutional Court expressed a similar view in *Hugo*[53] in the following terms:

> At the heart of the prohibition of unfair discrimination lies a recognition that the purpose of our new constitutional and democratic order is the establishment of a society in which all human beings will be accorded equal dignity and respect regardless of their membership of particular groups.

At another place, the same court stated:

> The South African Constitution is primarily and emphatically an egalitarian Constitution. The supreme laws of comparable constitutional states may underscore other principles and rights. But in the light of our own particular history, and our vision for the future, a Constitution was written with equality at its centre. Equality is our Constitution's focus and its organising principle.

The *Hugo* case concerned the president of South Africa granting a special remission of sentence, inter alia, to "all mothers in prison on 10 May 1994 with minor children under the age of 12 years." [54] A father of a minor child under the age of twelve years (the applicant) challenged the president's action and claimed that it discriminated against him on the grounds of sex and gender, and indirectly, against his son because his incarcerated parent was not a female. The majority of the judges of the Constitutional Court decided that the action in question did not unfairly discriminate against the applicant on the grounds of sex and gender. The dissenting judgment of Judge Kriegler is, however, also worth noting in so far as it concerns gender issues. The judge argued that the action of the president transgressed the constitutional principle of equality. He criticized the majority decision for upholding gender stereotyping, which he believed to be the "root cause of women's inequality in our society [and] both a result and cause of prejudice; and societal attitudes which relegate women to a subservient, occupationally inferior yet increasingly onerous role."[55] Although the majority ruled against the applicant in this case, one can still say that the principle of gender equality is not only firmly entrenched in the South African constitution, but is also strongly supported by the highest court in the country. This is evident from *Fraser* as well as from other cases in which the Constitutional Court has addressed the issues of equality and non-discrimination.[56] Moreover, one hopes that the views of Judge Kriegler will, in due course, become standard measure in gender equality jurisprudence.

The Namibian constitution prohibits discrimination on grounds of sex and also advances gender in another important direction.[57] With regard to the latter, it provides specifically for affirmative action[58] and "equality of opportunity for women to enable them to participate fully in all spheres of Namibian society."[59] Furthermore the constitution exceptionally provides for gender equality in family law. It gives all men and women of full age the right to marry and to found a family. It also gives equal rights to men and women "as to marriage, during marriage and at its dissolution."

In contrast, the Zambian and Zimbabwean constitutions are less generous with regard to gender equality. While the Zambian constitution provides for the right to the protection of the law, it does not provide for the equality of everyone before the law or for equal protection of the law.[60] Neither does it include gender among the grounds on which discrimination is prohibited.[61] The Zimbabwean constitution does not mention sex or gender among the grounds on which discrimination is prohibited.[62] An even more serious limitation on the equality provisions in both constitutions concerns the special protections accorded family law and customary law in the non-discrimination provisions. The provisions outlawing discrimination[63] are qualified in relation to family law and customary law. Discrimination is allowed in any law so far as that law makes provision with respect to adoption, marriage, divorce, burial, devolution of property on death, or other matters of personal law. Discrimination is also allowed in any law that makes provision for the application of customary law.[64] In what has been condemned as taking the women's movement back to the 1960s, the Supreme Court of Zimbabwe has recently decided that such limitations on the constitutional principles of equality and non-discrimination are valid.[65]

The protection against gender discrimination in these constitutions does not, therefore, extend to the private area of family law, customary law generally, and the allocation of land under customary law. Yet these are all areas in which gender discrimination is endemic. And as Kankasa-Mabula so aptly observes, this kind of limitation on gender equality in the constitutional provisions also flies in the face of the protection of gender equality by international conventions, which these countries have ratified.[66] It is to these instruments that the discussion will now turn.

Gender Equality in International Human Rights Instruments

Southern African countries have signed and/or ratified a number of human rights instruments that have a bearing on gender equality in many fields of law. These instruments will not be discussed in any great detail, as they are the subject of existing scholarly literature on human rights in Africa.[67] They include the United Nations Universal Declaration of Human Rights,[68] CEDAW,[69] the African Charter on

Human and People's Rights,[70] the Convention on the Rights of the Child,[71] the International Covenant on Economic, Social and Cultural Rights,[72] and the International Covenant on Civil and Political Rights.[73]

This chapter singles out CEDAW, for two reasons. First, this convention has the most comprehensive provisions on the rights of women and is considered to provide for "human rights standards that are specifically applicable to women on a general basis."[74] Second, it is the most commonly referred to convention in the emerging African jurisprudence on women's rights, as evident from court decisions.[75]

In its breadth, the convention places an obligation on governments to eliminate discrimination against women and to promote equality through constitutional, legal, and other appropriate means.[76] It defines discrimination as,

> Any discrimination, exclusion or restriction made on the basis of sex which has the effect or purpose of impairing or nullifying the recognition, enjoyment or exercise by women, irrespective of their marital status, on a basis of equality of men and women of human rights and fundamental freedoms in the political, economic, social, cultural, civil or any other field.

The comprehensive nature of CEDAW's coverage can be further seen in its very last provision, concerning gender equality in family law.[77] This article requires governments to take all appropriate measures to eliminate discrimination against women and to ensure equality of men and women in their family laws (customary, religious, and civil) in all matters relating to marriage, parent-child relationship, personal consequences of marriage, and ownership of property. Thus, not only do women have a right to enter into marriage on the same basis as men, but they have equal rights with their husbands over the guardianship of their children, ownership and control of marital property during marriage, the right to share such property on divorce, and a right to divorce on the same grounds.

This convention is undoubtedly critical to the advancement of gender equality in family law in those countries (like Zambia and Zimbabwe) where the constitutions do shield customary law from the effect of the Bill of Rights, and also lack provisions ensuring equality before the law or provisions prohibiting discrimination on grounds of gender or sex. The convention is also crucial in countries that do not provide for equality in family law in their Bills of Rights. This includes all of the countries under review except Namibia. Since the courts tend to resort to international conventions in interpreting domestic law, as already stated, the deficiencies concerned in the constitutional provisions of these countries may be remedied by the provisions of this and other relevant international conventions.

Gender Equality and the Instrumentality of Law

Gender inequalities exist in different degrees in all systems of law in the southern African region. The equality norms just considered provide the framework within which all systems of law and state policies are to be interpreted and developed. The application of these human rights norms should, therefore, in classical liberal fashion, eventually weed out all gender inequalities in the various components of national legal systems.

In a liberal philosophical view of society, law is a vital starting point in addressing problems of gender inequality. The abolition of discriminatory laws, the guarantee of gender neutrality in the law, and the availability of enforcement mechanisms are all important steps toward the equality of all and enjoyment by all of the rights sponsored by the state. Moreover, law may be seen both as a symbolic force and a potential social force in as much as it can be mobilized as a vehicle to fight for change. This perspective of law, obviously, presupposes the existence of the "right" kind of law and its actual use by the social groups concerned. The latter is largely outside the legislators' and courts' direct influences; it is a much broader social project to which different groups, persons, and institutions can contribute in different ways.

Patricia Crotty sums up law's potential as a tool for equality generally, and for gender equality particularly, as follows:

> No matter what type of law is involved or how closely it reflects a nation's culture, law can serve as a first step in transforming social realities and fostering equal rights. It can validate injuries and, in some cases, deter or redress them. It can help redistribute power and increase the number of voices that are heard. Legal rights are means for women to achieve equality, not ends in themselves. If women are to be equal, therefore, all laws are important. And in the interplay between law and culture, changing the law has the potential to change cultural practices.[78]

The relevance to gender of human rights equality provisions, discussed in the previous section, is viewed within this framework. Indeed, individual women and men have challenged gender inequalities within this very framework. For example, the women and men in the *Fraser, Hugo, Dow,* and *Longwe* cases have used the law to challenge sex or gender discrimination in various areas of the law.[79] Furthermore, activist women's rights organizations in southern Africa have lobbied for gender equality and the improvement of women's positions in law[80] within the liberal framework. For example, the Women and Law in Southern Africa (WLSA) Research Project, which is one of the most active NGOs in this area in the region, has as its stated objective and purpose of existence the use of the law to empower women.[81]

A more specific way of assessing the instrumentality of human rights law in relation to gender equality in southern Africa, however, is to examine the legislation and court decisions made within the context of human rights contained in domestic and international human rights instruments. In this regard, important decisions have been made by the courts outlawing gender inequality in various areas of the law, as shown in *Dow, Longwe, Fraser,* and by the minority judgment in *Hugo* discussed earlier. In the following section we elaborate on this theme by focusing on instances of legislation and court decisions drawn specifically from family law, including succession law.

The Impact of Human Rights in Family Law: Legislation and Court Decisions

The examples in this section are drawn from the consequences of customary marriages and from customary succession law. This discussion is limited to what has been called "official" customary law as opposed to "living" customary law. Official customary law is the law applied by state courts and other official agencies. It owes its creation and construction to these institutions, as well as to gender and generational conflicts.[82] Thus although it is said to be derived from indigenous customary law, it has little or nothing in common with the customary law practiced by the people. The origin of this constructed version of customary law is traced to the African colonial era.[83] However, it continues to flourish in the post-independence period, as many of the factors that contributed to its origin continue to exist.[84] On the other hand, living customary law consists of customs practiced by the people in their daily lives. It is the version of law that applied in informal forums of dispute settlement, such as the family. Research in most countries of southern Africa has shown that in areas of family law the official versions of customary law are "extensively contradicted by the living customary law."[85] More will be said later about the notions of official and living customary law.

The Consequences of Customary Marriages

One of the major sites of gender inequality in family law involves the consequences of marriage. In many African customary law systems, a married woman, unlike her male counterpart, is deemed to be a minor under the guardianship of her husband as long as she lives with him.[86] Thus married women cannot enter into contracts, acquire or dispose of property, or sue in court in their own names. Under some of these systems of law, married women also have no right to the guardianship of their minor children once bridewealth (lobola or lobolo[87]) has been paid for the marriage. The children in such cases are considered to be children of the husband and his family. Bridewealth itself is a requirement for validating the marriage contract. Since the majority of women in Africa marry under customary law, only a few women (i.e., those who contract marriages under the received common law systems) have capacity equal to that of their husbands in their legal relations with the outside world.[88]

South Africa has recently taken a leap toward the elimination of gender inequality in these areas of family law. In 1998, it enacted a law that, while recognizing customary marriages, removes the major discriminatory aspects of these marriages.[89] This law was the culmination of the investigation by the South African Law Commission that was aimed at finding a way of giving recognition to customary marriages that would meet the constitutional imperatives of equal treatment of all individuals regardless of their race, sex, gender, social origin, and so on.[90] The law in question puts wives on an equal footing with their husbands in terms of their legal capacity.

Furthermore, the recognition of customary marriages as legal marriages for all purposes[91] means that certain laws, which previously applied only to civil law marriages will, once the law comes into force, also apply to the consequences of customary marriages. These include laws that give equal guardianship to parents of minor children born in wedlock.[92] Thus *lobola* will no longer be a decisive factor in defining the rights of men and women in regard to the guardianship of their children born in customary marriages.

A further attack on the discriminatory effects of *lobola* is evident in court decisions that have drawn upon the human rights of children. For example, in *Hlophe*[93] the High Court for South Africa decided that the principle that "the best interests of the child are of paramount consideration in all matters concerning the child," enshrined in the Bill of Rights, took precedence over the principle of *lobola,* with regard to the custody of children under customary law. The court stated in this connection that

> the issues relating to the custody of a minor child cannot be determined . . . by the mere delivery or non-delivery of a certain number of cattle [as *lobola* payment] . . . Any doubt as to the applicable legal principles that might have existed in this regard was . . . effectively removed by the promulgation of the . . . Interim Constitution of South Africa . . . in as much as it provides [that] " . . . a child shall mean a person under the age of 18 years and in all matters concerning such child his or her best interest shall be paramount."

In reaching this decision the court relied also on the provision of the interim constitution that stated that

> In the interpretation of any law and the application and development of the common law and customary law, a court shall have due regard to the spirit, purport and objects of [the Bill of Rights of the Constitution].

The court accordingly applied the principle of the best interests of the child rather than customary law in this case, in which the father sought to assert his right to the custody of a minor child. The father's claim was based on his alleged payment of *lobola* upon his marriage to the child's mother under Swazi customary law. The child's custody was ultimately awarded to the father, and not to the child's maternal grandparents[94] who were contending for custody. However, this was done on the basis that awarding custody to the father would serve the best interest of the child and not simply on the basis that he paid *lobola* for the child's mother. By the same token, a mother may be given custody (or guardianship) if that is in the best interests of the child, regardless of whether or not any *lobola* was paid by the child's father.

This case shows that in those countries that have entrenched the principle of the best interests of the child in their Bills of Rights, the enforcement of children's rights may have a bearing on the achievement of gender equality in the family. This may, however, also be so in the case of those countries that have ratified the Convention on the Rights of the Child, since it incorporates the principle of the best interests of the child.[95] All the countries under review have ratified this convention, and the courts may, therefore, resort to this convention in the interpretation of domestic law, as shown above.[96]

Customary Succession Law

In the area of succession, the customary intestate succession laws of all African communities of southern Africa following patrilineal systems of succession[97] discriminate between men and women with regard to rights to inherit. Applying the principle of primogeniture, these systems of succession prefer males (sons and other male relatives of the deceased person) to females (daughters and other female relatives of the deceased person as well as his widow) as heirs to the estate of the head of the family, who is always a male. This rule has recently been affirmed in Zimbabwe by the Supreme Court in *Magaya*.[98] The court decided that the deceased's daughter (from his first marriage) could not be appointed heir to her father's estate when there was a male (her younger half-brother, born of a marriage between her late father and his second wife). The court reasoned that matters of personal law, including succession and issues relating to the application of customary law, were specifically excluded from the anti-discrimination provisions of the constitution.[99]

As was to be expected, this decision was followed by a series of protests from various sections of the community, especially human rights groups in Zimbabwe, accusing the Supreme Court of setting a "very retrogressive precedent, greatly undermining women's rights."[100] Despite the protests, the decision remains good law until it is reversed by the Supreme Court itself or by legislation. This is because the Supreme Court is the highest court in the land. The positive side, however, is that although the decision is said to affect a significant number of women, its ambit is restricted to women in cases of estates that are governed by customary law and cases in which the deceased died before 1 November 1997.[101] From this date on, a lot of other deceased estates of indigenous Africans that would otherwise have been governed by customary law are administered and distributed in accordance with the new law.[102] Even those estates that continue to be governed by customary law are, according to this law, subject to a degree of supervision and control by the courts and other state officials. The aim of the new law is to remove the iniquities created by antiquated versions of customary law "which excluded widows and daughters from inheriting from their husbands and fathers respectively."[103] Thus although flawed in various respects,[104] the new law represents an initial attempt in Zimbabwe to achieve a measure of equality within the family in succession matters. Such an attempt is a significant development in the search for gender justice.

In South Africa, the High Court in *Mthembu*[105] dealt with the principle of primogeniture within the framework of the constitutional principle of non-discrimination itself. The case concerned intestate succession to a deceased African male's estate. The widow, whom the deceased had married under customary law, applied to the High Court for a declaration that the deceased's only child, a seven-year-old girl, was the sole heir to his estate. Her application was opposed by the deceased's father, who claimed that according to the relevant customary law governing the estate he, and not the deceased's daughter, was the heir. The relevant customary law, which the court accepted, was said to involve the principle of primogeniture. The widow contended further that this customary law discriminated between persons on grounds of sex or gender, and that the principle of primogeniture placed women in a subservient role under the guardianship of the heir who is their guardian. The court decided that the rule of primogeniture did not unfairly discriminate on the grounds of sex or gender, because of the associated duty of support placed upon the heir to maintain the deceased person's surviving family dependents.

It is interesting that the High Court in this case placed a high premium on the duty of the heir to support. Presumably, this rule is premised on the heir actually discharging the duty concerned toward the deceased's dependents. But research in other countries in southern Africa has shown that under conditions of change, the deceased's heir often acquires the assets of the estate without assuming any of the customary responsibilities toward the deceased's dependents.[106] This phenomenon, which has come to be characterized as "property grabbing," is a result of a combination of factors that have changed the contexts within which the customary rules developed in the traditional pre-colonial and pre-capitalist African societies. These factors include the weakening of traditional social security or support systems in modern conditions,[107] as well as problems of poverty and the ensuing struggles for scarce resources among family members.[108] If the phenomenon of "property grabbing" does exist in South Africa,[109] then the principle of primogeniture may long have lost the redeeming features attributed to it by the court.[110]

The differences between official customary law and living customary law create the need for the courts to grapple with issues of the sources of the customary law they apply, as well as with the broader social, economic, and historical contexts in which these rules have developed. To ignore this imperative is to risk the courts "immortalizing" as constitutional outdated versions of customary law, which only serve to perpetuate gender inequalities built into these rules, particularly in the colonial periods of African societies.[111] This argument is developed further in the next section.

Challenges of Implementing Gender Equality

A study of the impact of human rights on gender relations would not be complete without a consideration of the specific challenges and problems concerning the implementation of legal rights in practice. De jure equality is one thing and the achievement of equality in practice is another. The following lament and indictments of one human rights activist in southern Africa[112] may serve to underline the problems considered in this section. The statement deplores African states' flagrant contempt and disregard of court decisions that have ruled against gender inequality:

> In the two years since the Court of Appeal reaffirmed the earlier High Court decision in favour of Unity [Dow], the government [of Botswana] has taken none of the necessary actions which should follow: it has not granted Botswana citizenship to Unity's children; it has not amended the Citizenship Act to provide gender equality in access to citizenship; it has not moved to amend all the other laws which are, by implication, similarly made unconstitutional by the court decision in the Unity Dow case. . . . There are close parallels in Zambia. In 1992 I myself got a High Court ruling that hotels' discrimination against unaccompanied women contradicts basic rights given in the Zambian Constitution; but this discrimination by hotels still continues. In 1990 Edith Nawakwi got a High Court ruling that it is unconstitutional for the government to require written permission from the father of her children before putting the children's names in her passport.[113] Four years later the Zambian government maintains the same discriminatory requirement. . . . As with the Unity Dow case these cases have . . . exposed the governments' lack of any ideological or legal legitimation for a state system of gender discrimination. But in each case the government behaves as if nothing has happened.

This statement highlights an apparent problem of lack of political will to enforce the principle of gender equality in the countries concerned. It also underlines the lack of respect for the rule of law and the independence of the judiciary. Thus the states' theoretical commitments to the implementation of gender equality do not translate into realities for those concerned. There are, however, other obstacles to the achievement of de facto gender equality in the southern Africa region. In the remaining part of this section, two of the most common problems and challenges in this area are examined. These are structural problems and the challenges posed by legal pluralism.

Structural Problems

The structural problems concerning the implementation of gender equality legal provisions relate to the accessibility of official institutions for the enforcement of equality rights, and the way these institutions apply the law. Much can be learned in this regard from the challenges of implementing ordinary laws concerning gender issues in the region.

The accessibility of official institutions for enforcement of rights is hampered by several factors. These include the people's ignorance of the law, including ignorance of the legal aid facilities for the poor; the cost of litigation and legal representation; and the attitudes and insensitivity of law enforcement agencies to gender issues and to women's rights generally. This is especially true in areas that are traditionally considered private domains, such as family relationships and the allocation of land under customary tenure. Studies of women and law in southern Africa[114] have shown that while both men and women are affected by these structural problems to the implementation of their rights, women are more adversely affected. This is partly because the systems of delivery of rights and justice generally are almost exclusively administered and controlled by gender-insensitive officials, many of whom are men. It may, for example, not come as a surprise that "maintenance laws suffer from administrative problems throughout the region because officials hesitate to apply a law which seems to them to run contrary to customary law."[115] Furthermore, these studies have shown that women suffer more than men from lack of knowledge of the laws because of their status, poverty, education, and location, which distance them from information and materials on the law.[116]

WLSA and other NGOs have, of course, made and continue to make, considerable contributions to the legal education of women and the general public about women's rights, as well as to the sensitization of court officials and law enforcement agencies on gender issues.[117] However, the fact that men continue to dominate the rights delivery system as judges, magistrates, court clerks, police officers, prosecutors, and other supporting staff is alone sufficient to prolong the battle for gender equality in southern Africa.

Legal Pluralism

The pluralistic nature of African legal systems is partly manifested by the existence of "living" and "official" versions of customary law, as already indicated. It is also worth noting that the newer constitutions of Malawi, South Africa, and Namibia recognize the right of "everyone to . . . participate in the cultural life of their choice."[118] This right to culture has been taken to mean that the people who are subject to customary law have the right to have that law applied to them by the courts.[119]

Presumably, the right to culture entitles the people concerned to having their living customary law applied to them rather than the official customary law. It is inconceivable that the framers of the constitutions in question could have intended to protect the rights to the application of obsolete versions of customary law. Yet both the South African and Zimbabwean courts in *Mthembu* and *Magaya* above applied the principle of primogeniture ascertained from the official versions of customary law recorded in academic works on customary law.

There are two major problems arising from the application by the courts of official customary law in cases involving gender equality. First, official customary law is not only considered to be more oppressive to women than living customary law,[120] but it is also perceived, in historical terms, as the embodiment of institutionalized gender inequality.[121] Second, official customary law focuses on formal rules rather than on the underlying values and morality of those rules and the context of their application. Consequently the courts end up applying rules that are outdated and inflexible to dynamic social relations. For example, among the important underlying values of intestate succession rules is the provision to be made for the family of the deceased, especially wives and minor children, from the deceased's property. It is this value that gives rise to the duty of the heir to support the deceased's family, supposedly connected to the principle of primogeniture adopted by the courts in *Mthembu*[122] and *Magaya*.[123] However, recent studies of customary succession law in southern Africa have shown that according to living customary law, the rules for giving effect to this value are not predetermined; they are flexible and capable of accommodating varying family circumstances.[124] For example, in the case of a married couple whose eldest son has left the village, under the patrilineal system, the property may be left in the hands of the widow. In other cases, the property may be left with the eldest daughter, rather than the son, if this would be the best way to give effect to the underlying values of the inheritance rules. There is, therefore, apparently no underlying discrimination in the rules of succession or predetermined rules of succession that favors men as preferred inheritors of property while women have only a right of support.

Thus the empirical studies by WLSA seem to show that the primogeniture principle itself exists only in ossified official versions of customary law. The studies further show that in the living customary laws of a number of southern African communities, the widow may be left in control of the matrimonial landholding (e.g., commercial farming land, communal tribal land, or urban housing). On the other hand, the disposition of movable property is need related.[125]

Indeed, even the academic work quoted by the courts in both *Mthembu* and *Magaya* as the source of the principle of primogeniture[126] acknowledges that "this verity [of the primogeniture principle being one of the most hallowed principles of customary law] has recently been challenged by a study of the inheritance patterns in a Lebowa village" [in South Africa].[127]

There is, therefore, apparently no basis for the courts applying the primogeniture principle, and perhaps many other principles that are at the heart of gender inequality, as strictly and inflexibly as they do.

Furthermore, Baerends has pointed out that emphasis on the formalistic aspects of customary rules by the courts has often resulted in an emphasis on the rules that deny the existence of obligations as preconditions for rights. This, in turn, has resulted in an emphasis on men's rights and a denial of women's secondary or derived rights—for example, in the area of ownership of land and rights to inheritance.[128]

Therefore, it can be argued that by applying official customary law in litigation concerning constitutional equality provisions, the courts transport this law's institutionalized gender inequalities and prejudices against women into the constitutional jurisprudence. These inequalities and prejudices are then "immortalized" by virtue of the supremacy of the constitution and constitutional precedents as sources of law, as already intimated. It appears from this that the application by the courts of "living" as opposed to "official" customary law in gender equality litigation is a pre-condition for the achievement of gender equality in African societies. The South African case of *Mabena*[129] can be cited as an illustration of what difference the application of living customary law (as opposed to official customary law) can make to the question of gender equality.

The case involved the existence or otherwise of a customary marriage of a woman whose husband had died. The woman's father did not consent to her marriage and was not involved in the negotiations regarding the *lobolo*. Instead, the woman's mother attended to these matters. The deceased's father denied the existence of a marriage between his late son and the woman. He argued that in terms of customary law a female (in this case the woman's mother) could not be a guardian of her child for the purposes of negotiating the child's marriage. Only a male person, in the ordinary course the father of the child, could play that role. It was contended, therefore, that the woman's marriage, having been negotiated by her mother, was not valid. The court acknowledged the fact that the (academic) authors on customary law cited to it agreed that only the father or other male relative and not the mother could validly consent to the marriage of a woman and receive *lobolo*. Nevertheless the court found that there were instances in practice where mothers negotiated for and received *lobolo,* and consented to the marriage of their daughters. The court accordingly decided that the woman's mother was in law entitled to negotiate for and receive *lobola* in respect of her daughter and that she was entitled to act as guardian and to consent to the marriage of her daughter.

It is interesting to note that the judge did not rely on established (academic) authorities to accept the existence of the rule that entitled the mother to negotiate and consent to the marriage of her daughter. Rather, he relied on the evidence of the existence of such a rule given by the woman in the proceedings.[130] In reaching its decision concerning the existence of the rule in question, the court also noted that customary law exists not only in the "official version" as documented by writers; there is also the "living law," denoting the law actually observed by "African communities," and a rule of the living law actually observed by the community and testified to by the woman in her evidence. Thus the rule applied by the court was the rule stated by the woman in the proceedings to be "their custom" (the living customary law).

By applying living law, or at least by not restricting itself to the application of customary law ascertained from written sources, the court in this case has shown, first, that the application of living customary law by the courts is feasible, and second, that gender equality may be advanced by the application of the more flexible, adaptable, system of living customary law than the ossified version of official customary law. There can be little doubt that the court's reticence about the application of official customary law to the case was influenced by its understanding that customary law could not fail to adapt to conditions in which women had become heads of families.[131] This is evident from the court's statement that "customary law is, as any system of law should be, in a state of continuous development . . . to [meet] the actual demands of society."[132]

It is also interesting that the judge in this case considered the recognition of the rule of living customary law concerned to "constitute a development in accordance with the spirit, purport and objects" of the Bill of Rights. Thus the application of living customary law is consistent with the constitution.

It cannot be denied that there are difficulties in the ascertainment of living customary law for the purposes of its application by the courts.[133] For it cannot be expected that courts will find it easy to ascertain and apply an unwritten system of law. However, this cannot justify the application of official customary law and the consequent perpetuation of gender inequalities inherent in it. The challenge for the courts, the litigants, and the legal system as a whole is to find ways to facilitate the ascertainment and proof of living customary law. The *Mabena* case has, indeed, broken the ground in this area, and it does demonstrate that this challenge can be addressed.

This chapter has attempted to show that substantial provision exists for gender equality in the domestic and international human rights instruments in force in southern Africa. These instruments provide the means through which the courts and various social groups have sought to weed out gender inequalities in law and to improve the legal position of women, and individual people's gender relations, hopefully, have been improved thereby. In particular, men and women have gained a foothold through human rights norms to challenge gender inequalities entrenched in the multiple laws of African legal systems. However, de facto gender equality has still not been achieved in southern Africa. The challenges posed by the sheer lack of political will, structural obstructions, and legal pluralism to the enforcement of state-sponsored rights seriously affect the translation into the lived experiences of men and women of the theoretical achievements in gender equality. Any attempt at making gender equality a reality will, therefore, have to acknowledge and address the problems of enforcement and the application of the law, as well as the broader social, economic, and historical contexts in which law has developed and operates.

NOTES

1. See for example, E. Baerends, *Changing Kinship, Family and Gender Relationships in Sub-Saharan Africa* (Leiden: Women and Autonomy Centre [VENA], Leiden University, 1994).

2. See P. M. Crotty, "Legislating Equality," *International Journal of Law, Policy and the Family* 10 (1996): 317–33, at 320–21.

3. Adopted by General Assembly Resolution 34/180 of 18 December 1979 (entered into force on 3 September 1981).

4. See T. Maluwa, "The Role of International Law in the Protection of Human Rights

under the Malawian Constitution of 1995," in A Yusuf, ed., *African Yearbook of International Law* (The Hague: Kluwer Law International, 1996), pp. 53–79, at 77–79.

5. Crotty, "Legislating Equality," p. 322.

6. Such as the Age of Majority Act no. 57 of 1972 and the Recognition of Customary Marriages Act no. 120 of 1998 (both of South Africa) and the Legal Age of Majority Act no. 15 of 1982 (Zimbabwe). The Recognition of Customary Marriages Act is discussed later.

7. Such as the Administration of Estates Amendment Act no. 6 of 1997 (Zimbabwe) discussed later.

8. These include the Republic of South Africa, Namibia, and Malawi.

9. See F. Banda, "Law Reform in Namibia," in A. Bainham, ed., *The International Survey of Family Law 1996* (The Hague: Martinus Nijhoff, 1998), p. 269.

10. These include Botswana, Swaziland, Lesotho, Zimbabwe, and Zambia.

11. Crotty, "Legislating Equality," pp. 318–19.

12. Ibid.

13. See A. Armstrong et al., "Towards a Cultural Understanding of the Interplay between Children's and Women's Rights: An Eastern and Southern African Perspective," *International Journal of Children's Rights* 3 (1995): 333.

14. See the judgment of Judge Kentridge in *Du Plessis and others v De Klerk and Another,* 1996 (5) BCLR 658 at 666ff.

15. See J. Sinclair, "From the Interim to the Final Constitution," in Bainham, ed., *International Survey of Family Law 1996*, pp. 435–49; T. Kankasa-Mabula, "The Enforcement of Human Rights of Zambian Women: Sara Longwe v Intercontinental Hotel Revisited," *Zambia Law Journal,* 21–24 (1989–92): 30–47; A. Cockrell, "The Law of Persons and the Bill of Rights," in *Human Rights Compendium* (Durban: Butterworths, 1996).

16. This is the highest court in the country.

17. Supra.

18. Act no. 200 of 1993.

19. At p. 692.

20. Sinclair, "From the Interim," p. 436.

21. Act no. 108 of 1996.

22. See Sinclair, "From the Interim," pp. 436–37.

23. Ibid., p. 437.

24. The relevant section is sec. 23(2) of the constitution of Zambia, act no. 1 of 1991. It prohibits discrimination by "any person acting by virtue of any written law or in the performance of the functions of any public office or public authority."

25. *Sara Longwe v Intercontinental Hotel,* 1992/HP/765. This case is discussed further in the next section.

26. See T. Kankasa-Mabula, "Enforcement of Human Rights." T. Maluwa, "Law Reform between Men and Women in Southern Africa: Some Recent Legal Developments" (paper presented at the Workshop on Transformations of Power and Culture in Africa, Center for Afroamerican and African Studies, University of Michigan, Ann Arbor, 11–20 November 1996), pp. 22–23.

27. Quoted by Kankasa-Mabula, "Enforcement of Human Rights," p. 35.

28. Kankasa-Mabula, "Enforcement of Human Rights."

29. See Cockrell, "Law of Persons."

30. The exception is Namibia, where all international treaties ratified by the republic

are self-executing. See Article 144 of the constitution of Namibia, which provides that unless otherwise provided by the constitution or act of parliament the general rules of public international law and international agreements binding upon Namibia under the constitution shall form part of the law of Namibia. (See Banda, "Law Reform," pp. 267–68 for a discussion of this article.)

31. See sec. 39(1)(b)(c) of the constitution of South Africa (1996). For a discussion of comparable provisions in Namibia, see G. J. Naldi, 1995, *Constitutional Rights in Namibia: A Comparative Analysis with International Human Rights* (Cape Town: Juta, 1995), pp. 10–12; Maluwa, "Law Reform," pp. 75–77.

32. See Maluwa, "Law Reform," pp. 75–77; B. A. Rwezaura, "Domestic Application of International Human Rights Norms: Protecting the Rights of the Girl-Child in Eastern and Southern Africa," in W. Ncube, ed., *Law, Culture, Tradition, and Children's Rights in Eastern and Southern Africa* (Aldershot, UK: Ashgate, 1998), pp. 28–46.

33. *Attorney General v Dow,* Civil Appeal 4/91 (Unreported). Fully documented in Unity Dow, *The Citizenship Case: The Attorney General of Botswana v Unity Dow Court Documents, Judgments, Cases and Materials* (Gaborone: Lentswe Lesedi, 1995).

34. Supra.

35. See Himonga, "Protection of Widows and Administration of Customary Estates in Zambia," in G. Ludwar-Ene and M. Reh, eds., *Focus on Women in Africa* (Bayreuth: Bayreuth African Studies, 1993), pp. 159–95 at 191.

36. For as noted by Sara Longwe: "Unity Dow successfully challenged the legitimacy of the Citizenship Act which denied Botswana citizenship to her children on the basis that her husband [was] a foreigner . . . but she did not stand in court merely for herself, or only for the women of Botswana who are married to foreigners. She also stood in court to represent all the women of Botswana who are treated as second class citizens under the various discriminatory laws. For the women of Africa Unity's victory is our victory" (foreword to Dow, *Citizenship Case,* p. viii).

37. This is the highest court in Botswana.

38. See T. Maluwa, "Implementing the Principle of Gender Equality through the Law: Some Lessons from Southern Africa," *International Journal of Discrimination and the Law* 3 (1999): 249–68 at 260.

39. Adopted at the eighteenth Assembly of Heads of State and Government of the Organisation of African Unity, 27 June 1981 (entered into force on 21 October 1986).

40. Supra.

41. Judicial Colloquium held in Bangalore, 24–26 February 1988.

42. See Rwezaura, "Domestic Application," p. 29.

43. See, for example, F. Kaganas and C. Murray, "The Contest between Culture and Gender Equality under South Africa's Interim Constitution," *Journal of Law and Society* 21 (1994): 409; *Du Plessis* case, supra.

44. See, for example, sec. 9 of the South African constitution (1996).

45. Sec. 7(1) of the constitution.

46. The relevant provisions state in part as follows: "Every person shall have the right to equality before the law and to equal protection of the law [and] no person shall be unfairly discriminated against . . . on one or more of the following grounds in particular: race, gender, sex, ethnic or social origin, colour, sexual orientation, age, disability, religion, conscience, belief, culture or language" (see sec. 9(3) of the constitution).

47. This is the highest court in the country in constitutional matters.

48. *Fraser v Children's Court, Pretoria North, and Others* 1997 (2) SA 261 (CC).

49. Sec. 18(4)(d) of the Child Welfare Act no. 74 of 1983.

50. I.e., the interim constitution of 1993 (sec. 8[2]).

51. Sec. 30 of the interim constitution also provided that in all matters concerning the child, his or her best interests were paramount.

52. At p. 272.

53. *The President of the Republic of South Africa and Another v Hugo,* 1997 (4) SA 1 CC.

54. See the Presidential Act 17 of 1994.

55. P. 37.

56. See, for example, the case of *Ryland v Edros,* 1997 2 SA 690 (C), and *Harksen v Lane, NO,* 1998 (1) SA 300 CC, where the test of non-discrimination has been fully developed and summarized by the Constitutional Court.

57. See sec. 10(2) of the constitution. (For a discussion of the equality and non-discrimination provisions, see Banda, "Law Reform," pp. 269–74.)

58. See Article 23(3) of the constitution, which provides that discrimination may be permitted in legislation and the application of any policy and practices if they are aimed at taking into account "the fact that women in Namibia have traditionally suffered special discrimination and they need to be encouraged and enabled to play a full, equal and effective role in the political, social, economic and cultural life of the nation."

59. See Article 96 of the constitution.

60. See chap. 3 of the constitution (Act no. 1 of 1991), the Bill of Rights.

61. See constitution of Zambia, Article 23(3).

62. The relevant provision is quoted in *Magaya v Magaya,* judgment no. S.C. 210/98, Civil Appeal no. 635/92 (Supreme Court of Zimbabwe), p. 5.

63. See sec. 23(1); sec. 23(1)(a)(b) of the constitution of Zimbabwe, as amended by sec. 9 of Act 14 of 1996 and sec. 23(2)(3) of the Zambian constitution. Sec. 23(3) of the Zambian constitution defines the expression "discriminatory" as affording different treatment to different persons attributable to the stated grounds.

64. See constitution of Zambia, sec. 23(4)(c)(d) and constitution of Zimbabwe, sec. 23(3)(b).

65. See *Magaya v Magaya,* supra, p. 6.

66. See Kankasa-Mabula, "Enforcement of Human Rights," p. 34.

67. See, for example, Maluwa, "Implementing the Principle"; C. Beyani, "Towards a More Effective Guarantee of Women's Rights in the African Human Rights System," in Rebecca Cook, ed., *Human Rights of Women: National and International Perspectives* (Philadelphia: University of Pennsylvania Press, 1994), pp. 285–306.

68. Adopted and proclaimed by General Assembly Resolution 217 A (III) of 10 December 1948.

69. Supra.

70. Supra.

71. Adopted by General Assembly Resolution 44/25 of 20 November 1989 (entered into force on 2 September 1990).

72. Adopted by General Assembly Resolution 2200A (XXI) of 16 December 1996 (entered into force on 3 January 1976).

73. Adopted by General Assembly Resolution 2200(XXI) of 16 December 1966 (entered into force on 23 March 1976).

74. Beyani, "Towards a More," p. 286.

75. See, for example, *Dow* and *Longwe* cases, supra.

76. See Article 2 of the convention.

77. See Article 16(1).

78. Crotty, "Legislating Equality," pp. 318, 331.

79. See also the cases of *Sakala v Attorney-General,* 1991/HP/2082, and *Nawakwi v Attorney General,* 1990/HP/1724 (both decided by the High Court for Zambia), in which individual women challenged the government's actions of discrimination in relation to conditions of employment and administrative procedures concerning the issuing of passports respectively.

80. See WLSA, *Regional Impact Study Report* (Harare, December 1996).

81. See J. Stewart and A. Armstrong, eds., *The Legal Situation of Women in Southern Africa* (Harare: University of Zimbabwe Publications, 1990), p. xi.

82. See M. Chanock, *Law, Custom and Social Order: The Colonial Experience in Malawi and Zambia* (Cambridge: Cambridge University Press, 1985).

83. Ibid.

84. Examples of such factors are the application of customary law by European and African professional judges, who know little or nothing about the nature of customary law; reliance by these judges on precedent and other written, ossified versions of customary law, including academic literature and codes of customary law; and the predominance of men as adjudicators in the courts.

85. See W. Ncube, "Muddling in the Quicksands of Tradition and Custom and Skating Down the Slippery Slopes of Modernity: The Reform of Marriage and Inheritance Laws in Zimbabwe," *Zimbabwe Law Review* 13 (1996): 1–19, at 5; Armstrong et al., "Uncovering Reality: Excavating Women's Rights in African Family Law," *International Journal of Law and the Family* 7, no. 3 (1993): 314–69.

86. See, for example, the provisions of the South African Black Administration Act 38 of 1927 (sec. 11(3)(b), which, among other statutes, regulates the application of customary law to black persons in South Africa.

87. These terms are readily understood by many ethnic groups in the region. However, different ethnic groups use different names for bridewealth. For example, *lobolo* (Zulu), *ikhazi,* (Xhosa), *bogadi, bohali* (Sotho-Tswana), *roora/rovoro* (Shona), and so on.

88. However, even women who marry under civil laws continue to suffer degrees of incapacity under the Roman Dutch common law systems of countries such as South Africa, Zimbabwe, and Botswana. These systems of law contain matrimonial property regimes that subject the wife to varied degrees of the husband's marital power. Marital power incapacitates the wife in law in various ways. (See A. Molokomme, "Marriage—What Every Woman Wants or 'Civil Death'? The Status of Married Women in Botswana," in A. Armstrong, ed., *Women and Law in Southern Africa* (Harare: Zimbabwe Publishing House, 1987), pp. 181–92. And although South Africa has abolished the marital power of the husband, there still remain some vestiges of this incidence of marriage that perpetuate inequality between husbands and wives. (See Sinclair, "From the Interim," p. 441.)

89. The Recognition of Customary Marriages Act, supra. The president of the republic assented to this act on 2 December 1998, but it will come into force only at a later date promulgated by the president.

90. See the South African Law Commission Project 90, Discussion Paper 74 (August 1997), p. 22.

91. See sec. 2 of the act.

92. For example, the Guardianship Act no. 192 of 1993.

93. *Hlophe v Mahlalela and Another,* 1998 (1) SA 449.

94. The mother of the child was dead.

95. See Article 3 of the Convention on the Rights of the Child, supra.

96. See discussion under sec. 2.2

97. This applies to all ethnic groups in South Africa and to major communities in Zimbabwe. In Zambia, the Ngoni of Eastern Province fall in this category, while the majority of the indigenous communities are matrilineal.

98. See *Magaya v Magaya*, supra.

99. At p. 6.

100. See the letter written by several women's rights groups to the minister of justice and parliamentary affairs, the chief justice, etc., reproduced in *WLSA Newsletter* 11, no. 2 (June 1999).

101. See E. Sithole, "It's Not Just a Case—It's about Justice and Equality before the Law or is it?" in *WLSA Newsletter* 11, no. 2 (June 1999).

102. See The Administration of Estates Amendment Act no. 6 of 1997, which came into force on 1 November 1997.

103. See Ncube, "Muddling in the Quicksands," p. 5.

104. Ibid., pp. 1–19.

105. *Mthembu v Letsela and Another,* 1997 (2) SA 936 (T).

106. See W. Ncube and J. Stewart, eds., *Widowhood, Inheritance Laws, Customs and Practices in Southern Africa* (Harare: WLSA, 1995).

107. See B. A. Rwezaura, "The Changing Role of the Extended Family in Providing Economic Support for an Individual in Africa," in M. T. Meulders-Klein and J. Eekelaar, eds., *Family, State and Individual Economic Security* (Bruxelles: E. Story-Scientia, 1988), pp. 167–85.

108. See B. A. Rwezaura et al., "Parting of the Long Grass: Revealing and Reconceptualising the African Family," *Journal of Legal Pluralism and Unofficial Law,* no. 35 (1995): 35.

109. In fact, the widow in *Mthembu*, supra, alleged that the deceased's father, the supposed heir, demanded that she and her daughter should leave the deceased's house where they had lived with the deceased and that she should give him all of the deceased's movable property. He also refused to assume maintenance responsibilities over the widow and the child, and denied the existence of any marriage between his deceased son and the widow. These allegations are typical of the "property grabbing" cases.

110. The widow's legal counsel argued that the redeeming features of the rule were non-existent in the urban areas. It is submitted that a dichotomy between rural and urban areas may be difficult to maintain in matters of this nature in present social and economic conditions.

111. See Chanock, *Law, Custom and Social Order.*

112. That is, Sara Longwe.

113. See *Nawakwi v Attorney General*, supra.

114. See, for example, C. N. Himonga, *Family and Succession Laws in Zambia: Developments since Independence* (Munster: LIT Verlag, 1995), pp. 237–49; A. Armstrong, *Struggling over Resources: Women and Maintenance in Southern Africa* (Harare: University of Zimbabwe Publications, 1992).

115. See WLSA, *Regional Impact Study Report* (Harare, December 1996), p. 8.

116. Ibid.; U. Wanitzek, "Legally Unrepresented Women Petitioners in the Lower Courts of Tanzania: A Case of Justice Denied?" *Journal of Legal Pluralism and Unofficial Law,* nos. 30/31 (1990–91): 255–71.

117. For the achievements of WLSA and other NGOs in this regard, see WLSA, Regional Impact Study Report (Harare, December 1996). The Law, Race and Gender Institute, located in the Faculty of Law at the University of Cape Town is also active in judicial education on gender and other issues.

118. See, for example, sec. 31 of the constitution of South Africa (1996).

119. See T. W. Bennett, *Human Rights and African Customary Law under the South African Constitution* (Cape Town: Juta, 1995), pp. 24–27. See also sec. 211(3) of the constitution of South Africa (1996).

120. A. Armstrong et al., "Uncovering Reality"; Baerends, *Changing Kinship,* pp. 85–86.

121. See Ncube, "Muddling in the Quicksands."

122. Supra.

123. Supra.

124. See J. Stewart, "Why I Can't Teach Customary Law" (and references therein to WLSA studies on inheritance), in J. Eekelaar and T. Nhlapo, eds., *The Changing Family: International Perspectives on the Family and Family Law* (Oxford: Hart Publishing, 1998), pp. 217–29.

125. The state of living customary law on these issues may be seen from the studies by WLSA on inheritance conducted in 1992–93 in six countries of southern Africa (Zimbabwe, Zambia, Swaziland, Lesotho, Mozambique, and Botswana) (Ncube and Stewart, eds., *Widowhood,* p. 5). The publications on these studies may be obtained from WLSA regional office in Harare.

126. That is, T. Bennett, *A Sourcebook of African Customary Law for Southern Africa* (Cape Town: Juta, 1991), p. 400.

127. Ibid., p. 400.

128. See Baerends, *Changing Kinship.*

129. *Mabena v Letsoalo,* 1998 (2) SA 1068. (This is a decision of the Transvaal Division of the High Court.)

130. Customary law in South Africa is considered to be partly a matter of fact rather than of law. Evidence must therefore be adduced to the court to prove the existence of any alleged rule of customary law, unless the court can take judicial notice of the rule concerned. (See sec. 1(1) of the Law of Evidence Amendment Act no. 45 of 1988.) The evidence of the rule in question in this case was given in evidence in terms of sec. 1(2) of the Law of Evidence Amendment Act, which states that a party may adduce evidence of the substance of a customary rule that is in issue in the proceedings. The judge, of course, stated that the woman's evidence lent support to what the authorities said. This cannot, however, be understood to suggest that the judge in fact recognized the rule he applied only because it was supported by the authorities, because none of the authorities cited said anything about the existence of the rule in question.

131. There was evidence before the court that the father of the woman, who according to official customary law should have negotiated her marriage and given consent to it, had abandoned the family, and that the mother had acted as head of the family.

132. At p. 1074.

133. See, for example, the case of *Hlophe v Mahlalela and Another,* 1998 (1) SA 449, in which the court tried to ascertain living customary law to apply to the case before it. But it received conflicting evidence of the law from witnesses, both of whom claimed to be well placed to know the customary law of the local community concerned.

12. Education in Southern Africa
The Paradox of Progress

Bruce Fuller and Allen Caldwell

Educational Progress Center Stage, Political Doubts Backstage

We endeavor to tell two paradoxical stories. We begin by detailing the very modern progress that southern African governments have made in steadily *expanding* primary and secondary schooling. Yet since the late 1970s, spirited debate has arisen over inattention to educational *quality* as mass schooling has spread like wildfire.

This first tale contains two important subplots. Indeed, rapid school expansion in the region has come at the expense of school quality, often in rather dramatic ways. Mass schooling—over the past half century—has been defined either as a crucial ingredient of modernization or as a vile means for reproducing a caste-like social structure. The result under both ideological frameworks has been to thin out classroom quality. This is not inevitable, as we discuss with the case of Botswana, which has expanded enrollments and advanced quality simultaneously. Yet Malawi is the more typical case, where the newly democratic state recently abolished school fees, then watched primary school enrollments rise at a startling pace.

The parallel subplot is that expansion has been motivated by different forces prior to and following the independence heydays of the 1960s. Competing political and economic ideologies have been rekindled in post-apartheid Namibia and South Africa. Apartheid regimes had aimed to cool out opposition and political resistance. At the continent's southern tip, we saw a dramatic case where mass expansion, with little concern for improving quality, was used as a tool *with intent* to reproduce stratification and inequality. This leads to the contemporary question of whether softer forms of economic and class reproduction are linked to newly democratic states' heightened interest in expanding mass schooling. It is the constructed *meaning* and *effects* of mass expansion that demand serious reflection. Every state in the region—as well as their international patrons—continues to debate the balance between school expansion and raising quality. But we rarely discuss the real meaning of and political interests linked to the faith-filled expansion of mass schooling.

A second story is beginning to surface throughout the region as doubts grow over the state's actual efficacy in raising the quality and effectiveness of mass schooling. The political Left worries over whether the central state can decisively redistribute school resources to poor communities, racially desegregate high-status white schools, and democratize the social relations of schools rather than reproduce "apartheid of the mind." The political Right raises doubts over whether the central state *should* be an effective institutional actor, or whether it should devolve authority to local governments and school-level councils, or adopt market remedies, like voucher schemes. Within multi-ethnic societies, such as South Africa or Namibia, we see localized chiefs and provincial leaders challenging the central state, seeking a federalist political structure organized along ethnic boundaries.

This tale captures a paradox that besets newly democratic states around the world—one that hits political actors with a vengeance in southern Africa, given the region's racial and cultural diversity and its quick post-1989 importation of pro-capitalist statism. To look modern and attract foreign capital—within the post–cold war institutional context—southern African governments must crisply signal a concern for school expansion and improvement in educational quality. The surface motivations underlying this constructed "public interest" must follow conventional human capital orientations: a functionalist commitment to skilling children through homogenous, bureaucratic schooling.

But over the past decade we have come to vividly see that the central state often has limited capacity to truly alter social relations found inside local institutions, such as schools.[1] Cultural resistance to the social norms and assimilationist agenda of government schools is often strong; or, central policies are quietly and tacitly subverted at the school level. Most recently, we have seen the liberal-democratic state—now a worldwide institution—being decentered and recast in core countries, including the United States and Britain. Reinventing the state in the West— with an emphasis on decentralizing public authority and market-oriented remedies— means that the economic and symbolic ways of "looking modern" in southern Africa also must undergo change to establish isomorphism and legitimacy both at home and abroad.[2]

Since the mid-1960s most southern African governments have made enormous progress in expanding mass schooling, working within the constitutive rules of a centralized bureaucratic state (be it in the service of a capitalist or caste economy). But now what it means to be "a modern state"—within an economic and political environment that demands federalist arrangements, decentralizing toward local ethnic groups, and reforming school quality with an eye toward the grass roots—is changing. The old emphasis on expansion and raising quality in secular, mechanical ways is no longer a sufficient political strategy. This is the paradox around which the second story revolves. The political contest that swirls around this second story holds important implications for the state's institutional future in the region—and the constrained utility of international agencies as they presently cast their work.

Organization of the chapter. Section 1 details the progress that southern African nations have made in expanding primary and secondary enrollments between 1965 and 1995. Primary school completion rates have improved. Reliable data are becoming available on indicators of school quality. We also will discuss the political discourse and varying motivations underlying the state's historical commitment to expand mass schooling. This helps to highlight commonalties and country-specific policy agendas. For example, South Africa and Malawi both used human capital conceptions of mass schooling's role in society to justify expansion. But Pretoria expanded Bantu education in ways that ensured reproduction of a racist class structure. Malawi, under Kamuzu Banda, structured the expansion of secondary schooling to preserve a sharp (multi-ethnic) class structure. Section 1 focuses on three nations—Malawi, South Africa, and Namibia—that manifest diverse political dynamics and education policy thrusts.

Section 2 reports on new political challenges and policy discourses that have flowed across the region since 1989. We focus on the emerging language of school reform heard in Namibia and South Africa since the end of the cold war. These countries have come on-line into the world economy most recently, quickly importing the cultural tenets of world institutions, including the state's role in expanding and improving mass schooling opportunities. This importation of policy frames has occurred even in direct repudiation of earlier ANC (African National Congress) and SWAPO (South West African People's Organization) commitments to the politicized ideals of Black Consciousness in the 1960s, the redistributive themes of the People's Education movement in the 1980s, and the ANC's earlier interest in advancing democratic social relations at the grass roots. Instead, the rapid importation of a policy discourse from the West, with only a residue of structural critique and attention to redistribution, has been truly remarkable.

At the same time, the West's own story line about mass schooling has been changing as transmitted through elite policy networks and international agencies, such as USAID (U.S. Agency for International Development) and the World Bank. We observe a stronger focus on decentralization, school choice, and measuring learning outcomes as a means of holding schools accountable. African policy elites rarely voice the earlier debates over how social relations within schools might become more democratic, what educational "quality" actually means in a multi-ethnic context, and whether the school should primarily serve an assimilationist agenda to help integrate labor markets.[3]

We conclude our analysis in section 3 by asking whether the old policy discourses around school expansion and quality improvement can be sustained, given shifts in world institutions *and* legitimate multi-ethnic contention within countries. The old policy discourse assumed the presence of an effective central state that could, for instance, build schools and ship more textbooks and teachers out to a unified school "system." The new world order now offers sacraments (and foreign aid) for states that decenter authority, move financing down to the school level, and advance market remedies. Ironically, this fits a post-modern, multi-ethnic agenda that challenges the central state's emphasis on cultural homogenization and assimilation. Modern statecraft is seen as eroding the cohesion of local communities and as subverting the authority of local ethnic leaders.

Together, decentralizing and multi-ethnic pressures on the state may further constrain its effectiveness to expand a uniform system of mass schooling. Indeed, the modern Durkheimian affection for "system" and "mass" is eroding in the West, a target of political attack from elements of the Left and Right since the 1960s. Considerable pressure is being put on the state to advance quality and accountability. We see this in the push for uniform curricular standards and more testing, which preserve the central state's utility. But we also see contention in multi-ethnic societies like South Africa over school choice (from desegregation advocates), culturally responsive curricula, and what languages and religious symbols are to be respected in classrooms. How the modern state remains credible and effective—and responds to these centrifugal forces—may be the defining frame for policy debates in the new century.

Progress in Expanding Schools and Raising Quality, 1965–95

We begin with three country cases, illustrating patterns of school expansion, definitions of quality, and the contrasting ideological and political foundations underlying these alternative pathways.

Malawi: Shaking Off Stark Stratification

Since independence in 1964, Malawi's government has identified the education sector as key in its efforts to reduce poverty. Under dictatorship and, more recently, a democratic regime, the state has made significant strides to develop mass schooling. Policy-makers have concentrated their efforts at expanding access to primary and (a stratified) secondary school system. State actors increasingly focus on raising the quality of education. The new, freely elected government is pressing a third policy goal: increasing the number of girls who attend secondary school.

For over thirty-five years Malawi has made substantial investments in its education sector, although the opportunity structure was tightly constrained in this very poor nation where GDP per capita is about $200 annually. Yet expectations are skyrocketing that education will deliver Malawi from the valley of poverty to the heights of development. Provided below are data that chronicle the expansion of schooling in Malawi, as well as proxies of educational quality. Numbers are given detailing the government's rising spending on education in Malawi since 1980. We also highlight policy pitfalls that threaten to undermine elements of the state's educational strategy.

Illustrated in Figure 12.1, over a thirteen-year period from 1980 to 1993, the

Figure 12.1 Gross Enrollment Ratio (%) Primary Level

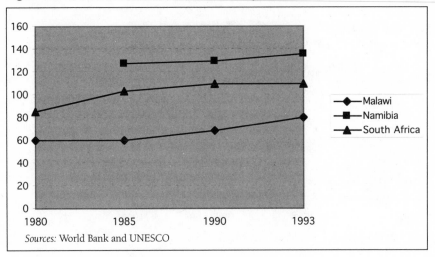

Sources: World Bank and UNESCO

Malawian state succeeded in raising the primary enrollment ratio by approximately 20 percent. It was in the following year, 1994, that access to primary school shot up exponentially. The 1994 expansion was fueled by the new, democratic government's decision to abolish school fees at the primary level. One year after the elimination, primary enrollment surged by 41 percent, from 1.9 million to 3.2 million children. Although abolishing primary school fees was consistent with the government's commitment to investing in human capital and signaling mass opportunity, the avalanche of additional students eroded educational quality and severely strained an already overburdened sector.[4]

The increase of over one million new students into the primary sector stimulated demand for new primary teachers. Although student enrollment expanded by 41 percent, the government was forced to recruit and hire 75 percent more primary teachers. Many of these new hires, 20,000, received minimal teacher training before being dispatched to the schools. The state estimates that an additional 38,000 new classrooms must be created to reach its goal of approximately 60 students per classroom. Malawi's schools continue to suffer from high grade repetition and dropout rates. In 1995, the average primary school student in Malawi required a decade and a half to complete the eight-year primary cycle: thirteen years for boys and sixteen years for girls.[5]

Although the primary gross enrollment ratio swelled after school fees were eliminated, the enrollment ratio at the secondary level remains stubbornly low. As depicted in Figure 12.2, over a thirteen-year period (1980 to 1993) the enrollment ratio failed to reach double digits. With the dual aim of boosting secondary enrollments and decreasing gender disparities, policy-makers have turned their attention to expanding access to secondary schooling for girls. As Figure 12.3 illustrates, the gross enrollment ratio for girls at the secondary level has crept upward

Figure 12.2 Gross Enrollment Ratio (%) Secondary Level

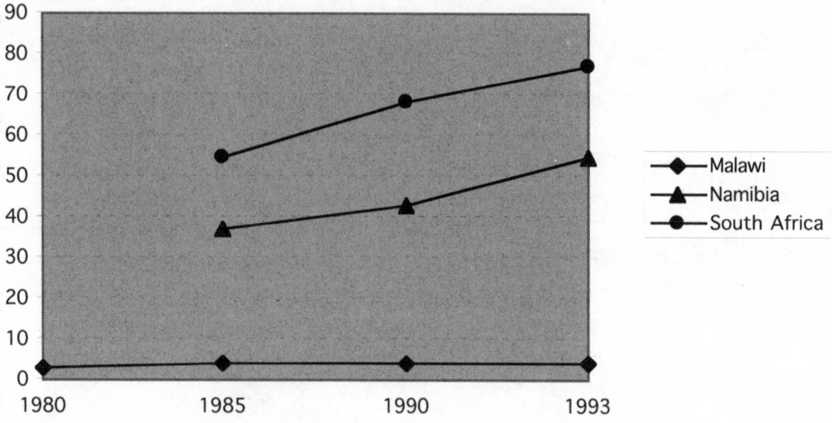

Sources: World Bank and UNESCO

over time, yet a disparity remains. In 1995, girls accounted for less than 39 percent of secondary enrollment. To address the problem, the new government has simply reserved 50 percent of all places in secondary school for girls.[6] Whether this quota approach is politically sustainable remains to be seen.

Rapid expansion has not come without costs. As seen in Figure 12.4, from 1985 to 1990 spending on education as a percentage of GNP jumped sharply, from 20 to 30 percent. After 1990, costs leveled off and remained fairly constant, hovering near the 30 percent mark. However, after the elimination of primary fees, educational costs rose again. The bill for the primary subsector alone mushroomed to account for 71 percent of all public spending on education. Still more alarming, within the five-year period from 1990 to 1995 the government's recurrent expenditures on education as a whole more than tripled, a level of spending that will be very difficult to sustain.[7] International agencies have applauded the new government's attempts to widen school opportunities. But the cost of this initiative means an ever-rising foreign debt burden.

If education is to play the prominent role that the new government intends, helping to alleviate the country's grinding poverty while simultaneously developing its human capital base, future education policy must address a basic paradox that has emerged. This involves the devilishly hard problem of expanding mass schooling while at the same time improving educational quality. If mass schooling is spreading like wildfire, as indeed it is in Malawi, the issue of quality represents the firebreak that very well could extinguish the blaze.

The paradox itself is riddled with internal complications. The complications stem from how policy-makers and members of the donor community define "quality" in the post-1989 world institutional context. Key policy players remain mired in me-

Figure 12.3 Girls Enrollment Share Secondary Level (%)

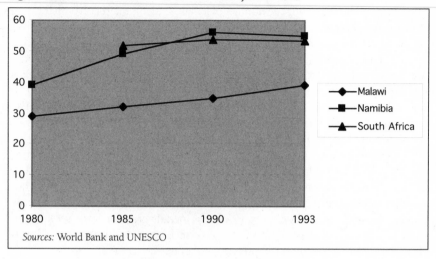

Sources: World Bank and UNESCO

Figure 12.4 Public Expenditure on Education as % of GNP

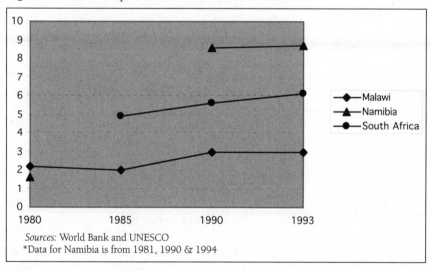

Sources: World Bank and UNESCO
*Data for Namibia is from 1981, 1990 & 1994

chanical, Durkheimian conceptions of quality. By this we mean that policies aimed at broadening access and boosting quality aim to incorporate peripheral groups into mass schooling and the nation-building agenda. But this will remain largely a symbolic exercise—unless school quality is sufficient to raise basic literacy and improve lives. For instance, the Malawian government is implementing a quota policy that will reserve half of all secondary school slots for girls. While the aim is laudable, the quota policy frame may prove problematic on two accounts. First, domestically a quota targeted on increasing the number of female students may clash with the democratic state's objective of devolving authority to regional and local education offices. Newly hatched democratic regimes are under great pressure to deliver promised results, including expanding mass opportunity. But this too contradicts the decentering of government to local agencies and tribal political structures. This counter-pressure comes in the wake of rejecting a dictatorial political structure. Some Western states also now push decentralization as a remedy for many ills. Yet strong policies aimed at reducing historical disparities, including but not limited to gender, require the retention of strong political authority at the center.

Second, it remains unclear whether new, more pluralistic conceptions of school quality will surface. Malawi remains committed to a conventional, British-style, exam-driven curriculum. But shifts away from this centralized system may be necessary. Even dictator Banda's textbook company published school readers in several mother tongues. Will democratic reforms include greater respect for local cultural and linguistic groups? Can more diverse forms of educational quality be explored when expansion is the pre-eminent policy concern?

Next we focus on post-apartheid South Africa, where the push for mass opportunity is intense and discourse over diverse forms of "school quality" is contentious.

South Africa: Attacking Gross Disparities in School Quality

In 1953 the engineers of apartheid decided that it was time to pave the dusty educational paths that black children were forced to travel upon. With the passage of the Bantu Education Act, the ascendant National Party formally began the state-sponsored process of constructing these new and broader roads of black education. But these roads were paved with the poorest of intentions: "natives will be taught from childhood to realize that equality with Europeans is not for them. . . . There is no place for him in the European community above the level of certain forms of labour."[8]

Not surprisingly, the engineers designed their educational road with a singular off-ramp: the exit of stunted learning outcomes and staggered educational aspirations. The spread of mass schooling for black and so-called coloured children was intended to signal educational opportunity but bound by narrow pathways that led to a stratified labor structure organized strictly by race. Engineered disparities in school quality would ensure that access to higher education would continue to be restricted for students of color.

Over forty years after passage of the Bantu Education Act, South Africa, in 1994, replaced the white engineers of apartheid with a National Government of Unity led by Nelson Mandela and the ANC. Mandela's party would garner 63 percent of all votes in the first all-race elections. It is hoped that the new educational policymakers will jackhammer and dismantle the old, inefficient educational system and replace it with a new one. A key question is whether the models of mass schooling and the school-reform discourse imported from the West—largely aiming to serve capitalist expansion—will match rising popular expectations and the vibrant ethnic pluralism that marks South African society.

The interplay between race, politics, and education in South Africa has always existed. Our statistical profile picks up the story in 1970. From 1970 to 1994, the apartheid regime did expand black access to primary schooling. The share of black children enrolled in school rose from about 50 to almost 90 percent. But the key point is not so much the expansion of primary schooling, but rather the pre-modern *political motivations* behind the expansion. In 1976, black resistance to Bantu education had violently erupted, culminating in the Soweto riots. The apartheid regime relied on a transparent political strategy to cool out black resistance to Bantu education: throughout the 1980s, the white government aggressively expanded black access to primary schooling (Figure 12.1). Then, as optimism grew in the early 1990s and following through to the 1994 democratic elections, the primary gross enrollment ratio climbed to over 100 percent.

The racist National Party also increased spending on education as a percentage of GNP between 1985 and 1993, as seen in Figure 12.4. Within a five-year period, from 1987 to 1992, the government's education budget nearly tripled, growing from R 9.9 billion to R 27.3 billion. This represents an annual increase of 5.2 percent. Just prior to the regime's demise in 1994, public outlays for education had surged to represent nearly one-quarter (24.4 percent) of total government spending.[9]

This was a distinctly pre-modern expansion of mass schooling within a starkly stratified opportunity structure. For the 1991 school year, the apartheid state was spending 4.2 times more per white primary school pupil than for each black pupil. In the same year, although whites made up only 13 percent of the population, 34 percent of the national education budget was allotted to them. Blacks made up 75 percent of the population, and the state was committing less than half (48 percent) of the national education budget to Bantu education.[10]

This stark stratification of school financing resulted in dismal school quality for black and coloured children. White schools were staffed with better-trained (white) teachers than were black and coloured institutions. In 1993, all white teachers possessed at least the minimum qualifications compared to 25 percent of all black teachers. Educational quality in black schools under apartheid was further diluted as a result of high student-teacher ratios. For instance, in 1987, black schools had a student-teacher ration of 41:1; the student-teacher ratio in white schools was 16:1.[11] Given that black schools were forced to operate on a shoestring budget, instructional materials were not only outdated but also in short supply.[12] With poorly trained teachers, overcrowded classrooms, and a dearth of materials, it was not surprising that in 1994 the matriculation exam pass rate for blacks was 48 percent compared to 97 percent for whites.

After the 1994 elections, the new ANC government—in truth, a federal system with the National and the Inkatha Freedom parties winning two provinces—was faced with the challenge of undoing a highly stratified school institution. Similar to the situation in Malawi, the paradox of expanding mass schooling while raising quality presents a huge problem. The expansion of mass opportunity involves more than merely opening more schools for historically marginalized groups. Opportunity is also linked to desegregation—that is, expanding black access to formerly all-white schools. White schools have had, and continue to be seen as having, higher quality and status than black schools. This fact has not been lost on black and coloured parents. They understand that formerly white schools have better-trained teachers and a rich array of materials. Concerns over access and quality also are evident at the level of higher education.

Moves to open access to high-status universities are met with concern over lowering quality. Yet the previously black and coloured colleges remain overcrowded, with inadequately trained faculties. Educational policy-makers must attempt to address the legacy of Bantu education with a mixture of modern policy frames. At one end of the policy spectrum resides a Durkheimian frame that emphasizes rationalizing the education system. The operative word is "system." Enhancing quality by consolidating the bureaucracy, buying more inputs like textbooks, and measuring achievement with standardized tests are examples from this end of the policy spectrum. School reform pushes for uniformity, greater efficiency, and more equitable distribution of school inputs. Mass schooling should become a coherent system.

At the opposite end of the spectrum are neo-liberal, market-inspired policy frames. Devolving authority to local actors, decentralizing financing to the provinces, and viewing students and parents as "consumers" of education all drive these market-inspired policy options. The ANC's policy agenda has been surprisingly pro-choice in character: encouraging student migration to white schools, tolerating religious curriculum in Muslim and other "public" schools, and devolving much authority over schools to the provincial governments. As the South African constitutional structure emerged as federalist in character, the local pressures of ethnicity and regional politics gained greater force—countering these Durkheimian tendencies of consolidating toward a single nation-building agenda.

Deciding which policy frame to apply to different education problems—while always attempting to deliver concrete results to assure impatient voters that the ANC state can make a difference—generates intense political tensions. Let's turn to an example from higher education to illustrate the dilemmas between mass expansion and quality improvement. This example illustrates how the historic and current interplay of ethnicity and social class continues to define the political stage upon which school reforms are contested. What's more, it may prove to be a litmus test of policy-makers' ability to reform South African education in the next century.

Much work remains to equalize the quality of secondary schools and racial disparities in attainment. But the most contentious dispute around widening access and the perceived threat to quality is situated in the higher education sector. Under apartheid, black students were tracked into the lowest quality of colleges. This ensured a low-status path into the labor structure. Many of these students refused to pay tuition as an act of resistance. The refusal to pay tuition was part of an overall battle plan adopted by student unions to topple apartheid. Although the war against apartheid proved successful, the tactics of resistance persist. In the "new South Africa" many black university students still refuse to ante up tuition. The apartheid-era strategy of resistance remains, while the adversary has literally switched skins.[13] How does the new government resolve the standoff? Not only are many black students refusing to pay their college bills, many black parents simply cannot afford to pay their children's tuition. The ANC government is itself strapped for cash.

To signal broader opportunity, the ANC substantially expanded admissions to black and coloured universities—without raising their budget commitment a commensurate level. The problem presents a political dilemma: on one side are students and parents who lack the necessary financial means to afford higher education; on the other side sits the ANC, which is politically beholden to black students and parents yet cannot afford to match rapidly rising expectations. It's a telling case of modern contradiction of a state that must preach faith in more schooling—as a highly institutionalized signal of mass opportunity. But the state can't afford to seriously reverse the erosion of quality. The result is the ongoing reinforcement of a race-based stratification structure that may return to haunt ANC policy-makers.[14]

Other examples abound in South Africa where the modern push to expand mass schooling and build a Durkheimian system just doesn't match the centrifugal dynamics of diversity. ANC policy-makers now push outcomes-based education (OBE), another avant-garde reform import from the West. The idea is to define uniform learning outcomes against which teachers and children are held accountable. Like the Thatcher reforms of the 1980s, it sharpens the central state's role in outcome standards and public accountability, while leaving school inputs and parental choice to local actors. But how the elegance of the OBE fits the linguistic, ethnic, and political pluralism of South Africa's societies is difficult to fathom. Once again, a mechanical conception of how to raise school quality is imported from the West and deemed *modern*. How it advances local participation and advancement of local forms of living are questions rarely posed by the new ANC.[15]

Namibia: Addressing Inequality in a Smaller Post-Apartheid State

Our final country case is Namibia, another young nation that illustrates the paradoxes of modern policy-making. Namibia shares this set of dilemmas involving the mass expansion of schooling while attempting to raise educational quality. The fragile, newly democratic state struggles to look modern in the post-1989 world institutional context. This requires a push to widen educational opportunity. Modern rules of democratic statecraft also require reducing disparities in quality, equally stark and organized along racial lines relative to South Africa. But Namibia—as a fledgling state—lacks the resources and organizational capacity to deliver on these modern policy fronts that must keep pace with ever-widening faith in the modern school. These conflicts, if left unresolved, may erode the state's legitimacy.

Since gaining independence from Pretoria in 1990, the Namibian government has attempted to reverse the decades-long educational neglect caused by apartheid. Beyond expanding access to schooling, the SWAPO-led government hopes to expand access to secondary schooling, desegregate white schools, and reduce race-based disparities in school quality at all levels. Similar to the ANC leadership in South Africa, SWAPO, led by Sam Nujoma, was rooted in the Black Consciousness and student movements of the 1960s and 1970s.

Figures 12.1 and 12.2 help to illustrate the SWAPO government's effort to expand access to schooling since Namibia's independence. We present enrollment ratios for both primary and secondary education. Although enrollment trajectories at both levels inched upward between 1985 and 1990—as the apartheid regime struggled for legitimacy in their southwest territory—it was after independence that enrollments rose sharply. While holding relatively steady at approximately 128 percent during the five-year period between 1985 and 1990, the gross enrollment ratio for the primary level jumped another 5 percent between 1990 and 1993. More impressive have been rising enrollments at the secondary level. The secondary enrollment ratio increased significantly between 1990 and 1993. During this three-year period, the gross enrollment ratio for the secondary level jumped nearly 28 percent. As in South Africa, the surge in optimism and expectations in the new Namibia was quickly followed by a jump in school enrollment. And again, a paradox emerges: if mass expansion erodes quality, then only symbolic opportunities are being granted by a regime that is eager to advance its own political legitimacy.

Identical to the spreading of schooling in Malawi and South Africa, skyrocketing costs have accompanied the expansion of schooling in Namibia. As Figure 12.4 indicates, public spending on education as a percentage of GNP was close to 9 percent in 1993, and climbing. In 1996, spending on education represented nearly 27 percent of the nation's recurrent budget. If the country's projected enrollment rates for the year 2010 are met, this share will explode to 40 percent. If the Ministry of Education is successful in its plan to raise the qualifications of all teachers by the year 2006, the education sector will consume approximately 46 percent of the national budget.[16] Such are the fiscal effects of a suddenly modern state that must gain legitimacy by appearing to deliver mass opportunity while struggling to exhibit more equal quality levels.

Both the SWAPO government and international agencies have committed substantial resources to expansion of mass schooling (at the secondary level) and improving quality, especially within the impoverished northern region. In 1991 approximately 1,234 schools were registered in Namibia; by 1997 that number has risen to 1,457, an increase of 18 percent. The majority of these new schools were started by black parents and other community stakeholders in rural Namibia.[17] The school-building initiatives of these two groups and the government's automatic financing of these new schools provide a window through which we can observe the issues central to this chapter.

A sizable majority of these new schools opened in response to parental and community initiative, marking the rising demand for schooling. Seemingly, parents and community stakeholders were motivated to build schools because they wanted their children to receive an education that the apartheid state had not provided. In other words, their motivation was not overtly political. The same, however, cannot be said for how the state responded.

The central state of Namibia responded to the parent-driven expansion of schooling politically: it folded the new schools into a national education system it is eagerly attempting to consolidate. Through its incorporation of the new, parent-initiated schools, the Namibian government was bringing the institutions under its political control. As Namibia is a newly independent and fragile state, political control translates into governmental oversight and regulation. Again we see a central state that institutionally must follow policy frames grounded in Durkheimian notions of a unified system. The Namibian government can now determine the qualifications of teachers, measure student learning outcomes, and exercise financial oversight of the schools. The system is seen as a necessary condition for addressing poor quality and inequities. Yet these political motivations of the state converge with the regulatory mechanisms used to monitor educational quality. And "quality" comes to be defined in the Western parlance of inefficiency, high grade retention, and the need to "continuously assess" student performance.[18] The previous SWAPO discourse over the political or participatory aims of schooling is squeezed out by this new modern discourse.[19]

Playing by Durkheimian rules of rationalizing the school organization and its symbolic meanings, however, leads to contradictions inherent in multi-cultural societies, be they newly democratic or less fragile ones. First, given the multi-ethnic composition of Namibian society, local political leaders may view consolidation of the school system as a power grab by central authorities. Second, the policy frames required to establish regulatory capacity and financial oversight may clash loudly with local customs and practices. For instance, will local actors interpret a government-designed curriculum as culturally sensitive and linguistically relevant? The SWAPO government's recent efforts to relocate teachers to advance equity has resulted in the dispatch of teachers from one ethnic group to teach in a community dominated by a different ethnic group. Playing by modern rules that emphasize national unity conflicts with a post-modern faith in ethnic-rooted community.

Third, parts of the Western donor community are coming to view the policy frames in which centralized governments are grounded as relics of a past era. With a growing emphasis on devolution of public authority and a decentering of the state, some foreign donors are beginning to push decentralization out to Namibia's weak regional agencies. Resorting to devolution and market remedies may buy legitimacy in the eyes of Western donors. However, whether such post-1989 policy shifts advance school quality or truly encourage democratic participation is doubtful. This is the key dilemma facing newly democratic states as the post-1989 world institutional norms shift toward decentralizing policy reforms.

The paradox confronts Namibia as it struggles to expand and improve its schools. With Namibia, a fragile state attempting to consolidate its political legitimacy, the largely democratic SWAPO regime has no choice but to take over parent-initiated schools. Similarly, the central ministry simultaneously is rationalizing national curricula and exams, reallocating resources to the impoverished north, and, at least symbolically, devolving authority to very fragile regional offices. But for the consolidation process to move forward, the central government must utilize policy frames that will likely meet resistance from local-tribal leaders and competing political parties. And on the horizon, policy frames emphasizing the *central* control of schools may undercut the state's legitimacy internationally in the post-1989 world institutional context. On the one hand, a classically modern Durkheimian policy frame enhances the central state's authority over a loose, far-flung collection of village schools now defined as a "system." Yet, this may incite resurgent ethnic leaders at the grass roots, as well as certain members of the international community, such as USAID and the World Bank. At the same time, market-oriented policy frames, aimed at decentralizing power to local agents of the state may fail to raise school quality or reduce gross inequalities, eroding SWAPO's long-term legitimacy.

In short, to the extent that "democracy" in Africa connotes a Jeffersonian emphasis on local participation, not only implying a centralized Durkheimian system, the old modern rules of statecraft may not be sufficient. But how to encourage democratic participation locally while institutionally constructing a unified nation-state—in the historical context of ethnic segmentation and stark class inequality—represents a long-term dilemma that will continue to plague SWAPO and ANC leaders.

After the Cold War: New Policy Frames That Challenge the Modern State

These old policy thrusts aimed at expanding mass schooling and mechanically raising quality will persist. They neatly fit a Durkheimian, post-war conception of a liberal-democratic state that is fairly centralized. This conventional agenda advances the symbols and occasional material rewards associated with expanding opportunity and economic integration as well as advancing the stock of human capital, consolidating nation-building, and the homogenization of language and culture. Even political parties that once articulated a socialist-marxist critique of capitalism—most notably the ANC—now preach the importance of attracting foreign investors, advancing free markets, and dedicating mass schooling to a classic human capital agenda bent on skilling the individual child.[20] Economic participation will be lopsided throughout the region until strong state policies can effectively reduce gross disparities. Consolidation of state authority is also required to nurture democratic institutions and provide the civil order so necessary to grow a capitalist economy.[21]

Isn't this what modern nation-building is all about?

Perhaps not. We have reviewed two post-1989 policy discourses that suggest a recasting of what "modern government" connotes. Both streams of ideology—indeed, a recasting of the ideal elements of a good, more pluralistic society—are affecting how we think about educational policy options and how the state crafts the governance and character of mass schooling. The first stream relates to contestation in the West over how centralized the liberal-democratic state should be. By becoming more classically liberal in an Adam Smith or Jeffersonian sense, social relations at the grass roots will become more democratic, so argue the advocates of decentralization and school choice. Thus, the institutional form of the state is up for grabs as government is "reinvented" in the West.

Second, we see new education issues floating to the top of political agendas *within* southern Africa, especially inside multi-ethnic nations, like South Africa and Namibia. This includes debate over the following issues: Which languages can be legitimately spoken in classrooms? Will school choice aid or subvert the desegregation of white schools? How can the state retain centralized authority to redistribute school resources while decentralizing other responsibilities? Will a greater emphasis on measuring learning outcomes, and importing the American love of testing, actually raise achievement, or simply make classrooms more stultifying and mechanical? This second stream of issues emanates from the region's own history and the peculiarities that characterize multi-ethnic, post-colonial societies.

Together, these two streams of discourse are seriously challenging the state's constitutive rules under which the old policy talk, centering on school expansion and quality improvement, seemed so sensible. These new education issues also raise questions about the central state's efficacy and wisdom in truly advancing forms of schooling that are inviting to local families and that advance democratic social relations at the grass roots. Can the state stretch beyond the political-economy imperatives of capitalist growth and democratization at the top to nurture more pluralistic forms of schooling that advance participatory ideals locally?

In short, modern progress in the education sector has led to a pair of telling contradictions. Rapid school expansion has served to undercut quality. Under apartheid regimes this inverse relationship was engineered with intent; Bantu education in South Africa and in what was then South West Africa (Namibia) aimed to cool out political opposition by opening up access for millions of black and coloured children to enter low-quality primary and secondary schools. Malawi continues to expand "day secondary schooling" mostly for poor children, while youngsters of middle-class parents enter the more prestigious boarding secondary schools, reproducing the class structure.[22] Only Botswana—buoyed by steady earnings from diamonds and foreign donors—has been able to simultaneously expand enrollments and improve quality at primary and secondary levels.[23] As the central state imports Western avant-garde means for raising school quality, such as South Africa's sudden affection for "outcomes-based education" and Namibia's ad option of "continuous assessment," we must ask whether such hyper-rationalized strategies can be implemented by fragile states or even deciphered by local teachers.

This bumps up against another paradox that besets central government in southern Africa, a contradiction that also flows from earlier progress linked to the logic of modernity. It is simply not clear that the new generation of debates around educational quality and local governance of schools, including particularistic forms of grassroots participation and accountability, can be effectively addressed by the central state. The problem here is that the arrival of democratic institutions at macro levels—multiple political parties, an elected parliament, a free press—bring politicized demands for *local* democracy and a decentering of political authority. Within intensely multi-ethnic societies, a uniform Durkheimian cultural frame for the nation-state can no longer be assumed.

Nowhere is this clearer than in South Africa, where a partially centralized federalist state attempts to balance competing demands from distinct ethnic groups.[24] The ANC government has been remarkably "pro-choice" in its school policies, allowing parents to choose any school to which their child can apply, permitting religious classes, and liberally allowing local schools to select their preferred language of instruction. To mediate multi-ethnic and pluralistic cultural interests, the state must mediate competing interests by becoming more liberally tolerant of competing cultural frames—a monumental departure from the strong state conception of nation-building that dominated discourse prior to 1989.

This internal shift blends almost inadvertently with the West's recent affection for "reinventing government" in ways that reduce central spending and devolve political authority down to provinces and local communities, from creating school site governing councils to experimenting with school vouchers.[25] Policy debates in the region no longer only focus on the limited institutional capacity of the central state apparatus. Government is now an active advocate of decentralization and is rearranging itself to accommodate cultural pluralism. The very meaning of *modern progress* is being deconstructed and pasted back together.

Next, we briefly describe how world institutions have shifted since the end of the cold war in 1989. By this we mean the renewed international legitimacy of capitalism, which leads to the virtual disappearance of a counter model of political-economy that socialist regimes tried to advance. The state institution and its tacit policy frameworks—imported from the West by southern African political leaders—now emphasize a balance between making elements of central government more efficacious through decentralization and adopting market-oriented reforms. These shifting conditions partially explain why the old discourse, assuming that a strong state would implement education policy, is giving way to something new. We then turn to the new policy debates that flow from the two paradoxes of how school expansion has led to erosion of quality and why the new debates over school effectiveness and local governance are difficult to contain within Durkheimian conceptions of the modern state.

The Contested Meaning of the Modern State

Our South African colleague Linda Chisholm reminds us that when we look toward Europe or the United States, it is difficult to reach out and grasp a single "Western model" of the state. Indeed the surging faith in markets and decentralized government, following the collapse of centralized socialism in 1989, has heightened contention over how the state should be organized. This shift in worldwide economic and institutional conditions directly shaped how Namibia and South Africa came on-line into the international network of states. In 1990, Sam Nujoma's SWAPO party won the first all-race elections in newly independent Namibia. Then, in 1994, Nelson Mandela's ANC swept into power with a strong popular mandate. Despite over three decades of commitment to socialist ideals and military struggle aimed at overthrowing white capitalist elites, these two men and their parties understood that after independence "reconciliation, reconstruction, and development" were required to maintain civil stability and spur economic growth. Nor would much foreign aid come from the collapsing bloc of socialist countries.

The materialist principles dominant in the West—including the school institution's potential contribution to "human capital accumulation"—now reigned supreme. The overall positioning of mass schooling in post-apartheid nations must be aimed at contributing to individual mobility and economic growth. The old ANC and SWAPO goals of linking education to democratic participation or a more critical consciousness quickly became secondary, now rarely mentioned in policy circles.[26]

Two contradictory policy frames—displaying competing ideologies and implementing technologies—are now transmitted from the West into the hearts and minds of policy-makers in southern Africa. This signaling process stems from intention-filled projects by foreign donors and development banks, as well as from inadvertent signals emanating from internal contention in the United States and Europe over how government can best improve public education. The first is the ongoing interest in strengthening the central state's technical capacity to expand or improve the quality of schooling, discussed in first section.

Even more rationalized forms of governance and planning have been pushed on ministries of education in recent years. Under USAID contracts, for instance, Florida State University has advocated what they call instructional systems design (ISD). Rooted in behaviorist principles of learning, ISD materials break down syllabi and textbooks to include discrete learning objectives and skills. Teachers are then required to "continually assess" students' mastery of this ladder of competencies. This curricular system allegedly will drive the content of new "competency based exams," allowing countries to move away from old-style British exams that focused on facts and imperial forms of knowledge, not basic skills and "higher order thinking skills."[27]

In one speech, soon after independence, President Nujoma (1991) praised this system of "learner-based education." His first minister of education insisted on calling students "learners" to combat the controlling and "teacher-centered" character of Bantu education.[28] Similarly, Mr. Mandela's Ministry of Education is pressing forward with "outcomes-based education," whereby even popular literacy curricula for adults is reduced to learning objectives and skills, stripped of the ANC's earlier political and participatory spirit that was attached to basic education and literacy programs.[29] This rationalized approach to teaching and classroom organization, neatly fitting a technocratic form of governance, has long been emphasized in development projects elsewhere in the region, including Botswana, Malawi, and Zambia. Many World Bank projects continue to support management information systems, the redesign of textbooks and examination systems, and consolidation of teacher-training programs via stronger central planning. But these highly standardized and technocratic approaches rest on the assumption of a strong state, precisely the foundational premise being shaken by neo-liberals in the West.

Challenges to Modern Statecraft and Policy-Making

Three sets of internal dynamics in Africa prompt additional questions over the central state's political legitimacy and technical capacity to tackle a new generation of educational-related problems:

- *The ethnic boundaries of public problems. Political* pluralism and a move toward federalist governing structures manifest new respect for *cultural* pluralism. This includes better understanding of how ethnic groups and their particular institutional histories manifest diverse problems *and* strengths that offer possible remedies.

- *Local constitutive rules that advance or constrain gender equity.* The spread of mass schooling has served to incorporate many girls and young women into a modern framework. But this enfranchisement abruptly ends for many during secondary school when traditional gender roles kick in. In addition, recent research shows that girls' persistence through secondary school, achievement levels, and downstream effects, such as lower fertility rates, are shaped by family-level factors that are difficult to touch from policy levels.[30]

- *The central state's inability to alter the tacit culture of schools and classrooms.* Governments and international agencies have rightly focused on raising the level of school resources and, occasionally, redistributing the level of school inputs toward poorer communities.[31] But the deeper we look inside schools and classrooms, the more we discover that social relations are far from participatory, or even inquisitive in their character. Student and teacher roles remain narrow, often passive and stuck in hierarchical organizations. Schools often act to inadvertently subvert the democratization of macro-political institutions. Technocratic tools for improving educational quality rarely recognize the cultural rules found inside schools.

Let's examine specific examples and recent research on these new dynamics, focusing on the past decade. We then will close this chapter by returning to the question: Can conventional, modern forms of statecraft and policy-making really speak to these emerging issues? If not, what new forms of central policy might advance the spirit of grassroots democracy and the pressing imperative of economic justice?

Ethnic archipelagos. Multi-cultural societies display various ways in which children are socialized at home, as well as diverse local conditions in which school institutions develop over time. Both sets of conditions influence what children learn and at what rate. Ethnic differences in children's achievement levels, for instance, often are sharp in societies with a history of caste-like structures of opportunity. This includes post-apartheid nations—Namibia and South Africa—as well as those with strict class structures that partially map against ethnic status, like Malawi. Where the development of local institutions differed systematically for different ethnic "homelands," as under Pretoria's *bantustan* system of coercive "local governance," we may see advantageous institutional conditions under which the achievement of children from certain ethnic groups, or within particular regions, is relatively high. But when policy-makers earnestly seek a universal remedy, they often ignore variation in local conditions on which the reform's effectiveness depends. Nor is the bureaucratic state very adept at identifying particular local conditions that help contribute to higher school achievement. This is a problem endemic to mechanical, input-oriented strategies for raising school quality. The nurturing or stifling facets of local settings are deemed irrelevant.

Recent research in southern Africa illuminates the importance of ethnic and regional boundaries as we diagnose disparities in student achievement. In South Africa, the education ministry each year publishes the passage rate for students taking the secondary school matriculation exam. In 1993, as in prior years, the pass rate varied dramatically across the old regions populated by different ethnic groups. Over 63 percent of students in the "homeland" that was called Bophuthatswana under the apartheid regime passed the matriculation exam, compared to 42 percent in KwaZulu-Natal and just 35 percent in the very impoverished Ciskei region.[32] We further explored these ethnic and regional variations in a 1993 household survey, involving interviews in 8,850 homesteads and a literacy exam (in English and mother tongues) for a subsample of families.[33]

Focusing on older and younger cohorts of black South Africans, we found that the apartheid regime's policy of expanding mass schooling had succeeded in raising mean school attainment levels. However, measurable literacy and numeracy rose more modestly and remained far below basic achievement levels of coloured and white graduates. More surprising, however, were the differences in literacy that we discovered among black ethnic groups. SeTswana-speaking youths, for example, showed literacy levels that were about 20 percent higher than in other large black groups (Xhosas and Zulus), after taking into account social class and home factors. This is consistent with the matriculation exam results: Bophuthatswana is populated primarily by Tswana families. We also found that children from the major black groups significantly outperformed youngsters from the smaller black groups (such as Vendas, Pidi, and Tsonga speakers). This pattern persisted even when looking at separate literacy assessments taken in their respective native language.[34]

Undoubtedly, institutional forces operating with this region—now called the

Northern Province—help to explain the Tswana advantage. The Bophuthatswana homelands administration, although lacking in political legitimacy, did mount initiatives to improve the quality of its schools. The Northern Province is depressed economically, which means the opportunity costs of staying in school are quite low, especially for girls. Another factor might be the historical strength of mission schools and the fact that the national headquarters of the AME (African Methodist Episcopal) church is situated in Mafikeng, the traditional capital of the Northern Province. Due to male labor migration to the cities, women often are the mainstays of local churches, reproducing an essential element of the community's infrastructure. Finally, cross-migration of Tswanas between this province and neighboring Botswana, where school attainment steadily increased since the 1960s, may have raised parents' expectations for how far their children should go in school.[35]

Similar ethnic differences in school achievement have been documented in Namibia, the second apartheid society where racial and ethnic groups were geographically segregated. This led to regional differences in the extent to which racial education authorities and *bantustan* administrations invested in school expansion and quality in the four decades prior to gaining independence from South Africa. Ethnic segregation in Namibia's schools—not just black-white but also between black groups—remains stark. Most Oshindonga-speaking children in the north attend schools with enrollments that are almost entirely from this ethnic group. Even in towns and commercial centers, black Nama-Damara children attend schools that are made up almost exclusively of this particular ethnic group.

We tracked the school performance of 2,650 primary school children over a three-year period, beginning in 1992, and found significant differences among black groups. The Nama-Damara children outperformed all other groups, although they still were far behind white Afrikaans-speaking youngsters (who continued to attend predominantly white schools). Even in the impoverished northern region, we found that the children of certain Owambo-speaking groups had achieved higher levels of literacy and numeracy by age twelve, relative to Oshindonga and Oshinkwanyama speakers.[36]

As with the South Africa findings, it is difficult to disentangle what is special about parenting practices or home environments across ethnic groups from regional differences in their institutional commitment to schooling. But the dynamics that affect children's learning appear to differ in important ways. Policy-makers' tendency to link all poor communities together, or to apply universal remedies and ignore such local variations, limit the effectiveness of their interventions.

Gender boundaries and inequality. Cutting across the ethnic borders of public problems are gender differences, both in how girls are raised at home and how schools set expectations about their futures. In countries like Namibia and Botswana, the spread of mass schooling has pulled girls into this modern institution. In more traditional pockets of the region, most notably Malawi, many young females remain disenfranchised. The central state's efficacy in making further inroads to reduce gender inequality is questionable. Unless policy-makers are willing to illuminate the *local* determinants of gender disparities—and home or school factors that advance equity—it is not clear that universal remedies alone will be very effective.

The recent empirical studies of ethnic differences in school achievement also reveal intriguing gender differences. For example, in Namibia we observed girls falling behind in math achievement as early as grade seven, even in rural areas where formal mathematics is an equally foreign body of knowledge for boys and girls.[37] In South Africa, we found that young Tswana females were the most literate group in the nation, among all black ethnic groups. Their level of secondary school completion was the highest, indicating either strong parental pressure to stay in school or very low opportunity costs within the depressed economy of the Northern Province.[38] Learning more about these kinds of factors could provide keys to raising female attainment and achievement for other groups.

Recent work in Botswana also points to family-level factors that influence girls' school attainment. Household studies in poor rural communities reveal that maternal education, the family's social structure, attitudes toward fertility, and a family's propensity to save and invest in their household help to predict daughters' school attainment. Counter to Western assumptions, it appears that the absence of the father or maternal control over resources, although associated with less income, may lead to *higher* school achievement for daughters.[39] Here again we observe very localized factors, emanating from within the family or local school, that are influential yet difficult to alter from a distant central state.

The cultural bounds of classrooms and schools. Mechanical means of raising quality are of crucial importance. Wide disparities persist throughout the region in terms of the availability of trained teachers and instructional materials. These inequities are structured by race and class. Only a strong central state will be able to steadily attack these inequalities through redistributional and input-oriented policies. But such conventional means of raising school quality will not be sufficient to alter the social relations of schools and classrooms that serve to suppress learning and undercut the local democratization of social relations. The very school inputs on which policy-makers focus represent the tools through which stultifying didactics and hierarchical social norms are reproduced. In an observational study of Soweto classrooms, Ntshingila-Khosa (1993) found that exercise books were used by students mainly to copy material off the blackboard written by the teacher. In Botswana, ethnographers Prophet and Rowell (1993) observed how science lessons were didactically presented with a focus on memorizing the English vocabulary; little was done to promote awareness of conceptual thinking or scientific inquiry. In Namibia, Nicodemus (1997) discovered that former exiles—often SWAPO freedom fighters who had fled to Zambia—are the most proficient English teachers in the north. But they also bring more liberal social mores and values, sparking concern among school principals who have been told by the ministry that instruction must be conducted in English, not in native languages. The tacit cultural norms of classrooms, enacted and re-enacted by teachers, tend to swamp the more participatory and Deweyan aims of earnest curriculum reformers.[40]

It is the hidden and tacit norms of classrooms and schools—reproduced at the grass roots far from national education ministries—that subvert the technocratic school reforms brought by foreign donors and swallowed by domestic policy elites. Outcomes-based education or continuous assessment represent avant-garde reforms that signal a central ministry is indeed modern and hip. But as these reforms bump into school cultures on the ground, they are easily, often inadvertently, deflected. Once again, government usually fails even to recognize the power of these processes, which are taken for granted inside schools and classrooms. The decentralization of school governance ironically may reinforce the legitimacy of these local norms and social rules, despite their distinctly un-modern and non-democratic character. Again, we hit a contradiction between first decentering the state, then expecting to see more democratic social relations inside schools. At the same time, central government rarely has a clue as to how to build from more indigenous norms and cultural structures found inside schools.

Thickening civil society, eroding universal policies and symbols. This fourth dynamic has received much less attention in southern Africa, although debate is growing in the United States over how grassroots democratization intersects multi-cultural forms of language, child-rearing, and schooling—what some refer to as "the culture wars." Again, we see contradictions stemming from resurgent interest in the liberal state's Jeffersonian side, with renewed emphasis on reinforcing local community. Under shifting world institutional conditions—with a greater emphasis on decentralized public authority and parental choice—we see greater policy attention placed on strengthening "intermediate institutions" that rest between the family and the state.[41]

Namibia, for instance, is investing heavily in local school boards. South Africa struggles with how best to support non-governmental organizations (NGOs). Malawi searches for ways to build civil society from scratch, following centuries of colonization and dictatorial rule. But as public authority and moral frames are deconcentrated back to local communities, we may see traditional tribal authorities, school principals, and church leaders regaining authority over schooling—an influence that they already exercise informally inside villages. This will result in a dilution of the "social facts," the universal tenets of social organization that Durkheimian statecrafters so eagerly attempt to protect. From the "official languages" permitted in classrooms to the religious and ethnic symbols sanctified by government schools, more pluralistic symbols and ways of raising children are sprouting through the bureaucratic concrete of mass schooling.

Conclusions: Who Will Define Educational Progress in the New Century?

African states and their policy-makers have made enormous progress in expanding mass education over the past four decades. Enrollment rates have steadily inched upward in most nations. Basic approaches to raising school quality and effectiveness often slide off the table, eclipsed by the policy obsession with expansion and infrastructure. Yet standard initiatives to raise quality—improving teacher preparation, lowering class size, even efforts to advance more stimulating pedagogies—do get placed back on the table. Until classrooms become more engaging places for learning, all the policy talk about educational progress will yield abundant symbolic returns for politicians but skimpy results for children.

Indeed, all the glowing claims of progress that take center stage in parliamentary sessions and in countless international meetings mask fundamental political doubts backstage. Whether fragile and technically constrained states can effectively address the public problems associated with family poverty, limited literacy, and a workforce with low educational attainment is a crucial worry. Efforts aimed at strengthening the institutional capacity of central governments and provincial education departments are vital.

Yet these tandem public problems of poverty and a semi-skilled workforce cannot be remedied by simply building more classrooms, hiring a larger number of teachers, and cleaning out school latrines. Infrastructure alone will not touch issues fundamentally rooted in post-colonial forms of authority, distinctly undemocratic social relations that are reproduced in local institutions. Earlier we focused on the new generation of problems linked to the character of African schooling and child socialization: the ethnic segmentation of educational and language problems, the persistence of gender inequalities, and the difficulties of altering the hierarchical and unstimulating nature of the classroom's social rules. Can fragile states move beyond their politically rewarding obsession with infrastructure to a new policy framework that rediscovers questions of local democracy and social participation?

We arrive at a final pressing question: Will policy-makers inside African nation-states really be the authors of educational policy? Will they be the ones defining benchmarks of educational progress?

Education policy-makers often are simply messengers, signaling to local communities and national elites that the state can make a difference by building schools, creating government (teaching) jobs, and distributing textbooks. But the audience for the work of domestic policy-makers and planners has become thoroughly global. The essential discourse around schooling focuses on advancing the nation's human capital stock by getting graduates ready for market. Even the earlier radical thinkers of the ANC or SWAPO now chant the dominant mantra: raise the efficiency of schools, delineate learning outcomes, and push for accountability of far-flung schools to the neo-liberal political center. Much of the policy talk around school reform is situated in world institutions—development banks, UN agencies, and foundations. It is rarely authored by policy-makers residing in southern Africa.

At the same time, domestic policy-makers must attend to centrifugal local forces, especially within the region's intensely multi-ethnic nations. Education leaders in Pretoria, for instance, must respond daily to cantankerous provincial legislatures or to ethnic communities that seek to protect their language or religion in "their" local schools. Or recurrent ministry efforts to advance gender equity now raise the hackles of local interest groups.

The rising commitment to decentralization and market-oriented remedies by the World Bank and other donors is fueling divergent political action in the provinces. Here the central state is pulled from both sides: international donors press for devolution of the domestic state, and grassroots constituencies press to decentralize budgets, as well. At the very same time that many political leaders in the West have become disaffected with modern Durkheimian notions of a "mass" public "system" of education, African states are still struggling to emulate this institutional model.

The Paradox of Progress

The region's three-decade-long catharsis has been painful since breaking free of foreign colonial rulers and the internal authors of apartheid. A liberal-democratic agenda—including further expansion of mass education and important ways of raising school quality—will continue to dominate political discourse. Schools will be pulled into alignment with neo-liberal capitalist goals with greater intensity. But these very modern forms of progress bring new challenges. The very definition of "school quality" is becoming more focused on altering gender roles, changing the fundamental social rules of classrooms, boosting tolerance for alternative languages of instruction and forms of decentralized school governance. As these policy frontiers are explored more vigorously, old forms of nation-building and modern conceptions of progress offer fewer signposts for guiding us through this unknown, potentially treacherous terrain.

NOTES

We wholeheartedly thank Linda Chisholm, Bekett Mount, Ndeshi Nicodemus, Francisco Ramirez, and Wes Snyder for thoughtful conversations over how the state touches, or fails to affect, local schools and how we must rethink this relationship. Jan Leno and Dzingai Mutumbuka spent considerable time to help us understand the World Bank's perspective on policy debates in the region. Bank staff generously shared recent education and budget statistics for several countries. Much of the evidence reported in this chapter stems from research projects supported by the U.S. Agency for International Development (USAID) and the World Bank. Interpretations stemming from this empirical work are solely our own, not necessarily the views held by these agencies.

1. J. Migdal, *Strong Societies and Weak States: State-Society Relations and State Capabilities in the Third World* (Princeton, N.J.: Princeton University Press, 1988); B. Fuller, *Growing up Modern: The Western State Builds Third World Schools* (New York: Routledge,

1991); Y. Bradshaw and B. Fuller, "Policy Action and School Demand in Kenya: When a Strong State Grows Fragile," *International Journal of Comparative Sociology* 37 (1996): 72–96.

2. B. Fuller, ed., *Government Confronts Culture: The Struggle for Local Democracy in Southern Africa* (New York: Garland Press, 1999).

Appreciation is expressed to Francisco Ramirez for his ideas on how world institutional theory does not necessarily depend on a conception of the "great rationalization project," an earlier more bureaucratic and formalized conception of the state and the school. As world institutions linked to the Western state evolve, the institutional environment shifts; lower-status nation-states then import a new set of tacitly held beliefs and features of what the state (in southern Africa) must look like to gain legitimacy.

3. L. Chisholm and B. Fuller, "Remember People's Education? Shifting Alliances, Statebuilding and South Africa's Narrowing Policy Agenda," *Journal of Education Policy* 11 (1996): 693–716.

4. World Bank, South Africa, *Education Sector: Strategic Issues and Policy Options* (Washington, D.C.: World Bank, 1995).

5. Ibid.

6. World Bank, Staff Appraisal Report, Malawi, Primary Education Sector (Washington, D.C.: World Bank, 1998).

7. World Bank, 1995.

8. "South Africa Survey," *Economist,* 20 May 1995 (special supplement), p. 14.

9. World Bank, 1995.

10. B. Fuller, P. Pillay, and N. Sirur, *Literacy Trends in South Africa: Expanding Education While Reinforcing Unequal Achievement?* (Cape Town: Department of Economics, University of Cape Town, 1995).

11. Ibid.

12. World Bank, 1995.

13. S. Daley, "University Insists That Tuition Be Paid. . . . or Else," *New York Times,* 31 March 1998, p. A3.

14. Fuller, *Growing up Modern.*

15. Chisholm and Fuller, "Remember People's Education?"

16. John Mendelsohn, *Basic Education in Namibia and SIDA Support* (Windhoek: Swedish International Development Agency, 1997).

17. Ibid.

18. Fuller, ed., *Government Confronts Culture.*

19. Chisholm and Fuller, "Remember People's Education?"

20. Ibid.

21. M. Bratton, *Democratic Experiments in Africa* (Cambridge: Cambridge University Press, 1997).

22. Fuller, *Growing up Modern.*

23. B. Fuller, H. Hua, and W. Snyder Jr., "When Girls Learn More Than Boys: The Influence of Instructional Time and Teaching Practices," *Comparative Education Review* 38 (1994): 347–76.

24. Migdal, *Strong Societies and Weak States.* B. Fuller, X. Liang, and H. Hua, "Did Black Literacy Rise after Soweto? Public Problems and Ethnic Archipelagos in South Africa," *International Journal of Comparative Sociology* 37 (1996): 97–120.

25. B. Fuller and R. Elmore, eds., *Who Chooses, Who Loses? Culture, Institutions, and the Unequal Effects of School Choice* (New York: Teachers College Press, 1996).

26. Chisholm and Fuller, "Remember People's Education?"

27. C. W. Snyder Jr. and P. T. Ramatsui, *Curriculum in the Classroom* (Gaborone, Botswana: Macmillan Botswana, 1990); Fuller, ed., *Government Confronts Culture.*

28. Fuller, ed., *Government Confronts Culture.*

29. Chisholm and Fuller, "Remember People's Education?"

30. Fuller, Pillay, and Sirur, *Literacy Trends.*

31. During the Mandela Administration's first year, education leaders successfully shifted about 3 percent of the national education budget from the more affluent to the poorer provinces. Both Namibia and South Africa have moved aggressively to equalize the ratio of pupils per teacher, redistributing posts from former white schools to schools in impoverished black or coloured communities.

32. Education Foundation, *Edusource Data News,* no. 5 (Durban, 1994).

33. Fuller, Pillay, and Sirur, *Literacy Trends.*

34. Fuller, Liang, and Hua, "Did Black Literacy Rise."

35. J. De Graaf and M. Lawrence, *Rural Parents and School Enrollment Patterns: Two Regions of Bophuthatswana* (Mafikeng: Institute of Education University of Bophuthatswana, 1986).

36. S. Grant Lewis, B. Fuller, and H. Hua, *How Much Do Namibia's Children Learn in School: The National Learner Baseline Assessment* (Windhoek: New Namibia Books, 1995).

37. Ibid.

38. Fuller, Liang, and Hua, "Did Black Literacy Rise."

39. B. Fuller, J. Singer, and M. Keiley, "Why Do Daughters Leave School in Southern Africa? Family Economy and Mothers' Commitments," *Social Forces* 74 (1995): 657–80.

40. B. Fuller and P. Clarke, "Raising Schools' Effects While Ignoring Culture?" *Review of Educational Research* 64 (1994): 119–57.

41. V. Havel, *Summer Meditations* (New York: Knopf, 1992); E. J. Dionne Jr., "Why Civil Society? Why Now?: The Reasons for This Issue and a (Very) Brief History of an Idea," *The Brookings Review* 15, no. 4 (1997): 5–8.

13. Health and Society in Southern Africa in Times of Economic Turbulence

Ezekiel Kalipeni

In spite of the raging AIDS epidemic, recent research in the field of health care in sub-Saharan Africa indicates that major improvements in health have been achieved in some countries since independence.1 Infant mortality rates have experienced dramatic declines, from 145 per 1,000 live births in 1970 to 104 per 1,000 in 1992. Other statistics such as increases in life expectancy, declines in maternal mortality, and widespread immunizations of children have been offered as indicators of success in the fight against disease in a number of countries in southern Africa, notably Malawi, Zimbabwe, Botswana, and South Africa. Nevertheless, these figures mask the worsening situation in parts of the region that recently were or are still plagued by political instability, for example, Mozambique and Angola.

More important than the above is the economic crisis that began in the early 1980s and was further exacerbated by the imposition of structural adjustment programs mandated by the IMF (International Monetary Fund) and the World Bank. The economic crisis has resulted in the collapse of health care delivery systems in poorer countries such as Angola, Malawi, Mozambique, and Zambia. Challenges in the provision of and access to health care are immense. The maternal mortality rate of 700 deaths per 100,000 live births for the region and the continent as a whole is double that of other low- and middle-income developing countries and more than forty times greater than in the industrial nations.[2]

This chapter examines the health and health care situation in southern Africa. It notes that, in general, southern Africa has made remarkable gains in reducing mortality levels and that if current trends continue, infant mortality could decline to a low of 26 deaths per 1,000 births by the year 2020. Life expectancy, which is currently at sixty-two for both sexes, could increase to a high of seventy-two by 2020. However, the chapter argues that these figures mask marked regional variations and inequalities within the southern African subcontinent, particularly in areas where high political instability has been the norm for most of the post-independence era. Specifically, the chapter examines the political ecology of diseases such as malaria, AIDS, Ebola, schistosomiasis, and other major causes of illness and death. A discussion of the health care system, particularly the problems faced by governments and other agencies in the provision of health care, is also offered. The discussion in this chapter centers upon the argument that the health status of any population depends on a complex set of social, political, and environmental factors. This set of complex factors includes economic situations, environmental deterioration, nutritional issues, safe water and sanitation, provision of basic education (especially to women), and the position of women in societal structures. In discussing health and society, this chapter leans heavily toward a more detailed examination of gender inequalities in access to health in southern Africa.

Current Demographic Situation

For the purposes of this chapter, the following countries are considered to be part of the southern African subcontinent: South Africa, Botswana, Swaziland, Namibia, Zimbabwe, Lesotho, Zaire, Zambia, Angola, Malawi, and Mozambique. As of 1994, estimates indicated that the combined population for these countries was about 146 million people. The country-specific distribution of this population ranged from a low of 0.8 million for Swaziland to 43.9 million for Zaire. Two countries, Zaire and South Africa, contain 58 percent of the total population of this region. Population growth rates also vary considerably from country to country but are generally on the higher end in comparison to the global population growth rate of 1.8 percent per annum. For example, the annual rate of natural increase ranges from 2.4 percent for South Africa to 3.7 percent for Zambia. It is interesting to note that the countries with the highest population densities (Malawi, Lesotho, and Swaziland) are also the most heavily dependent on agriculture. Considering the widespread shortage of cultivable land, the low productivity of the farming techniques employed by most of the smallholder farmers in the region, and the rising costs of living, many of the people living in this region are finding it increasingly difficult to make a decent living.[3]

In terms of fertility, South Africa has the lowest total fertility rate (4.0), while Malawi has the highest rate (7.1). Zimbabwe and Botswana, the two countries in the region with evidence of rapidly declining fertility rates, have total fertility rates of 5.1 and 4.7, respectively. Although most of the countries in this region have experienced substantial declines in mortality, mortality rates are still very high by world standards. Infant mortality is lowest in South Africa (51) and highest in Malawi (147). In Angola, Mozambique, and Zambia, infant mortality rates exceed 100. Botswana has the second lowest infant mortality rate (55), followed by Swaziland (63), Lesotho (79), and Zaire (94) (see Tables 13.1 and 13.2).

Maternal mortality rates are also alarming for some of the countries in this region. For example, Angola and Mozambique have a maternal mortality rate of 1,500

Table 13.1. Demographic and Health Indicators, 1994

Country	Maternal Mortality Rate (per 100,000 Live Births)	Infant Mortality (per 1,000 Live Births)	One-Year-Olds Fully Immunized Against		AIDS Cases (per 100 People)	Total Fertility Rate	Crude Birth Rate	Crude Death Rate	Total Pop. (Mil.)	Pop. per Doctor
			Tuberculosis	Measles						
South Africa	230	51	95	76	12.91	4.0	30.7	8.6	40.6	—
Botswana	250	55	81	68	25.10	4.7	36.6	11.8	1.4	4,762
Swaziland	—	72	—	—	18.50	4.7	38.5	10.1	0.8	9,091
Namibia	370	63	94	69	19.94	5.1	37.0	11.9	1.5	4,545
Zimbabwe	570	70	95	74	25.84	5.1	40.5	14.4	10.9	7,692
Lesotho	610	79	59	74	8.35	5.1	36.5	11.1	2.0	25,000
Zambia	940	110	63	69	19.07	5.8	43.4	18.5	7.9	11,111
Angola	1500	120	40	32	2.12	7.2	50.7	18.5	10.5	—
Malawi	560	147	91	70	14.92	7.1	50.2	22.7	9.6	50,000
Mozambique	1500	116	58	40	14.17	6.5	45.0	18.6	16.6	33,333

Source: Compiled from United Nations Development Programme, *Human Development Report 1997* (New York: Oxford University Press, 1997), pp. 194–95.

Table 13.2. Indicators of Human and Economic Development for Southern African Countries, 1994

Country	HDI Rank Globally (175 Nations)	HDI Rank within Southern Africa	Life Expectancy at Birth (Years)	Adult Literacy Rate (%)	Real GDP per Capita	Life Expectancy Index	Education Index	GDP Index	Human Develop. Index Value
Angola	157	9	47.2	42.5	1600	0.37	0.39	0.25	0.335
Botswana	97	2	68.1	98.0	2726	0.72	0.90	0.43	0.684
Lesotho	137	6	57.9	70.5	1109	0.55	0.66	0.17	0.457
Malawi	161	10	41.1	55.8	694	0.27	0.60	0.10	0.320
Mozambique	166	11	46.0	39.5	986	0.35	0.35	0.15	0.281
Namibia	118	4	55.9	40.0	4027	0.52	0.55	0.65	0.570
South Africa	90	1	63.7	81.4	4291	0.64	0.81	0.69	0.716
Swaziland	114	3	58.3	75.2	2821	0.55	0.74	0.45	0.582
Zambia	143	8	42.6	76.6	962	0.29	0.67	0.14	0.369
Zimbabwe	129	5	49.0	84.7	2410	0.44	0.68	0.38	0.500

Source: Compiled from United Nations Development Programme, *Human Development Report 1997* (New York: Oxford University Press, 1997), pp. 146–48.

deaths for every 100,000 live births. Rates of other countries range from a low of 230 for South Africa to a high of 940 for Zambia. In short, there is tremendous diversity in the demographic and socio-economic experiences of countries in the southern African region. It should be noted that the indicators of development, which are given at the national level, mask intra-country diversity among regions and between rural and urban areas. In short, the southern African subregion is far from being homogeneous, and one cannot overgeneralize the demographic and health experiences of countries in this region. Some countries seem to be well on the path to an irreversible socio-economic and demographic transition, while others continue to experience difficulties in resuscitating their ailing economies and health care delivery systems. For example, Botswana, Zimbabwe, South Africa, and Namibia have the most favorable demographic, socio-economic, and health care indices, while Angola, Malawi, and Mozambique are at the bottom of the scale (see Tables 13.1 and 13.2).

The Historical Context of Health Care in Southern Africa

Understanding the contemporary pattern of health services in southern African countries is impossible without reference to the pre-colonial and colonial experiences. During the pre-colonial era, full or part-time traditional medical practitioners provided healing. Due to the large number of healers, almost every extended family had one practitioner,[4] medical services were well distributed, and basic care was available to everyone. As Twumasi and Oppong note,[5] healers often held positions of power in society, and usually knew the cultural, social, and physical environments of their patients, and thus the context of the diseases they treated.

Traditional Medical Systems

As many scholars have contended, traditional medicine was and is effective for a number of reasons. First, it has been argued that traditional medicine is rooted in the past, with the gift of healing handed down parent to child. Ancestors are therefore thought to be the ultimate cause of disease, and to determine this cause the healer consults the ill person's ancestors. Second, it has been pointed out that traditional medicine is rooted in nature and natural remedies and that living close to the earth reinforces a culture and world view that understands the cosmos as constant and humans and their actions as ephemeral. Third, traditional medicine is rooted in systems of morality and normative social order that are homogeneous and strongly reinforced. Fourth, traditional medicine is rooted in social systems based on the extended family and the reciprocal obligation of living in harmony with broad networks of blood kin.[6]

Other advantages of traditional medical practitioners include their cultural acceptability, willingness to adapt, the performance of several (primarily psychological and sociological) functions, the possession of a large body of indigenous knowledge, and the treatment of a wide range of diseases.[7] Although most traditional medical systems and practices continue to be widely used and constitute the only health resource in many isolated areas, they have often been marginalized and have not fully been integrated into the official health care systems.[8] However, it needs to be pointed out that traditional medicine also has its weaknesses, which include the lack of standardized training for traditional medical practitioners, dosage imprecision, and lack of elementary understanding of the functions of hygiene and sanitation.[9]

Modern Biomedical Systems

Right at the outset of colonial rule in the early 1880s, the British and Portuguese colonists introduced Western-style health services in administrative centers to provide health care for themselves and their employees. Different health facilities tended to exist for Africans and Europeans, with better official health facilities reserved for Europeans and concentrated in urban areas and mining centers where most Europeans lived.[10] In South Africa the segregation of health care facilities was at its pinnacle during apartheid,[11] which came to an end in the early 1990s. Similarly in Zimbabwe, segregation was the norm until 1980 when black majority rule took over from minority European control of the government. During the early days of colonial rule, small hospitals of twenty to thirty beds were built in administrative centers.[12] On the other hand, missionaries overwhelmingly provided health care in rural areas, with curative rather than preventive medicine being fostered.[13]

The new Western-oriented medical system immediately began to contest the hegemony of the traditional medical system, resulting in an unprecedented challenge to the legitimacy, integrity, and character of traditional medicine. Aided by missionaries, colonial authorities vigorously repressed and officially banned some organized religious therapy systems. Suddenly, sound medical and health beliefs became "superstitious," and laws were promulgated to criminalize the practice of traditional medicine.[14] Biomedicine provided dramatic results for some diseases that traditional medicine had not been able to manage. But modern health care facilities were spatially concentrated in cities and towns, making them inaccessible to the majority of rural inhabitants. Several generations of Africans educated in colonial government and mission schools and colleges were taught that traditional healers were savage and primitive.[15] Consequently, traditional healing lost its prestige and was stigmatized; healers became persona non grata.[16] Yet, because these efforts did not rid the continent of devastating epidemics, traditional healers continued to practice illegitimately, in secrecy and isolation.[17]

The failure of the expensive urban-based Western medical system to root out most diseases was, in part, due to its heavy reliance on treatment rather than on prevention. A careful examination of the major causes of morbidity and mortality in Zambia and Malawi during the 1980s reveals that most deaths are due to diseases that can generally be controlled through preventive measures.[18] These measures include provision of adequate water supply, proper sanitation, public health education, and vector and rodent control, as well as the availability of health care facilities. With the exception of the provision of health care facilities, very little was done during the colonial era to promote effective primary health care for prevention purposes.

After independence, governments in the region have attempted to provide bio-medicine to everyone, focusing on hospitals, dispensaries, and medical schools centered in urban areas, to the neglect of rural areas. Biomedical health facilities have typically been based in urban settings beyond the reach of many rural dwellers. To obtain formal biomedical health care, rural residents have to travel long distances, sometimes on foot, to urban centers where they have to endure a long wait before finally seeing a biomedical practitioner. The inconvenience and hassles involved, particularly when patients are illiterate and unable to communicate meaningfully with doctors, are formidable. The strange and usually impersonal cultural environment in which biomedical services are provided frequently leads to patients vowing not to repeat the experience.[19] In a village-level study of primary health care in Malawi, Kalipeni and Kamlongera revealed that villagers were unwilling to use modern health care facilities for a variety of socio-cultural reasons.[20] Among the problems the villagers identified were the long walk to the clinic, and spending the whole day to get to such facilities only to find the medical superintendent out, or encountering relatively unhelpful personnel who, under pressure of work, made snap and unhelpful diagnoses. Some of the villagers found such centers both imposing and threatening.

In recent years, increasing deterioration in the economy has meant little money for maintaining existing health infrastructure. Countries such as Malawi and Zambia have been hardest hit by the economic crisis that began in the early 1980s and was exacerbated by the imposition of structural adjustment programs, which we discuss in greater detail later in this chapter. Cutbacks in health expenditure have resulted in large layoffs, significant salary reductions (due to inflation), and closure of many facilities.[21] Most health workers have been compelled to take second jobs to make ends meet, resulting in absenteeism and poorer health care. For example, in Zambia, the departure of a large number of expatriate doctors due to declining economic conditions in the late 1980s and early 1990s has created a wide gap in the availability of doctors, particularly in the Copperbelt and Southern provinces.[22] In addition, because of poor conditions of service, even Zambian doctors are leaving the country for Zimbabwe, Botswana, and other countries of southern Africa. In Malawi the health care situation has become desperate, with severe scarcities of medicines in government hospitals and health centers throughout the country. One expatriate doctor working at a hospital in Northern Malawi recently lamented:

> the hospital stays busy here, still mostly with malaria, malnutrition and AIDS, the big three for us—as well as complicated obstetrics of course. We hear that there is bubonic plague or some close cousin to it down in Kasungu with 110 cases re-

333

ported but no deaths. We have a team of malaria experts here rather unexpectedly studying our Fansidar resistance which is rather depressingly (but not too surprisingly) at 10%. . . . We have been out of Bactrim and Tylenol and chloroquine for two months and this morning ran out of alcohol so the lab guys are using a paraffin lamp to dry the slides.[23]

To try to counter the growing scarcity of medications and the deteriorating health care delivery system, most governments have begun to introduce user charges. Dubbed the "Bamako Initiative," African ministers of health met in September of 1987 in Bamako, Mali, and decided to introduce a small fee for health care services for cost recovery purposes. However, concerns have been raised about the deleterious effects on health care utilization that have been noted in many instances where user charges or cost recovery attempts have been introduced.[24] For example, in Ghana, the imposition of user fees under structural adjustment has drastically reduced access to health care, compelling users to forgo or delay treatment and seek alternatives to biomedical services.[25] In southern Africa, when Swaziland imposed user fees, attendance at health facilities declined by 32 percent in government facilities and 10 percent in mission clinics. Furthermore, visits for childhood vaccination and treatment of sexually transmitted diseases fell by 17 percent and 21 percent, respectively.[26]

In Angola and Mozambique, health care facilities were drastically affected by the prolonged civil wars during the 1970s and 1980s. During the civil war many peripheral health units were destroyed, which represented 31 percent of the total primary health care network in these countries. Although in the post-war period many health posts have been reopened and expansion has continued, the overall effect has been to halt the previous rapid expansion in the number of peripheral health units. Patients in hospitals were sometimes massacred, which scared most sick people away from hospitals. By 1987, over 4 million Mozambicans had lost access to health care facilities as a result of direct destruction, looting and forced closure of health units, displacement of people, and kidnapping of health care workers.[27]

The Ecological Context of Disease

The physical and ecological structure of southern Africa is as varied as the population densities and demographic characteristics. The altitude ranges from zero to over two thousand meters above sea level. Several major biomes characterize this region, including tropical rain forests in Zaire, patches of montane forest, moist and dry savanna, semi-desert and desert conditions, and temperate grasslands.[28] The political environment, poverty, and the generally low levels of well-being for the majority of the people in this region combine with the varied climatic conditions, vegetation, and biogeography to explain the prevalence of disease-causing organisms, or pathogens, such as bacteria, viruses, and worms.[29] Indeed, in most parts of southern Africa the main causes of mortality continue to be infectious and vectored diseases such as tuberculosis, measles, and malaria. The prevalence of these causes of mortality is a testimony to the low levels of development in this region. According to the epidemiologic transition model, as a nation develops, the pattern of the disease burden and the prime causes of morbidity and mortality shift from communicable to old-age diseases such as cancer and cardiovascular diseases. With the exception of South Africa, most countries in Southern Africa are in the early stages of the epidemiologic transition dominated by infectious diseases, which I briefly describe below.

The major cause of infant and childhood mortality in this region is malaria, which is also responsible for many miscarriages and babies born underweight.[30] Malaria is a problem that appears to be worsening in much of southern Africa. The increase in malaria is attributed to the collapse (owing to managerial, institutional, and financial constraints) of the malaria control programs in many countries, together with the increasingly widespread resistance of malaria vectors to the available insecticides and of malaria parasites to the available chemoprophylactic agents.[31] Today almost all countries in southern Africa have chloroquine-resistant *Plasmodium falciparum,* the most common and lethal of the malaria parasites.

While malaria is widespread throughout southern Africa, it is more prevalent in more humid and low-lying areas. For example, malaria is not a serious problem in South Africa except along the eastern and northern parts of the country where it borders with Mozambique, Swaziland, and Zimbabwe, and along the coastal subtropical region inland of the Indian Ocean.[32] This is also true of countries such as Malawi, Mozambique, and Zambia, where malaria is most acute in the lowlands. In Malawi, colonial occupation was restricted to the Shire Highlands precisely because of the presence of malaria in the low-lying plains and valleys throughout the rest of the country. Furthermore, the region experiences seasonal malaria epidemics due to the variations in temperature and rainfall during the dry season and the rainy season. Malaria cases are at their peak during the rainy season.

Schistosomiasis is another debilitating and widespread environmental disease, which leads to chronic ill health. During contact with river or pond water through everyday activities such as washing, the parasites enter a person via body openings. Infected people pass eggs through urine or feces that hatch into flukes, which then infest water snails before emerging into their final form to infect other people. In southern Africa, malaria and schistosomiasis can be thought of as gender-biased diseases, in that women, who are in contact with water through their daily household chores of washing and cooking, are more likely to be infected than men. Malaria is also likely to be fatal among those who are undernourished, and women and children are most likely to be undernourished. Stock notes that the resurgence of malaria throughout Africa is partly attributable to the decline in nutritional status among the poor in both urban and rural areas.[33]

The most troubling and recent scourge to hit the population of southern Africa is the AIDS pandemic. As shown in Table 13.1, Namibia and Zimbabwe stand out in AIDS cases, with rates of about 119 per 100,000. Botswana, Malawi, and Zambia have rates ranging from 35 to 47 per 100,000 people. The AIDS epidemic is creating a major health crisis. Medical systems, already overwhelmed by the numerous tropical diseases, cannot cope with the new and massive onslaught of AIDS cases. The disease could reverse the little development that has so far been attained by a number of countries in this subregion. It will have major socio-economic and demographic consequences. Some projections show that if current AIDS/HIV infection rates continue, life expectancies could decline to less than thirty years, and infant and adult mortality rates will begin to increase in the first decade of the twenty-first century.[34] Of concern here is the tragic impact of this disease on the lives of many women in this region. The impact of the pandemic on women and children will be discussed in greater detail in a later section on AIDS in southern Africa. As if the above was not enough, there is another newly emerging disease consanguine to AIDS, named Ebola.

Some parts of the tropical rain forest patches throughout the world possess a remarkable diversity of animals, plants, and microbes and are quite often the natural nidus of hitherto unknown vectored diseases. As people have flown the terror of war and retreated into more marginal regions, the potential of encountering a previously unknown virus such as Ebola has grown higher.[35] Indeed, most emergent viruses are zoonotic (communicable from animals to humans under natural conditions), with natural animal reservoirs a frequent source. The Ebola virus is a member of a family of viruses known as filoviruses, with rodents as the main hosts of many of the filoviruses. However, for Ebola, the animal hosts are not known with certainty. The Ebola virus was discovered in 1976 and was named after the Ebola River in Zaire, where it was first detected. After exposure to the virus, onset of symptoms (usually fever and muscle pains) begins in four to twenty-one days and can progress into acute respiratory problems, severe bleeding, kidney problems, shock, and eventual death. Ebola kills its victims by slowly "dissolving" their organs, blood cells, and connective tissue.[36] The disease is spread through personal contact with infected people. The recent outbreak in Zaire killed 244 of a total of 315 infected people, a disease mortality rate of 77 percent.[37] In other reported outbreaks, from 50 to 90 percent of the cases have been fatal.[38] Different strains of the virus have been detected in Zaire, Gabon, Sudan (Ebola Sudan), and the Ivory Coast (Ebotai). Knowing no boundaries, the disease was detected in one patient in South Africa. We should also caution that the disease is not constrained to the tropical rain forest patches of Africa alone but has been identified in other parts of the world, notably South America and Asia.[39]

The above are a few of the many diseases people in this region have to contend with in the face of declining health care services. Other preventable diseases such as tuberculosis, cholera, tetanus, respiratory infections, diarrheal diseases, measles, and pneumonia, as well as anemia and nutritional deficiencies, continue to take precious infant and adult lives. It has been estimated that peri-natal infections and parasitic illnesses are responsible for 75 percent of infant deaths and 71 percent of childhood deaths in Africa.[40] Data in the 1991 book *Disease and Mortality* suggests that an African child has a 10 percent chance of suffering from diarrhea on any given day and a 14 percent chance of dying from a severe episode. This is significant, since diarrhea accounts for 25 percent of all childhood deaths worldwide and 37 percent of all childhood deaths in sub-Saharan Africa, being one of the foremost causes of childhood mortality in this part of Africa. In southern Africa, recent demographic and health survey (DHS) data indicate that 20 to 40 percent of children suffer from attacks of diarrhea characterized by cramping, abdominal pain, nausea, vomiting, and often death.[41]

Southern Africa's Mortality Transition

A recent World Bank study notes that health in sub-Saharan Africa has improved dramatically in the decades since independence.[42] Infant mortality rates have declined by one-third from a high of 145 infant deaths per 1,000 live births in 1970 to 104 per 1,000 in 1992. The mortality rate for children under five years fell 17 percent between 1975 and 1990. In Botswana and Zimbabwe, for example, the under-five mortality declined by 41 percent between the late 1970s and the late 1980s. Adult mortality rates have also seen major declines during the post-independence era in most countries of southern Africa. Life expectancy at birth is currently estimated to be fifty-two for men and fifty-five for women and has increased approximately by four years every decade since the 1950s.[43] The crude death rate has declined to a very low level of 13 deaths per 1,000 for the whole region.

In spite of these remarkable gains, challenges in the provision of and access to health care are immense. The risk of death remains markedly higher at all ages in southern Africa than in other parts of the world. Life expectancy at birth is four years less than in southern Asia and fourteen years less than in Latin America.[44] Among the countries in the world where life expectancy in 1990 was lower than fifty years, five were in southern Africa.[45] Infant and childhood mortality are generally higher than in any part of the world. In certain countries that have endured deteriorating economies during the last decade, child mortality levels are virtually identical to those prevailing ten years ago. For example, one of the most striking findings from the Zambia Demographic and Health Survey of 1992 was the apparent recent downturn in child survival prospects. From 1977 to 1991, under-five mortality rose by 15 percent from 152 to 191 per 1,000 live births. Much of this increase resulted from an increase in mortality under the age of one year. Both neonatal and post-neonatal mortality increased by 35 percent in the fifteen-year period before the survey. In this same period, child mortality increased by 20 percent.[46] Similarly, in countries such as Angola and Mozambique, infant, childhood, and adult mortality rates increased as a result of prolonged civil war and subsequent economic downturns.

It has been reported that African women of reproductive age have the highest death risk from maternal causes of any women in the world.[47] Boerma concludes that national levels of maternal mortality in sub-Saharan Africa most likely vary from 250 to 700 per 100,000 live births. For the southern African subregion, as shown in Table 13.1, the range is from 230 for South Africa to 1,500 for Angola and Mozambique. On average, the regional maternal mortality rate is 740, which

Figure 13.1 Age-Specific Death Rates by Gender, Malawi 1987

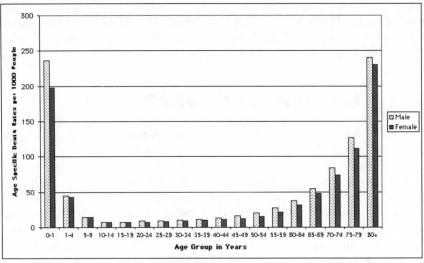

(Data from National Statistical Office. 1991. *Malawi Housing and Population Census.* 1987. Zomba: Government Printer.)

is above the African average of 700. In industrialized countries, women live on average seven years longer than men due to an inbuilt biological superiority.[48] As a
matter of fact, life expectancy is consistently greater for women at all ages in developed countries. On the other hand, in developing countries a disadvantage ac-
crues to women from their double burden of household production and reproduction, which results in high maternal mortality rates due to complications of
pregnancy and childbirth.[49]

In southern Africa, insights into the actual differences between the health of
women and men can be gained by comparing sex differentials in mortality in countries that are at different stages of development. In Malawi, where life expectancy
is shorter, sex differentials in mortality are less pronounced, particularly in the childbearing age range (see Figure 13.1). The most marked divergence between women
and men can be seen after age fifty, with women experiencing lower mortality. For
a low-income country like Malawi, women of childbearing age experience similar
mortality to men due to the greater risks associated with reproduction. This is also
true of other low-income countries in this region such as Angola, Mozambique,
and Zambia. On the other hand, an examination of a country such as South Africa
shows slightly larger sex differentials in favor of women. But even in South Africa
one has to take into consideration the great inequality in access to health services,
with the better-off (mainly the white population) enjoying access to a private health
service comparable to that of a developed country. Differences in life expectancy
also support the assertion that economically better-off countries in the region are
beginning to show a growing gap between the life expectancies of women and men
in favor of women. Countries at the bottom of the economic development ladder,

Figure 13.2 Life Expectancy by Gender, 1994

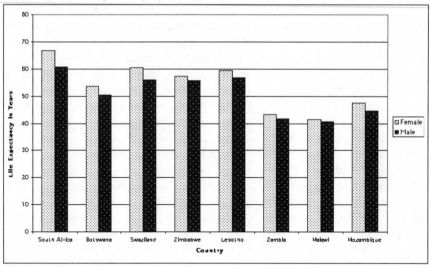

(Data from UNDP 1997.)

like Malawi and Mozambique, show no significant differences in life expectancy between men and women (see Figure 13.2). This finding also holds true in other parts of Africa. A recent study by Klasen gives evidence of large and, in some parts, rising mortality disadvantages for women and girls, which have been traced to the intra-household allocation of resources.[50]

Explanations for these differentials lie in the triple burden of household chores, nutritional intake, and access to health care resources. As Santow and Svedberg point out, one way in which gender distinctions are maintained and reinforced is through differential allocation of food.[51] It is quite common for women to eat less, and less well, than men. The high fertility rate even in those countries where fertility has begun to decline means that women have to undergo frequent pregnancies and giving birth, which take a toll on their health status.

It has been argued that sub-Saharan Africa has not yet experienced a genuine demographic transition and that it is doubtful whether the continent will achieve the transition in a timely fashion.[52] The main factor in achieving a timely transition is socio-economic development. The demographic transition postulates a necessary causal link between modernization and sustained mortality reduction.

Although mortality has declined rapidly in Southern Africa over the past fifty years, the declines have occurred not because of socio-economic development but mainly because of the importation of medical technologies from the industrialized world. Therefore, as I have argued elsewhere,[53] declining infant mortality rates and crude death rates are due largely to superficial demographic and epidemiological social changes. Sustainable socio-economic development has yet to take root in the southern African subregion. Infectious, parasitic, diarrheal, respiratory, and nutritional diseases continue to dominate the causes of death, an indication that this region and other parts of Africa are still in the age of famine and pestilence, as postulated by the epidemiologic transition. According to the epidemiologic transition, the main causes of death are related to the levels of economic and institutional development. The changes in the health problems that come with economic and social advancement or a shift in the most common causes of death in a society as it accumulates wealth are often called the mortality or epidemiological transition. Pessimists contend that deep-rooted cultural forces may prevent southern Africa from ever achieving a sustained mortality and fertility transition. However, in this paper we contend that the disadvantaged position of the African continent within the global international economy is largely to blame for the retrogression of the continent and its subregions. It should also be pointed out that it took Europe well over two hundred years to achieve the demographic transition; mortality declines in Africa began only about fifty years ago. Given more time and a fair share of the international development cake, the transition may not be out of reach for southern African countries.

Southern Africa's Fertility Transition

Recent data from the demographic and health surveys of the late 1980s and early 1990s seem to indicate that southern Africa in general may have begun to experience both fertility and mortality transitions.[54] Countries such as South Africa, Namibia, Botswana, and Zimbabwe are experiencing a fertility transition largely believed to be due to structural changes in social, economic, and environmental conditions. The beginning of the fertility transition in the region has initiated a shift in the thinking of many demographers toward explaining the uniqueness of the few countries where the transition has commenced.[55] Caldwell, who has been one of the strongest advocates in attributing the region's lag in fertility decline to cultural factors, has argued that the transition in the four countries "throws light on the erosion of traditional supports of high fertility."[56] However, the extent to which the fertility decline going on in the above-mentioned countries can be attributed to the alleged crumbling of the cultural supports of high fertility is yet to be empirically established. As a matter of fact, much of the credit for the fertility decline in Botswana and Zimbabwe has been attributed to the greater access to contraceptives by women of reproductive age, which has been made possible through the effectiveness of the government-sponsored family planning programs.[57] The adoption of contraceptives in these countries has been further facilitated by declining infant mortality rates and the increasing status of women. Increased literacy rates, life expectancy, participation in the political arena, and other avenues support the assertion that female autonomy and status is crucial to the improvement of lives of women and children and the society in general.

Other scholars have argued that the decline in fertility that is being experienced

Table 13.3. Gender-Related Indices of Development (Mortality, Education, and Income), 1994

Country	Life Expectancy (Yrs)			Adult Literacy Rate (%)			GDI
	Female	Male	Diff.	Female	Male	Diff.	
Angola	—	—	—	—	—	—	—
Botswana	53.7	50.5	3.2	58.0	79.3	21.3	0.652
Lesotho	59.4	56.8	2.6	60.9	80.3	19.4	0.446
Malawi	41.5	40.6	0.9	40.4	71.7	31.3	0.310
Mozambique	47.5	44.5	3.0	22.1	55.8	33.7	0.262
Namibia	—	—	—	—	—	—	—
South Africa	66.8	60.8	6	81.2	81.4	0.2	0.681
Swaziland	60.5	56.0	4.5	73.3	76.4	3.1	0.563
Zaire	—	—	—	—	—	—	—
Zambia	43.3	41.7	1.6	69.3	84.4	15.1	0.362
Zimbabwe	57.3	55.8	1.5	60.7	79.8	19.1	0.503

Source: Compiled from United Nations Development Programme, *Human Development Report 1997* (New York: Oxford University Press, 1997), pp. 149–51.

in Zimbabwe and Botswana has been precipitated by crises led by worsening economic conditions and a growing scarcity of resources, such as land shortages.[58] The greater availability of contraceptives has, thus, only helped couples to meet the demand for birth control created by the difficult economic conditions. Zulu notes that although the fertility transition provides hope to other countries in the region that the so-called "cultural inhibitors" of contraceptive use can be overcome, there is substantial agreement in demographic circles that the prospects for seeing such a decline in the near future in these countries are not very bright.[59] This view is somehow supported by the fact that the few "super performers" (namely Zimbabwe, Botswana, and South Africa) have stronger economies, higher levels of education (particularly female education), lower infant mortality rates, and greater government and political leadership on family planning and gender-empowerment issues. Indeed composite measures of human development and gender-specific measures such as the Gender Empowerment Index and the Gender Related Development Index are much higher in these countries than in other countries in the region (see Tables 13.3, 13.4, and 13.5).

This brings me to the importance of female status and autonomy in ensuring better health for both women and children. The critical ingredient in ensuring better female autonomy is education. Female literacy is a key indicator of human development, alongside infant and child mortality and access to safe water. Studies during the past twenty years or so indicate that there exists a very significant relationship between high levels of infant and child mortality and low levels of maternal education.[60] For example, Cleland and Van Ginneken note that, on average,

Table 13.4. Gender-Related Indices of Development:
Measures of Gender Empowerment, 1994

Country	Rank on Gender-Empowerment Measure	Seats Held in Parliament (% Women)	Administrators and Managers (% Women)	Professional and Technical Workers (% Women)	GEM Value
Angola	—	—	—	—	—
Botswana	39	8.5	36.1	61.4	0.455
Lesotho	41	11.2	33.4	56.6	0.450
Malawi	80	5.6	4.8	34.7	0.255
Mozambique	43	25.2	11.3	20.4	0.430
Namibia	—	—	—	—	—
South Africa	22	23.7	17.4	46.7	0.531
Swaziland	61	8.4	14.5	54.3	0.366
Zaire	89	5.0	9.0	16.6	0.211
Zambia	71	9.7	6.1	23.1	0.273
Zimbabwe	45	14.7	15.4	40.0	0.429

Source: Compiled from United Nations Development Programme, *Human Development Report 1997* (New York: Oxford University Press, 1997), pp. 152–54

each one-year increment in mothers' education corresponds with a 7–9 percent decline in under-five mortality.[61]

As Caldwell points out, female education has a direct impact on female autonomy.[62] A marked degree of female autonomy is central to exceptional mortality declines, especially in poor countries like Malawi. When there is no scandal about girls assuming roles outside the house even when they are unmarried but have reached puberty, or about older women appearing in public on their own initiative, then girls are more likely to take action about sick children or about themselves. When necessary, they will travel to health centers, wait in queues of mixed sex, and argue even with male physicians.[63] In a study on the determinants of infant mortality in Malawi, Kalipeni found a very strong inverse relationship between levels of infant mortality and female literacy rates at district level.[64] Districts with higher levels of female literacy rates exhibited lower levels of infant mortality.

Although a review of a broad range of studies relating education to fertility has shown that the relationship is not as uniform as is generally believed, female education has been found to have a significant inverse relationship with fertility.[65] Cochrane has noted that there exists a definite relationship between fertility and education but that this relationship is indirect, with education operating through other variables to effect fertility reduction.[66] A United Nations study of relationships between fertility and education, comprising a comparative analysis of World Fertility Survey data for twenty-two developing countries, concluded that generally education has a negative effect on fertility.[67]

Browne and Barrett provide a framework within which to view the relationship

Table 13.5. Regional Comparisons of Human Development Values, 1994

Country	Human Development Index	Gender-Related Development Index	Gender-Empowerment Development Index	HDI Value as % of Highest in Region	GDI Value as % of Highest in Region	GEM Value as % of Highest in Region
South Africa	0.716	0.681	0.531	100	100	100
Botswana	0.673	0.652	0.455	94	96	86
Swaziland	0.582	0.563	0.366	81	83	69
Namibia	0.570	—	—	80	—	—
Zimbabwe	0.513	0.503	0.429	72	74	81
Lesotho	0.457	0.466	0.450	64	68	85
Zaire	0.381	—	0.211	53	—	40
Zambia	0.369	0.362	0.303	52	53	57
Angola	0.351	—	—	49	—	—
Malawi	0.320	0.310	0.255	45	46	48
Mozambique	0.281	0.262	0.430	39	38	81

Source: Compiled from United Nations Development Programme, *Human Development Report 1997* (New York: Oxford University Press, 1997), p. 155

Figure 13.3 The Linkage between Female Education, Human Development, and Economic Development

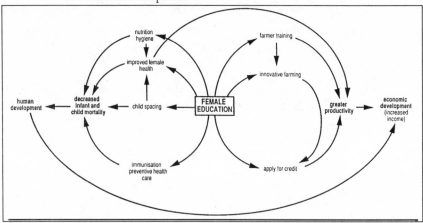

(Browne and Barrett 1991, p. 277.)

between female education, on the one hand, and infant mortality and fertility on the other.[68] Their framework is reproduced here in Figure 13.3. As this figure shows, there are many complex and varied intervening mechanisms that explain this relationship. Better educated mothers are more likely to use preventive and curative health service and make more timely use of them, have better knowledge of hygiene and nutrition, and have reduced fertility.[69] Schooling itself imparts new values and makes mothers more receptive to modern ideas on child care. These values persist into adulthood and influence the health of mothers and children without any conscious intent.

In spite of these obvious benefits, girls in southern Africa face an uphill battle in educational and job opportunities. A number of studies have documented the under-representation of girls in schooling both in southern Africa and elsewhere in the world.[70] Phiri looked at the under-representation of female students in technical education and vocational training in Zambia.[71] He noted that boys accounted for almost 80 percent of the students accepted by the Department of Technical Educational and Vocational Training in Zambia for the teaching of middle-level technical skills. In Ghana, Weis has documented the striking inequalities in recruiting girls and boys to post-primary education.[72] Recent studies in other parts of Africa substantiate the precarious position of girls in their access to schooling.[73] A number of factors constitute barriers to girls' full participation in schooling. Some of these barriers are "formal" in that they are linked to institutional policies, practices, and procedures; others are "informal," being mainly socio-cultural in nature and arising from stereotyped attitudes and beliefs about women's roles and capabilities.[74] In order to devise effective policies that deal directly with the issue of female access to education, it is imperative that policy-makers and researchers grasp the workings and complexities of these "formal" and informal barriers to female education, especially in the African context, which we have addressed elsewhere.[75] The most important thing to note here is that female education is the key to a healthy nation. The link between health, female autonomy, and development works both ways: a healthy nation will be able to develop faster, while development brings its own rewards in health.[76] A study by Over and colleagues highlights the effect of adult ill health on families. Where the mother falls ill or dies, children have higher mortality rates and perform less well in school.[77] Raising the status of women and empowering them will generate numerous benefits over and above the obvious one of improving individuals.

AIDS in Southern Africa

More recently there has been an explosion of heterosexually transmitted AIDS in southern Africa. The hardest hit countries in this subregion include Malawi, Zimbabwe, Namibia, and Botswana (see Table 13.1). Stanecki and Way note that repeated studies of pregnant women conducted in African countries generally show a consistent and rapid increase in HIV seroprevalence.[78] For example, in Botswana, HIV seroprevalence increased from less than 10 percent to more than 30 percent in Francistown, and from 6 percent to 19 percent in Gaborone between 1990 and 1993.[79] In the following paragraphs, I use Malawi to highlight salient features of the AIDS pandemic in southern Africa.

Current estimates for Malawi indicate that about one in every ten Malawians is HIV positive and that certain sectors of the population (e.g., commercial sex workers, pregnant women, truck drivers, and soldiers) have alarming HIV infection rates. Small surveys conducted in the early 1980s indicated a 2 percent HIV-positive rate in otherwise fit pregnant women in ante-natal clinics, and in blood donors.[80] In the case of pregnant women, this figure rose dramatically to 8 percent in 1987, 19 percent in 1989, 23 percent in 1990, and is currently estimated to be about 35 percent.[81] Although the data has to be used with caution due to issues of reliability, representativeness, and quality, there is sufficient evidence to suggest that within a very short period the disease has rapidly diffused throughout southern Africa. In Malawi, the cumulated number of reported fully blown AIDS cases has also exploded, from almost zero in 1985 to 40,000 in 1995.[82] One must keep in mind that this is a gross underestimate of the true magnitude of the disease, since the data is based on hospital cases and most people do not go to hospitals.

From a geographic point of view, throughout southern Africa and Africa in general, urban areas have been hit hardest by the epidemic in comparison to rural areas.[83] Estimates compiled from blood donors, women coming to ante-natal clinics, and people undergoing testing when applying for life insurance reveal that well over 30 percent of the adult population in the major urban areas of Blantrye and Lilongwe may have been infected by the virus.[84] While urban areas lead in rates of infection, it must be pointed out that the disease is spreading rapidly in rural areas, propelled by rural-urban linkages and the lack of knowledge of the disease in rural areas. Rural and urban areas in Malawi are closely intertwined with a constant two-way flow of people, facilitating the HIV/AIDS exchange. In addition, rural Malawi has traditionally sent thousands of its young men to work in the mines of South Africa on two- to three-year contracts. Upon their return to Malawi, these migrant workers spend a week or so in the cities of Blantyre and Lilongwe having a "good time" before going back to their home villages in the countryside.[85] It is estimated that nearly half of the mine workers returning to the rural areas of the country after a work stint in South Africa are infecting their wives and other women.[86] Indeed, the rapid diffusion of the disease in this region has been ascribed to a high level of "sexual mobility"—to such factors as men's premarital and extramarital sexual activity during frequent work-related absences from home, institutionalized prostitution in the towns, the lack of other economic opportunities for divorcees and widows, polygyny, and related post-partum sexual abstinence for wives but not husbands.[87]

In fact, conventional prevention measures, including education, are ill-focused because they do not deal with poverty. As Oppong argues,[88] expecting people to abandon behaviors that bring pleasure and immediate gratification is unreasonable, especially when it gives them power or income, even while posing unacceptable risks to personal family health and community. People should be rewarded with tangible benefits, not penalized through loss of income, for changing unacceptable behavior. Providing opportunities for young women to prevent them from turning to prostitution for economic survival may be as important as any educational measure in the fight against AIDS.[89] Indeed we concur with Oppong that without such a reorientation in focus, we may very well be fighting a losing battle with AIDS in Africa.

Regarding gender, data compiled by the Malawi AIDS Control Programme shows some interesting trends in the age and sex distribution of the AIDS cases.[90] The age and sex distribution in rural and urban areas are quite similar. The majority of the AIDS cases are in the twenty to forty-nine age group. The lowest rates are in the five to fourteen age range. The zero to four age group shows significantly higher numbers of infection, an indication that infants are being infected either in the womb before birth or while being taken care of by infected mothers (see Figure 13.4). One interesting trend in the data is that women appear to be exposed to the disease at earlier ages than men. For example, there is a preponderance of females in the age range fifteen to twenty-four, while men are slightly more predominant in the age groups above thirty years. The "sugar daddy" phenomenon can be invoked here as a plausible explanation for the age/sex mismatch. Researchers elsewhere in Africa frequently reveal one particularly insidious aspect of the pandemic: namely, older men going for schoolgirls. As middle-aged men have begun to realize the real and quite personal danger of intercourse with their usual "girlfriends," they are enticing young girls ten to fifteen years of age, hoping that they will be relatively free of infection. The age-sex disparities shown in Figure 13.4 seem to support this assertion. Throughout the world, the ratio of female to male cases is rising, but women in southern Africa and elsewhere in Africa are at greatest risk, and show the highest seroprevalence.

Figure 13.4 Age/Sex Distribution of AIDS Cases in Malawi, 1990

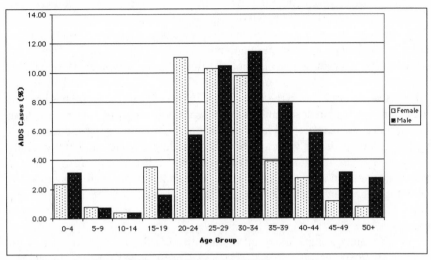

(Data from Malawi National AIDS Control Programme 1996.)

Health and Political Instability

The people of Angola and Mozambique suffered greatly from the prolonged civil wars in these countries during the post-independence era.[91] The violence that usually produces refugees has complex and multiple direct and indirect effects on health and disease, particularly for women and children who make up the greatest proportion in refugee populations. First, it disrupts livelihoods, including agricultural production and food supplies, leading to famine and widespread malnutrition. Health service provision is similarly affected as health workers flee for their lives, or disruption of medical supplies creates shortages that result in closure of health facilities. Second, expenditure on war usually results in drastic reductions in health expenditure and health services at a time of increased demand for health services. Third, fleeing the prevailing anarchy of war puts refugees into refugee camps—an environment where poor sanitation, contaminated food and water, and overcrowding make suffering and disease bloom. The combined effect of these is escalated morbidity and mortality, frequently from infectious and vaccine-preventable diseases such as measles.

During the war in Angola many health units were destroyed, resulting in shortages of drugs and equipment, low morale and productivity of health workers, high levels of absolute poverty, and chronic malnutrition affecting more than 50 percent of the children.[92] In several places health workers fled the violence, creating staff shortages. Similarly, between 1982 and 1986, war destroyed more than 40 percent of Mozambique's health centers and left about two-thirds of the country's 2 million primary school children without classrooms.[93] The Mozambican war also had a devastating effect on water supplies, especially in rural areas. For many years, routine maintenance of hand pumps was impossible, and many water sources were deliberately poisoned or destroyed during the war.[94]

Sexual violence and exploitation are a shockingly frequent experience for refugee women before or during flight and even in refugee camps. Before flight, sexual violence is routinely an element of the persecution of women. During flight, sexual exploitation or violence may be part of their experience with border officials, other refugees, or people in the host region. In recent years the world has listened in horror as women in Bosnia and Rwanda have recounted stories of rape, resulting in unwanted pregnancies and high rates of unsafe, sometimes self-induced abortions. In some raids in Rwanda during the appalling genocide of 1994, virtually every adolescent girl who survived the attack was subsequently raped.[95] Rape is also widespread in many refugee camps. Women have seen their spouses killed in front of them and then been raped. Thus, separated from husbands, fathers, and family, refugee women are vulnerable to attack both in war situations and in camps.[96]

Unfortunately, a high risk of infection with sexually transmitted diseases including HIV/AIDS accompanies all sexual violence against women and girls. Yet, refugee women commonly lack even the most basic elements of reproductive health care while facing unwanted pregnancies, unsafe abortions, and other risks such as sexually transmitted diseases. The breakdown of health services worsens the impact of such diseases and the chances for treatment, and escalates the risk involved in pregnancy. At many refugee camps, most of those who become pregnant are considered to be in high-risk groups—adolescents, women over forty, women with many existing children, and women who are physically and emotionally exhausted and undernourished.

AIDS is a major problem facing many refugee populations. In instances such as Rwanda where AIDS was a problem in the original community, social instability, poverty, and vulnerability usually accelerate the spread of the virus in two major ways—sexual activity and blood transfusion. Exchanging sex for money to buy food is common in or around refugee camps, putting both sex workers and their clients at high risk. Mixing of populations in refugee camps compounds the problem. Sexual contact between people who have fled from areas with high HIV rates and others from areas with low HIV rates spreads the virus among all groups. In the Rwandan emergency of 1994–95, some refugees fleeing to the camps in Zaire were from Kigali, where HIV rates preceding the crisis ranged between 20 and 30 percent. Others were from rural areas with much lower infection rates (1–9 percent). Materials for HIV prevention, such as condoms, typically are lacking, and access to health services, including treatment of sexually transmitted diseases, is severely limited. Yet, untreated STDs augment the spread of HIV. Moreover, a serious but frequently overlooked danger is the spread of HIV through transfusions of HIV-tainted blood. Blood transfusions are often needed in large numbers in situations of war and strife, and because of the poor nutritional status of women and children.[97]

Structural Adjustment and Health

As pointed out earlier, a recent book by the World Bank titled *Better Health in Africa: Experience and Lessons Learned,* highlights that major improvements in health have been achieved in Africa in the years since independence, notably, dramatic declines in the infant mortality rate from 145 per 1,000 live births in 1970 to 104 per 1,000 in 1992. Other statistics such as increases in life expectancy, declines in maternal mortality, and widespread immunizations of children are offered as evidence of success in the fight against disease throughout the African continent in the post-independence era. But these figures mask the worsening situation in southern Africa. In spite of the remarkable gains, in this study the World Bank acknowledges that challenges in the provision of and access to health care are immense. The risk of death remains markedly higher at all ages in Africa than in other parts of the world, more so in the case of women and children. What the World Bank study fails to note is that in certain countries that have endured deteriorating economies during the last decade, child mortality levels are virtually identical to those prevailing ten years ago. The book seems to lay the blame for the deteriorating health care infrastructure squarely on African governments, noting the inefficiency and waste in the supply of drugs and other health-related services. In reading this book I found it ironic that the bank fails to be self-critical in the evaluation of its programs, particularly the famous structural adjustment programs, which seem to have caused more harm than good throughout the continent.

As the economies of poor southern African countries such as Malawi, Zambia, and Angola failed in the 1980s, financial and technical assistance from multi-lateral organizations such as the World Bank was conditioned by the World Bank's structural adjustment program (SAPs). The SAPs were initiated to adjust malfunctioning economies and promote greater economic efficiency and economic growth to make sub-Saharan economies more competitive in today's global economy.[98] As Aryeetey-Attoh notes, candidates for structural adjustment were those with budget deficits, balance-of-payment problems, high inflationary rates, ineffective state bureaucracies, inefficient agricultural and industrial production sectors, overvalued currencies, and inefficient credit institutions.[99] The SAPs have a number of features that have negatively affected the position of the urban poor, women, and children. The major features include trade liberalization, government expenditure reduction, devaluation of currencies, reduction of controls over foreign currency, and trade union restrictions.

Evidence indicates that SAPs have had far-reaching deleterious effects on health and social services throughout Africa. Living conditions for urban and rural populations have deteriorated, the educational infrastructure crumbled, and the health care services are in dire straits.[100] For example, Lensik notes that the number of people between the ages of six and twenty-three who received education decreased during the 1980s, and the number of people per doctor and per nurse increased strongly.[101] Generally adjustment programs have had dramatic negative effects on quality of care, health service utilization due to the imposition of user fees, search for alternative sources of health care, changes in mortality and morbidity, and nutritional status. We have already touched on some of these issues, and I will briefly discuss the major findings from southern Africa with reference to these issues.

In many countries, even those that have stronger economies, governments have had to reduce expenditure on health care. Tevera clearly demonstrates that in the course of the 1980s government funding for the health sector in Zimbabwe became inadequate for the provision of basic health services, and even more so for the support of community-based health care.[102] Zimbabwe is one of the few countries in southern Africa that managed to increase government health expenditure in real terms during the 1980s.[103] However, this policy of consistent real increases in public financing of health services could not be sustained under the conditions of the SAP that started in 1991. As a result, real per capita public expenditure on health dropped by a total of 35 percent between 1991 and 1994.[104]

Tevera notes that the health sector in Zimbabwe has suffered from across-the-board cuts in government expenditures since 1991 and that these cuts have reversed the upward trend in expenditure that had occurred since independence.[105] The end result of the cuts in Zimbabwe's health care expenditure was a 10 percent decline in the number of nurses per person employed by the Ministry of Health and Child Welfare between 1991 and 1992, from more than 9 per 10,000 to just over 8 per 10,000 population. By mid-1992 about 800 health workers had been retrenched and 400 nursing posts had been abolished. This was followed by a substantial decline in the public funding of drugs and the imposition of user fees as part of cost recovery. The stringent implementation of fee collection together with the requirement of advance payment, particularly for maternity care, has already had a deterrent effect in terms of utilization of government services in Zimbabwe.[106] Drugs are in short supply, and their costs have increased sharply and are beyond the reach of most of the low-income earners. Perhaps the most tragic consequence in Zimbabwe is a steady increase in deaths from diseases that in the past had been brought under control. This is in large part because of the indirect effects of structural adjustment on nutrition, unhealthy living conditions, and poverty. Similar narratives can be told for health care delivery systems in Botswana, Malawi, Zambia, Zaire, Angola, and Mozambique.[107]

Poverty is now a major national problem in Zambia, where it is estimated that as much as 42 percent of the urban population lives below the poverty line.[108] Prices of basic commodities, such as chicken, have increased more than tenfold during the past decade, whereas in the same period wages only doubled. Studies suggest that the consumption pattern in poor households is changing from relatively protein- and energy-rich food toward less expensive, bulkier foods, with a decreasing number of meals per day.[109]

This process of impoverishment hits women harder than men, in particular because SAPs reinforce an already existing process of marginalization of women's production. Where SAPs lead to an increase in production, they stimulate the production of cash crops for export—such as cotton, cocoa, tea, and coffee—often to the detriment of household consumption.[110] The increase in cash crop production, usually controlled by men, also leads to increase in workloads for female family members. Further, women must bear the brunt of the social consequences of adjustment measures. Since they are also responsible for social and health aspects within the family, it is they who must cope with the increased burden of disease and hunger. In short, SAPs have had a disproportionate impact on increasing their workload while often yielding very few health and economic benefits.

There is growing evidence of the impact of structural adjustment on the health of mothers and infants. Costello and colleagues argue that most of the child mortality rates presented in World Bank tables should be viewed with suspicion, as such data are based on extrapolation rather than direct measurements.[111] Directly measured estimates for Zambia show a rise in infant mortality from 176 to 190 per 1,000 live births in the period between 1975 and 1992. As already indicated above, the Zambia Demographic and Health Survey data confirm this finding. In Zimbabwe, infant and child mortality exhibited a downward trend throughout the early and mid-1980s. Infant mortality declined from between 120 and 150 per 1,000 live births before 1980 to 61 by 1990, whereas the child mortality rate (children one to five years of age) declined from around 40 per 1,000 to 22 per 1,000 during the same period.[112] However, as UNICEF data indicate, evidence is accumulating that both indicators began to rise in the late 1980s and 1990s.[113] In addition to economic decline, deteriorating health services, and drought, the impact of HIV/AIDS is suspected to have contributed significantly to the observed changes in infant, childhood, and maternal mortality rates in countries such as Zimbabwe, Zambia, Botswana, and Malawi.

Rising to the Challenge

The World Bank, a latecomer in promoting better health care but an organization that has the means to make a difference, has recently produced a number of encouraging policy documents. The bank notes that substantial health improvements in sub-Saharan Africa are not only imperative but also feasible.[114] The bank has set forth a new vision of health improvement that challenges countries and their external partners to rethink current health strategies. The discussion in this paper, although critical of the current health care conditions, would like to offer a complementary outlook to that espoused by the World Bank. Although the problems seem to be insurmountable, it is our strong conviction that through commitment societies in southern Africa can turn the tide in their favor.

Health care is a very high priority for poor rural communities. Policies should be implemented that reduce barriers to access imposed by cost. The training of health personnel should emphasize interpersonal skills and cultural sensitivity. The supply of drugs to rural clinics should be improved. One of the options to improve health care in rural areas is to implement a policy of decentralization in a more practical manner, with each region getting its fair budgetary allocation. This was implemented in Zimbabwe during the early days of independence with remarkable results. There is need for urgent reform in the provision of health care facilities. As countries in sub-Saharan Africa liberalize their political systems with some success, it is time to turn attention to health.

It should be recognized that health and development are intimately interconnected. The linkage of health, the environment, and socio-economic improvements requires intersectoral efforts.[115] Each country should marshal the limited resources and utilize expertise in education, housing, public works, and community groups, including businesses, schools and universities, and religious, civic, and cultural organizations. The gist of the approach is to enable local communities to ensure sustainable health care and development. Of greater significance should be the inclusion of prevention programs rather than relying solely on remediation and treatment.[116] It is in this spirit that we suggest the following three target areas for immediate consideration in the health reform task. This is a reiteration of some of the points raised at the 1992 United Nations Conference on Environment and Development.

Primary Health Care for Rural Communities

Governments and international organizations such as the World Bank and World Health Organization (WHO) should channel their energies to the provision of basic primary health care by supplying the necessary specialized environmental health services, and coordinating the involvement of citizens, the health sector, the health-related sectors, and relevant non-health sectors. Rural needs should be high on the agenda, and the primary health care approach should be developed and strengthened in an innovative manner. These should be community based, practical, socially and culturally acceptable, and appropriate to the needs of the community.

Protection of Vulnerable Groups

In addition to meeting basic health needs, organizations should place specific emphasis on protecting and educating vulnerable groups, particularly infants, children, women, and the very poor. As noted earlier, in developing countries the health status of women and infants remains unacceptable, and poverty, malnutrition, and ill health appear to be on the increase for these vulnerable groups. Thus there is an urgent need to strengthen basic health care services for women and children in the context of primary health-care delivery, including prenatal care, breast-feeding, immunization, and nutritional programs. Women's groups should be actively involved in decision-making at the national and community levels to identify health risks and incorporate health issues in national action programs on women and development. The education of girls should be promoted at all levels of the educational system.

Eradication of Communicable Diseases

The only way African countries are going to move through the various stages of the epidemiologic transition is by eradicating communicable diseases on a sustainable basis. As noted earlier in this paper, advances in the development of vaccines and chemotherapeutic agents have brought many communicable diseases under control. But, as the discussion on the major causes of illness and death points out, many important communicable diseases such as cholera, diarrheal diseases, malaria, tuberculosis, measles, schistosomiasis, and a host of other parasitic infections continue to pester the peoples of Africa. The effects of the AIDS epidemic have also been amply highlighted above. The impact of many of these diseases can be lessened through serious environmental control measures, especially through the provision of safe water and sanitation. The environmental control measures, either as an integral part of the primary health care approach or undertaken outside the health sector, form an indispensable component of overall disease control strategies together with health and hygiene education.[117] In the case of AIDS, since a cure or vaccine appears to be a remote and unattainable possibility, governments should vigorously implement and enhance educational programs

Concluding Remarks and Policy Options

This chapter has attempted to highlight the major facets of society and health in southern Africa. The critical observations highlighted in preceding sections notwithstanding, data seem to indicate that southern Africa in general has made remarkable gains in reducing mortality levels across gender. If current trends continue, infant mortality could decline to a low of 26 deaths per 1,000 births by the year 2020. Figure 13.5 shows the trends in the Human Development Index (HDI) for selected countries in southern Africa. It is encouraging to see that even for a poor country like Malawi the trend in the HDI is increasing over time. Life expectancy, which is currently at sixty-two for both sexes, will increase to a high of seventy-two by 2020. However, these figures mask marked intra-country and regional variations within the southern African subcontinent. For example, Angola, Mozambique, Zambia, and Malawi stand out in having extremely high maternal, infant, and childhood mortality. Although under-five mortality rates have declined over the past decade, they have done so very slowly, from 258 deaths per 1,000 live births during the 1978–82 period to 234 deaths per 1,000 live births for the 1988–1992 period. In other words, one in four children do not live to see their fifth birthday. On the optimistic side, countries such as Botswana and Zimbabwe have the lowest level of under-five mortality in East and southern Africa as revealed by the DHS data. Namibia, Zimbabwe, Botswana, and South Africa have under-five mortality rates that range from a low of 40 per 1,000 for South Africa to a high of about 90 per1,000 for Zimbabwe. Indeed gender-related measures of development and empowerment seem to have improved dramatically in these countries.

Figure 13.5 Trends in Human Development Index (HDI)

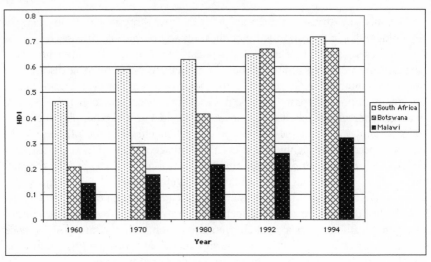

(Data from UNDP 1997.)

In short, the future of southern Africa in terms of gender differentials in mortality, disease, and health seems to be a mixed bag.

The key to a more equitable future is increased levels of female education and autonomy. Given the inequitable access to educational facilities, it is no wonder that women in southern Africa occupy a disadvantaged position. Although women make up 70 percent of full-time smallholder farmers, they have little or no access to necessary resources to improve agricultural output.[118] Due to their inferior social status, they suffer heavier seasonal weight losses than do men (2–4 kg versus 1–3 kg), suggesting that they receive less adequate diets relative to food requirements than do men.[119] The educational discrimination against girls reported in research on education in this region inevitably results not only in lower employment and earning opportunities for women, but also subsequently affects the health and welfare of their children and families.

As noted earlier, the benefits of educating women seem quite obvious. If provided quality education that does not discriminate by gender, men and women would be able to complement each other for the general good of the society in southern Africa. Among some of the visible benefits directly related to female education are lower fertility rates, lower infant and maternal mortality rates, improved nutrition for children, increases in economic productivity, and more participation of women in the labor market.

As pointed out earlier, Kalipeni found a very strong relationship between levels of infant mortality and female literacy rates at the district level.[120] Districts that had higher levels of female literacy rates consistently exhibited lower rates of infant mortality. Data from the 1984 Family Formation Survey and the recent Demographic and Health Survey show generally lower fertility levels for women with increasing levels of education. Women with secondary school education have the lowest levels of fertility, irrespective of their place of residence, followed by women with primary school education. Those without schooling display the highest fertility levels, as measured by average number of children ever born. Extended formal education of women also has the effect of raising the age at first marriage, which in turn has the effect of limiting the period of women's effective exposure to childbearing.[121] One can cite many other benefits of high female levels of education.

The implications and policy options are therefore self-evident. We reiterate here the program of action of the Cairo International Population Conference that the empowerment of women and improvement of their status is an important end in itself and is essential for the achievement of sustainable development in all its manifestations.[122] The governments of this region should endeavor to achieve equality and equity between men and women and enable women to realize their full potential. Women should be involved fully in policy and decision-making processes and in all aspects of economic, political, and cultural life as active decision-makers, participants, and beneficiaries. All women, as well as men, should receive the education required to meet their basic human needs and to exercise their human rights. As the Cairo program of action recommends, mechanisms for women's equal participation should be established, and women's education, skill development, and employment should be vigorously promoted. But more importantly, full measures need to be taken to eliminate all forms of exploitation and discrimination against women.

Indeed most governments in southern Africa are aware of the serious impact on family welfare of the disadvantaged position of women in society, and have made strong efforts to redress it, but the increasingly difficult economic circumstances could reverse any gains made in this respect. Numerous non-governmental organizations (NGOs) and donors are also helping to fund projects that directly benefit women by relieving the double burden of household production and reproduction. These efforts need to be applauded and should be intensified. Both strategic and practical solutions should be applied to the precarious position in which women currently find themselves. Strategic or long-range solutions include attempts to reduce the gap between boys and girls in educational attainment by increasing school enrollment ratios for girls. In keeping with the arguments discussed in this paper, changes that would greatly help to bridge the gender gap in education include reducing the cost of school for girls, making school mandatory, changing the attitudes of teachers toward girls, and making the curriculum more gender sensitive.

NOTES

1. Ties Boerma, "Health Transition in Sub-Saharan Africa," *Population and Development Review* 20, no. 1 (1994): 206–9.

2. Wendy J. Graham, "Maternal Mortality: Levels, Trends, and Data Deficiencies,"

in Richard G. Feachem and Dean T. Jamison, eds., *Disease and Mortality* (New York: Oxford University Press, 1991), pp. 101–6. (Published for the World Bank.)

3. E. Zulu, "Sociocultural Factors Affecting Reproductive Behavior in Malawi" (Ph.D. diss., Population Studies Center, University of Pennsylvania, 1996).

4. W. M. Gesler, *The Cultural Geography of Health Care* (Pittsburgh: University of Pittsburgh Press, 1992); and J. Oppong, "The Medical Consequences of Social Change: A Political Ecology of Health Care in Contemporary Ghana" (paper presented at the Department of Geography Friday Colloquium, University of Illinois at Urbana-Champaign, 30 January 1998).

5. P. A. Twumasi, *Social Foundations of the Interplay Between Traditional and Modern Medical Systems* (Accra: Ghana University Press, 1988); and Oppong, "Medical Consequences of Social Change."

6. See, for example, Charles Good, *Ethnomedical Systems in Africa* (New York: Guilford Press, 1987); J. Oppong, "Medical Geography of Sub-Saharan Africa," in Samuel Aryeetey-Attoh, ed., *Geography of Sub-Saharan Africa* (Upper Saddle River, N.J.: Prentice-Hall, 1997), pp. 147–81; Z. A. Ademuwagun, *African Therapeutic Systems* (Waltham, Mass.: Crossroads Press, 1979); and C. O. Airhihenbuwa and I. E. Harrison, "Traditional Medicine in Africa: Past, Present, and Future," in P. Conrad and E. B. Gallagher, eds., *Health and Health Care in Developing Countries* (Philadelphia: Temple University Press, 1993), pp. 122–34.

7. Oppong, "Medical Geography of Sub-Saharan Africa."

8. P. A. Twumasi, *Social Foundations;* Helmut Kloos, "The Poorer Third World: Health and Health Care in Areas That Have Yet to Experience Substantial Development," in David R. Philips and Yoda Verhasselt, eds., *Health and Development* (London: Routledge, 1994), pp. 199–215; and B. Hyma and A. Ramesh, "Traditional Medicine: Its Extent and Potential for Incorporation into Modern National Health Systems," in Philips and Verhasselt, *Health and Development,* pp. 65–82.

9. Charles Good, *Ethnomedical Systems in Africa;* and Oppong, "Medical Geography of Sub-Saharan Africa."

10. Kloos, "Poorer Third World"; and Bose Folasade Iyun, "Health Care in the Third World: Africa," in Philips and Verhasselt, *Health and Development.*

11. Cedric De Beer, *The South African Disease: Apartheid Health and Human Services* (London: Catholic Institute for International Relations, 1986); and Thomas R. De Gregori and William A. Darity, "Surplus People and Expendable Children: The Structure of Apartheid and the Mortality Crisis in South Africa," *The Review of Black Political Economy* 15 (1987): 47–62.

12. Michael King and Elspeth King, *The Story of Medicine and Disease in Malawi* (Blantyre: Montfort Press, 1992).

13. Ibid.

14. H. Fabrega, "The Scope of Ethnomedical Science," *Culture, Medicine and Psychiatry* 1: 201–25; Gesler, *Cultural Geography of Health Care;* C. O. Airhihenbuwa and I. E. Harrison, "Traditional Medicine in Africa: Past, Present, and Future," in Conrad and Gallagher, *Health and Health Care;* and Oppong, "Medical Geography of Sub-Saharan Africa."

15. Ademuwagun, *African Therapeutic Systems.*

16. Oppong, "Medical Geography of Sub-Saharan Africa."

17. J. M. Janzen, *The Quest for Therapy in Lower Zaire* (Berkeley: University of California Press, 1978).

18. Helmut Kloos and Zein Ahmed Zein, eds., *The Ecology of Health and Disease in Ethiopia* (Boulder, Colo.: Westview Press, 1993); E. Kalipeni and J. Oppong, "The Refugee Crisis in Africa and Implications for Health and Disease: A Political Ecology Approach," *Social Science and Medicine* (1998). In press.

19. E. Kalipeni and P. Thiuri, "Africa's Superficial Epidemiologic Transition," in E. Kalipeni and P. Thiuri, eds., *Issues and Perspectives on Health Care in Contemporary Sub-Saharan Africa* (Lewiston, N.Y.: Edwin Mellen Press, 1997), pp. 1–20; and Oppong, "Medical Consequences of Social Change."

20. E. Kalipeni and C. Kamlongera, "The Role of 'Theater for Development' in Mobilizing Rural Communities for Primary Health Care: The Case of Liwonde PHC Unit in Southern Malawi," *Journal of Social Development in Africa* 11, no. 1 (1996): 53–78.

21. Toyin Falola, "The Crisis of African Health Care Services," in Toyin Falola and Dennis Ityavyar, eds., *The Political Economy of Health in Africa* (Athens, Ohio: Ohio University Center for International Studies, 1992).

22. Helmut Kloos and Zein Ahmed Zein, "The Poorer Third World: Health and Health Care in Areas That Have Yet to Experience Substantial Development," in Philips and Verhasselt, eds., *Health and Development;* and Rais Akthar and Nilofar Izhar, "Spatial Inequalities and Historical Evolution in Health Provision: Indian and Zambian Examples," in Philips and Verhasselt, eds., *Health and Development,* pp. 216–33.

23. Norm McCracken, "Letter from Embangweni," NYASANET Discussion Group, 23 April 1998. (Posted letter from a Dr. Loomis stationed at Embangweni Hospital in Northern Malawi.)

24. Kloos and Zein, "Poorer Third World."

25. C. Anyinam, "The Social Cost of the IMF's Adjustment Programs for Poverty: The Case of Health Care in Ghana," *International Journal of Health Services* 19 (1989): 531–47; and Oppong, "Medical Geography of Sub-Saharan Africa."

26. B. McPake, "User Charges for Health Services in Developing Countries: A Review of the Economic Literature," *Social Science and Medicine* 36, no. 11 (1993): 25–30.

27. For a detailed discussion of the Mozambican and Angolan tragedies, see Mozambique Health Assessment Mission, *Mozambique Health Assessment Mission: Final Report* (Indianapolis: Woodrow E. Myers [Distributor] and Indiana State Board of Health, Division of Media and Publications, 1988); and United States Committee for Refugees, *Uprooted Angolans: From Crisis to Catastrophe* (Washington, D.C.: American Council for Nationalities Services, 1987).

28. See Robert Stock, *Africa South of the Sahara: A Geographic Interpretation* (New York: Guilford Press, 1995).

29. Kloos and Zein, eds., *Ecology of Health and Disease in Ethiopia.*

30. D. J. Bradley, "Malaria," in Feachem and Jamison, eds., *Disease and Mortality.*

31. Ibid.; Oppong, "Medical Geography of Sub-Saharan Africa."

32. David Le Sueur, Carrin Martin, Sipho Ngxongo, and Brian Sharp, "Geographic Information System (GIS) and the National Malaria Research Programme, South Africa," in Kalipeni and Thiuri, *Issues and Perspectives,* pp. 375–88.

33. Stock, *Africa South of the Sahara.*

34. E. Kalipeni, "The AIDS Pandemic in Malawi: A Somber Reflection," *21st Century Afro Review* 1, no. 2 (1995): 73–110; and Charles M. Becker, "The Demo-Economic Impact of the AIDS Pandemic in Sub-Saharan Africa," *World Development* 18 (1990): 1599–1619.

35. Kalipeni and Oppong, "Refugee Crisis in Africa."

36. Oppong, "Medical Geography of Sub-Saharan Africa."

37. J. C. Butler, et al., "Perspectives in Fatal Epidemics," *Infectious Diseases Clinical (North America)* 10, no. 4 (1996): 917–37.

38. L. A. Cole, "The Specter of Biological Weapons," *Scientific American* 275, no. 6 (1996): 50–60; and D. Pimentel et al., "Increasing Disease Incidence: Population Growth and Environmental Degradation" (David Pimentel, Cornell University, Ithaca, N.Y.).

39. K. J. Payling, "Ebola Fever," *Professional Nurse* 11, no. 12 (1996): 798–99.

40. Feachem and Jamison, eds., *Disease and Mortality*.

41. Puume Katjianjo, Stephen Titus, Maazuu Zauana, and J. Ties Boerma, *Namibia Demographic and Health Survey 1992* (Windhoek, Namibia: Ministry of Health and Social Services; Columbia, Md.: Macro International, 1992); Kwesi Gaise, Anne R. Cross, and Geoffrey Nsemukila, *Zambia Demographic and Health Survey 1992* (Lusaka: University of Zambia and Central Statistical Office; Columbia, Md.: Macro International, 1993); National Statistical Office of Malawi, *Malawi Demographic Health Survey, 1992* (Zomba: National Statistical Office; Columbia, Md.: Macro International, 1994); Lesetedinyana T. Lesetedi, Gaboratanelwe D. Mompati, Pilate Khulumani, Gwen N. Lesetedi, and Naomi Rutenbert, *Botswana: Family Health Survey II: 1988* (Gaborone: Central Statistics Office; Columbia, Md.: Institute of Resource Development/Macro Systems, 1989).

42. World Bank, *Better Health in Africa: Experience and Lessons Learned* (Washington, D.C.: World Bank, 1994).

43. Population Reference Bureau, *World Population Data Sheet* (Washington, D.C.: Population Reference Bureau, 1992); and African Development Bank, *African Development Report 1992* (Abidjan, Ivory Coast: African Development Bank, 1992).

44. Population Reference Bureau, *World Population Data Sheet*.

45. United Nations Development Programme, *Human Development Report* (New York: Oxford University Press, 1997).

46. Gaise et al., *Zambia Demographic and Health Survey*.

47. Bimal Kanti Paul, "Maternal Mortality in Africa: 1980–87," *Social Science and Medicine* 37, no. 6 (1993): 745–52; and Ties Boerma, "The Magnitude of the Maternal Mortality Problem in Sub-Saharan Africa," *Social Science and Medicine* 24, no. 6 (1987): 551–58.

48. G. Santow, "Gender Differences in Health Risks and Use of Services," in United Nations, ed., *Population and Women* (New York: United Nations, 1996), pp. 125–40.

49. See, for example, Priscilla Cunnan, "Family Planning in an Informal Settlement: The Case of Canaan, Durban, South Africa," in Kalipeni and Thiuri, eds., *Issues and Perspectives*, pp. 165–78; Vadi Moodley and Busi Zama, "The Health Status of Women in a Southern African Peri-Urban Settlement: The Case of Amadawe, Durban, South Africa," in Kalipeni and Thiuri, eds., *Issues and Perspectives*, pp. 179–94; and M. Hoffman, W. M. Pick, D. Cooper, and J. E. Myers, "Women's Health Status and Use of Health Services in a Rapidly Growing Peri-Urban Area of South Africa," *Social Science and Medicine* 45, no. 1 (1997): 149ff.

50. Stephan Klasen, "Nutrition, Health and Mortality in Sub-Saharan Africa: Is There a Gender Bias?" *Journal of Development Studies* 32, no. 6: 913ff.

51. Santow, "Gender Differences in Health Risks"; and Peter Svedberg, "Undernutrition in Sub-Saharan Africa: Is There a Gender Bias?" *Journal of Development Studies* 26 (April 1990): 469–86.

52. Kalipeni and Thiuri, "Africa's Superficial Epidemiologic Transition."

53. See "The Fertility Transition in Africa," *Geographical Review* 85, no. 3 (1995): 287–301.

54. Katjiunjo et al., *Namibia Demographic and Health Survey 1992;* Gaise, Cross, and Nsemukila, *Zambia Demographic and Health Survey 1992;* National Statistical Office, *Malawi Demographic Health Survey, 1992;* and Lesetedi et al., *Botswana: Family Health Survey II: 1988.*

55. Zulu, "Sociocultural Factors."

56. J. C. Caldwell and P. Caldwell, "The Cultural Context of High Fertility in Sub-Saharan Africa," *Population and Development Review* 13, no. 3 (1987): 409–37; J. C. Caldwell, I. O. Orubuloye, and P. Caldwell, "Fertility Decline in Africa: A New Type of Transition," *Population and Development Review* 18, no. 2 (1992): 211–42; and J. C. Caldwell, "Fertility in Sub-Saharan Africa: Status and Prospects," *Population and Development Review* 20 (1994): 179–87.

57. Zulu, "Sociocultural Factors"; Kalipeni, "Fertility Transition."

58. K. Ekouevi and A. Adepoju, "Adjustment, Social Sectors, and Demographic Change in Sub-Saharan Africa," *Journal of International Development* 7, no. 1 (1995): 47ff; I. O. Orubuloye, "The Demographic Situation in Nigeria and Prospects for Fertility Transition," *Journal of International Development* 7, no. 1 (1995): 135–44; N. C. Onuoha and I. M. Timaeus, "Has a Fertility Transition Begun in West Africa?" *Journal of International Development* 7, no. 1: 93–116; M. Lockwood, "Development Policy and the African Demographic Transition: Issues and Questions," *Journal of International Development* 7, no. 1 (1995): 1–23; and John Blacker, "Some Thoughts on the Evidence of Fertility Decline in Eastern and Southern Africa," *Population and Development Review* 20 (1994): 200–205.

59. Zulu, "Sociocultural Factors."

60. J. C. Caldwell, "Education as a Factor in Mortality Decline: An Examination of Nigerian Data," *Population Studies* 33 (1979): 395–413; J. C. Caldwell, "Routes to Low Mortality in Poor Countries," *Population and Development Review* 12 (1986): 171–220; J. G. Cleland and J. K. Ginneken, "Maternal Schooling and Childhood Mortality," *Journal of Biosocial Science,* Suppl. 10 (1989): 13–34; H. Y. Aly and R. Grabowski, "Education and Child Mortality in Egypt," *World Development* 18 (1990): 733–42; E. Kalipeni, "Determinants of Infant Mortality in Malawi: A Spatial Perspective," *Social Science and Medicine* 37, no. 2 (1993): 183–98; and G. T. Bicego and G. Fegan, "Maternal Education and Child Survival: A Comparative Analysis of DHS Data," *Demographic and Health Surveys World Conference: Proceedings,* vol. I (Columbia, Md.: IRD/Marco International, 1991), pp. 177–204.

61. Cleland and Van Ginneken, "Maternal Schooling."

62. Caldwell, "Routes to Low Mortality."

63. Ibid.

64. Kalipeni, "Determinants of Infant Mortality."

65. J. Bongaarts, O. Frank, and R. Lesthaeghe, "The Proximate Determinants of Fertility in Sub-Saharan Africa," *Population and Development Review* 10, no. 3 (1984): 511–37; K. O. Mason, "The Impact of Women's Social Position on Fertility in Developing Countries," *Sociological Forum* 1 (1987): 718–45; Caldwell and Caldwell, "Cultural Context"; M. M. Kritz and D. T. Gurak, "Women's Economic Independence and Fertility Among the Yoruba," in *Demographic and Health Surveys World Conference: Proceedings,* vol. I, pp. 73–88; Caldwell, Orubuloye, and Caldwell, "Fertility Decline in Africa."

66. S. Cochrane, "The Relationship Between Education and Fertility," in H. Ware, ed., *Women, Education and Modernization of Family in West Africa* (Canberra: Department of Demography, Australian National University, 1981), pp. 154–78.

67. United Nations, *Relationships Between Fertility and Education: A Comparative Analysis of World Fertility Survey Data for Twenty-two Developing Countries,* Doc. St/ESA/SER.R/48 (New York: United Nations, 1983).

68. A. W. Browne and H. R. Barrett, "Female Education in Sub-Saharan Africa: The Key to Development?" *Comparative Education* 27, no. 3 (1991): 275–85.

69. See, for example, ibid.

70. See, for example, D. Elder and S. Parker, "The Cultural Production and Re-production of Gender: The Effect of Extracurricular Activities on Peer-Group Culture," *Sociology of Education* 60 (1987): 200–213.

71. E. L. Phiri, "Do Girls Face Inequality in Technical Education and Vocational Training in Zambia?" *Zambian Educational Journal* 1, no. 8 (1981): 14–25.

72. L. Weis, "Education and the Reproduction of Inequality: The Case of Ghana," *Comparative Education Review* 23, no. 1 (1979): 41–51; and L. Weis, "Women and Ed-ucation in Ghana: Some Problems of Assessing Change," *International Journal of Women's Studies* 3, no. 5 (1991): 41–51.

73. See, for example, G. Kelly, "Research on the Education of Women in the Third World: Problems and Perspectives," *Women's Studies International Quarterly* 46 (1978): 1–9; C. Robertson, "Women's Education and Class Formation in Africa," in C. Robert-son and I. Berger, eds., *Women and Class in Africa* (New York: Africana Publishing, 1986): 92–116; A. Milton and S. Kuppenbach, "Gender and Access in the African School," *International Review of Education* 33, no. 4 (1987): 437–53; K. H. Lee, "Universal Primary Education: An African Dilemma," *World Development* 16 (1988): 1481–91; S. Leigh-Doyle, "Increasing Women's Participation in Technical Fields: A Pilot Project in Africa," *International Labor Review* 130, no. 4 (1991): 427–44; and E. Kalipeni, "Gender and Regional Differences in Schooling Between Boys and Girls in Malawi," *East African Ge-ographical Review* 19, no. 1 (1997): 14–32.

74. G. Engelhard and J. Monsaas, "Academic Performance, Gender, and the Coop-erative Attitudes of Third, Fifth, and Seventh Graders," *Journal of Research and Devel-opment in Education* 22 (1987): 13–17.

75. See Kalipeni and Thiuri, "Africa's Superficial Epidemiologic Transition."

76. A. Whiteside, "Health, Education, and Productivity," in Gavin Maasdorp, ed., *Can South and Southern Africa Become Globally Competitive Economies?* (New York: St. Martin's Press, 1996).

77. M. Over, R. Ellis, J. Huber, and O. Solon, "The Consequences of Adult Ill-Health," in R. Feacher, T. Kjeastrom, C. Murray, M. Over, and M. Phillips, eds., *The Health of Adults in the Developing World* (New York: Oxford University Press, 1992).

78. K. A. Stanecki and P. O. Way, "The Dynamic HIV/AIDS Pandemic," in Jonathan M. Mann and Daniel J. M. Tarantola, eds., *AIDS in the World II: Global Dimensions, So-cial Roots, and Responses* (New York: Oxford University Press, 1996), pp. 41–56.

79. Ibid., p. 43.

80. King and King, *The Story of Medicine and Disease in Malawi.*

81. P. B. Bloland, J. J. Wirima, R. W. Steketee, and B. Chilima, "Maternal HIV In-fection and Infant Mortality in Malawi: Evidence for Increased Mortality Due to Pla-cental Malaria Infection," *AIDS* 9, no. 7 (1995): 551–58; P. A. Reeve, "HIV Infection in Patients Admitted to a General Hospital in Malawi," *British Medical Journal* 298 (1989): 1567–68; J. K. Kristensen, "The Prevalence of Symptomatic Sexually Transmitted Dis-eases and Human Immunodeficiency Virus Infection in Outpatients in Lilongwe, Malawi," *Genitourinary Medicine* 66 (1990): 244–46; H. E. J. Kool, D. Bloemkolk, P. A.

Reeve, and S. A. Danner, "HIV Seropositivity and Tuberculosis in a Large General Hospital in Malawi," *Tropical and Geographic Medicine* 42, no. 2 (1990): 128–32; King and King, *The Story of Medicine and Disease in Malawi*; and G. B. Namanja, D. Sokal, G. Dallebetta, and B. Chimera, *A Preliminary Report of Sexually Transmitted Diseases (STD) and Human Immuno-Deficiency Virus (HIV) Seroprevalence Survey in Rural Ante-natal Women in Malawi* (Lilongwe: Malawi National AIDS Control Programme and AIDSTECH, Family Health International, 1993).

82. Malawi AIDS Control Programme, *AIDS Statistics 1994* (Lilongwe: Malawi National AIDS Control Programme, 1995).

83. April A. Gordon, "Population Growth and Urbanization," in April A. Gordon and Donald L. Gordon, eds., *Understanding Contemporary Africa* (Boulder, Colo.: Lynne Rienner, 1996), pp. 167–94.

84. P. Miotti, G. A. Dallabeta, J. D. Chiphangwi, G. Liomba, and A. J. Saah, "A Retrospective Study of Childhood Mortality and Spontaneous Abortion in HIV-1 Infected Women in Urban Malawi," *International Journal of Epidemiology* 21, no. 4 (1992): 792–99.

85. Kalipeni, "AIDS Pandemic in Malawi."

86. Peter Gould, *The Slow Plague: A Geography of the AIDS Pandemic* (Oxford: Blackwell, 1993).

87. Catherine Campbell, "Migrancy, Masculine Identities and AIDS: The Psychosocial Context of HIV Transmission on the South African Gold Mines," *Social Science and Medicine* 45, no. 2 (1997): 273–81; Michael Carael, "Women, AIDS and Sexually Transmitted Diseases in Sub-Saharan Africa: The Impact of Marriage Change," in United Nations, ed., *Population and Women*, pp. 125–140; and A. Chilivumbo, "Malawi: Cultural Consequences of Population Growth," in *The Consequences of Population Change*, a report on a seminar held in Bucharest, Romania, 14–17 March 1974 (Washington, D.C.: Center for the Study of Man, Smithsonian Museum, 1975).

88. "Medical Geography of Sub-Saharan Africa."

89. Ibid.

90. *AIDS Statistics 1994.*

91. See Julie Cliff and Abdul Razak Noormahomed, "The Impact of War on Children's Health in Mozambique," *Social Science and Medicine* 36, no. 7 (1993): 843ff.

92. UNICEF, *State of the World's Children Report* (New York: Oxford University Press, 1996); and United States Committee for Refugees, *Uprooted Angolans.*

93. UNICEF, *State of the World's Children Report;* and Allison Beattie, Laetitia Rispel, and Michelle Booysen, "Problems and Prospects for Health Sector Links in the Southern African Region: The Role of South Africa" *Social Science and Medicine* 37, no. 7 (1993): 927–35.

94. K. Wilson, "Internally Displaced Refugees and Returnees from and in Mozambique" (Uppsala, Sweden: Nordiska Afrikainstitutet, 1994).

95. UNICEF, *State of the World's Children Report.*

96. B. N. Hackett, *Pray God and Keep Walking: Stories of Women Refugees* (Jefferson, N.C.: McFarland, 1996); W. R. Smyser, *Refugees: Extended Exile* (New York: Praeger, 1987); R. F. Gorman, *Coping with Africa's Refugee Burden: A Time for Solutions* (Dordrecht, Netherlands: M. Nijhoff, 1987); and O. Dunbar and B. Harrell, "Africa Rights Monitor: Who Protects the Human Rights of Refugees?" *Africa Today* 34, nos. 1/2 (1987): 105–25.

97. For a detailed discussion on the subject of refugees, health, and political instability in Africa, see Kalipeni and Oppong, "Refugee Crisis in Africa."

98. Samuel Aryeetey-Attoh, "Geography and Development in Sub-Saharan Africa,"

in Aryeetey-Attoh, ed., *Geography of Sub-Saharan Africa;* and Sheena Asthana, "Economic Crisis, Adjustment and the Impact on Health," in Philips and Verhasselt, eds., *Health and Development.*

99. Aryeetey-Attoh, "Geography and Development."

100. Deborah Potts, "Shall We Go Home? Increasing Urban Poverty in African Cities and Migration Processes," *The Geographical Journal* 16 (1995): 245–64; R. Lensink, *Structural Adjustment in Sub-Saharan Africa* (Harlow, Essex: Longman, 1996); and Daniel S. Tevera, "Structural Adjustment and Health Care in Zimbabwe," in Kalipeni and Thiuri, eds., *Issues and Perspectives.*

101. *Structural Adjustment in Sub-Saharan Africa.*

102. "Structural Adjustment and Health Care."

103. J. Cabot, J-W. Harnmeijer, and P. H. Streetfland, eds., *African Primary Health Care in Times of Economic Turbulence* (Amsterdam: Royal Tropical Institute, 1995).

104. M. Chisvo and L. Munro, "A Review of Social Dimensions of Adjustment in Zimbabwe, 1990–1994" (unpublished paper, 1994).

105. "Structural Adjustment and Health Care."

106. Ibid.

107. See McPake, "User Charges for Health Services."

108. K. Kalumba, "Impact of Structural Adjustment Programmes on Household Level Food Security and Child Nutrition: The Zambian Experience" (unpublished paper, University of Zambia, 1990).

109. P. Streefland, J-W. Harnmeijer, and J. Chabot, "Implications of Economic Crisis and Structural Adjustment Policies for PHC in the Periphery," in Chabot, Harnmeijer, and Streetfland, eds., *African Primary Health Care.*

110. Ibid.

111. A. Costello, F. Watson, and D. Woodward, *Human Face or Human Façade? Adjustment and the Health of Mothers and Children* (London: Centre for International Development, 1994).

112. J. Chabot, et al., *African Primary Health Care.*

113. UNICEF, *State of the World's Children Report 1994;* UNICEF, *State of the World's Children Report 1996.*

114. World Bank, *Better Health in Africa.*

115. United Nations, *In Our Hands, Earth Summit: United Nations Conference on Environment and Development, Rio de Janeiro, Brazil, 1–12 June 1992* (New York: Department of Public Information, 1992).

116. Ibid.

117. Ibid.

118. World Bank, *Malawi Population Sector Study, Vol. I: Main Report* (Washington, D.C.: Population and Human Resources Division, Southern Africa Department, World Bank, 1992).

119. Ibid.

120. "Determinants of Infant Mortality in Malawi."

121. W. R. M'manga and M. L. Srivastave, *Socioeconomic and Demographic Determinants of Family Size in Malawi: A Multivariate Analysis* (Zomba: Demographic Unit, University of Malawi, 1991).

122. S. Johnson, *The Politics of Population: The International Conference on Population and Development, Cairo 1994* (London: Earthscan, 1995).

14. | Economic Integration in Southern Africa

Sue Kell and Troy Dyer

Introduction: Background and History

"The countries of Sub-Saharan Africa expect regional cooperation and integration to reverse the continent's economic decline, promote development and strengthen Africa's position in the world at large. Up to the present these expectations have been disappointed."[1]

With few exceptions the economies of sub-Saharan Africa are characterized by small populations and low per capita incomes: the entire subcontinent had a GNP of $290 billion in 1995, a little bigger than Argentina and a little smaller than Switzerland. Thus regional groupings are deemed imperative. There have been a number of attempts at cooperation of various kinds since the early 1960s, most of which have failed; but the drive toward integration in Africa has been given even greater impetus by the formation of the major trading blocs of the EU (European Union), NAFTA (North American Free Trade Agreement), and ASEAN (Association of South East Asian Nations) countries.

The primary objective of integrations is to obtain the benefits of international specialization of production via economies of scale. The relationships between participating countries may range from a loose association of trade partners to full integration of production and macro-economic policies.

Economic integration in the southern African subregion consists of three groupings at present. The broadest based is COMESA, the Common Market for Eastern and Southern Africa, which, despite its name, is aiming to become a free-trade area, and which consists of twenty-three countries (excluding South Africa and Botswana) containing 314 million people. COMESA has inherited from its predecessor, the Preferential Trade Area of Eastern and Southern Africa, structural weaknesses: too-similar economies, poor intra-regional links, and the lack of at least one stronger more sophisticated economy to be the locomotive or lead goose.[2] Intra-regional trade amounts to only about 6 percent of the total trade of the constituent economies. Despite these drawbacks, tariffs in the region have fallen 70 percent, and intra-regional trade is growing by over 10 percent per annum. However, further development may be constrained by significant political instability in several members' countries, together with the actual and threatened withdrawal of several members of the Southern African Development Community (SADC).

The second and smallest grouping is the Southern African Customs Union (SACU), within which goods and services move free of tariffs or any other hindrance, and which has a common external tariff. Originally formed in 1910 and thus the world's oldest customs union, its members are South Africa, Botswana, Lesotho, Swaziland, and Namibia. The existing treaty has been in place for nearly thirty years and is presently being re-negotiated to resolve issues pertaining to revenue distribution, intra-SACU trade, and the overwhelming influence of South Africa's domestic policies on those of its much smaller partners. The Common Monetary Area, consisting of the same members except Botswana, complements SACU. The common currency is the South Africa rand, into which all the other members' currencies are freely weighed by the advantages of full access to the sophisticated South African financial markets. The combination of customs union and monetary integration places SACU well on the road to full economic union.

The rest of this analysis of economic integration in southern Africa will be focused on the third, wider grouping of the SADC. It was originally constituted in 1980 as the SADCC (Southern African Development Coordination Conference), an association of the nine so-called frontline states—Botswana, Swaziland, Lesotho, Angola, Zimbabwe, Zambia, Mozambique, Malawi, and Tanzania; Namibia joined the group in 1990 after its independence from South Africa—formed to provide a bulwark against South Africa's apartheid regime and its economic dominance, by forging links and mobilizing resources to bring about "functional" economic integration via infrastructural and sectoral coordination.

The SADCC became SADC in 1992, when the Treaty of Windhoek incorporated broader objectives for the organization, notably a program of development integration (as opposed to development coordination) to alleviate poverty, support the socially disadvantaged, and maximize productive employment by combining policy cooperation, sectoral coordination, and trade integration. The treaty goes beyond the vision of economic integration to include the promotion of peace and security, and the consolidation of historical, social, and cultural affinities.[3] South Africa became a member in 1994, after the successful democratic election, and Mauritius joined in 1995. The number of member countries rose to fourteen in 1998 with the addition of the Democratic Republic of Congo (DRC, formerly Zaire) and the Seychelles.

SADC is a vision common to many if not most of the policy-makers in southern Africa, but progress toward the defined objectives has been very limited to date, for reasons relating to political dilemmas arising out of domestic interests, weak institutional capacity, and the slow pace of consensus building. There is a concern that the whole venture is a triumph of political idealism over economic reality. This report will show that the structure and potential of the participating economies present some formidable impediments to regional integration, but that the development of the region to its full potential will not occur without such integration.[4]

Part A: The Vision and the Reality

The stated objective of the SADC is a high degree of economic cooperation and integration, but, as noted in the introduction, the characteristics of the constituent economies are likely to make the achievement of that goal a complex process.

The Vision

The existing state of all the SADC countries encompasses poverty, inequality, economic stagnation, underdevelopment of physical and especially human capital, and marginalization in a globalizing world. Thus the declared purpose of the SADC is to enable the countries of southern Africa to "achieve their full potential through close cooperation in the exploitation of natural resources in a coordinated fashion, the pooling of technical expertise, the harmonization of trade practices and the promotion of economies of scale. . . . [The] vision for the Southern African region [is] the highest possible degree of economic cooperation, mutual assistance where necessary and joint planning of regional development initiatives leading to integration consistent with socio-economic, environmental and political realities."[5] Political and economic stability in the region is to be achieved through free trade and infrastructural links initially, leading to a common market. Full economic union is too distant a goal as yet.

The envisaged future for the region consists of economic and social integration, creating peace and prosperity for all the inhabitants of the region, which will thus attain a demonstrably stronger position in the world at large.

The Current Reality

The following analysis and discussion covers eleven aspects of the economy of the region, in order to present as comprehensive a picture as space allows of the structure, trends, and potential that constitute the parameters of the strategic analysis in part B.

GDP and Growth Rates

The SADC is a substantial economic player in the context of Africa south of the Sahara. The GDP (gross domestic product) of the region is nearly 60 percent of that of sub-Saharan Africa, per capita incomes are double, and the SADC accounts for well over half the foreign trade of the subcontinent. In a broader context, south-

Table 14.1. SADC Gross Domestic Product by Country

	GDP ($ mil.), 1995	GDP Growth (% p.a.), 1990–95	GDP per Capita ($), 1995	GDP per Capita Growth (% p.a.), 1985–95	% Contribution to GDP		
					Agriculture	Industry	Services
Angola	4,422	-4.1	410	-6.1	12	59(3)	28
Botswana	4,381	4.2	3,020	6.1	5	46(4)	48
DRC	5,313	-10.0	120	-8.5	30	34(11)	36
Lesotho	1,519	5.0	770	1.2	10	56(18)	34
Malawi	1,622	0.7	170	-.7	42	27(18)	31
Mauritius	3,815	5.2	3,380	5.4	9	33(23)	58
Mozambique	1,353	5.5	80	3.6	33	13(—)	55
Namibia	3,098	3.8	2,000	2.5	14	29(9)	56
Seychelles	487	5.0	6,620	4.2	—	—	—
South Africa	130,918	0.6	3,160	-1.1	5	31(24)	64
Swaziland	1,051	2.1	1,170	0.6	13	49(46)	38
Tanzania	3,703	3.2	120	1.0	58	17(8)	24
Zambia	3,605	-0.2	400	-.8	22	40(30)	37
Zimbabwe	5,933	1.0	540	-.6	15	36(30)	48
SADC total	171,220		973				

ern Africa represents 0.6 percent of world GDP. However, it must be borne in mind that South Africa contributes about 80 percent of the SADC's GDP; the collective GDP of the rest of the region amounted to $40 billion in 1995, equivalent to that of Algeria or Hungary. Zimbabwe's economy ranks second to that of South Africa in size, but at $6.5 billion is only 5 percent of that of its large southern neighbor. Six of the economies have national incomes of $3–4 billion, while Lesotho, Malawi, and Mozambique trail well behind at $1–1.5 billion.

In 1995 the per capita income in the SADC region was $973, compared with $490 for the whole of sub-Saharan Africa. That average encompasses a range within the region from $90 per person in Mozambique, through the low $100s in Tanzania and the DRC and $300–600 in the countries in the central part of the region, up to $2,000 in Namibia, $3,000 in Botswana, and peaking at $3,160 in South Africa. The considerable variation reflects, in the main, the production structure of the various economies. The three poorest countries are those in which agriculture still contributes a large proportion of the national income; many of the mid-range economies are dependent on exports of metals and minerals and thus subject to the vagaries of international commodity markets. (See Table 14.1 for details.) Two of the higher-income countries benefit from substantial diamond value-adding services. In the other SADC countries, industry consists largely of local raw materials processing and import-substituting manufactures of food, beverages and tobacco, textiles and clothing, and construction.

The level of and growth in national income are indicative of three characteristics of the region that affect integration. First, the entire region is small by global standards. Second, comparisons of the member countries reveal rather more similarities than complementarities. It is the third characteristic—the contrasts between countries within the region—that gives rise to consideration of convergence. Economic convergence is the tendency for poor countries to catch up over time with richer ones, as a result of technological leapfrogging, openness to trade, or willingness to integrate into the global economy. Importantly, it appears that, "as economies converge, structures of production and demand within individual countries diversify. . . ." Jenkins and Thomas show that in the period 1960–90 there was no convergence in per capita incomes of SADC countries; if anything there has been slight divergence.[6] In contrast, there has been strong convergence among SACU member countries.

Convergence has not increased overall in recent years. Average GDP growth in the region in the first half of the 1990s was around 2.3 percent per annum, which means that average per capita incomes barely rose. Again, there is a wide range among countries, with Botswana and Mozambique well in the lead at 6 percent and 4 percent per person per year, respectively. Angola and the DRC suffered grievously from internal turmoil. Several of the others were affected by some combination of drought, weak export markets, and structural adjustment programs (SAPs). Growth increased noticeably between 1995 and 1997 (6 percent for the region in 1996), partly through the cyclical benefits of good rains and higher commodity prices, but also due to structural changes instituted to attract foreign investors, such as privatization in Zambia and Mozambique and plans for massive infrastructural development.[7] Above all, there was a perceptible change in the policy climate in response to the imperatives of globalization. However, these developments have yet to show up in the narrowing of the relative gap between richer and poorer states in the region.

The initial forecasts for 1998 and beyond were relatively optimistic, primarily because of the policy momentum established in the preceding couple of years, the end of conflict in Angola and the DRC, and the fact that the impact of the El Niño weather phenomenon was not as bad as originally feared. Most of the countries, apart from Zambia and South Africa, were set to grow 4–5 percent. However, even the initial impact of the Asian crisis caused the IMF (International Monetary Fund) to scale back its forecast for sub-Saharan Africa from 4.7 percent to 3 percent. The subsequent waves of the crisis and recent developments in the Russian political economy have negatively affected the currencies and financial markets of all emerging economies and commodity markets, reducing further the short- and medium-term growth prospects of the region.

In summary, analysis of the causes and patterns of growth shows that most of the countries in the region are undergoing significant structural change, which is overlaid by temporary but deeply felt factors such as periodic drought, and by exogenous shocks of a medium-term nature such as the Asian crisis. The important point is that all the economies are affected in much the same way, so there are no compensating mechanisms to modify the resulting business cycles. For example, ten of the member countries have textile industries that are vulnerable to imports considerably cheapened by the depreciation of the South East Asian currencies. Drought affects exports of agricultural commodities from several members, the food-processing industries of almost all of the economies, and most importantly the incomes and poverty levels in the region. There are seven minerals producers in the region, all susceptible to the same softening world markets.

A notable but unquantified factor in southern Africa is the role of the informal sector, and consequent undercounting of the national income. There are three segments of the informal sector: first, hawking and micro-retail and service enterprises are expanding rapidly in response to lack of formal sector employment and to the rapid pace of urbanization (especially in the form of informal squatter settlements). Second, new enterprises are established for purposes of second incomes or tax evasion. Third, crime at both the local and international syndicate level is creating uncounted income for some. The first category, the small, micro, and medium enterprises (SMMEs), is by far the biggest and most significant of the three, and there is considerable debate as to whether growth in the region is in fact more robust than the official statistics show. That same debate has also not yet yielded conclusions as to whether the informal sector activity in these countries is a springboard to value-added manufacturing and production sectors, or whether it keeps the participants permanently in a rut of low-level output in the service and distribution sectors. Rough estimates put the uncounted economy at 20–25 percent of GDP in countries at this level of development. The significance of the informal sector is that it is growing fast both in absolute and relative terms, but by its nature is survivalist, very locally oriented, and inward-looking, and thus produces few if any incentives for regional integration.

Poverty and Development Indicators

Real per capita income is considered to be the best available proxy for the level of development of an economy, and the per capita incomes detailed in Table 14.1 point to a wide disparity in the development levels of the members of the SADC. The more broadly based Human Development Index (HDI) calculated for the UN Development Program incorporates not only income but life expectancy and literacy as well. The 1994 HDI shows South Africa ranking top in the region, with an HDI of .72 (out of possible 1.00, and compared with the average industrial country HDI of .91) and Mozambique at the bottom with an HDI of .288. The average for the region is .46, rather higher than the .38 for sub-Saharan Africa, but considerably below South America's average of .76.[8]

The HDI is still an inadequate indicator of poverty in southern Africa, largely because of the patterns of income distribution in some of the countries. Gini coefficients measure concentration and thus inequality. They are available for only five of the SADC countries (see Table 14.2), and among these five there is a direct relationship between higher average per capita incomes and higher Gini coefficient, indicating greater inequality. To give some perspective to the income distribution, first the figures for South Africa, Lesotho, and Zimbabwe are comparable with those in a number of South American countries, led by Brazil whose coefficient is 63. Tanzania's distribution is similar to that of a number of Central and Western African countries. Second, the HDI of the white, historically richer population in South Africa is estimated to be the same as that of the industrialized countries, .91, while that of historically disadvantaged black South Africans is around .52. The intra-regional differences in poverty levels, life expectancy, and calorie supply are detailed in Table 14.2.

Another aspect of structural development is physical infrastructure, a relatively non-controversial focus of the functional integration referred to earlier. In global terms, it should be noted that the entire region, including South Africa, has less than half the number of telephones of Hong Kong. Intra-regionally, the five SACU members have 88 percent of the electricity output of the SADC region, 62 percent of the rail tracks, 61 percent of the paved roads, 72 percent of the air traffic, and 90 percent of the telephones.

These indicators serve to emphasize the fact that the developmental imperatives of the member states are similar in principle: a substantial increase in standards of living, which will require, among other things, huge investment in human capital and reduced balance of payments constraints. However, those imperatives differ considerably in degree and thus in the opportunity costs of relevant policy choices.

Table 14.2. Poverty and Development Indicators

	HDI Ranking (out of 175)	Gini Coefficient	% of Pop. Below National Poverty Line	Life Expectancy at Birth	Calorie Supply as % of Average Industrial Countries
Angola	157	—	—	47	59
Botswana	97	—	35	52	73
DRC	142	—	41	52	66
Lesotho	137	56	26	58	71
Malawi	161	—	50+	41	59
Mauritius	61	—	11	71	87
Mozambique	166	—	50+	46	54
Namibia	118	—	45	56	—
Seychelles	52	—	—	72	—
South Africa	90	58	48	64	87
Swaziland	114	—	—	58	—
Tanzania	149	38	50	50	65
Zambia	143	46	86	43	62
Zimbabwe	129	57	26	49	64

The latter fact has a significant bearing on the willingness and ability of the member states to integrate to the envisaged extent.

Demography

The population of the SADC region is just over 180 million, comparable with Indonesia's 193 million, and totaling about one-third that of sub-Saharan Africa. Table 14.3 shows that the largest individual countries are South Africa and the DRC, with over 40 million people each, followed by Tanzania and Mozambique. Four other countries cluster around 10 million, and three others have only 1–2 million people. These figures constitute one of the strongest arguments for integration of the region, since combining the economies would yield a population two-thirds that of the United States. Extrapolation of historical trends indicates a potential market of 250 million people by the year 2010, even with the average population growth rate falling from 2.7 percent per annum to 2.4 percent in the next decade.

The age structure is similar throughout the region (excluding South Africa): over 45 percent of the population is fifteen years old or younger. This, coupled with an average life expectancy at birth of fifty years, means that the median age (which divides the population into two halves) is less than twenty years, in comparison with the thirty-five years characteristic of the aging population of developed countries. The level of urbanization in the region as a whole is 33 percent (29 percent excluding

Economic Integration in Southern Africa

Table 14.3. Demography

	Total Pop. (in 1000s)	Pop. Growth (% p.a.), 1990–95	% of Pop. under 15 Years	Urban Pop. as % of Total
Angola	11,500	2.8	45	31
Botswana	1,550	3.3	45	27
DRC	43,500	3.0	48	29
Lesotho	2,000	2.7	41	23
Malawi	10,000	3.3	47	15
Mauritius	1,130	0.9	—	41
Mozambique	18,000	2.9	44	30
Namibia	1,600	3.0	44	36
Seychelles	80	0.9	—	50
South Africa	41,000	2.3	38	50
Swaziland	950	3.5	48	28
Tanzania	29,000	3.0	47	25
Zambia	9,500	3.2	47	43
Zimbabwe	11,200	2.7	45	32

South Africa), which compares with 31 percent for sub-Saharan Africa as a whole and 75 percent in industrial countries. Urbanization is proceeding apace (see details in Table 14.3), and of the thirty largest cities in Africa, ten are in southern Africa.

The level and rate of urbanization in the region as a whole is encouraging in respect to concentration of markets, synergies in economic activities, and lower unit costs of infrastructural service provision. However, the distribution of the urbanization is not yet providing an incentive for integration. Four of those ten largest cities are in South Africa, which for reasons that emerge in later discussion, is ambivalent about opening up its borders to its northern neighbors. Three others of the large cities are Kinshasa, Luanda, and Maputo, all of which are suffering from the widespread economic destruction consequent on prolonged civil war, and all three are located in countries with the lowest per capita incomes in the region, which inhibits their ability to act as economic locomotives.

The patterns of urbanization, the massive reconstruction requirements, and the social expenditure requirements of a young, generally poor population result in similar demands on the fiscus and on the balance of payments of all the member countries (discussed in more detail in the relevant sections below). Those same demographic characteristics are the foundations of the stock of and potential for human capital in the region, and thus the prospects for employment and for competitive advantage in the globalized world economy. The future demographic structure of the region will be significantly affected by two factors not yet considered, namely AIDS and migration. By far the greatest number of HIV-infected people are in sub-Saharan Africa, which also accounts for half of the world's tally of new infections every day. Malawi, Tanzania, Zambia, and Zimbabwe are the worst affected in the southern Africa. Indications are that at least 25 percent of the population will be HIV positive within a decade. Available medication is financially unobtainable: a typical triple cocktail of drugs costs about $15,000 a year. "At that price, the entire per capita health budget of Kenya would buy six hours of coverage."[9] The consequent deaths from AIDS will bring down life expectancy by ten years or more, and it is estimated that the number of AIDS deaths will cause Zimbabwe's population growth rate to fall to zero by the year 2002. Similar predictions have been made about Zambia. The group most affected is the 25–45-year-olds, into which group fall the most productive and the most skilled. As President Mandela pointed out at the Davos meetings in early 1998, "AIDS kills those on whom society relies to grow the crops, work in the mines, run the schools and hospitals . . . thus increasing the number of dependent persons. It creates new pockets of poverty when parents and breadwinners die and children leave school earlier to support the remaining children."[10] It is estimated that GDP growth will fall 1–5 percent per annum in the region, which will aggregate to 20–25 percent of GDP over a twenty-year period.

The relevance of these developments to integration is that, first, intra-regional migration is helping to spread the disease. Second, the structure of the labor forces in the individual economies is being affected in the same way, thus inhibiting compensating distribution of skills around the region. Human capital is the factor in shortest supply, and is now the one under most threat, impacting the potential competitiveness and future ability to overcome the trade gap discussed below.

There are three patterns of migration observable in the region at present. The first is the net emigration from South Africa to industrialized countries of those who are internationally mobile by virtue of skills or wealth. The second is the movement of highly skilled professional and academic staff from the rest of Africa to South Africa, in response to the perceived opportunities for advancement, higher incomes, and higher standards of living.[11] The third, and numerically by far the greatest group, is the inflow of illegal immigrants into South Africa from neighboring countries. Estimates of the number of such immigrants vary widely, ranging from 2 to 8 million people, that is, up to 20 percent of the population. The main reasons for the flow are civil wars in the immigrants' own country, poverty, and destitution, often resulting from unemployment, in other words, "forced ecomigration."[12]

The inflow of so-called illegal aliens is a source of intra-regional conflict, in that South Africans resent to the point of xenophobia the immigrants taking up jobs and entrepreneurial opportunities, and both the population and governments of the other countries in the region criticize South Africa for not sharing its wealth, and not taking responsibility as a member of SADC for those outside its borders. The South African government is caught between the rock of its avowed policies of human rights and the hard place of its increasingly daunting responsibilities for creating jobs for its own citizens ahead of those of other countries. Analysts and commentators are all agreed that the only sustainable solution to the problem is regional economic development—and a necessary, though not sufficient, condition for that development is integration.

Table 14.4. Fiscal Indicators

	Government Expenditure as % of GDP	Fiscal Deficit (Surplus) as % of GDP	Public Debt to GDP	Aid as % of GDP
Angola	—	–18	—	11
Botswana	48	(6)	14	2
DRC	18	–15	104	—
Lesotho	50	–6	68	9
Malawi	26	–8	117	38
Mozambique	51	–5	—	101
Namibia	37	–5	12	5
South Africa	31	–5	55	0
Swaziland	33	–4	12	5
Tanzania	38	–9	—	30
Zambia	35	–4	128	21
Zimbabwe	36	–8	70	10

Government Revenue and Expenditure

The role of government in a developing economy is subject to opposing forces. The countries are characterized by inadequate physical and social infrastructure, and a number of developmental analysts and practitioners consider that the government should be pro-active in effecting structural development of and fundamental redistribution in the economy. However, the revenue base is often narrow and volatile; and there is unremitting pressure from international lending institutions and international investors to keep the fiscal deficit under strict control, in conformity with the widespread neo-liberal policy paradigm encompassed in the Washington Consensus. The ability of the SADC members to reconcile these forces varies widely.

Government expenditures as a proportion of national expenditures range from 18 percent to 51 percent of GDP, as shown in Table 14.4. The median is 36 percent, and the extremes consist of those countries where war has thrown the entire economy into complete disarray, or where the economy is disproportionately dependent on one sector, as in Botswana and Lesotho. Details of the composition of expenditure are patchy, but interest on public debt is a large item in some budgets. Importantly, as Table 14.5 shows, the expenditure on health and education (which represent investment in human capital) amounts to 17–33 percent of the total, with a median of 24 percent, which compares with an average of 20 percent for developed countries.

The composition of government revenue reflects the broader tax bases indicative of the greater development of the South African and Zimbabwean economies. Indirect sales taxes are important sources of revenue in a number of the member

Table 14.5. Further Fiscal Indicators for Selected Countries (Averages 1991–95)

	% of Total Current Revenue			% of Total Expenditure	
	Income Tax	Sales Tax/ VAT	Tariffs and Excise	Interest on Debt	Health and Education
Botswana	30	3	19	2	26
Lesotho	15	16	55	7	33
Malawi	35	32	19	—	18
Namibia	26	27	34	1	40
South Africa	51	35	3	15	33
Tanzania	29	55	10	—	17
Zambia	33	42	19	18	23
Zimbabwe	44	26	19	15	27

states. Both of these items in the budget of the less industrialized economies in the region are vulnerable to fluctuations in agricultural output and commodity prices. However, the fiscal feature most relevant to integration is the substantial dependence on tariff revenues in the majority of countries, especially the members of SACU. In view of the fact that several of the countries are committed to fiscal discipline under the conditions of SAPs, reductions in revenue may be difficult to contemplate. The overall impact depends on the proportion of each country's imports coming from other SADC members, a topic explored in more depth below.

The fiscal deficit is one area where there has been some convergence among the SADC states, due in part to the SAPs and in part to the necessity of creating a policy environment that encourages inflows of foreign capita. By 1996 the deficit had narrowed to between 1 and 6 percent of GDP in all but Angola, the DRC, Tanzania, and Zimbabwe. The ratio of total government debt to GDP is higher than the internationally desirable 60 percent in the DRC, Lesotho, Malawi, Zambia, and Zimbabwe, pointing to interest payments remaining a burden on the fiscus and constraining the development of social infrastructure. Aid constitutes a significant portion of GDP in Angola, Malawi, Mozambique, Tanzania, and Zambia.

In summary, the unremitting demands for developmental expenditure by the public sector in all of the SADC states and the continual need in each country for inflows of foreign capital will contribute to the tension between national and regional interests.

Financial Market Structure

Development, industrialization, and private foreign capital flows are assisted and encouraged to a considerable degree by functional financial markets, comprising the banking sector, the capital markets, and eventually stock markets.

Financial reforms are being introduced slowly and unevenly into many of the sub-Saharan Africa banking systems, which are in disarray because of the proliferation of state-owned banks, often characterized by inadequate management and governance, and over-exposure to unprofitable public enterprises and thus bad debts. The institutional capacity of central banks is generally weak, and lack of risk management expertise results in inadequate surveillance. In fact, in some of the SADC countries, the central bank is regarded and used as just an extension of treasury of the central government. Clearing and settlement systems are underdeveloped and subject to long delays, especially in places like Angola and Mozambique, which in turn lead to liquidity problems and poor risk assessment.

However, some banks are responding to the forces of international integration and global competitiveness. The increasing liberalization of African economies is encouraging inflows of private foreign capital, with concomitant pressure for more efficient financial markets and institutions, leading to the deregulation of interest rates and credit expansion, for example, in Central African countries including Malawi. Nonetheless the capital adequacy of state-owned banks, such as those in Tanzania, is still a major concern.

Southern Africa is still characterized by a widespread cash-carrying culture, even in large parts of the financially sophisticated South Africa, but banks in Zimbabwe, Botswana, and the SACU countries have introduced electronic banking. There is a discernible movement toward a broader range of services and toward depth and breadth of cross-border financial transactions. Symptomatic of that trend is the northerly migration of South African banks, which are now operating in a number of SADC and other sub-Saharan African countries, bringing global sophistication together with local knowledge, and high levels of technology.[13]

An important facet of financial markets in southern Africa is reaching the so-called unbanked population—those whose deposits are too small to be financially viable in conventional banking and whose borrowing cannot meet even minimum requirements of prudential banking. Informal financial institutions in the form of small unregistered savings pools, deposit takers, and micro-lenders are filling those needs throughout much of the region.[14]

Under these circumstances it is appropriate that, as a part of the SADC Finance and Investment Protocol, a committee of central bank governors was established, whose task it is among other things to develop the quality of and capacity for proper bank regulation and supervision, to revise banking levels, and to encourage central banks where necessary to withdraw themselves from private banking activity. In general, the aim is to build effective institutional frameworks for the financial system.[15]

Ghon Rhee shows that the integration of national capital markets into the international market consists of four stages, depending on the stage of development of the country.[16] First, markets are entirely closed and interest rates and exchange rates fully controlled. The second phase is a partially open market with unilateral capital flows—that is, inflows are encouraged but outflows severely restricted. Further development gives rise to a partially open market with multi-lateral capital flows, as both exchange controls are progressively eased and interest and exchange rates gradually decontrolled. The final phase is a fully open market. The southern

African economies fall into the second and third phases of this classification, with South Africa on the verge of the final phase. Such opening up encourages inward international investment and intra-regional investment, but may be a particularly sensitive point of potential conflict between national and regional interests, in respect of infection by other countries' mismanaged exchange or interest rates, as demonstrated by the long debate over the monetary integration of the EU, despite the fact that those economies were converging.[17]

Stock markets are less developed in Africa than in other LDCs (less developed countries) because economies are relatively small, capital markets are generally underdeveloped and dominated by bank-based finance, there tend to be wide-ranging government controls, and in recent years priority has been given to economic crises, stabilization, and structural adjustment.[18] There are stock markets in nine of the SADC countries: those in Botswana, Mauritius, Namibia, Swaziland, South Africa, and Zimbabwe have been established for varying periods. Zambia, Malawi, and Tanzania's stock markets opened recently. All of these except South Africa's are characterized by limited trading and low level of liquidity. However, the positive impact in recent years of policy reform, structural adjustment, and liberalization has been significant, resulting in market capitalization of the sub-Saharan African markets (excluding South Africa) rising from $5 billion in 1989 to $43 billion in 1996, although the ratio of market capitalization to GDP is still low in comparison with other emerging economies.[19]

Greater attention has been given to development of stock markets recently because of the increasing importance of the financial sector in economic development in the wake of the forces of globalization. Stock markets constitute a new source of finance for private corporate investment, encourage higher levels of savings, have an impact on institutional savers, attract inward portfolio investment, and very importantly are a vehicle for privatization. However, the small size of African stock markets suggests that their impact is likely to be limited in the near and medium term. Botswana and Zimbabwe have performed well in recent years but are considered to be insignificant in size and difficult to access.

The stock markets could become a focal point of integration in the region. Plans are in place to link the listing and financial requirements of the nine regional stock exchanges, to grant the smaller exchanges access to the sophisticated electronic systems of the Johannesburg Stock Exchange, and thus to attract global investors to share in the region's resources and growth prospects, and importantly allow for cross-border equity flows to underpin the growing intra-regional investment. Takirambudde[20] considers the stagnation in FDI (foreign direct investment) inflows into southern Africa, excluding South Africa, to be bleak enough that southern Africa "must look to its own resources and design an enabling environment for domestic capital mobilization, in particular an integrated capital market."[21] However, the removal of capital controls and alignment of regulations and fiscal system necessary for such integration would require considerable convergence and coordination of macro-economic policies, of which there is little evidence thus far.

Table 14.6. Inflation

	Average (% p.a.), 1990–94	1996	1997	1998
Angola	870	1,650	—	—
Botswana	13	10	9	9
DRC	6.3 bil.	659	176	—
Lesotho	14	10	9	—
Malawi	20	10	38	—
Mozambique	44	17	7	—
Namibia	12	8	9	—
South Africa	12	7	9	7
Swaziland	12	12	8	—
Tanzania	24	21	16	15
Zambia	130	43	25	24
Zimbabwe	27	22	19	30

Inflation

Inflation is one of the areas of convergence in the SADC. The rather wide divergences of the early 1990s (see Table 14.6) had narrowed somewhat by 1996, when seven of the members had inflation rates of less than 12 percent per annum The SACU countries were in line with the anti-inflationary monetary policy pursued by the South African policy-makers, and the rates in Mozambique and Tanzania seem set to continue falling. However, the former war zones of Angola and the DRC are still facing enormous price spirals, and Zambia and Zimbabwe are coping with the inflationary aftermath of massive currency depreciation and, in the case of the latter, inflationary fiscal policy. The variations in inflation will affect relative cost structures in the region and thus industrial diversification unless exchange rates fully compensate for the differentials.

Structural Adjustment Programs

There is a strong consensus about the need for structural adjustment in much of sub-Saharan Africa, and about the objectives of the programs instituted by the World Bank and IMF: the shorter-term restoration of macro-economic stability and longer-term structural adjustment via supply-side policies, export-led growth, and market deregulation so that prices fully reflect relative scarcities[22]. However, experience has shown, first, that weak implementation capacity has resulted in adjustment taking much longer than the five years originally anticipated for such programs, and second, that more account must be taken of social dimensions such as the impact on the poor and the delivery of basic social services.

Six SADC countries have SAPs in place—Lesotho, Malawi, Mozambique, Tanzania, Zambia, and Zimbabwe. South Africa's macro-economic policy framework constitutes in many respects a voluntary SAP. The downside, as far as regional integration is concerned, is that, as both Hope and Kayira and Mwanza[23] show, the results of the programs in these countries have been mixed to negative, especially in respect to growth. Even export-led growth depends on the prevailing weather and international commodity prices, and the development of manufactured exports may be hampered by de-industrialization in the wake of trade liberalization. There are consequent constraints on the development of strong regional demand and on the diversification of the manufacturing sector throughout the region.

The advantages of the SAPs are, first, potential convergence among countries with macro-economic indicators in line with SAP parameters, and second, increasing confidence of international investors in the face of policy reform.

Micro-economic Aspects

The micro-economic structure and trends in southern Africa reflect the region's rather uneven progress on the liberalization and deregulation fronts. State-owned enterprises have constituted a significant share of economic activity in Africa, where their share in GDP has averaged around 14 percent, compared with 11 percent for developing countries as a whole and 10 percent in Latin America. Similarly, by the early 1990s, parastatals accounted for over 20 percent of total employment, double the level of developing countries.[24] The globalization-driven emphasis on competitiveness, together with the demonstrably poor performance of the state-owned enterprises, has led recently to policies more attractive to the private sector.

In the Global Competitiveness Report,[25] South Africa ranked 44th and Zimbabwe 51st out of 53 countries. In the more recent African Competitiveness Report,[26] South Africa ranked 7th and Zimbabwe 20th out of 23 countries. Of the other SADC economies, Mauritius, Botswana, and Namibia ranked 1st, 3d, and 4th, respectively. Competitiveness is calculated as an average of six indices—openness, government, finance, labor, infrastructure, and institutions. More specifically, surveys of businesspeople, both national and potential international investors, indicate that taxes, corruption, and especially uncertainty about and changes in regulations are important barriers to investment and commerce. There are differences in the other barriers to trade in the region. In the less-developed SADC countries, infrastructures, availability of financing, and foreign currency regulations are considered problematic. In South Africa, these are of little or no account, but labor regulations are considered a significant hindrance.[27]

Trade and the Balance of Payments

Generally LDCs suffer from two gaps—the savings investment gap and the trade gap. The latter has been identified as a dominant constraint to growth in southern Africa.[28] The trade structures of the constituent economies of SADC are very sim-

Table 14.7. Foreign Trade and Balance of Payments

	Imports and Exports as % of GDP	Primary Exports as % of Total	Terms of Trade (1987 = 100)	Current Account Balance as % of GDP	Foreign Reserves: Months' Imports
Angola	132	95	86	–18	1
Botswana	101	98	152	+8	23
DRC	—	98	—	(1990) –7	1
Lesotho	138	—	—	+14	5
Malawi	69	76	87	–35	2
Mozambique	102	—	124	–31	3
Namibia	110	95	—	+2	1
South Africa	44	70	111	–2	2
Swaziland	154	—	—	–4	32
Tanzania	96	79	83	–12	2
Zambia	71	90	85	–12	2
Zimbabwe	74	56	84	–7	2

Note: Most of the data pertains to 1995, and after a short-lived improvement in 1996, most countries' current account positions have deteriorated.

ilar. Minerals, metals, or oil constitute the main exports in seven out of twelve countries, and agricultural products do the same in the other six countries. Manufactured exports from countries other than South Africa account for a small proportion of exports, and that in only three of the states. Consumer goods are the major import into Angola, Lesotho, Mozambique, Namibia, and Tanzania, and manufactured and capital goods feature largely in the import structure of all the countries. The main destination of exports for most of the countries is the developed industrial countries of Europe and the United States, with South Africa being an important market for the SACU countries and Malawi and Zimbabwe. South Africa features much more strongly as an origin of imports in nine of the SADC countries. Overall, intra-regional trade amounts to only 5 percent of the total external trade in the region; this proportion falls to 3 percent among non-SACU members.

The importance of external trade to the region is summed up in the fact that imports plus exports amount to 100 percent or more of GDP in eight of the countries, as indicated in Table 14.7; only in South Africa is the ratio less than 50 percent. However, the growth of exports in real terms has been very uneven across the region, and the majority of countries have suffered from declining terms of trade, with the result that, in spite of SAP-induced reductions in imports, substantial current account deficits and low levels of foreign exchange reserves render almost all the states (with the exception of Botswana) similarly vulnerable to balance of payments constraints and exogenous shocks.

The second defining characteristic of trade patterns in the region is the imbalance in trading relationships with the dominant South Africa. Of total SACU imports, only 2 percent originate in SADC countries, in spite of substantial year on year growth in such imports. In contrast, 11 percent of SACU exports go to SADC countries, as a result of even more substantial one-year growth. Thus exports to the SADC exceeded imports by about $2.5 billion in 1996. Since South Africa accounts for over 85 percent of the SACU imports and exports, by far the bulk of the trade surplus accrues to South Africa, which is a cause of tension within the region, particularly since, as noted below, capital flows are by no means compensating for the trade gap.

Maasdorp makes the point that there are three groups of countries within the SADC with respect to intra-regional trade.[29] The first is the SACU countries. The second consists of the five SADC members (Malawi, Mauritius, Tanzania, Zambia, and Zimbabwe) who are participating in the fourteen-country Cross-Border Initiative (CBI), which is fast tracking toward the elimination of tariffs on intra-regional trade and the harmonization of external tariffs. Angola and Mozambique are committed to trade liberalization under the World Trade Organization (WTO) and COMESA, but are not involved in any immediate moves toward free trade.

Todaro reaffirms the thinking that effective regional blocs can provide a buffer against the negative effects of globalization, while still permitting the dynamic effects of specialization and reduced inequalities.[30] The preconditions for successful integration are, however, relatively equal stages of industrial development, similar market sizes, and a regional rather than national orientation. With respect to the first two criteria, the SADC countries in fact fall into three tiers: South Africa (and SACU with it), Zimbabwe and Zambia, and the others. Proff makes the point that the patterns and compositions of intra-regional trade of the smaller SADC members are similar to their total trade, whereas South Africa's trade with the rest of the world is similar to that of a developed country.[31] This contributes significantly to the perception of South Africa as a hegemon rather than a partner in a region.[32] Proff follows Krugman in outlining the four-stage process in bringing about integration. The first is the political will toward integration; the second stage involves establishing the overall gains from trade to be expected; the third is concerned with the distribution of those gains among the partner countries; and the final stage is setting the agenda.

In the SADC, the political will extended to the drawing up of a trade protocol in 1996, which envisaged a free-trade area in the region by 2004. However, few of the member states have signed the protocol. Research indicates that the overall gains from trade arising from economic integration will enhance welfare in the region. Models of the distribution of gains from trade applied to the SADC indicate that regional integration between unequal partners tends to bias the distribution toward the more advanced partner, because the manufacturing sector is able to reap much greater benefits than the primary sectors, which would inhibit economic convergence. An extended theoretical framework suggests that the gains depend on the structure and competitiveness of the industrial sector in each participating country.[33] SADC countries, apart from South Africa, suffer from poor diversification of industrial activities. As discussed earlier, intra-regional trade is low; similar resource endowments and consequently reduced scope for specialization mean that the level of inter-industrial trade is low; and the level of intra-industrial trade is also low because the level of industrial development is low. The theory posits that the higher the intra-industrial trade, the more the smaller countries benefit from regional integration. Despite these potential tensions, Proff recommends that integration proceed because the mutual benefits certainly exist in the opening up of the South African market to smaller SADC members, in larger markets for South African manufactures, and in the start of a reduction in eco-migration. Carim concurs that South Africa's role in rehabilitating regional infrastructure and promoting balanced industrial development will counter the more obvious bias of benefits toward South Africa.[34]

Investment

According to Dr. Chris Stals, governor of the South African Reserve Bank: "The region of SADC is gradually becoming an attractive place for foreign investors. Its potential for economic development is vast, and undeveloped human resources and the exploding demand for goods and services emanating from people who are now being absorbed for the first time in a real market economy must lure many multi-national institutions to the southern Africa region. It depends on us (the central bankers) how attractive we can make our own region for the outside world as a place for long-term durable and productive investment."[35]

Dr. Stals's optimism is based on the future potential for the region, not historical trends. Net FDI inflows into all developing countries in 1996 were $109 billion. Of that, a mere $2.6 billion was directed to sub-Saharan Africa, and of that amount $1.2 billion ended up in the SADC region, compared with nearly $10 billion flowing into the major South American economies.[36] The recipient countries constituted a small number of the region's members: South Africa, Angola, and Tanzania received two-thirds of the SADC total. So the risk-reward balance in southern Africa as a whole did not compete with that in other emerging countries and regions (see Table 14.8).

It is generally agreed that the determinants of FDI flows are market growth, as measured by per capita GDP, the level of competitiveness of the economy, and the propensity to export, which reflects the degree of openness of the economy. FDI comes in two forms: (1) investment in a business to serve the local market, or (2) to set up an export business, based either on the country's natural resources or on manufacturing made globally competitive by location advantages such as low wages.[37] Factors that have inhibited investment in sub-Saharan Africa include civil strife, macro-economic instability, low growth and small domestic markets, inward orientation, slow progress on privatization, poor infrastructure, and high wages relative to productivity.[38]

Investment patterns in the region so far exhibit four trends. First, a large part of the investment flowing into the region has been connected with mining, but there is early evidence that some multi-nationals are looking at the potential of in-

Table 14.8. Foreign Debt and Foreign Direct Investment (FDI)

	External Debt, 1996 ($ bil.)	Debt as % of GNP, 1996	Debt as % of Total Exports	Inward FDI as % of GDI*, 1995
Angola	11.5	300	311	48
Botswana	0.6	16	20	5
DRC	13.1	250	1,300	—
Lesotho	0.6	45	400	4
Malawi	2.2	132	675	6
Mozambique	5.8	427	1,080	4
Namibia	0.4	12	30	7
South Africa	32.9	25	95	0.1
Swaziland	0.2	22	25	30
Tanzania	7.4	198	536	14
Zambia	7.1	196	539	19
Zimbabwe	5.0	82	160	3

*gross domestic investment

frastructural development in the SADC in the new millennium, in areas such as power, water, and transport. Second, a number of investors are making preliminary investments in South Africa with a view to expanding into the regional market. Third, investment in the manufacturing sector for purposes of export has been confined almost exclusively to South Africa, and to a narrow range of industries, notably motorcar components. This kind of investment is considered to be vital to the future development of the region.

The fourth trend is the dominance of South Africa in intra-regional flows. Most FDI flows from South Africa to other SADC states are the result of natural resource endowments rather than location efficiency, and are thus not contributing materially to the restructuring of economic activity toward manufacturing. The largest non-mining investors are retailers and banks. Furthermore, of the total South African FDI stock in SADC in 1996, over 90 percent was in the SACU countries whose links have been long established.[39] The situation is exacerbated by a perception that a number of the SADC states encourage inward investment only if it does not compete with established domestic corporate interests. However, there is pressure on South Africa to increase cross-border investment to balance the trade surpluses that it runs with the other member states.

The factors that support Dr. Stals's optimism noted earlier are that investor-friendly reforms have been under way for a while, in the wake of the SAPs, in the form of lower trade barriers, removal of price controls, fiscal discipline, lower inflation, liberalization of financial markets, and infrastructural development. Against these positive and far-reaching changes must be set the negative images of corruption and civil war in a few of the states. Investment incentive schemes exist piecemeal in a few of the states, and there are EPZs (export processing zones) in Namibia and Zimbabwe, and industrial free zones in Mozambique; there is not yet a region-wide program to promote investment.[40] Further, the view has been expressed that the money required for incentive schemes would be more constructively spent on worker training and infrastructure, to minimize the enclave effects and maximize the trickle-down effects of such investment.[41]

In summary, the region is more attractive than individual countries, and thus investment issues are likely to be the source of more cooperation than conflict, particularly in respect to the cross-border infrastructural projects. However, perceptions of risk differentials among the member countries will remain until integration is much further advanced, and consequently the distribution of FDI may not change materially for a while.

Employment

The very youthful population noted in the section on demography results in high dependency ratios—the number of non-working children plus the aged versus the economically active population. In sub-Saharan African countries, only about half the population falls into the potential labor force age group of 15–64 years, in contrast to the 66 percent characteristic of developed countries and even the 60 percent found in other developing countries. Labor force participation rates are even lower in those countries where not all the women work and where tertiary education is available (see Table 14.9). The average participation rate in southern Africa is about 45 percent. Three important factors affect employment in the region. First, in seven of the twelve countries an average of 78 percent of the population is engaged in agriculture, an indicator of the level of development, the dependency on primary production, and the immediately accessible skill level of the workforce. In the other five countries—Botswana, Lesotho, Namibia, South Africa, and Zambia (again, largely SACU countries)—the average is 29 percent, corresponding to more developed manufacturing and service sectors. Productivity levels vary accordingly. Unger notes that the average worker in the world produces over $10,000 of GDP per annum, almost four time the $2600 produced in southern Africa.[42] The range within that average will reflect both the 29–78 percent gap just noted and the differential levels of education and training.

Second, the growth in the labor force between 1990 and 1995 in the region averages 2.5 percent per annum, with a relatively low variation, between 2.2 and 2.9 percent. Thus each of the member states faces unremitting pressure to create jobs, in order (a) to alleviate poverty, since fiscal redistribution is limited as discussed above, (b) to contribute to the greatly needed growth of the economy, and (c) to increase the quantity and quality of human capital, the resource in shortest supply in the countries concerned.

The existing economic structure of the majority of the members, in particular the relative lack of export-oriented manufacturing industry, inhibits the job-creating capacity of the economy. Not only has the growth in the labor supply exceeded the growth in formal sector employment, but formal sector employment has actually declined in most countries since the 1980s, and several studies have shown that

Table 14.9. Employment and Potential Skills Structure

	Labor Force as % of Pop., 1995	Labor Force Growth Rate (% p.a.), 1990–95	Employment by Sector, 1995			Combined 1st-, 2d-, 3d-Level Gross Enrollment Ratio (%), 1997	Adult Literacy, 1997
			Agriculture	Industry	Services		
Angola	45	2.8	73	10	17	27	45
Botswana	33	2.5	28	11	61	70	74
DRC	37	—	71	13	16	39	77
Lesotho	50	2.3	23	33	44	58	82
Malawi	50	2.5	87	5	8	75	58
Mozambique	50	2.4	85	7	8	25	41
Namibia	50	2.5	43	22	35	82	80
South Africa	39	2.4	13	25	62	93	84
Swaziland	—	—	74	9	17	73	77
Tanzania	50	2.9	85	5	10	33	72
Zambia	44	2.8	38	8	54	49	75
Zimbabwe	45	2.2	71	8	21	78	91

real wages in the non-agricultural sector have been falling for years. The informal sector, discussed in the section on GDP and growth above, has expanded enormously in response to the lack of formal jobs and lack of state-supplied material welfare. The informal sector now absorbs a large part of the labor force in southern Africa—80 percent of the urban workers in Zambia, 50 percent in Tanzania, and even in South Africa it accounts for perhaps 20 percent of the economically active population.[43] The role of the informal sector as a labor sponge is crucial throughout the region, but there are questions about its ability to contribute to future per capita income growth to well above survival levels, and to the skills base of the country and the region.

Third, the education levels of the existing labor force are low throughout the region. The mean period of schooling achieved by the population over twenty-five years of age in the early 1990s ranged between 1.5 and 4 years. The situation is changing, with gross enrollment in 1997 averaging 75 percent of the applicable population in the SACU countries, 78 percent in Zimbabwe, but only 41 percent in the other six, as shown in Table 14.9. Literacy levels reflect the education structures. Given the restricted opportunity for formal skill acquisition, the need for on-the-job training and experience is even greater, and such skill acquisition depends on employment opportunities.[44]

Therein lies the problem for regional integration. Unemployment in all the member states is difficult to measure, but is estimated to be at least 30 percent, often ranging up to 50 percent or more. Almost all the unemployment is of a structural nature, arising from the imbalance between the requirements of an industrializing economy in a highly competitive world environment and the skill levels of the workforce. Given the imperative to create jobs, noted above, governments of individual countries find it very difficult to put regional priorities ahead of domestic needs when jobs are at stake. A clear example of this dilemma is the textile and clothing industries. Regionally, Zimbabwe has a comparative advantage in textile production, while South Africa has a comparative advantage in more sophisticated manufacturing industries. However, there is enormous resistance from trade unions and employers in the textile industry in South Africa to the regionally rational policy option to allow Zimbabwean textiles free access to South African markets. The industry employs about 250,000 people in South Africa, where the unemployment rate of around 30 percent is causing significant socio-political problems. This is the same underlying reason for the reluctance to allow foreign companies in to compete with domestic companies, as noted in the section on investment. Similarly, the need to employ and upgrade local workers at all levels gives rise to affirmative action programs, and to resistance to the expatriate employee arrangements that often accompany inward FDI. This is as true of intra-regional labor movements as of inward flows from outside the region.

The more developed labor markets in the region tend to be inflexible, as a result of redistributive government policies giving rise to minimum wage levels or strong union pressure. Additionally, as Sachs and Warner have shown, economies abundantly endowed with natural resources, particularly minerals, tend to have higher labor costs per unit of output than those with few or no such resources, notably in Asia.[45] The result of these developments is that in the more industrialized states in the region, especially South Africa and Zimbabwe, relatively high labor costs have led to mechanization and automation, thus reducing the labor-absorbing capacity of the economy. Downsizing and re-engineering in the wake of the drive toward global competitiveness and of SAPs have led to retrenchments even of those who are employed in the formal sector.

Intra-regional tensions are heightened by the fact that formal sector wages are lower in several southern African countries than in South Africa, reflecting in part the lower productivity in the former, and working conditions are considerably inferior. Trade unions in South Africa are concerned that regional integration will allow companies to locate production elsewhere in the region and thus bring about lower wages and working conditions in South Africa. For example, the minimum wage in the mining sector in South Africa is nearly four times the comparable wage in Zimbabwe.

Although rates of unemployment are high throughout the region, they are by no means uniform, as illustrated by the patterns of migration noted earlier: migrants move from areas of higher unemployment to those perceived to supply more jobs. In general, unemployment is below 40 percent in the recipient states and above 50 percent in the supplier states. Low economic growth and the corresponding poor prospect of any mitigation of the job crisis induce large numbers of migrants to move into the relatively richer countries, particularly South Africa in spite of the absolute level of unemployment there.[46] Proff suggests that integration would benefit all members of the SADC. He quotes the example of NAFTA, noting that only by developing Mexico could the United States reduce the illegal immigration of Mexico's poor. It should be remembered, however, that the United States could command resources surplus to its domestic requirements, which South Africa cannot.

High rates of unemployment may seem to be alleviated by the spread of AIDS in the region. However, the loss of scarce skilled workers and the sheer costs of AIDS in the workplace will outweigh any potential benefits of reduced numbers.

In summary, the issues are as follows: Are the economic structures different enough to provide the full range of employment opportunities across the region, and are the labor forces mobile enough to respond to regional differences? Will regionalism solve the enormous problems of employment and underemployment more effectively than the individual countries will? The answers have to be yes, but as with the gains from trade, the distribution of jobs will be unequal, at least in the short to medium term.

Part B: Strategic Analysis

The countries of the SADC region are characterized by similar policy dilemmas. Each has to balance the prevailing global ideology as manifest in the Washington

Consensus with domestic development and restructuring; there are marked, if not extreme, inequalities and disparities at every level of society; each country has to overcome the distortions induced by the colonial or apartheid past; in most of these countries, political democracy has occurred ahead of economic democracy, which gives rise to very different relationships between the government, business, and labor sectors than were evident in the Asian economies, for example. All these factors can be subsumed into the widespread debate within the region about economic growth versus redistribution of income and wealth, or competitive production efficiency versus equity in employment and social services. The ensuing policy conflicts in individual countries and in the region as a whole impinge strongly on the strategic choices to be made by the member states.

Implications of the Gap between Vision and Reality

The substantial gap between the vision and the reality of the SADC—or any other form of southern African regional integration—means that member nations still have a choice: to persevere with integration or to opt out. Unlike the EU, where so much has already been invested in the process of integration, thus precluding any reversal, SADC still consists more of words and rhetoric than resources.[47]

If the SADC is at a crossroads in its development, it is as well to revisit briefly those forces encouraging economic integration, and those hindering it. The overriding reason for integration is the small size of the constituent economies. Economic union at any level will open up opportunities for economies of scale, increased efficiency of production, improved terms-of-trade, enhanced integration into growth-generation world trade, and increased attraction for inward foreign direct investment with its concomitant technology. Overall, integration should result in faster growth, higher standards of living, reduced inequalities, and a buffer against the negative effects of globalization. There is a general consensus among economists that the economic gains for the region as a whole are unequivocal, and among socio-political commentators that the consequence of not integrating would be downward spiral into increasing regional conflict.

However, the distribution of gains among individual members is a far more complex issue. In broad summary, theory and experience elsewhere indicate that although all members ultimately will be better off in the union than on their own, the gains will accrue disproportionately to the most advanced members. The existing hindrances to integration include gross inequalities in economic and human resources development among members; vertical integration into the northern developed economies via the primary export–manufactured import structure; national interests overriding regional interests, particularly in respect to political fragility, which undermines any confidence in ceding sovereignty to the regional authority; and heavy reliance on tariff revenues. Therefore, "it becomes logical for member states to keep the process at the level of triumphalist rhetoric, while underneath doing everything possible to undermine it."[48]

Methods of Closing the Gap

The economic imperatives of globalization and possible upsurge in protectionism in the wake of the world market turmoil of mid-1998 may result in economic priorities taking precedence over socio-political concerns in the region, in which case the SADC may move ahead with renewed determination. Future success will depend on a number of factors, among which are the following:

All members perceive that they will gain from the arrangement.

There are means to counter the concentration of manufacturing production in the most advanced country.

The economic systems, with regard to the role of the market, are broadly aligned.

A regional mindset is developed, perhaps as part of the African Renaissance.

The regional institutions are restructured in such a way that the regional authority has substantive leadership and real power to make governments implement regional policies; that is, the governments are prepared to cede enough national sovereignty to the supra-national body.

Priorities must be agreed upon and explicitly stated, first in respect to the balance between the security aspects of the region and the economic aspects, as the scarce resources of the region do not permit the two to be pursued simultaneously. Second, the common vision should be articulated in measurable terms, as in, for example, the Malaysian 2020 long-term plan. This will enable negotiators to anticipate trade-offs and begin to seek win-win solutions, in order to avoid crisis management. Part of the vision would be the stages of the integration, moving from, say, sectoral cooperation (in respect to energy, water, transport and communications, finance), through functional integration of labor markets and capital markets to facilitate industrial diversification, and finally into fully free trade. It is the business sector that actually conducts intra-regional trade, and it can do so effectively only if telephones work, if business travel is not hampered by visa and residence permit problems, and if delivery vehicles pass quickly and without bureaucratic hindrance through border posts.

The potential difficulties in the choice between the ordering of trade and multisectoral linkages and the resultant gains for individual members are the subject of several analyses.

Mayer and Thomas summarize the situation and pose an important question as follows:

> the critical constraint to intra-regional trade is structural: the lack of diversification in all SADC countries except South Africa and Zimbabwe, and the concomitant lack of complementarity in their productive base. While the prevailing trade imbalances in the region may be somewhat diminished by demand side measures in the form of intra-regional tariff liberalization—in particular enhanced access to South Africa's market—the structural problems underpinning these inequities

will only be removed if the region collectively endeavors to foster industrial development. The critical issue is whether the trade protocol is an adequate instrument to bring about structural change.[49]

Mayer and Thomas's own answer to the question is that it is the diversification and development of industrial capabilities that will influence trade patterns, not the reverse, and that this will best be achieved by strengthening multi-sectoral linkages. Kritzinger van Niekerk concurs, stating that emphasis on sectoral cooperation is a precondition for trade integration because it will reduce unsustainable trade balances.[50]

Jenkins argues that considerable research worldwide concludes that there is an unambiguous relationship between openness to trade and higher rates of economic growth.[51] Regional trade liberalization enables members to take advantage of the gains from trade in larger markets while limiting exposure to non-regional competition. There is evidence that the poorer members of the region are then able to catch up or converge with the richer members. This has been true of the SACU members and points to the potential for the SADC once the free-trade protocol is ratified and takes hold in the region. Jenkins considers a number of gains to the smaller members and concludes that open trade within the region will lead to industrial development and diversification. In the short term, the trade gains for South Africa will exceed those for the other countries, but the other countries can still expect to grow more rapidly because of higher levels of investment and exports. However, Jenkins expands the argument to show that convergence may limit the growth of the richest member of the group, and it is in the interests of all in the SADC for South Africa to grow as fast as possible. Thus South Africa should be as accommodating as possible in allowing access to its markets, and it should retain the ability to negotiate in its own interests with third parties, such as the EU. In this way, South Africa will not be limited by the smallness and lack of diversity in production of its neighbors.

Choices Facing SADC Members

1. Other members need South Africa as the lead goose and the major market for their non-primary goods. However, they are in danger of being overwhelmed by South Africa hegemony. They must be satisfied that, even if South Africa gains proportionately more, they will still be better off than they would otherwise have been.
2. South Africa's growth may be hindered by regional considerations, because it will have to carry a disproportionate share of the burden of providing resources for the region's development. However, the South African stance is also influenced by the fact that economically and political stable neighbors are of far greater benefit than the reverse, and that there already exist strong regional links in the supply and distribution of water and energy. Further, foreign investors are applying pressure on South Africa to play a leading role in the region.

SOURCES FOR STATISTICS

The volatility of economic circumstances in southern Africa results in the statistics varying quite significantly among sources, for reasons relating largely to differing time periods and different dollar conversion rates, where applicable. The tables represent the authors' combination of attainable levels of consistency, reliability, and timeliness of data.

The authors have drawn on a wide range of sources, including the following:

1. *Africa at a Glance 1997/98.* Africa Institute, Pretoria, 1998.
2. *World Development Report 1997.* The World Bank, Oxford University Press, 1997.
3. *Human Development Report 1997.* United Nations Development Programme, Oxford University Press, 1998.
4. *Human Development Report 1999.* United Nations Development Programme, Oxford University Press, 1999.
5. *World Investment Report 1997.* United Nations, 1997.
6. *The Africa Competitiveness Report.* World Economic Forum, Geneva, 1998.
7. *IMF International Financial Statistics.* International Monetary Fund, various issues.
8. Jenkins and Thomas (see n. 6).
9. *African Quarterly.* Standard Chartered Bank, various issues.
10. *Quarterly Bulletin.* South African Reserve Bank, various issues.
11. *Quarterly Review.* LSE Centre for Research into Economics and Finance in Southern Africa (CREFSA).
12. Local media: daily, weekly, and monthly newspapers, financial magazines and journals.

NOTES

1. E. Leistner, "Regional Cooperation in Sub-Saharan Africa, With Special Reference to Southern Africa," *Africa Insight* 27, no. 2 (1997): 112–23.

2. The flying geese model was originated in Japan and refers to a process of regional economic integration where several groups of countries followed each other through stages of economic development. The lead goose constantly develops new industries and passes on to the next tier of countries those industries in which in which it has lost comparative advantage in the wake of changing labor costs and productivity. UNCTAD, *World Investment Report 1997* (New York: United Nations, 1997).

3. Leistner, "Regional Cooperation." R. Davies, "South Africa and Southern Africa" in A. Handley and G. Mills, eds., *South Africa and Southern Africa: Regional Integration and Emerging Markets* (Johannesburg: South African Institute of International Affairs, 1998).

4. Not that all analysis and comment in this chapter refers to continental southern Africa; that is, it excludes the Indian Ocean islands of Mauritius and Seychelles, on the grounds that they, especially Mauritius, are very different from the other SADC economies in history and structure, and that the economies are so small that their omission does not materially alter the results of the analysis.

5. DFA, opening address delivered by the Director General of the South Africa Department of Foreign Affairs at a SADC workshop for academics (Foreign Service Institute, Pretoria, January 1997, mimeograph), pp.1–2.

6. C. Jenkins and L. Thomas, *Is Southern Africa Ready for Regional Monetary Integration? Convergence, Divergence and Macroeconomic Policy in SADC*, Research Paper, no. 10 (London: Centre for Research into Economics and Finance in Southern Africa, London School of Economics, 1997).

7. Notably the Maputo Corridor linking South Africa's industrial heartland with Maputo on the Mozambique coast, the Trans-Kalahari Highway from Botswana to the Namibian coast, the Cahora Bassa hydro-electric scheme between South Africa and Mozambique, and the Lesotho Highlands Water Scheme making water available to the industrial center of Gauteng in South Africa.

8. United Nations Development Programme, *Human Development Report 1997* (New York: Oxford University Press, 1997).

9. D. Pilling, "Battle Against AIDS Not Nearly Won," *Business Day* (Johannesburg), 9 July 1998.

10. "AIDS: Time Is Running Out," *Mail and Guardian* (Johannesburg), 30 May 1998.

11. O. Saasa, "Migration and the Brain Drain," in G. Maasdorp, ed., *Can South and Southern Africa Become Globally Competitive Economies?* (London: Macmillan, 1996), pp. 61–66.

12. W. B. Wood, "Forced Migration: Local Conflicts and International Dilemmas," *Annals of the Association of American Geographers* 84 (1994): 607–34, quoted in B. Maharaj and R. Rajkumar, "The 'Alien Invasion' in South Africa: Illegal Immigrants in Durban," *Development Southern Africa* 14, no. 2 (1997): 255–73.

13. M. Siddiqui, "Banking in Africa," *African Business,* October 1997, pp. 8–14.

14. A. Gillingham, "Banking in Southern Africa," *Business Day,* suppl. August 1996.

15. C. Stals, "The Role of Financial Cooperation in the Development of the Southern African Development Community," *South African Reserve Bank Quarterly Bulletin* 204 (June 1997): 35–38.

16. S. Ghon Rhee, "Internationalism of Capital Markets," in Maasdorp, ed., *Can South and Southern Africa,* pp. 137–47.

17. Jenkins and Thomas, *Is Southern Africa Ready?*

18. K. R. Jefferis, "The Development of Stock Markets in Sub-Saharan Africa," *South African Journal of Economics* 63, no. 3 (1995): 346–63.

19. M. Siddiqi, "The Birth of a New Star?" *African Business,* June 1998, pp. 28–31.

20. P. Takirambudde, "Financial, Corporate and Tax Harmonization for Capital Market Development in Southern Africa," *Development in Southern Africa* 12, no. 3 (1995): 379–400.

21. Ibid., p. 384

22. World Bank, *Adjustment in Africa* (New York: Oxford University Press, 1994). World Bank, *Africa's Experience with Structural Adjustment,* World Bank Discussion Paper, no. 288 (Washington, D.C.: World Bank, 1995). P. Strydom and F. Fiser, "Structural Adjustment Programmes," *Development in Southern Africa* 12, no. 3 (1995): 321–32. K. R. Hope and G. Kayira, "Developmental Policies in Southern Africa: The Impact of Structural Adjustment Programmes," *The South African Journal of Economics* 65, no. 2 (1997): 258–74.

23. A. Mwanza, "Structural Adjustment Programmes: Theory and Reality," *Southern African Political and Economic Monitor* 11, no. 4 (1998): 21–24.

24. World Bank, *Bureaucrats in Business-Summary* (Washington, D.C.: World Bank, 1995), pp. 9–10.

25. World Economic Forum, *The Global Competitiveness Report 1997* (Geneva: World Economic Forum, 1997).

26. World Economic Forum, *The Africa Competitiveness Report 1998* (Geneva: World Economic Forum, 1998).

27. M. Kaunda and K. Miti, "Promotion of Private Enterprise and Citizen Entrepreneurship in Botswana," *Development in Southern Africa* 12, no. 3 (1995): 367–78. D. Davies, "Blows to Trade Flows," *Business in Africa,* June/July 1998, pp.15–17.

28. S. Mainardi, "Southern Africa in a Comparative Context: Development Pattern and Growth Constraints," *The South African Journal of Economics,* 62, no. 2 (1994): 107–22.

29. G. Maasdorp, "Can Regional Integration Help Southern Africa?" in Maasdorp, ed., *Can South and Southern Africa,* pp. 45–52.

30. M. P. Todaro, *Economic Development,* 6th ed. (London: Longman, 1997).

31. H. V. Proff, "Distributions of Gains from Trade in an Unequal Environment: Gains from Trade in the SADC," *The South African Journal of Economics* 65, no. 4 (1997): 482–99.

32. F. Ahwireng-Obeng and P. McGowan, "Partner or Hegemon? South Africa in Africa," *Journal of Contemporary African Studies* 16, no. 1 (1998): 5–38.

33. Proff, "Distributions of Gains."

34. X. Carim, "Multilateral Trading, Regional Integration and the Southern African Development Community," *The South African Journal of Economics,* 65, no. 3 (1997): 334–53.

35. Stals, "Role of Financial Cooperation."

36. F. Hu, "FDI and Market Growth" in World Economic Forum, *The Global Competitiveness Report 1997,* p. 29.

37. H. Shatz, "What Attracts FDI?" in World Economic Forum, *The Global Competitiveness Report 1997.*

38. A. Bhattacharya, P. J. Montiel, and S. Sharma, "How Can Sub-Saharan Africa Attract More Private Capital Inflows?" *Finance Africa,* November/December 1997, pp. 12–14.

39. UNCTAD, *World Investment Report 1997.*

40. L. Sachikonye, "Rethinking about Labour Markets and Migration in Southern Africa," *Southern African Political and Economic Monitor* 11, no. 4 (February 1998): 11–20.

41. R. Jamie, "Future Imperfect," *South,* November 1997, pp. 21–23.

42. M. Unger, "Effective Investment and Competitiveness," in Maasdorp, ed., *Can South and Southern Africa,* pp. 172–81 .

43. K. R. Hope and G. Kayira, "The Economic Crisis in Southern Africa: Some Perspective on Its Origin and Nature," *Development Southern Africa* 13, no. 6 (1996): 881–94.

44. T. Godana, "Returns to Education in the Manufacturing Sector in Zimbabwe: Some Empirical Evidence," *The South African Journal of Economics* 65, no. 1 (1997): 99–113.

45. J. D. Sachs and M. Warner, "Natural Resources and Economic Growth," Development Discussion Paper 517a (Cambridge, Mass.: Harvard Institute for International Development, 1995).

46. L. Sachikonye, "Rethinking about Labour Markets."

47. Political tensions regarding military intervention in the renewed civil war in the DRC at the time of writing have exposed to an even greater extent the fragility of the region's apparent unity. Some analysts considered that the Mauritius summit in September 1998 "could determine whether the SADC evolves into a prosperous and harmonious economic community or degenerates into a club of squabbling military adventurers" (P. Fabricius, *Sunday Independent* [Johannesburg], 13 September 1998, p.1). The subsequent actions and reactions of various SADC members to the war in the DRC and the more recent renewal of hostilities in Angola has taken the community midway between the two extremes, with members disagreeing about the appropriate stance, but avoiding interference in each other's decisions, except for attempts at peace-mongering.

48. F. Goncalves, "Is SADC Ready?" *Southern African Economist*, February 1998, p. 7.

49. M. J. Mayer and R. H. Thomas, "Trade Integration in the Southern African Development Community: Prospects and Problems," *Development in Southern Africa* 14, no. 3 (1997): 327–54.

50. L. Kritzinger van Niekerk, "Towards Strengthening Multisectoral Linkages in SADC" (Development Bank of Southern Africa, 1997, mimeograph).

51. C. Jenkins, "Regional Integration Is Not Enough," *Quarterly Review* (LSE CREFSA), April 1997, pp. 15–21.

15. Compendium of Data for the Quantitative Analysis of Southern Africa

Liezell Bradshaw

Studies of Africa have not been known for their quantitative focus. In the past, scholars typically offered one (or more) of the following explanations for this fact: lack of data on Africa, inadequate statistical training for Africanists, poor computer equipment across Africa, and a general "suspicion" of the utility of quantitative research. Although most research on Africa remains "qualitative," a growing number of studies use statistical methods. Some studies use multivariate statistical techniques to test data for a large sample of African countries; some use time-series analysis to test annual data for a single country and, in rare cases, more than one country; and some use quantitative analysis to test data collected through surveys or questionnaires.[1] There is a new generation of Africanists who comfortably use statistical methods in their research on African development.[2]

The purpose of this chapter is to provide a compendium of data for southern Africa in order to facilitate more quantitative research on the region. Along with presenting the data, I offer brief examples about how the data have been used in quantitative research on Africa and other regions (not just southern Africa). Even if researchers are not quantitatively oriented, however, they will still benefit from the descriptive data on southern Africa. I include only the most recent year for each variable. If researchers need time-series data, they can trace the data source and collect data for the years required.

Data in Table 15.1 clearly underscore the inequality in development across southern Africa. The single best indicator of quality of life, argues UNICEF, is the under-five mortality rate.[3] Three southern African countries—Angola, Malawi, and Mozambique—exhibit some of the highest rates in the world, exceeding 200 deaths before age five per 1,000 births. Zambia is not far behind. Poverty, disease, and the HIV/AIDS situation are to blame for the dismal statistics. In fact, the AIDS emergency is partly responsible for a current life expectancy in southern Africa that, in

394

Table 15.1. Quality of Life

Country	Mortality Rates		Life Expectancy at Birth (Yrs), 1997	Child Malnutrition % of Children 1992–97	AIDS Orphans No. of Children Under Age 5 per 10,000 1994–97
	Under 5 Per 1,000 Live Births, 1997	Maternal Per 100,000 Live Births, 1990–97			
Angola	209	1,500	47	35	30
Botswana	88	250	47	27	390
Malawi	224	620	43	30	580
Mozambique	201	1,100	46	26	180
Namibia	101	220	56	26	110
South Africa	65	230	65	9	110
Zambia	189	650	43	24	890
Zimbabwe	108	280	53	16	700

Source: World Bank, *World Development Report 1999/2000* (Washington, D.C.: World Bank), 1999; UNICEF, *The State of the World's Children, 1999* (New York: UNICEF, 1999); UNICEF, *The Progress of Nations, 1999* (New York: UNICEF, 1999).

some cases, is lower than its 1980 levels. Zambia's life expectancy is now only 43; in 1980, it was 50.[4] Another startling reminder of the AIDS crisis is displayed in the table, where we see the number of children (under age fifteen) orphaned by AIDS. Developed countries have fewer than 1 child out of every 10,000 orphaned by this disease. By contrast, southern African countries have among the highest rates in the world: Zambia, Zimbabwe, and Malawi are among the world leaders in this category. An incredible 9 percent of all children in Zambia are AIDS orphans, and the numbers continue to increase.[5]

A number of quantitative studies have utilized cross-national data to test the global determinants of child/infant mortality and other indicators of quality of life.[6] Some studies use regional samples of Africa and others focus exclusively on specific African countries.[7] One of the most interesting quantitative studies of AIDS has been completed by Njeri Mbugua in a recently completed Ph.D. dissertation. She administered detailed surveys to more than 500 Kenyan schoolgirls and utilized the data to examine their knowledge of HIV/AIDS and their behaviors in light of this knowledge. There will be more statistical studies of quality of life in Africa given the growth in new data related to this topic.

The figures in Table 15.2 continue to underscore the inequality across southern Africa with respect to development indicators. High rates of fertility and low rates of contraception are still the rule across the region. Moreover, there are relatively high rates of urbanization in some southern African countries—the most urbanized part of Africa. Two-thirds of the population of Botswana lives in urban areas, while half of the South African population and nearly half of the Zambian reside in cities.

Starting in the early 1980s, there have been a fairly large number of quantita-

Table 15.2. Population and Urbanization

Country	Total Population (in Mill.), 1998	Fertility Rate — Births per Woman, 1997	Contraceptive Rate — % of Women Aged 15–49, 1990–98	Urban Population — % of Total Population, 1997	Access to Sanitation in Urban Areas — % of Urban Population, 1995
Angola	12.0	6.8	1	33	71
Botswana	1.6	4.3	33	68	91
Malawi	10.5	6.4	22	15	94
Mozambique	16.9	5.3	6	38	68
Namibia	1.7	4.9	29	39	77
South Africa	41.3	2.8	69	50	78
Zambia	9.7	5.6	26	44	66
Zimbabwe	11.7	3.8	48	34	96

Source: World Bank, *World Development Report, 1999/2000* (Washington, D.C.: World Bank, 1999); UNICEF, *The State of the World's Children, 1999* (New York: UNICEF, 1999).

tive, cross-national studies of the impact of urbanization (and "over-urbanization") on development.[8] The most recent study, authored by Bradshaw and Schafer,[9] examines the causes and effects of over-urbanization in different regions, including Africa. Other authors have utilized detailed survey data to complete individual-country studies of urbanization, such as Zamberia, who examined the provision of water and sanitation in an urban slum in Kenya.[10]

Investing in education, especially girls' education, is probably the best investment a developing country can undertake.[11] Scholars have utilized quantitative data to examine a wide range of education concerns in Africa and beyond (see Table 15.3). Most recently, Schafer used cross-national data (with a regional look at Africa) to show that international non-governmental institutions have enhanced education in developing regions.[12] Buchmann also used cross-national data to demonstrate that the international debt crisis has particularly harmful effects on female enrollment.[13] Statistical studies of individual countries have also been instructive. Fuller, Liang, and Hua used detailed household data from South Africa to show that, although enrollment rates increased substantially following the Soweto uprising in 1976, black literacy increased only slightly.[14] Fuller, Singer, and Keiley used household data to investigate why daughters leave school in southern Africa.[15] Bradshaw and Fuller used time-series data from Kenya to show that the Kenyan state was highly effective at increasing enrollments, but not effective in enhancing educational quality.[16] And Buchmann used survey data from Kenya to examine the determinants of whether girls receive schooling at the same rate as boys (they do not).[17]

Table 15.3. Education

Country	Public Expenditure on Education % of GNP, 1996	Net Enrollment Ratio % of Relevant Age Group Primary, 1996	Secondary, 1996	% of Cohort Reaching Grade 5, 1996	% of Adults Literate, 1996
Angola	—	—	—	34	42
Botswana	10.4	81	45	90	79
Malawi	5.5	68	6	94	56
Mozambique	—	40	6	46	40
Namibia	9.1	91	36	76	76
South Africa	7.9	96	51	76	82
Zambia	2.2	75	17	—	78
Zimbabwe	8.3	91	47	90	85

Source: World Bank, *World Development Report, 1999/2000* (Washington, D.C.: World Bank, 1999); UNICEF, The State of the World's Children, 1999 (New York: UNICEF, 1999); supplemented by UNICEF studies of individual countries.

Table 15.4. Size and Structure of the Economy

Country	Gross National Product $ bil., 1998	Rank in World, 1998	GNP per Capita $, 1998	Rank in World, 1998	% of Gross Domestic Product Agriculture 1998	Industry 1998	Services 1998
Angola	4.1	121	340	178	14	54	32
Botswana	5.6	107	3,600	82	4	46	51
Malawi	2.1	144	200	202	39	19	41
Mozambique	3.6	130	210	199	34	18	48
Namibia	3.2	131	1,940	106	10	34	56
South Africa	119.0	32	2,880	92	4	38	57
Zambia	3.2	132	330	180	16	30	55
Zimbabwe	7.1	99	610	156	18	24	58

Source: World Bank, *World Development Report, 1999/2000* (Washington, D.C.: World Bank, 1999).

Africa's economic woes are underscored by data in Table 15.4. Although Namibia, Botswana, and South Africa have appreciably higher GNP per capita levels than the rest of southern Africa (and, indeed, all of sub-Saharan Africa), these levels are still low from a global perspective. Botswana, the wealthiest southern African country, has a GNP per capita that places it only 82nd in the world. I discuss quantitative studies of economic growth and development after the next table.

There are three interesting and important points about the data in Table 15.5. First, the region continues to receive relatively little foreign investment. Second,

Table 15.5. Aid and Financial Flows

Country	Foreign Direct Investment $ mil., 1997	External Debt $ mil., 1997	External Debt % of GNP, 1997	Official Development Assistance $ per Capita, 1997	Official Development Assistance % of GNP, 1997
Angola	350	10,160	206	37	10.2
Botswana	100	562	9	81	2.4
Malawi	2	2,206	45	34	13.7
Mozambique	35	5,991	135	58	29.6
Namibia	137	-	-	102	5.0
South Africa	1,725	25,222	19	12	0.4
Zambia	70	6,758	136	65	16.7
Zimbabwe	70	4,961	52	29	4.1

Source: World Bank, *World Development Report, 1999/2000* (Washington, D.C.: World Bank, 1999).

southern Africa—like the rest of Africa—is heavily indebted. Three countries—Angola, Mozambique, and Zambia—have an external debt that is much more than 100 percent of their entire GNP. And third, the region continues to receive little development assistance, especially considering its underdeveloped and indebted status. In fact, the entire continent of Africa receives only about 12 percent of all U.S. non-military foreign assistance.[18]

There is an extensive quantitative literature dealing with the impact of foreign investment and aid, as well as external debt. A number of quantitative, cross-national studies have examined the effect of foreign investment on quality of life.[19] Recently, however, other scholars have argued that a "new dependency" is created by growing external debt and the accompanying structural adjustment policies mandated by the International Monetary Fund (IMF).[20] As noted by Ramphal, "For nearly two decades, the debt crisis has had a crippling impact on some of the world's poorest countries, hobbling economic growth and draining scarce resources from health, education and other vital services. Can the campaign for debt relief be translated into effective action, ensuring that children of the new millennium are freed from the chains of debt and poverty?"[21]

The economic gap between rich and poor countries is substantial. The technological gap is enormous (see Table 15.6). South Africa, the most technologically advanced country in Africa, has 41.6 personal computers for every 1,000 people and 34.7 Internet hosts for every 10,000 people. This is above the numbers for the average middle-income country, which has rates of 32.4 and 10.15, respectively.[22] Still, South Africa's numbers are far below those of the average upper-income country, which has rates of 269.4 and 470.12, respectively. Without more personal computers and Internet hosts, Southern Africa will continue to fall further behind in education, business, health, and other sectors.

Table 15.6. Communication and Technology

Country	Per 1,000 people					Per 10,000 people
	Daily Newspapers, 1996	Television Sets, 1997	Telephone Main Lines, 1997	Mobile Telephones, 1997	Personal Computers, 1997	Internet Hosts, 1999
Angola	12	91	5	1	0.70	0.00
Botswana	27	27	56	0	13.40	4.18
Malawi	3	2	4	0	0.50	0.00
Mozambique	3	4	4	0	1.60	0.08
Namibia	19	32	58	8	18.60	15.79
South Africa	30	125	107	37	41.60	34.67
Zambia	14	80	9	0	0.50	0.31
Zimbabwe	18	29	17	1	9.00	0.87

Source: World Bank, *World Development Report, 1999/2000* (Washington, D.C.: World Bank, 1999).

Although there have been few quantitative studies of the effects of technology on development in southern Africa (or other regions), the topic would make a fascinating research topic. I expect such studies in the future as more and more statistical data become available.

Useful Web Sites

An increasing amount of data and other resources are available on-line. I do not attempt an exhaustive inventory of relevant Web sites in this article. Instead, I provide several key sites that researchers might find useful.

Two excellent Web sites for data are the following:

World Bank data: www.worldbank.org/

This Web site provides a link to the *World Development Report* and other exceptional resources.

United Nations Children's Fund (UNICEF) data: www.unicef.org/

This Web site provides a link to *The Progress of Nations*, *The State of the World's Children*, and other excellent UNICEF resources.

There is also a Web site for each southern African government, or at least a Web site that contains extensive information relevant to government:

Angola: www.angola.org/

Malawi: www.malawi.com/

Mozambique: www.mozambique.mz/

Namibia: www.republicofnamibia.com/

South Africa: www.polity.org.za/

Zambia: www.statehouse.gov.zm/

Zimbabwe: www.mother.com/~zimweb/

Again, these are not all the Web sites available—just a sampling of what is deemed important by each government in the region. Readers may also want to consult the *Europa World Year Book,* which contains a list of ministries for each country in the region. Some of the Web pages listed above have links to government and private-sector data, especially in the economic sector. Not surprisingly, South Africa has a large number of Web sites, some endorsed by the government and some not. A particularly useful site is a list of on-line addresses:

South African servers: www.southafrica.net/servers/

This site even contains a link to one of my favorite sites: a site dedicated to homesick South Africans.

Another good Web site is by IDASA, Institute for Democracy in South Africa:

IDASA: www.idasa.org.za/

This site even contains information related to democracy in South Africa, as well as information on IDASA itself.

An excellent Web site for African newspapers and media is the following:

Newspapers: www.hanszell.co.uk/nlink.htm

This site does not list every newspaper in Africa, but it does provide an out-standing selection of some of the major newspapers. For researchers attempting to follow current events, and possibly code them, this is a very useful Web site.

NOTES

1. For a detailed review of quantitative research relating to Africa, see York W. Bradshaw, Paul J. Kaiser, and Stephen N. Ndegwa, "Rethinking Theoretical and Methodological Approaches to the Study of African Development," *African Studies Review* 38 (1995): 39–65.

2. Claudia Buchman, "The Debt Crisis, Structural Adjustment and Women's Education: Implications for Status and Social Development," *International Journal of Comparative Sociology* 37 (1996): 5–30; Paul N. Mbatia, "Provision of Health Care by the State in Kenya: A Fragile State Versus Civil Society" (Ph.D. diss., Department of Sociology, Indiana University, 1996); Njeri Mbuga, "Effective Strategies for Prevention of Sexual Transmission of HIV/AIDS among High School Students: The Case of Kenya" (Ph.D. diss., Department of Sociology, Indiana University, 1999); Agostino Zamberia, "The State-Civil Society Partnership in the Provision of Water and Sanitation for the

Urban Poor: The Case of Kibera, Kenya" (Ph.D. diss., Department of Sociology, Indiana University, 1999).

3. United Nations Children's Fund (UNICEF), *The State of the World's Children, 1999* (New York: UNICEF, 1999).

4. Ibid., p. 26.

5. United Nations Children's Fund (UNICEF), *The Progress of Nations 1999* (New York: UNICEF, 1999), p. 1.

6. See York W. Bradshaw, Rita Noonan, Laura Gash, and Claudia Buchmann, "Borrowing against the Future: Children and Third World Indebtedness," *Social Forces* 71 (1993): 629–56.

7. Ezekiel Kalipeni, "Determinants of Infant Mortality in Malawi: A Spatial Perspective," *Social Science and Medicine* 37 (1993): 183–98.

8. Bruce London, "Structural Determinants of Third World Urban Change: An Ecological and Political Economic Analysis," *American Sociological Review* 52 (1987): 28–43.

9. York W. Bradshaw and Mark Schafer, "Urbanization and Development: The Emergence of International Nongovernmental Organizations amid Declining States" *Sociological Perspectives,* forthcoming.

10. Zamberia, "State-Civil Society Partnership."

11. Kenneth Hadden and Bruce London, "Educating Girls in the Third World: The Demographic, Basic Needs, and Economic Benefits," *International Journal of Comparative Sociology* 37 (1996): 31–46.

12. Mark J. Schafer, "International Non-governmental Organizations and Third World Education in 1990," *Sociology of Education* 72 (1999): 69–88.

13. Buchman, "Debt Crisis."

14. Bruce Fuller, Xiaoyan Liang, and Haiyan Hua, "Did Black Literacy Rise After Soweto? Public Problems and Ethnic Archipelagos in South Africa," *International Journal of Comparative Sociology* 37 (1996): 97–120.

15. Bruce J. Fuller, J. Singer, and M. Keiley, "Why Do Daughters Leave School in Southern Africa? Family Economy and Mothers' Commitments," *Social Forces* 74 (1995): 657–80.

16. York Bradshaw and Bruce Fuller, "Policy Action and School Demand in Kenya: When a Strong State Grows Fragile," *International Journal of Comparative Sociology* 37 (1996): 72–96.

17. Claudia Buchmann, "Family Background, Parental Perceptions and Labor Demand: The Determinants of Educational Inequality in Contemporary Kenya" (paper presented at the International Sociological Association meetings, Montreal, Canada, 1998).

18. York Bradshaw and Michael Wallace, *Global Inequalities* (Thousand Oaks, Calif.: Pine Forge Press, 1996), pp. 42–43.

19. Bruce London and Bruce A. Williams, "Multinational Corporate Penetration, Protest, and Basic Needs Provision in Non-Core Nations: A Cross-National Analysis," *Social Forces* 66 (1988): 747–73; Bruce London and Bruce A. Williams, "National Politics, International Dependency, and Basic Needs Provision: A Cross-National Analysis," *Social Forces* 69 (1990): 565–84; Dale W. Wimberly, "Investment Dependence and Alternative Explanations of Third World Mortality: A Cross-National Study," *American Sociological Review* 55 (1990): 75–91.

20. John Walton and Charles Ragin, "Global and National Sources of Political

Protest: Third World Responses to the Debt Crisis," *American Sociological Review* 55 (1990): 876–90; Bradshaw et al., "Borrowing against the Future."

21. Shridath Ramphal, "Debt Has a Child's Face," in *The Progress of Nations 1999* (New York: UNICEF, 1999), p.1

22. World Bank, *World Development Report 1999/2000* (Washington, D.C.: World Bank, 1999), p. 267.

CONTRIBUTORS

LIEZELL BRADSHAW has worked for the Foundation for Research and Development in Pretoria, South Africa. Her research has examined the role of non-governmental organizations in the development process, both in southern African and other world regions.

YORK BRADSHAW is professor and chair of sociology at the University of Memphis. He has conducted substantial research in eastern and southern Africa. He is author of *Global Inequalities* (with Michael Wallace), *Education in Comparative Perspective, Understanding Societies in a Global Age* (with Joseph Healey, forthcoming), and many articles in social science and Africa-related journals.

ALLEN CALDWELL is a Ph.D. student at the University of California, Berkeley, Graduate School of Education. His academic interests include comparative education and international human rights. Professionally, he has worked in public and private sectors, the NGO community, and multilateral agencies. He intends to complete work on his doctorate within the next two years.

HORACE G. CAMPBELL is professor of African American studies and political science at Syracuse University, Syracuse, New York. He has taught at the University of Dar es Salaam, Tanzania, at Northwestern University, and at Sussex University in the United Kingdom. His research has focused on militarism and transformation in Southern Africa. He has written extensively on the search for peace in southern Africa. He is on the board of the Southern Africa Regional Institute for Policy Studies (SARIPS) in Harare, Zimbabwe.

CONTRIBUTORS

DAVID B. COPLAN is professor, chair, and head of the Department of Social Anthropology at the University of the Witwatersrand in Johannesburg. He is known for his writing on urban and popular performing arts in Africa, in particular South Africa. Recently his research has focused on the social experience and expressive culture of labor migrants from Lesotho to South Africa, and his current interest is a social history of the Lesotho–Free State border. His publications include *In Township Tonight! South Africa's Black City Music and Theatre* (1986), *In the Time of Cannibals: The Word Music of South Africa's Basotho Migrants* (1994), *Lyrics of the Basotho Migrants* (1995), and numerous articles, chapters, and occasional papers.

STAFFAN DARNOLF is assistant professor of political science at Södertörn University College in Sweden. On obtaining his Ph.D. in political science from the Göteborg University in Sweden, he went to the Johns Hopkins School of Advanced International Studies (SAIS) in Washington, D.C., as a visiting scholar. His main area of interest is electioneering in southern Africa, and the administration of elections in emerging democracies. Darnolf has published several articles and contributed to edited books on development in southern Africa. He is currently co-authoring a book on electoral management in young democracies as well as co-editing a book on development in Zimbabwe since independence.

JEAN DAVISON is adjunct professor of sociology at American University and president of International Development and Education Associates, a consulting firm in the Washington, D.C., area. Prior to this, Dr. Davison was a research scholar at Stanford University and was assistant professor of sociology at the University of Malawi where she coordinated the design and implementation of a graduate program on gender and development (1989–92). Her current research interests are on the role of NGOs and their relationships with CBOs in southern Africa. She is the author of three books: *Agriculture, Women and Land: The African Experience* (1988), *Voices from Mutira: Change in the Lives of Rural Gikuyu Women* (1989, 1996), and *Gender, Lineage and Ethnicity in Southern Africa* (1997).

TROY DYER is a consultant in strategy and business development, active in Internet-based information services for professional entrepreneurs, and in the raising of venture capital and private equity financing for entrepreneurial high-growth businesses. He is a part-time lecturer on strategy and entrepreneurship at the Wits Business School, Johannesburg. Armed with an accounting degree and a Wharton MBA, he previously worked as a management consultant for two major international consulting companies.

JOSHUA BERNARD FORREST is associate professor of political science at the University of Vermont; he has served as a fellow of the American Philosophical Society and as a Fulbright Faculty Research Scholar in Namibia.

Contributors

His recent work includes *Namibia's Post-Apartheid Regional Institutions: The Founding Year* (1998) and articles on Namibia in the *Journal of Democracy, World Policy Journal*, and the *Journal of Commonwealth and Comparative Studies*. In addition, he has published articles on state-building in Africa in *Comparative Politics, Studies in Comparative International Development, The Journal of Modern African Studies*, and in edited volumes including *Comparing Nations: Concepts, Strategies, Substance and the African State at a Critical Juncture*. He was also an Ira J. Kukin Scholar at the Harvard Academy of International and Area Studies, where he wrote *Guinea-Bissau: Power, Conflict, and Renewal in a West African Nation* (1992).

BRUCE FULLER is professor of education and public policy at the University of California, Berkeley. His current work focuses on how decentralization of the state affects school and child care organizations in different kinds of ethnic communities. Fuller has worked at the World Bank and USAID on school quality and family poverty issues. His most recent book is *Government Confronts Culture: The Struggle for Democracy in Southern Africa*.

KENNETH W. GRUNDY is the Marcus A. Hanna Professor of Political Science at Case Western Reserve University in Cleveland. He has also served as visiting senior lecturer at Makerere University College (University of East Africa) in Uganda; as visiting scholar at the Institute of Social Studies (The Hague) and the University of Pretoria (South Africa); as visiting Fulbright professor at both the University of Zambia and the National University of Ireland, Galway; as university fellow twice at Rhodes University, South Africa; and as the first Bradlow Fellow at the South African Institute of International Affairs in Johannesburg. His books include *Guerrilla Struggle in Africa* (1972), *Confrontation and Accommodation in Southern Africa* (1973), *Ideologies of Violence* (co-author, 1974), *Evaluating Transnational Programs in Government and Business* (co-editor, 1980), *Soldiers without Politics: Blacks in the South African Armed Forces* (1983), *The Militarization of South African Politics* (1986; revised ed., 1988), and *South Africa: Domestic Crisis and International Challenge* (1991). Professor Grundy has also written some two dozen book chapters and more than forty scholarly articles. In August 1998 he was named director of Case Western Reserve University's newly formed Center for Policy Studies.

CHUMA HIMONGA is associate professor at the University of Cape Town, South Africa. Her previous research has focused on Zambian family and succession laws. She has published considerably on issues of women's and children's rights, customary law, and family law in southern Africa. These areas of law continue to be her main areas of research and teaching.

JOHN D. HOLM is professor of political science and executive director of International Services and Programs at Cleveland State University. He has written extensively on various aspects of Botswana politics over the last thirty years. He was co-editor of *Democracy in Botswana* (1989), has authored several monographs on citizen participation in African democracies, and has published articles on Botswana in a wide range of journals, including *Development and Change, African Studies Review,* and *African Affairs.* He was co-founder of the Botswana Democracy Project, which has become within Africa a model of university-community partnership concerned with political development.

EZEKIEL KALIPENI is a population/medical/environmental geographer interested in demographic, health, environmental, and resource issues in sub-Saharan Africa. He has carried out extensive research on the population dynamics of Malawi and Africa in general, concentrating on fertility, mortality, migration, and health issues. His most recent works are *Population Growth and Environmental Degradation in Southern Africa; Issues and Perspectives on Health Care in Contemporary Sub-Saharan Africa,* edited with Philip Thiuri; *Sacred Spaces and Public Quarrels: African Cultural and Economic Landscapes,* edited with Paul Tiyambe Zeleza; and *AIDS, Health Care Systems, and Culture in Sub-Saharan Africa: Rethinking and Reappraisal* (a special issue of the journal *African Rural and Urban Studies*), edited with Joseph Oppong (forthcoming).

SUE KELL hails from Zimbabwe and is a part-time lecturer in general and international economics and the economics of financial markets at Wits Business School, Johannesburg. She has had many years of experience as a business economist (first at a large mining house with extensive interests in the southern African subcontinent and then in the banking sector in South Africa). She is the author of articles on the development of Namibia, the development of financial markets in South Africa, and world financial markets, and has presented conference papers on reconstruction and development in South Africa and on the impact of globalization and knowledge industries on developing economies.

COLIN LEGUM was previously editor of the *Observer* (London) and the *Africa Contemporary Record.* He is an independent journalist presently living in South Africa.

STEPHEN N. NDEGWA is associate professor of government at the College of William and Mary, Williamsburg, Virginia. His previous research has focused on Kenya, civil society, and democracy, and his current research is on land reform in southern Africa. He is the author of the *Two Faces of Civil Society* (1996). His other publications have appeared in journals such as the *American Political Science Review, African Studies Review,* and *Africa Today.*

M. ANNE PITCHER is associate professor of political science at Colgate University, Hamilton, New York. She is the author of *Politics in the Portuguese Empire: The State, Industry, and Cotton, 1926–1974* (1993) and has also published articles in *African Studies Review, Journal of Southern African Studies,* and the

Contributors

Journal of Modern African Studies. She is currently preparing a manuscript that analyzes the politics of privatization in Mozambique. Her research interests include comparative study of economic transitions, the agrarian question in Africa, and women's rights to natural resources.

MASIPULA SITHOLE is professor of political science at the University of Zimbabwe. He has written extensively on Zimbabwean politics.

INDEX

Action Christian National Party (ACN), 111n2

activism: for gender equity, 285; in Namibia, 96–97; for women's rights, 275

affirmative action, 56–58

African Charter on Human and People's Rights, 280, 283–284

African Episcopal Methodist Church, 320

African Jukebox (television), 227

African National Congress (ANC): affirmative action, 57; alliance fissures, 51–54; budget expenditures, 16; citizenship for refugees, 20; Code of Conduct, 47; corruption handling, 46–47; education reform, 309–310; freedom of press, 144; future considerations, 59–62; in GNU, 42–43; National Land Commission, 261; negotiations in exile, 34–36; negotiations with NP, 36–39; parliamentary majority, 256; popular mandate, 317; power sharing, 43; predecessors, 31; promises, 47–49, 61–62; provincial power, 44–45; reduced government role, 60; release of prisoners, 35; rhetoric vs. performance, 60; sabotage of support, 193; UDM alliance against, 220; unbanning, 34; under pressure, 20; union leadership association, 144

African Peacekeeping Initiative, 17

Africanists, 54

Afrikaner farmers settling in north, 19–20

Afrikaner Nation, in evolution, 29–30

Afrikaner Weerstandsbeweging (AWB), 41

agriculture: commercialization in South Africa, 28; communal gardens, 263; decline in Mozambique, 189; genetic engineering, 183; hybrid seeds, 107; improvement in Mozambique, 197; land redistribution, 104–105; Lenyene case study, 262–264; livestock programs, 102; Mozambique government policies, 191; Namibian development, 98, 105–107; North Pondoland case study, 264–266; over-grazing in Namibia, 105; and population density, 328; productivity in South Africa, 60; subsistence in Angola, 162

AIDS: Botswana, 118, 148n3, 335, 345; cost of treatment, 372; female impact, 336, 346; and future demographic structure, 371–372; life expectancy impact, 336, 372, 394–395; Malawi, 335, 345–346; mortality rate impact, 351; Namibia, 335, 345; orphaned children, 395; quantitative studies, 395; Rwanda, 348; and sexual mobility, 346; and sexual violence, 348; southern Africa, 329t, 335–336, 345–346; Zambia, 335, 372; Zimbabwe, 335, 372

Albright, Madeleine, 171

Alvor peace agreement, 169

amnesty, in South Africa, 55–56

androcentrism, 174–176

INDEX

Index

INDEX

KwaZulu-Natal: autonomy demands, 39; murder as employment source, 220; violence in, 39, 41, 42, 56

Kwelagobe, Daniel, 140, 141

Ladysmith Black Mambazo, 227

land: *bantustans* for indigenous development, 255; customary land, 238–241; deliberations in Zimbabwe, 248–255; freehold land, 241–242; gender equity in South Africa, 255–256; historical antecedents of control, 236–237; laws governing, 237–238, 242; leasehold land, 241–242; Lenyene case study, 262–264; marital status and claims, 242–248; Namibian issues, 104–107; North Pondoland case study, 264–266; Ratidzai case study, Zimbabwe, 252–254; redistribution, 104–105; reform, 108, 271n49; state farm division in Mozambique, 200

land mines, 168, 180

language: Afrikaans on television, 224–225; in Namibia, 99, 112n34; political battles, 10; separation on radio, 225–226; Southern Soto on television, 225; vernacular radio stations, 228

language cultures, 218–219

Lara, Lucio, 163

Lawry, S. W., 245

League of Independent Women of Angola (LIMA), 174, 177

Lekota, Patrick "Terror," 54

Lenyenye, South Africa, 262–264

Lerner, Gerda, 174–175

Lesotho: gross domestic product, 367; marital status and land claims, 244–245; patrilineal precepts, 244; population, 328

Levin, R., 259, 260–261

Liberation War Collaborators Association, 85–86

Liberation War Veterans Association, 84, 85–86

life expectancy: Botswana, 118; impact of AIDS on, 336, 372, 394–395; quantitative data, 395t; southern Africa, 327, 330t, 337–338

Liga de Mullheres Independentes de Angola. *See* League of Independent Women of Angola (LIMA)

Linchwe II, 134

literacy: Botswana, 136, 147; Mozambique, 189; South Africa, 319; southern Africa, 330t; and women's health, 341–342, 344–345

living standards, Botswana, 123

lobolo (bridewealth), 286–287, 293

Lomé Accord, 12

Longwe, Sarah, 235, 280–281, 296n36. See also *Sara Longwe v Intercontinental Hotel*

Love and Crime in Johannesburg (theater), 223

Lozi ethnic group, 102

Lusaka Protocol, 152, 165, 166, 169–172

Maasdorp, G., 380

Mabena v Letsoalo, 293, 294

Mabuse, Sipho, 227

Machel, Josina, 172

Machel, Samora: death, 193; diplomatic leadership, 20–21; on female liberation, 175; groundwork for ties with West, 195; negotiation with South Africa, 193; perceptions of, 167; urban resettlement, 191

Machungo, Mario, 200

Madikizela-Mandela, Winnie, 54

Mafwe ethnic group, 102

Magaia, Americo, 199–200

Magaya v Magaya, 288, 291–292

Maharaj, Mac, 18

Makeba, Miriam, 227

Malan Accord, 36

malaria, 334–335

Malawi: British-style school curriculum, 308; ethnic educational differences, 319; gross domestic product, 367; Land Act, 240; Lands Acquisition Act, 240; legal pluralism, 291; marital status and land claims, 243; matrilineal precepts, 243; patrilineal precepts, 243; population, 328; Registered Land Act, 241–242; school enrollment rates, 304–307; student dropout rates, 305; women's access to land, 240

malnutrition, quantitative data, 395t

Malope, Rebecca, 228

Mandela, Nelson: on AIDS, 372; in Angola peace process, 171; call for cooperation with government, 61; on crime, 50–51; diplomatic leadership, 21; election, 27, 256, 308; on gender inequities, 257–258; handling of corruption, 46–47; on majority rule, 42; mentioned, 3; outcomes-based education, 317; popular mandate, 317; presidential succession, 58–59; release from prison, 34, 35, 256; and Savimbi, 177; in secret talks with NP, 34–35; in talks with National Party, 36–38; unbanning political organizations, 195; and white South Africans, 261

Manuvakola, Eugenio Ngolo, 171, 178

416

Index

INDEX

Mugabe, Robert (*continued*)
88–89; as prime minister, 91n22; Sandura Commission, 82; as socialist, 75; in unity accord, 71; unpopularity of, 10; War Victims Compensation Fund, 83–84; and Zimbabwe Congress of Trade Unions, 85

Multi-Party Negotiating Forum, 38

Murphy, C., 259, 261

music styles, 227–228

Mussanhene, Egas, 199–200

Mutasa, Dydimus, 77, 91n27

Muyongo, Mishake, 95, 96, 102

Muzorewa, Abel, 90n15

Mwanza, A., 378

Nama-Damara ethnic group, 320

Nama ethnic group, 102

Namibia: bureaucratic bourgeoisie, 103; Commercial Land Reform Act, 104; Communal Land Reform Bill, 105; constitutional adherence, 110; constitutional gender equity provisions, 281, 283, 297n58; Council of Traditional Leaders, 101; economic development, 103–108; ethnic educational differences, 319, 320; food crop programs, 106–107; fragile political culture, 109; governmental framework, 94–99; grain crops, 106; import dependence on South Africa, 107; independence, 166, 169–170; in international network of states, 317; Labor Code, 98; land reform, 108; Legal Aid Center (LAC), 98; legal pluralism, 291; livestock farming, 106–107; local school boards, 322; mass schooling, 312–313; micro-level businesses, 106; National Assembly, 95, 97, 108; National Council, 97–98; National Land Policy, 105; national reconciliation policy, 100; natural resource management, 5; one-party dominant political system, 96; parliamentary democracy, 94–95; political disenfranchisement, 100–101; political variables, 99–103; racial heritages, 8–9; racial representation, 100–102; school enrollment rates, 312; school expansion vs. quality, 315; village-level authority, 103; white flight, 6

Namibia Defence Force (NDF), 98

Namibia National Front, 111n2

Namibian Meat Board, 106

National Assembly, South Africa, 41

National Council of Provinces, 44

National Party (NP): attrition, 29–30; Bantu Education Act, 308–309; cosmetic changes, 30; election of 1994, 39–41; national negotiations with ANC, 36–39; power sharing, 43; power shifts, 28; state of emergency, 256

National Patriotic Front (NPF), 111nn2,10

National Security Review of the United States, 155

National Union for the Total Independence of Angola (UNITA): Angolan deployment, 166; cease-fire violations, 169; Congo Brazzaville resupply base, 160; defeat at Cuito Cuanavale, 166; demobilization by UN, 165; diamond revenues, 163–165; disintegration, 177–178; exploitation of women, 174; famine as weapon, 181; food aid for, 181; foreign weaponry, 178; humanitarian efforts for, 185; information warfare, 177; isolation, 163; negotiations with WFP, 184; oil installation attacks, 162; political divisions, 178; relief food manipulation, 181–182; siege of civilians, 151–152, 179; total war concept, 175; UN sanctions, 164–165, 171–172; U.S. support, 170, 171; at war with MPLA, 157; weapons expenditures, 153, 164; women's organization, 174; Zambian deployment, 166

National Union of Steelworkers of South Africa, 52

natural resource governance, 5

Nawakwi, Edith, 290

Ncube, Welshman, 75, 249–250, 251

Ndebele, Cyril, 76–77, 91n27, 92n35

Ndebele ethnic group, 70, 77, 90n10

Nehova, Kandindima, 97–98

New National Party, 29, 43

Nkomati Accord, 193, 194

Nkomo, Joshua, 71, 73, 91n16

non-governmental organizations (NGOs): food aid for UNITA, 181; in Mozambique, 202; in Namibia, 98, 110; in South Africa, 322; WFP agreement, 182

North Korea, 73

North Pondoland, South Africa, 264–266

Nujoma, Sam: assertion of power, 99; election as president, 95; managerial style, 109; support for Kabila, 98; third-term presidency, 96, 108–109; under criticism, 110; victory in all-race elections, 317

Nyerere, Julius, 20

Nzinga, Queen, 172

Nzo, Alfred, 16

Index

oil companies, in Angola, 161
The One-Party State and Democracy: The Zimbabwe Debate, 82
Oppong, J., 331, 346
Organization of Angolan Women (OMA), 153, 173
Orphans of the Cold War (Anstee), 170, 177
Oshindonga ethnic group, 320
Oshinkwanyama ethnic group, 320
ostrich export niche, 106
outcomes-based education, 311, 315, 317
Ovambo ethnic group, 100–102
Ovimbundu ethnic group, 152
Owambo ethnic group, 320

Pan Africanist Congress (PAC), 31, 41, 43
Pankhurst, D., 240
Parson, J., 126
Participatory Poverty Assessment, 266
Patel, Kekobad, 201
peace: in Angola, 8, 165–166, 169–172; Bicesse accord, 169–170, 171; D. F. Malan Accord, 36; Lomé Accord, 12; Lusaka Protocol, 152, 165, 166, 169–172; in Mozambique, 8, 195–196; negative definitions, 157; Nkomati Accord, 193; RENAMO with FRELIMO, 195; Tripartite Accords, 169
People's Liberation Army of Namibia (PLAN), 98
Pepetela, 174
Peters, P., 239
PF-ZAPU: absorption by ZANU(PF), 74–75; denigration of election symbol, 91n16; destruction, 72–73; formation, 71; gains in cabinet shuffles, 75; support threshold, 81. *See also* Zimbabwe African People's Union (ZAPU)
Phiri, E. L., 344
Pohamba, Hifikepunye, 109, 113n41
political action, in South Africa, 31–32
political change, 6–7
political conflict, and warfare, 7–8
political elites, in South Africa, 61–62
political murders, 49–50, 74, 76
political pluralism, in Namibia, 99, 100
popular culture: aural genres, 217; debate over, 215–217; dependent on reconciliation and development, 219; moments of freedom, 216; and nationalism, 218; ongoing transformation, 221; recording industry, 228–229; television soap opera, 224
Popular Forces for the Liberation of Angola (FAPLA), 170

Popular Movement for the Liberation of Angola (MPLA): corruption, 162–163; for liberation of women, 173; at war with UNITA, 157; women in liberation process, 172–173
popular music, 227–228
popular musical theater, 221–223
Porter, G., 259, 265–266
Portugal: African nationalists against fascism, 167; Angolan liberation wars, 167; colonialism in Angola, 158–159; departure of traders from Mozambique, 190; investment in Mozambique, 197–198
post–cold war policy, 314–322
poverty: and crime, 50; indicators in southern Africa, 369–370; in Malawi, 306; and quality of life, 394; in South Africa, 60; in Zambia, 350
power: concentration in Namibia, 99; gender gap in Zimbabwe, 252–254; global changes, 32–33; manipulation of custom and tradition, 254; national vs. provincial in South Africa, 44–45; of Nujoma, 99; sharing in GNU, 43; shifts, 9–10, 27–32; shifts in South Africa, 27–32
present study, 4
President of the Republic of South Africa and Another v Hugo, 282–283, 285
Pretoria Minute, 36
Price, Robert M., 33
primogeniture, 288–289, 291–292, 299n110
Proff, H. V., 380
Progressive Federal Party, 29
property grabbing, 289, 299n109
protectionism, 5
protest theater, 221–222
protests, in South Africa, 30–31
public opinion polls, 141
Puna, Nzau, 177

racial heritages, 8–9
racial inequality, 57, 61
radio: in Botswana, 133, 150n35; language separation, 225–226; music diversification, 228; popular music, 228; programming diversification, 225; in South Africa, 217, 225–226; vernacular language stations, 228
Ramaphosa, Cyril, 37, 38, 58
Ramphal, Shridath, 398
Ramphele, Mamphela, 262
Ranger, T., 259
rape, in refugee camps, 348
Ratidzai case study, Zimbabwe, 252–254

INDEX

Index

INDEX

Southern Africa Customs Union (SACU), 17, 107
Southern Africa Development Coordination Conference (SADDC), 206, 364
Southern African Development Community (SADC): about, 14, 16, 364–365; balance of payments, 378–381, 379t; challenges, 389; demographics, 370–372, 371t; development indicators, 369–370; Finance and Investment Protocol, 375; financial market structure, 374–376; foreign debt and investment, 382t; government revenue and expenditure, 373–374; gross domestic product, 365–369, 366t; inflation, 377; interests, 12; investment, 381–383; micro-economic structure, 378; objectives, 365; policy dilemmas, 387–388; poverty indicators, 369–370; ratification of protocols, 15t; Savimbi declared war criminal, 178; structural adjustment programs, 377–378; structural change, 368; trade, 378–381, 379t; value-added exports, 17
Southern African Human Rights Foundation (SAHRF), 78
Southwest Africa Territorial Force (SWATF), 98
Soweto uprising, 29
Spatial Development Initiative (SDI), 18
Stals, Chris, 381–382
Stepan, Alfred, 68–69, 70, 74, 78, 86, 88
Stock, Robert, 335
stock markets, 61, 376
strikes: civil service strike in Zimbabwe, 83; by health workers in Angola, 154; by teachers in Angola, 154; women in Angola, 153–154
student unrest, 81, 86
Suharto, 86, 88
Svedberg, Peter, 339
Swaziland: marital status and land claims, 244–245; monarchy crisis, 220; patrilineal precepts, 244; population, 328; women's access to land, 239–240

Taiwan, 21
Takirambudde, P., 376
Tanzania, naval support, 17
Taylor, Charles, 167
Tayob, Abdul Gani, 199
teachers, 154, 305
technology, 160, 398, 399t
Tekere, Edgar, 71, 76, 77–78, 83
telecommunications, integrating, 19
television: advertising, 224; in Botswana, 144, 150n35; cultural studies, 224; pay-per-view services, 224–225; political self-expression, 224; programming in South Africa, 225; reform and diversification in South Africa, 226–227; satellite reception, 224–225; in South Africa, 217, 223–224; as threat to social morality in South Africa, 226
Terre'blanche, Eugene, 39
Tevera, Daniel, 350
theater: popular musical theater, 221–223; protest theater, 221–222; as socially embedded art form, 222–223; township theater, 221–223
Third World Bunfight Company, 221–222
Thomas, L., 367
Thomas, R. H., 388–389
Tjitendero, Mosé, 95, 101
Todaro, M. P., 380
tourist industry: "authentic" Soweto tours, 221; fear of crime in South Africa, 51; safaris in Botswana, 117
township theater, 221–223
traditional medicine, 331–332
Transparency International, 46, 81
tribal Africa view, 155, 179
tribal homeland policy, 29
Tripartite Accords, 169
Truth and Reconciliation Commission (TRC), 54–56
Tsvangirayi, Morgan, 87, 93n47
Tswana ethnic group, 116, 125–126, 140, 148n1, 319–320, 321
tuberculosis, 334–335
Tutsis, 21, 70
Tutu, Desmond, 46
Twala, Sello, 227
Twusami, P. A., 331

UANC/United Parties, 81
ukuhlonipha gender concept, 259
Ulenga, Ben, 96, 108
Umkhonto we Sizwe (MK), 39
Unger, M., 383
União Nacional para a Independência Total de Angola. See National Union for the Total Independence of Angola (UNITA)
unions: and ANC, 144; and apartheid, 144; in Botswana, 108, 131, 132–133, 146; in corporate restructuring, 61; in South Africa, 52–53; in Zimbabwe, 81
UNITA. See National Union for the Total Independence of Angola (UNITA)

Index

UNITA Renovado, 171

United Democratic Front (UDF), 31, 37, 111nn2,10, 167

United Democratic Movement (UDM), 38, 43, 220

United Nations: Angolan peace process, 170, 178–179; apartheid as crime against humanity, 169; Convention on the Elimination of All Forms of Discrimination Against Women (CEDAW), 250, 275, 279–281, 283–284; demobilization of armies in Mozambique, 195, 202; elections in Mozambique, 203; Human Development Index, 118, 369, 370t; Human Development Report, 168; humanitarian programs in Angola, 181; Namibia-brokered peace, 94; negotiation in Angola, 166; peacekeeping missions, 74; presence in Mozambique, 202; sanctions on UNITA, 164–165, 171–172; and Savimbi, 166, 169, 171, 177, 179–180; Special Relief Program for Angola, 181; trade sanctions against Rhodesia, 190; troops in Angola, 166; UNAVEM missions, 169–170; UNITA demobilization, 165; UNOMOZ peacekeeping force, 196; World Food Programme (WFP), 181–185

University of Botswana, Democracy Project, 135

U.S. Institute for Peace, 166

Valentim, Jorge, 178

value-added exports, 17

van Eck, Jan, 17

Van Ginneken, J. K., 341–342

Victims of Apartheid, 262

Viljoen, Constand, 39

Vines, A., 194

violence: against women in Angola, 168; Boipatong massacre, 37; culture of, 220–221; in KwaZulu-Natal, 39, 41, 42, 56; sexual violence, 348;

War Victims Compensation Fund, 83

warfare: civil war spillover in Botswana, 137; in civilian areas, 151–152; in Democratic Republic of Congo, 98; and diamonds in Angola, 163–165; endemic to Africa, 155; food as weapon in Angola, 180–185; gendered nature in Angola, 157; history in Angola, 154, 157–158; human displacement in Angola, 168, 181; internal in Mozambique, 192–195; Kuito siege, 151–152; linked with weapons expenditures, 155;

and peace accords in Angola, 169–172; and political conflict, 7–8; political economy in Angola, 158–163; rules of engagement, 178; siege of civilians, 151–152, 171, 172, 179; total war concept, 175, 193; women in Angolan war, 171

Warner, M., 385–386

water: access in Mozambique, 189, 197; access in Namibia, 105; Angola resources, 158–159; and disease, 335; drilling in Botswana, 123; lobbying for in Namibia, 97; provision of adequate in southern Africa, 333; regional plans, 19

weapons: arms industry, 17; foreign in Angola, 178; foreign in Mozambique, 195; gun availability in South Africa, 50; markets, 165, 178

Web sites, 399–400

Weiner, D., 259, 260–261

Weis, L., 344

welfare reform, 7

whistle-blowers, 47

White, Landweg, 236

white flight, 6, 103

whites, percentage of population in Zimbabwe, 70

Windrich, Elaine, 177

witchcraft, 192, 221

women: in Angolan war, 171; autonomy, 342; Botswana coalitions, 144; boycotts in Africa, 153–154; education and development linkage, 344f; ethnic stamping, 174; exposure to AIDS, 346; in failure of Savimbi, 152–153; in informal sector in Angola, 162; in *kgotla* meetings, 148n11; land access strategies, 239–240; land control, 236–237; in liberation process, 172–175; literacy and health, 341–342, 344–345; in Mozambique politics, 257; objectified as victims, 233; in population percentages, 255, 257; protest by withholding labor, 272n78; role in Angolan economy, 156; in siege of Kuito, 152; social change, 7; South Africa coalitions, 144; in South African National Assembly, 257t; in South African politics, 256–258; into South African workforce, 57–58; stridency, 231; strikes in Angola, 153–154; UN anti-discrimination convention, 250; as victims, 173–174; as war booty, 173–174; war hardships in Angola, 168

Women and Law in Southern Africa (WLSA), 285, 291, 292

423

INDEX

Women in Development approach, 233
Worby, E., 238–239
World Bank, 206, 327, 349, 351, 377
World Food Programme (WFP), 181–185
World Health Organization (WHO), 352
World Trade Center occupation, 39
World Trade Organization (WTO), 380
World Wide Web sites, 399–400

Xiaoyan Liang, 396

Young, T., 190
Young Directors Festival, 223
YWCA, 130

Zaire, 328, 336
Zambia: Bill of Rights, 278, 295n4; constitutional gender equity provisions, 281, 283, 290; Demographic and Health Survey, 337; Movement for Multi-Party Democracy (MMD), 85; population, 328; privatization, 368; women's access to land, 240
ZANU(Ndonga), 80, 81
ZANU(PF): absorption of PF-ZAPU, 74–75; active opposition to, 81; authoritarianism establishment, 71–73; coercive apparatus, 73–74; in constitutional reform, 88; decline in elite cohesion, 76–78, 86, 92n35; electoral hegemony, 80; formation, 71; headquarters attacked, 84; and liberation war collaborators, 85–86; stoking racial resentment, 10; support threshold, 81; sympathetic to strikers, 83. *See also* Zimbabwe African National Union (ZANU)
Zimbabwe: Agricultural Finance Corporation (AFC), 253; change in recent decades, 3; civil war spillover in Botswana, 137; colonial authoritarian regime, 70; commercial farm tenure issues, 252; Communal Areas, 239, 240, 250–251, 267; consolidating authoritarianism, 71–73; constitutional gender equity provisions, 281, 283; constitutional reform, 87–88, 92n34, 93n53; customary practices, 254; customary succession law, 288; Electoral Act of 1990, 80; erosion of authoritarianism, 74–75; ethnic division, 70–71; forced population movements, 216; freehold land, 241; gross domestic product, 367; health spending, 350; Indigenous Commercial Farmers' Association, 253; land laws, 242; land tenure and inheritance, 249–250; Land Tenure Commission, 248–252, 254–255, 267; legal pluralism, 291–292; manipulation of custom and tradition, 254; marital status and land claims, 246; marriage laws, 246; National Constitution Assembly (NCA), 87; National Multi-Party Consultative Conference, 78, 80; one-party state, 71, 90n11; opposition party coalition, 80–81; parliamentary election results, 1979–1995, 79t; patriarchy, 246; patrilineal precepts, 246, 250; Political Parties (Finance) Act, 72, 80, 90n14; post-colonial authoritarian regime, 70; racial resentment, 10; Ratidzai land case study, 252–254; Resettlement Areas, 251–252; Roman Dutch common law system, 298n88; salary averages, 92n42; segregation of health care facilities, 332; socialism, 75; turning point, 84–85; Unified Civil Service Negotiating Committee (UCSNC), 83; weak opposition parties, 78, 80, 92; white flight, 6; women's access to land, 240. *See also* Rhodesia
Zimbabwe African National Liberation Army (ZANLA), 70, 73
Zimbabwe African National Union (ZANU), 70, 193
Zimbabwe African People's Union (ZAPU), 70
Zimbabwe Catholic Commission for Justice and Peace (ZCCJP), 81–82, 87
Zimbabwe Congress of Trade Unions (ZCTU), 81–82, 84, 85, 87, 93n47
Zimbabwe Council of Churches (ZCC), 81–82, 87
Zimbabwe Human Rights Association (Zimrights), 81, 82, 87
Zimbabwe Law Society, 81
Zimbabwe National Army (ZNA), 73–74
Zimbabwe People's Revolutionary Army (ZIPRA), 70, 73
Zimbabwe Union of Journalists, 81
Zimbabwe Unity Movement (ZUM), 71, 76, 81, 92n36
Zimbabwe Women's Resource Centre and Network (ZWRCN), 249, 250, 251, 255
Zulu, E., 341
Zvobgo, Eddison, 76, 88